# STRATEGIC MARKETING IN TOURISM SERVICES

# STRATEGIC MARKETING IN TOURISM SERVICES

EDITED BY

## RODOULA H. TSIOTSOU
*University of Macedonia, Greece*

## RONALD E. GOLDSMITH
*Florida State University, USA*

United Kingdom – North America – Japan
India – Malaysia – China

Emerald Group Publishing Limited
Howard House, Wagon Lane, Bingley BD16 1WA, UK

First edition 2012

**British Library Cataloguing in Publication Data**
A catalogue record for this book is available from the British Library

ISBN: 978-1-78052-070-4

ISOQAR certified
Management Systems,
awarded to Emerald for
adherence to Quality
and Environmental
standards ISO 9001:2008
and 14001:2004,
respectively

Certificate Number 1985
ISO 9001
ISO 14001

INVESTOR IN PEOPLE

*To all the Professors who guided, shined and stigmatized my academic experience and career: Professor Euthimios Kioumourtzoglou, Professor Catherine Brown, Professor Charles Imwold, Professor Ronald E. Goldsmith and Professor Yiorgos Zotos.*

Rodoula H. Tsiotsou

*For my family, teachers, students and colleagues, to all of whom I am deeply indebted.*

Ronald E. Goldsmith

# Acknowledgements

We are indebted to the contributors of the book who submitted their chapters and brought them up after revisions to a high quality level. We appreciate the opportunity to include the best of their work in the book.

We also wish to thank the distinguished panel of academics that assisted with the rigorous double-blind reviewing process for this edition. Specifically, the editorial review board of the book consisted of:

| | |
|---|---|
| *Professor Mike Bosnjak* | Free University of Bozen-Bolzano, Italy |
| *Professor Eileen Bridges* | Kent State University, USA |
| *Professor Evaggelos Christou* | Technological Educational Institution of Thessaloniki, Greece |
| *Professor Leisa Flynn* | The University of Southern Mississippi, USA |
| *Professor Simon Hudson* | University of South Carolina, USA |
| *Professor Rob Law* | The Hong Kong Polytechnic University, Hong Kong |
| *Dr Xiang (Robert) Li* | University of South Carolina, USA |
| *Nathaniel Line* | The University of Tennessee-Knoxville, USA |
| *Dr Sacha Matthews-Joseph* | University of the Pacific, USA |
| *Professor Bill Merrilees* | Griffith University, Australia |
| *Professor Mike McCall* | Ithaca College, USA |
| *Stacey Robinson* | Florida State University, USA |
| *Dr Marianna Sigala* | University of the Aegean, Greece |
| *Dr Claire Haven-Tang* | University of Wales Institute Cardiff, UK |
| *Dr Cleopatra Veloutsou* | University of Glasgow, UK |
| *Dr Ipkin A. Wong* | Institute For Tourism Studies, Macau |
| *Professor Arch Woodside* | Boston College, USA |
| *Professor Jorge Zamore* | University of Talca, Chile |

We would like to express our gratitude to the Emerald Group Publishing Limited Development Editors, Mary Miskin and Kieran Booluck, for their support and guidance in editing and managing this book. We are also grateful to the doctoral candidates Evaggelia Chatzopoulou and Alkiviadis Karagiorgos for assisting in the format of the chapters.

Rodoula H. Tsiotsou
Ronald E. Goldsmith
*Editors*

# CONTENTS

About the Editors                                                      xiii

About the Authors                                                        xv

List of Contributors                                                   xxiii

PREFACE                                                                xxvii

INTRODUCTION TO STRATEGIC MARKETING
   IN TOURISM                                            xxxi

**PART I – TARGET MARKETING**

1.  Target Marketing and Its Application to Tourism                       3
   *Rodoula H. Tsiotsou and Ronald E. Goldsmith*

2.  The Role of Market Segmentation in Strategic Tourism Marketing      17
   *Sara Dolnicar*

3.  Social Interactions as Basis for Segmenting the
   Tourism Market                                          35
   *Rodoula H. Tsiotsou, Andreas Mild and D. Sudharshan*

**PART II – BRANDING**

4.  Destination Branding Development: Linking Supply-Side
   and Demand-Side Perspectives                             51
   *Giacomo Del Chiappa and Ilenia Bregoli*

5.  Place Branding: The Issue of a Narrowed Tourism Perspective         63
   *Sebastian Zenker and Suzanne C. Beckmann*

6. Destination Imagery: Examining Online Representative
   Dissonance in India                                          79
   *Deepak Chhabra*

7. Destination Brand Equity Modelling and Measurement — A
   Summer Tourism Case From Sweden                              95
   *Matthias Fuchs, Tatiana Chekalina and Maria Lexhagen*

8. Local Stakeholders' Image of Tourism Destinations: Outlooks
   for Destination Branding                                     117
   *Danielle Fernandes Costa Machado,*
   *Mirna de Lima Medeiros and João Luiz Passador*

**PART III – RELATIONSHIP MARKETING**

9. Implementing Relationship Marketing in Hospitality and
   Tourism Management                                           139
   *Ronald E. Goldsmith and Rodoula H. Tsiotsou*

10. Customer Value in Tourism Services: Meaning and Role
    for a Relationship Marketing Approach                       147
    *Martina G. Gallarza, Irene Gil-Saura*
    *and Morris B. Holbrook*

11. Identifying the Major Determinants of Loyalty in Tourism    163
    *Ana María Campón Cerro, José Manuel Hernández*
    *Mogollón and Helena Maria Baptista Alves*

12. Familiarity and Experience in Tourist Satisfaction
    and Loyalty Development                                      185
    *Ramón Rufín Moreno, Cayetano Medina Molina,*
    *José Luis Roldán Salgueiro and Manuel Rey Moreno*

**PART IV – EXPERIENTIAL MARKETING**

13. Introduction to Experiential Marketing                      207
    *Ronald E. Goldsmith and Rodoula H. Tsiotsou*

14. Tourist Experience Development: Designed Attributes,
    Perceived Experiences and Customer Value                    215
    *Lihua Gao, Noel Scott, Peiyi Ding and Chris Cooper*

15. The Service-Dominant Logic Approach to Tourism
    Marketing Strategy                                              231
    *Sun-Young Park and Stephen L. Vargo*

16. Marketing the Rural Tourism Experience                         247
    *Elisabeth Kastenholz, Maria João Aibéo Carneiro and*
    *Carlos Peixeira Marques*

17. Destination Cross River                                        265
    *Alvin Rosenbaum*

**PART V – E-MARKETING**

18. An Overview of the Main Innovations in E-Marketing            289
    *Maria Elena Aramendia-Muneta*

19. Information and Communication Technologies in Tourism: A
    Comparison for Travel Agents, Hotels and Restaurants          299
    *Irene Gil-Saura, María-Eugenia Ruiz-Molina and*
    *Gloria Berenguer-Contrí*

20. Exploring the Potential of Travel Reviews: Implications
    for Strategy Formulation and Implementation                   321
    *Antonella Capriello*

21. Mobile Marketing in Tourism Services                          339
    *Shintaro Okazaki, Sara Campo and Luisa Andreu*

EPILOGUE                                                          359

Appendix                                                          363

Index                                                            369

# About the Editors

**Rodoula H. Tsiotsou** (PhD) obtained her PhD from Florida State University and is currently assistant professor of marketing at the Department of Marketing & Operations Management, University of Macedonia, Greece. She has published in a variety of international scientific journals such as *Journal of Business Research*, *The Service Industries Journal*, *Journal of Business & Industrial Marketing*, *Journal of Marketing Management*, *Journal of Services marketing*, *Journal of Marketing Communications*, *International Journal of Retail and Distribution Management*, *Applied Financial Economics Letters*, *Journal of Vacation Marketing*, *Journal of Hospitality and Leisure Marketing*, *Journal of Travel & Tourism Marketing* and *Journal of Sport Management*. She serves at the editorial boards of *The Service Industries Journal* and the *International Review on Public and Nonprofit Marketing*. Her research interests include services marketing (focused on tourism and sports), brand management, relationship marketing, non-profit marketing and e-marketing.

**Ronald E. Goldsmith** (PhD) is the Richard M. Baker Professor of Marketing in the College of Business at Florida State University where he teaches consumer behavior and marketing research. Most of his research focuses on personality's role in consumer behavior and measurement issues, especially in the areas of diffusion of innovations, consumer involvement and services marketing. Since 1991 he has been a co-editor (North America) for *The Service Industries Journal*. He has published over 140 articles in such journals as *The Journal of the Academy of Marketing Science*, *The Journal of Business Research*, *The Journal of Services Marketing*, *The Journal of Consumer Behaviour*, *The Journal of Advertising*, *The European Journal of Marketing* and *The Journal of Social Psychology*. His book co-authored with Gordon Foxall entitled *Consumer Psychology for Marketing* was first published in 1994 and appears in Chinese, Polish, Russian and Korean editions.

# About the Authors

**Luisa Andreu** is associate professor of marketing at the University of Valencia (Spain) where she obtained her PhD. She also holds master of science in tourism management and marketing from the International Centre for Tourism at Bournemouth University. Her publications include papers in *Annals of Tourism Research, European Journal of Marketing, Tourism Management, Journal of Travel and Tourism, Spanish Journal of Marketing Research ESIC, Cuadernos de Economía y Dirección de Empresas, Revista Europea de Dirección y Economía de la Empresa* and *Universia Business Review*. She is an active member of European Academy of Marketing (EMAC) and Spanish Association of Scientific Experts in Tourism (AECIT). She has participated in conferences organized by the Academy of Marketing Science, European Marketing Conference (EMAC), Tourism: State of the Art II and EuroCHRIE, among others. She has been co-chair of the congress Advances in Tourism Marketing Conference in 2005, 2007 and 2011 editions. Her research interests include the analysis of consumer behaviour, tourism marketing, corporate social responsibility and online marketing.

**Maria Elena Aramendia-Muneta** is a lecturer in marketing at the Business Administration Department of the Public University of Navarra, Spain. She has been a guest lecturer in different universities of Italy, Slovenia, Latvia and Lithuania, among others. Aramendia-Muneta's primary research fields are consumer behaviour in an international environment, e-marketing and e-business.

**Helena Maria Baptista Alves** is university professor at the Department of Management and Economics, Faculty of Social and Human Sciences, University of Beira Interior (Portugal). She is also researcher at the Center for Research on Business Sciences. She obtained a PhD in management and is the author of various papers in Portuguese and international journals, books and chapters in collective works. Her research interests include services marketing and tourism.

**Suzanne C. Beckmann** is professor at the Department of Marketing, Copenhagen Business School. Her research interests focus on integrated marketing communications, brand management and consumption studies. Her publications include several books, numerous conference papers and journal articles in, for example the

*International Journal of Research in Marketing*, *Journal of Marketing Management*, *Journal of Business Research* and *Psychology and Marketing*.

**Gloria Berenguer Contrí** is professor in the Marketing Department of University of Valencia. She has been a visitant researcher at different universities and her studies are published in several international journals. Her current research interests are consumer behaviour and services marketing.

**Ilenia Bregoli** was awarded her PhD in management (research field Marketing) at the Catholic University of Milan (Italy) in March 2011. She worked as teaching fellow in management at the University of Milan-Bicocca and she is now lecturer in marketing at the University of Northampton (UK). Her research interests are related to destination management and destination branding from a supply side perspective.

**Maria João Aibéo Carneiro** is assistant professor of tourism at the University of Aveiro (Portugal), where she is also coordinator of the degree programme in tourism and researcher at the GOVCOPP Research Unit. She holds a degree in tourism management and planning, an MBA and a PhD in tourism from the University of Aveiro. Her research interests include consumer behaviour in tourism and tourism destination marketing.

**Sara Campo** received her PhD in marketing from the Universidad Autónoma de Madrid (Spain) where she works as associate professor of marketing in the College of Economics and Business Administration. Her research interests lie in tourism marketing, service marketing, retailing and pricing, and new technology adoption. She has participated in a number of national congresses, such as ATMC, EuroChrie Congress, ESADE and ESCP-EAP, among others. Her work appears in leading tourism and marketing journals, including *Progress in Tourism Marketing*, *International Journal of Service Industry Management*, *Tourism Management*, *Tourism Economics*, *Journal of Business-to-Business Marketing*, *Journal of Travel Research*, *International Journal of Tourism Research*, *Tourism Analysis* and *International Journal of Culture, Tourism and Hospitality Research*, among others.

**Ana María Campón Cerro** is university professor at the Department of Business Management and Sociology, Faculty of Business Administration and Tourism, University of Extremadura (Spain). She graduated in market research and techniques and is the author of various papers in Spanish and international journals, books and chapters in collective works. Her research interests include marketing and tourism management.

**Antonella Capriello**, PhD, is assistant professor in marketing at the Università del Piemonte Orientale in Novara (Italy). She has received awards from the Italian Academy of Management in 2007, from the Piedmont Region in 2007 and 2009, and from the *International Journal of Contemporary Hospitality Management* in Alanya, Turkey in 2008. She has over 40 publications including articles in *Tourism Management*, *Journal of Business Research*, *Journal of Hospitality Marketing and Management* and *Tourism Review*.

**Tatiana Chekalina** in 2007 defended the PhD thesis in the field of human geography at Immanuel Kant State University of Russia in Kaliningrad. In November 2008, Tatiana started the doctoral studies in business administration and tourism science at the European Tourism Research Institute (ETOUR), Mid-Sweden University. Tatiana's main focus is destination marketing and branding.

**Deepak Chhabra** teaches at Arizona State University, USA. She also holds the position of a 'senior sustainability scientist' in the Global Institute of Sustainability at Arizona State University. Her research interests include sustainable marketing and ethical consumption of tourism.

**Chris Cooper**, pro vice-chancellor and dean of School of Business, Oxford Brookes University. Chris is co-editor of 'Current Issues in Tourism' and the author of numerous leading tourism texts and research volumes.

**Danielle Fernandes Costa Machado** (MSc) obtained a bachelor's degree in tourism from Universidade Federal de Minas Gerais (UFMG) in 2006 and obtained her master degree in administration also from UFMG in 2010. She is currently doing her PhD studies at Universidade Federal do Rio Grande do Sul (UFRGS). She is also an assistant professor of the tourism course at Universidade Federal de Juiz de Fora (UFJF).

**Mirna de Lima Medeiros** (MSc) obtained a bachelor's degree in tourism from Universidade Federal de Minas Gerais (UFMG) in 2008. In early 2011, she obtained her Master of Science in administration from Universidade de São Paulo (USP). She is currently doing her PhD studies at USP and participating in a study group on Contemporary Management and Public Politics (GPublic/USP).

**Giacomo Del Chiappa** is assistant professor in marketing at the Faculty of Economics, University of Sassari (Italy). He lectures in the areas of 'Tourism Marketing and Management' and 'Destination Management' and his research topics relate to destination management and branding and consumer behaviour in tourism. He is on the editorial board of *Tourism Analysis*.

**Peiyi Ding**, senior research officer, University of Queensland. Peiyi received his BSc degree from Xinjiang University and MSc degree from the Chinese Academy of Sciences in China, and his PhD from the University of New England in Australia. He was a visiting research fellow at the Department of Geography and Environmental Sciences at the University of Melbourne, and a postdoctoral research fellow at The

University of Queensland. His main research area is environmental management for tourism development with a particular focus on environmental auditing for tourism organizations.

**Sara Dolnicar** is a professor of marketing at the University of Wollongong and director of the Institute of Innovation in Business and Social Research. Sara's key research interests are measurement and segmentation methodology in the social sciences in general and tourism in specific.

**Matthias Fuchs** (PhD), since 2008 he is full professor at the European Tourism Research Institute (ETOUR), Mid-Sweden University. Previously he was the director of the e-Tourism Competence Centre Austria (ECCA) where he also supervised four large-scale industry projects in the area of mobile information systems, online auctions, technology impact and diffusion as well as e-learning. His research interests are on e-commerce and e-tourism, tourism management and destination economics.

**Martina G. Gallarza** (PhD) lectures in the Marketing Department of University of Valencia (Spain). She has formerly taught at Catholic University of Valencia, where she has been dean of the Faculty of Business. Her research interests include consumer behaviour and services marketing. She has published in *Annals of Tourism*, *Tourism Management*, *International Journal of Culture, Tourism and Hospitality Research*, *Journal of Consumer Behaviour* and *Tourism Review*.

**Lihua Gao** is a doctoral candidate at the University of Queensland studying the design of experiences in China.

**Irene Gil-Saura** is professor of marketing at the University of Valencia. Her main teaching and research interests include business-to-business marketing, services marketing, consumer behaviour and retailing. She has published articles in several journals as the *Annals of Tourism Research*, *Industrial Marketing Management*, *Tourism Management*, *Industrial Management & Data Systems*, *The Service Industries Journal*, among others.

**José Manuel Hernández Mogollón** is university professor at the Department of Business Management and Sociology, Faculty of Business Administration and Tourism, University of Extremadura (Spain). He holds a PhD in economics and business management and is the author of various papers in Spanish and international journals, books and chapters in collective works. His research interests focus on marketing and tourism management.

**Morris B. Holbrook** is the recently retired W. T. Dillard Professor Emeritus of Marketing in the Graduate School of Business at Columbia University in New York City. His research and teaching have covered a wide variety of topics in marketing and consumer behaviour with a special focus on issues related to communication in general and to aesthetics, semiotics, hermeneutics, art, entertainment, music, jazz, motion pictures, nostalgia and stereography in particular.

**Elisabeth Kastenholz** is assistant professor at the University of Aveiro, researcher at the GOVCOPP Research Unit and currently coordinates the doctoral programme of marketing and strategy at the University of Aveiro (in collaboration with University of Minho and Beira Interior). Holding an MBA and a PhD in tourism, her research focuses on rural tourism, consumer behaviour, destination marketing and sustainable destination development.

**Maria Lexhagen** is a lecturer at European Tourism Research Institute, Mid Sweden University, and holds a PhD in business administration and tourism with a special interest in marketing and new technology. Her research covers both business practice and consumer behaviour. She has published in both tourism journals and technology focused journals. Her current research deals with pop culture tourism, social media use in tourism, destination branding and destination information systems.

**João Luiz Passador** (PhD) obtained a bachelor's degree in administration from Fundação Getúlio Vargas (FGV) in 1988 and in law from Universidade de São Paulo (USP) in 1992. He obtained his master degree in public administration in 1993 and a PhD degree in administration in 2000 from FGV. He is currently a full professor at Universidade de São Paulo (USP) and coordinates a study group on Contemporary Management and Public Politics (GPublic/USP).

**Carlos Peixeira Marques**, MBA and PhD in management, is assistant professor at the University of Tras-os-Montes and Alto Douro and principal researcher at the Centre for Transdisciplinary Development Studies, Vila Real, Portugal. His recent research focuses on consumer behaviour, quantitative methods of market research and destination marketing.

**Andreas Mild** received his PhD from Vienna University of Economics and Business (WU Wien), where he is now an associate professor at the Department of Information Systems and Operations. His research interests include the application of pricing models and the analysis of consumer preferences in various industries. He is also interested in methods for the efficient aggregation of distributed information. His previous research appeared in journals such as *Management Science, Marketing Science, MIS Quarterly* or the *Journal of Retailing and Consumer Services*. He has been guest professor and lecturer in Frankfurt, Germany, Sydney, Australia, Bangkok, Thailand and Istanbul, Turkey.

**Cayetano Medina Molina** received his PhD degree in business administration from UNED in 2006. This work was honoured with the University's award for the best doctoral research during the years 2006/2007. He has written many papers and contributions in the field of strategic marketing, relationship management, distribution and tourism.

**Manuel Rey Moreno** received his PhD degree in business administration and economy from the University of Seville (Spain). He was visiting professor in the University of Pinar del Río, Cartagena de Indias, and in York St. John University. As a practitioner, he was in charge of the Business Studies Centre, director of the 'Tourism in Seville' Consortium and Board of Urbanism at Seville City Hall.

**Ramón Rufín Moreno**, PhD, is full professor and head of the Marketing Research Group at the Spanish University of Distance Teaching (UNED), where he has tutored many doctoral theses. He also serviced as an adviser for the Spanish Ministry of Commerce and Tourism in developing the Strategic Tourism Program (1995–1996). He has written several books and many articles in the field of tourism.

**Shintaro Okazaki** received his PhD in marketing from the Universidad Autónoma de Madrid (Spain) where he works as associate professor of marketing in the College of Economics and Business Administration. His research focuses on mobile commerce, consumer generated media and cross-cultural issues in marketing communications. His work has appeared in the *Journal of Advertising, Journal of Advertising Research, International Journal of Advertising, Journal of International Marketing, Journal of Business Research, Journal of World Business, Psychology & Marketing, European Journal of Marketing, International Marketing Review, Tourism Management, Information & Management, The Service Industries Journal, Journal of Computer-Mediated Communication, Computers in Human Behavior* and *Internet Research*, among others. He serves on the editorial boards of the *Journal of Advertising* (associate editor), *Journal of Advertising Research, International Journal of Advertising, Journal of Public Policy & Marketing, Electronic Markets* (Associate editor), *International Marketing Review, Internet Research* and *Journal of Marketing Communications* (former deputy editor), among others. He is also on the executive board of the European Advertising Academy (EAA). He is a recipient of the 2008 Best Academic of the Year from the Mobile Marketing Association.

**Sun-Young Park** is an assistant professor at the School of Management of University of San Francisco. She studies and teaches courses on sustainable business models, corporate social responsibility, strategic service management and marketing. She taught at University of Hawaii at Manoa upon completing her PhD at Texas A&M University. While pursuing her PhD, she produced reports that evaluated the Texas State agencies' marketing programmes including tourism marketing. She was a management consultant at a multinational firm, working with various companies and national government agencies in Asia Pacific and the US on business strategy, knowledge management, and national/regional tourism destination marketing.

**Alvin Rosenbaum** is an international tourism consultant and regional planner. He is a senior research scholar, International Institute of Tourism Studies at the George Washington University. Rosenbaum was team leader for CDC Development Solutions for the subject of this case study, recognized in 2010 by the Africa Travel Association for Outstanding Achievement in Development of Responsible Tourism in Africa.

**María-Eugenia Ruiz-Molina** is associate professor in the Marketing Department of University of Valencia, where she earned her PhD in business administration and management. Her studies are published in several international journals. Her current research interests are consumer behaviour, retailing and ICT business solutions.

**José Luis Roldán Salgueiro** is associate professor of management at the Faculty of Economics and Business Administration, University of Seville. His recent contributions have been published in *International Small Business Journal, Computers in Human Behavior, Handbook of Partial Least Squares, Industrial Marketing Management, International Journal of Technology Management* and *Internet Research.*

**Noel Scott**, associate professor, University of Queensland. Noel is the author of several tourism books, and has published over 130 academic papers. He has extensive experience as a senior tourism manager and researcher and over 25 years in industry research positions. He holds a doctorate in tourism management and master's degrees in marketing and business administration and is an associate professor at The University of Queensland, Brisbane, Australia. His research interests involve aspects of destination management and marketing.

**D. Sudharshan,** B.Tech from IIT, Madras and a PhD from the University of Pittsburgh, served as dean of the Gatton College 2003–2011. From 1982 to 2003, he was on the Faculty of the College of Business Administration at the University of Illinois at Urbana-Champaign. He has published extensively in major international journals such as: *Marketing Science, Management Science, Journal of Marketing, Journal of Marketing Research, Journal of Service Research, Strategic Management Journal, Managerial and Decision Economics, European Journal of Operational Research, Journal of Innovation and Management* etc., and authored 2 books, including the first eBook in marketing: *Market Thinker*, and has edited several books.

**Stephen L. Vargo** is a Shidler distinguished professor and professor of marketing at the University of Hawaii at Manoa. His primary research areas are marketing theory and thought and consumers' evaluative reference scales. He has had articles published in the *Journal of Marketing*, the *Journal of the Academy of Marketing Science*, the *Journal of Service Research* and other major marketing journals and serves on six editorial review boards, including the *Journal of Marketing, Journal of the Academy of Marketing Science* and the *Journal of Service Research*. Professor Vargo has been awarded the *Harold H. Maynard Award* by the American Marketing

Association for 'significant contribution to marketing theory and thought' and the *Sheth Foundation Award* for 'long term contributions to the field of marketing'.

**Sebastian Zenker** is postdoctoral researcher at the Erasmus School of Economics, Erasmus University Rotterdam. His research interests are mainly place brand management, the measurement of place brands and changes in place brand perceptions. His work has been presented at various international conferences, as well as in book chapters and international journals, for example the *Journal of Business Ethics*, the *Journal of Place Branding and Public Diplomacy* and the *Journal of Place Management and Development*.

# List of Contributors

| | |
|---|---|
| *Luisa Andreu* | University of Valencia, Spain |
| *Maria Elena Aramendia-Muneta* | Departamento de Gestión de Empresas, Universidad Pública de Navarra, Pamplona, Spain |
| *Helena Maria Baptista Alves* | Department of Business and Economics, University of Beira Interior, Portugal |
| *Suzanne C. Beckmann* | Department of Marketing, Copenhagen Business School, Copenhagen, Denmark |
| *Gloria Berenguer-Contrí* | Marketing Department, University of Valencia, Valencia, Spain |
| *Ilenia Bregoli* | Northampton Business School, University of Northampton, Northampton, UK |
| *Maria João Aibéo Carneiro* | Department of Economics, Management and Industrial Engineering (DEGEI), University of Aveiro, Aveiro, Portugal |
| *Sara Campo* | Universidad Autónoma de Madrid, Spain |
| *Ana María Campón Cerro* | Department of Business Management and Sociology, University of Extremadura, Spain |
| *Antonella Capriello* | Dipartimento di Studi per l'Economia e l'Impresa, Università del Piemonte Orientale, Novara, Italy |
| *Tatiana Chekalina* | The European Tourism Research Institute (ETOUR), Mid-Sweden University, Sweden |
| *Deepak Chhabra* | School of Community Resources & Development, Arizona State University, Phoenix, AZ, USA |
| *Chris Cooper* | School of Business, Oxford Brookes University, Oxford, UK |
| *Danielle Fernandes Costa Machado* | Escola de Administração da Universidade Federal do Rio Grande do Sul, Porto Alegre – RS and Escola de Turismo da Universidade Federal de Juiz de Fora, Juiz de Fora – MG, Brazil |

Mirna de Lima
Medeiros

Faculdade de Economia, Administração e
Contabilidade de Ribeirão Preto, Universidade de
São Paulo (USP), Ribeirão Preto - SP, Brazil

Giacomo Del Chiappa

Faculty of Economics, University of Sassari, Italy

Peiyi Ding

School of Tourism, The University of Queensland,
St Lucia, Queensland, Australia

Sara Dolnicar

Institute for Innovation in Business and Social
Research, University of Wollongong, Wollongong,
New South Wales, Australia

Matthias Fuchs

The European Tourism Research Institute
(ETOUR), Mid-Sweden University, Sweden

Martina G. Gallarza

Faculty of Economics, University of Valencia,
Valencia, Spain

Lihua Gao

School of Tourism, The University of Queensland,
St Lucia, Queensland, Australia

Irene Gil-Saura

Faculty of Economics, University of Valencia,
Valencia, Spain

Ronald E. Goldsmith

Department of Marketing, Florida State University,
Tallahassee, FL, USA

José Manuel
Hernández Mogollón

Department of Business Management and Sociology,
University of Extremadura, Spain

Morris B. Holbrook

Graduate School of Business, Columbia University,
New York, NY, USA

Elisabeth Kastenholz

Department of Economics, Management and
Industrial Engineering (DEGEI), University of
Aveiro, Aveiro, Portugal

Maria Lexhagen

The European Tourism Research Institute
(ETOUR), Mid-Sweden University, Sweden

João Luiz Passador

Faculdade de Economia, Administração e
Contabilidade de Ribeirão Preto, Universidade de
São Paulo (USP), Ribeirão Preto - SP, Brazil

Carlos Peixeira
Marques

Department of Economics, Management and
Sociology, University of Trás-os-Montes and Alto
Douro, Vila Real, Portugal

Andreas Mild

Department of Information Systems and Operations,
Vienna University of Economics and Business,
Austria

| | |
|---|---|
| *Cayetano Medina Molina* | Centro Andaluz de Estudios Empresariales, Spain |
| *Manuel Rey Moreno* | University of Seville, Spain |
| *Ramón Rufín Moreno* | Universidad Nacional de Educación a Distancia, Spain |
| *Shintaro Okazaki* | Universidad Autónoma de Madrid, Spain |
| *Sun-Young Park* | School of Management, University of San Francisco, CA, USA |
| *Alvin Rosenbaum* | International Institute of Tourism Studies, School of Business, The George Washington University, Washington, DC, USA |
| *María-Eugenia Ruiz-Molina* | Marketing Department, University of Valencia, Valencia, Spain |
| *José Luis Roldán Salgueiro* | Faculty of Economics and Business Sciences, University of Seville, Spain |
| *Noel Scott* | School of Tourism, The University of Queensland, St Lucia, Queensland, Australia |
| *D. Sudharshan* | Gatton College of Business and Economics, University of Kentucky, Lexington, KY, USA |
| *Rodoula H. Tsiotsou* | Department of Marketing & Operations Management, University of Macedonia, Greece |
| *Stephen L. Vargo* | Shidler College of Business, University of Hawaii, Manoa, Honolulu, HI, USA |
| *Sebastian Zenker* | Erasmus School of Economics, Erasmus University Rotterdam, Rotterdam, the Netherlands |

# Preface

Strategic marketing in tourism companies around the world is confronted with unparalleled challenges and exciting opportunities in the twenty-first century. Fierce global competition, turbulent markets, recession, wars, diseases, technological advances and demanding customers constitute strategic marketing an inevitable responsibility and direction of every tourism firm. Providing superior customer value, developing unique capabilities, responding to current economic, social and environmental challenges and differentiating from competitors are only a few initiatives that tourism firms need to take in order to gain and sustain a competitive advantage.

*Strategic Marketing in Tourism Services* aims to provide some strategic directions in how tourism firms could respond to contemporary challenges and compete effectively in today's turbulent global business environment. The book provides a comprehensive coverage of the most emerging marketing strategies employed by tourism firms which have not been presented all together before in a tourism marketing book. The book demonstrates not only the development of tourism marketing, but more importantly illustrates current strategic marketing practices in the tourism sector. The book focuses on marketing strategies that have been or could be implemented in tourism services. *Strategic Marketing in Tourism Services* presents the application of specific marketing strategies such as Target Marketing, Branding, Relationship Marketing, Experiential Marketing and E-Marketing in tourism. Furthermore, it presents the strategic responses of each of the tourism sub-sectors — hospitality, air transport, tour operation, travel agencies and tourism destinations — from various countries all over the world.

*Strategic Marketing in Tourism Services* has four main objectives:

(1) To introduce tourism marketing scholars, students and practitioners, and related fields to pertinent strategic approaches in tourism marketing and to illustrate their applications and benefits (and limitations) with the help of a combination of conceptual and empirical papers as well as case studies related to all tourism sub-sectors.
(2) To advance our understanding of the causal mechanisms underlying the formation and implementation of contemporary marketing strategies in tourism services.
(3) To encourage further research that draws on the same strategies, modifies them or introduces superior strategies.
(4) To respond to current calls for more academic work on strategic marketing issues in tourism.

*Strategic Marketing in Tourism Services* is a collection of papers on various marketing strategies in tourism written by well-known academics from all over the world. The book is a compilation of various points of view expressed by the various authors contributing to the book representing several different places all over the world. Contributors of the book come from Australia, the United Kingdom, the United States, Brazil, Italy, Germany, Greece, Sweden, Spain and Portugal. The book combines conceptual and empirical papers in order to stimulate its readers' thinking on emerging strategic issues in tourism marketing and provide the grounds for future developments, theoretical and practical, in the field.

In addition to an Introduction and an Epilogue section, the book consists of five parts: Part I: Target Marketing, Part II: Branding, Part III: Relationship Marketing, Part IV: Experiential Marketing and Part V: E-Marketing. The first chapter of each Part is an introductory chapter while the remaining chapters are conceptual or empirical papers. The introductory chapters present an overview of each marketing strategy (theoretical framework and research findings related to tourism) in order to familiarize the reader and facilitate reading of the papers included in every part.

The *Introduction* chapter defines the role of strategic marketing in tourism and briefly describes the unique features of the tourism industry that need to be taken into account before deciding on a marketing strategy and planning the strategic marketing process, from analysis and strategy formulation to implementation techniques.

*Part I: Target Marketing* incorporates an introductory chapter and two main chapters. The introductory chapter describes the steps that need to be taken for implementing this strategy, named segmentation, targeting and positioning. The second chapter proposes an analytic technique that integrates market segmentation, positioning and competition strategy. The third chapter discusses the influence of social interactions in the formation of tourism segments and proposes a new technique that could be implemented in identifying these segments.

*Part II: Branding* includes an introductory chapter and four main chapters. The introductory chapter proposes a model of brand development that combines supply-side and demand-side perspectives, and analyses the main conditions for successful destination branding. The second chapter shows the needs for an integrated approach to communicate with both internal and external target groups when branding a city. The third chapter examines online destination images portrayed by different agents of tourism in India to determine if representative dissonance exists in the self-representations at the nationwide and localized levels. The fourth chapter proposes a holistic approach to measure destination brand equity. The fifth chapter presents an empirical study of the image of a tourism destination from the perception of all the relevant stakeholders.

*Part III: Relationship Marketing* consists of an introductory chapter and three main chapters. The introductory chapter presents the main tenets and goals of relationship marketing while it presents the application of this strategy in tourism. The second chapter analyses the role and meaning of customer value in tourism-service settings, with a focus on providing positive recommendation and/or repeat behaviour. The third chapter examines the factors that generate loyalty to tourism destinations while the fourth chapter examines the role of familiarity and adjusted expectation in developing loyalty to a destination.

*Part IV: Experiential Marketing* includes an introductory chapter and four main chapters. The introductory chapter discusses experiential marketing and the dimensions of a customer experience as applied in tourism. The second chapter seeks to provide an understanding of the theoretical linkage between experience attributes and customer value in tourism. The third chapter proposes the application of service-dominant (S-D) logic in tourism by first presenting the foundational premises of S-D logic and then showing how these can be applied to tourism. The fourth chapter discusses the total experience, with reference to its main constituents, from the perspective of the tourist, the service providers, the host communities and the rural destination's core resources. The last chapter is a case study that examines the marketability of experiential products based on authenticity and visitor readiness to attract travellers to a destination.

*Part V: E-Marketing* incorporates an introductory and three main chapters. The introductory chapter summarizes through the use of concept maps (CM), the main innovations in online marketing that have an influence on the tourism industry. The second chapter examines the application of information technologies in various tourism sub-sectors. The third chapter analyses the potential of travel reviews to identify e-marketing strategies for tourism and travel firms. The last chapter discusses the application of mobile marketing in tourism and proposes a conceptual framework of mobile internet based on two primary factors, the stage of tourism information search (pre-travel, on site, and post-travel) and the degree of ubiquity.

The *Epilogue* chapter closes the book by summing up the most important issues in strategic marketing in tourism services and providing directions for future developments.

*Strategic Marketing in Tourism Services* is intended for use in undergraduate tourism marketing strategy courses and master's courses of tourism marketing and advanced strategy in tourism services. Tourism marketing academics and practitioners as well as students have little inkling of the many and different strategies that can be applied to tourism firms. The book is a comprehensive work in strategic tourism marketing by incorporating all the vital marketing strategies in tourism services. It provides useful theoretical overviews, tools, examples and empirical results of contemporary marketing strategies such as experiential marketing, relationship marketing, e-marketing, branding and target marketing. *Strategic Marketing in Tourism Services* is an essential reading for students in tourism and marketing as well as for various tourism services managers.

# Introduction to Strategic Marketing in Tourism

Tourism constitutes one of the largest industries worldwide, contributing 6 trillion dollars annually to the global economy (or 9% of global gross domestic product) with nearly 260 million jobs worldwide — either directly in the industry or in related sectors. According to the March 2011 report of the World Travel & Tourism Council, global travel and tourism are expected to grow by an average 4% per year between 2011 and 2021. By 2021, tourism is predicted to account for 69 million more jobs — almost 80% of which will be in Asia, Latin America, the Middle East and Africa (World Travel & Tourism Council, 2011). Moreover, the United Nations World Tourism Organization (2011) expects that international tourist arrivals will reach 1.8 billion by 2030. International tourism will continue to grow in the period 2010–2030, but at a more moderate pace than the past decades, with the number of international tourist arrivals worldwide increasing by an average 3.3% a year.

Tourism services all over the world are currently facing new challenges and rapid changes owing to recession, market globalization, intensified competition and the dynamic evolution of new technologies. International events such as terrorist attacks, wars and severe diseases (i.e. SARS, influenza A-H1N1) have resulted in diminishing tourist demand and consequently decreased their business. Moreover, it is expected that tourism will be one of the industries that will be mostly affected by the current recession. Increasingly demanding tourism consumers, rapid technological advances, the increased emphasis on sustainability issues along with economic, social, political and environmental developments have altered the way businesses are executed in the tourism sector (Tsiotsou & Ratten, 2010). Tourism services are increasingly integrating marketing principles in their management and are becoming more market oriented (Tsiotsou, 2010; Tsiotsou & Vlachopoulou, 2011). This book is premised on the assumption that the most effective response tourism firms can make to these challenges is through integrated marketing strategies. However, to do this successfully, tourism managers must recognize and adapt to the unique features of the tourism industry.

## The Unique Features of the Tourism Industry and Tourism Services

Tourism products are considered services (Fyall & Garrod, 2005) and like all services are characterized by intangibility, heterogeneity, inseparability and perishability (Zeithaml, 1981). These characteristics imply the increased involvement of consumers in the service process of production and consumption. In addition to the features related to their service nature, the 'particularities' of the tourism industry named seasonality, globalization, low levels of loyalty, complexity (including multiple sub-sectors such as food and beverage, accommodation, transportation, recreation and travel) and cross and income elasticity demand need to be taken into account before making any marketing decision.

*Seasonality* in tourism has been defined as: 'a temporal imbalance in the phenomenon of tourism, which may be expressed in terms of dimensions of such elements as number of visitors, expenditure of visitors, traffic on highways and other forms of transportation, employment and admission to attractions' (Butler, 2001, p. 5). Seasonality is considered a severe problem in tourism because it leads tourism firms to hire part time personnel, therefore limiting their ability to develop distinct capabilities. Moreover, the constant need to hire new seasonal employees leads to increased training and other costs associated with employee turnover. Thus, seasonality has been linked to low returns on investment, underutilization of facilities and limited access to capital (Butler, 2001). In some cases, 80% of tourism income occurs within a two-month period. Therefore, it has been suggested that destinations with extreme seasonality should develop policies to overcome extremes of seasonality while tourism enterprises should adopt marketing strategies to cope with the problem (Lundtorp, 2001).

*Globalization* in tourism means that tourism businesses have the ability to operate and market themselves not only locally but globally as well, while many of them have opted for a competitive strategy of internationalization. Nowadays, tourism firms consider the world as their operating environment and establish both global strategies and global market presence (Knowles, Diamantis, & El-Mourhabi, 2001, p. 177). In tourism, globalization affects both the supply and the demand side in various ways. In the supply of tourism services, the most common trends refer to the development of large worldwide suppliers (e.g. transnational corporations such as Disney and Club Méditerranée) and intermediaries (e.g. TUI), which lead to oligopolies. Another development refers to the creation of virtual travel agencies, which jeopardize (owing to disintermediation) the traditional intermediate function of offline travel agencies (Tsiotsou & Ratten, 2010). On the demand side, globalization has been linked to decreasing costs of air travel, access to new and low-priced destinations, as well as relatively low social standards.

Moreover, tourism is characterized by *low levels of customer loyalty*. If developing loyalty in services is difficult (Tsiotsou & Wirtz, 2012), then achieving loyalty in tourism is a feat. Because consumers search for new experiences by visiting various places and destinations all over the world, it is very difficult to develop loyalty, for example, in destinations or accommodation services. Therefore, the task here is to develop loyalty to global service brands so customers trust and purchase services from the same service providers (usually transnational corporations) no matter which destination they travel to.

Tourism is a *complex industry* because it is a compilation of various services such as accommodation, transportation, dining, recreation and travel. All these services comprise the tourism experience. Often these services are not offered by one provider who has control over them, but by different providers who might not communicate or collaborate with the remaining providers. Thus, a delayed flight might stigmatize the whole customer tourism experience, resulting in dissatisfaction not only with the particular service provider but with all the others as well (e.g. hotel and restaurants).

Finally, tourism services are characterized of a *cross elasticity demand* meaning that a trip can be easily replaced by the purchase of another product (e.g. buying a car might lead consumers postpone their travelling for one or more year until they entirely pay for their car) and *income elasticity demand,* where a reduction in customers' income could lead to significant decrease in demand for tourism services.

## The Necessity of Employing Strategic Marketing in Tourism

The long-term existence and effectiveness of tourism services in such a fierce competitive and financially difficult global environment depends not only on their ability to satisfy customers' needs and desires but to strategically respond to current challenges. Therefore, strategic marketing becomes a necessary practice for contemporary tourism services firms.

In this sense, marketing strategies have been adopted by tourism firms in order to respond to current challenges, to achieve competitive advantage and to increase their effectiveness. Strategic marketing has been defined as 'an organization's integrated pattern of decisions that specify its crucial choices concerning products, markets, marketing activities and marketing resources in the creation, communication and/or delivery of products that offer value to customers in exchanges with the organization and thereby enables the organization to achieve specific objectives' (Varadarajan, 2010, p. 128). A marketing strategy refers to a set of specific ideas and actions that outline and guide a firm's decisions on managing in the most effective manner its marketing mix and sustain competitive advantage. Strategic marketing decisions encompass resource commitments and tradeoffs, complement other strategic decisions and are made at the higher management level (Varadarajan, 2010).

Owing to its benefits and advantages, strategic marketing in the tourism industry is increasingly becoming important, from both theoretical (academic) and applied (practitioner) perspectives. However, a lack of work on strategic marketing issues in tourism has been identified in the literature (Bagnall, 1996; Riege & Perry, 2000; Tsiotsou & Ratten, 2010). The key reason for this is that, until recently, marketing for tourism services has focused not on the consumer but on the destination or outlet, with marketing strategies being related to the products offered (Williams, 2006). As marketing within the sector has advanced, however, the attention to the offer has diminished owing to the heterogeneity of consumers' needs, desires, preferences, motivations and behaviours and to the changing global economic and social environments. Nowadays, consumers are more knowledgeable and perceptive in their judgements, demanding superior value from tourism services. In addition, technological advances (e.g. Web 2.0 and Web 3.0) have transformed tourism consumers to active producers of tourism services (prosumers) (Tsiotsou & Ratten, 2010) and co-creators of value (Vargo & Lusch, 2004). Thus, tourism firms and destinations understand that they need to modify their strategies to respond effectively to these changes (Tsiotsou & Ratten, 2010).

## Applying Strategic Marketing in Tourism

Successful marketing strategies require the recognition and understanding of global business challenges, the development and leverage of distinctive capabilities, the provision of superior customer value and immediate response to competitors' actions. A marketing strategy should make the most of a company's strengths (capabilities) and matches them to the customer value requirements. Furthermore, a marketing strategy should be flexible in order to respond to changes in consumers' needs, desires and preferences and be able to identify new market segments and target them successfully. Then, a marketing strategy can lead to superior business performance and sustainable competitive advantage.

Tourism firms need to be cognizant of the factors influencing their marketing strategy such as resources and competencies they possess, or should acquire the opening and closing of strategic windows, the nature of competition in the tourism industry and the stage of the marketing or industry life cycle. A competitive marketing strategy also requires decisions on the product market in which a tourism firm competes, the level of investment needed, the functional area strategies (product line, positioning, pricing, distribution, information technology, segmentation and global strategy), the strategic assets, competencies and synergies matched with the functional area strategies and the allocation of resources among the business units (Proctor, 2008). A competitive strategy refers to 'developing a broad formula for how a business is going to compete, what its goals should be and what policies will be needed to attain these goals. Competitive strategy is a combination of the ends or goals for which the firm is striving and the means or policies by which it is seeking to get there' (Proctor, 2008, p. 13).

A general process for implementing strategic marketing in a tourism firm as well as in every other type of a service company is presented in Figure 1. The process consists of three major phases: Planning, Implementation and Control. Each phase includes several activities and steps that need to be taken.

During the *Planning Phase*, tourism firms need to conduct a number of analyses such as industry, market, competition, business and customer analyses in order to understand the economic and market environment in which they operate, evaluate their capabilities, identify opportunities and set goals that are realistic and achievable. By analysing the external environment (threats and opportunities), and the internal environment (weaknesses and strengths), tourism firms can use this information to think about the focus strategy and other supporting or complementary strategies

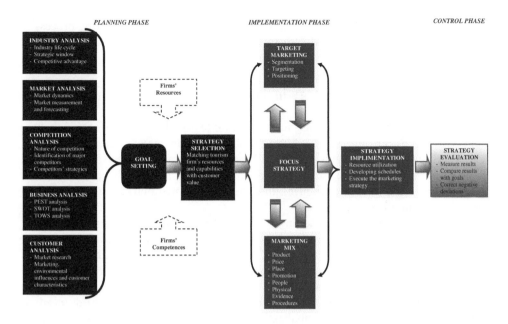

Figure 1: The strategic marketing process in tourism services.

they could adopt. Moreover, when selecting the appropriate marketing strategy, tourism firms need to consider their available resources and capabilities as well as the new assets they need to acquire and the new skills they need to develop in order to implement the strategy efficiently and effectively.

After selecting the marketing strategy, the next step is *Strategy Implementation*. The focus strategy selected should influence both the target marketing strategy (segmentation, targeting and positioning) as well as the marketing mix of the tourism firm. At the same time, both target marketing and the marketing mix can influence the implementation of the selected strategy. Target marketing refers to *strategic launch decisions* whereas marketing mix decisions refer to *tactical launch decisions* (Crawford & Di Benedetto, 2008). Target marketing and marketing mix are considered here as a baseline marketing strategy and tactic, respectively, that all tourism firms need to embrace. Due to differences in consumers' needs, preferences and desires, target marketing is considered a prerequisite strategy implemented in tandem with any other marketing strategy. The current marketing mix of the firm also should influence strategy implementation while at the same time it should be modified to serve the purposes of the selected strategy. Thus, a tourism firm should execute the selected marketing strategy by making use of all the available resources and competencies.

The process ends with the *Control Phase* where the selected strategy is evaluated. This stage involves measurement of the marketing strategy results, comparing the outcomes with the goals set and correcting negative performance deviations. This phase provides feedback to the previous phases of the strategic marketing process in order to make the necessary adjustments.

## Developing a Global Strategy in Tourism

Nowadays, markets are becoming increasingly integrated and, therefore, globalization is seen as an imperative business strategy (Ghemawat, 2010). However, globalization is not a strategy employed by only large multinational businesses but from firms of all sizes (Knight & Cavusgil, 2009). Tourism industry consists of both large and medium to small size firms and, therefore, global marketing strategies can be employed in all of them.

In addition to the focus marketing strategy selected, tourism firms need to decide about their degree of domestication or globalization (Table 1). Globalization depends on industry characteristics and on specific industry globalization drivers such as market, competition, cost and government (Lovelock & Yip, 1996). Tourism is an industry global in scope and, therefore, with potentials to employ globalization strategies. In order to develop effective global strategies, tourism firms need to systematically analyse their globalization drivers (e.g. common customer needs, global customers, global channels, use of ICTs and global economies of scale) that might influence the tourism industry and identify its distinctive features (Lovelock & Yip, 1996).

Based on the EPRG framework (ethnocentrism, polycentrism, regiocentrism and geocentrism), it is proposed that tourism firms have several options when choosing their degree of internationalization. If they decide to have a domestic focus, then all the activities described above should be concentrated in the home market. If they aim to remain with a home focus but export their services (enthnocentric), then they need to adapt an international strategy. However, if they can collaborate with one or more other service firms from other countries, then all partners need to adapt their marketing mixes to their overseas operations (polycentric). An international approach refers to a simple extension of exporting, whereby the marketing mix is simply adapted in some way to take into account differences in consumers and segments. Finally, if a tourism firm would like to operate globally, then it needs to create value by extending its services and focus on serving emerging global markets (geocentric). This strategy involves recognizing that markets around the world consist of similarities and differences and that it is possible to develop a global strategy based on similarities to obtain scale economies. Globalization is a combination of extension, adaptation and creation strategies (Wind, Douglas, & Perlmutter, 1973).

As Table 1 indicates, global marketing is an evolutionary process and adapting a global strategy should take place gradually. First, tourism firms need to enter to proximate and familiar markets while gradually expand into more distant markets as they become more experienced and knowledgeable of international markets (Contractor, 2007). Douglas and Craig (1989) have proposed three phases that a

Table 1:  From domestication to globalization of tourism firms.

| | *Stage one* Domestic | *Stage two* International | *Stage three* Multinational | *Stage four* Global |
|---|---|---|---|---|
| **Marketing strategy** | Domestic (ethnocentrism) | Extension (polycentrism) | Adaption (regiocentrism) | Extension (geocentrism) |
| **Orientation** | Home country orientation | Host country orientation | Regional orientation | Global orientation |
| **Location of operations** | Operate in home country and target mainly local customers | Operate in a country and target customers from other countries | Operate in several countries and target customers from specific regions | Target customers globally |
| **Marketing mix** | Marketing mix for the home customers Overseas operations are considered of secondary importance | Exporting activities with a small adaption of the marketing mix | Subsidiaries are established in overseas markets and develop their own marketing mixes | A global marketing mix is developed |

firm should go about in becoming global: initial market entry, local market expansion and global market rationalization. Moreover, due to market convergence and divergence, it has been proposed recently that a semi-global marketing strategy might be more appropriate because it 'involves following different directions in different parts of the world, resulting in greater autonomy at the global level' (Douglas & Craig, 2011, p. 82). Thus, the biggest challenge of tourism firms is to decide on their marketing strategies, and be able to manage the diversity of these strategies in order to be successful.

## Conclusion

It has been suggested that market-driven strategies focusing on the market and the customers that comprise the market should become the starting point of any business (Cravens & Piercy, 2009). Thus, any major strategy should be market driven and can be furthered by complementary strategies. Moreover, several of the above-mentioned unique characteristics of the tourism industry can be treated with certain marketing strategies. For example, in dealing with seasonality and globalization issues related to consumers, tourism firms could employ target marketing in identifying specific global groups of consumers who, for example, would like to take vacations in off-peak periods by paying lower prices. In order to attract more tourists, destinations could employ experiential marketing that differentiate their products/services from competing destinations and provide sustainable competitive advantage (Prahalad & Ramaswamy, 2004). Moreover, loyalty could be achieved in tourism by implementing marketing strategies such as customer relationship marketing where strong customer–tourism firm relationships can be developed (Shoemaker & Bowen, 2003; Tsiotsou & Ratten, 2010).

In sum, tourism firms need to recognize the unique characteristics of their services and the drivers of their industry, be aware of the recent social, economic and technological developments, and adopt the most appropriate marketing strategy or combination of strategies that suits better to their available resources, competencies and business goals. The purpose of this book is to help them achieve these goals.

Rodoula H. Tsiotsou

## References

Bagnall, D. (1996). Razor gang creates tourism jitters. *The Bulletin*, 25, 46.

Butler, R. W. (2001). Seasonality in tourism. Issues and implications. In T. Baum & S. Lundtorp (Eds.), *Seasonality in tourism* (pp. 5–21). Advances in Tourism Research Series. Amsterdam: Pergamon.

Contractor, F. J. (2007). Is international business good for companies? The evolutionary or multi-stage theory of internationalization vs. the transactional cost perspective. *Management International Review*, *47*(3), 453–475.

Cravens, D. W., & Piercy, N. F. (2009). *Strategic marketing* (9th ed.). New York, NY: McGraw Hill.

Crawford, M., & Di Benedetto, A. (2008). *New products management* (9th ed.). New York, NY: McGraw Hill.

Douglas, S. P., & Craig, C. S. (1989). Evolution of global marketing strategy: Scale, scope and synergy. *Columbia Journal of World Business*, *24*(3), 47–58.

Douglas, S. P., & Craig, C. S. (2011). Convergence and divergence: Developing a semiglobal marketing strategy. *Journal of International Marketing*, *19*(1), 81–101.

Fyall, A., & Garrod, B. (2005). *Tourism marketing: A collaborative approach*. Clevedon, UK: Channel View Publications.

Ghemawat, P. (2010). Finding your strategy in the new landscape. *Harvard Business Review*, *88*(3), 54–60.

Knight, G. A., & Cavusgil, S. T. (2009). *Born global firms: A new breed of international enterprise*. New York, NY: Business Expert Press.

Knowles, T., Diamantis, D., & El-Mourhabi, J. B. (2001). *The globalization of tourism and hospitality: A strategic perspective*. London: Continuum.

Lovelock, H. C., & Yip, G. S. (1996). Developing global strategies for service businesses. *California Management Review*, *38*(2), 64–86.

Lundtorp, S. (2001). Measuring tourism seasonality. In T. Baum & S. Lundtorp (Eds.), *Seasonality in tourism* (pp. 23–50). Advances in Tourism Research Series. Amsterdam: Pergamon.

Prahalad, C. K., & Ramaswamy, V. (2004). Co-creation experiences: The next practice in value creation. *Journal of Interactive Marketing*, *18*(3), 5–14.

Proctor, T. (2008). *Strategic marketing: An introduction* (2nd ed.). London: Routledge.

Riege, A. M., & Perry, C. (2000). National marketing strategies in international travel and tourism. *European Journal of Marketing*, *34*(11/12), 1290–1304.

Shoemaker, S., & Bowen, J. (2003). Loyalty: A strategic commitment. *Cornell Hotel & Restaurant Administration Quarterly*, *44*(4/5), 47–52.

Tsiotsou, R. (2010). Delineating the effect of market orientation on service performance: A component-wise approach. *The Service Industries Journal*, *30*(3), 357–403.

Tsiotsou, R., & Ratten, V. (2010). Future research directions in tourism marketing. *Marketing Intelligence & Planning*, *28*(4), 533–544.

Tsiotsou, R., & Vlachopoulou, M. (2011). Understanding the effects of marketing orientation and e-marketing on services performance. *Marketing Intelligence & Planning*, *29*(2), 141–155.

Tsiotsou, R., & Wirtz, J. (2012). Consumer behavior in a service context. In V. Wells & G. Foxall (Eds.), *Handbook of new developments in consumer behavior*. Edward Elgar Publishing.

United Nations World Tourism Organization. (2011, December 20). *Economic impact research (Tourism Towards 2030)*. Retrieved from http://www.wttc.org/research/economic-impact-research/.

Varadarajan, R. (2010). Strategic marketing and marketing strategy: Domain, definition, fundamental issues and foundational premises. *Journal of the Academy of Marketing Science*, *38*, 119–140.

Vargo, S. L., & Lusch, R. F. (2004). Evolving to a new dominant logic for marketing. *Journal of Marketing*, *68*(1), 1–17.

Williams, A. (2006). Tourism and hospitality marketing: Fantasy, feeling and fun. *International Journal of Contemporary Hospitality Management, 18*(6), 482–495.

Wind, Y., Douglas, S. P., & Perlmutter, H. V. (1973). Guidelines for developing international marketing strategies. *Journal of Marketing, 37*(April), 14–23.

World Travel & Tourism Council. (2011, December 20). *Economic impact research.* Retrieved from http://www.wttc.org/research/economic-impact-research/

Zeithaml, V. A. (1981). How consumer evaluation processes differ between goods and services. In J.A. Donnelly & W.R. George (Eds.), *Marketing of services* (pp. 186–190). Chicago, IL: American Marketing Association.

# PART I
# TARGET MARKETING

Chapter 1

# Target Marketing and Its Application to Tourism

*Rodoula H. Tsiotsou and Ronald E. Goldsmith*

The recognition that consumers have different needs, wants, resources, preferences and purchase behaviours led marketing to move away from mass marketing and embrace target marketing. Kotler and Armstrong (2008) describe target marketing as a customer-driven marketing strategy because its goal is to create value for targeted customers. Thus, target marketing provides the necessary knowledge and tools for developing 'the right relationships with the right customers' (Kotler & Armstrong, 2008, p. 184). Target marketing involves three major steps: market segmentation, targeting and positioning (Figure 1.1).

## 1.1. Market Segmentation

Market segmentation has become one of the main practices in marketing that assists in identifying distinct groups of consumers. These groups have similar needs, wants, attitudes, shopping habits, media usage, price sensitivity and other characteristics. The goal of segmentation is to identify homogeneous groups of consumers in order to satisfy their needs, desires and preferences more specifically than a mass marketing strategy could do while at the same time increasing marketing efficiency and effectiveness. The information gathered through market segmentation is crucial in the strategic marketing planning process because managers can develop products and services for specific groups of consumers, thereby gaining competitive advantage. Thus, marketing actions are more efficient and effective.

There are two types of segmentations, *a priori* and *post hoc* segmentation. *A priori* segmentation is when the variable used as a criterion to divide a market is known in advance, whereas *post hoc* segmentation is when there is no knowledge about distinct consumer groups, and a set of variables is used as the base for segmentation (Chen, 2003).

Strategic Marketing in Tourism Services
Copyright © 2012 by Emerald Group Publishing Limited
All rights of reproduction in any form reserved
ISBN: 978-1-78052-070-4

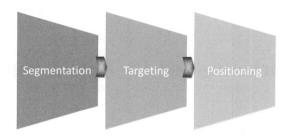

Figure 1.1: The three stages of target marketing.

Marketers have used various criteria as the bases of segmentation. The most often used criteria for segmenting consumer markets are demographic (age, gender, family status, income), geographic, behavioural (benefits, frequency of use, loyalty) and psychographic (lifestyle, personality characteristics) (Kotler, 2000). Usually, marketers use multiple segmentation criteria in order to identify more homogeneous groups of consumers. In addition to 'domestic market segmentation', international firms engage in *international market segmentation*. That is, they need to identify distinct international segments based on segmentation criteria such as geographic location (e.g. grouping countries by region), economic, political, legal and cultural factors. Travel and tourism firms engage in international market segmentation since they target not only their domestic markets but also mostly international markets. Thus, a tourism destination might target consumers from specific countries (e.g. German and/or French consumers) or regions (e.g. consumers from the Middle East). Another approach some international companies are taking is *intermarket segmentation* (Kotler & Armstrong, 2008, p. 193). In this case, international firms develop consumer segments with similar needs and buying behaviours although the tourists come from different countries. For example, in tourism, destinations focusing on developing extreme sports aim to attract tourists from all over the world who are interested in experiencing extreme activities.

## 1.2. Market Targeting

This step involves the evaluation of market segments and the selection of target market segments. When evaluating various market segments, firms should examine the market segment size (e.g. number of consumers), growth (e.g. sales and expected profitability) and structural attractiveness (e.g. competitors, suppliers, substitute products and buyers' power) of each segment while taking into account their resources and strategic goals. These evaluation criteria assist companies in deciding the number and which segments they can better and/or most profitably serve. Firms have several choices: to use undifferentiated marketing (target the whole market with one offer), differentiated marketing (target several segments with different offers for each segment), concentrated/niche marketing (target one or few small segments/niches having a large share) and micromarketing (tailoring offers to specific individual consumers or locations). In tourism, differentiated marketing is the most common market targeting approach nowadays.

## 1.3.  Positioning

The last step of target marketing involves a company's decision on its value proposition to the targeted segment(s). According to Kotler (1997), 'Positioning is the task of designing a company's offering and image so that they occupy a meaningful and distinct competitive position in the target customers' minds' (p. 295). Thus, companies need to decide how they will develop differentiated value for their target segments and how important attributes of the value proposition will be positioned in the minds of the consumers comprising those segments relative to competitors' products. Marketers need to decide positions that will provide competitive advantage, develop marketing mixes that correspond to the aimed positions and, finally, deliver and communicate the selected position to the target segments.

Positioning should take a strategic approach by 'doing things differently from competitors, in a way that delivers a unique type of value to customers' (Porter, 2001, p. 70). However, marketing strategy cannot be based only on product differentiation, which will only give the marketer a horizontal share of a broad and generalized market (Smith, 1995). Effective market segmentation constitutes a prerequisite of a successful marketing strategy as it creates depth in the market positioning (Smith, 1956). There are various positioning strategies. Positioning by attributes, by use, by user, by benefits, by product category, by price/quality and competitive positioning are the most well-known approaches (Aaker & Shansby, 1982). According to O'Sullivan (1991, p. 58), target marketing strategies reflect the degree to which the market segments the organization wishes to target are homogeneous or diverse, the firm's mission and goals, and the type of competition facing the organization and its scope.

However, as Kotler (1997) argues, regardless of the initial success of a brand positioning strategy, firms may need to reposition it later. In line with this reasoning, Trout and Rivkin (2010) propose that nowadays brands require more repositioning than positioning owing to the dynamic economic and marketing environment. Depending on the situation, repositioning might involve a number of implications such as redefining or enlarging segments or reshaping the entire marketing plan (Brassington & Pettitt, 1997).

Market segments are dynamic in nature resulting in changes in relation to their size, composition and buying behaviour. Thus, a large and profitable segment might become smaller and have reduced sales because consumers' needs and preferences change or competitors offer a more attractive value proposition.

Consumer preferences might change because of their experiences (McFadden & Train, 1996), and interaction between customers does change preferences (Janssen & Jager, 2001). Because the needs, wants and preferences of consumers change over time owing to changes in demographics and lifestyle or more attractive competitors' products, target marketing and its steps should be performed all over again after a certain time period.

## 1.4.  Tourism Research on Target Marketing

### 1.4.1.  Segmentation

Market segmentation is the most investigated area in target marketing research in tourism. Segmentation is used to identify distinct groups of tourists because, like any other market, tourists do not respond homogeneously to marketing activities. Diverse services and customers in tourism make segmentation a necessary tool for responding to changes and to competitors' pressure.

A recent review of literature on segmentation studies in tourism (Dolnicar, 2006) revealed that psychographic variables are the most often used segmentation criteria (75%) followed by behavioural (21%) and mix of both (4%). The most often used bases for segmenting tourists are demographics, socioeconomic and lifestyle variables. Specifically, the variables recommended for tourist segmentation are demographic characteristics (Chen, 2000; Sung, 2004; Tsiotsou, 2006), activities (Sung, 2004; Sung, Morrison, & O'Leary, 2000), travel expenditure (Mok & Iverson, 2000), benefits (Frochot, 2005; Frochot & Morrison, 2000) and motivation (Sellick, 2004). Table 1.1 summarizes recent studies and the segmentation criteria used in travel and tourism.

Demographic segmentation studies report inconsistent findings. For example, age and occupation differed significantly among Norwegian tourist segments (Chen, 2000); gender, age and marital status were found to be significantly different among adventure trip segments (Sung, 2004); and age differed between heavy and light spenders (Mok & Iverson, 2000). However, it has been also found that marital status, gender and occupation did not differ significantly among expenditure-based segments (Mok & Iverson, 2000), neither age, education, marital status and income among risk taking–sensation seeking tourist segments (Pizam et al., 2004). It seems that it is not clear whether demographics act as discriminating factors among segments or not. Further research is needed to identify in which occasions demographics are important in segmenting tourists. Moreover, it might be that similar demographic groups seek different benefits from their tourism experiences, so that demographics alone might be poor bases on which to segment.

Activities have been often used to segment tourists of different trip type, age and national origin. It has been suggested that tourists who prefer certain activities are likely to differ from others who participate in different types of activities (Jeffrey & Xie, 1995; Tsiotsou & Vasioti, 2006). However, activities are not well

Table 1.1: Summary of selected segmentation studies in tourism.

| City/Country | Segmentation variables | Statistical analysis | Tourism market | No. of segments | References |
|---|---|---|---|---|---|
| Various countries | Propensity to travel<br>Propensity to spend | Correlation discriminant | International tourists from various countries | 9 | Oyewole (2010) |
| N/A | Demographics<br>Moral obligation<br>Environmental attitudes<br>Environmental concerns | Stepwise forward binary regression $\chi^2$ test | N/A | 2 | Dolnicar (2010) |
| Caribbean | Benefits<br>Sightseeing<br>Sports<br>Nightlife<br>Beach<br>Park and arts | Non-hierarchical cluster<br>ANOVA | Various countries | 4 | Huang and Sarigollu (2007) |
| Greece | Ski experience<br>Overall satisfaction<br>Income<br>Frequency of visit | Classification with discriminant | Ski resorts customers | 2 | Tsiotsou (2006) |
| Greece | Satisfaction<br>Leisure activities<br>Demographics | Factor discriminant | Adventure visitors | 2 | Tsiotsou and Vasioti (2006) |

Table 1.1: *(Continued)*

| City/Country | Segmentation variables | Statistical analysis | Tourism market | No. of segments | References |
|---|---|---|---|---|---|
| Austria | Summer activities Demographics Socioeconomic Behavioural Psychographic | Bagged cluster | International visitors | 3–5 | Dolnicar and Leisch (2004) |
| South Africa | Demographics Socioeconomic Geographic | Self-organizing neural networks | Urban visitors | 3–4 | Bloom (2004) |
| Spain | Emotions Satisfaction Loyalty | Cluster (*K*-means) | Museum theme park visitors | 2 | Bigne and Andreu (2004) |
| Scotland | Benefits Socioeconomic Behavioural | Cluster (*K*-means) | Rural tourists | 4 | Frochot (2005) |
| Virginia, USA | Sentiments Demographics Trip characteristics | $\chi^2$ automatic interaction detection | Residents | 4 | Chen (2003) |
| New Zealand | Expenditures Lifestyle | Cluster | International tourists | 6 | Becken (2003) |

| Moravia, Czech Republic | Demographics<br>Destination choice | MANOVA cluster | National tourists<br>International tourists | 6 | Tureckova (2002) |
|---|---|---|---|---|---|
| Guam, Taiwan | Expenditures<br>Demographics<br>Trip purpose<br>Travel behaviour | One-way ANOVA | National tourists | 3 | Mok and Iverson (2000) |
| Balearic Islands | Sociodemographics | $\chi^2$ | International tourists | 2 | Juaneda and Sastre (1999) |
| United Kingdom | Participation patterns<br>Destination determinants<br>Sociodemographics<br>Ski level | $\chi^2$ | Ski resorts customers | 3 | Richards (1996) |

*Source:* Tsiotsou (2006).

defined in the travel and tourism literature. More often, the term refers to physical activities (or sport activities) and sometimes to cultural or other activities such as shopping.

Sung et al. (2000) identified six physical activity segments (soft nature, risk equipped, question marks, hard challenge, rugged nature and winter snow) and suggested that 'activity sets are associated with distinct groups of customers who have varying demographic and travel characteristics' (p. 17). They further argued that activities should be taken into account when studying adventure traveller segments because they are associated with consumer preferences. Adventure trip segments differ in trip-related characteristics and demographic and socioeconomic characteristics (Sung, 2004). Similarly, it has been found that high risk taking–sensation seeking tourists score significantly higher in physical activities than low risk taking–sensation seeking tourists of 11 different countries (Pizam et al., 2004). Thus, it becomes evident that physical activities can discriminate among different tourist segments.

In *post hoc* segmentation, the identification of 'physical activity' segments is very common. In most segmentation studies, at least one segment is characterized by its preference in active participation for physical activities. Preference for active participation in physical activity (sports) was the main factor along with age and social class that distinguished the 'actives' from the other segments of rural tourists in Scotland (Frochot, 2005), the 'active individual tourists' of Austria (Dolnicar & Leisch, 2004) and the 'carefree wellness tourists' in Czech Republic (Tureckova, 2002). Even in senior tourist segments physical activity as travel motive is different among segments. The 'enthusiastic-connectors' segment of Sellick's (2004) study scored higher in physical activity than the other three segments of senior tourists. Similarly, the 'physicals' (seniors who travelled so they participate in a physical activity) were one of the segments identified by Astic and Muller (1999).

Another aspect of tourism segmentation being studied is the role of the length of a trip. Neal (2003) categorized tourists as 'short-term visitors' (those who stayed from one to six nights) and 'long-term visitors' (those who stayed seven or more nights). Significant satisfaction differences have been identified between 'short-term' and 'long-term' visitors, and first-time and repeated visitors (Baloglu, Pekcan, Chen, & Santos, 2003; Neal, 2003; Tsiotsou, 2006). Short-term visitors are less satisfied with perceived service quality and perceived reasonableness of the cost of their travel destination than are long-term visitors (Neal, 2003), while repeat visitors score higher in satisfaction than first-time visitors (Baloglu et al., 2003). Furthermore, overall satisfaction varies according to the length of stay, gender and decision horizon (Huh & Uysal, 2003). Andereck and Caldwell (1994) show that satisfaction and enjoyment demonstrate significant differences among segments in tourism markets while demographic variables display little difference.

Chapter 2 provides six principles that tourism firms should use in order to use tourism segmentation as a strategic tool that could assist in obtaining sustainable competitive advantage. Moreover, the chapter describes in detail nine steps that destination managers should take in order to perform an effective data-driven tourism market segmentation.

### 1.4.2. Targeting

In addition to segmentation, the literature suggests a number of benefits result from targeting well-defined segments of tourists. These benefits are (1) developing new tourism products that better satisfy the needs and wants of specific tourist segments; (2) the design of more effective marketing programmes to reach and satisfy the defined tourist segments; and (3) a more efficient and effective allocation of marketing resources (Chandra & Menezes, 2001). Thus, target marketing is a necessary strategy not only for obtaining competitive advantage but for also achieving cost-effective marketing.

A good application of market segmentation and targeting is the case of the National Tourism Organization of Australia, called Tourism Australia. After undertaking an extensive research initiative, Tourism Australia aimed at identifying the 'ideal visitor segment' for Australia that would help in achieving its business objectives. Instead of using the traditional segmentation criteria in tourism such as country of origin, mode of travel, style of travel and distribution channels, Tourism Australia applied psychographic criteria such as personal motivations and lifestyle. Thus, it employed *intermarket segmentation* in order to identify global segments that would be most receptive to the Australian experience. The ideal group of tourists identified was the 'Experience Seekers'. Research assisted Tourism Australia to assess the size of this segment, profile it and identify means for communicating with it. Thus, it was found that the targeted segment constitutes around 30–50% of all potential long-haul outbound travellers from key source markets (e.g. Germany, the United Kingdom, Japan, China and the United States). 'Experience Seekers' are international travellers who seek out and enjoy authentic personal experiences, involve themselves in holiday activities, are adventurous, acquire a variety of experiences on any single trip and seek out for value (a balance between cost and benefits) on their trips. Finally, this segment is familiar with new technologies, makes selective view of TV (usually views programmes that meet its lifestyles and motives) and likes to learn from and share information with peers (Tourism Australia, 2011).

Thus, a campaign named 'Australian Invitation' was developed aiming to attract 'Experience Seekers' and increase demand for Australia from this segment. To target these consumers, the campaign media schedule and the messaging strategy included the following elements:

- The Australian invitation was presented in media used by the 'Experience Seekers' within each market.
- The core media were supported by programmes providing detailed destination information on Discovery and National Geographic channels.
- Interactivity and information were provided with a number of digital programme and web activity.
- Public relations event activities further informed and promoted major Australian experiences.
- Direct programme and contact points were developed to achieve immediacy.

- Local Tourism Australian offices were established in major markets, providing information to the 'Experience Seekers' (Tourism Australia, 2011).

### 1.4.3.  Positioning

In tourism, positioning has not attracted the same research attention as segmentation. Positioning is the last stage of target marketing and involves the creation of a distinctive image for a given destination or tourism firm in the minds of potential tourists that distinguishes them from competing destinations or tourism companies and is linked to the destinations assets. A successful positioning strategy should provide a sustainable competitive advantage to a destination (Chandra & Menezes, 2001). For example, a tourist destination such as Greece, with its rich cultural heritage, has positioned itself to appeal to tourists across several countries who are interested in history, culture and historical architecture.

A tourist destination or firm may be positioned on a number of different bases, such as positioning by benefit, use and users, activities, price, quality, direct comparison etc. Positioning by benefit should be practiced with caution. It has been suggested that the dominant attribute selected for positioning should represent something realizable (O'Shaughnessy & O'Shaughnessy, 2000) while the use of multiple benefits to position a tourism destination or firm should be exercised with caution because it might dilute the brand position and confuse the related stakeholders (Chandra & Menezes, 2001; Harrison-Walker, 2011).

Thus, countries, regions, cities and tourism firms employ various positioning strategies in order to compete effectively with their counterparts. For example, France has positioned itself as the country of the arts, such as film, music, art and literature. According to the Anholt GfK Roper Nation Brands IndexSM 2008 Highlights Report, France was ranked first in terms of cultural heritage and people's appreciation for contemporary culture. Another example is Scotland that positioned itself as 'Scotland — Silicon Glen' (Kotler & Gertner, 2001) in an effort to associate itself with Silicon Valley, the southern part of the San Francisco Bay Area. Silicon Valley is known for its large number of silicon chip innovators and manufacturers and high-tech businesses.

Like brands, tourist destinations may have to be repositioned, too. An interesting example of repositioning is that of Club Med. Originally, Club Med resorts were positioned to appeal to the single, city residents who wished to escape the stressful city life. Later, Club Med repositioned itself to appeal to families by offering amenities such as telephones, TV, fax machines and computer facilities.

Another repositioning case is that of Canada with the campaign 'Brand Canada'. Initially, Canada was perceived as one-dimensional and nature-based destination that was not attractive to tourists. The Brand Canada campaign resulted from information gathered via online surveys that took place in 2005 and positioned Canada by the experiences of the visitors. Brand Canada was officially launched in 2007 and targeted to the emotions of tourists resulting from their own adventures.

The slogan used reflected directly this experiential approach: 'Come to Canada: Create extra-ordinary stories of your own' (Hudson & Ritchie, 2009).

A recent study of ski resorts conducted by Frochot and Kreziak (2008) suggests that marketers should examine the primary and the secondary images of a destination in order to identify the most effective positioning strategy. Primary images reflect the core values and attributes of tourism services (e.g. ski resorts) and are common to all destinations of the same type. Secondary images actually differentiate tourism services (e.g. ski resorts positioned on extreme skiing, on ski variety or as relaxing) and provide them competitive advantage.

In sum, 'the decision about how to position or reposition a tourist destination should be made on the basis of market segmentation and targeting analysis in tandem with positioning analysis. The position selected should match the preferences of the targeted market segment and the positioning of competing tourism services' (Chandra & Menezes, 2001, p. 92).

## 1.5. Conclusion

Changes in consumer habits, interests or preferences or the rise of new attractive destinations make target marketing a necessary strategic approach that travel and tourism firms should take. Moreover, owing to changes in the size and composition of target segments, the major steps of target marketing should be repeated on a regular basis in order for tourism companies to operate efficiently and effectively. The rise of new technologies and social media that facilitate user-generated content and travel reviews will play a significant role in developing consumer preferences and choices of tourism services and destinations. Thus, social influences might in the future come to play a more significant role in changing consumers' desires, preferences and buying behaviours resulting in changing tourism segments.

## References

Aaker, D. A., & Shansby, J. G. (1982). Positioning your product. *Business Horizons, 25*(3), 56–62.

Andereck, K. L., & Caldwell, L. L. (1994). Variable selection in tourism market segmentation models. *Journal of Travel Research, 33*(2), 40–46.

Astic, G., & Muller, T. E. (1999). Delighting the senior tourist. *Journal of Consumer Satisfaction, Dissatisfaction and Complaining Behavior, 12*, 71–80.

Baloglu, S., Pekcan, A., Chen, S., & Santos, J. (2003). The relationship between destination performance, overall satisfaction and behavioral intention for distinct segments. *Journal of Quality Assurance in Hospitality and Tourism, 4*(3/4), 149–165.

Becken, S. (2003). *An integrated approach to travel behaviour with the aim of developing more sustainable forms of tourism.* Landcare Research Internal Report. New Zealand. Retrieved from http://www.landcareresearch.co.nz/research/sustain_business/tourism/integrated_approaches.asp

Bigne, E. J., & Andreu, L. (2004). Emotions in segmentation: An empirical study. *Annals of Tourism Research, 31*(3), 682–696.

Bloom, J. Z. (2004). Tourist market segmentation with linear and non-linear techniques. *Tourism Management, 25*(6), 723–733.

Brassington, F., & Pettitt, S. (1997). *Principles of marketing*. London: Prentice-Hall.

Chandra, S., & Menezes, D. (2001). Applications of multivariate analysis in international tourism research: The marketing strategy perspective of NTOs. *Journal of Economic and Social Research, 3*(1), 77–98.

Chen, J. S. (2000). Norwegians' preferences for U.S. lodging facilities: Market segmentation approach. *Journal of Travel & Tourism Marketing, 9*(4), 69–82.

Chen, J. S. (2003). Market segmentation by tourists' sentiments. *Annals of Tourism Research, 30*(1), 178–193.

Dolnicar, S. (2006). Data-driven market segmentation in tourism — Approaches, changes over two decades and development potential. In *CD Proceedings of the 15th International Research Conference of the Council for Australian University Tourism and Hospitality Education (CAUTHE)*, Australia.

Dolnicar, S. (2010). Identifying tourists with smaller environmental footprints. *Journal of Sustainable Tourism, 18*(6), 717–734.

Dolnicar, S., & Leisch, F. (2004). Segmenting markets by bagged clustering. *Australasian Marketing Journal, 12*(1), 51–65.

Frochot, I. (2005). A benefit segmentation of tourists in rural areas: A Scottish perspective. *Tourism Management, 26*(3), 335–346.

Frochot, I., & Kreziak, D. (2008). Customers' perceptions of ski resorts' images: Implications for resorts' positioning strategies. *Tourism and Hospitality Research, 8*(4), 298–308.

Frochot, I., & Morrison, A. M. (2000). Benefit segmentation: A review of its applications to travel and tourism research. *Journal of Travel & Tourism Marketing, 9*(4), 21–45.

Harrison-Walker, J. L. (2011). Strategic positioning of nations as brands. *Journal of International Business Research, 10*(2), 135–147.

Huang, R., & Sarigollu, E. (2007). Benefit segmentation of tourists to the Caribbean. *Journal of International Consumer Marketing, 20*(2), 67–83.

Hudson, S., & Ritchie, B. J. R. (2009). Branding a memorable destination experience: The case of "Brand Canada". *International Journal of Tourism Research, 11*(2), 217–228.

Huh, J., & Uysal, M. (2003). Satisfaction with cultural/heritage sites: Virginia historic triangle. *Journal of Quality Assurance in Hospitality and Tourism, 4*(3/4), 177–194.

Janssen, M. A., & Jager, W. (2001). Fashions, habits and changing preferences: Simulation of psychological factors affecting market dynamics. *Journal of Economic Psychology, 22*(6), 745–772.

Jeffrey, D., & Xie, Y. (1995). The UK market for tourism in China. *Annals for Tourism Research, 22*(4), 857–876.

Juaneda, C., & Sastre, F. (1999). Balearic Islands tourism: A case study in demographic segmentation. *Tourism Management, 20*(4), 549–552.

Kotler, P. (1997). *Marketing management* (9th ed.). Upper Saddle River, NJ: Prentice-Hall.

Kotler, P. (2000). *Marketing management: Millennium edition* (10th ed.). Upper Saddle River, NJ: Prentice-Hall.

Kotler, P., & Armstrong, G. (2008). *Principles of marketing* (12th ed.). Upper Saddle River, NJ: Pearson Prentice Hall.

Kotler, P., & Gertner, D. (2001). Country as brand, product, and beyond: A place marketing and brand management perspective. *Brand Management, 9*(4–5), 249–261.

McFadden, D., & Train, K. (1996). *Mixed multinomial logit models for discrete response.* University of California Working Paper, Berkeley, CA.

Mok, C., & Iverson, T. J. (2000). Expenditure-based segmentation: Taiwanese tourists to Guam. *Tourism Management, 21*(3), 299–305.

Neal, J. D. (2003). The effect of length of stay on travelers' perceived satisfaction with service quality. *Journal of Quality Assurance in Hospitality and Tourism, 4*(3/4), 167–176.

O'Shaughnessy, J. O., & O'Shaughnessy, N. J. (2000). Treating the nation as a brand: Some neglected issues. *Journal of Macromarketing, 20*(1), 56–64.

O'Sullivan, E. O. (1991). *Marketing for parks, recreation, and leisure.* State College, PA: Venture Publishing.

Oyewole, P. (2010). Country segmentation of the international tourism market: Using propensity to travel and to spend abroad. *Journal of Global Marketing, 23*(2), 152–168.

Pizam, A., Jeong, G. H., Reichel, A., van Boemmel, H., Lusson, J. M., Steynberg, L., ... Montmany, N. (2004). The relationship between risk-taking, sensation-seeking, and the tourist behavior of youth adults: A cross-cultural study. *Journal of Travel Research, 42*(3), 251–260.

Porter, M. (2001). Strategy and the Internet. *Harvard Business Review, 79*(3), 63–78.

Richards, G. (1996). Skilled consumption and UK ski holidays. *Tourism Management, 17*(1), 25–34.

Sellick, M. C. (2004). Discovery, connection, nostalgia: Key travel motives within the senior market. *Journal of Travel & Tourism Marketing, 17*(1), 55–71.

Smith, W. (1956). Product differentiation and market segmentation as alternative marketing strategies. *Journal of Marketing, 21*(1), 3–8.

Smith, W. (1995). Product differentiation and market segmentation as alternative marketing strategies. *Marketing Management, 4*(3), 63–65.

Sung, H. Y. (2004). *Predicting the likelihood of selecting different adventure trip types: A product-driven approach for segmenting the U.S. adventure travel market.* Retrieved from http://www.ttra.com/pub/uploads/017.pdf. Accessed on November 15, 2004.

Sung, H. Y., Morrison, A. M., & O'Leary, J. T. (2000). Segmenting the adventure travel market: From the North American industry providers' perspective. *Journal of Travel & Tourism Marketing, 9*(4), 1–20.

Tourism Australia. (2011). *A uniquely Australian invitation: The experience seeker.* Retrieved from http://www.tourism.australia.com/en-au/documents/Corporate%20-%20Marketing/marketing_experience_factsheet.pdf. Accessed on October 1, 2011.

Trout, J., & Rivkin, S. (2010). *Repositioning: Marketing in an era of competition, change and crisis.* USA: McGraw-Hill.

Tsiotsou, R. (2006). Using visit frequency to segment ski resort customers. *Journal of Vacation Marketing, 12*(1), 15–26.

Tsiotsou, R., & Vasioti, E. (2006). Satisfaction: A segmentation criterion for "short-term" visitors of mountainous destinations. *Journal of Travel & Tourism Marketing, 20*(1), 61–74.

Tureckova, O. U. R. (2002). Segmenting the tourism market using perceptual and attitudinal mapping. *Agriculture Economy, 48*(1), 36–48.

Chapter 2

# The Role of Market Segmentation in Strategic Tourism Marketing

*Sara Dolnicar*

## 2.1. Introduction

Market orientation is a key factor of business success (Narver & Slater, 1990) because it informs strategic planning. It is defined as 'the organisation-wide generation of market intelligence pertaining to current and future customer needs, dissemination of the intelligence across departments, and organisation-wide responsiveness to it' (Kohli & Jaworski, 1990, p. 6). As such, it represents the basis of, and justification for, any marketing action.

Essentially, market orientation is about understanding and responding to consumer needs. Consumer needs, however, are heterogeneous: that is, different consumers have different needs. The key strategic marketing tool driven by the motivation to understand consumer needs, thus ensuring market orientation, is market segmentation. Market segmentation also accounts for the fact that in most markets consumers differ in their needs. As Lilien and Rangaswamy (2003) put it:

> Segmentation is best viewed as the first step in a three-step process of segmentation, targeting and positioning (STP). Segmentation groups customers with similar wants, needs, and responses. Targeting determines which groups a firm should try to serve (and how). Positioning addresses how the firm's product will compete with others in the target segment. (p. 63)

One would expect, therefore, that organisations in general — and specifically tourism destinations and businesses — would be very familiar with market segmentation and use it in close conjunction with other aspects of strategic marketing as a basis for their marketing activities. A number of authors have pointed out, however, that this is not the case and that there is in fact a significant theory–practice divide that prevents organisations from utilising market segmentation effectively as a strategic tool (Dibb, 2005; Dibb & Simkin, 1994; Greenberg & McDonald, 1989). A recent survey with

167 marketing managers (Dolnicar & Lazarevski, 2009) confirmed these concerns empirically: 68% of marketing managers agreed that segmentation analyses are like a black box to them and that they do not understand what actually happens in the process of segmenting respondents, 65% stated that they have had difficulties interpreting segmentation solutions in the past and 30% believe that segmentation strategy is independent of positioning and competition strategy.

Given the importance of segmentation and the apparent shortcomings in its application, the aims of this chapter are to

(1) place market segmentation in the context of strategic marketing rather than treating it as an isolated marketing tool;
(2) provide a systematics of basic segmentation approaches and criteria relevant to tourism;
(3) illustrate the entire process of tourism market segmentation step by step, highlighting potential difficulties and alternative ways of addressing them to arrive at valid segmentation solutions;
(4) point to an analytic, perceptions-based market segmentation (PBMS) strategy that offers a methodological framework for integrating market segmentation with other areas of strategic marketing in order to most effectively harvest the benefits of segmentation; and
(5) make market segmentation more transparent to data analysts and users of segmentation solutions in tourism, thus reducing the theory–practice divide.

## 2.2.  The Role of Market Segmentation in Strategic Marketing

Hooley, Saunders, and Piercy (2004), in their book on marketing strategy, propose a few basic principles to guide marketing action (pp. 23–26):

*Principle 1* — Focus on the customer.
*Principle 2* — Only compete in markets where you can establish a competitive advantage.
*Principle 3* — Customers do not buy products (they buy solutions to their problems).
*Principle 4* — Marketing is too important to leave to the marketing department.
*Principle 5* — Markets are heterogeneous.
*Principle 6* — Markets and customers are constantly changing.

This set of principles helps to develop a model of the role market segmentation plays in strategic marketing. Market segmentation 'consists of viewing a heterogeneous market … as a number of smaller homogeneous markets' (Smith, 1956, p. 6) and thus represents the direct response to *Principle 5* (markets are heterogeneous).

Market segmentation is also directly in line with *Principle 1* (focus on the customer) because the focus is on understanding the consumer, without focusing on *all* consumers in the market. Rather, the aim is to identify an attractive market segment (a part of the market) that matches the tourism organisation's or destination's strengths. The alignment with an organisation's or a destination's strength implies that competition has to be accounted for when selecting target segments. Selecting a segment that can be catered to more successfully by another tourism organisation or destination is unlikely to present the opportunity for a sustainable competitive advantage, which, however, is necessary for long-term success (*Principle 2*: only compete in markets where you can establish a competitive advantage). To have a sustained competitive advantage in a market described by a high level of competition, as the tourism market is, a tourism organisation or destination must not only focus on its strength, but it also needs to develop a positioning strategy that will ensure that the strengths are clearly formulated and can be communicated to internal and external stakeholders as well as to customers.

Whether or not market segmentation complies with *Principle 3* (customers do not buy products; they buy solutions to their problems) depends mainly on the nature of the segmentation approach taken. Benefit segmentation, for example, uses the stated benefits derived from the consumption of a product or service; it thus implicitly accounts for the fact that tourism offers solutions to people, and should therefore offer different solutions for different people. For example, some tourists seek a change of environment as a key benefit from tourism activity. The problem they may be solving is boredom at home or boredom with the everyday routine of work life and home responsibilities.

Finally, *Principle 4* states that marketing is too important to leave to the marketing department. This principle applies without any doubt to the entire area of strategic marketing, including market segmentation. All areas of strategic marketing represent very fundamental organisational or destination management decisions and require a mindset of customer orientation to be adopted by all members of the organisation. Strategic marketing, or single areas of strategic marketing, such as market segmentation, therefore cannot be outsourced to an operative department. The worst-case scenario in the context of market segmentation is that an operational market research department is told to collect data without a clear brief of what this data needs to contain in order to produce a valid segmentation solution down the track. The data is then e-mailed to a consulting company that runs a segmentation analysis. The consulting company chooses one solution and presents key features of segments to the operational marketing department. The operational marketing department makes a recommendation to the executive. The executive, as a result of the process or multiple outsourcing, has little understanding of how the segmentation solution presented to him or her has emerged and if it represents a valid basis to develop — typically long term — segmentation strategies. Such problems occur regularly in the tourism industry because, in many countries, national tourism organisations conduct large guest surveys and commission segmentation studies. The results of these studies (but no explanation of the rationale and the parameters of the analysis) are then passed on to regional tourism organisations and businesses with the recommendation to focus on these segments. In such a situation, the end user of the segmentation solution has hardly any understanding of how the segmentation solution was developed and is therefore not in the position to assess if it indeed represents the strategically optimal choice for them.

*Principle 6* postulates that markets and customers are constantly changing. This principle has major implications for market segmentation in tourism. Because the market is dynamic, segmentation (as well as competition and positioning) strategies need to be reviewed regularly. A market segmentation study conducted at a certain point in the past reflects merely the segment structure at that particular point in time. To ensure market dynamics are not neglected, market segmentation analyses, as well as competition analysis and positioning strategies, need to be regularly assessed and, if necessary, modified to suit changed market circumstances. For example, tourism planning has changed dramatically since the Internet has become a key platform for obtaining travel-related information. Mobile technologies have further changed the timing and mode of information search and travel decision making. A tourism segmentation solution based on an information search that was conducted 10, or even 2, years ago is therefore very unlikely to provide a strong basis for strategic decision making, such as segment selection.

Many authors view market segmentation as the first step in strategic marketing, followed by targeting, positioning and competitive analysis (e.g. Lilien & Rangaswamy, 2003). However, when deriving the role of market segmentation from Hooley et al.'s (2004) principles, it becomes clear that, in reality, these three key areas of strategic marketing need to be assessed simultaneously (as illustrated in Figure 2.1).

Unless a destination or organisation knows what its strengths are (which implies a certain positioning), it is impossible to decide on the best market segment to target. For example, even if adventure tourists emerge from a segmentation study as the most attractive segment, a destination that is famous for its museums and art galleries would not be well advised to target adventure tourists. Clearly, such a destination would need to identify an attractive segment of the tourist market that is interested in cultural activities when selecting its holiday destination. A less obvious case is that of the growing number of destinations claiming to be 'green'

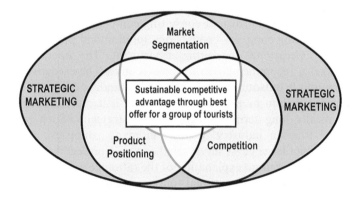

Figure 2.1: The role of market segmentation in strategic marketing.

(environmentally sustainable or friendly). The question that would have to be asked is whether being 'green' is indeed something they are perceived to be, and whether the people who seek what they have to offer — which could be remoteness — are even interested in environmental sustainability.

The opposite also holds: no matter what the destination's or organisation's strengths are, if the market, or at least a segment of the market, does not appreciate this strength, then competitive advantage and success are unlikely. The same is the case with competition: the preferred market segment that perfectly matches an organisation's or destination's strength may also be the one most other competitors are trying to attract, thus forcing an organisation or destination to rethink its target segment. For example, some nations have an abundance of a certain kind of tourist attraction. Australia has a large number of coastal destinations, all of which have long, sandy beaches, good surf, friendly locals and, predominately, good weather. Most of these destinations not only are attractive for families but also are in the position to host events or small conferences. From a competitive point of view, it is therefore not ideal for an Australian coastal destination to position itself as a 'friendly coastal destination that hosts events and conferences'. This sort of position lacks a unique selling proposition because it does not differentiate one coastal destination from the many others in Australia, and therefore makes the destination substitutable and vulnerable to competition. On the other hand, if competition becomes the dominant factor in assessing market opportunities, organisations or destinations may miss interesting market niches that, despite competition, may be worth targeting.

To the best of the author's knowledge, only one segmentation technique has been proposed to date that accounts for segmentation, positioning and competition simultaneously. This technique, referred to as PBMS, has been developed by Mazanec and colleagues (Buchta, Dolnicar, & Reutterer, 2000; Mazanec & Strasser, 2000) and will be discussed in more detail later in this chapter.

It must be concluded that market segmentation plays a key role in strategic marketing. However, its role is not to be the first, second or last in a sequence of strategic decisions. Instead, all aspects — segmentation, positioning and competition — need to be considered simultaneously before committing to strategic decisions.

## 2.3. Basic Segmentation Approaches and Criteria

The two most fundamental approaches to grouping heterogeneous consumers into homogeneous market segments are referred to as: (1) *a priori* (Mazanec, 2000) or commonsense segmentation (Dolnicar, 2004); and (2) *post hoc* (Myers & Tauber, 1977), *a posteriori* (Mazanec, 2000) or *data-driven* (Dolnicar, 2004) segmentation.

Commonsense segmentation implies that the manager of a tourism destination or business knows in advance which criterion is most relevant for creating a grouping. For example, an operator of a local petting zoo may assume — rightly or wrongly — that the family life cycle is the single most informative segmentation criterion. No sophisticated data analysis is required; consumers can simply be split into families with babies and toddlers, families with pre-school aged children, families with primary school aged children and families with high school aged children. Each of these segments is described in as much detail as possible in order to understand which services provided by the zoo best satisfy their needs. For example, families with babies and toddlers will require shaded spaces from where they can view the animals, with a toilet and nappy-changing facility in close proximity. Families with primary school aged children may want signage or guides or audio tapes with information about the animals so their children can learn.

Commonsense segmentation is often criticised for not being 'sophisticated', especially by academics. Yet, for many destinations and tourism businesses, this is all that may be needed to best satisfy the customers who are interested in their service in a way that provides them with a competitive advantage. Segmentation criteria that have been used in the past include, for example, age, heavy versus light users (e.g. Goldsmith & Litvin, 1999; Horneman, Carter, Wei, & Ruys, 2002) and visitors with and without a disability (Israeli, 2002). Arguably, the single most frequent commonsense segmentation used in the tourism industry is tourists' countries of origin. This makes a lot of sense when destinations cater for tourists from different linguistic and cultural backgrounds, such as European destinations where for obvious reasons the marketing messages need to be customised to the country of origin.

Data-driven segmentation also requires input from management, but in a less specific way. Management may suspect that people's vacation activities, their motivations to undertake a vacation, their vacation budget, or any other criterion, could lead to a managerially useful grouping of tourists. These constructs are then measured in a survey, and each one of them — typically comprising a number of variables — can be used as a so-called segmentation base to identify or create market segments (Dolnicar & Leisch, 2010).

Another way of classifying segmentation studies is by the segmentation base used. The segmentation base in such cases tends to determine how the segmentation study is identified. Examples include 'benefit segmentation' (customers are segmented based on the benefits they seek), 'activity segmentation' (segmentation based on the holiday activity desired; see, e.g. Moscardo, Pearce, Morrison, Green, & O'Leary, 2000), 'demographic segmentation' (segmentation based on the demographic profiles of customers; see Dodd & Bigotte, 1997) and 'psychographic segmentation' (segmentation based on customer motivations, as illustrated by Bieger & Laesser, 2002). Typical segmentation bases that have been used to group tourists in the past include benefits sought, motivations, travel activities, travel-related attitudes, trip characteristics, product attributes and expenditure patterns (Zins, 2008). A detailed description of the data-driven segmentation process is provided in the following section.

## 2.4.  Data-Driven Market Segmentation, Step by Step

Figure 2.2 provides an overview of all the steps that need to be taken when a market segmentation study is conducted. Note that this model is not specific to the tourism industry; it is a general model relevant to any market segmentation application.

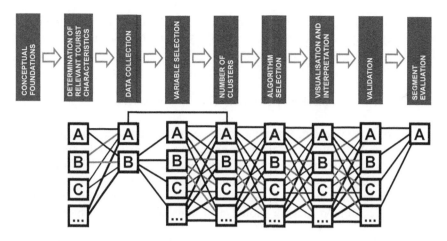

Figure 2.2: Data-driven market segmentation, step by step.

Positioning and competition need to be considered in a number of these steps: when the relevant characteristics for grouping tourists into market segments are determined (Step 2), when data is collected (Step 3), when results are visualised and interpreted (Step 7), when segments are validated (Step 8) and when segments are evaluated and a target segment chosen (Step 9).

In the following sections, each of these steps is discussed briefly, key issues are raised and interactions with other areas of strategic marketing are highlighted.

### 2.4.1.  Step 1: Conceptual Foundations

Step 1 is not, strictly speaking, a step in the actual process of market segmentation. It is included here, however, because many of the misunderstandings between academics and practitioners result from a lack of understanding of the basic principles of segmentation analysis. The conceptual foundations of market segmentation are as follows:

- Analyses need to be conducted with all other strategic considerations in mind, especially positioning and competition.
- Keep it as simple as possible. If simple commonsense segmentation using a single splitting variable to group tourists into segments (e.g. age or gender) is expected to lead to managerially useful target segments, this approach can be used. There is no need to use more complex data-driven approaches unless there is reason to believe that using them will lead to a better outcome.
- Data-driven market segmentation is an exploratory process. Repeated computations can, and frequently do, lead to different solutions (Dolnicar & Leisch, 2010). It is therefore not sufficient to run one computation with one algorithm because the result could well be random.

- Usually only one good segment is needed. It is therefore not the quality of the overall segmentation solution that matters, but the quality of the segment ultimately chosen as the target segment.

### 2.4.2.  Step 2: Determination of Relevant Tourist Characteristics

Before any data is collected, the users of the segmentation solution (optimally high-level managers in a tourism destination or business), not the data analyst, need to decide which characteristics of tourists they consider to be most informative for a managerially useful segmentation solution. This decision needs to be in line with the strengths and the current or aspired positioning of the destination or business. In making this decision, managers should also consider areas in which competition occurs.

For example, if the management of Destination A come to the conclusion that tourists can engage in nature-based activities at Destination A that they cannot undertake in many other places in the country, then nature-based activities would represent an interesting segmentation base. Using a well-developed questionnaire, the management of Destination A may gain insight into not only which segments have a particular interest in those activities but also whether these segments perceive Destination A as being able to offer nature-based activities (positioning) and whether other destinations are perceived to offer similar, inferior, or perhaps even superior, nature-based activities (competition).

Users of the segmentation solution may identify a number of relevant segmentation bases, in which case all of them can, and should, be included in the questionnaire. It is critical, however, to identify and select survey questions very carefully, because the number of variables that can be analysed given a certain sample size is limited (Formann, 1984). Including redundant items is counter-productive, as it just shifts the challenge of item selection to a later stage in the segmentation process (from Step 3 to Step 4).

Finally, the answer options provided in the questionnaire are critical in order to avoid capturing response styles (Paulhus, 1991) and to ensure that a valid distance measure is available to use in the actual segmentation process. For these two reasons, binary answer formats (offering respondents the answer options 'yes' and 'no') are a good choice (Dolnicar, 2003; Dolnicar, Grün, & Leisch, 2011).

### 2.4.3.  Step 3: Data Collection

Two key recommendations can be made with respect to data collection in market segmentation studies. First of all, it is important that data is collected specifically with the segmentation study in mind. Often pre-existing data sets do not optimally identify the target markets being sought and therefore should not be used; far better results will be found by replacing old data sets with data collected specifically to capture the segment identified by management.

Second, when collecting data for segmentation studies, one key aspect relating to sample selection needs to be considered: if tourism organisations or destinations want to understand market segments in the broader market, as opposed to understanding only their current customers, then they need to make sure that their sample includes non-customers. This typically has not been the case in tourism segmentation studies (Zins, 2008).

### 2.4.4.   *Step 4: Item (Variable) Selection*

This step is not required if a data-driven segmentation study is conducted on the basis of a data set which was specifically collected for the purpose of market segmentation. In such a case it can be assumed that survey questions used as segmentation base have been carefully formulated and chosen.

If, however, data analysts find themselves in the unfortunate situation that the data set was not actually collected with the segmentation study in mind, or that too many questions were asked thus leaving the data analyst with too many variables given the sample size (Formann, 1984), then it is necessary to reduce the number of variables in the segmentation base.

Reducing the number of variables is frequently achieved using a procedure referred to as 'factor-cluster segmentation', where original responses are first factor analysed, and then only the factor scores (each representing a number of variables in the original data set) are used as a segmentation base. As a consequence of this two-step procedure, a substantial amount of information contained in the original data is lost because the data is effectively compressed and the segments are identified in a transformed space, not the actual space of interest as defined by the survey questions asked (Arabie & Hubert, 1994; Dolnicar & Grün, 2008; Ketchen & Shook, 1996; Milligan, 1996; Sheppard, 1996). Factor-cluster segmentation is therefore not recommended.

Optimally, experts (e.g. the users of the segmentation base) should assess the content of the variables and try to eliminate any redundant or irrelevant ones. If redundancy cannot be eliminated in this way, then factor analysis can be conducted, but only to determine the grouping of variables. After having grouped them, a subset of variables assigned to each factor should be chosen and used in its original form (as opposed to using factor scores).

### 2.4.5.   *Step 5: Number of Clusters*

In the case of most segmentation algorithms, the number of clusters has to be specified in advance. This is a major decision in the data analysis process because the number of clusters chosen has a huge impact on the final segmentation solution derived.

Although a large number of indices have been proposed in the past to help the data analyst with this decision (Dimitriadou, Dolnicar, & Weingessel, 2002), the author's experience is that indices are of little value if the data set is not well structured, which is typically the case with consumer data.

An alternative way to determine which number of clusters may be most suitable is to conduct data structure analysis to gain insight into the shape of the data and base the number of clusters decision on this knowledge. This can be done by manually repeating computations with different numbers of clusters and different algorithms to see which leads to the most stable solution. Alternatively, an automated procedure can be used that has been proposed by Dolnicar and Leisch (2010): the segmentation analysis is computed many times with different bootstrap samples of the original data. It is then assessed, using the Rand Index (Rand, 1971), with respect to its stability over repeated replications. The most stable solution is recommended.

### 2.4.6.   Step 6: Algorithm Selection

The selection of the algorithm will depend on the nature of the segmentation. If the interaction of a set of dependent variables and an independent variable is being grouped (as is the case in response-based clustering), then finite mixture models (Wedel & Kamakura, 1998) represent the typical analytical approach chosen.

If a set of variables is clustered without accounting simultaneously for response variables (as is the case with, e.g. benefit segmentation and activity segmentation), then a large number of hierarchical and partitioning algorithms will be available to choose from. If the data is highly structured, then it is likely that all algorithms will correctly identify such naturally existing segments. This is rarely the case with survey data, however. When data sets are highly unstructured, different segmentation algorithms impose structure on the data. It is therefore critical to understand which algorithm has which effect on the data. Some guidance is provided by Everitt, Landau, and Leese (2001).

### 2.4.7.   Step 7: Visualisation and Interpretation

After the 'mechanical' work is completed, the resulting segments have to be visualised and interpreted. Although it is not necessary to visualise the segments, it is easier to understand differences between segments if they are well visualised. One example for an activity segmentation of winter tourists is provided in Figure 2.3.

In Figure 2.3, the line indicates the responses of all respondents and the bars indicate the distribution of responses within the segment. The distribution is available in this case because a bagged clustering algorithm was used (Dolnicar & Leisch, 2003), whereas usually only the average response of the segment for each variable is available. Wherever the bar is higher than the line, it means that members of the segment engage in these winter tourism activities more than the total tourist population. These variables are called 'marker variables' and can be interpreted as

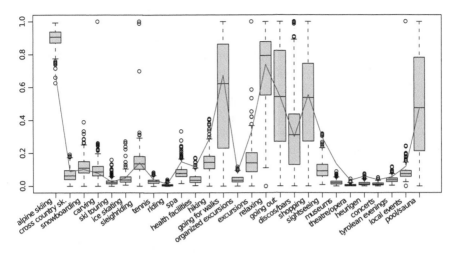

Figure 2.3: Visualising market segments. *Source*: Adapted from Dolnicar and Leisch (2003, p. 287). Copyright 2003 by the SAGE. Reprinted with permission.

the key characteristics of the segment. In this particular case, members of the segment depicted in Figure 2.3 all engage in alpine skiing a lot more than the total sample of respondents. They also like to relax more. Cultural activities, on the other hand, are of no interest to this segment at all.

The interpretation stage is where the integration with other strategic issues becomes extremely important again. It could well be that a very attractive segment is identified, but that this segment has been identified by competitors and therefore does not represent an opportunity to develop competitive advantage. For example, the segment depicted in Figure 2.3 is likely to be the focus of many alpine regions that have the infrastructure required for alpine skiing. Consequently, it may be difficult to customise discount offers to this segment without constant competition from similar destinations in the fight over market share for this segment of tourists.

It could also be the case that a very attractive segment is identified, but it does not match the tourism destination's strengths. For example, Vienna, which is known for its culture, is unlikely to select the segment depicted in Figure 2.3 because segment members have no interest in cultural activities and Vienna is not an alpine skiing destination.

### 2.4.8. Step 8: Validation

Up to and including Step 7, the only variables that have been considered were those chosen to form the segmentation base. At the validation stage additional information available from respondents is included in the process. In an optimal situation, members of segments will differ not only in the segmentation base (e.g. vacation activities in Figure 2.3) but also with respect to other characteristics, such as general travel behaviour, travel motivations or socio-demographics. Of particular interest are differences in travel information search behaviour (e.g. some people use the Internet to find travel information, while others rely on visits to a travel agent), because such differences can be exploited to effectively target communication messages.

Validation is conducted by testing differences between segments with respect to information other than that included in the segmentation base. This can be achieved by using Bonferroni-corrected analyses of variance, chi-square tests, discriminant analysis or regression analyses.

### 2.4.9.   Step 9: Evaluation

After the validation stage, a full picture of the segments becomes apparent. This is the point where it is possible to assess which of the resulting segments, if any, should be chosen to become the target segment for a tourism destination or business.

The segmentation literature proposes a number of criteria to guide users of segmentation solutions in selecting their target market. For example, Wedel and Kamakura (1998) recommend that the target segment should: (1) be large enough to generate enough revenue (substantiality); (2) have identifiable members (identifiability), which is easy if the segments are gender based, but not so trivial in the case of benefit segments; (3) be reachable (accessibility) to ensure that information can be successfully communicated; and (4) be stable in the medium term (stability) so that the segment does not change before marketing action targeting the segment can be implemented. Wedel and Kamakura (1998) also recommend that: (5) members of the segment should be expected to respond in a unique way to marketing action taken (responsiveness); and finally, and of most importance from the point of view of integrating all aspects of strategic planning, (6) the selected target segment should be actionable — marketing activities developed to target the segment must be in line with the core competencies of the tourism destination or tourism business.

## 2.5.   Perceptions-Based Market Segmentation

One of the key problems of market segmentation as it is conducted currently, by both academics and practitioners, is that it tends to be used in isolation from other strategic marketing tools, thus ignoring the inherent connection between choosing a suitable target segment, knowing one's strengths and positioning oneself by emphasising those strengths while accounting for competitive threats. The fact that segmentation analysis is a stand-alone analysis contributes to this problem, giving the impression that segmentation on its own is a useful exercise.

PBMS (Buchta et al., 2000; Mazanec & Strasser, 2000) is a segmentation approach — to the author's knowledge the *only* segmentation approach — that does not treat segmentation as an isolated strategy, but automatically integrates the aspects of segmentation, positioning and competition.

The basic idea of PBMS is to take advantage of the three-way structure of destination or brand image data. What is meant by three-way structure is that every person (dimension 1 on the data) is assessing every brand or destination (dimension 2) along every attribute (dimension 3). For example, 1000 tourists were asked to assess 5 destinations using 10 attributes such as fun, expensive, cultural, clean, safe, etc. The three-way nature of the data allows management to simultaneously gain market insight about brand positioning, market segmentation and competition. The main advantage of this approach is that the process happens simultaneously, rather than by the more typical sequential approach, which can lead to mistakes. Imagine, for example, a tourist destination deciding first on the target segments. They choose a very attractive segment in terms of high expenditures. Then they move on to the positioning aspect and realise that their destination actually has nothing to offer these tourists because, for example, this segment loves cultural events, whereas the destination is an old mining town by the sea. Examples of applications of PBMS that illustrate this particular approach are provided by Dolnicar, Grabler, and Mazanec (1999a, 1999b) and Dolnicar and Grabler (2004).

## 2.6. An Illustration in Tourism

In this section, we provide an illustration of the strategic aspects discussed in this chapter and how they need to be considered as a part of solving the same strategic problem. Table 2.1 contains three pieces of information: the left shaded area shows our positioning as a destination. As can be seen, we have no cultural attractions, no wineries and no bush or wilderness, and we are not 'off the beaten track'. We do, however, have sea and sandy beaches, family attractions and shopping opportunities, and we are a safe place for tourists to spend their vacations.

The columns in the middle of Table 2.1 illustrate the benefits sought by three segments, which resulted from a data-driven segmentation study. Segment 1 can be roughly described as 'culture tourists', who seek cultural attractions, wineries, shopping opportunities and safety, and who spend a substantial amount of money when on vacation. Segment 2 can be described as 'family tourists'. They want sea and sandy beaches, family attractions and shopping opportunities, they care about safety, and they spend an average amount of money on vacation. Segment 3 could be labelled 'adventure tourists'. They do not care about safety; they are interested in the sea and sandy beaches, bush and wilderness, and want to spend their vacation 'off the beaten track'.

The two right columns show the positioning of two competing tourist destinations. Destination 1 has the profile of a culture tourism destination, offering a wide range of man-made tourist attractions. Destination 2 is a safe beach destination with shopping opportunities.

Looking only at the market segments in an isolated manner, we would have concluded that Segment 1 (culture tourists) is the most attractive to any tourism destination: they undertake vacations both on- and off-season and they spend a lot of

Table 2.1: Hypothetical example of the integration of market segmentation, positioning and competition strategy.

| Tourism destination attributes | Our positioning | Segment 1 benefits sought | Segment 2 benefits sought | Segment 3 benefits sought | Competing destination 1 | Competing destination 2 |
|---|---|---|---|---|---|---|
| Many cultural attractions | No | Yes | No | No | Yes | No |
| Sea and sandy beaches | Yes | No | Yes | Yes | No | Yes |
| Family attractions | Yes | No | Yes | No | Yes | No |
| Wineries | No | Yes | No | No | Yes | No |
| Many shopping opportunities | Yes | Yes | Yes | No | Yes | Yes |
| Bush and wilderness | No | No | No | Yes | No | No |
| Season | | On and off | On | Off | | |
| Vacation expenditure level | | Very high | Medium | Low | | |
| Off the beaten track | No | No | No | Yes | No | No |
| Safe | Yes | Yes | Yes | No | Yes | Yes |

money at the destination. However, we are aware of our own destination's positions and strengths and the fact that we are not in a very strong position to offer this segment anything that could be attractive to them other than some shopping opportunities. This knowledge identifies culture tourists as a bad strategic target segment choice in view of our positioning. The inspection of competitors further supports this conclusion because Competing Destination 1 is in a much stronger competitive position than we are with respect to satisfying the needs of members of the culture tourists segment. Segment 3, the adventure tourists, is also not a suitable target segment given what our destination has to offer. However, Segment 2, the family segment, basically represents a perfect match: our destination offers everything this segment wants. Competing Destination 2 is likely to target this segment as well, indicating their threat as a possible competitor in future; however, as Competing Destination 2 does not currently have any specific family attractions, we have a competitive advantage which we can build on to stay ahead of Competing Destination 2 in future.

## 2.7.   Conclusion

Market segmentation is a key strategic instrument of tourism marketing. It embraces the concept of market orientation by using consumer needs and wants as a starting point for strategic decision making. The benefits market segmentation has to offer cannot, however, be fully exploited if segmentation is treated in isolation from other strategic marketing areas, especially positioning and competitive strategy.

The key to the successful use of market segmentation therefore lies in

(1) Good integration with the strengths of tourism business or those of destination — segments must want what the tourism destination or business is particularly good at.
(2) Good integration with consumers' perceptions of the tourism business or of the destination's perceived strengths and weaknesses — tourists must be able to determine the strength of tourism businesses or that of destination. It is the responsibility of management to develop a positioning strategy that communicates strengths effectively to the market in general and, specifically, to the chosen target segment.
(3) Good integration with competitive strategy, ensuring long-term competitive advantage with respect to the chosen target segments — the strengths the tourism business or destination chooses to focus on and communicate to tourists should be chosen in a way that differentiates it from other tourism businesses or destinations.
(4) Rigorous use of market segmentation methodology — market researchers and data analysts within the tourism industry need to be knowledgeable enough in segmentation analysis to at least understand what they are buying when commissioning a segmentation study. This is the only way they can make sure the

best possible segmentation solution has been chosen (remember, the best solution usually does not naturally emerge from the statistical analysis!), and that they fully understand the implications of the segmentation analysis, which is critical for translating it into marketing action.

(5) Close collaboration between data analysts/consultants/market research companies and business or destination management to ensure that a rigorous segmentation study is undertaken that at the same time fulfils all the requirements of being managerially useful and relevant. A segmentation study, ultimately, is only as good as the tourism manager who provides input into it.

## Acknowledgement

The author thanks the Australian Research Council for ongoing funding of methodological research projects relating to market segmentation.

## References

Arabie, P., & Hubert, L. (1994). Cluster analysis in marketing research. In R. Bagozzi (Ed.), *Advanced methods of marketing research* (pp. 160–189). Cambridge: Blackwell.

Bieger, T., & Laesser, C. (2002). Market segmentation by motivation: The case of Switzerland. *Journal of Travel Research, 41*(1), 68–76.

Buchta, C., Dolnicar, S., & Reutterer, T. (2000). *A nonparametric approach to perceptions-based market segmentation: Applications.* Interdisciplinary Studies in Economics and Management (Vol. 2). Berlin: Springer Verlag.

Dibb, S. (2005). Market segmentation implementation barriers and how to overcome them. *The Marketing Review, 5*(1), 13–30.

Dibb, S., & Simkin, L. (1994). Implementation problems in industrial market segmentation. *Industrial Marketing Management, 23*(1), 55–63.

Dimitriadou, E., Dolnicar, S., & Weingessel, A. (2002). An examination of indexes for determining the number of clusters in binary data sets. *Psychometrika, 67*(1), 137–159.

Dodd, T., & Bigotte, V. (1997). Perceptual differences among visitor groups to wineries. *Journal of Travel Research, 35*(3), 46–51.

Dolnicar, S. (2003). Simplifying three-way questionnaires — Do the advantages of binary answer categories compensate for the loss of information? In *Australia and New Zealand Marketing Academy: Proceedings of the ANZMAC 2003 Adelaide conference*, Adelaide (pp. 1647–1652). Retrieved from http://www.anzmac.org

Dolnicar, S. (2004). Beyond "commonsense segmentation" — A systematics of segmentation approaches in tourism. *Journal of Travel Research, 42*(3), 244–250.

Dolnicar, S., & Grabler, K. (2004). Applying city perception analysis (CPA) for destination positioning decisions. *Journal of Travel & Tourism Marketing, 16*(2/3), 99–111.

Dolnicar, S., Grabler, K., & Mazanec, J. A. (1999a). Analysing destination images: A perceptual charting approach. *Journal of Travel & Tourism Marketing, 8*(4), 43–57.

Dolnicar, S., Grabler, K., & Mazanec, J. A. (1999b). A tale of three cities: Perceptual charting for analyzing destination images. In G. I. Crouch, A. G. Woodside,

M. Oppermann, M. Y. Sakai & J. A. Mazanec (Eds.), *Consumer psychology of tourism, hospitality and leisure* (pp. 39–62). New York, NY: CAB International.

Dolnicar, S., & Grün, B. (2008). Challenging "factor-cluster segmentation". *Journal of Travel Research, 47*(1), 63–71.

Dolnicar, S., Grün, B., & Leisch, F. (2011). Quick, simple and reliable: Forced binary survey questions. *International Journal of Market Research, 53*(2), 231–252.

Dolnicar, S., & Lazarevski, K. (2009). Methodological reasons for the theory/practice divide in market segmentation. *Journal of Marketing Management, 25*(3–4), 357–373.

Dolnicar, S., & Leisch, F. (2003). Winter tourist segments in Austria — Identifying stable vacation styles using bagged clustering. *Journal of Travel Research, 41*(3), 281–293.

Dolnicar, S., & Leisch, F. (2010). Evaluation of structure and reproducibility of cluster solutions using the bootstrap. *Marketing Letters, 21*(1), 83–101.

Everitt, B., Landau, S., & Leese, M. (2001). *Cluster analysis*. London: Arnold.

Formann, A. K. (1984). *Die latent-class-analyse: Einführung in die theorie und anwendung*. Weinheim: Beltz.

Goldsmith, R. E., & Litvin, S. W. (1999). Heavy users of travel agents: A segmentation analysis of vacation travelers. *Journal of Travel Research, 38*(2), 127–133.

Greenberg, M., & McDonald, S. S. (1989). Successful needs/benefits segmentation: A user's guide. *Journal of Consumer Marketing, 6*(3), 29–36.

Hooley, G. J., Saunders, J. A., & Piercy, N. F. (2004). *Marketing strategy*. London: Prentice-Hall.

Horneman, L., Carter, R. W., Wei, S., & Ruys, H. (2002). Profiling the senior traveler: An Australian perspective. *Journal of Travel Research, 41*(1), 23–37.

Israeli, A. A. (2002). A preliminary investigation of the importance of site accessibility factors for disabled tourists. *Journal of Travel Research, 41*(1), 101–104.

Ketchen, D. J., & Shook, C. L. (1996). The application of cluster analysis in strategic management research: An analysis and critique. *Strategic Management Journal, 17*(6), 441–458.

Kohli, A. K., & Jaworski, B. J. (1990). Market orientation: The construct, research propositions, and managerial implications. *Journal of Marketing, 54*(2), 1–18.

Lilien, G. L., & Rangaswamy, A. (2003). *Marketing engineering*. Upper Saddle River, NJ: Prentice-Hall.

Mazanec, J. (2000). Market segmentation. In J. Jafari (Ed.), *Encyclopedia of tourism*. London: Routledge.

Mazanec, J., & Strasser, H. (2000). *A nonparametric approach to perceptions-based market segmentation: Foundations*. Berlin: Springer.

Milligan, G. W. (1996). Clustering validation: Results and implications for applied analyses. In P. Arabie & L. J. Hubert (Eds.), *Clustering and classification* (pp. 341–375). River Edge, NJ: World Scientific Publications.

Moscardo, G., Pearce, P., Morrison, A., Green, D., & O'Leary, J. T. (2000). Developing a typology for understanding visiting friends and relatives markets. *Journal of Travel Research, 38*(3), 251–259.

Myers, J. H., & Tauber, E. (1977). *Market structure analysis*. Chicago: American Marketing Association.

Narver, J. C., & Slater, S. F. (1990). The effect of a market orientation on business profitability. *Journal of Marketing, 54*(4), 20–35.

Paulhus, D. L. (1991). Measurement and control of response bias. In J. P. Robinson, P. R. Shaver & L. S. Wrightsman (Eds.), *Measures of personality and social psychological attitudes* (pp. 17–59). San Diego, CA: Academic Press.

Rand, W. M. (1971). Objective criteria for the evaluation of clustering methods. *Journal of the American Statistical Association, 66*(336), 846–850.

Sheppard, A. G. (1996). The sequence of factor analysis and cluster analysis: Differences in segmentation and dimensionality through the use of raw and factor scores. *Tourism Analysis, 1,* 49–57.

Smith, W. (1956). Product differentiation and market segmentation as alternative marketing strategies. *Journal of Marketing, 21*(1), 3–8.

Wedel, M., & Kamakura, W. A. (1998). *Marketing segmentation: Conceptual and methodological foundations.* Boston, MA: Kluwer Academic Publishers.

Zins, A. H. (2008). Market segmentation in tourism: A critical review of 20 years' research effort. In S. Kronenberg, M. Muller, B. Peters, B. Pikkemaat & K. Weiermair (Eds.), *Change management in tourism: From old to new* (pp. 289–301). Berlin: Erich Schmidt Verlag.

Chapter 3

# Social Interactions as Basis for Segmenting the Tourism Market

*Rodoula H. Tsiotsou, Andreas Mild and D. Sudharshan*

## 3.1. Introduction

Market segmentation is a fundamental part of marketing thinking, action and research. A number of chapters in this book (e.g. Chapters 1 and 2) have provided superb introductions, overviews and approaches to segmentation for the tourism industry. In this chapter, we take an agent provocateur approach by suggesting a different way to think about market segmentation in tourism. So far, tourism research, and consequently tourism segmentation research, has been mainly focused on the (economic) impact of tourism on tourism destinations and communities neglecting the effect of tourism on the tourists (Moscardo, 2009). Since segmentation is a grouping of individuals on a basis of their similarity, our insight is that social interaction behaviour before, during and after a trip forms and shapes segments. Because social interactions in tourism take place at various stages of a trip, segments are not considered static but dynamic in nature. Moreover, market segments exposed to and interacting with members of various other groups in order to co-create value (Vargo & Lusch, 2004: see also Chapter 15) can become even more dynamic due to the influences of these social agents. This insight came as a result of asking the question as to why and how segments emerge. At the very least, this chapter will suggest some questions to the reader and may perhaps even put forward a different approach to strategic thinking about tourism segmentation.

The application of new technologies has changed not only the way in which tourism businesses operate today but also the attitudes and behaviours of tourism consumers. There are three major trends that lead us to our approach. The first is that a growing volume of tourism-related information search, information sharing, recommendations and perhaps even purchasing takes place on the Internet (Buhalis & Law, 2008; Tsiotsou & Ratten, 2010; Werthner & Ricci, 2004). Next-generation information systems such as intelligent systems promise to supply tourism consumers and service providers with 'more relevant information, greater decision-support, greater mobility, and, ultimately, more enjoyable tourism experiences. They currently encompass a wide range of technologies relevant for tourism contexts such as recommender systems, context-aware systems, autonomous agents searching and mining Web resources, and ambient intelligence' (Gretzel, 2011, p. 758). Werthner and Ricci (2004) point out to the increasing 'informatization' of the entire tourism value chain, emphasizing that information and communication technologies (ICTs) have become essential elements of value-generating strategies in tourism.

The second development is the growth in social networking on the Internet that has had consequences even for 'in-person' social networks (Sigala, 2010). Innovations such as Web 2.0 applications and location-based services are currently driving value generation and influence the manner in which tourism information is created, exchanged and evaluated. 'Various web 2.0 applications such as collaborative trip planning, social and content sharing networks result in new products/services and travelers' involvement within business operations. Thus, these new tools transform travelers from passive consumers to active prosumers (producers and consumers) of travel experiences' (Tsiotsou & Ratten, 2010, p. 537). Because these technological innovations encourage social interactions between consumers, relationships can be formed and maintained (Law, Fuchs, & Ricci, 2011).

The third trend refers to 'tourism experiences' which are ever more both vividly shared and shareable in real time (e-mailed videos, photos, tweets, blogs), and stored for posterity. For example, social media allow tourists to communicate with not only tourism providers (e.g. hotel) but also tourists in real time who have previously experienced the services offered by the specific tourism provider. Thus, tourists have the opportunity to gather information first-hand from other tourists and make decisions about the tourism supplier or the experience. Blogging has also expanded the way in which information sharing and communication takes place via the Internet. Tourists can post their stories about their tourism experiences on their personal Internet site, the operator's site or a networked site. This is a simple way of both communicating with others and gathering information.

All three of the trends affect a wider and wider range of individuals. New technologies have elevated the importance of tourists' social interactions as a market force. The growth of social networking via websites and new ICTs facilitates marketers in initiating and managing social interactions (Godes et al., 2005) while tracking consumption behaviour by studying these social interactions.

## 3.2. Social Interactions in Tourism

Initially, tourism was perceived as an individual activity related to leisure time. However, gradually tourism has been considered as social relation due to its social–cultural impacts. Tourism is an inherently social phenomenon (Cohen, 1979) and previous research has explored many of its social aspects including the host–guest interactions (Dogan, 1989), social interactions (Murphy, 2001), the commoditization and consumption of culture (Waitt, 2000), community-based tourism (Reed, 1997) and voluntourism (Wearing, 2001). According to Smith (1989), tourism is the social interaction between tourists as 'guests' and residents in the tourist destination as 'hosts'. Tourism has been also viewed as a social system in which three main actors are involved: the traveller-generating region, the travel and tourism industry and the tourist destination region (Leiper, 1979).

Two major perspectives have been used to explain the social interactions between tourists and other entities:

- Social exchange theory (Gursoy & Rutherford, 2004) which tries to understand 'the exchange of resources between individual and groups in an interaction of situation' where 'actors supply one another with valued resources' (Ap, 1992, p. 668).
- Social representations theory which is concerned 'with describing and understanding how and what people think in their ongoing everyday experiences and how a wider social reality influences these thoughts' (Pearce, Moscardo, & Ross, 1996, p. 39). The theory argues that social representations are created through social interactions with the aim of assisting in social communication (Moscovici, 2001).

Tourism provides several opportunities to tourists to interact with various other groups of consumers and non-consumers. Figure 3.1 shows the various interactions and the 'actors' involved in these interactions. During a trip tourists can interact with travel partners, with other tourists, with tourist services personnel and with local residents. Social interactions and conversations are important to tourists because they play a significant role in reducing the anxieties associated with the terrain and the circumstances in which tourists find themselves (White & White, 2009). Therefore, social interactions during travelling constitute a major tourist consumer motive (Thyne, Davies, & Nash, 2005). Tourism consumers are often observed to travel together, have vacations together, eat together at restaurants and participate in physical activities together. In each of these examples, consumers may differ in their preferences but prefer to coordinate the decisions to yield either social or economic benefits (Hartmann, 2010).

Interactions between tourists can take place before, during and after travelling offline and online. The opportunities for social interactions might play a significant role in selecting a type of trip. For example, it has been found that anticipated opportunities for social interaction with other travellers are an important factor in choosing to backpack (Richards & Wilson, 2004). During a trip, tourist-to-tourist offline interactions can have a significant impact on their tourism experiences. Interactions with other tourists provide a range of benefits such as the opportunity to find and share information (Harrison, 2003; Wang, 1999) and to affirm mutual understandings of shared, common experiences of social and cultural landscapes (Harrison, 2003). Thus, interactions between tourists not just contribute to the production of the travel experience but also give meaning to these experiences. Tourism satisfaction is often derived by other tourists as tourism consumption takes place in the presence of other tourists.

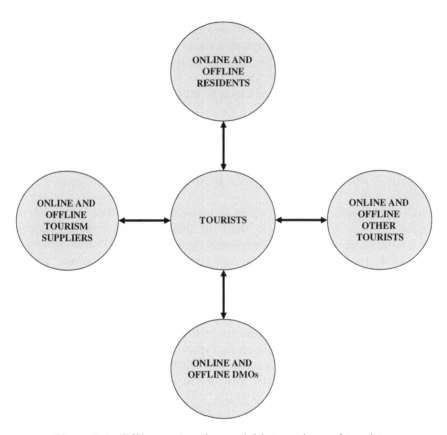

Figure 3.1: Offline and online social interactions of tourists.

Despite the importance of interactions between tourists in shaping the tourism experiences, the topic has attracted limited research attention (Huang & Hsu, 2010; Levy, Getz, & Hudson, 2011). A recent online survey examined interactions between tourists on cruise vacations and its impact on the cruise experience and vacation satisfaction. The findings of the study indicate that the quality of tourist-to-tourist interactions had positive direct impacts on the cruise experience as well as indirect effects on vacation satisfaction, mediated by cruise experience (Huang & Hsu, 2010).

Online interactions among tourists have attracted recent research attention. Online communities help dedicated travellers in planning their trips and sharing travel experiences in forums or blogs while they offer a comfortable means of booking trips and accommodation. In addition to sharing information and experiences, web-based tourist communities can serve as cultural production and political participation outlets. The study of Rokka and Moisander (2009) shows that web-based tourist communities may bring about new forms of environmental dialogue and create a political space where consumers can participate in the construction of active consumer citizenship for sustainable development via 'ethical' ecological consumption practices during their travel and tourism. Thus, via tourism consumption — not political parties — 'people have come to voice their interests and demands for a sustainable and just global order' (Rokka & Moisander, 2009, p. 199).

Moreover, tourists might interact with local residents of a tourism destination. Both parties are influenced by these interactions in terms of their attitudes and behaviour. Local residents have been linked to the sustainability of a destination because their attitude towards the tourists is one of the most important factors contributing to the attractiveness of a destination (Gursoy & Rutherford, 2004) and affecting tourists' choices (Hoffman & Low, 1981). In line with the social exchange theory, a recent study conducted in Taiwan showed that residents economically depended on tourism and having frequent and quality interactions with tourists tended to have more positive attitudes towards the tourism industry (Chuang, 2010). Prior research regarding the interactions between residents and tourists was conducted in offline settings. There is limited research devoted in examining residents as information sources to potential tourists such as in online travel communities. A recent study examined the influence residents may have on travel decisions and identify the types of travel decisions they influence. Moreover, it compared the influence residents have on travel decisions with other online community members (i.e. experienced travellers). The findings revealed that nearly one-third of the communication threads (including 1699 postings from 713 contributing members) have been influential for members. Residents were more influential in accommodations and food and beverage recommendations, whereas experienced travellers were more influential in the destination information category (Arsal, Woosnam, Baldwin, & Backman, 2010).

In terms of the interactions between tourists and tourism suppliers, the majority of the existing literature in an offline context is focused on the relational exchanges between tourists and tourism service encounters such as hotels (Kim, Han, & Lee, 2001), restaurants (Lin & Mattila, 2010) and tour groups (Conze, Bieger, Laesser, & Riklin, 2010). Tourists like any other consumers derive important social benefits through these interactions such as friendship, personal recognition and enjoyable connections with tourism providers (Gwinner, Gremler, & Bitner, 1998). Tourism services, on the other hand, can also benefit from their interactions with tourists. For example, Butcher (2005) found that café customers were significantly more likely to return if they felt at ease with and could relax around employees. In addition, interactions between tourism service providers and their customers are facilitated by the use of ICTs.

Online tourism services have changed the role of service providers and their intermediaries as well as their interactions with tourism consumers. The role and influences of tourism consumers are currently enhanced through the use of Web 2.0 tools that empower the voice of customers and enable them to form and collaborate in peer-social groups. Online communities serve travellers in gathering more and better quality of travel information in terms of information timeliness, completeness, structure and personalization (Schwabe & Prestipino, 2005). Research exploring the customer benefits and value of online tourism communities indicates that users of Web 2.0 (e.g. social tools, online communities and geocollaborative portals) derive all types of relational benefits such as functional, social, hedonic and psychological (Chung & Buhalis, 2008; Yoo & Gretzel, 2008).

Geocollaborative portals have also added a social aspect to the online trip planning process (Sigala, 2009) by not only providing social intelligence but also facilitating and encouraging members' interactions and intersupport (Sigala, 2010). Virtual, free of charge web maps, called geoportals, such as Yahoo Maps, Google Maps and Microsoft Live Maps, have introduced new collaborative ways for developing, searching, reading, sharing and disseminating geographical information and services (Sigala, 2010). According to Sigala (2010), geoportals provide four social benefits: '*social search* that enables users to search for geo-content based on other users' content such as profiles, geo-tags, personal maps, favourites, reviews, feedback etc.; *social mapping* referring to the dissemination and sharing of maps within social networks; *social publishing* referring to the collaborative creation and publication of a map within a social network and/or amongst a group of users; and *social administration* referring to the collaborative development of new value-added mapping services through the combination (mashing-up) and the collaborative administration of multiple geo-information and services' (p. 422). Sigala (2010) studied the role and functionality of geocollaborative portals in assisting collaborative trip planning processes. Her findings provided evidence of the existence of both 'give' (risk, time and effort to use the system) and 'get' (functional, social and emotional) customer values.

## 3.3.   Social Interaction as Basis for Segment Formation and Change

Recently, Sudharshan and Mild (2011) studied the formation and evolution of market segments using computer simulations. As pointed out by Sudharshan and Mild (2011), two fundamental forces drive social behaviour according to the behavioural science literature (a recent edition of the *Handbook of Social Psychology* provides an encyclopaedic collection of readings in the area, e.g. Gilbert, Fiske, & Lindzey, 1998). The first force is a conforming or an imitation force and is a function of the interactions within a group. The second is the desire to be unique and since uniqueness is a relative quality, it is a force that again is set relative to a social group. The strength of these forces varies from individual to individual, but there seems to be a systematic effect of culture on these forces. This cultural effect is evident from the cross-cultural psychology literature which differentiates cultures based on the degrees of collectivism or individualism they exhibit (Hofstede, 1980; Triandis, 1983).

## 3.4.   Using Social Network Analysis to Segment the Tourism Market

Computer simulations like the one used in Sudharshan and Mild (2011) can be considered as so-called agent-based models (ABM). Such models endeavour to explain phenomena appearing on the macro-level of a system (such as the emergence and development of various consumer segments) by simulating the behaviour of the elements (agents) of that system on the micro-level. Agents in such a model are typically described by (1) an agent's characteristics (e.g. preferences and knowledge), (2) a decision heuristic (often, such agents are assumed to act boundedly rational, i.e. they have only limited information about the system), (3) a rule governing interactions between agents and (4) a rule for the adaption of agents' knowledge. Clearly, to decide if the learning from a highly abstract simulation model can be transferred to and applied in the tourism industry, first, the assumptions on which the model is grounded must be compared to reality. The model assumes that changes in consumer preferences or attribute importance are influenced by the interaction of individuals with others. In particular, individuals are assumed to adjust their preferences to the mean preference of a reference group governed by a certain degree of willingness to adapt to or to differentiate from the mean preference. In this model, an individual's reference group consists of other individuals with similar preferences.

Arguably, reference groups based on similar preferences are increasingly supported by various applications on the Internet. For example, for many topics such as ecological concerns in tourism or backpacking tourism one can find a discussion forum where people from all over the world with similar interests can meet. In addition, the expanding amount of information on the web has made automated tools necessary that assist consumers in a variety of information-seeking and decision-making tasks. So-called recommender systems make use of consumers' preferences that have been expressed explicitly or implicitly. This can be booking data from an online travel agency or hotel, field reports from (un)satisfied customers on a retailer's homepage or browsing habits of online shoppers. The application of such models enables sellers to recommend products/services based on consumers' purchasing history and satisfaction with these products or services. The travelling platform booking.com, for example, shows consumer ratings for hotels grouped by traveller characteristics which are expected to have influence on a customers' preferences (young couple, old couple, alone, group, family with young/older kids). For each group, satisfaction with a variety of measures (cleanness, convenience, location, personnel, service and value) is reported. Finally, social networks such as Facebook or Google encourage users to disclose their preferences by implementing features like Facebook's 'like button'. By doing so, a user's preference is immediately spread around his or her personal network. We therefore conclude that at least a fraction of consumers is influenced by the interaction with other consumers. In a next step towards the application of the model to the real world, we will have a look at the data used.

In the model, consumer preferences are modelled as a continuous metric variable in two-dimensional space. Real-world data will often show preference for certain products than the importance of certain product characteristics. Simplicity of interfaces (such as Facebook) or the nature of interaction (purchase data) will often provide binary data which have to be taken into account when choosing an algorithm for analysis.

A final prerequisite for the application of the model is the proper measurement of additional parameters used in the model, that is, the force of adaption and the size of the reference group. Some platforms might provide interesting variables for the measurement of the size of the reference group, such as the number of 'friends' on a social platform. When automated recommendation engines are used, the size of the neighbourhood must be configured directly. The propensity to adapt or individualize might be measured *ex post* or collected via a survey.

Clearly, the identification of a proper number of segments (or clusters) is both a question of academic research and a practical problem every market researcher is confronted with. However, as the model is mainly concerned about the development of preference structures over time, the trend of the number of clusters (derived by application of any automated selection criterion) is more important than its absolute value.

Future empirical research could therefore use the following propositions and conjectures derived from observations from the ABM applied in Sudharshan and Mild (2011) to formulate hypotheses for empirical testing (all the following propositions have a *ceteris paribus* or unless acted upon by an external force condition attached to them).

**Proposition 1.** Markets will smoothly move to a steady number of segments.

**Proposition 2.** In the case of populations with uniform distribution of preferences, the number of segments will increase over time.

**Proposition 3.** In the case of populations with normal distribution of preferences, the number of segments will decrease over time.

- *Conjecture 1*: If the modality of the distribution of preferences of a population changes, it has an impact on whether the number of segments increases or decreases. For example, increase of modality from 1 (e.g. normal) to infinite (e.g. uniform) implies that at a certain critical value for the number of modes, the number of segments over time will switch from declining over time to increasing over time.
  - *Implication 1: For new markets in which the interactions about the subutilities are just beginning, it is important to know the modality of the initial distribution as the modality will determine whether the number of segments will decrease or increase. And correspondingly the number of major product variants will increase or decrease. This clearly has implications for whether one should introduce a diverse product line and then prune it, or introduce a single product and then add breadth to the product line.*

**Proposition 4.** Knowing the type of initial distribution, the variation in the properties of number of segments, concentration of markets and compactness of segments can be forecasted.

**Proposition 5.** In the case of populations with uniform distribution of preferences, the market share concentration of major variants will decrease over time. That is, initially strong products will get weaker.

**Proposition 6.** In the case of populations with normal distribution of preferences, the market share concentration of major variants will increase over time. That is, initially strong products will get stronger.

- *Conjecture 2*: There exists a critical value for the number of modes above which market concentration will start decreasing over time and below which market concentration will increase over time. This conjecture may have applications for both marketing managers and public policy officials.
  - *Implication 2: First-mover advantage, that is, persistently higher market shares and/or profits accruing to early entrants, is more likely in markets with normal distributions of preferences (or low-mode distributions) as opposed to markets with uniform (or high-mode) distributions.*

**Proposition 7.** Increasing the size of reference groups (except when it is very small) increases the number of segments but only up to a maximal value.

- *Conjecture 3*: As networking communication technologies add to the size of reference groups, the number of segments will increase in cultures where the reference group size had shrunk due to specialization of labour, disruption of traditional (tribal/village) ties or long commuting times (and thus reduced time for social interactions).
- *Conjecture 4*: No matter how much networking communication technologies add to the size of reference groups, the number of segments will not increase beyond a certain maximal point (around 20).
  - *Implication 3: Reference group size should be a focus of attention of social media management efforts to manage product line strategies.*

**Proposition 8.** However strong the conformity force, markets will not collapse to a single segment. This is due to the likely presence of at least a very small error in knowing the preferences of the reference group, if not the presence of the need for differentiation.

**Proposition 9.** Market power can be gained by increasing conformity — this seems to be very intuitive.

**Proposition 10.** Market power can be gained by increasing uncertainty (the alpha effect) in normal markets, whereas uncertainty has the opposite effect in uniform markets.

- *Conjecture 5*: There exists a critical value for the number of modes above which market concentration will start decreasing with increasing uncertainty and below which market concentration will increase with increasing uncertainty. This conjecture may have implications for competitive models in marketing which include customer uncertainty.

○ *Implication 4: It is important for marketing research professionals to provide information on the preference distributions to product managers as this information impacts the expected uncertainty in the appropriate product line width for a market and through this uncertainty it has an impact on risk management.*

## 3.5. Implications for Practitioners

Using social networking data (name sources — tourism firms) we should develop machine learning algorithms combined with social network analysis to identify segments, and identify how individuals switch, when they do. For each segment we could identify the first few who choose their tourism sites for a given season and use that as a basis to develop offerings for that segment.

To develop offerings, practitioners should keep in mind that to effectively manage exchange with customers based on the values that they seek requires a firm to manage its exchange entities that in turn consist of its offerings, transaction facilitators and the mode of its relationship (Sudharshan, 1995). The exchange relationship depends on the values (functional, social, emotional, epistemic and conditional) that customers seek, and the exchange entities that are provided by firms (Sheth, Newman, & Gross, 1991).

OK, let us face it, the purpose of marketing strategy is to create a monopoly — a monopoly in serving a customer's needs better than anybody and thus earning their business at a profitable price. Since from scale requirements a minimum size may be necessary, it becomes necessary to find customers who can be served by a common set of exchange entities — perhaps with some fine-tuning for each customer (mass customization). So choosing a set of exchange entities for a segment requires a thorough understanding of the customers as well as the customers' customers — depending on the focal firm's position in the value (supply) chain. Not only does the focal tourism firm have to satisfy the customers' needs, but it also needs to do it differently and better than its competitors.

Creativity is what provides defensible differentiation. If all you do is to offer a lower price than your competitors, it will not be long before they lower their prices (including, as appropriate, changing their own sourcing to obtain lower costs). Same logic prevails if you increase a little bit on the length of stay etc. However, if you make a qualitative change, such as arranging with a cruise ship to exclusively provide a differentiated cabin experience only for a firm's clients, changing the internal customer digital entertainment environment (e.g. Emirates), owning a destination island/facility etc., it will be near impossible or at least very difficult for a firm's differentiation edge to be eroded.

The dimensions (exchange entity elements) on which creativity may be brought to bear to differentially serve client needs are provided in detail in Sudharshan (1995). The elements of exchange entities are offerings, relationship modes and transaction facilitators. In a more extensive form they are shown in Table 3.1.

Table 3.1: Exchange entities from the firm's side.

| Offering | Relationship mode and quality[a] | Transaction facilitators |
|---|---|---|
| Function | Structure<br>• Flexibility<br>• Formality<br>• Openness | Information |
| Form | Control<br>• Accountability<br>• Responsibility<br>• Knowledge<br>• Accuracy of information<br>• Sufficiency of resources<br>• Ease of operation<br>• Responsiveness to the customers' need for information, needs and changes | Service |
| Price | Emotion<br>• Trustworthiness<br>• Fairness<br>• Respect<br>• Approval<br>• Satisfaction<br>• Bonding — comfort level and a mutual feeling of commitment to a partnership | Financing/risk management |

[a]*Source*: Musgrave and Anniss (1996).

While a firm designs its marketing strategy and its exchange entities, it may be worth bearing in mind the 'second economy' that Arthur (2011) posits and describes in his recent article in which he estimates that this second economy will equal or surpass the physical (first) economy by 2025. What is the second economy? In Arthur's own words, 'The second economy ... is vast, silent, connected, unseen, and autonomous (meaning that human beings may design it but are not directly involved in running it). It is remotely executing and global, always on, and endlessly configurable. It is concurrent ... everything happens in parallel. It is self-configuring, meaning it constantly reconfigures itself on the fly, and increasingly, it is also self-organizing, self-architecting, and self-healing'.

Arthur also provides two examples to frame his discourse. The first asks the readers to consider all that happens between the time they insert a credit card into a self-serve check in kiosk at an airport and the time that the boarding pass is printed out. Prior to the digital revolution all this processing was done by humans. Now it is part of the second economy.

The second example is from supply chain management where the paperwork regarding the international shipment of freight is carried out through a series of 'conversations' between various servers at light speed and not by humans at snail mail speed.

> In both these examples, and all across economies in the developed world, processes in the physical economy are being entered into the digital economy, where they are 'speaking to' other processes in the digital economy, in a constant conversation among multiple servers and multiple semi-intelligent nodes that are updating things, querying things, checking things off, readjusting things, and eventually connecting back with processes and humans in the physical economy. So we can say that another economy — a second economy — of all of these digitized business processes conversing, executing, and triggering further actions is silently forming alongside the physical economy. (Arthur, 2011, pp. 2–3)

It is thus worth pausing and asking the key question: 'in a world where the second economy is growing rapidly, how can the tourism industry proactively create customer value and differentiate their exchange entities and be it known that it is theirs?'

# References

Ap, J. (1992). Residents perceptions on tourism impacts. *Annals of Tourism Research, 19*(4), 665–690.

Arsal, I., Woosnam, K. M., Baldwin, E. D., & Backman, S. (2010). Residents as travel destination information providers: An online community perspective. *Journal of Travel Research, 49*(4), 400–413.

Arthur, B. W. (2011). The second economy. *McKinsey Quarterly, 4*(October), 1–9.

Buhalis, D., & Law, R. (2008). Progress in information technology and tourism management: 20 years on and 10 years after the Internet — The state of eTourism research. *Tourism Management, 29*, 609–623.

Butcher, K. (2005). Differential impact of social influence in the hospitality encounter. *International Journal of Contemporary Hospitality Management, 17*(2), 125–135.

Chuang, S.-T. (2010). Rural tourism: Perspectives from social exchange theory. *Social Behavior and Personality, 38*(10), 1313–1322.

Chung, J. Y., & Buhalis, D. (2008). Information needs in online social networks. *Information Technology & Tourism, 10*(4), 267–281.

Cohen, E. (1979). A phenomenology of tourist experiences. *Sociology, 13*(2), 179–201.

Conze, O., Bieger, T., Laesser, C., & Riklin, T. (2010). Relationship intention as a mediator between relational benefits and customer loyalty in the tour operator industry. *Journal of Travel & Tourism Marketing, 27*(1), 51–62.

Dogan, H. Z. (1989). Forms of adjustment – Sociocultural impacts of tourism. *Annals of Tourism Research, 16*(2), 216–236.

Gilbert, D., Fiske, S. T., & Lindzey, G. (1998). *The handbook of social psychology* (4th ed.). Boston, MA: McGraw-Hill.

Godes, D., Mayzlin, D., Chen, Y., Das, S., Dellarocas, C., Pfeiffer, B., … Verlegh, P. (2005). The firm's management of social interactions. *Marketing Letters, 16*(3–4), 415–428.

Gretzel, U. (2011). Intelligent systems in tourism. A social science perspective. *Annals of Tourism Research, 38*(3), 757–779.

Gursoy, D., & Rutherford, D. G. (2004). Host attitude toward tourism: An improved structural model. *Annals of Tourism Research, 31*, 495–516.

Gwinner, K. P., Gremler, D. D., & Bitner, M. J. (1998). Relational benefits in service industries: The customer's perspective. *Journal of the Academy of Marketing Science, 26*(2), 101–144.

Harrison, D. (Ed.). (2003). Themes in Pacific Island tourism. In *Pacific Island tourism.* New York, NY: Cognizant.

Hartmann, W. R. (2010). Demand estimation with social interactions and the implications for targeted marketing. *Marketing Science, 29*(4), 585–601.

Hoffman, D. L., & Low, S. A. (1981). An application of the probit transformation to tourism survey data. *Journal of Travel Research, 20*(2), 35–38.

Hofstede, G. (1980). *Culture's consequences.* Beverly Hills, CA: Sage.

Huang, J., & Hsu, C. H. C. (2010). The impact of customer-to-customer interaction on cruise experience and vacation satisfaction. *Journal of Travel Research, 49*(1), 79–92.

Kim, W. G., Han, J. S., & Lee, E. (2001). Effects of relationship marketing on repeat purchase and word of mouth. *Journal of Hospitality & Tourism Research, 25*(3), 272–288.

Law, R., Fuchs, M., & Ricci, F. (2011). *Information and communication technologies in tourism.* Vienna, Austria: Springer Verlag.

Leiper, N. (1979). The framework of tourism towards a definition of tourism, tourist, and the tourist industry. *Annals of Tourism Research, 6*, 390–407.

Levy, S. E., Getz, D., & Hudson, S. (2011). A field experimental investigation of managerially facilitated consumer-to-consumer interaction. *Journal of Travel & Tourism Marketing, 28*(6), 656–674.

Lin, I. Y., & Mattila, A. S. (2010). Restaurant servicescape, service encounter, and perceived congruency on customers' emotions and satisfaction. *Journal of Hospitality Marketing and Management, 19*, 819–841.

Moscardo, G. (2009). Tourism and quality of life: Towards a more critical approach. *Tourism and Hospitality Research, 9*(2), 159–170.

Moscovici, S. (2001). Why a theory of social representations? In K. Deaux & G. Philogene (Eds.), *Representations* (pp. 8–35). Oxford: Blackwell.

Murphy, L. E. (2001). Exploring social interactions of backpackers. *Annals of Tourism Research, 28*(1), 50–67.

Musgrave, J., & Anniss, M. (1996). *Relationship dynamics: Theory and analysis.* New York, NY: Free Press.

Pearce, P. L., Moscardo, G., & Ross, G. F. (1996). *Tourism community relationships.* Oxford: Pergamon.

Reed, M. G. (1997). Power relations and community-based tourism planning. *Annals of Tourism Research, 24*(3), 566–591.

Richards, G., & Wilson, J. (Eds.). (2004). *The global nomad: Backpacker travel in theory and practice* (pp. 3–42). Clevedon, UK: Channel View Publications.

Rokka, J., & Moisander, J. (2009). Environmental dialogue in online communities: Negotiating ecological citizenship among global travellers. *International Journal of Consumer Studies, 33*, 199–205.

Schwabe, G., & Prestipino, M. (2005). How tourism communities can change travel information quality. Paper presented at the 13th European conference on information systems (ECIS 2005), 18–21 June 2005, Regensburg, Germany.

Sheth, J., Newman, B. A., & Gross, B. L. (1991). *Consumption values and market choices: Theory and applications.* Cincinnati, OH: South-Western Publishing.

Sigala, M. (2009). Geoportals and geocollaborative portals: Functionality and impacts on travellers' trip planning and decision making processes. Paper presented at the annual International Council for Hotel, Restaurant and Institutional Education (I-CHRIE) convention (I-CHRIE 2009 annual conference), organised by I-CHRIE in San Francisco, CA, 29 July – 1 August 2009.

Sigala, M. (2010). Measuring customer value in online collaborative trip planning processes. *Marketing Intelligence & Planning, 28*(4), 418–443.

Smith, V. L. (Ed.). (1989). *Hosts and guests: The anthropology of tourism* (2nd ed.). Philadelphia, PA: University of Pennsylvania Press.

Sudharshan, D. (1995). *Marketing strategy: Relationships, offerings, timing and resource allocation.* Upper Saddle River, NJ: Prentice Hall.

Sudharshan, D., & Mild, A. (2011). *Changes in customer preference heterogeneity patterns.* Working Paper.

Thyne, M., Davies, S., & Nash, R. (2005). A lifestyle segmentation analysis of the backpacker market in Scotland: A case study of the Scottish Youth Hostel Association. *Journal of Quality Assurance in Hospitality and Tourism, 5*(2), 95–119.

Triandis, H. C. (1983). Some dimensions of intercultural variation and their implications for community psychology. *Journal of Community Psychology, 11*, 285–302.

Tsiotsou, R., & Ratten, V. (2010). Future research directions in tourism marketing. *Marketing Intelligence & Planning, 28*(4), 533–544.

Vargo, S. L., & Lusch, R. F. (2004). Evolving to a new dominant logic for marketing. *Journal of Marketing, 68*(1), 1–17.

Waitt, G. (2000). Consuming heritage: Perceived historical authenticity. *Annals of Tourism Research, 27*(4), 835–862.

Wang, N. (1999). Rethinking authenticity in tourism experience. *Annals of Tourism Research, 26*(2), 349–370.

Wearing, S. L. (2001). *Volunteer tourism: Experiences that make a difference.* Oxon, UK: CABI Publishing.

Werthner, H., & Ricci, F. (2004). E-commerce and tourism. *Communications of the ACM, 47*(12), 101–105.

White, N. R., & White, P. B. (2009). The comfort of strangers: Tourists in the Australian outback. *International Journal of Tourism Research, 11*, 143–153.

Yoo, K. H., & Gretzel, U. (2008). What motivates consumers to write online travel reviews? *Information Technology & Tourism, 10*(4), 283–295.

# PART II
# BRANDING

# Chapter 4

# Destination Branding Development: Linking Supply-Side and Demand-Side Perspectives

*Giacomo Del Chiappa and Ilenia Bregoli*

## 4.1. Introduction

Two of the most important factors influencing the competitiveness of a destination are *destination governance* and *destination branding* (Dwyer & Kim, 2003). Destination governance is instrumental in managing the fragmented and complex nature of tourist destinations effectively, while destination branding is important because it enhances a destination's positioning and exerts considerable influence over tourists' choices and their satisfaction. The relationship between destination governance and destination branding, however, has not been investigated in depth. This omission occurred because in recent decades the literature on destination branding has mainly adopted a demand-side rather than a supply-side perspective (Konecnik & Go, 2008), whereas both should be taken into consideration for destination brand plannin.g and positioning to be effective (Cai, 2002). Indeed, keeping in mind both these perspectives helps managers develop a coherent method of execution and to achieve consistency and cohesiveness in brand positioning (Freire, 2007).

This chapter addresses the above point. It defines the concepts of a destination brand and destination branding, proposes a dynamic model of brand development that combines supply-side and demand-side perspectives, and analyses the main conditions for successful destination branding. The chapter concludes by arguing that, when considering how destination governance affects destination branding, three layers of governance should be examined: the internal governance of a Destination Management Organization (DMO), the governance of the relationship between stakeholders and the governance of the relationship between the DMO and stakeholders. This model therefore draws destination managers' attention to the necessity of carrying out both internal and external marketing and branding operations when trying to achieve a unique destination brand positioning.

Strategic Marketing in Tourism Services
Copyright © 2012 by Emerald Group Publishing Limited
All rights of reproduction in any form reserved
ISBN: 978-1-78052-070-4

## 4.2.  The Concept of Destination Branding: An Overview

Initially, destination branding borrowed the definition given by the American Marketing Association (Ritchie & Ritchie, 1998). According to this definition, a brand can be defined as 'a multidimensional assortment of functional, emotional, relational, and strategic elements that collectively generate a unique network of associations in consumers mind' (Aaker, 1996, p. 68; Keller, 1993, 2003). More recently, a destination brand is considered as a relational network developed by a destination between itself and certain target markets and stakeholders in order to affirm its own offer (Del Chiappa, 2008; Hankinson, 2004; Kavaratzis, 2005). This means that a destination brand exists only if it is able to stake out a position in the tourist's mind and not because it has a recognized name, distinctive logo, tagline or symbol.

Broadly speaking, destination branding can be defined as the dynamic process of drawing support and cooperation from different stakeholders so that 'the brand will be accepted, communicated and manifested through official and unofficial publicity and products' (Ooi, 2004, p. 109). Overall, the objective of destination branding is 'to select a consistent mix of brand elements to identify and distinguish a destination through positive image building' (Cai, 2002, p. 734).

Destination branding has been recognized as a critical element for destinations wishing to cope with fierce competition from other destinations and changes to tourists' behaviour and expectations (Beerli & Martin, 2004). It describes the development of a unique identity and its promotion, with the aim of creating a positive image in the minds of targeted tourists (positioning), so that a destination can gain a differential advantage over its competitors (Deslandes, Goldsmith, Bonn, & Joseph, 2006; Greaves & Skinner, 2010). Destination image (one of the components of a destination branding) influences tourists' behaviour before and after they visit the destination. On the one hand, it influences tourists' initial perceptions about the destination and their choice as to where to spend their holidays (Byon & Zhang, 2010). On the other hand, destination image plays a significant role after tourists have visited the destination as it is the benchmark against which tourists compare both their initial perceptions and what they really experienced during their stay (Konecnik & Gartner, 2007; Pike, 2007). It follows that the more positive the brand of a destination, the greater the likelihood that the destination will attract more travellers than its competitors. Therefore, it can be argued that effective destination branding improves destination positioning and competitiveness. For example, the case of New Zealand with its '100% Pure' tourism campaign has been considered highly successful in reinforcing the country's 'clean and green' positioning (Morgan, Pritchard, & Piggott, 2002).

Destinations function as a brand even if they are not managed under a conceptual brand framework (Freire, 2007) but, as previous research emphasizes, the responsibility for directing the process of destination branding should be given to a DMO (Gartrell, 1994; Hankinson, 2007) to reach consistency. Then, the DMO becomes responsible for the management and marketing of the destination as a whole. Place branding can occur across multiple spatial scales, involving DMO at different levels (local, regional, national etc.) and creating significant issues for the governance and management of place brand architecture (Hall, 2010). A dynamic model of destination branding that considers both demand-side and supply-side branding perspectives is therefore necessary to highlight the roles that different stakeholders have in developing the destination brand.

## 4.3.   A Dynamic Model of Destination Branding

Previous tourism literature mainly focuses on the definition of destination branding, looking at the static dimensions of a brand and its functions/advantages, while neglecting its dynamic dimensions (e.g. Deslandes & Goldsmith, 2002). Recently, several authors have proposed a model of destination brand equity that describes the dynamic process of destination brand creation, development and assessment (Konecnik & Gartner, 2007). Moreover, as Konecnik and Go (2008) emphasize, most tourism literature analyses the success of specific tourist destinations from a demand-side perspective, while the supply-side perspective has remained largely unexamined. On the contrary, it could be argued that, for destination brand planning and positioning to be effective, it is necessary to adopt a perspective that evaluates brand identity and brand image at the same time (Cai, 2002). Indeed, as research carried out in fields other than tourism has found, it can be argued that tourist operators not only represent an important and significant stakeholder group but are also the original source of brand equity (Burmann, Zeplin, & Riley, 2009). Therefore, it becomes necessary to study how a destination brand is perceived by both local stakeholders and tourists. Figure 4.1 displays a dynamic model of destination brand development, obtained using research from literature on general branding (Kapferer, 1995).

According to this model, to create and develop a unique brand positioning, the DMO should first seek and shape the destination brand identity based on the resources, both tangible (e.g. hotel facilities, beaches etc.) and intangible (e.g. myths, friendly people), that really exist within the tourist area. These resources create a natural tourist vocation for the destination and based on these, the DMO should define the destination's identity. Destination identity refers to the essence of a place. In particular, Zenker and Braun (2010), cited in Zenker (2011, p. 42), consider place identity as 'the visual, verbal and behavioural expressions of a place, which are embodied in the aims, communication, values and general culture of the place's stakeholders and the overall place design'.

To sum up, according to Freire (2007) tourism destinations should develop a system of brand management focused on their identity with DMOs identifying a 'unique set of brand associations that the brand strategist aspires to create or maintain' (Aaker, 1996, p. 68). When defining the destination identity, DMOs should involve both the stakeholders who provide services to tourists (accommodation, restaurants, transport providers, visitor attractions, shops etc.) and the local community, so that they become committed to the brand values that are delivered

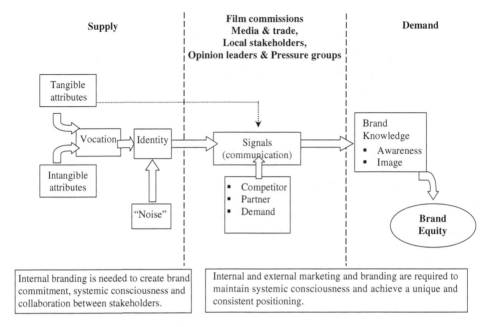

Figure 4.1: A model of destination brand creation and development. *Source*: Del Chiappa (2008).

to the market. In the process of brand development, the DMO should not only establish the destination's brand identity based on the real essence of the place but also try to harmonize the different views that stakeholders have about the brand identity to be promoted. (In Figure 4.1, these different views refer to 'noise'.) This is necessary because the more divergent these views are, the greater the difficulties that the DMO will have to face when shaping the destination's identity and the greater the likelihood that stakeholders will deliver divergent messages to the market through their own promotional activities. By harmonizing the different views, the DMO can reach a consensus-based collaborative strategy, and it becomes possible to align the image that tourists have of the destination before and after they visit it, meaning that tourist satisfaction and loyalty can be addressed (Konecnik & Gartner, 2007). Indeed, local people are relevant because they influence how consumers experience the destination. This is particularly true when local people working in tourism sector are considered. As Freire (2007) stated, the degree of tourists' satisfaction is linked to the behaviour and attitudes of people working within the tourist service providers.

Once the DMO has decided upon the destination's brand identity, the brand development process enters the second phase of the model, during which the brand is communicated in three different ways: primary (architecture and real place offering), secondary (formal communication through official media) and tertiary (word of mouth reinforced by the media and residents) (Kavaratzis, 2005). At this stage, the DMO is the main organization responsible for brand promotion. However, other 'image formation agents' are able to influence, both positively and negatively, the brand image formation process and tourists' decision making (Deslandes et al., 2006; Gartner, 1993). According to Gartner (1993), these agents can be organic (non-commercial sources of information, such as family and friends) and induced (commercial sources of information, such as travel agencies), with destination marketers having less control over the former than over the latter (Deslandes et al., 2006; Greaves & Skinner, 2010). Our model considers the following: (a) film commissions trying to attract motion media production crews (movies, TV and commercial films) in their respective localities, contributing significantly to the destination image and interest in visiting a place (Beeton, 2005; Mercille, 2005); (b) media (both visual and non-visual) that can strongly influence a destination image through the message they deliver to their audience (Roesch, 2009); (c) intermediaries (such as tour operators and travel agencies) that can influence the destination image formation process, based on how they promote destinations and specific tourist packages to their customers; (d) local stakeholders delivering services to tourists (hotel facilities, restaurants, transport providers, visitor attractions, shops etc.) who are able to influence the destination image formation process through the promotional activities they run to market their own businesses (Gallarza, Saura, & Garcìa, 2002) and by how they interact with visitors once they are at the destination (Freire, 2007); and (e) opinion leaders (tourism journalists, archaeologists etc.) and pressure groups (environmental groups) who can influence the way tourists perceive a destination image by the opinions they express. Furthermore, the destination's image formation process can be influenced by its competitors, that is, other destinations competing to attract tourist flows (Echtner & Ritchie, 1993; Hankinson, 2004), and by its partners. The latter includes other organizations (tourism related or not, such as other tourism destinations, companies, airlines, producers of typical foods etc.) with whom a destination could develop co-marketing activities aimed at creating new products and/or strengthening its brand positioning (Cai, 2002).

The destination identity that the DMO and stakeholders try to deliver to the market does not necessarily conform to the image perceived by tourists (Greaves & Skinner, 2010). This occurs because macro-promotional activities delivered by the DMO can be interpreted differently by tourists, according to their sociocultural background (Mercille, 2005) and/or distorted by the aforementioned 'agents' (film commissions, media and trade etc.). As a result, destination managers should systematically carry out market research to determine if there is any inconsistency between identity and image (Pike, 2007), in order to understand the reasons for such a misalignment and decide how to correct it.

Regarding the third stage of the model, which covers the demand side of the process, it must be stressed that brand knowledge consists of brand awareness and brand image, that is, the sources of destination brand equity (Keller, 2003). The former is 'reflected by consumers' ability to identify the brand under different conditions' (Keller, 1993, p. 3) and can be considered as being the first step in a purchase behaviour model. Awareness is a necessary but not a sufficient step leading to an initial trial and then to repeat purchases (Konecnik & Gartner, 2007). Image is another decisive factor and can be defined 'as the sum of beliefs, ideas and impressions that a person has of a destination' (Crompton, 1979, p. 18). According to customer-based brand equity perspective (Keller, 2003), destination brand assessment can be carried out by comparing the awareness and image of a destination with those of its competitors (Konecnik & Gartner, 2007). Hence, the higher the level of brand awareness and brand image, the higher the likelihood of brand choice (Pike, 2007). By and large, brand success can be measured through business-based criteria (profitability, market share, overnight stays etc.), consumer-based criteria (brand awareness and image, loyalty etc.) (de Chernatony, Dall'Olmo, & Harris, 1998; Deslandes et al., 2006) and citizen/stakeholders-based criteria (Zenker & Martin, 2011).

## 4.4.  The Relationship between Destination Governance and Destination Branding

The model presented in Figure 4.1 highlights the existence of a relationship between destination governance and branding, with the former influencing the latter through internal marketing and branding activities (Del Chiappa & Bregoli, 2011).

On the one hand, destination governance refers to the way in which relationships between players are regulated (Palmer, 1998) and, from a tourism perspective, it 'consists of setting and developing rules and mechanisms for a policy, as well as business strategies, by involving all the institutions and individuals' (Beritelli, Bieger, & Laesser, 2007, p. 96). On the other hand, destination branding is the dynamic process of drawing support and cooperation from different stakeholders (Hankinson, 2004). It could be argued that an effective governance is needed in order to enhance the collaboration between local stakeholders (both public and private) and involve them in the destination brand strategy, so that they can feel themselves engaged, attached and committed to a unique and consistent destination identity to be delivered to the market. This collaboration, in turn, creates the pre-condition for reaching a unique and consistent brand positioning (Sheehan & Ritchie, 2005), since it contributes to eliminating, to some extent, conflicting brand messages delivered by the marketing and communication activities of the single stakeholders and the DMO.

When considering the way destination governance affects destination branding (Del Chiappa & Bregoli, 2011), three elements should be taken into account: (1) the internal governance of a DMO; (2) the relationship among stakeholders; and (3) the relationship between the DMO and stakeholders.

The first element refers to the rules regulating internal functioning of DMOs. In particular, two aspects affect the destination branding strategy, namely the organizational structure of the DMO and the DMO's funding strategies. The former is represented, for instance, by the number of positions on a board, the number of people sitting on each board and the number of institutions represented on the various boards (Beritelli et al., 2007). The latter refers to the strategies adopted by the DMO to obtain the necessary funds for carrying out its activities, such as raising funds through tourism and hotel taxes, through fees paid by members or from the public sector (Ritchie & Crouch, 2003).

The second element refers to relationships developed between destination stakeholders who are engaged in offering complementary services to tourists. As far as the network structure is concerned, relevant dimensions include embeddedness, network centrality and density. Embeddedness refers to the fact that firms are embedded in a network of interpersonal relationships (Bhat & Milne, 2008). Network centrality refers to the position that an organization has within the network, as a consequence of the power it acquires through the network. The central role played by an individual organization in a network influences the coordination of the network itself (Scott, Cooper, & Baggio, 2008). Finally, network density refers to the number of ties between stakeholders, and it is suggested that dense networks ensure high certainty because there is an increased access to both information and resources (Scott et al., 2008).

Finally, the third element addresses the relationships between DMOs and their stakeholders. These relationships are developed through internal branding and communication. Internal branding, communication of the brand identity and coordination are not necessary to increase the collaboration and integration between local stakeholders, but they are essential in committing the stakeholders towards the destination's brand identity. Moreover, they allow the DMO to gain the authority and leadership to shape and guide the operations of local stakeholders, so that these can converge and create a unique and consistent destination brand (Del Chiappa & Bregoli, 2011). In particular, the tools that a DMO can use to cultivate its relationship with stakeholders include developing coordination mechanisms, such as regular communications and meetings, socialization processes, staff training, interlocking directorates and selection systems (Beritelli et al., 2007; Mowforth & Munt, 2003).

Internal governance of a DMO and the relationship between the DMO and stakeholders are pivotal in destination brand development. Therefore, it is advisable that rules regulating the internal operation of a DMO might require that destination stakeholders are involved in the process of creation and management of the destination brand. At the same time, the DMO's funding strategy might influence marketing activities towards developing a destination brand. Finally, the way through which different destination stakeholders are coordinated is fundamental to avoid the delivering of divergent brand messages.

## 4.5. Conditions for Successful Destination Branding

The creation and development of a destination brand are more likely to be successful when the project is managed bottom-up rather than top-down (Gnoth, 2002). Furthermore, the success of a destination brand strategy depends on the involvement of all public and private stakeholders (Jamal & Getz, 1995; Lodge, 2002). The role of the DMO as a convener is crucial because it has the power to identify all the significant stakeholders who should be involved (Sheehan & Ritchie, 2005). In so doing, the DMO should favour stakeholders who are perceived by other players as having the legitimacy to participate in the partnership (Wood & Gray, 1991). Nevertheless, some studies highlight that a full involvement of stakeholders in destination brand creation and development is not always the optimal solution (Bhat & Milne, 2008). Furthermore, a brand-oriented organizational culture must exist in the DMO and departmental coordination and process alignment must be established in order to shape and share brand values and then to secure commitment to them (Hankinson, 2007).

Moreover, it is necessary that the DMO should be able to exercise effective, strong and visionary leadership and manage the partnerships in order to minimize conflicts between partners and satisfy their needs. Recent research on destination governance and branding emphasizes that the degree of authority and trustworthiness DMO managers exert depends on their personal characteristics and previous experience (Marzano & Scott, 2009). Research in the field of network and stakeholder theory shows that strong authority and leadership are essential in destination branding while those responsible must work together on the brand development process to regulate the relationships between stakeholders, prevent conflicts and make the most of the opportunities for networking (Palmer, 1998).

## 4.6.  Conclusions

To sum up, the proposed model views destination branding as a dynamic process and takes into account both the internal (supply-side) and external (demand-side) perspectives of brand creation. It also underlines the fact that destination branding basically means managing the network of relationships between public and private operators who work at the destination. Destination branding is mainly about integrating marketing communication and is difficult to manage because stakeholders are interested in making their own brand and brand campaigns serving their own needs (Ooi, 2004). Consequently, the main objective of destination branding should be to enhance the collaboration between the different stakeholders (Hankinson, 2004), thereby eliminating, to some extent, the conflicting brand messages they might deliver. The proposed model of destination branding turns the attention of destination managers to the necessity of carrying out internal and external marketing and branding operations, making them mutually consistent, in order to reach a holistic and effective destination brand positioning. Internal branding and coordination activities are necessary to increase collaboration and integration between local stakeholders, to make them committed towards the chosen destination brand identity. Moreover, they enable DMOs to take over a leadership role they need to shape and guide the activities of local stakeholders so that the latter can converge in creating a unique and consistent destination brand identity. Internal branding and coordination of operations are essential to reach internal brand strength, which synthesizes the extent to which stakeholders internalize the brand values and adopt them in their daily job when interacting with visitors (Bregoli & Del Chiappa, 2011). Finally, external branding is necessary to develop a unique destination brand, thereby differentiating one destination from another and gaining a competitive advantage (Prayag, 2010).

# References

Aaker, D. A. (1996). *Buildings strong brands*. New York, NY: Free Press.

Beerli, A., & Martin, J. D. (2004). Tourists' characteristics and the perceived image of tourist destinations: A quantitative analysis — A case study of Lanzarote, Spain. *Tourism Management, 25*(5), 623–636.

Beeton, S. (2005). *Film-induced tourism*. Clevedon: Channel View.

Beritelli, P., Bieger, T., & Laesser, C. (2007). Destination governance: Using corporate governance theories as a foundation for effective destination management. *Journal of Travel Research, 46*(1), 96–107.

Bhat, S. S., & Milne, S. (2008). Network effects on cooperation in destination website development. *Tourism Management, 29*(6), 1131–1140.

Bregoli, I., & Del Chiappa, G. (2011). Destination governance and internal branding as antecedents of destination brand development: An exploratory study on Edinburgh. In *Proceedings of 2011 advances in hospitality and tourism marketing and management conference*, Istanbul, Turkey (pp. 254–260).

Burmann, C., Zeplin, S., & Riley, N. (2009). Key determinants of internal brand management success: An exploratory empirical analysis. *Journal of Brand Management, 16*(4), 264–284.

Byon, K. K., & Zhang, J. J. (2010). Development of a scale measuring destination image. *Marketing Intelligence & Planning, 28*(4), 508–532.

Cai, L. A. (2002). Cooperative branding for rural destinations. *Annals of Tourism Research, 29*(3), 720–742.

Crompton, J. L. (1979). Motivations for pleasure vacation. *Annals of Tourism Research, 6*(4), 408–424.

de Chernatony, L., Dall'Olmo, F., & Harris, F. (1998). Criteria to assess brand success. *Journal of Marketing Management, 14*(7), 765–781.

Del Chiappa, G. (2008). The brand building process of a convention destination. In *Marketing Trends Association: Proceedings of the VII international congress "marketing trends"*, Venice, Paris. Retrieved from http://www.marketing-trends-congress.com/sites/default/files/papers/2008/2008_it_DelChiappa.pdf.

Del Chiappa, G., & Bregoli, I. (2011). Destination governance and branding: The Portofino case study. In *Athens tourism symposium: Proceedings of the 2011 Athens tourism symposium: International scientific congress on current trends in tourism management and tourism policy*, Athens, Greece.

Deslandes, D. D., & Goldsmith, R. E. (2002). Destination branding: A new concept for tourism marketing. In *Academy of Marketing Science: Proceedings of the 2002 AMS annual conference*, Sanibel Island, FL (pp. 130–137).

Deslandes, D. D., Goldsmith, R. E., Bonn, M., & Joseph, S. (2006). Measuring destination image: Do the existing scales work? *Tourism Review International, 10*(3), 142–153.

Dwyer, L., & Kim, C. (2003). Destination competitiveness: Determinants and indicators. *Current Issues in Tourism, 6*(5), 369–414.

Echtner, C. M., & Ritchie, B. (1993). The measurement of destination image: An empirical assessment. *Journal of Travel Research, 31*(4), 3–13.

Freire, J. R. (2007). 'Local people' a critical dimension for place brands. *Journal of Brand Management, 16*(7), 420–438.

Gallarza, M. G., Saura, I. G., & Garcìa, H. C. (2002). Destination image: Towards a conceptual framework. *Annals of Tourism Research, 29*(1), 56–78.

Gartner, W. (1993). Image formation process. *Journal of Travel & Tourism Marketing, 2*(2–3), 191–216.

Gartrell, R. (1994). *Destination marketing for convention and visitor bureaus.* Dubuque: Kendall/Hunt.

Gnoth, J. (2002). Leveraging export brands through a tourism destination brand. *The Journal of Brand Management, 9*(4–5), 262–280.

Greaves, N., & Skinner, H. (2010). The importance of destination image analysis to UK rural tourism. *Marketing Intelligence & Planning, 28*(4), 486–507.

Hall, C. M. (2010). Tourism destination branding and its effects on national branding strategies: Brand New Zealand, clean and green but it is smart? *European Journal of Tourism, Hospitality and Recreation, 1*(1), 68–89.

Hankinson, G. (2004). Relational network brands: Towards a conceptual model of place brands. *Journal of Vacation Marketing, 10*(2), 109–121.

Hankinson, G. (2007). The management of destination brands: Five guiding principles based on recent developments in corporate branding theory. *Journal of Brand Management, 14*(3), 240–254.

Jamal, T. B., & Getz, D. (1995). Collaboration theory and community tourism planning. *Annals of Tourism Research, 22*(1), 186–204.

Kapferer, J. N. (1995). *Les marques. Capital de l'entreprise.* Paris: Éditions d'organisation.

Kavaratzis, M. (2005). Place branding: A review of trends and conceptual models. *The Marketing Review, 5*(4), 329–342.

Keller, K. L. (1993). Conceptualizing, measuring, and managing customer-based brand equity. *Journal of Marketing, 57*(1), 1–22.

Keller, K. L. (2003). *Strategic brand management: Building, measuring, and managing brand equity* (2nd ed.). Upper Saddle River, NJ: Pearson Education, Inc.

Konecnik, M., & Gartner, W. C. (2007). Customer-based brand equity for a destination. *Annals of Tourism Research, 34*(2), 400–421.

Konecnik, M., & Go, F. (2008). Tourism destination brand identity: The case of Slovenia. *Journal of Brand Management, 15*(3), 177–189.

Lodge, C. (2002). Success and failure: The brand stories of two countries. *Journal of Brand Management, 9*(4), 372–384.

Marzano, G., & Scott, N. (2009). Power in destination branding. *Annals of Tourism Research, 36*(2), 247–267.

Mercille, J. (2005). Media effects on image: The case of Tibet. *Annals of Tourism Research, 32*(4), 1039–1055.

Morgan, N., Pritchard, A., & Piggott, R. (2002). New Zealand, 100% pure. The creation of a powerful niche destination brand. *Journal of Brand Management, 9*(1–5), 335–354.

Mowforth, M., & Munt, I. (2003). *Tourism and sustainability. Development and new tourism in the third world.* London: Routledge.

Ooi, C. (2004). Poetics and politics of destination branding: Denmark. *Scandinavian Journal of Hospitality and Tourism, 4*(2), 107–128.

Palmer, A. (1998). Evaluating the governance style of marketing groups. *Annals of Tourism Research*, *25*(1), 185–201.

Pike, S. (2007). Consumer-based brand equity for destinations: Practical DMO performance measures. *Journal of Travel & Tourism Marketing*, *22*(1), 51–61.

Prayag, G. (2010). Brand image assessment: International visitors' perceptions of Cape Town. *Marketing Intelligence & Planning*, *28*(4), 462–485.

Ritchie, J. R. B., & Crouch, G. I. (2003). *The competitive destination: A sustainable tourism perspective*. Wallingford: CABI Publishing.

Ritchie, J. R. B., & Ritchie, R. J. B. (1998). The branding of tourism destination: Past achievements and future challenges. In P. Keller (Ed.), *Destination marketing — Scope and limitations. International Association of Science Experts in Tourism: Proceedings of 48th annual congress AIEST*, Marrakech, Morocco (pp. 89–116).

Roesch, S. (2009). *The experiences of film location tourists*. Clevedon: Channel View.

Scott, N., Cooper, C., & Baggio, R. (2008). Destination networks: Four Australian cases. *Annals of Tourism Research*, *35*(1), 169–188.

Sheehan, L. R., & Ritchie, J. R. B. (2005). Destination stakeholders: Exploring identity and salience. *Annals of Tourism Research*, *32*(3), 711–734.

Wood, D. J., & Gray, B. (1991). Toward a comprehensive theory of collaboration. *Journal of Applied Behavioral Science*, *27*(2), 139–162.

Zenker, S. (2011). How to catch a city? The concept and measurement of place brands. *Journal of Place Management and Development*, *4*(1), 40–52.

Zenker, S., & Braun, E. (2010). Branding a city — A conceptual approach for place branding and place brand management. In *European Marketing Academy: Proceedings of the 39th EMAC*, Copenhagen, Denmark. Retrieved from http://www.placebrand.eu/mediapool/85/857874/data/Zenker_Braun_EMAC2010.pdf

Zenker, S., & Martin, N. (2011). Measuring success in place marketing and branding. *Place Branding and Public Diplomacy*, *7*(1), 32–41.

Chapter 5

# Place Branding: The Issue of a Narrowed Tourism Perspective

*Sebastian Zenker and Suzanne C. Beckmann*

## 5.1. Introduction

Cities around the world increasingly compete with each other for the attention of tourists, investors, companies and new citizens (Anholt, 2007; Hospers, 2003; Kavaratzis, 2005; Zenker, 2009). Place marketers therefore focus on establishing the city as a brand (Braun, 2008), trying to promote their city to its many different target groups. Quite often, these campaigns are grounded in the belief that a city brand is a controllable and fully manageable communication tool and that one place brand 'fits all' — an external as well as an internal target audience. Yet a brand is, by definition, a network of associations in the minds of individual people (Keller, 1993) and is therefore — on an aggregated level — based on the perceptions of different groups. Hence, the perception of a city (brand) can differ significantly given the various stakeholders' different perspectives and interests (e.g. between residents and tourists). These different perceptions are a challenge for place brand communication because different associations have to be communicated.

   Thus, we argue that place branding should increasingly focus on the city brand perception of its different stakeholders; consequently, brand managers should develop strategies for how to build *target group-specific place brand architecture.* The current academic discussion shows considerable shortcomings in this respect (Govers & Go, 2009; Zenker, 2011), since it mainly focuses on the explorative description of a certain city brand without distinguishing properly between external and internal target groups. The aim of our study is therefore to assess whether significant discrepancies exist between the internal and external stakeholders' mental representations of the city brand, using the city of Hamburg as a case study. Based on our findings, we suggest a model of place brand architecture, the *Place Brand Centre* (Zenker & Braun, 2010), that has the potential to address these discrepancies.

Strategic Marketing in Tourism Services
Copyright © 2012 by Emerald Group Publishing Limited
All rights of reproduction in any form reserved
ISBN: 978-1-78052-070-4

## 5.2. Place Marketing and Branding

### 5.2.1. Defining Place Marketing and Branding

As a matter of fact, branding places (and cities in particular) has gained popularity among city officials in recent years. This is illustrated by the development and popularity of city brand rankings such as the *Anholt-GMI City Brands Index* (Anholt, 2006) or the *Saffron European City Brand Barometer* (Hildreth, 2011). Places are eager to garner positive associations in their stakeholders' mind and the number of interesting contributions is growing: Medway and Warnaby (2008) observe that places are being more and more conceptualized as brands, referring to the work of Hankinson (2004) and Kavaratzis and Ashworth (2005) in particular. Recently, Ashworth and Page (2011) have discussed the progress of urban tourism research, highlighting that place marketing (also in tourism) increasingly uses branding techniques, while Lucarelli and Berg (2011), as well as Gertner (2011), published first meta-analyses of the research domain.

The current research particularly highlights the important role of actual residents in place branding, since residents are simultaneously vital participants and audience of the process; in fact, it is a field where the exclusion of residents (internal stakeholders) is not an option. Freire (2009), for example, has discussed the role of local people in place branding, showing that they are indeed a critical dimension for the formation of place brands. His research on British users of the Algarve and Costa del Sol place brands demonstrates that local people are 'used' for a multitude of purposes in the formation of place brands. More specifically, he found that local people are used as an indicator for the evaluation of place brands, as a justifier for place brand consumption and as a differentiating factor between places. For instance, Freire (2009) reveals that the perceived degree of friendliness in local peoples' attitudes is a crucial element in destination evaluation. Furthermore, Freire (2009) contends that many of the perceived characteristics that make local people friendly — and therefore a positive and reinforcing factor of a successful place brand — are not necessarily culturally embedded. Rather, they are taught as part of an effective tourism service delivery process, which leads to the conclusion that local people can be considered a manageable asset within place branding.

Nevertheless, in practice as well as in theory, the definitions and concepts of place marketing and place branding often lack a consistent usage. As a result, place marketing is often mistakenly understood as 'place selling' (for a more thorough discussion, see Berglund & Olsson, 2010), concentrating solely on the promotional aspects while disregarding the more general objectives and range of place marketing and branding. Although the original aim of marketing is to understand and satisfy the consumer's needs (demand orientation), place selling is more concerned with trying to find the right consumers for an existing product (supply orientation). While the two may work in conjunction, they cannot be used interchangeably.

In general, place marketing is 'the coordinated use of marketing tools supported by a shared customer-oriented philosophy, for creating, communicating, delivering, and exchanging urban offerings that have value for the city's customers and the city's community at large' (Braun, 2008, p. 43). Place marketing is thus a customer-oriented approach, which aims at integrating all the existing and potential 'customers' of a given place. It therefore includes the concept of destination marketing, which is concerned exclusively with external target groups and their attraction to a place. In other words, place marketing targets not only tourists or one favourable group but also many different stakeholders (in contrast to destination marketing, which focuses on tourists).

From a theoretical point of view, the core stakeholder groups in place marketing and place branding are (1) visitors; (2) residents and workers; and (3) business and industry (Kotler, Haider, & Rein, 1993). However, the groups actually targeted in recent marketing practice are much more specific and complex. Tourists, for example, can be divided into business and leisure time visitors (Hankinson, 2005) as well as professional visitors such as archaeologists and architects, while residents can be separated into an internal target group (current residents) and an external group (potential residents). Within these groups, specific target audience segments are found such as students or the so-called creative class (Braun, 2008; Florida, 2004). A third generic group of stakeholders consists of public services, private business and non-governmental organizations such as environmental groups or grass-root organizations. Again, with the exception of civil service, all these groups can be both internal and external. A final stakeholder group is composed of media (e.g. Avraham, 2004) in a broad sense, covering everything from travel books to in-flight magazines, TV, daily newspapers and so forth. Figure 5.1 illustrates the different stakeholders in more detail.

As already mentioned, these stakeholders differ not only in their perceptions of a place but also foremost in their place needs and demands. Leisure time tourists, for example, are searching for leisure time activities like shopping malls or cultural events; business visitors, however, are more interested in logistics and facilities for their business meetings, while residents search for an attractive living environment. It

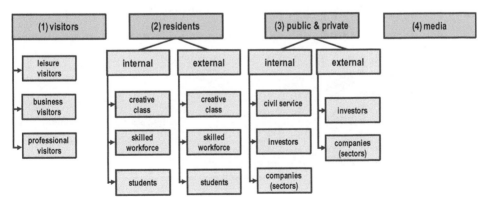

Figure 5.1: Stakeholders in place branding.

is therefore inevitable that both conflicts and synergies arise between the needs and wants of different stakeholders. Therefore, brand communication for a city's different and diverse target groups should be developed with these diverse expectations in mind.

Zenker and Braun (2010) also highlight the individual perception of the target audience in their place brand definition: 'a place brand is a network of associations in the consumer's mind based on the visual, verbal, and behavioral expression of a place, which is embodied through the aims, communication, values, and general culture of the place's stakeholders and the overall place design' (p. 3). The definition additionally asserts that a brand is not the communicated expression or 'place physics', but the perception of those expressions in the minds of the target group(s).

According to Kavaratzis (2008), the perception of a place is formed by three types of city communication: (1) primary communication that includes the architecture and real place offerings, as well as the place's behaviour, and therefore constitutes place physics; (2) secondary communication that includes the formal communication through official channels, like all forms of advertising or public relations, and is therefore called place communication; and (3) tertiary communication that refers to word of mouth reinforced foremost by media and the residents themselves and thus represents place word of mouth. Together they lead to a model of place brand perception that explicates how the place brand is built through the identity of a place and how its image differs between target groups. Those perceptions ultimately engender brand effects (Zenker & Martin, 2011), as shown in Figure 5.2.

The largest difference in place perceptions is expected to be found between the internal and external stakeholders, mainly because of the different needs and knowledge levels of the target audience. Furthermore, as proposed in Tajfel and Turner's (1979) Social Identity Theory, individuals define themselves as parts of social groups according to, for example, their value setting or geographical closeness. The residence or home of a person thereby determines a strong part of the person's self, distinguishing strongly between the *We* (In-Group, e.g. residents of Hamburg) versus *Them* (Out-Group, e.g. tourists). Because of this so-called

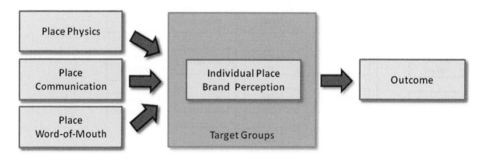

Figure 5.2: The concept of place brand perception. *Source*: Zenker (2011, p. 43).

*In-Group/Out-Group Effect* (Hogg, 2003; Tajfel & Turner, 1979) and the difference in knowledge structures based on different levels of experience, the Out-Group (external target audience) should show more common and stereotyped associations, while the In-Group (internal target audience) should possess a more diverse and heterogeneous place brand perception. Hence, brand communication for those two target groups should also differ.

Even though these different perceptions illustrate the urgent need for a place communication distinguishing between internal and external target groups, many locations are relevant for several stakeholders simultaneously; therefore, the place offering is not a single location but a package of locations. Consequently, an offering for tourists in Hamburg such as a local shopping street, for instance, overlaps to some extent with the offering for the city's residents. This simple example illustrates that even though brand communication should distinguish between different target groups, it must also be, to some extent, integrated in the brand communication since place customers cannot necessarily be separated from each other. Hence, a complex brand architecture is called for and will be discussed later in this chapter.

### 5.2.2. Measuring Place Brand Perceptions

In general, brand perception measurement can be divided into three main approaches: (1) elicitation of free brand associations from target customers with qualitative methods (e.g. Garrod, 2008; Supphellen, 2000); (2) rating of attributes with quantitative methods like standardized questionnaires on different brand dimensions (e.g. J. Aaker, 1997); and (3) mixed methods such as multidimensional scaling (MDS), the laddering technique based on means-end chain theory (e.g. Grunert & Grunert, 1995) or network analysis that combines qualitative research with quantitative methods (e.g. Henderson, Iacobucci, & Calder, 2002).

The extant place branding literature mainly represents the first two approaches, measuring place (brand) associations with qualitative methods (e.g. focus group discussions) or quantitative methods (e.g. rating place attributes with standardized questionnaires on different location factors; Zenker, 2011). The third approach of mixed methods is not yet widely used, even though these methods have the potential to overcome general shortcomings of the two other approaches (for one of the few examples, see McDonald, Thyne, & McMorland, 2008). While qualitative methods have the advantage of open questions and therefore allow researchers to explore unique associations with a city or a brand in general, it is nearly impossible to compare two different cities (brands) or target groups with this type of data. However, measuring the perception of a city with the help of a standardized questionnaire invites other problems. The results are strongly affected by the selection of attributes and thus could be biased by leaving out important dimensions (Zenker, 2011), making a comparison of cities with the help of those rankings partly a result of each study's respective focus. Additionally, this kind of direct measurement is strongly vulnerable to different kinds of social bias like the response bias (Fazio & Olson, 2003). Hence, a mixed method would allow both capturing the unique associations of the target group members and translating those into a comparable brand perception structure in a reliable and valid manner. Therefore, we chose the method of network analysis for our empirical study.

## 5.3. Empirical Study

### 5.3.1.  The Case of Hamburg

Hamburg is the second largest city in Germany with 1.8 million inhabitants (metropolitan region including Hamburg: 4.3 million). The city area comprises 755 km$^2$, including 75 km$^2$ of harbour (the second largest European harbour). Hamburg calls itself the green metropolis of Europe with 4700 ha of wooded area (16.8% of the city area, although nearby competitor Berlin maintains 18.1% of green areas). It is also a city at the waterfront, with 8% of the city area covered with water drawn from three rivers and some smaller canals. Additionally, Hamburg enjoys a healthy tourism industry, with over 8.95 million overnight stays in 2010. Favourite tourist attractions include the harbour and its fish market; the Reeperbahn (the former red light district that is nowadays more famous for clubbing); the vibrant restaurant and bar scene; and the very diverse cultural offerings such as theatres, musicals and museums. Furthermore, Hamburg attracts important economic powers by playing host to numerous headquarters from the top 500 German companies. Combined with international trade, Hamburg's gross domestic product in 2009 was €85.76 billion. With a foreigner's population percentage of 13.5, the city features an international touch: nearly 100 different consulates reside in the city, as do a high percentage of second-generation foreigners (who are not included in the foreigner statistics because of their German passports). Last, but not least: the city is a students' town, with 18 different universities and about 72,000 students (Federal Statistical Office of Hamburg and Schleswig-Holstein, 2011; Hamburg Marketing GmbH, 2009).

### 5.3.2.  Procedure and Sample

Since we wanted to assess both unique place brand associations and the comparability of place perception between the internal and external target audiences, we chose the method of network analysis (Henderson et al., 2002), which uses data from qualitative research and analyses it quantitatively. The method calculates the centrality of an association within the network of associations (e.g. by the numbers of interconnections between associations) and the result is a network of brand associations for each group, which can then be compared with each other. The objective is to identify top-of-mind brand associations that are strongly connected in the image network and to assess the differences in the perception of internal versus external stakeholders.

Data was collected via an online survey in which participants were randomly selected from a representative joint online research panel hosted by the University of Hamburg and the University of Cologne at the end of 2009. The image associations of the city of Hamburg brand were assessed via an open-ended questionnaire, which asked the participants to identify their three to five top-of-mind associations for the city of Hamburg. Additionally, we measured the familiarity with the city of Hamburg using an adaptation of the 7-point Likert brand familiarity scale (Kent & Allen, 1994). Afterwards, all qualitative mentions ($N = 1.437$) were coded into 85 different associations by three independent coders. The coder agreement was 96%, which is deemed very good (Neuendorf, 2002). The structures of the associations were analyzed with the help of network analysis and the top 20 brand associations were calculated by their degree centrality in the network (Henderson et al., 2002).

The sample consisted of 334 participants, with 174 participants who have lived or are still living in Hamburg (group A: internal residents) and 160 participants who have never been to Hamburg or only gone for a short visit (group B: external visitors). For group A, the average age was 37.8 years ($SD = 15.36$), 46.6% were male, and the average familiarity with the city of Hamburg was very high ($M = 5.46$; $SD = 1.20$). For group B, the average age was 34.5 years ($SD = 14.93$), 49.4% were male, and the average familiarity with the city of Hamburg was much lower than that in group A ($M = 2.63$; $SD = 1.44$).

### 5.3.3. Results

The 20 core associations for both target groups are shown in Table 5.1. The differences in the rankings are shown in bold if the discrepancy in the centrality within the network was more than 10 ranks. In total, 13 strong discrepancies were found. For the internal target group, the associations with Hamburg are much more diverse, covering the many different offerings of the city. Moreover, seven associations were exclusively found in this group, such as 'nature and free space', 'home' and 'good universities'.

As expected, the view of the Hamburg brand for the external target group is much more based on a tourist-stereotypical picture of the city (and actually includes the association of 'ocean' even though Hamburg is located more than 100 km away from the sea). Additionally, 'harbour' and 'Reeperbahn' are strongly connected in this group. Figures 5.3 and 5.4 illustrate the brand association network of both target groups. The unique associations are highlighted by using a different node shape (diamonds). In comparison with the external target group (Figure 5.4), the internal target group (Figure 5.3) shows a much stronger network of associations (in terms of more connections between the associations).

Table 5.1: Top 20 core associations of the Hamburg brand by degree centrality.

| No. | Group A (internal) | Group B (external) |
|-----|--------------------|--------------------|
| 1 | Harbour | Harbour |
| 2 | Alster (river) | Reeperbahn (red light and party district) |
| 3 | Elbe (river) | Alster (river) |
| 4 | Michel/churches (flagship — tourist attraction) | **Fish market (weekly market — tourist attraction)** |
| 5 | Reeperbahn (red light and party district) | **Musicals** |
| 6 | **Nature and free space** | St. Pauli (vibrant district and local soccer club) |
| 7 | Beautiful | Elbe (river) |
| 8 | City at the waterfront | Michel/churches (flagship — tourist attraction) |
| 9 | HSV (local soccer club) | HSV (local soccer club) |
| 10 | Shopping | Hanse (historic trade union) |
| 11 | **Home/a place to settle down** | City at the waterfront |
| 12 | **Open and tolerant** | **Fish** |
| 13 | **Hamburg city hall** | **Northern** |
| 14 | Harbour city/harbour store houses | Shopping |
| 15 | St. Pauli (vibrant district and local soccer club) | Beautiful |
| 16 | Hanse (historic trade union) | **Rich and expensive** |
| 17 | **Cultural offerings** | Major city |
| 18 | Major city | Harbour city/harbour store houses |
| 19 | **Good universities** | Friends and family |
| 20 | **Opera and theatres** | **Ocean** |

*Note*: Order by Freeman's degree centrality measurement; strong differences are given in bold.

## 5.4.  How to Communicate Place Brands?

### 5.4.1.  *Diverse Perceptions of Place Brands*

A limited focus on tourists in place (destination) branding often leads to a narrow brand communication, which disregards the complexity of the place marketing target audience and the different brand perceptions of the various stakeholders. The present study shows that the perception of tourists differs significantly from that of residents. For visitors, the image of the city of Hamburg was much more based on stereotypes ('fish' or 'ocean') than for the resident target group, which revealed a much more heterogeneous image of their city (brand), including 'theatres', 'universities' or

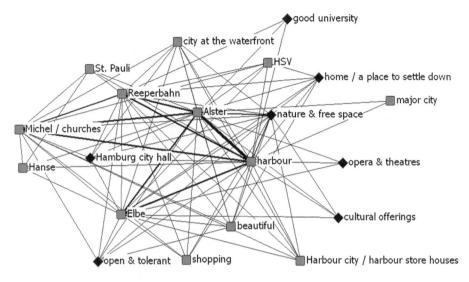

Figure 5.3: Perception of the city of Hamburg brand by internal target group.

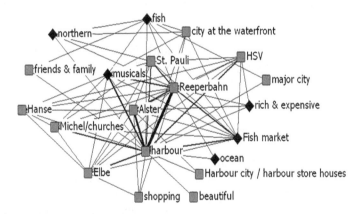

Figure 5.4: Perception of the city of Hamburg brand by external target group.

Hamburg as an 'open and tolerant' value setting. These results importantly call for a more differentiated brand communication that takes stakeholder differences explicitly into account in order to align the perceptions of the target audience with the place communication.

According to Kotler et al. (1993), one of the aims of place marketing is to 'promote a place's values and image so that potential users are fully aware of its distinctive advantages' (p. 18). Since an effective brand communication is based on the existing positive images of the city brand, it is crucial to assess the existing brand associations of the various stakeholders and then to highlight the distinctive advantages of the place. In the case of the city of Hamburg, place marketers so far mainly concentrate on the image of Hamburg as a 'city on the waterfront', a 'shopping city', a 'business place' and a city with a lot of cultural offerings like 'musicals' (Hamburg Marketing GmbH, 2009). This image strongly fits the perception of Hamburg for its visitors, but it neglects the image held by most of the city's actual residents (e.g. associating more with 'theatres' when thinking about cultural offerings) — a circumstance that results in low identification with the Hamburg brand and even public protest about place marketing activities, such as the 'Not in our Name' campaign from Hamburg residents (Gaier, 2010; Oehmke, 2010). Due to the focus on attracting tourists, a big mistrust occurred between the city marketing and large parts of the population.

Consequently, this example demonstrates the urgent need for a more differentiated brand communication, as well as a stronger resident involvement and participation in the place branding process, since residents simultaneously fulfil different roles in such a process: they not only are targets of place marketing itself but also function as ambassadors for their place brand and therefore 'make or break' the branding process for tourists (Freire, 2009; see also Chapters 4 and 7). A more complex brand architecture, featuring a place umbrella brand and different target group–specific sub-brands, would be able to communicate a more heterogeneous picture for the Hamburg brand. For example, the association 'university' (important for students) could be included in one sub-brand, while the 'musicals' association, which seems important for tourists, could be retained in a tourist sub-brand. This approach would likely lead to more authentic communication and higher identification with the Hamburg brand among all target groups.

### 5.4.2.  A Place Brand Architecture

Unfortunately, this customer-centred view — an essential part of the general marketing discussion (Webster, 1992) — is not yet common sense in the public sector (Buurma, 2001), or in place marketing practice. However, place marketers could find strong parallels in the development of corporate marketing organization and from there learn how to deal with the complexity of the multiple target groups.

D. A. Aaker and Joachimsthaler (2000) show for the corporate context hierarchical structures of brands using a brand architecture with different strategies for multiple target groups: for example, the *branded house* approach, consisting of a corporate umbrella brand and independent sub-brands that are still marked with the umbrella brand (Petromilli, Morrison, & Million, 2002). The aim is to build a strong overall umbrella brand with the help of the target group-specific product sub-brands. This approach should not be limited to product and company brands, however: it could be effectively extended to product or company brands that include a place brand (Uggla, 2006), or fully extended to the place branding context (Dooley & Bowie, 2005; Iversen & Hem, 2008; Therkelsen & Halkier, 2008). In contrast, Zenker and Braun (2010) do not use brand architecture in the context of an umbrella (country) brand and regional or provincial (city) sub-brands, but suggest a brand management structure with target group-specific sub-brands and a place (e.g. city) umbrella brand. The argument follows that the marketing structure of places should be organized by their target groups (Braun, 2008), very much like the modern organizational structures of marketing departments in companies (Homburg, Workman, & Jensen, 2000), as shown in Figure 5.5.

In their *Place Brand Centre* model, Zenker and Braun (2010) include a branded house approach with target group-specific sub-brands for all different groups chosen to be targeted, and a place umbrella brand that is represented by the overall place brand perception shared by the entire target audience. This place umbrella brand perception is built by the communicated place umbrella brand, by the place physics and finally by the perception of the different sub-brands.

In the context of our example, the city of Hamburg should use its shared associations (e.g. 'harbour', 'city at the waterfront' and 'major city') for its umbrella brand communication. Another Hamburg sub-brand could aim to strengthen the identity of the current residents (e.g. using the 'theatres' association), while associations like 'musicals' would be helpful for establishing a strong tourism sub-brand. Other sub-brands (e.g. for investors or students) should also be included. Of course, these sub-brands also influence the perception of the other place sub-brands and the place umbrella brand. A communicated tourist brand with a focus on 'musicals', for example, will also influence the perception of potential new residents or companies. Hence, brand communication must be aware of those associations that

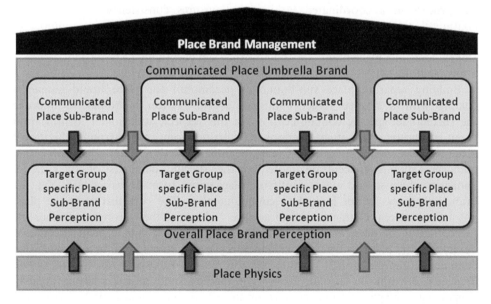

Figure 5.5: The Place Brand Centre. *Source*: Zenker and Braun (2010, p. 4).

could be problematic for other stakeholders — for instance, those that could be helpful for business and industry (e.g. 'industrial harbour') could lower the credibility of other associations for residents (e.g. 'nature and green spaces').

Another advantage of creating target group-specific sub-brands involves the already established organizational structure in city governments. For example, in city structures the tourism office is typically separated from the business development office. By employing the sub-brand approach discussed here, policy-making procedures and place sub-brand management could be very efficient, since no new structures are needed. Furthermore, all of the experience and knowledge about specific target groups within the organization can be utilized. Consequently, this approach will lead to new tasks for the place brand management of the place umbrella brand: namely the coordination, monitoring and communication between the sub-brand units as key aspects of the process.

### 5.4.3.   The Future of Place Branding

If branding — as a process of reduction — tries to simplify messages to the consumers (Anholt, 2009), it may not be as useful as managers think in cases of high complexity, such as with places. As mentioned, it could even be that communication that is too simple and merely focuses on an external target audience can prove very dangerous for a general place branding process. Dealing with complex brands calls for brand managers to moderate the different interest groups (sub-brands) and mitigate interest conflicts. Another crucial issue is the optimal number of sub-brands. Is there a limit to the optimal number of sub-brands? In terms of managing the process in a coordinated fashion that ensures consistency, coherence and continuity, there certainly is. Yet the decision about the appropriate number of sub-brands depends to a large extent on the assessment of who the relevant stakeholders of a place brand are and how they can eventually be grouped together in a meaningful way.

Building separate place sub-brands is paramount for place brand managers dealing with a diverse target audience, as this action is bound to improve the stakeholder-specific communication. In this respect, stakeholder identification is an important, yet often overlooked, starting point to determine the target groups of place communication (Currie, Seaton, & Wesley, 2009). Place sub-brand managers should concentrate more on the specific demands of their target audience, which should make identifying place competitors an easier task. Yet, the branding process is not limited to communication. The core feature is the place physics — the real characteristics of a place — because they strongly influence the perception of the place brand. In this regard, place brand management also means developing the place to meet the stakeholders' expectations, and, in a second step, communicating an honest picture of the place (Ashworth & Voogd, 1990; Trueman, Klemm, & Giroud, 2004). The method used in our study is actually supporting strategic decisions concerning these two steps, since it both assesses the place perceptions of stakeholders at a given point of time in terms of place characteristics and, given the measurement of the associations' centrality, indicates important topics for the content of the communication strategy. In this sense, place brand management as suggested in our stakeholder model embraces important features of relationship marketing management (Gummesson, 2002), especially the aspects of networks and interaction that signify the dynamics of places and their stakeholders.

For academia, we recommend two different main directions for further empirical research: first, researchers should empirically assess whether a target group-specific place brand has a stronger impact on dependent outcomes (e.g. place satisfaction or place identity) than does a simple 'one-for-all' place brand. Second, taking the actual discussion in Hamburg as an example, the complexity of the phenomenon of diverse place brand stakeholders warrants more research about the general question of place brand management in relation to governance situations (see also Chapter 4).

# References

Aaker, D. A., & Joachimsthaler, E. (2000). *Brand leadership*. New York, NY: The Free Press.

Aaker, J. (1997). Dimensions of brand personality. *Journal of Marketing Research, 34*(3), 347–356.

Anholt, S. (2006). *Anholt city brand index — "How the world views its cities"* (2nd ed.). Bellevue, WA: Global Market Insight.

Anholt, S. (2007). *Competitive identity — The new brand management for nations, cities and regions*. New York, NY: Palgrave Macmillan.

Anholt, S. (2009). Should place brands be simple? *Place Branding and Public Diplomacy, 5*(2), 91–96.

Ashworth, G., & Page, S. J. (2011). Urban tourism research: Recent progress and current paradoxes. *Tourism Management, 32*(1), 1–15.

Ashworth, G., & Voogd, H. (1990). *Selling the city: Marketing approaches in public sector urban planning*. London: Belhaven.

Avraham, E. (2004). Media strategies for improving an unfavorable city image. *Cities, 21*(6), 471–479.

Berglund, E., & Olsson, K. (2010). Rethinking place marketing — A literature review. In *European Regional Science Association: Proceedings of the 50th ERSA congress 2010*, Jönköping, Sweden.

Braun, E. (2008). *City marketing: Towards an integrated approach*. Rotterdam: Erasmus Research Institute of Management (ERIM).

Buurma, H. (2001). Public policy marketing: Marketing exchange in the public sector. *European Journal of Marketing, 35*(11/12), 1287–1300.

Currie, R. R., Seaton, S., & Wesley, F. (2009). Determining stakeholders for feasibility analysis. *Annals of Tourism Research, 36*(1), 41–63.

Dooley, G., & Bowie, D. (2005). Place brand architecture: Strategic management of the brand portfolio. *Journal of Place Branding, 1*(4), 402–419.

Fazio, R. H., & Olson, M. A. (2003). Implicit measures in social cognition research: Their meaning and use. *Annual Review of Psychology, 54*, 297–327.

Federal Statistical Office of Hamburg and Schleswig-Holstein. (2011). *Statistisches Jahrbuch Hamburg 2010/2011* [*Annual statistical report for Hamburg 2010/2011*]. Hamburg: Federal Statistical Office of Hamburg and Schleswig-Holstein.

Florida, R. (2004). *The rise of the creative class*. New York, NY: Basic Books.

Freire, J. R. (2009). Local people: A critical dimension for place brands. *Journal of Brand Management, 16*(7), 420–438.

Gaier, T. (2010). *Not in our name, Marke Hamburg!* [Web log post]. Retrieved from http://www.buback.de/nion/

Garrod, B. (2008). Exploring place perception: A photo-based analysis. *Annals of Tourism research, 35*(2), 381–401.

Gertner, D. (2011). Unfolding and configuring two decades of research and publications on place marketing and place branding. *Place Branding and Public Diplomacy, 7*(2), 91–106.

Govers, R., & Go, F. (2009). *Place branding: Glocal, virtual and physical identities, constructed, imagines and experienced.* Basingstoke: Palgrave Macmillan.

Grunert, K. G., & Grunert, S. C. (1995). Measuring subjective meaning structures by the laddering method: Theoretical considerations and methodological problems. *International Journal of Research in Marketing, 12*(3), 209–226.

Gummesson, E. (2002). *Total relationship marketing* (2nd ed.). Oxford: Butterworth Heinemann.

Hamburg Marketing GmbH. (2009). *Discover Hamburg — The city on the waterfront.* Hamburg Marketing.

Hankinson, G. (2004). Relational network brands: Towards a conceptual model of place brands. *Journal of Vacation Marketing, 10*(2), 109–121.

Hankinson, G. (2005). Destination brand images: A business tourism perspective. *Journal of Services Marketing, 19*(1), 24–32.

Henderson, G., Iacobucci, D., & Calder, B. J. (2002). Using network analysis to understand brands. *Advances in Consumer Research, 29*(1), 397–405.

Hildreth, J. (2011). *The Saffron European City Brand Barometer.* Report. Retrieved from Saffron Brand Consultants, Saffron Brand Consultants website: http://saffron-consultants.com/news-views/publications/

Hogg, M. A. (2003). Social identity. In M. R. Leary & J. P. Tangney (Eds.), *Handbook of self and identity* (pp. 462–479). New York, NY: Guilford.

Homburg, C., Workman, J. P., & Jensen, O. (2000). Fundamental changes in marketing organization: The movement toward a customer-focused organizational structure. *Journal of the Academy of Marketing Science, 28*(4), 459–478.

Hospers, G.-J. (2003). Creative cities in Europe: Urban competitiveness in the knowledge economy. *Intereconomics, 38*(5), 260–269.

Iversen, N. M., & Hem, L. E. (2008). Provenance associations as core values of place umbrella brands. *European Journal of Marketing, 42*(5/6), 603–626.

Kavaratzis, M. (2005). Place branding: A review of trends and conceptual models. *The Marketing Review, 5*(4), 329–342.

Kavaratzis, M. (2008). *From city marketing to city branding: An interdisciplinary analysis with reference to Amsterdam, Budapest and Athens.* Doctoral dissertation, Rijksuniversiteit Groningen.

Kavaratzis, M., & Ashworth, G. (2005). City branding: An effective assertion of identity or a transitory marketing trick? *Tijdschrift voor Economische en Sociale Geografie, 96*(5), 506–514.

Keller, K. L. (1993). Conceptualizing, measuring, and managing customer-based brand equity. *Journal of Marketing, 57*(1), 1–22.

Kent, R. J., & Allen, C. T. (1994). Competitive interference effects in consumer memory for advertising: The role of brand familiarity. *Journal of Marketing, 58*(3), 97–105.

Kotler, P., Haider, D. H., & Rein, I. (1993). *Marketing places: Attracting investment, industry, and tourism to cities, states, and nations.* New York, NY: The Free Press.

Lucarelli, A., & Berg, P. O. (2011). City branding: A state-of-the-art review of the research domain. *Journal of Place Management and Development, 4*(1), 9–27.

McDonald, S., Thyne, M., & McMorland, L. (2008). Means-end theory in tourism research. *Annals of Tourism Research, 35*(2), 596–599.

Medway, D., & Warnaby, G. (2008). Alternative perspectives on marketing and the place brand. *European Journal of Marketing, 42*(5/6), 641–653.

Neuendorf, K. A. (2002). *The content analysis guidebook.* Thousand Oaks, CA: Sage.

Oehmke, P. (2010). Stadtentwicklung: Stadt der Gespenster [*City development: The city of ghosts*]. *Der Spiegel,* January (1/2010), pp. 94–98.

Petromilli, M., Morrison, D., & Million, M. (2002). Brand architecture: Building brand portfolio value. *Strategy and Leadership, 30*(5), 22–28.

Supphellen, M. (2000). Understanding core brand equity: Guidelines for in-depth elicitation of brand associations. *International Journal of Market Research, 42*(3), 319–338.

Tajfel, H., & Turner, J. C. (1979). An integrative theory of intergroup conflict. In W. G. Austin & S. Worchel (Eds.), *The social psychology of intergroup relations* (pp. 33–57). Monterey, CA: Brooks Cole.

Therkelsen, A., & Halkier, H. (2008). Contemplating place branding umbrellas. The case of coordinated national tourism and business promotion in Denmark. *Scandinavian Journal of Hospitality and Tourism, 8*(2), 159–175.

Trueman, M., Klemm, M., & Giroud, A. (2004). Can a city communicate? Bradford as a corporate brand. *Corporate Communications: An International Journal, 9*(4), 317–330.

Uggla, H. (2006). The corporate brand association base — A conceptual model for the creation of inclusive brand architecture. *European Journal of Marketing, 40*(7/8), 785–802.

Webster, F. E. (1992). The changing role of marketing in the corporation. *Journal of Marketing, 56*(4), 1–17.

Zenker, S. (2009). Who's your target? The creative class as a target group for place branding. *Journal of Place Management and Development, 2*(1), 23–32.

Zenker, S. (2011). How to catch a city? The concept and measurement of place brands. *Journal of Place Management and Development, 4*(1), 40–52.

Zenker, S., & Braun, E. (2010). Branding a city — A conceptual approach for place branding and place brand management. In *European Marketing Academy: Proceedings of the 39th EMAC annual conference,* Copenhagen, Denmark. Retrieved from http://www.placebrand.eu/publications.html

Zenker, S., & Martin, N. (2011). Measuring success in place marketing and branding. *Journal of Place Branding and Public Diplomacy, 7*(1), 32–41.

Chapter 6

# Destination Imagery: Examining Online Representative Dissonance in India

*Deepak Chhabra*

## 6.1. Introduction

Destination images can perform a crucial role in the strategic marketing planning of tourism because they are an inherent and prominent component of a tourists' decision-making process and also influence their preferences, expectations and ultimate behaviour and satisfaction once at the destination (Joppe, Martin, & Waalen, 2001; Lin & Huang, 2009; Van Raaij & Francken, 1984). Fakeye and Crompton (1991) describe destination images as mental constructs drawn from a selection of impressions out of an infinite range of expressions impinged daily on the audience. Bandyopadhyay and Morais contend that they are an embodiment of 'all objective knowledge, impressions, prejudice, imaginations, and emotional thoughts an individual or group might have of a particular place' (2005, p. 1009). This chapter examines online destination images (textual and visual) portrayed by different agents of tourism in a developing country (India). It takes an initiative to decipher how India is represented by agents internal to India especially in the context of online imagery. The aim is to critically construe differences between India's national self and its local self and between the government and the trade media marketing endeavours. This line of inquiry is important because online imagery comparisons between the induced tourism agents (external and internal to the region) are still sparse (Bandyopadhyay & Morais, 2005; Echtner & Prasad, 2003). This investigation is also significant in that existence of imagery dissonance has the potential of creating serious implications on tourist satisfaction at the visited destination and causes inconsistent behaviour with potential for serious negative impacts for the host region. Strategic marketing efforts, therefore, require unveiling of imagery discrepancies so that they can be removed or minimized.

Strategic Marketing in Tourism Services
Copyright © 2012 by Emerald Group Publishing Limited
All rights of reproduction in any form reserved
ISBN: 978-1-78052-070-4

## 6.2.   Review of Literature on Destination Image

This section describes destination image making and delineates it into its various components. It presents predominant classifications of image formation agents as noted extensively in documented literature. Next, a more discursive view is offered of the induced agents. A travel trade media perspective follows and the section concludes with a brief overview of studies on Indian destination representations by the travel trade and the visitors.

### 6.2.1.   Destination Image Perspectives

Henderson describes destination images 'as an amalgam of the knowledge, feelings, beliefs, opinions, ideas, expectations, and impressions people have about a named location' (2007, p. 262). Image is a crucial factor in promotion strategies and 'destinations with clearly delineated and appealing images are better positioned than those about which little is known or which seem unattractive' (Henderson, 2007, p. 262). The multifaceted nature of images implies that it has cognitive, affective and conative connotations. The cognitive perspective is represented by a person's beliefs or knowledge about characteristics of a destination, whereas the affective component refers to the emotions a person holds for a destination (Alcaniz, Garcia, & Blas, 2009). The conative perspective refers to the intention to visit and the travel behaviour. The cognitive dimension is represented by factors such as natural environment, cultural heritage, tourist infrastructures and atmosphere. More recent studies suggest a multidimensional framework in the form of a cognitive–affective sequence (Kim & Richardson, 2003; Martin & Bosque, 2008). Some studies have further divided the cognitive dimension into functional and psychological elements. The functional aspect refers to tangible perceptions of scenery, accommodation or price levels, whereas the psychological perspective focuses on being informed of the intangible characteristics such as atmosphere and friendliness (Bigne, Sanchez, & Sanchez, 2001).

Furthermore, extant literature recognizes that both stimulus and personal factors contribute to the formation of destination images. Stimulus factors refer to information sources and agents, whereas personal factors focus on social and psychological attributes. Several classifications of destination image sources or agents exist. The most commonly used classification by Gunn consists of two main classifications of image: organic and induced. According to Henderson, 'the former are evolved over time and are founded on information sources such as the media, popular culture and schooling while the latter are a consequence of exposure to advertisements and guidebooks' (2007, p. 262). Apparently, the key basis of differentiation between the two is the extent of control a destination is able to exercise over what and how they are represented. Organic images emanate from unbiased external sources such as books, travel experiences and television documentaries, whereas induced agents arise from source of origin — 'the destination itself and its marketing and promotion materials' (Choi, Lehto, & Morrison, 2007, p. 119).

Further classifications of induced image formation agents were presented by Gartner (1993): overt induced I, overt induced II, covert induced I and covert induced II. The overt induced I agents refer to conventional forms of advertising such as television, radio, brochures, billboards and print media advertising to showcase selected images in the minds of tourists. Overt induced II image formation agents refer to information obtained or requested from mediating agents such as tour operators, wholesalers and organizations with a vested concern in the travel decision-making process. Covert induced I agents make use of a familiar and famous spokesperson to stress credibility of their destination. Covert induced II refers to unbiased sources that have no inherent personal or commercial interest in promoting travel to the destination. Examples within this category include newspaper reviews.

### 6.2.2. Developing Destination Images

Congruent to the perspective of induced agents, destination images are a creative way of generating dreams for potential tourists, and it often rests on a destination marketing organization (DMO)/national tourism office (NTO) and the travel trade media to make decisions on the promotional content so that preferred messages are delivered to the target markets (Entman, 1993; Martin & Bosque, 2008; Phelps, 1986). Hence, in essence, destination image frames formulated by induced agents rely on sanitized expressions (Cohen, 2001). Aligned with this view, Wang, Hawk, and Tenopir (2000) imply that the formulation of destination images involves preference, exclusion and accentuation of certain images. The point stressed here is that the tourism industry agents develop destination images to cater to the needs of the popular market segments and these representations are often incongruent with the actual complexity prevailing in the destination (Chon, 1992; Gartner, 1993; Wang et al., 2000). In other words, some aspects of a perceived reality are framed to 'make them more salient in a communication context' (Entman, 1993, p. 52) with the purpose of capturing audience attention and influencing perceptions.

The relevance of framing aspects of perceived reality is all the more substantiated and visible in the tourism promotion media of developing world destinations in that they are mystified to make them more attractive to the western audience (Echtner & Prasad, 2003; Silver, 1993). The developing countries are often projected, especially by the western media, as problem-free, primitive, untouched and with frozen and simpler past (Bhattacharyya, 1997; Chaudhary, 2000). Such selected representations make these destinations devoid of sense of place and distinct identity and reflect power configurations (Sturma, 1999). Thus, akin to the past era of selected expressions of Orientalism (colonialism) and imperial subjugations, it is claimed that the contemporary discourse carries forward the colonial perspective and favouring the 'West's pleasure periphery' and claim of superiority (Echtner & Prasad, 2003). Such trends have provided fuel to the Orientalism ideologies as Echtner and Prasad explain that the 'touristic representations tend to portray destinations as stagnant in a state of unchanged Orientalism, open to all the exotic fantasies, and as primitive and backward' (2003, p. 166). Moreover, it has also been claimed that projected expressions have socio-political connotations. That is, they display evidence of ongoing power struggles and preferred identity (Pritchard & Morgan, 2001). Bandyopadhyay and Morais (2005) and Palmer (1994) echo this view in their assertion that preferred signs of nationhood help to build a sense of national identity within the mind of the western visitor. Central to this contention is the argument that 'tourism representations do not exist in isolation but are inexorable intertwined in a circuit of culture whereby representations utilize and reflect identity and in which images are continuously produced and consumed' (Pritchard & Morgan, 2001, p. 168).

Aligned with the aforementioned view, Cohen argues that different travel trade media sources narrate different versions of preferred stories (Cohen, 2001). For instance, western media projections of a developing country and media projections by the developing country itself are not similar.

### 6.2.3. The Demand Perspective

Using a demand perspective, Chaudhary (2000) had presented foreign tourists' perspective of a developing country (India). The author identified strengths and weaknesses of India's tourism-related image dimensions. Positive images of the country related to inexpensive destination, diversity in arts and rich cultural heritage, whereas attributes that fell short of expectations were poor quality of roads, petty crimes and poor guide services. The author suggested that the promotional images should use arts and heritage as their main plank to portray India as an attractive destination to foreign tourists. Suggestions were also made in regard to improvement in services, safety from petty crimes and better infrastructure. In another study, Bhattacharyya (1997) conducted a semiotic analysis of popular tourism guidebooks to understand how Indian images are mediated. The author reported an emphasis on 'past glory' and 'exotic present'. The results revealed how selected images of India were reinforced in addition to unfolding preferred relationship with the indigenous Indians. Evidence of ongoing power struggles and preferred identity was uncovered.

Although extant literature exists on destination image, most studies to date have centred on visitor perceptions and resulting behaviour based on destination image responses (MacKay & Fesenmaier, 2000; Sirgy & Su, 2000; Tapachai & Waryszak, 2000). For instance, Tasci and Gartner (2007) reported that destination images have significant influences on consumer behaviour before, during and after a trip, all the more so in the case of tourism because of its intangible nature and restricted consumer ability to comprehend and examine the actual product before purchase. Therefore, images from reliable induced destination agents are often regarded as reliable and these affect the intentions and decisions of potential consumers (Aguilar, 2009). However, investigation of destination image structures, especially digital, remains meagre, although exhaustive research has confirmed the significance and pronounced domination of Internet in projecting and influencing destination image formulations (Choi et al., 2007). It is an accepted fact that digital sources of information offer great opportunities and a broad gamut of online information sources today formulates destination images and revolutionary progress of Internet has made communications between suppliers, distributors and consumers more complex and dynamic (Echtner & Ritchie, 1993). Multiple identities are communicated via Internet, thereby blurring the competition thresholds (Govers & Go, 2003). It is argued that there is a crucial need to discern both textual and visual information 'to understand the complete structure of destination image formation in the online market space' (Choi et al., 2007, p.119). Choi et al. argue that 'visual images are powerful marketing tools which enable a destination to communicate diverse images in a compressed format' (2007, p. 119). They are a simplified and condensed form of numerous materials and pieces of information and hence likely to generate a deeper impact by holding attention and interest (MacKay & Couldwell, 2004).

### 6.2.4. Tourism in India

This study focuses on online destination images. India is selected as it has become one of the major tourism destinations in Southeast Asia with an unprecedented increase in the number of international and domestic tourists over the past decade. It is the seventh largest country in the world and stretches over an area of 3.3 million square kilometres. It is also the second most populated country in the world with a population of approximately 1.2 billion. Approximately 16 major languages are spoken in India with Hindi being national language spoken by 45% of the total population. The official language of communication is English. Almost 50% of the population is under 25 years of age. Over the past several years, India has witnessed an unprecedented growth in both domestic and international tourism. It consists of 7 union territories (sub-national administrative divisions) and 28 states and all but 5 union territories (which are directly ruled by the centre) have elected governments and legislatures.

Tourism is the largest service industry and makes a contribution of 6.23% to the nation's GDP (Ministry of Tourism, 2009). It also contributes to 8.8% of the total employment in the country. According to the tourism statistics report, India annually received more than 5.1 million foreign tourist arrivals and approximately 650 million domestic tourists in 2009. Total economic benefits in 2008 were accrued to the amount of US$100 billion. Top international markets for India are the United States and the United Kingdom and top five states to receive international tourists in 2009 were Rajasthan, Tamil Nadu, Maharashtra, Delhi and Uttar Pradesh. Top states for domestic tourism are Andhra Pradesh, Uttar Pradesh and Tamil Nadu (Ministry of Tourism, 2010). Ministry of Tourism is the primary agency responsible for the formulation of policies and agenda for the development and promotion of tourism at the national level. It is the task of the Ministry to consult and collaborate with other stakeholders in the sector including various central ministries/agencies, the state governments/union territories and the representatives of the private sector. This central agency is responsible for the development and promotion of tourism in India and is currently focussing on 'Incredible India' campaign. According to the World

Travel and Tourism Council, India will become one of the most popular tourism destinations by 2018.

It is the objective of this study to provide an insightful view into the manner in which India is projected online by induced destination agents. In sum, the following research questions guide the key objectives of this study: How is India positioned at the national and state levels by the Indian government? What are the positioning strategies adopted by the Indian trade media? Does representative dissonance exist between the government and trade media representations?

## 6.3.  Method

This study is anchored in three sets of data: Indian government representations at the national level, state government representations and popular travel magazine representations. Two key sources of representations employed by the government are examined: the Ministry of Tourism's newsletter and the official tourism website of India at the national level. Also, the content of the official tourism websites at the statewide level is examined. Featured articles for 2010 from the *Express Travel & Tourism* (online now and offers one issue per month) related to India were examined. Bandyopadhyay confirms that this magazine is the leading source of information on travel and 'the only national tabloid on the travel industry and reaches major travel agencies, tour operator, hotel and resort owners and airlines and publishes statements and interviews of foremost tourism personalities in the country, from both private sector as well as the Indian Tourism Ministry' (2009, p. 58).

Additionally, Indian public representations were assimilated from the online version of the premier magazine of India at the national level, the *Outlook Traveller* (Bandyopadhyay, 2006). It is published once a month and introduces interested audience to unknown places while informing readers about unknown facts of familiar and popular destinations. According to Bandyopadhyay, this magazine is represented by 'travel writers from different religious backgrounds who sometimes travel to remote places of the country and describe the history of a temple or mosque or church which is unknown to people. Also, sometimes they narrate their unique experiences of visiting a place' (2006, p. 59). Additionally, content of online versions of other popular magazines, such as *Travel Express* and *Tourism India*, was examined.

Time frame of this study was 2010. Because all published material was in English, data was collected in English. A qualitative technique was employed to collect data in the form of content analysis. Content analysis of marketing material helped identify recurrent destination image themes at the national and statewide levels. It is argued that effective content analysis can help develop appropriate themes or classifications which can be independently verified and tested for reliability. A systematic comparison of the online content between the three induced agents of tourism was conducted to identify predominant themes and determine if representative dissonance exists at the national and statewide levels and between travel magazines and government representations. It is important to point out here that the data does not represent an exhaustive selection of travel trade representations such as images portrayed by the promotional material employed by travel agents and tour operators operating inside India. Also, because of time and budget constraints, the focus was on 2010 and an extended time frame analysis could not be employed.

Two independent coders were used in this study to test inter-coder reliability. Bias was minimized by following three steps: (1) the websites were examined in their entirety by both the coders who took notes about possible themes; (2) list of codes was gleaned and frequency was calculated for each coded theme independently; and (3) themes were described based on the assembling and examination of text coded under each theme. The coders belonged to different backgrounds: one was a native citizen of India and the second one was a native of the United States. Different backgrounds can help identity cultural nuances within the assimilated data (Bandyopadhyay, 2006; Pritchard & Morgan, 2001). Reflexivity technique was used to address the personal bias associated with the researcher's identity as one of the coders was a citizen of India. The coder exercised self-reflection techniques to eliminate personal bias.

## 6.4. Research Findings

### 6.4.1. National-Level Government Representations

A systematic analysis of the Indian government's representations at the national level revealed emphasis on the following themes in order of most recurrence: history and architecture, wellness, royal treatment, natural beauty, and arts and crafts. These themes were, respectively, drawn from the government's description of India as a country with ancient heritage and exquisite Mughal architecture; spirituality, medicinal wellness and rejuvenation; royal retreats and luxury; and offer of abundant nature-based attractions such as deserts, cool retreats, beaches and wildlife. Emphasis on art work demonstrations focused on painting and handicrafts and crafts.

A comparison with Bandyopadhyay and Morais's report, which focused on a 1998–2003 time frame, revealed both similarities and differences in terms of prominent footage. The authors had reported personal enlightenment and wellness to be the most recurrent theme while this 2010 study reveals that history and architecture are showcased most predominantly. Wellness-related themes are significantly featured next. Cultural diversity and richness stand third on Bandyopadhyay and Morais's chart, whereas they fail to feature in a prominent manner in this study. Natural beauty receives similar secondary footage. However, royalty and luxury dominate the 1998–2003 time frame charts in order of fourth most recurrent theme, whereas these feature in terms of third highest recurrence in the most recent period. The expressions related to richness of arts and crafts appear in the year 2010 but failed to feature on Bandyopadhyay and Morais's top list. These results illustrate reinforcement of preferred images by the tourism agents. From the demand perspective, it is interesting to note that rich cultural heritage and arts and crafts had featured most prominently in contributing to the foreign tourists' high satisfaction levels during visit to India in the results reported by Chaudhary (2000). With regard to the pictorial representations, some of the pictures on the national website were aligned with the recurrent themes in the textual self-representations. Pictures portrayed natural landscapes of India highlighting themes such as sunset, adventure sports (e.g. scuba diving and white water rafting), camping, spiritual feel and being pampered through a head massage, reflecting, local traditional transportation (e.g. a rickshaw) and traditional recreation activities (e.g. flying kites and washing elephants) in addition to well-being examples through Ayurvedic treatment and display of architectural evidence through monuments and forts. In short, these visual demonstrations communicated India as a country with natural beauty, rich in adventure sport offerings, a place for the enhancement of physical health, mental well-being and spirituality, a busy bazaar, traditional animals, ancient history and architectural beauty. Additionally, sport-related themes which were given pronounced attention were exemplified by the commonwealth mascot. A closer match between the textual and visual content reveals that pictures offer more variety of attractions and themes. However, they showcase items (such as adventure sports) that fail to feature prominently in textual representations.

Content analysis of the 'Incredible India' campaign identified the following themes in order of recurrence: wellness, primitiveness (featured by a description of rural India), luxury (illustrated through luxury trains and royal treatment), cultural heritage and nature (illustrated through description of beaches and cool retreats and wildlife). Additionally eco-experiences and MICE were featured. Most predominant attention was given to natural beauty followed by royal treatment and luxury. According to Bandyopadhyay and Morais, the 'Incredible India' campaign focuses on the western audience. For this reason, comparing these predominant themes with the most recurrent themes of attention in the western media requires attention. The authors had identified the following six most recurrent themes in order: cultural diversity, cultural richness, spirituality and wellness, simple life, natural beauty and luxurious treatment. Evidently, the ordering of themes in terms of most frequent recurrence varies. The most recent version of the campaign emphasizes most on wellness-related opportunities and attractions followed by stereotype west-driven images of primitive/poor and untouched simpler India, thereby feeding the western notions of superiority and power. Luxury is also given a higher degree of importance by offering images of luxurious forms of transportation and royal welcome and experience.

### 6.4.2. Statewide Level Government Representations

Evidenced by Table 6.1, the self-representations at the state level differed across different regions. The most recurrent themed representations in order were associated with natural beauty, cultural richness and diversity, history and architecture, wellness, religion and sports. Least attention was accorded to colonial past, royal treatment and luxury and primitiveness. Some states extensively highlighted natural beauty while others highlighted their attractiveness to tourists in terms of cultural richness and diversity. Natural beauty was predominantly described in the form of tea gardens,

Table 6.1: Dominant themes represented by the state governments.

| State | Cultural richness/ diversity | Natural beauty | History and architecture | Royal treatment | Wellness and Ayurveda | Art and dance | Religion | Custom holiday | Cuisine | Sports | Colonial | Mystique | Primitive |
|---|---|---|---|---|---|---|---|---|---|---|---|---|---|
| Andhra Pradesh | 3 | 2 | 1 |  | 4 |  |  | 1 |  |  |  |  |  |
| Arunachal Pradesh | 1 | 1 |  |  |  | 1 |  |  |  |  |  |  |  |
| Assam |  | 5 | 2 |  | 1 |  | 1 |  |  | 1 |  | 1 |  |
| Bihar |  |  | 3 |  | 1 |  | 4 |  |  |  |  |  | 1 |
| Chattisgarh | 2 | 2 | 1 |  |  | 1 | 1 |  |  |  |  | 1 | 1 |
| Goa | 2 | 2 | 4 |  | 6 | 1 |  |  |  |  |  | 1 |  |
| Gujarat | 4 |  | 1 |  | 1 |  | 1 |  | 1 | 2 |  | 1 | 1 |
| Haryana | 2 | 1 | 1 |  |  |  | 2 |  | 1 | 2 |  |  |  |
| Himachal Pradesh | 2 | 4 | 1 |  | 1 |  |  |  |  |  | 1 |  |  |
| Jammu & Kashmir | 4 | 6 |  |  |  |  |  | 2 | 4 |  |  |  |  |
| Karnataka | 1 | 3 | 1 |  | 3 | 2 | 1 |  |  | 1 |  | 1 |  |
| Kerala | 4 | 2 |  |  | 1 | 1 | 1 | 1 | 1 |  |  |  |  |
| Maharashtra | 5 | 5 | 2 |  | 1 | 1 | 2 |  |  |  |  |  |  |
| Meghalaya | 4 | 1 | 1 |  |  | 1 |  |  |  |  |  |  |  |
| Manipur | 2 | 2 | 2 |  |  | 2 |  | 1 |  | 1 |  |  |  |
| Mizoram | 6 |  | 6 |  |  | 1 |  |  |  |  |  |  |  |
| Orissa | 2 |  | 2 |  |  | 2 |  | 1 |  |  |  |  |  |
| Rajasthan | 2 | 2 | 5 | 4 | 1 | 3 | 1 |  | 1 |  |  |  |  |
| Sikkim | 6 | 7 | 1 |  | 5 |  |  | 1 |  |  |  |  | 1 |
| Tamil Nadu | 3 | 3 | 4 |  |  |  |  |  |  | 1 |  |  |  |
| Tripura | 6 | 3 | 2 |  |  | 1 | 1 |  |  |  |  | 1 | 1 |
| Uttar Pradesh | 2 |  |  |  |  |  | 3 |  |  |  |  |  |  |
| Andaman & Nicobar | 3 | 12 | 4 |  |  |  |  |  |  | 2 |  | 1 |  |
| Chandigarh |  | 4 | 6 |  |  |  |  | 1 |  |  |  |  |  |
| Dadar & Nagar Haveli | 1 | 4 | 1 |  |  |  | 1 |  |  | 1 |  |  |  |
| Daman & Diu | 1 | 3 | 1 |  |  |  | 2 |  |  | 1 |  | 1 |  |
| Delhi | 1 | 2 | 2 |  | 1 |  | 2 |  | 1 | 1 |  |  |  |
| Lakshadweep | 1 | 5 | 1 |  |  |  | 2 |  |  |  |  |  |  |
| Total | 70 | 81 | 54 | 4 | 26 | 17 | 25 | 8 | 8 | 11 | 1 | 7 | 5 |

lakes, ocean, mountains, national parks, river cruise, wildlife, forests, mineral resources, ancient caves, hill stations, scenic beauty, exquisite gardens, remote Himalayan valleys, beautiful seasons, spectacular waterfalls, sanctuaries, abode of clouds, flora and fauna, songbird, wildlife such as camels and elephants, birds and wetlands, organic, coastline, trees and plants, and coral reefs. Also under this category were included several sustainable themes such as ecotourism, eco-destinations and green paradise.

Cultural variety and richness were illustrated in the form of fairs and festivals, warm and colourful communities, cultural exuberance of people, traditional hospitality, homestay tourism experiences, different languages, people, traditional bazaars, indigenous people, cultural customs, cross-cultural vibrancy, obtaining new friends, friendly community, rich harmonious culture, beat of tribal drums and inhabitation by tribals. History and architecture was emphasized by different states through description of monuments, ongoing excavations, splendour of forts, pulsating history, sculptures, architecture, ancient monuments, city of palaces, construction plan of buildings and roads, city of twin forts, glorious tales of ruins, and lighthouses. Personal enlightenment and wellness appeared next on the list. Noted illustrations under this theme were offerings of alternative medicine, rejuvenation therapy, traditional healing systems, spiritualism, Ayurvedic centres, wellness, medicine, herbs, yoga and health. Religion also received pronounced attention through the use of keywords such as temples, monasteries, Buddha, shrines, trail of pilgrimages, Hindu and Buddhist sculptures, timeless temples, land of Buddha, bhakti, pilgrims and religious festivities. Arts and crafts also somewhat appeared prominently in statewide representations. The states described the arts and crafts kaleidoscope in the form of souvenirs, traditional dances, classical art forms, cave paintings, handloom and handicrafts, music and tribal drums.

Sports were portrayed in the form of air balloon rides, white water rafting, adventure sports, golf, water sports centre, trekking and camping. Mystique appears to be de-emphasized and noted on only two websites. Primitiveness illustrated through narrative content was associated with rural and farm life and simple holi-days and untouched/frozen India. However, these supposedly pronounced repre-sentations of India in the western media received marginal attention in India. Three states claimed to offer customized services to cater to personal preferences and established claim for shopping opportunities. Other less recurrent themes were associated with resorts, highway stops and colonial charm. Celebrity and religious icons such as Gandhi, Jawaharlal Nehru and Buddha appeared extensively to elicit the attention of tourists. Emerging attention in few states centred on MICE and promotion of more responsible and sustainable forms of tourism. Additionally, some state website offered tourism statistics and an insight into the perceptions and experiences of the tourists in the form of guest feedback.

In contrast, the national image of India is portrayed by history and architecture, wellness, royal treatment, natural beauty, and arts and crafts and does not accord highest degree of prominence to natural attractions. It appears that the national-level positioning projects India through a fascinating landscape of historic richness and architectural splendour followed by wellness. However, an aggregate focus at the state level centres on cultural richness and diversity. History and architecture is given a somewhat lower focus. Also, although being visible, wellness opportunities are not given pronounced attention. Departing from the preferred nationwide expressions, the state-level data promotes themes centred on religion and sports. Dissonance also existed between national and state on arts and crafts representations. The later received more emphasis at the statewide representations while the national positioning includes arts and crafts among the most highlighted images. Information on sustainable use of resources, tourism statistics and positive feedback from visitors can enhance the credibility of the destinations and make them more attractive. Some states demonstrate this sophistication, although it lacks universality. The development of pre-trip image is relevant to tourists' destination choice and hence a high level of engagement should be achieved by appealing to both cognitive and affective needs of the desired audience.

Next, as acknowledged earlier, pictures also seek to construct a desired portrait of India (Bhattacharyya, 1997). State-level visual representations offer striking images in terms of natural beauty (44 times), history and architecture (25 times), art, crafts and dance (13 times), followed by cultural richness and diversity (11 times). These themes were collectively exemplified through illustrations of wildlife, dances, rural farms, wellness, Buddha, mela, paintings, temple, Gandhi statue, gardens, people, monastery, forts, excavation, Amarnath yatra, rural village, hotel, massage, tiger, rhino, music, city lights, festivals, sunset, indigenous people, fort, palace, heritage hotel, folk music, snow mountain, sun set at river, monument, boats, train, rickshaw, Taj Mahal, sculpture, holy Ganges, ocean, island, park, rock garden, lake, church, roads, trees, lighthouse, cruise, water sports and marine life. Visuals related to sports appeared four times and wellness, poverty, royal treatment and luxury appeared twice. Additionally, city view and lights appeared three times. A textual and visual match of themes reveals a richer and more diverse visual projection of India and highlight of themes not recurrently reported in textual content. Hence, dissonance in pictorial and textual representations is noted.

### 6.4.3. *Representations by the Indian Travel Magazines*

Content analysis of travel magazines revealed that nature-based descriptions were stressed in the most recurrent manner. Next, arts and crafts and cuisine featured prominently in order of frequent recurrence. Other prominently featured representations related to luxury, primitiveness, and history and architecture followed by colonial illustrations. The remaining themes such as cultural diversity and richness, wellness, mystique and religion were showcased in a mild manner. All magazines appeared to be on the same page with respect to positioning India as a nature-based destination in a highly pronounced manner. However, arts and crafts are not prominently showcased in the state-level representations. This highlighted projected image of India is more aligned with the nationwide image. Cuisine appears to be showcased in a predominant manner and by doing so, the travel trade media depart from both the national- and state-level preferred image representations and impressions by highlighting a different theme.


## 6.5. Discussion

The purpose of this study was to examine online destination imagery portrayed by a variety of tourism agents in India. Table 6.2 offers a comparison between the representations of different induced agents. Examination of the representations at the national level reveals efforts to project India by celebrating first its history and architecture followed by (in order of recurrence) wellness opportunities, royal treatment offers, natural attractions, and arts and crafts. Somewhat similar emphasis is also visible in the 'Incredible India' slogan in that it promotes India in terms of its wellness and personal enlightenment opportunities and 'luxury for less' themes. Also, the primitive features of India are prominently projected. Both nationwide information agents appear to appeal to the western audience because their depictions support the dominant narratives portrayed in the west. As mentioned earlier, the western media and travel trade prefer to project India as a place of simplicity, frozen, rural, poor, timeless and simple, thereby providing fodder for the stereotype images of India in the west. Bandyopadhyay and Morais (2005) note that the self-representations by the Indian government and the ones by the western media are similar to some extent because of the government's desire to attract tourists from the west.

There is a tendency to mystify India and project it as timeless, untouched, rural and primitive to make it more attractive to the west. Similar views were substantiated by Cohen (2001) and Santos (2004). Cohen (2001) is of the view that preferred tourism representations by different countries are driven by controversial and complex

Table 6.2: Comparative representations.

| Themes in order of most frequent recurrence | Indian magazines | Incredible India campaign | Nationwide representations | Statewide representations |
|---|---|---|---|---|
| 1 | Natural beauty | Wellness | History and architecture | Natural beauty |
| 2 | Arts and crafts | Primitiveness | Wellness | Cultural richness and diversity |
| 3 | Cuisine | Luxury | Royal treatment | History and architecture |
| 4 | Luxury | Cultural heritage | Natural beauty | Wellness |
| 5 | Primitiveness | Natural beauty | Arts and crafts | Religion |

processes and need to attract the attention of desired audience. Said's (1979) seminal work had argued that the developing countries' representations are often portrayed as contrasting to the west to feed the western need of seeking a world different from their day-to-day lives. In other words, the tourism discourse of the non-west 'justifies the exploitation of the Orient as the West's pleasure periphery and stagnant in a state of unchanged Orientalism, open to all the exotic fantasies and as primitive and backward' (Echtner & Prasad, 2003, p. 168).

Therefore, results suggest that at the national level, Indian tourism identity is shaped by political discourses, although a shift of emphasis is noted in terms of extended attention offered today to ancientness (year 2010) from wellness and personal enlightenment (years 1998–2003). Luxury-based text also appears more frequently. An emerging theme celebrating India's arts and crafts is also noted in a predominant manner. This aspect of India was not highlighted by Bandyopadhyay and Morais (2005) which goes to show that the self-representations of India at the national level have changed over time. However, 'the arts and crafts' theme was supported by an early demand-based study in Chaudhary's (2000) work, thereby showing the western tourists' preference for arts and crafts. A closer analysis of narrative content reveals that the cognitive information is supplanted by the use of affective expressions such as nostalgia, rejuvenation and immersion to appeal to the emotional side of the desired audience.

Next, in contrast to the nationwide representations, the statewide level emphasizes natural beauty followed by cultural diversity and richness and history/architecture. A mix of affective expressions is also noted here, for example, curiosity and use of words such as exquisite, rejuvenation, peaceful, surprise, exotic, pulsating, drench, rejoice, once-in-a-lifetime experience and silent. The leading travel trade magazines also feature nature and in the most pronounced manner. Evidently, with regard to the highlighted representations by the travel magazines and state-level projections, travel magazine promotions appear to be more aligned with key positioning theme across all states based on nature-based attractions, thereby demonstrating substantial congruity and harmony in the manner India's core essence is portrayed in its natural beauty. Also, worthy of note is Indian's trade media and state government's resistance to the colonial images by highlighting valour of Indian freedom fighters against the British rule. Evidence of this effort exists in the promotion of local icons who sacrificed their lives in the struggle for independence.

Therefore, traces of discrepancy are noted between national-level representations and statewide projections. At the state level, there is a less tendency to please the western audience. For instance, royal treatment and luxury are not highlighted in a predominant manner. The states try to show how they want to be seen and appear to be more focused on domestic markets by highlighting cuisine, religion and adventure sports. In other words, the intrusion of the west is resisted and countered by India' internal and more domestic-driven representations. Hence, evidence exists of the effort to deny western's stereotype projections of itself, thereby emphasizing preference for the postcolonial and counter-colonial discourse. Such findings lend credence to the theory of representative dissonance between western and localized images and unfold a more serious dialogue and mediated internal resistance towards western representations empowerment.

In conclusion, all three sources of self-representations differ in their desired positioning of India and depict a multitude of images to describe India, thereby portraying their preferred versions and presenting a somewhat dissonant view of India. As appropriated by Bruner (1996), destination representations are often besotted by dynamic and often aggressive disagreements among the different tourism agents who are only interested in their version of the story. Such discrepancies can relate to imagery inconsistencies. This area of inquiry commands ongoing attention so that self-awareness of the existing or ongoing discrepancies can be generated. It can serve as a tool for 'understanding the conflicting ideological forces that shape destination images' (Bandyopadhyay & Morais, 2005). This dissonance can be blamed on the power struggles between local and national groups with different motivations and preference for their versions of the story or image to be shared.

Representative dissonance of destination images is likely to create confusion in the minds of the audience, influence their decision-making behaviour and impede the long-term success of tourism agents' marketing efforts. In other words, contrasting themes can evoke dissatisfaction among tourists searching the dossier of different agents for information. Credibility of the agents can thus be damaged in addition to the risk of possible negative impacts on the host region because of fake expectations. Therefore, a strategic marketing stance centred on ongoing research on destination image and long-term view can help plan satisfactory tourist experiences which are realistically aligned with the actual destination product in addition to reducing the gap between realistic tourist expectations and satisfaction once at the site. It is important to mention at this point that the results of this study are subject to several limitations. Data limitations include focus on a small selection of leading Indian magazines identified by previous studies. It is also likely that the themes gleaned from online content are not as comprehensive as the ones from printed copies. Hence, caution should be exercised in generalizations and universal application of the results. Furthermore, the focus is on the most recent year — 2010. Because of budget and time constraints, longitudinal comparisons were not possible.

Nevertheless, this study is one of the few to simultaneously examine the narratives of key agents responsible for disseminating preferred images of India. Nevertheless, this study makes important contribution in that it offers important implications for both the public and private mediators of Indian representations. In the contemporary era, desire for an authentic experience dominates the wish list of travellers, both domestic and international. Previous studies have noted that discordant and conflicting images of a destination, by various sources considered reliable and legitimate, can have a dampening effect on travel behaviour decisions. Contemporary markets demand sincere narrations to diminish the gap between expectations and actual experience once at the destination. Hence, comparative accounts of destination image representations can unpack similarities, discrepancies and gaps between the real and projected. A further insight can also unfold the dynamics and complexities of preferred narrations in the context of power relations and authority. This study calls for a further discourse on the complexities associated with representational dynamics and politics.

# References

Aguilar, M. (2009). *Examining destination marketing from the lens of sustainability.* Unpublished Master's thesis, Arizona State University, Phoenix.

Alcaniz, E., Garcia, I., & Blas, S. (2009). The functional-psychological continuum in the cognitive image of a destination: A confirmatory analysis. *Tourism Management, 30,* 715–723.

Bandyopadhyay, R. (2006). *Representative dissonance in heritage tourism in India.* Unpublished Ph.D. dissertation, Pennsylvania State University, Pennsylvania.

Bandyopadhyay, R. (2009). The perennial western tourism representations of India that refuse to die. *Tourism Preliminary Communication, 57*(1), 23–35.

Bandyopadhyay, R., & Morais, D. (2005). Representative dissonance: India's self and western image. *Annals of Tourism Research, 32*(4), 1006–1021.

Bhattacharyya, D. (1997). Mediating India: An analysis of a guidebook. *Annals of Tourism Research, 24*(2), 371–389.

Bigne, J., Sanchez, M., & Sanchez, J. (2001). Tourism image evaluation variables and after purchase behavior: Inter-relationship. *Tourism Management, 22*(6), 607–616.

Bruner, M. E. (1996). Tourism in Ghana: The representation of slavery and the return of the black diaspora. *American Anthropologist, 98*(2), 290–304.

Chaudhary, M. (2000). India's image as a tourist destination — A perspective of foreign tourists. *Tourism Management, 21,* 293–297.

Choi, S., Lehto, X., & Morrison, A. (2007). Destination image representation on the web: Content analysis of Macau travel related websites. *Tourism Management, 28,* 118–129.

Chon, K. (1992). Tourism destination image modification process: Marketing implications. *Tourism Management, 12,* 68–72.

Cohen, E. (2001). Ethnic tourism in Southeast Asia. In D. Pearceand & R. Butler (Eds.), *Tourism research* (pp. 36–69). London: Routledge.

Echtner, C., & Prasad, P. (2003). The context of third world tourism marketing. *Annals of Tourism Research, 30,* 660–682.

Echtner, C., & Ritchie, J. (1993). The measurement of destination image. *Journal of Tourism Studies, 2*(2), 2–12.

Entman, R. (1993). Framing: Toward clarification of a fractured paradigm. *The Journal of Communication, 43*(4), 51–58.

Fakeye, P., & Crompton, J. (1991). Image differences between prospective, first-time and repeat visitors to the lower Rio Grande Valley. *Journal of Travel Research, 30*(2), 10–16.

Gartner, W. (1993). Image formation process. *Journal of Travel & Tourism Marketing, 2*(2/3), 191–215.

Govers, R., & Go, F. (2003). Deconstructing destination image in the information age. *Information Technology and Tourism, 7*(2), 13–29.

Henderson, J. (2007). Uniquely Singapore? A case study in destination branding. *Journal of Vacation Marketing, 13,* 261–265.

Joppe, M., Martin, D., & Waalen, J. (2001). Toronto's image as a destination: A comparative importance–satisfaction analysis by origin of visitor. *Journal of Travel Research, 39*(3), 252–260.

Kim, H., & Richardson, S. (2003). Motion picture impacts on destination images. *Annals of Tourism Research, 30*(1), 216–237.

Lin, C., & Huang, Y. (2009). Mining tourist imagery to construct destination image position model. *Expert Systems with Applications, 36,* 2513–2524.

MacKay, K., & Couldwell, C. (2004). Using visitor-employed photography to investigate destination image. *Journal of Travel Research, 42*(4), 390–396.

MacKay, K., & Fesenmaier, D. (2000). An exploration of cross-cultural destination image assessment. *Journal of Travel Research, 38*(4), 417–423.

Martin, H., & Bosque, I. (2008). Exploring the cognitive–affective nature of destination image and the role of psychological factors in its formation. *Tourism Management, 29,* 263–277.

Ministry of Tourism. (2009). *Tourism statistics at a glance.* Government of India. Retrieved from http://tourism.gov.in/writereaddata/CMSPagePicture/file/marketresearch/New/2010.pdf

Ministry of Tourism. (2010). *Annual report 2009–2010.* Government of India. Retrieved from http://tourism.gov.in/

Palmer, C. (1994). Tourism and colonialism: The experience of the Bahamas. *Annals of Tourism Research, 21,* 792–811.

Phelps, A. (1986). Holiday destination image: The problem of assessment — An example developed in Minorca. *Tourism Management, 7*(3), 168–180.

Pritchard, A., & Morgan, N. (2001). Culture, identity and tourism representation: Marketing Cymru or Wales? *Tourism Management, 22,* 167–179.

Said, E. (1979). *Orientalism.* New York, NY: Vintage Books.

Santos, C. (2004). Framing Portugal: Representational dynamics. *Annals of Tourism Research, 31,* 122–138.

Silver, I. (1993). Marketing authenticity in third world countries. *Annals of Tourism Research, 20,* 302–318.

Sirgy, M., & Su, C. (2000). Destination image, self-congruity, and travel behavior: Toward an integrative model. *Journal of Travel Research, 38,* 340–352.

Sturma, M. (1999). Packaging Polynesia's image. *Annals of Tourism Research, 26,* 712–715.

Tapachai, N., & Waryszak, R. (2000). An examination of the role of beneficial image in tourist destination selection. *Journal of Travel Research, 39,* 37–44.

Tasci, A., & Gartner, W. (2007). Destination image and its functional relationships. *Journal of Travel Research, 45*(4), 413–425.

Van Raaij, W., & Francken, D. (1984). Vacation decisions, activities and satisfaction. *Annals of Tourism Research, 11*(1), 101–112.

Wang, P., Hawk, W., & Tenopir, C. (2000). Users' interaction with World Wide Web resources: An exploratory study using a holistic approach. *Information Processing and Management, 26*(2), 229–251.

Chapter 7

# Destination Brand Equity Modelling and Measurement — A Summer Tourism Case From Sweden

*Matthias Fuchs, Tatiana Chekalina and Maria Lexhagen*

## 7.1. Introduction

As a core marketing concept, brands are broadly defined as the 'physical representation of a set of benefits that companies offer to customers to satisfy their needs' (Kotler & Keller, 2009). In doing so, brands are considered as being more than just names and symbols, rather 'they are the key element in a company's relationships with consumers representing consumers' perceptions and feelings about a product and its performance — everything that the product or service means to consumers. In the final analysis, brands exist in the heads of consumers' (Armstrong & Kotler, 2009). This particularly customer-centric brand perspective is traced back to the new service marketing paradigm (Gummesson, 2002; Vargo & Lusch, 2004, 2008), thereby focusing on relationships with customers who 'do not look for goods or services per se; [rather] they look for solutions that serve their own value-generating processes' (Grönroos, 2000).

The topic of customer-based brand equity (CBBE) development and related validation has only recently attracted attention by tourism researchers (Boo, Busser & Baloglu, 2009; Konecnik & Gartner, 2007; Pike, Bianchi, Kerr, & Patti, 2010). However, as argued by Boo et al. (2009), Pike (2009) and Gartner (2009), the enormous complexity and multi-dimensionality of tourism destinations compared to single goods or services products substantially complicate the measurement of CBBE in a tourism context.

Therefore, this study aims at contributing to the further development of the CBBE concept in a tourism destination setting based on previous discussions and findings in the marketing and tourism literature. Particularly, it is proposed that the customer's evaluation of destination benefits, which include the transformation of functional destination attributes into experiential (i.e. intangible) destination characteristics, constitutes the core component of the CBBE in a tourism destination context.

## 7.2.   The Customer-Based Brand Equity Model

The power of a brand mainly consists of the 'differentiation effect' the customers' brand knowledge has on their response towards a product and is quantified by 'brand equity' (Gartner, 2009). Keller (2008) identifies four stages of brand development that correspond to the CBBE model consisting of six brand building blocks and five CBBE dimensions (see Figure 7.1).

The first stage comprises the establishment of brand identity and corresponds to brand salience, thus, having brand awareness as the branding objective (e.g. brand recognition as consumer's ability to recognize the name of the brand). Typical metrics are brand recall, top-of-mind awareness (*TOMA*), brand knowledge and brand opinion (Aaker, 1996). The second stage concerns the creation of brand meaning attached to product performance and its intangible outcome (i.e. imagery).

Brand association is the second stage of the brand development, which refers to the customer's ability to identify and evaluate brand attributes and benefits. Particularly, Keller (1993) defines customer benefits from brands as the 'personal value consumers attach to the product or service attributes', thereby including functional, experiential and symbolic benefits; functional and experiential benefits are linked to product and service attributes to satisfy consumers' basic needs connected with problem removal or avoidance. Experiential benefits relate to feelings evoked by the use of the product or service, thus, satisfying needs as sensory pleasure or cognitive stimulation. Finally, symbolic benefits concern non product-related attributes, such as social approval or personal expression.

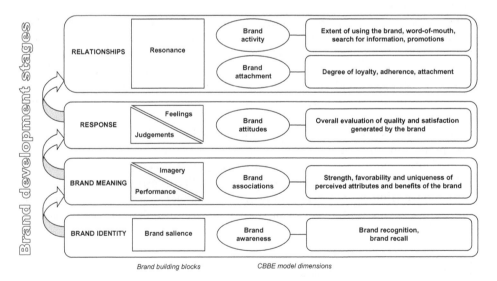

Figure 7.1: Hierarchical model of brand development and CBBE formation (Aaker, 1996; Keller, 2008).

The third stage of the brand development comprises the response aiming at receiving positive reactions towards the brand and consists of judgements and feelings related to brand attributes. Keller (1993) classifies brand attributes as product-related (category-specific characteristics of product/service performance or function) and non product-related brand attributes (e.g. price, visual information, user and usage imagery including customer's associations about other brands and consumption contexts). Finally, resonance is the brand building block at the top of the CBBE process labelled as 'relationships' aiming at the establishment of active and intense forms of customer loyalty.

So far, marketing research has brought forth a range of competing CBBE models. However, although CBBE models are extensively elaborated on a theoretical and empirical level, further development and harmonization of related metrics remains an acute issue. For instance, Lehmann, Keller, and Farley (2008) identified six brand performance factors: (1) *comprehension* (presence, awareness and knowledge: 'how much is the brand seen and thought of'); (2) *comparative advantage* (difference, esteem, performance and advantage: 'how favourably and differentiated is the branded product?'); (3) *interpersonal relations* (prestige, service and innovation: 'interpersonal and social aspects'); (4) *history* (heritage and nostalgia: 'past brand-related events, episodes and emotions'); (5) *preference* (bonding, loyalty, value for money, overall attitude, extension potential: 'consumer attitudes toward the brand and its purchase'); and (6) *attachment* (persistence and activity: 'how strongly consumers connect to and interact with the brand'). Finally, in the course of the analysis of relationships between these factors four stages of brand performance were identified: (1) awareness, (2) image and associations (represented by comparative advantage, interpersonal relations and history), (3) preference and (4) attachment (Lehmann et al., 2008).

To summarize, brand evaluations are based on customer's beliefs about brand attributes and related benefits and form the basis for consumer behaviour (Keller, 1993). According to Aaker (1996), loyalty should be used as the endogenous dimension of brand equity. Hence, predecessor variables of the brand equity model should be assessed based on their specific ability to influence customer loyalty (e.g. willingness to pay a premium price, repurchase and/or recommend).

The topic of destination branding and, particularly, the issue of CBBE modelling and validation in a tourism destination context has only recently attracted attention by tourism researchers (Boo et al., 2009; Gnoth, 2007; Konecnik & Gartner, 2007; Morgan, Pritchard, & Pride, 2004; Pike et al., 2010). The following section summarizes major development steps of the CBBE model and its core dimensions as reported in the tourism literature. Particularly, the measurement of the CBBE model dimensions is in focus, including image, quality, value, satisfaction and loyalty.

## 7.3. Brand Equity Modelling for Tourism Destinations

Since destination branding was introduced in the early 2000s (Deslandes & Goldsmith, 2002) it became the 'hottest topic in the field of destination marketing research' (Morgan et al., 2004). A destination brand is defined as a 'name, sign or symbol representing the core values of a place offered for tourism consumption' (Gnoth, 2007). Core values are cultural, social, natural and economic dimensions of destination resources utilized to produce services experienced by tourists on a functional (basic needs), experiential (emotions and senses) and symbolic level. Thus, as tourism brands represent 'benefits of services tourists are promised to receive' (Gnoth, 2007) they similarly show functional, experiential and symbolic brand dimensions.

It is argued that the issue of destination brand equity measurement has only recently attracted attention in tourism research (Gartner, 2009; Pike, 2009). This lack of research is explained by the complexity and multi-dimensionality of tourism destinations, thus, being also the reason why measurement scales developed for consumer products cannot be directly applied to a destination context (Deslandes, Goldsmith, Bonn, & Joseph, 2006). Moreover, until recently the topic of destination branding was shadowed by destination image studies (Konecnik & Gartner, 2007; Pike, 2009). Consequently, tourism research adopted a definition of brand image that reflects the reasoned or emotional perceptions attached to specific brands by consumers and is widely acknowledged as a central source of brand equity (Boo et al., 2009). For instance, Echtner and Ritchie (1993) conceptualized destination image as a continuum between 'common' functional and psychological characteristics versus 'unique' characteristics, like sights, local events, special feelings and auras that form a very specific holistic destination impression. Gallarza, Saura, and Garcia (2002) followed this idea by developing attribute-based image metrics organized along a functional (tangible attributes)/psychological (intangible attributes) axis. The empirically most frequently observed attributes in tourism destinations are 'residents' receptiveness', 'landscape and surroundings', 'cultural attractions', 'sports facilities' and 'price, value and costs'.

Research indicates that the perception of destination attributes plays a crucial role in tourism-related decision-making processes. As being the first, Crompton (1979) distinguishes between tourists' 'internal' socio-psychological needs (push motivation factors) including motives of escape, exploration, novelty seeking, relaxation, social recognition and interaction and 'external' drivers of destination choice (pull motivation factors) comprising destination image characteristics and attributes. Recent studies identified significant relationships between destination image and satisfaction as well as tourists' loyalty behaviour (Bigne, Garcia, & Blas, 2009; Faullant et al., 2008; Yoon & Uysal, 2005). However, according to Konecnik and Gartner (2007), destination image should not be viewed as a single explanatory factor in determining tourism decision-making processes. Rather, image should be considered along with other isolated dimensions of the CBBE model, including destination awareness, quality and loyalty. Therefore, Konecnik and Gartner (2007) specify the CBBE model for tourism destinations as a multi-dimensional higher-order construct. Their first destination equity measurement model was conceptualized and empirically validated as the 'sum of factors or dimensions contributing to a brand value in the consumer's mind'.

Boo et al.'s (2009) study was the next step towards the elaboration of a CBBE model in a tourism destination context. The authors complemented Konecnik and Gartner's (2007) approach with the additional dimension of destination brand value, arguing for its particular relevance in creating customer loyalty. Their study was also the first one that also investigated causal relationships between CBBE dimensions in tourism destinations. Particularly, the authors reveal that tourists' previous experience overshadows the model's image dimension, while the importance of the value dimension on tourist's loyalty increases. Thus, an alternative model has been tested, which empirically supports the existence of four first-order constructs, namely (1) awareness, (2) experience, (3) value and (4) loyalty.

Pike et al.'s (2010) study is the most recent example for empirical validation of the CBBE model in tourism. They examined and empirically identified structural relationships between four model dimensions, namely brand salience, brand image, perceived quality of destination attributes and destination loyalty.

So far, Boo et al.'s (2009) and Pike et al.'s (2010) studies are the only ones that examine (causal) relationships within the CBBE model in a tourism destination context. At the same time, both studies differ in terms of both the selection and operationalization of the CBBE model constructs. However, in order to develop effective destination branding strategies causal structures responsible for the formation of destination brand equity should be well understood. Nevertheless, tourism literature has accumulated a number of topical studies examining specific relationships between selected CBBE constructs (see, e.g. Chen & Tsai, 2007; Chi & Qu, 2008). Furthermore, existing studies examining relationships between destination loyalty (as the endogenous construct) and its antecedents, like brand awareness and destination image, destination quality, value and satisfaction, vary significantly in terms of construct selection, model design and measurement scales used. Thus, before proposing and validating a holistic CBBE model for tourism destinations, crucial destination brand equity dimensions and related causal relationships will be deconstructed, critically discussed and synthesized in the next section (Gartner, 2009; Li & Petrick, 2008).

## 7.4. A Meta-Comparison of CBBE Models in Tourism

In order to deduce a testable model, main results from a previously published meta-comparison of empirically validated CBBE models in tourism are summarized. (Chekalina & Fuchs, 2009a). In this attempt, the following criteria for inclusion of studies have been applied: (1) empirical relationships between model constructs are considered; (2) customer loyalty is the endogenous construct (i.e. intention to return and recommend or cognitive, affective and/or behavioural loyalty); (3) tourist's judgement of destination performance is the antecedent of customer loyalty.

As a result, we identified 11 destination brand studies fitting with the defined criteria (see Table 7.1, column 1). Although construct labels varied significantly, the meta-comparison revealed that destination loyalty is (directly or indirectly)

Table 7.1: Attribute-based and holistic items in measurement of destination brand performance.

Columns 1–15 are grouped as **Functional Attributes**; columns 16–28 are grouped as **Intangible/Psychological Attributes**.

| Authors | 1. Various Activities | 2. Nature and Landscape | 3. Culture and Built Environment | 4. Knowledge and Learning | 5. Nightlife and Entertainment | 6. Shopping Facilities | 7. Information availability | 8. Sport and Spa | 9. Transportation | 10. Accommodation | 11. Gastronomy | 12. Infrastructure | 13. Price, Value, Cost | 14. Time and Effort Value | 15. Physical and Emotional Needs | 16. Climate | 17. Relaxation vs. Crowdedness | 18. Accessibility | 19. Safety | 20. Quality of Life | 21. Social Interaction | 22. Lifestyle | 23. Resident's Receptiveness | 24. Personality | 25. Manageable Size, Coziness | 26. Cleanliness | 27. Service Quality | 28. Staff | 29. Holistic Items | Total Number of Items |
|---|---|---|---|---|---|---|---|---|---|---|---|---|---|---|---|---|---|---|---|---|---|---|---|---|---|---|---|---|---|---|
| Bigne et al. (2001) | | | | | | | | | | | | | | | | | | | | | | | | | | | 1 | | 4 | 5 |
| Back and Parks (2003) | | | | | | | 2 | | | | | | | | | | | | | | | | | | | | | | 11 | 13 |
| Yoon and Uysal (2005) | 3 | 8 | 6 | | 3 | 1 | | | | 2 | 4 | 1 | | 1 | 14 | 1 | 1 | 1 | 1 | 1 | | 2 | | | | | | | 6 | 56 |
| Chen and Tsai (2007) | 1 | 5 | 1 | | 1 | 1 | | | 2 | 1 | 4 | | 1 | 2 | 1 | 2 | | | 2 | | 2 | 1 | 1 | 2 | 1 | 1 | 1 | 1 | 3 | 37 |
| Jang and Feng (2007) | 1 | | 2 | 1 | | | | | | | 1 | | 1 | | | | | | | | | | 1 | | | | 3 | | 4 | 14 |
| Lee, Yoon, and Lee (2007) | | | | | | | | | | | | | 4 | | | | | | | | 2 | | | | | | | | 14 | 20 |
| Chi and Qu (2008) | 5 | 6 | 9 | | 3 | 5 | 1 | 3 | 5 | 6 | 7 | | 3 | | 2 | | 2 | 2 | 2 | 2 | | | 2 | 1 | 1 | 1 | 2 | | 3 | 73 |
| del Bosque and Martin (2008) | 3 | 4 | 4 | 1 | | 1 | | | | 1 | 1 | 2 | 1 | | | 1 | 2 | 1 | 2 | | | | 1 | 4 | | 2 | 1 | | 18 | 50 |
| Faullant, Matzler, & Füller (2008) | 1 | | | | 1 | | | 1 | | | | | | | | 1 | | | | | | | 1 | 3 | | | | | 4 | 12 |
| Boo et al. (2009) | | | | | | | | | | | | | 5 | | 1 | | | | | | | | | 1 | | | | | 11 | 18 |
| Hutchinson, Lai, and Wang (2009) | | | | | | | | | | | | | 1 | | | | | | | | 2 | | | | | | 1 | 5 | 12 | 21 |
| **Total** | 14 | 23 | 22 | 2 | 8 | 8 | 3 | 4 | 7 | 10 | 17 | 3 | 16 | 3 | 18 | 5 | 5 | 4 | 7 | 3 | 6 | 3 | 6 | 11 | 2 | 4 | 9 | 6 | 90 | 319 |
| *Image items* | *9* | *19* | *13* | *1* | *6* | *5* | | *3* | *3* | *4* | *6* | *1* | *4* | | *4* | *4* | *4* | *2* | *4* | *2* | | *1* | *4* | *9* | *2* | *3* | *1* | | *4* | *118* |

*Source:* Chekalina and Fuchs (2009a).

determined by a total of 12 (first-order) constructs: pull and push motivation, novelty seeking, awareness, image, expectations, quality, experience, equity, value, disconfirmation, positive and negative emotions and satisfaction. These labels fully correspond to Lehmann et al.'s (2008) stages of brand performance. Secondly, at the level of measurement-items a list comprising 319 items emerged (see Table 7.1).

Interestingly, Table 7.1 clearly reflects a predominance of attribute-based items, while only 90 out of 319 items belong to the group of holistic items (column 29). Moreover, 118 items labelled as 'image metrics' include only 4 holistic items measuring overall destination image. More precisely, attribute-based items are used for measuring push motivation (30 items labelled as 'push motivation' are associated with 10 destination attributes), quality (2 holistic items and 58 items associated with 21 destination attributes) and attribute value (8 items, 5 destination attributes) (Chekalina & Fuchs, 2009a). By contrast, value is measured by 12 items representing value for money and 3 items representing time and effort value. Finally, items labelled as satisfaction or loyalty exclusively belong to the group of holistic items. A comparison of destination brand performance constructs allowed us to group them together in order to reveal unique constructs and, thus, preserve them as distinct model dimensions.

This leads to the final step of the analysis, namley to provide a comprehensive overview of significant empirical relationships among brand-related constructs as found in the tourism literature (Back & Parks, 2003; Bigne, Sanchez, & Sanchez, 2001;

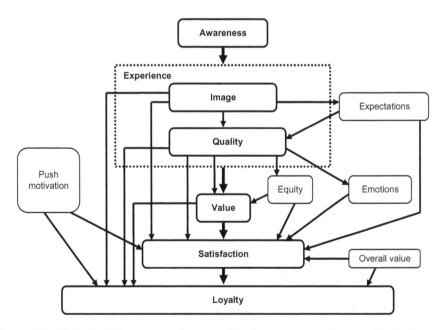

Figure 7.2: Relationships among brand-related constructs. *Source*: Chekalina and Fuchs (2009a).

Boo et al., 2009; Chen & Tsai, 2007; Chi & Qu, 2008; del Bosque & Martin, 2008; Faullant et al., 2008; Hutchinson et al., 2009; Jang & Feng, 2007; Lee et al., 2007; Yoon & Uysal, 2005; see Figure 7.2).

The final assessment of survey-based brand metrics offers a valuable framework for the selection of model constructs, the operationalization of model dimensions and the formulation of measurement items. In doing so, it is assumed that the CBBE concept does not contradict the major propositions of the relationship-based or service-dominant marketing approach (Andersson, 2007; Larsen, 2007; Mossberg, 2007; Pike, 2009; Vargo & Lusch, 2008).

## 7.5. A Customer-Based Destination Brand Equity Model

Based on the literature discussed in Section 7.3, a customer-based destination brand equity (CBDBE) model is proposed. It is hypothesized that customers' awareness-based experience of common and unique functional (tangible) destination attributes directly influences the perceived quality of experiential (intangible) destination characteristics. In turn, the latter affect destination loyalty via the 'intermediary' construct 'overall satisfaction' (Reisinger & Turner, 1999). Finally, it is hypothesized that destination loyalty is affected by the CBDBE dimension 'value for money', which is again mediated by the 'overall satisfaction' construct (Konecnik & Gartner, 2007). Before going on to operationalize and empirically test the proposed CBDBE model a set of literature-based hypotheses is formulated and summarized graphically (Figure 7.3).

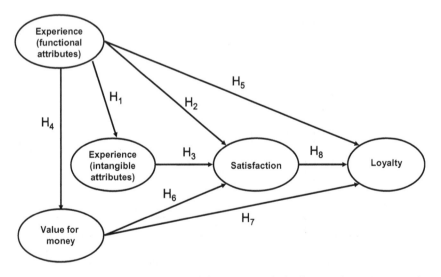

Figure 7.3: Proposed CBDBE model. *Source*: Chekalina and Fuchs (2009b).

**H1.** The more positive the perception of *functional destination attributes*, the more positive the perception of *intangible destination characteristics* (Gallarza et al., 2002).

**H2.** The more positive the perception of *functional destination attributes*, the higher the degree of *customer satisfaction* (Chi & Qu, 2008).

**H3.** The more positive the perception of *intangible destination attributes*, the higher the degree of *customer satisfaction* (Chi & Qu, 2008).

**H4.** The more positive the perception of *functional destination attributes*, the higher the degree of *value for money* (Chen & Tsai, 2007).

**H5.** The more positive the perception of *functional destination attributes*, the higher the degree of *customer loyalty* (Chi & Qu, 2008).

**H6.** The higher the degree of perceived *value for money*, the higher the degree of *customer satisfaction* (Chen & Tsai, 2007; Hutchinson et al., 2009; Lee et al., 2007).

**H7.** The higher the degree of perceived *value for money*, the higher the degree of *customer loyalty* (Boo et al., 2009; Hutchinson et al., 2009).

**H8.** The higher the degree of *customer satisfaction*, the higher the degree of *customer loyalty* (Back & Parks, 2003; Bigne et al., 2001; Chi & Qu, 2008; del Bosque and Martin, 2008; Faullant et al., 2008; Hutchinson et al., 2009; Lee et al., 2007; Yoon & Uysal, 2005).

## 7.6. Method

### 7.6.1. Study Area-the Swedish Destination of Åre

The study has been conducted in collaboration with Åre, which is a leading Swedish mountain destination currently transforming its brand image from a winter ski resort to an all-year-round destination.

The history of Åre as a winter sport destination started in 1910, when the first ski lift was constructed. In 1954, Åre hosted the World Ski Championships, which resulted in more international attention to the destination. In early 1970s the government recognized Åre as one of the main recreational areas in Sweden, and the destination received significant support on the national and regional level. The 1980s was the period of extensive development of the ski resort infrastructure. Since then the role of the private actors in the development of Åre gradually increased and in late 1980s the majority of the ski lift infrastructure was transferred into the ownership of private stakeholders. The bank and real estate crisis of the early 1990s drastically changed the business landscape of the destination and in the late 1990s SkiStar became the main private stakeholder owning ski areas, ski rentals, ski schools, the destination booking system and parts of the accommodation facilities, while Åre became a ski resort within the system of winter destinations run by SkiStar in Sweden and Norway (Nordin & Svensson, 2007).

In 2004 Holiday Club opened in Åre and became the second largest business actor in the destination. Nordin and Svensson (2007) assume that the presence of two strong dominating private stakeholders boosted the willingness of numerous smaller firms to be involved into the destination planning and development process and effectively use the collaboration platform of the local business association counting about 200 members. The informal Vision 2011 group consisting of representatives of local authorities, SkiStar, Holiday Club and small businesses achieved significant results. For instance, a number of strategic development goals for Åre have been identified and various decisions regarding infrastructure investments have been made. The destination also attracted EU funding as an additional financing base to implement its infrastructural plans. Finally, the holding of the Alpine Ski World Championship in 2007 was a great international success.

The strategic goals identified by the Vision 2011 were quite ambitious. First of all, Åre aims at becoming the most attractive winter destination in Europe. Secondly, Åre plans to transform from a winter sport destination to an all-year-round destination. The resort aims a 50% increase of guests up to 225,000 per year, while a 50% increase in the number of tourists is expected in the snow-free season. Moreover, ensuring tourists' loyalty is an important goal (e.g. the frequency of repeated visits should increase by 50% by 2011). Finally, the development strategy envisages the provision of professional and memorable experiences for tourists and a financially, ecologically and socially sustainable growth for the local community. Thus, the infrastructural improvements are part of the larger strategy and planning activities (e.g. Ski Master Plan, survey plan and design programme) and development of the brand profiling (Nordin & Svensson, 2007). More recently the strategy was updated and the overall target identified by Vision 2020 is to develop Åre as 'the most attractive European alpine all-year-round destination'.

### 7.6.2.  *Operationalization of the CBDBE Model*

In accordance with Echtner and Ritchie's (1993) destination concept which considers common and unique destination characteristics as well as Gallarza et al.'s (2002) continuum of functional (tangible) and psychological (intangible) destination attributes, the customer 'awareness-based experience' construct is operationalized by attribute-based items typical for summer mountain destinations (Chekalina & Fuchs, 2009b; Fuchs & Weiermair, 2004; Stepchenkova & Morrison, 2008). By contrast, for the two CBDBE constructs 'satisfaction' and 'loyalty' a holistic measurement approach is applied. Finally, 'customer value' is conceptualized as 'value for money' and is operationalized on an attribute-base and on a holistic level (Keller, 1993, 2008). Thus, from a measurement perspective the measurement instrument considers both quality and price dimensions of common (e.g. accommodation, dining, shopping etc.) and unique (e.g. hiking, Åre cable-car,

Åre Bike Park etc.) functional destination attributes (Echtner & Ritchie, 1993). Furthermore, the survey instrument includes a list of intangible attributes found in the literature reviewed in Sections 7.2 and 7.3, which are particularly relevant for summer destinations.

More precisely, this part of the measurement instrument contains items measuring intangible aspects of destination performance, like family friendliness, safety, service quality, peaceful and restful atmosphere as well as interaction quality with employees and locals (Chi & Qu, 2008; Weiermair & Fuchs, 1999). Moreover, the operationalization of the customer's response construct includes metrics that measure overall satisfaction with the summer destination and the emotional outcome of the visitation in terms of enjoyment with the stay as well as the overall impression of Åre as a summer destination (Bigne et al., 2001; Bigne, Andreu, & Gnoth, 2005; Lee et al., 2007; Yoon & Uysal, 2005). By contrast, the price-based value of the destination visitation is measured through attribute-based performance metrics (Boo et al., 2009; Chen & Tsai, 2007; Hutchinson et al., 2009; Lee et al., 2007). Finally, the operationalization of the loyalty construct corresponds to the cognitive–affective–conative structure of loyalty formation proposed by Oliver (1997, 1999) and applied by Keller (2008) in their CBBE model conceptualization. More precisely, destination loyalty is measured by the items 'willingness to return to the destination in summer within a two year period' and the 'willingness to recommend the summer destination to friends and relatives' (Back & Parks, 2003; Chi & Qu, 2008; del Bosque & Martin, 2008; Faullant et al., 2008; Hutchinson et al., 2009). Finally, all multi-items were measured by using a five-point Likert scale (from 1 = strongly disagree to 5 = strongly agree).

### 7.6.3. *Data Collection*

Data was collected in Åre in the course of a questionnaire-based survey during July 2009. While the destination understands its winter product fairly well, the summer product is still in its early stage of development. Although the destination offers summer tourists a wide variety of attractions and activities, the configuration of destination resources actually contributing to the summer destination experience remains largely unknown and can, thus, only be hypothesized by managers in the destination. The final choice and wording of measurement items in the survey instrument as well as the overall structure of the questionnaire is arranged on the basis of discussions with representatives from major stakeholders of the Åre destination, namely Åre Destination AB (the destination management organization, DMO), SkiStar Åre (a major lift infrastructure and facility provider) and Holiday Club Åre (an accommodation and restaurant chain).

Since the summer destination product is in the very early stage of its development, Åre's destination management has only little awareness about the summer visitors' population profile, what makes it difficult to apply advanced (probability) sampling techniques (e.g. random or stratified sampling). Thus, a non-probability-based convenience sampling technique was employed (Finn, Elliott-White, & Walton, 2000).

Finally, data collection is organized in collaboration with Åre Destination AB, thereby utilizing a convenience sampling method. More precisely, the DMO's interviewers approached the summer guests during their stay in Åre by disseminating both English and Swedish questionnaires in local accommodation facilities. In August 2009, the total number of compiled questionnaires was 214. However, as respondents were allowed to skip questions if they had no opinion, missing values reduced the number of usable questionnaires. Moreover, after having identified also cases with outliers, data on destination brand perception and its attitudinal consequences of a total of 159 summer guests is utilized for data analysis.

### 7.6.4.   Testing the CBDBE Model

In order to empirically test the constitutive measurement constructs of the proposed CBDBE model, in a first methodological step *confirmatory factor analysis* (CFA) was employed by using the AMOS (version 18) software package (Hair, Black, Babin, Anderson, & Tatham, 2006). By doing so and after considering only signifcant measurement items and allowing a second-order construct which captures functional destination attributes (Gallarza et al., 2002), the estimated model shows fairly satisfactory measurment results (Table 7.2): firstly, values for *composite reliabilities* (CRs) approve the model, but two of the proposed constructs rank below the recommended threshold amounting at 0.7 (Hair et al., 2006); secondly, all estimated (standard) regression weights (factor loadings) are relatively high and significant (*t* values); thirdly, *squared multiple correlations* (SMC) demonstrate respectable portions and finally, for two of the proposed seven model constructs, *average variance extracted* (AVE) ranks below the recommended threshold value amounting at 0.5 (Hair et al., 2006).

In order to empirically test the significance of the hypothesized relationships among the CBDBE constructs reflecting the 'mechanic' of the proposed model, a linear structural equation modelling (SEM) approach using maximum likelihood (ML) estimation was applied (Hair et al., 2006; Steenkamp & Baumgartner, 2000).

Figure 7.4 displays the obtained SEM results. First of all, normed-$\chi^2$ statistics ($\chi^2$/df) and incremental (CFI, NFI) as well as absolute fit indices (GFI, RMSEA, SRMR) rank well above recommended thresholds (Hair et al., 2006). Secondly, the CBDBE model behaves well according to theory (only H2 and H7 are rejected), hence, showhing satisfactory nomologic validity. Thirdly, the model accounts for a substantial proportion of the variance (explanation power: $R^2$) in the endogenous constructs (Figure 7.4). Thus, although only a rather small sample size was used ($N = 159$) and relatively few variables were considered in the empirical analysis, based on the gathered results the proposed approach and the related instrument to measure brand equity-related constructs in a tourism destination context can be considered as plausible, reliable and valid (Reisinger & Turner, 1999).

Table 7.2: Testing of the CBDBE measurement model.

| Constructs | | Scale Items | Composite Reliability | Standardized Loadings | t-Value (CR) (Non-Standard Loadings) | SMC | AVE |
|---|---|---|---|---|---|---|---|
| Experience (functional attributes) | Urban | Accommodation. Quality | 0.626 | 0.434 | – | 0.188 | 0.309 |
| | | Restaurants and catering. Quality | | 0.371 | 3.266 | 0.137 | |
| | | Åre Kabinbana. Quality | | 0.632 | 4.301 | 0.399 | |
| | | HC Pool and Sauna World. Quality | | 0.715 | 4.424 | 0.511 | |
| | Nature | Hiking. Quality | 0.697 | 0.778 | – | 0.605 | 0.536 |
| | | Experiencing nature. Quality | | 0.683 | 3.988 | 0.467 | |
| | Bike | Åre Bike Park. Quality | 0.833 | 0.744 | – | 0.554 | 0.717 |
| | | Cykling. Quality | | 0.938 | 4.793 | 0.879 | |
| Experience (intangible attributes) | | Åre has peaceful and restful atmosphere | 0.847 | 0.610 | – | 0.372 | 0.444 |
| | | Åre has a good name and reputation | | 0.681 | 6.757 | 0.464 | |
| | | Employees were friendly and professional | | 0.628 | 5.997 | 0.394 | |
| | | While visiting Åre, I received good service | | 0.556 | 5.825 | 0.309 | |
| | | Åre is a family-friendly destination | | 0.716 | 6.891 | 0.513 | |
| | | Åre is clean and tidy | | 0.656 | 6.579 | 0.431 | |
| | | I feel safe and secure in Åre | | 0.790 | 8.283 | 0.625 | |

Table 7.2: (*Continued*)

| Constructs | Scale Items | Composite Reliability | Standardized Loadings | t-Value (CR) (Non-Standard Loadings) | SMC | AVE |
|---|---|---|---|---|---|---|
| Value | Compared to other summer destinations, visiting Åre is a good value for the money | 0.815 | 0.932 | – | 0.870 | 0.691 |
| | Overall Åre as a summer destination has reasonable prices | | 0.717 | 6.561 | 0.514 | |
| Sat | I have really enjoyed visiting Åre in summer | 0.925 | 0.879 | – | 0.773 | 0.805 |
| | Overall I am satisfied with my summer holidays in Åre | | 0.940 | 17.574 | 0.883 | |
| | My expectations about summer holidays in Åre have been fulfilled | | 0.871 | 15.228 | 0.759 | |
| Loy | I think I will come back to Åre in summer within 2 years period | 0.869 | 0.829 | – | 0.687 | 0.770 |
| | I will encourage relatives and friends to visit Åre in summer | | 0.923 | 10.681 | 0.852 | |

–, Indicates paths fixed to one to estimate parameters.

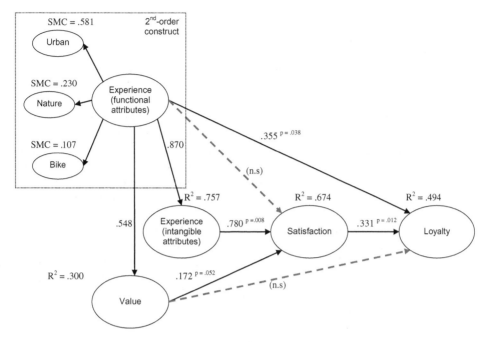

Figure 7.4: Testing of the CBDBE structural model.

*Model Fit Statistics:* $\chi^2 = 189.8$, df $= 183$, $\chi^2/\text{df} = 1.037$, $p = 0.350$, GFI $= 0.910$; CFI $= 0.996$; NFI $= 0.895$; RMSEA $= 0.015$ (LO-90 $= 0.000$, HI-90 $= 0.039$).

More precisely, the testing of the CBDBE model revealed that tourists' perception of functional destination attributes postively affects the perception of intangible attributes (SPC $= 0.870$, $R^2 = 0.757$) and value for money (SPC $= 0.548$, $R^2 = 0.300$). In turn, customers' overall satisfaction with the destination experience is exclusively affected ($R^2 = 0.674$) by the (i.e. emotional) perception of intangible attributes (SPC $= 0.780$) and value for money (SPC $= 0.172$). Finally, next to tourists' quality experience related to functional destination attributes (SPC $= 0.335$), the intermediary model constructs 'intangible attributes', 'value for money' and 'overall satisfaction' (SPC $= 0.331$) significantly explain the loyalty behaviour of tourists visiting a summer tourism destination ($R^2 = 0.494$).

## 7.7. Conclusion

The results gathered from the reported CBBE model test confirm the positive relationship between customer satisfaction and loyalty, which is fully consistent with previous findings in the tourism literature (e.g. Back & Parks, 2003; Bigne et al., 2001; Chi & Qu, 2008; del Bosque & Martin, 2008; Faullant et al., 2008; Hutchinson et al., 2009;

Lee et al., 2007; Yoon & Uysal, 2005). Moreover, the study at hand also confirms that customers' perception of functional destination attributes has a positive direct effect on both value for money (Chen & Tsai, 2007) and destination loyalty (Chi & Qu, 2008). By contrast, the hypothesis about the direct positive relationship between value for money and destination loyalty (Boo et al., 2009; Hutchinson et al., 2009) is not supported. However, the relationship between value for money and loyalty is mediated by customer satisfaction as reported by Chen and Tsai (2007), Lee et al. (2007) and Hutchinson et al. (2009). Finally, the direct positive relationship between experience of functional attributes and satisfaction (Chi & Qu, 2008) is not significant. Rather, it is mediated by tourists' experience of intangible destination attributes, which demonstrates the transformation of destination resources into an emotional component of the value-in-use of destination visitation for tourists (Vargo & Lusch, 2004, 2008).

For the leading Swedish tourism destination of Åre it has been shown that the proposed CBDBE modelling approach can be recommended to measure and strategically assess CBBE: the model's explanation power is relatively high and the gathered SEM results support six of eight previously formulated hypotheses concerning customers' process of destination brand equity formation and related (i.e. affective and behavioural) consequences. From these insights various managerial implications for both, strategy evaluation and strategy building at tourism destinations can be deduced and are discussed next.

On the general level, destination managers gain strategically relevant knowledge through the assessment of functional and experiential dimensions of destination experience (Andersson, 2007). More precisely, by monitoring the proposed brand equity dimensions proposed in the study at hand destination management can (a) implement effective brand development strategies and (b) control customer loyalty through *functional* destination attributes. For instance, for the Swedish tourism destination of Åre the urban environment is composed by the functional destination attributes accommodation and restaurant services, cable cars (*Åre Kabinbana*) and Holiday Club's public pool and sauna world. By contrast, the summer destination's natural environment is compound by hiking trails and the various outdoor opportunities for experiencing nature. Of particular interest for the destination management of Åre, the biking domain (Åre Biking Park, biking trails) emerged as being of crucial functional significance (see Table 7.2). Moreover, destination management may (c) evaluate and upgrade its marketing measures and, finally, (d) discover innovation potentials to improve experience intensive destination offers showing a predominance of *intangible* destination attributes mainly responsible for tourists' emotional destination experiences (Mossberg, 2007). For the Swedish tourism summer destination of Åre it can be shown that the following intangible destination attributes are of crucial relevance to the customer, in descending order of significance: safety and security, family friendliness, brand name and reputation, cleanliness and tidiness as well as the peaceful and restful atmosphere at the tourism destination (see Table 7.2).

The present study shows various limitations that should, thus, be addressed in future research studies. First of all, the proposed CBDBE model can only be viewed as a first step towards the definition of a fully validated measurement approach. As CR and AVE revealed, in the present study the experience constructs for tangible and intangible attributes could not yet satisfactorily be validated. Thus, based on the presented study, future research should focus on the more reliable measurement of tourist experience on an attributive base in the context of a CBDBE modelling approach.

Secondly, respondents were approached during destination stay. However, Palmer (2010) argues that customers' attitudes adjust over time, wherefore the widely adopted approach to evaluate service experiences during (or immediately after) service consumption is criticized. To avoid this drawback and in order to approach tourists after they returned home, it is proposed to employ web-based surveys in future research.

Thirdly, the proposed CBDBE model does not include a construct to measure destination awareness since the model is validated based only on data collected from tourists who have already arrived at the destination. Tourism literature suggests that the depth of destination-based brand knowledge builds on a variety of information sources, such as brochures, independent publications in media, travel agencies, relatives and friends as well as previous visits (Baloglu, 2001; Baloglu & McCleary, 1999; Beerli & Martin, 2004). However, at the same time, Gartner and Konecnik (2010) argue that in the case of repeat visitation destination awareness becomes less important compared to other CBBE dimensions. Finally, Aaker (1996) points at the various difficulties associated with the operationalization and measurement of the awareness construct for situations of repeat purchase (e.g. the irrelevance of TOMA). Thus, as this issue so far is inadequately represented in the tourism literature, there is a need to properly conceptualize the construct of destination awareness relevant to both, repeat and new customers. Consequently, a CBDBE model that incorporates destination awareness needs to be similarly tested based on data comprising repeat and first-time visitors. However, this raises the question about the specificity of branding and brand performance measurement for tourism destinations on differing geographical levels. Although not yet intensively discussed in the literature, but basically supported by the results gathered in the study at hand, the CBDBE dimension 'awareness' is assumed to be relatively more important for a destination country, while for local or regional tourism destinations functional destination characteristics are most critical.

Fourthly, the presented CBDBE model rests upon current tourism research in the emerging field of destination branding and destination loyalty studies. However, as pointed by Li and Petrick (2008) tourism marketing literature developed within a goods-centric paradigm should be revisited in light of the new service logic. Thus, for future research it is proposed to revisit the theoretical conceptualization behind the CBBE model by taking into account a service marketing perspective thereby focusing on the co-created value-in-use of a tourism stay (Grönroos, 2000, 2006; Vargo & Lusch, 2004, 2008). For this aim, it is particularly suggested to employ metrics for value-in-use from destination stay on the base of qualitative operationalization methods, such as the means-end analytical approach (Klenosky 2002; Klenosky, Gengler, & Mulvey, 1993) in order to relate functional and experiential destination attributes with valued outcomes from the process of the destination stay.

Furthermore, recent service marketing literature suggests that a brand and what is branded should be alienated and, therefore, a brand has a value-in-use of its own (Merz, He & Vargo, 2009). This, particularly, implies that the value-in-use of tourism destination brands does not have to be directly related to destination visitation. Thus, the CBDBE model of the future should integrate other dimensions, which not only reflect the value-in-use of the destination communicated by the brand, but also the value-in-use of the brand beyond destination visitation, such as, for instance, the symbolic value of tourism destination brands for the customer.

Finally, since the purpose of destination brand equity measurement primarily is about comparative evaluations of competitive brand positions (Boo et al., 2009), having tested the CBDBE model for only one tourism destination is an obvious limitation of the present study. Therefore, it is finally suggested to empirically test the proposed CBDBE model also within a set of competing tourism destinations of a similar type (e.g. summer destinations, winter sports destinations) in future research.

## Acknowledgements

This research project has been financed by the EU Structural Fund objective 2 project no. 39736 and the European Tourism Research Institute (ETOUR), Mid-Sweden University. The authors would like to thank the CEOs Lars-Börje Eriksson (Åre Destination AB), Niclas Sjögren Berg (SkiStar Åre) and Marketing Assistant Hans Ericson (Holiday Club Åre) for their excellent co-operation.

## References

Aaker, D. A. (1996). *Building strong brands.* New York, NY: The Free Press.

Andersson, T. D. (2007). The tourist in the experience economy. *Scandinavian Journal of Hospitality and Tourism, 7*(1), 46–58. doi: 10.1080/15022250701224035

Armstrong, G., & Kotler, P. (2009). *Marketing — An introduction* (9th ed.). NJ: Pearson Prentice Hall.

Back, K. J., & Parks, S. C. (2003). A brand loyalty model involving cognitive, affective and conative brand loyalty and customer satisfaction. *Journal of Hospitality and Tourism Research, 27*(4), 419–435. doi: 10.1177/10963480030274003

Baloglu, S. (2001). Image variations of Turkey by familiarity index: Informational and experiential dimensions. *Tourism Management, 22,* 127–133. doi: 10.1016/S0261-5177(00)00049-2

Baloglu, S., & McCleary, K. W. (1999). A model of destination image formation. *Annals of Tourism Research, 26*(4), 868–897. doi: 10.1016/S0160-7383(99)00030-4

Beerli, A., & Martin, J. D. (2004). Factors influencing destination image. *Annals of Tourism Research, 31*(3), 657–681. doi: 10.1016/j.annals.2004.01.010

Bigne, J. E., Andreu, L., & Gnoth, J. (2005). The theme park experience: An analysis of pleasure, arousal and satisfaction. *Tourism Management*, *26*, 833–844. doi: 10.1016/j.tourman.2004.05.006

Bigne, J. E., Garcia, I. S., & Blas, S. S. (2009). The functional-psychological continuum in the cognitive image of a destination: A confirmatory analysis. *Tourism Management*, *30*(6), 715–723. doi: 10.1016/j.tourman.2008.10.020

Bigne, J. E., Sanchez, M. I., & Sanchez, J. (2001). Tourism image, evaluation variables and after purchase behaviour: Inter-relationship. *Tourism Management*, *22*, 607–616. doi: 10.1016/S0261-5177(01)00035-8

Boo, S., Busser, J., & Baloglu, S. (2009). A model of customer-based brand equity and its application to multiple destinations. *Tourism Management*, *30*(2), 219–231. doi: 10.1016/j.tourman.2008.06.003

Chekalina, T., & Fuchs, M. (2009a). An assessment of survey-based brand metrics for tourism destinations. In L. Dioko & L. Xiang (Eds.), *Proceedings of the 3rd international conference on destination branding and marketing*, Macau (pp. 130–141).

Chekalina, T., & Fuchs, M. (2009b). Tourism destination brand equity — An empirical assessment from Sweden. *Proceedings of the consumer behaviour in tourism symposium, December15–19, 2009*, Brunico, South Tyrol, Italy.

Chen, C. F., & Tsai, D. (2007). How destination image and evaluative factors affect behavioral intentions. *Tourism Management*, *28*(4), 1115–1122. doi: 10.1016/j.tourman.2006.07.007

Chi, C. G. Q., & Qu, H. L. (2008). Examining the structural relationships of destination image, tourist satisfaction and destination loyalty: An integrated approach. *Tourism Management*, *29*(4), 624–636. doi: 10.1016/j.tourman.2007.06.007

Crompton, J. L. (1979). Motivations for pleasure vacation. *Annals of Tourism Research*, *6*(4), 408–424. doi: 10.1016/0160-7383(79)90004-5

Del Bosque, I. R., & Martin, H. S. (2008). Tourist satisfaction-a cognitive-affective model. *Annals of Tourism Research*, *35*(2), 551–573. doi: 10.1016/j.annals.2008.02.006

Deslandes, D., & Goldsmith, R. E. (2002). Destination branding: A new concept for tourism marketing. In E. Harlan & H. E. Spotts (Eds.), *Developments in marketing sciences: Proceedings of the annual conference of the academy of marketing sciences* (pp. 130–137). Coral Gables, FL: Academy of Marketing Science.

Deslandes, D. D., Goldsmith, R. E., Bonn, M., & Joseph, S. (2006). Measuring destination image: Do the existing scales work? *Tourism Review International*, *10*(3), 141–153.

Echtner, C. M., & Ritchie, J. R. B. (1993). The measurement of destination image: An empirical assessment. *Journal of Travel Research*, *31*(Spring), 3–13. doi: 10.1016/j.tourman.2003.06.004

Faullant, R., Matzler, K., & Füller, J. (2008). The impact of satisfaction and image on loyalty: The case of Alpine ski resorts. *Managing Service Quality*, *18*(2), 163–178. doi: 10.1108/09604520810859210

Finn, M., Elliott-White, M., & Walton, M. (2000). *Tourism and leisure research methods: Data collection, analysis, and interpretation*. Harlow, UK: Longman.

Fuchs, M., & Weiermair, K. (2004). Destination benchmarking-an indicator-system's potential for exploring guest satisfaction. *Journal of Travel Research*, *42*(3), 212–225. doi: 10.1177/0047287503258827

Gallarza, M. G., Saura, I. G., & Garcia, H. C. (2002). Destination image-towards a conceptual framework. *Annals of Tourism Research*, *29*(1), 56–78. doi: 10.1016/S0160-7383(01)00031-7

Gartner, C. (2009). Deconstructing brand equity. In *Tourism branding: communities in action. Bridging Tourism Theory and Practice* (Vol. 1, pp. 51–63). doi:10.1108/S2042-1443(2009)0000001006.

Gartner, W. C., & Konecnik, M. K. (2010). Tourism destination brand equity dimensions: Renewal versus repeat market. *Journal of Travel Research*. doi:10.1177/0047287510379157.

Gnoth, J. (2007). The structure of destination brands: Leveraging values. *Tourism Analysis*, *12*(5/6), 345–358. doi: 10.1016/j.tourman.2008.12.007

Grönroos, C. (2000). *Service management and marketing. A customer relationship management approach* (2nd ed.). UK: Wiley.

Grönroos, C. (2006). Adopting a service logic for marketing. *Marketing Theory*, *6*(3), 317–333. doi: 10.1177/1470593106066794

Gummesson, E. (2002). *Total relationship marketing* (2nd ed.). Oxford: Butterworth Heinemann.

Hair, J. F., Black, W. C., Babin, B. J., Anderson, R. E., & Tatham, R. (2006). *Multivariate data analysis* (6th ed.). NJ: Prentice Hall.

Hutchinson, J., Lai, F. J., & Wang, Y. C. (2009). Understanding the relationships of quality, value, equity, satisfaction, and behavioral intentions among golf travelers. *Tourism Management*, *30*(2), 298–308. doi: 10.1016/j.tourman.2008.07.010

Jang, S. S., & Feng, R. M. (2007). Temporal destination revisit intention: The effects of novelty seeking and satisfaction. *Tourism Management*, *28*(2), 580–590. doi: 10.1016/j.tourman.2006.04.024

Keller, K. L. (1993). Conceptualizing, measuring and managing customer-based brand equity. *Journal of Marketing*, *57*(January), 1–22. Retrieved from http://www.jstor.org/stable/1252054.

Keller, K. L. (2008). *Strategic brand management building, measuring and managing brand equity* (3rd ed.). NJ: Pearson Education.

Klenosky, D. B. (2002). The "Pull" of tourism destinations: A means-end investigation. *Journal of Travel Research*, *40*(4), 385–396. doi: 10.1177/004728750204000405

Klenosky, D. B., Gengler, C. E., & Mulvey, M. S. (1993). Understanding the factors influencing Ski destination choice: A means-end analytic approach. *Journal of Leisure Research*, *25*(4), 362–379.

Konecnik, M., & Gartner, W. C. (2007). Customer-based brand equity for a destination. *Annals of Tourism Research*, *34*(2), 400–421. doi: 10.1016/j.annals.2006.10.005

Kotler, P., & Keller, K. (2009). *Marketing Management* (13th ed.). NJ: Pearson Prentice Hall.

Larsen, S. (2007). Aspects of a psychology of the tourist experience. *Scandinavian Journal of Hospitality and Tourism*, *7*(1), 7–18. doi: 10.1080/15022250701226014

Lee, C. K., Yoon, Y. S., & Lee, S. K. (2007). Investigating the relationships among perceived value, satisfaction, and recommendations: The case of the korean DMZ. *Tourism Management*, *28*(1), 204–214. doi: 10.1016/j.tourman.2005.12.017

Lehmann, D. R., Keller, K. L., & Farley, J. U. (2008). The structure of survey-based brand metrics. *Journal of International Marketing*, *16*(4), 29–56. doi: 10.1509/jimk.16.4.29

Li, X., & Petrick, J. F. (2008). Tourism marketing in an era of paradigm shift. *Journal of Travel Research*, *46*(February), 235–244. doi: 10.1177/0047287507303976

Merz, M. A., He, Y., & Vargo, S. L. (2009). The evolving brand logic: A service-dominant logic perspective. *Journal of the Academy of Marketing Science*, *37*, 328–344. doi: 10.1007/s11747-009-0143-3

Morgan, N. J., Pritchard, A., & Pride, R. (Eds.). (2004). *Destination branding: Creating the unique destination proposition* (2nd ed.). Oxford: Elsevier.

Mossberg, L. (2007). A marketing approach to the tourist experience. *Scandinavian Journal of Hospitality and Tourism, 7*(1), 59–74. doi: 10.1080/15022250701231915

Nordin, S., & Svensson, B. (2007). Innovative destination governance: The Swedish ski resort of Åre. *Entrepreneurship and Innovation, 8*(1), 53–66. doi: 10.5367/000000007780007416

Oliver, R. L. (1997). *Satisfaction: A behavioral perspective of the consumer.* New York, NY: McGraw-Hill.

Oliver, R. L. (1999). Whence consumer loyalty? *The Journal of Marketing, 63*(Special Issue), 33–44. Retrieved from http://www.jstor.org/stable/1252099

Palmer, A. (2010). Customer experience management: A critical review of an emerging idea. *Journal of Services Marketing, 24*(3), 196–208. doi: 10.1108/08876041011040604

Pike, S. (2009). Destination brand positions of a competitive set of near-home destinations. *Tourism Management, 30*(6), 857–866. doi: 10.1016/j.tourman.2008.12.007

Pike, S., Bianchi, C., Kerr, G., & Patti, C. (2010). Consumer-based brand equity for Australia as a long-haul tourism destination in an emerging market. *International Marketing Review, 27*(4), 434–449. doi: 10.1108/02651331011058590

Reisinger, Y., & Turner, L. (1999). Structural equation modelling with LISREL: Application in tourism. *Tourism Management, 20*(2), 71–88.

Steenkamp, J.-B. E. M., & Baumgartner, H. (2000). On the use of structural equation models for marketing modelling. *International Journal of Research in Marketing, 17*(2), 195–202. doi: 10.1016/S0167-8116(00)00016-1

Stepchenkova, S., & Morrison, A. (2008). Russia's destination image among American pleasure travellers: Revisiting Echtner and Ritchie. *Tourism Management, 29*(3), 548–560. doi: 10.1016/j.tourman.2007.06.003

Vargo, S. L., & Lusch, R. F. (2004). The four service marketing myths: Remnants of a goods-based, manufacturing model. *Journal of Service Research, 6*(4), 324–335. doi: 10.1177/1094670503262946

Vargo, S. L., & Lusch, R. F. (2008). Service-dominant logic: Continuing the evolution. *Journal of the Academy of Marketing Science, 36*(1), 1–10. doi: 10.1007/s11747-007-0069-6

Weiermair, K., & Fuchs, M. (1999). Measuring tourist judgments on service quality. *Annals of Tourism Research, 26*(4), 1004–1021. doi: 10.1016/S0160-7383(99)00037-7

Yoon, Y., & Uysal, M. (2005). An examination of the effects of motivation and satisfaction on destination loyalty: A structural model. *Tourism Management, 26*(1), 45–56. doi: 10.1016/j.tourman.2003.08.016

Chapter 8

# Local Stakeholders' Image of Tourism Destinations: Outlooks for Destination Branding

*Danielle Fernandes Costa Machado, Mirna de Lima Medeiros and João Luiz Passador*

## 8.1. Introduction

Owing to the intangibility and inseparability between the moment of production and the moment of consumption of tourism services, destination image is considered a key factor that contributes to the process of destination choice and visitor choice behaviour (Chen & Tsai, 2007; Echtner & Ritchie, 1991; Martín & Bosque, 2008). However, it was not until 1990, with the publication of seminal works such as Echtner and Ritchie's (1991), that academic research started placing more emphasis on the adoption of approaches that could contribute to a better understanding of mental representations involved in image perception. Even so, it is still possible to identify gaps left by previous studies regarding the comprehension of the symbolic and subjective universe implied in the way stakeholders of local tourism trade portray destination image. These gaps formed the basis for the formulation of an empirical study whose results and discussions are presented in this chapter.

The main aim of the study was to analyse the image of a tourism destination based on the perceptions of the host community, as well as those of visitors and public administrators. The guiding question for the research was: Are there any differences among the image internalized by residents, the image induced by the public services and the image perceived by visitors regarding destination that may affect marketing strategies and actions? This question is based on the General Model for Images in Tourism formulated by Santana (2009) and also on studies suggesting that destination image is a multi-dimensional construct, which therefore has a plural and relativist character (Bonn, Joseph, & Daí, 2005; Chi & Qu, 2008; Frías, Rodríguez, & Castañeda, 2008; Gallarza, Saura, & García, 2002; Gartner, 1993; Hunter, 2008).

Based on this question, the research suggests a holistic approach to the process of forming and publicizing destination image, acknowledging the role of social stakeholders in such a process. Therefore, the study attempts to shed light on the importance of identifying attributes and values perceived from the destination image. Identifying such attributes and values helps to form and maintain a brand that is consistent with the brand positioning, something that is desired by destination public managers and that meets the social interests of stakeholders.

The Brazilian town of Diamantina is the destination chosen for the analysis. It is situated in Minas Gerais State, and was recognized as a World Heritage Site by UNESCO in 1999. A few comparisons were made with two other historical towns, Ouro Preto and Tiradentes. Both as well as the former are considered to be international induction centres for tourism by the Brazilian Ministry of Tourism. The comparison between Diamantina and the other two historical towns took into consideration the premise that creating a competitive differential position requires not only the recognition of elements associated with the image of a given destination in isolation but also in comparison with its counterparts. Therefore, it is understood that, even though these places may look similar at first sight, it is essential to demonstrate that they are different and to avoid creating standardized images that, instead of enhancing the value of the destination, merely homogenize landscapes and do not add value to the product.

## 8.2.   Conceptual Framework

### 8.2.1.   Process of Image Formation and Destination Choice

Destination image is a complex concept because it allows several interpretations and does not have a single definition that can cover all its meaning. Despite this difficulty, the present study adopts a widely used definition suggesting that destination image can be understood as a set of beliefs, ideas and impressions of a certain place that result in an internally accepted mental construct.

There is certain consensus that destination image is a multi-dimensional construct composed of indissoluble interconnections of a whole unit (Kastenholz, 2002; Martín & Bosque, 2008). From this perspective, Gartner (1993) emphasizes that destination image is composed of cognitive, affective and conative components. Echtner and Ritchie (1991) suggest a model for the dimensions of a place's image based on three continuous bipolar dimensions: (1) holistic-attribute (image is composed of the perception of specific attributes of the destination, added to general impressions on the place); (2) functional-psychological (refers to tangible characteristics, such as tourism attractions and accommodation, or more abstract ones such as hospitality and reputation); (3) common-unique (relates either to frequently encountered characteristics or to those which are peculiar).

The way these components are captured by individuals depends on the place's process of image formation. Crompton and Fakeye (1991) suggest that this process involves three stages: organic image, induced image and complex image. The *organic image* is formed by means of exposure to information that is not geared towards tourism such as newspaper and magazine articles, friends' and relatives' opinions and other non-specialized information. The *induced image* is made up of specifically promoted information, which is not influenced by the organizations operating in the area, for instance, traditional advertising methods (travel ads and posters) or information supplied by tour operators. In the last stage, after visitation, the visitor develops a *complex image* that results from his/her contact with the area.

This process of image formation is defined as being one of the key factors in tourism destination choice. Consequently, a large part of models for destination choice found in the literature emphasizes that, for a potential visitor to consider going to a particular destination, he/she must have some previous exposure to it.

Since it cannot be tried prior to the trip, the tourism 'product' requires subjective judgements. Based on that constraint, Tapachai and Waryszak (2000) suggest that the power of destination image and the visitor's choice of this particular destination are influenced by five consumption values associated with the place's image: (1) Functional — relates to consumer's choice being based on appealing physical and utilitarian attributes of the destination, for instance, beautiful scenery, tropical beaches, etc.; (2) social — associates the choice with its alignment to aspirations and wishes of the group the tourist belongs to, as when the choice is made based on the fact that the place caters for activities for young people, and also on the destination popularity and prestige, etc.; (3) emotional — linked with feelings, affection and desires, for instance, the search for quiet, relaxing atmosphere; (4) epistemological — related to the search for knowledge, interest in or desire for something new or different, as in trips to experience different cultures or to attend courses; and (5) conditional — in this, the alternatives have their functional or social value highlighted by contingencies (e.g. proximity, events), without which they would not have such a value. These five values might be crucial to destination choice, and decisions might be influenced by at least one or even by all of them simultaneously.

### 8.2.2. *Promotion of Tourism Image*

The image of a tourism destination is a subjective interpretation of reality that partially results from a process managed by promoters and administrators in tourism marketing (Kotler, Armstrong, Saunders, & Wong, 1999) who attempt to increase the chances of forming a desirable image that will attract tourists from the destination's target public. As for managing destination impressions, several authors point out the ethics issue. Mendonça and Amantino-de-Andrade (2003) state that a definition of authentic management of impressions is necessary. The place must look for the proximity between the way it longs to be seen and its self-image (identity). Kotler, Gertner, Rein, and Haider (2006) highlight that identity is the way a locality identifies and positions itself or its services, and image is the way the public sees the locality and its services. Hence, perceptions of destination image involve a universe of relations, where there are spaces with subjective and diverse meanings to groups that interact with it. Therefore, the approach from the perception of various stakeholders becomes pertinent.

There are some examples of studies that investigated the image of a destination by gathering data from various stakeholders and found differences in image perceptions: amongst visitors and residents (Ryan & Cave, 2005); visitors and travel agents (Grosspietsch, 2006); visitors and non-visitors (Stepchenkova & Morrison, 2008); and amongst distinct segments of the same group of stakeholders (visitors from different countries, domestic and overseas visitors and tour operators who sell the destination).

Based on this very same perception, Santana (2009) suggests a model composed of seven sub-processes of global image, which would be interconnected but operationally separable both in their analysis and in implementation. According to the author, it is important not only to focus image formation on the visitor/consumer's perspective, but also to include the perceptions of other stakeholders involved in the creation of the destination's imagery. The author proposes that the incorporation of *self-image* — the image residents have of themselves and of the spaces-territories — can give an authentic character to the marketing campaigns. This self-image can also pose limits to development or to tourism exploration of particular areas.

The physical, social and cultural elements of the territories that can be promoted in order to attract visitors form the *sales image*, which must serve the interests of local institutions, businesspeople and residents. This image will materialize in promotion campaigns, forming the *promoted image* in publicity materials. Despite this fact, this promoted image may not be the image consumed by visitors. This occurs because tour companies can modify the image while planning travel packages, establishing a *re-created image*. When this re-created image reaches travel agencies, which are the last channel before the consumer, it can still go through some alterations, which will define the *sold image*.

It is thought that disparities may exist between the induced image (the set of promoted images, re-created images and sold images), and the image that will be perceived by the visitor, since this is a whole set of beliefs, ideas and impressions on the visited place (Crompton, 1979) that overlay stereotyped images and accumulated expectations of the pre-visit phase. Satisfaction with the place is influenced by the confrontation between the image perceived by the visitor and a set of unpredictable and stereotypical expectations that result from organic and induced images (Bigné, Sanchez, & Sanchez, 2001).

Owing to all this complexity that involves tourism promotion, the creation of a strong image is frequently considered to be one of the main purposes of the brand. According to Cai (2002), the brand of a destination can be defined as the perceptions of a place reflected by means of associated images captured in visitors' memories. The building of a destination brand suggests the selection of a mix of elements that are coherent with its identity and distinction, before the construction of a positive image that aims at helping market segmentation. Furthermore, it may help reduce the intangibility effect, which is the risk perceived from the fact that the purchaser is not able to touch the item that is purchased.

Although it seems to be easy to create a marketing message, such a task can become complicated if the multi-faceted and complex character of destination is to be considered. In this respect, Bramwell and Randing (1996) state that if a place stresses a distinct attribute or its combination with a general image, the message is clear and easily understood. But when the attempt is to capture the place's diversity, the result is an image similar to those of other places, which may lead to the creation of stereotypes.

According to Bignami (2002), a stereotype is a widely accepted, highly misleading and fairly simplified image of something. It brings in itself a fixed idea about a subject and it hinders promotional efforts to differentiate images of destinations, mainly of those that have similar physical characteristics and tourism potentiality. Such places are at risk of having their diversity and differences overlooked by the release of stereotyped images, which are in most cases distortions of reality. For this reason, brand differentiation efforts are much more geared towards psychological factors evoked by the brand than towards its physical attributes (Aaker, 2007).

This set of physical and psychological attributes associated with the brand form the brand personality of the destination. The brand or destination personality refers to a set of human characteristics associated with it (Hosany, Ekinci, & Uysal, 2006). Tourism destinations are rich in terms of symbolic values and personality characteristics as they comprise a package of tangible and intangible components associated with private values, stories and feelings. Tourists' perceptions of the destination's brand personality may be an important variable influencing their purchasing behaviour since, according to Sirgy's (1982) theory of self-concept, consumers are encouraged to purchase certain products because of these products' symbolic values, assessing the degree of similarity between the personality characteristics the products convey and the personality they want to project of themselves. Therefore, products are more likely to be adopted if there is coherence between the brand personality of the destination and some characteristics of an individual's self-image.

The perception of the destination brand personality is influenced by filters created by demand, supply and autonomous agents, which increase the complexity of the study of destination image. However, few studies analyse these agents' activities. In order to meet the demand for such studies, the present work aims to answer the question: Are there any differences between the images internalized by the residents, induced by the public sector and perceived by the visitors about the destination that can affect strategies and marketing actions?

## 8.3. Research Method

The research work consisted of a case study using a qualitative approach. In order to facilitate access to representations and meanings attributed to destination image by different stakeholders, three data collection techniques were used: interviews, photoethnography and document research. The choice for this set of methods took into consideration the principle of the use of multiple sources of evidence, which, according to Yin (1984), is a very important characteristic that can help researchers approach the case from a broader and more comprehensive perspective, in addition to facilitating cross-checking of information.

Data were collected by means of primary and secondary sources. Primary data were collected *in locus* from stakeholders of the tourism trade — tourists, host community (residents and businesspeople in tourism sector) and local public sector in an intentional, non-probabilistic way. The total number of respondents was defined by answers saturation — 27 interviews were conducted: (a) 12 with visitors who stayed in Diamantina for at least 2 days and who had previously been to other historical destinations; (b) 4 with local public sector representatives, including all managers of the municipal public departments directly linked to the tourism promotion of the destination. (Although these figures may seem small, the number of respondents is representative of the staff appointed to tourism activities, since these departments have lean organizational structures.); (c) 11 with residents of the destination studied, who, after analyses, were put in two sub-groups: 5 businesspeople with professional experience in the field of tourism and 6 residents working in tourism. The selection of these residents was made in accordance with the snowball method. Individuals working in tourism for the longest periods and the most socially, economically engaged ones were chosen in preference to others.

The interviews were guided by a semi-structured plan containing traditional and projective open-ended questions, such as word association and sentence completion. In word association technique, terms like 'tourism' and 'Diamantina' were utilized as inductive expressions. As for the completion technique, respondents were asked to complete a set of eight unfinished sentences (e.g. 'People who visit Diamantina are ...' — 'If Diamantina was a person, he/she would be ...'). The photoethnography technique itself was utilized by means of asking respondents to choose a picture that illustrated their general impressions on the destination. Later, the respondents were asked to justify their choices.

The secondary data consisted of analysis of promotional materials, designed and managed by public institutions in charge of promoting the destination. Altogether 12 brochures were analysed (8 informative folders, 1 route plan, 1 map, 1 postcard and 1 events calendar used by public institutions to publicize the destination in events and at the town's Tour Information Centre). In addition, official websites run by public institutions were analysed.

After all these phases, the data were submitted to content analysis (CA), which supplies a logical analytical structure and also makes it possible to access subjective realities of symbolic representations involved in the perception of the image of the tourism destination. The organization of the analysis followed the three-phased model described by Bardin (1977): pre-analysis, material exploration and treatment of data and interpretations.

The analytical categories were defined according to the themes that emerged from both the respondents' narratives and the destination's promotional materials. In order to do so, we used the mixed model of categorization suggested by Laville and Dionne (1999). Therefore, some initial categories were pre-defined, based on the research theoretical reference and other categories were inserted, taking into consideration all the themes that proved to be significant.

Data interpretation followed the pattern-matching technique, which consisted of associating collected data with a theoretical model so that comparisons could be made. Additionally, criteria with precision, exhaustion, pertinence and legitimacy were used to guarantee scientific validity of the categories formulated. The latter criterion was met by following the procedure suggested by Bauer (2007), which defends content interpretation by the researcher in two distinct intervals in order to verify the agreement regarding the categories formulated or otherwise. The proposed categorization was then submitted to an expert panel, and the final grouping of categories was achieved. NVivo computer-aided, quantitative data analysis software was utilized in order to facilitate data interpretation.

## 8.4. Results and Discussions

### 8.4.1. Image Induced by Public Sector

For the study of induced image, all the publicity materials made available to visitors by public organizations in charge of the tourism promotion of Diamantina were analysed (websites and folders with information on tour packages, maps and event calendars). The analysis of photographs and figures in the materials made it possible to categorize themes and their frequencies, according to Table 8.1.

Table 8.1: Themes of figures used to promote Diamantina's image induced by public sector.

| Figure themes | Frequency (%) | Absolute no. (*n* = 94) | Main elements |
|---|---|---|---|
| Natural landscape | 15 | 14 | Waterfalls, mountains, roads/trails, Slaves Route, Saltpetre Cave |
| Architectural assets | 60 | 56 | Churches, Gloria House, Old Market, museums, colonial houses |
| Craft | 5 | 5 | Jewellery of gold and coconut shell, 'sempre-vivas', paper mache, wood |
| Popular manifestations | 6 | 6 | Marujada dance, religious events, music band |
| Events | 3 | 3 | Vesperata, carnival |
| Tourist activities (man–environment interaction) | 8 | 7 | Climbing, hiking, tourist mining, tourist watching the environment |
| Gastronomy | 3 | 3 | Log stove with tropeiro beans, 'tutu', chicken, 'bamba de garimpo', and cheese |

Apart from revealing the themes mentioned, content analysis also showed that 75% of the pictures analysed did not portray people. This absence of people grants the destination a 'museum-like' character, a scenario-town. According to Galí and Donaire (2005), this characteristic of tourism advertising is associated with the preservation of a romantic model that can be perceived through the use of pictures that illustrate areas deprived of any sign of everyday life and of decontextualized and non-temporal images. Consequently, guides and leaflets address a sort of visitor who does not consider tourism as a ritualistic activity based on collective consumption.

If, on one hand, the figures used to represent the place's heritage emphasize the idea of 'museum-town', on the other hand, those which are supposed to denote natural attractions retain the romantic style. Even in illustrations with human presence, individuals are portrayed in romantic attitudes (of relaxation, reflection or cheerfulness). The romantic style present in Diamantina's publicity is illustrated by the similarity of one photograph in the folder of the Circuito dos Diamantes/'The Diamonds Circuit' (Figure 8.1) to a painting by Caspar David Friedrich from 1817 (Figure 8.2).

Following the analysis of the figures, we analysed the contents of the written messages. Table 8.2 presents the main themes, associated words and expressions, and their frequency.

Figure 8.1: Sample of the use of romantic concept in publicity. Author: Henry Yu; *Source*: Image extracted from a folder of the Diamonds Circuit.

Figure 8.2: The wanderer above the mists. Author: Caspar David Friedrich; *Source*: Photopedia. (http://www.fotopedia.com/items/flickr-523677142)

The 'Historical Diamantina' (36%) refers to publicity items that focus on the town's historical past and its importance in the heyday of gold and diamond mining throughout the 18th century. Publicity appeal concentrates on the historical centre's architectural assets. In 'Diamantina of traditions and mineiridade' (36%), the town is highlighted as a locus of traditional and popular manifestations and of the strong association with the 'mineiridade' stereotype, usually described in characteristics like hospitality, religiosity, typical food and historical figures. 'Ecological Diamantina' (18%) refers to the effort, still prompt and unconscious, to present the town as a destination combining history and nature, which is summarized in the slogan 'Natureza e história em um só lugar' ('Nature and history in a single place'). Finally, 'Musical Diamantina' (10%) relates to the musical qualities present in the town or conveyed by it, due to a rich and varied musical programme in its events calendar.

Based on the features observed in destination promotion and in tourism publicity classification suggested by Jean-Didier (1999), we can suggest that the image presented by public sector is still limited to stylistic patterns belonging to the first communicational phase, that is, it emphasizes the description of the destination's physical characteristics. Apart from this interpretation, according to what we can infer from some extracts from interviews with public administrators, the public sector seems to find it difficult to define a positioning for destination brand departing from the creation of a strong and differentiated image:

> ... Despite all the tourism importance of our town, we don't even have a marketing plan. It makes things difficult because we don't have research or guidelines; we end up not knowing what to advertise. To whom? How? (Public administrator 3)

This situation leads to a collapse in the management of destination brand. The public sectors not getting involved leads to the image being induced by external agents, as pointed out by one of the respondents:

> The town itself hasn't defined well the image it wants to project. It is left up in the air, and what is up in the air is induced either by us or by others. But the problem is that we are the ones who are supposed to receive visitors. We are the ones who have to be concerned about preserving a positive image of the town because otherwise, Diamantina itself will be affected by a bad image. It is the destination after all. The travel agency may well sell other places. (Public administrator 4)

This hindrance to destination brand management reveals the complexity of the study of the image and the importance of trying to understand the outlook of several stakeholders involved in the process of image formation. In this respect, to perceive an image through someone's eyes becomes essential not only to identify the existing bottlenecks found in the promotion of induced images, but also to identify the blindness that prevents tourism promotion from becoming more authentic and less stereotyped.

In the present study specifically, the public sector's lack of promotional planning seems to have as its central reaction, the maintenance of the projection of a stereotyped image of 'Mineira historical town', which has been constructed throughout the years by public opinion. World Heritage Site, Brazilian baroque, steep roads, churches, museums, large houses, Minas Gerais–style tables, all these elements build up the 'Mineiridade' stereotype, which is praised by Diamantina's tourism promotion.

### 8.4.2. Stakeholders' Perceptions and Their Implications in Destination Branding

Data interpretation made it possible to identify different meanings and the interpretations that groups of local stakeholders have of the town, making visible the social relations, territoriality and collective imagination behind the elements that comprise the individuals' global understanding of the town's image. Among the most emphasized elements regarding the holistic dimension of the destination are the colonial architecture, liveliness of the relations amongst visitors–town–residents, nature and a peaceful atmosphere.

Table 8.2: Frequency of themes found in the promotion of Diamantina's image by public sector.

| Themes | Most common words and expressions | Frequency (%) |
|---|---|---|
| *Historical Diamantina* | Churches | 7 |
| | Large houses | 6 |
| | Mining/diamond/gold | 6 |
| | History/witness/memory | 4 |
| | Architectural asset and monuments | 4 |
| | Colonial/baroque | 3 |
| | Humanity's cultural and historical heritage site | 3 |
| | Museums | 2 |
| | A travel in time/back to the past | 1 |
| | *Total historical* | *36* |
| *Diamantina of mineiridade traditions* | Religious festivals/faith/religiosity | 7 |
| | Cultural and popular manifestations | 7 |
| | Craft/art/artisans | 5 |
| | Mineira personalities: JK and Chica da Silva | 4 |
| | Traditions/customs/originality | 3 |
| | Typical food/log stoves | 3 |
| | Socializing/tales/chat and coffee/fair | 3 |
| | Winding streets and alleys | 2 |
| | To receive well/welcoming people | 1 |
| | Jequitinhonha | 1 |
| | *Cultural traditions and total mineiridade* | *36* |
| Ecological Diamantina | Hills/Espinhaço Mountains/mountain ranges/observatories | 5 |
| | Paths/hiking/trails | 4 |
| | Waterfalls/rivers/lakes | 4 |
| | Natural parks/reserves/ecological diversity | 2 |
| | Nature/natural beauty | 2 |
| | Eco-tourism/sport/adventure | 1 |
| | *Total green* | *18* |
| *Musical Diamantina* | Vesperata/serenade/concerts/bands/choirs | 3 |
| | Music/musical streets/musical culture | 7 |
| | *Total musical* | *10* |

Pictures taken by visitors using photoethnography technique could be put into categories under two fundamental themes: (a) supporting the model of historical town and (b) broadening the tourism experience. The first refers to images that illustrate the physical aspects of urban landscape, with highlights to elements that form the stereotype of Mineira historical town. This finding confirms the statement that the induced image produced by tourism publicity may build up emblematic representations from which visitors can hardly escape. Therefore, a casual everyday scene gains a host of stereotyped meanings, as the following statement illustrates (Figure 8.3):

> This photo shows an alley, which is the typical structure of a historical town. There is also a sign that reads Café Mineiro. Every visitor to a Mineira town would like to have some coffee, wouldn't they? Besides, this lady sitting in the street conveys the image of a typical Mineira person. (Tourist 2)

The elements highlighted by the visitor's account serve the purpose of illustrating the relevance of cultural and historical attributes to the understanding of functional and epistemological values associated with destination image. As the eyes look around the streets in order to identify characteristics that reinforce the imagination built up around Mineira historical towns, the visit becomes a pleasurable way to acquire knowledge about Brazil's colonial history.

Although it can be noticed that the search for elements that aim at confirming the expectations induced by tourism publicity, some photographs taken by visitors reveal

Figure 8.3: Quitanda alley. *Source*: Research Data. Picture taken by Tourist 2.

aspects that are little explored by such publicity, which can serve as competitive differential to the destination. Amongst the expectations, interest in the everyday life of the destination and the possibility of interacting with the town and its people can be highlighted. The interest in gaining new cultural experiences and the desire to experience a quite inland town's lifestyle are related to the epistemological consumption value of the image, but also turn out to be important attributes of the emotional value, as they converge on the idea of peace and quiet, well-being/cheerfulness and safety.

The emotional value of tranquillity was mentioned by visitors almost as often as tangible characteristics of the historical centre. This fact confirms a multi-dimensional character of destination image and its cognitive and emotional components. However, it can be inferred that to position destination only by considering its tangible attractions is not enough, it is equally important to position it by taking into consideration its affective components, which in many cases can serve as one of the main key factors to reinforce the place's competitive differential.

Instead of centralizing the look at stereotyped elements, several visitors, mainly those who had stayed the longest at the destination, highlighted the liveliness of the town as being the factor that gave it most of its enchantment and authenticity. Therefore, the perception of the town reveals a place full of vivacity, different from the lifeless photographs that portray it as a museum-like town in folders and tourism sites. The town's architectural assets, however, seem to function as a backdrop to the place, as tourists' eyes focus entirely on the people who partake of the space and interact with it and in it (Figure 8.4).

Figure 8.4: Bars and church. *Source*: Research Data. Picture taken by Tourist 5.

I've taken this photo because it shows the church, which symbolizes religiosity, but at the same time, it shows people in the streets, fun, and cheerfulness. Diamantina is a 'crazy' town. As soon as I arrived here, I went for a walk and suddenly the church bells started to toll. It was because of a cortege of a Bishop. I walked on as far as the Old Market and a great party was taking place there. (Tourist 5)

The perception of Diamantina's liveliness added to its popularity makes up one of the factors that contribute to the social dimension of the decision on Diamantina. This confirmation arises from the high frequency of words such as 'everybody talks about it', 'my friends say' — words spoken by visitors who were interviewed. This revealed their wishes to join in particular groups by visiting the destination.

From the local community's perspective, pictures taken by residents tend to confirm visitor–resident interaction and the sharing of particular spaces by the two groups. Apparently, this social and spatial interaction is harmonious, except during specific events such as carnival.

The conditional consumption value associated with the participation in events fosters, in some cases, such a strong motivation that it can overlay visitor's interest in the tourism destination in the first place. Despite this fact, visitors, who had gone to the town to participate in some kind of event or for personal convenience (visit to friends or study visit), said to have been surprised and enchanted. Such a fact can show that induced image may present some flaws while delivering its attractiveness message.

Another aspect regarding residents' photographs, which draws researchers' attention, is the fact that they are connected with places of memory. The meanings attributed to the Old Market, for instance, are very distinct from each other. In the view of tourist 9, the market is a symbol of commerce and community life, whereas in the viewpoint of resident 5, it is an icon of the gold mining period. The association of the Old Market with the gold mining is only possible because the residents keep the memory of the town. Therefore, two significance systems co-exist, one arises from new social demands created by tourism, and the other arises from the everyday life of the host community, which has to be protected from the effects of touristification caused by the sharing of these spaces.

Owing to the different interpretations of the town, although the natural landscape was not stressed in any of the photographs taken by visitors, it was the highlight of those taken by some residents and public managers, which reinforces the existence of territorialities that configures in tourism destination. That is, there are areas, territories, which are restricted to or are only perceived by certain groups, according to their references, as mentioned by Benevides and García (1997).

Two other inferences arose from the photographs: (a) the space for tourism consumption is still very much limited to Diamantina's historical centre and (b) the combination of historical tourism and eco-tourism is considered by public managers to be tourism potential. Public managers also consider Diamantina to be extremely important as a regional induction centre for tourism.

In order to verify image attributes that may enhance the reach of Diamantina's competitive differential, the research subjects were invited to compare the town with two other historical destinations with similar tourism inclinations. By doing so, the respondents found it easier to report the most latent characteristics of the town they kept in their minds, emphasizing the benefits, the deficiencies and the psychological dimensions of the personality of each destination.

From the research data, it was possible to infer that both towns chosen for such a comparison (Ouro Preto and Tiradentes) are destinations whose brands are strong in the viewpoints of visitors to Diamantina. These comparisons are especially valid to help in the task of structuring Diamantina's competitive differential, apart from helping define guidelines to promote induced image. The results are summarized in Table 8.3.

Although functional attributes related to each destination are very similar amongst themselves (colonial houses, baroque, churches, etc.), the way they are presented in tourism promotion can be different and can serve the purpose of differentiating destinations. While tangible elements in the other towns are mainly associated with churches, the elements most put forth by visitors and residents in Diamantina are the historical houses, the narrow alleys and the flow of people along the stone-paved streets. This fact shows that they recognize the town's preservation, beauty and harmony with its surroundings. Because of this movement, we believe that the emphasis on landscape harmony and the aesthetic of Diamantina's architectural assets can be more useful to the town's tourism promotion than the emphasis on churches, which are more associated with Ouro Preto's image.

Furthermore, it is stressed that psychological characteristics of destination image play a central role in differentiating destinations. Respondents projected the following characteristics of Diamantina: a middle-aged woman, in tip-top shape, beautiful, welcoming, charismatic, convivial, tranquil and cultured. Spontaneous associations were also common between the perceived image of Diamantina and the historic figures who lived in the town, as illustrated below:

> I think of Diamantina and I remember the time of former president JK and the serenade. I belong to Belo Horizonte's bohemia, so I feel somehow at home with this. (Tourist 9)

The association of historical figures with the image of the town and the individual's self-image can present itself as an effective strategy for destination promotion and heritage interpretation. Once promotional strategies evolve and become more effective, while they become more 'humanized', the use of these relations in tourism communication can facilitate the formation of a relationship with the consumer (Ekinci & Hosany, 2006).

In the local community's descriptions of Diamantina's psychological dimension, there were statements of negative characteristic with the use of remarks like: 'a woman with lots of highs and lows, but that is worthwhile'; 'a beautiful look, but with contradictions'; 'a little bit cross, but a good person'. Residents are able to identify dimensions of the town that are not so easily perceived by visitors and, many times, are intentionally camouflaged by tourism promotion. Nonetheless, the

Table 8.3: Image of competitor destination.

| | **Ouro Preto** | **Tiradentes** | **Diamantina** |
|---|---|---|---|
| *Strength of destination brand* | Very strong, with a lot of media publicity | Strong | Average |
| *Historical centre* | Monumental and very expressive | Small with little attractiveness, but well structured | Medium size, but well-kept and expressive |
| *Atmosphere* | Dense, reflective, agitated, conservative, introspective | Charming, cosy, relaxing, sophisticated and romantic | Cheerful, light, peaceful, traditional |
| *The town per se* | Scenario town, monument town | Colonial shopping centre | 'Life' town |
| *Quality of services and tourism infrastructure* | Good structure | Excellent, with high standards | Deficient |
| *Associated events* | Winter festival, carnival | Gastronomy festival, cinema festival | Vesperata, winter festival, carnival and religious festivals |
| *Figures* | Tiradentes, Aleijadinho, slaves | Tiradentes and the 'inconfidentes' | Xica da Silva and JK |
| *Associated images* | Churches, baroque, colonial Brazil, slavery, gold | Craft shops, good gastronomy, comfortable inns, 'Inconfidência Mineira' | Quotidian spontaneity of cultural manifestations, colonial houses, nature and combined cultural traditions |
| *Tourist–resident involvement* | Restricted to commercial relations | Extremely restricted to commercial relations | Permeated by commercial relations, but amicable |
| *Main landscape icons* | Churches and Tiradentes square | Steam locomotive | Gloria House and Municipal Market. |
| *Unique attractions, most cited singularities* | Carnival, Inconfidência Museum, Pilar/São Francisco/Rosário Churches, Casa dos Contos, Tiradentes square, carnival | Not mentioned by respondents | Vesperata, municipal market, Gloria House, JK House, Biribiri Village, carnival |

recognition of residents' view is vital to guarantee veracity to tourism promotion, preventing created image from becoming unauthentic and caricatured.

Hospitality and liveliness shape themselves as strong characteristics in Diamantina. In contrast, Ouro Preto is described as a gloomy, grey and introspective atmosphere, while Tiradentes is portrayed as a relaxing, sophisticated and romantic town. Therefore, it is the combination of Diamantina's tangible assets with the liveliness of its social relations that makes it different from the other towns. These differences can be extremely appropriate to create competitive advantage. Ouro Preto, for instance, profits from these characteristics and highlights its baroque mysticism and its mysterious atmosphere. In Diamantina, publicity could value more the people and the preservation of the town's traditions. The use of images portraying empty and lifeless streets seems not to be adequate for the purposes of creating and maintaining a strong and well-positioned brand in the competitive tourism market of historical towns.

## 8.5. Conclusions

The chapter has brought a case that illustrates the importance of social stakeholders' apprehension of the perception of destination image so as to build a strong destination brand. It is therefore assumed that the possibilities of exploring the theme can become more advantageous when perspectives from different groups are jointly taken into consideration, with the following contributions: (a) providing for better understanding of the way a host community perceives its territory, facilitating the development of tourism communication closely related to the cultural and identity values of the place; (b) assessing the efficiency of messages and images released during tourism promotion and (c) helping to identify values and characteristics that may contribute to the creation of a more realistic image that enhances the value of the destination's singularities as competitive differentials.

From the theoretical-managerial point of view, the study revealed the existence of several gaps in tourism promotion. It is believed that these communication flaws may be due to the lack of guidance from public managers to destination marketing that is still very little explored by the destination. They can also be the consequence of neglecting the social stakeholders' perceptions of the place. Yet, it is relevant to socialize the issue of images perceived by these individuals, understand them and highlight their contents not only as a scientific attitude but also as an attitude towards constructing local citizenship.

Another aspect of the study points out that visitors tend to emphasize specific characteristics of the destination such as liveliness, the wish to interact more closely with locals, a sense of group belonging (tribalism) by making trips in search for well-being and authentic experiences in the everyday life of the visited place. All these characteristics show some similarities to what Kotler, Kartajaya, and Setiawan (2010) call 3.0 marketing, which conjectures that marketing must be addressed to bountiful human beings, who are made of soul, spirit, mind and heart. Yet, there seems to be a gap between what constitutes the aspirations of visitors in Diamantina (would they be 3.0 tourists?) and the destination promotion addressed to them. Further investigations may analyse this correlation in other contexts.

Destination stereotype, as it can be noticed, may prevent marketing communication from being more effective. This issue seems to be a challenge to be faced by many other destinations. Finally, it is vital to stress that further research may be conducted to better investigate the association found with the personality of historical figures, visitors' self-concept and the destination brand personality.

From the methodological point of view, the approach utilized proved to be adequate to the research purposes. Therefore, it can be applied to other contexts and destinations. It can be emphasized that the use of projective techniques and photoethnography to identify psychological attributes of destination image is adequate and especially useful for the development of authentic destination brand personality. Yet, it is necessary to recognize that the content analysis, despite presenting a host of advantages to the aims of this work, is a technique that depends a lot on hermeneutic efforts and subjective judgement. Moreover, the possibility that the selection of individuals for the research may have created some biases in the analysis cannot be rejected.

## Acknowledgements

We are grateful to all respondents who have collaborated and supported the research conducted in Diamantina, and to Henry Yu, a very talented photographer, for his permission to reproduce one of his photographs in this chapter.

## References

Aaker, D. A. (2007). *Construindo marcas fortes.* Porto Alegre, Brazil: Bookman.

Bardin, L. (1977). *Análise de Conteúdo.* Lisboa, Portugal: Edições 70 LDA.

Bauer, M. W. (2007). Análise de conteúdo clássica: uma revisão. In M. W. Bauer & G. Gaskell (Eds.), *Pesquisa qualitativa com texto, imagem e som: Um manual prático.* Petrópolis, Brazil: Vozes.

Benevides, I. P., & García, F. E. S. (1997). Imagens urbanas depuradas pelo turismo: Curitiba e fortaleza. In A. B. Rodrigues (Ed.), *Turismo, modernidade e globalização* (pp. 66–79). São Paulo, Brazil: Hucitec.

Bignami, R. (2002). *A imagem do Brasil no turismo.* São Paulo, Brazil: Aleph.

Bigné, J. E., Sanchez, M. I., & Sanchez, J. (2001). Tourism image, evaluation variables and after purchase behavior: Inter-relationship. *Tourism Management, 22*(6), 607–616.

Bonn, M. A., Joseph, S. M., & Dai, M. (2005). International versus domestic visitors: an examination of destination image perceptions. *Journal of Travel Research, 43*(3), 294–301. doi: 10.1177/0047287504272033

Bramwell, B., & Randing, L. (1996). Tourism marketing images of industrial cities. *Annals of Tourism Review, 23*(1), 200–221.

Cai, L. (2002). Cooperative branding for rural destinations. *Annals of Tourism Research, 29*(3), 720–742.

Chen, C., & Tsai, D. (2007). How destination image and evaluative factors affect behavioral intentions? *Tourism Management, 28*(4), 1115–1122.

Chi, C. G., & Qu, H. (2008). Examining the structural relationships of destination image, tourist satisfaction and destination loyalty: An integrated approach. *Tourism Management, 29*(4), 624–636.

Crompton, J. L. (1979). Motivations of pleasure vacations. *Annals of Tourism Research, 6*(4), 408–424.

Crompton, J. L., & Fakeye, P. C. (1991). Image differences between prospective, first-time, and repeat visitor to the lower Rio Grande Valley. *Journal of Travel Research, 30*(2), 10–16.

Echtner, C. M., & Ritchie, J. R. B. (1991). The meaning and measurement of destination image. *Journal of Tourism Studies, 2*(2), 2–12. Retrieved from http://www.jcu.edu.au/business/public/groups/everyone/documents/journal_article/jcudev_012328.pdf

Ekinci, Y., & Hosany, S. (2006). Destination personality: An application of brand personality to tourism destinations. *Journal of Travel Research, 45*(2), 127–139.

Frías, D. M., Rodríguez, M. A., & Castañeda, J. A. (2008). Internet vs. travel agencies on previsit destination image formation: An information processing view. *Tourism Management, 29*(1), 163–179.

Galí, N., & Donaire, J. A. (2005). The social construction of the image of Girona: A methodological approach. *Tourism Management, 26*(5), 777–785.

Gallarza, M. G., Saura, I. G., & García, H. C. (2002). Destination image: Towards a conceptual framework. *Annals of Tourism Research, 29*(1), 56–78.

Gartner, W. (1993). Image formation process. *Journal of Travel and Tourism Marketing, 2*(3), 191–215.

Grosspietsch, M. (2006). Perceived and projected images of Rwanda: Visitor and international tour operator perspectives. *Tourism Management, 27*(2), 225–234.

Hosany, S., Ekinci, Y., & Uysal, M. (2006). Destination image and destination personality: An application of branding theories to tourism places. *Journal of Business Research, 59*(5), 638–642.

Hunter, W. C. (2008). A typology of photographic representations for tourism: Depictions of groomed spaces. *Tourism Management, 29*(2), 354–365.

Jean-Didier, U. (1999). Parler à l'autre avant de parler de soi-même. Évolution de la publicité touristique. *Les Cahiers Espaces* (64), 40–42.

Kastenholz, E. (2002). *The role and marketing implications of destination images on tourism behaviour: The case of Northern Portugal.* Unpublished PhD dissertation, Universidade de Aveiro/Portugal. Retrieved from UMI dissertation service. Available at http://ria.ua.pt/bitstream/10773/1838/1/2005001493.pdf

Kotler, P., Armstrong, G., Saunders, J., & Wong, V. (1999). *Principles of marketing.* London: Prentice Hall.

Kotler, P., Gertner, D., Rein, I., & Haider, D. H. (2006). *Marketing de lugares.* São Paulo, Brazil: Prentice Hall.

Kotler, P., Kartajaya, H., & Setiawan, I. (2010). *Marketing 3.0: As forças que estão definindo o novo marketing centrado no ser humano.* Rio de Janeiro, Brazil: Elsevier.

Laville, C., & Dionne, J. (1999). *A construção do saber: manual de metodologia de pesquisa em ciências humanas.* Belo Horizonte, Brazil: UFMG.

Martín, H. S., & Bosque, I. A. R. (2008). Exploring the cognitive: Affective nature of destination image and the role of psychological factors in its formation. *Tourism Management, 29*(2), 263–277.

Mendonça, J. R. C., & Amantino-de-Andrade, J. (2003). Gerenciamento de impressões: Em busca de legitimidade organizacional. *RAE, 43*(1), 36–48. Retrieved from http://www.scielo.br/pdf/rae/v43n1/v43n1a05.pdf

Ryan, C., & Cave, J. (2005). Structuring destination image: a qualitative approach. *Journal of Travel Research, 44*(2), 143–150.

Santana, A. (2009). *Antropologia do Turismo: Analogias, encontros e relações.* São Paulo, Brazil: Aleph.

Sirgy, J. (1982). Self-concept in consumer behaviour: A critical review. *Journal of Consumer Research, 9*(3), 287–300.

Stepchenkova, S., & Morrison, A. M. (2008). Russia's destination image among American pleasure travelers: Revisiting Echtner and Ritchie. *Tourism Management, 29*(3), 548–560.

Tapachai, N., & Waryszak, R. (2000). An examination of the role of beneficial image in tourist destination selection. *Journal of Travel Research, 39*(1), 37–44.

Yin, R. (1984). *Case study research: Design and methods.* Newbury Park, CA: Sage.

# PART III
# RELATIONSHIP MARKETING

Chapter 9

# Implementing Relationship Marketing in Hospitality and Tourism Management

*Ronald E. Goldsmith and Rodoula H. Tsiotsou*

## 9.1. Introduction

The idea of relationship marketing, creating a long-term connection or involvement with consumers, stands in contrast to the practice of *transaction marketing*, or making many one-time sales (Ferrell & Hartline, 2005, p. 12). 'Relationship marketing can be defined as attracting, maintaining and — in multi-service organizations — enhancing customer relationships' (Berry, 2002, p. 61). The benefits of creating and maintaining relationships with customers are many. Among these are (1) the costs of keeping existing customers are lower than the costs of attracting new customers; (2) managers who get to know what their customers are like can better satisfy them; (3) engaged customers spread positive word of mouth and can strongly promote the destination to others. First introduced by Berry, Shostack, and Upah (1983), the concept has played a major role in transforming marketing theory and practice over the last three decades. Accordingly, a huge literature has accumulated consisting of journal articles, special journal issues, conference proceedings, white papers, presentations, books, webinars and so forth. At least two journals, *The Journal of Relationship Marketing* and *The International Journal of Relationship Marketing and Management*, are devoted to the topic.

Today, creating and maintaining long-term relationships with customers is considered one of the most important tasks of marketing managers, regardless of whether their products are tangible goods, intangible services or any combination. Thus, relationship marketing should be a guiding principle for hospitality and tourism managers, for not only the obvious benefits derived from returning visitors, but even when the likelihood that a tourist will only visit once, maintaining a long-term good relationship will pay off in positive recommendations to others (Schmitt, Bernd, & van den Bulte, 2011). More over, in a crowded tourism market, successful relationship marketing should provide powerful competitive advantages to its practitioners.

Strategic Marketing in Tourism Services
Copyright © 2012 by Emerald Group Publishing Limited
All rights of reproduction in any form reserved
ISBN: 978-1-78052-070-4

Relationship marketing has stimulated a variety of managerial innovations since its inception. These include an emphasis on relationships not just with customers, but with all important stakeholders, such as suppliers and distributors, as well (Kotler, 2000). This idea is especially crucial in the tourism business, where many different institutions, firms and service providers can be involved in the total destination experience. Relationship marketing has also drawn attention to the key idea of *customer lifetime value*. This means that the firm should view a customer as a revenue stream, a source of profits, during a long-term set of repeated transactions. Establishing relationships with customers can increase their lifetime profitability. These managerial insights have also drawn attention to the importance of attracting and retaining the most profitable customers. All marketers are aware of the 80/20 rule that states that 20% of customers provide 80% of profits. Thus, attracting the most profitable customers has become one of the most important goals of tourism marketing strategy.

In addition, the imperative to form relationships has spawned an entire industry centred on the notion of *customer relationship management* (CRM). This broad term means different things to different people, but a comprehensive definition proposed by Payne and Frow (2005) argues that CRM includes at least three related perspectives. The first derives from a narrow information technology (IT) focus that emphasizes using IT to solve particular problems related to managing customer relationships. Frequency marketing programmes such as frequent flyer miles and reward cards are examples. The second meaning of CRM seems to be a wide range of customer-oriented IT and Internet solutions. Currently, tourism managers use many such applications. Finally, CRM can mean an overall organizational perspective that recommends managing all the firm's functions and activities to satisfy and retain customers. Since a major aim of relationship marketing and CRM in particular is to create value for customers, it is important to understand what customer value in tourism really is.

## 9.2.  The Goals of Relationship Marketing

One way to summarize the importance of CRM is to present it as a set of interrelated goals that tie together many of the disparate ideas that make it up. Goldsmith (2010) proposes that these goals represent five sequential stages in managing customer relationships. Table 9.1 summarizes these goals and their implications for strategic tourism management.

The first stage is to *acquire* customers. Like most marketing strategies, tourism marketing often begins with advertising, promotion and word of mouth intended to entice visitors to the destination. For example, the frequent 'Visit Jamaica' TV ads familiar to most Americans seek to entice tourists with images of a tropical paradise and friendly people. Relationship marketing shares this goal with traditional, transactional marketing, but instead of stopping here, proceeds with customer acquisition as only the first step, employing the usual strategies and tactics of promotion. It is important to note that feedback from subsequent stages in the CRM

Table 9.1: An overview of the proposed CRM model.

| Stage in CRM | Before consumption | During consumption | After consumption |
|---|---|---|---|
| | Customer acquisition | Customer retention | Customer development | Customer consultation | Customer conversion |

| Stage in CRM | Before consumption | During consumption | During consumption | After consumption |
|---|---|---|---|---|
| | Customer acquisition | Customer retention | Customer development | Customer consultation | Customer conversion |
| Example | Super bowl advertising | Satisfaction with the product | Additional sales to satisfied customers | Seek input from customers for new products | Encourage customers to become brand advocates |
| Management recommendation | Target the most profitable customers | Segment customers for different strategies | Up sell and cross sell; develop personalized new products | Get input from customers to improve the relationship | Facilitate customer efforts to win new customers |
| Research recommendation | Segmentation and positioning | Why do these customers switch brands? | What additional products and services would meet the needs of these customers? | What is the best way to allow customers to co-produce this brand? | What would encourage and assist this customer in becoming an advocate? |
| Social policy concern | When is this effort become irritating? | When does this effort become intrusive? | When does this effort become harassment? | When does this effort become an invasion of privacy? | When does this become exploitation of customers? |

*Source:* Goldsmith (2010).

process improves customer acquisition by enabling managers to target customers effectively and motivate them to try the product. This ability is an important aspect of the relationship marketing/CRM approach that distinguishes it from transactional marketing.

Perhaps the core of CRM and the area where it most connects to relationship marketing is the second goal/stage. Once they acquire customers, firms must *retain* them. Customer *retention* is 'the continuing, active relationship with a customer that yields a stream of revenue from the sale of the initial product or service' (Heskett, Sasser, & Schlesinger, 1997, p. 61). The concept of customer retention goes beyond the traditional idea of customer loyalty in that it focuses on loyalty as the outcome of managerial actions that create satisfaction and an emotional bond with the brand. The growth of the concept of customer or brand *engagement* is a direct outcome of the relationship marketing revolution because in order to create a relationship and encourage loyalty, firms find that they must promote engagement or conscious emotional and cognitive reaction to marketing stimuli (Goldsmith, 2012). Retaining customers in the tourism context suggests repeat visits. An example of a successful customer retention strategy, for example, can be seen in the case of several Romanian hotels that use rewards, rebates, appreciation, partnerships and affinity programmes to engage their visitors and encourage their loyalty (Vlad, Laura, & Maria, 2008). Beyond the vital role played by satisfaction in securing repeat purchasing (Heskett et al., 1997), repeat visits by the same tourists surely implies developing new experiences and benefits that will entice them to come back.

Stage three of the model, *development*, proposes that firms and customers can benefit when managers engage more completely with their customers by offering them additional benefits associated with the primary product. This goes beyond the tried and true tactics of bundling, up selling and cross selling to imply that customers should be given the opportunity to purchase additional products, especially if they can co-create them. For example, cruise ships have long promoted on-board spending, and many destinations feature a variety of additional or add-on experiences for tourists. These experiences do not only provide additional revenue, they may form an essential part of value created by the tourism experience.

The fourth stage of the model, *customer consultation*, is consistent with recent theoretical developments in marketing management theory (Vargo & Lusch, 2004), which emphasize the key role in customer participation in creating the value of the product, termed co-creation. Marketers have long been urged to seek input from customers to help them develop new products and improve old ones. Sheraton's 'Belong' website is an example. Studies of tourism show that many customers do actively participate in creating the tourism product. For example, Dwivedi (2009, p. 231) analysed online postings to show that 'consumers are actively constructing their own destination image of India which is shared via the internet and available to a large audience through search engines'. The latest manifestation of this recommendation is to actually permit customers to participate in the creation of the product, following a strategy of personalization (Goldsmith, 1999). Evidence from the field of behavioural economics suggests that when people have a hand in creating something, it takes on additional value for them (Ariely, 2011).

The final stage in the model, *customer conversion*, builds upon the practice of some companies to enlist some of their customers as zealots, evangelists or missionaries who go forth to convert other consumers into customers of the brand (McConnell & Huba, 2003). As some customers become highly engaged with brands and more involved with their development, management and marketing, they take ownership of them as co-creators (Vargo & Lusch, 2004) and promoters. Because the influence of other customers is often stronger than the influence of marketing campaigns, these efforts by individuals can have a huge impact on the sales of brands. In the tourism context, strategies that enable and encourage satisfied visitors to 'spread the word' and promote the destination should reap huge benefits to sponsoring destinations. Such evangelistic activities by engaged tourists are especially important given the growing importance of social media on all aspects of contemporary consumer behaviour. For example, websites such as TripAdvisor enable tourists to post comments about their trips that can strongly influence other tourists. Destination managers should proactively try to create online travel communities of engaged visitors who will create positive word of mouth that encourages other visitors.

## 9.3.  The Application of Relationship Marketing in Tourism

Tourism is at the forefront of other industries adopting relationship marketing as indicated by practices such as airline frequent flyer programmes (Liu, Wall, & Westlake, 2000), hotel frequent guest programmes (Palmer, Beattie, & Beggs, 2000) and car rental company customer preference programmes (Chadee & Mattsson, 1996). Several recent published studies attest to the growing importance of relationship marketing in the hospitality and tourism industries. Research on CRM in tourism focuses on the degree tourism firms have embraced CRM strategies, on firm-to-consumer relationships and on business-to-business relationships.

Gan, Sim, Tan, and Tan (2006) studied the use of the Internet as a tool for facilitating CRM in the hotel sector in Singapore. They categorized CRM into four levels: (1) information provision, (2) database collection, (3) personalization and (4) community relationships. They found that the majority of Singapore hotels are in 'level 2', the stage of database collection. They also examined the relationship between the level of online CRM and the star rating of the hotels, the number of rooms and the locality of the hotels' web domain, respectively. Their findings showed that the level of online CRM adoption is positively related to the hotel rating and to the number of rooms, but negatively related to the local web domain.

Fyall, Callod, and Edwards (2003, p. 644) analysed the degree of implantation of relationship marketing in two contrasting destinations: Stockholm and Barbados. Their study concludes that 'the peculiarities of the destination product complicate the building of relationships with the tourist and diminish the suitability and value of such efforts, while promoting the value of greater interorganizational collaboration'. Similarly, Sigala (2008) studied electronic customer relationship management (eCRM 2.0) adoption and use among Greek tourism firms to determine usage and readiness to implement. She identified five styles of co-creation that allow and encourage customers to participate in the tourist value-creation process. These are prosumerism (e.g. creating and sharing travel videos, reviews); team-based co-learning (e.g. collaborative creating of travel guides); mutual innovation (e.g. firms and customers collaboration in such activities as creating a new hotel); communities of creation (e.g. social networking websites and blogs); and joint intellectual property (e.g. mash-up: combine resources from different partners for new business development). According to Sigala (2008, p. 469), the relationship marketing literature proposes that 'eCRM 2.0 strategies should aim at exploiting both the networking and social intelligence/customer knowledge of Web 2.0 applications by integrating and engaging customers and their communities (i.e., as co-marketers, co-producers, co-designers) along value chain operations'. Her empirical findings, however, revealed low adoption rates of all types of eCRM practices by Greek tourism firms, and those who did adopt seemed to focus more on defensive rather than proactive practices. Changing this situation requires both greater investments in IT as well as cultural and managerial changes by these businesses.

Although relationship marketing in terms of developing loyal customers to a destination or hotel or restaurant is considered a limitation of the tourism sector because tourists are seeking new experiences, some studies report that many tourists chose to repeat their holidays' destination, indicating a certain degree of loyalty (Fyall et al., 2003; Oppermann, 1998). According to these studies, five factors determine such loyalty behaviour: risk reduction, meeting the same people, the emotional affection to a specific place, a better exploration of the place and the desire to show the place to other people (Fyall et al., 2003; Oppermann, 1998). Loyalty programmes seem to boost such firm–customer relationships, as a study on worldwide hotel chains has shown (Barsky & Nash, 2006).

In a business-to-business setting, Roberts-Lombard and Steyn (2008) studied relationship marketing practices of travel agencies in the Western Cape province of South Africa. Their research revealed a fragmented and uncoordinated situation involving travel agencies and hotel groups and car rental companies. This situation blunts the impact of relationship marketing strategy because CRM involves not just a firm and consumers, but a firm and all its partners who must coordinate their marketing efforts to create a single, seamless process connecting suppliers, the firm and its customers (Kotler, 2000).

## 9.4.   The Future of Relationship Marketing in Hospitality and Tourism

What is the future of CRM in hospitality and tourism? Given the importance of this strategic management tool, we are likely to witness a continued growth in the number of firms that adopt some form of CRM as part of their marketing strategy. Moreover, the policies and practices of CRM are likely to spread to smaller and smaller hospitality and tourism enterprises as they struggle to compete with the larger ones. Simplified, easier to use and cheaper CRM products will facilitate this spread.

Another CRM change that is beginning in other commercial areas but has not yet spread widely in the hospitality and tourism field is variously called CRM 2.0 or Social CRM. This development adapts to and incorporates the recent growth of the social web in its many forms, to form a new type of CRM. While there are various definitions of Social CRM, they all touch upon the key ideas that it is an extension of traditional CRM strategy that incorporates aspects of the social networks enabled by the Internet to facilitate relationships with customers. Social CRM seeks collaborative conversations with customers, acknowledging that they are in charge, so as to improve the value of the product for the customer, decrease costs to the firm, encourage loyalty and promote favourable word of mouth. Social CRM engages customers to build their trust and solicit their co-creation of the product. Social CRM seems to be perfectly suited to the goals of strategic management in the hospitality and tourism industries because of the heavy involvement of the customer in creating the tourism experience. As more and more managers of destinations adopt sophisticated management strategies, Social CRM should become a standard component of them.

## 9.5.  Conclusion

In conclusion, given the tremendous importance relationship marketing and CRM have attained in contemporary marketing theory, research and management, the spread of these concerns into the hospitality and tourism field is inevitable. Tourism management has already firmly embraced the key marketing ideas of segmentation and targeting. It is hoped that the chapters in this book will promote the acceptance of relationship marketing and customer relationship management with equal enthusiasm.

## References

Ariely, D. (2011). *The upside of irrationality*. New York, NY: Harper Perennial.

Barsky, J., & Nash, L. (2006). Companies update loyalty programs, increase effectiveness. *Hotel & Motel Management, 22*(11), 28–29.

Berry, L. L. (2002). Relationship marketing of services — Perspectives from 1983 and 2000. *Journal of Relationship Marketing, 1*(1), 59–77.

Berry, L. L., Shostack, G. L., & Upah, G. D. (1983). Emerging perspectives on service marketing. In L. L. Berry (Ed.), *Relationship marketing* (pp. 25–38). Chicago, IL: American Marketing Association.

Chadee, D., & Mattsson, J. (1996). An empirical assessment of customer satisfaction in tourism. *Service Industries Journal, 16*(3), 305–320.

Dwivedi, M. (2009). Online destination image of India: A consumer based perspective. *International Journal of Contemporary Hospitality Management, 21*(2), 226–232.

Ferrell, O. C., & Hartline, M. D. (2005). *Marketing strategy* (3rd ed.). Mason, OH: Thompson South-Western.

Fyall, A., Callod, C., & Edwards, B. (2003). Relationship marketing: the challenge for destinations. *Annals of Tourism, 30*(3), 644–659.

Gan, L., Sim, C. J., Tan, H. L., & Tan, J. (2006). Online relationship marketing by Singapore hotel websites. *Journal of Travel & Tourism Marketing, 20*(3), 1–19.

Goldsmith, R. E. (1999). The personalized marketplace: Beyond the 4 ps. *Marketing Intelligence and Planning, 17*(4), 178–185.

Goldsmith, R. E. (2010). The goals of customer relationship management. *International Journal of Customer Marketing and Management, 1*(1), 16–27.

Goldsmith, R. E. (2011). Brand engagement and brand loyalty. In A. Kapoor, & C. Kulshrestha (Eds.), *Branding and sustainable competitive advantage: Building virtual presence.* (pp. 1–294). IGI Global, Web. 4 March 2012. doi: 10.4018/978-1-61350-171-9

Heskett, J. L., Sasser, J. W. E., & Schlesinger, L. A. (1997). *The service profit chain.* New York, NY: The Free Press.

Kotler, P. (2000). *Marketing management* (Millennium ed.). London, UK: Prentice Hall International.

Liu, A., Wall, G., & Westlake, J. (2000). Marketing through frequent flyer programmes: The example of China airlines. *Tourism Economics, 6*(3), 233–249.

McConnell, B., & Huba, J. (2003). *Creating customer evangelists: How loyal customers become a volunteer sales force.* Chicago, IL: Dearborn Trade Pub.

Oppermann, M. (1998). Destination threshold potential and the law of repeat visitation. *Journal of Travel Research, 37*(2), 131–137.

Palmer, A., Beattie, U., & Beggs, R. (2000). A structural analysis of hotel sector loyalty programmes. *International Journal of Contemporary Hospitality Management, 12*(1), 54–60.

Payne, A., & Frow, P. (2005). A strategic framework for customer relationship management. *Journal of Marketing, 69*(4), 167–176.

Roberts-Lombard, M., & Steyn, T. F. J. (2008). The relationship marketing practices of travel agencies in the Western Cape province. *South African Journal of Business Management, 39*(4), 15–26.

Schmitt, P., Bernd, S., & van den Bulte, C. (2011). Why customer referrals can drive stunning profits. *Harvard Business Review, 89*(6), 30.

Sigala, M. (2008). Developing and implementing an eCRM 2.0 strategy: Usage and readiness of Greek tourism firms. In P. O'Connor, W. Höpken & U. Gretzel (Eds.), *Information and communication technologies, in tourism 2008* (pp. 463–474). Vienna.

Vargo, S. L., & Lusch, R. F. (2004). Evolving to a new dominant logic for marketing. *Journal of Marketing, 68*(1), 1–17.

Vlad, S. D., Laura, P. A., & Maria, S. O. (2008). Loyalty programs which influence the decision process in choosing tourism destination, Facultatea de Stiinţe Economice, Universitatea Din Oradea, Romania, *17*(4), 1165–1169.

Chapter 10

# Customer Value in Tourism Services: Meaning and Role for a Relationship Marketing Approach

*Martina G. Gallarza, Irene Gil-Saura and Morris B. Holbrook*

## 10.1. Introduction

The concept of value has been recognized as fundamental to our understanding of marketing management (Day, 1999; Gale, 1994; Nilson, 1992) and has also influenced various paradigm shifts in marketing thought that have embraced the fundamental importance of consumer value (Gallarza, Gil-Saura, & Holbrook, 2011). Among these new paradigms, relationship marketing is one of the most closely linked to the role of customer value.

Relationship marketing has inspired a stream of research that reflects a managerial orientation focused on customer loyalty (Grönroos, 1997). As a key basis for the firm's long-term viability, customer loyalty is an important goal in the consumer-marketing community. Understanding better how customers value consumption experiences derived from various market offerings can provide insights into the determinants of long-run customer retention.

Thus, much or most of relationship marketing is based on a newly understood concept of value, placing value at the core of the contemporary approach to serving customers (Lin & Wang, 2006; Peck, Payne, Christopher, & Clark, 1999; Ravald & Grönroos, 1996). In particular, the value-based relationship marketing perspective emphasizes both the affective commitment to a service provider and repeat-purchase or repatronage intentions. As both perspectives underlie a comprehensive understanding of loyalty behaviour (Dick & Basu, 1994), perceived value is very often viewed as a positive influence on loyalty (Cronin, Brady, & Hult, 2000; Grace & O'Cass, 2005; Oh, 2003; Oliver, 1999) in both academic research (Parasuraman & Grewal, 2000) and marketing management (Bolton, Kannan, & Bramlett, 2000).

These findings have been shown to be particularly true within tourism services, where value is considered 'a very important component of the consumer decision-making process' (Bojanic, 1996, p. 20) and has been 'recognized in the literature as one of the most salient determinants of purchase intentions and repeat purchase behavior' (Jayanti & Ghosh, 1996, p. 5). Both perspectives — affective commitment to a service or destination as an attitudinal aspect of loyalty and repatronage intentions as a behavioural aspect — have been fully studied, jointly or separately, in the tourism literature and can be understood as key managerial objectives of a truly customer-oriented tourism firm.

The present chapter aims to provide a comprehensive approach to the role of customer value in tourism-oriented service settings so as to present value as a key driver of competitiveness for tourism organizations. This approach will be filtered through a consumer behaviour prism because, as stated in the introduction to this handbook, *until recently marketing for tourism services has been focused not on the consumer but, rather, on the destination or outlet with marketing strategies being related to the products offered rather than to the consumer who experiences the service.* Accordingly, we offer a brief state-of-the-art review of both conceptual and empirical research on customer value within the tourism literature. First, with the help of Figure 10.1 — representing the links between value and other constructs such as quality, satisfaction and loyalty — we highlight what has already been done and achieved. Second, we consider why value has far-reaching implications as a key driver for enhancing the competitiveness of tourism services. Finally, as future guidelines for the role and meaning of customer value in the tourism sector, we suggest managerial implications for targeting and positioning tourism services.

## 10.2.  Value and Relationship Marketing

Value is a two-fold notion, useful for both consumer behaviour assessments and marketing management prescriptions. In a consumer behaviour framework, consumer value — often called 'perceived value' — refers to the possession and consumption of products and services. For marketing strategy — as a way of achieving brand differentiation (commonly named 'customer value') — value focuses on the assessment made by the customer of his or her purchase. Clearly, one meaning cannot be separated from the other because 'understanding the salient antecedents and consequences of consumer value can probably be considered as the most fundamental prerequisite for sustainable competitive advantage' (Jensen, 1996, p. 60).

The conceptual and methodological links among the components of value and loyalty deserve further development from marketing academics in general and from the tourism industry in particular. As Chu and Shiu (2009, p. 99) declare, 'the two (value and loyalty) coexist for a mutual goal of building a close relationship with customers'. Searching for a comprehensive understanding of this close relationship, the services literature has examined the connections between value and loyalty in many ways. Some works deal with the value creation process in building profitable commercial relationships (e.g. Anderson, 1995; Day, 1999) or retaining customers (e.g. Chu & Shiu, 2009; Feng & Morrison, 2007; Gale, 1994). Other conceptual models offer loyalty-and-value linkages (e.g. Chaudhuri & Holbrook, 2001;

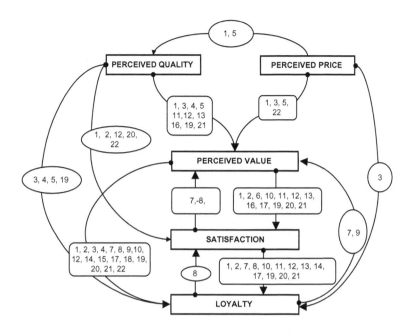

Figure 10.1: Means-end models of value in the tourism literature: a review since 1999.

| Authors and Services | | | |
|---|---|---|---|
| 1. Oh (1999) | Luxury hotel | 13. Chen and Tsai (2007) | Coastal Destination |
| 2. Tam (2000) | Restaurant | 14. Lee et al. (2007) | War-related destination |
| 3. Kashyap and Bojanic (2000) | Hotel | 15. Feng and Morrison (2007) | Travel club |
| 4. Murphy, Pritchard, and Smith (2000) | Destination | 16. Yuan and Wu (2008) | Coffee Shop |
| 5. Oh (2000) | Hotel | 17. Ryu et al. (2008) | Quick-causal Restaurant |
| 6. Babin and Kim (2001) | Destination | 18. Chen and Tsai (2008) | TV travel product shopping |
| 7. Petrick et al. (2001) | Entertainment Destination | 19. Hutchinson et al. (2009) | Golf resort |
| 8. Petrick and Backman (2002) | Golf resort | 20. He and Song (2009) | Packaged tour |
| 9. Oh (2003) | Upscale hotel | 21. Gallarza et al. (2009) | Volunteering in events |
| 10. Duman and Mattila (2005) | Cruise | 22. Brodie, Whittome, and Brush (2009) | Airline |
| 11. Gallarza and Gil (2006) | Packaged tours & Destination | 23. Chen and Chen (2010) | Destination (heritage) |
| 12. Um et al. (2006) | Destination | 24. Kim, Kim, and Goh (2011) | Food events |

Grewal, Iyer, Krishnan, & Sharma, 2003; Parasuraman & Grewal, 2000). All such investigations are of interest to the tourism industry.

Further, in a relationship marketing approach, the notions of value and loyalty suggest unexploited insights in tourism contexts when dealing with other stakeholders different from customers. A relationship value approach like the one proposed by Payne, Holt, and Frow (2001) — where employees, shareholders and customers are integrated — is needed for an integrative view of tourism services. In that sense, we encourage further studies of value in B2B contexts, employees' perceived value of the service delivered and comparisons of value perceptions held by managers and customers, as explored in the case of hotels by Nasution and Mavondo (2008). These comparative approaches can obviously reduce marketing myopia — a major threat in the tourism setting — all the more because the tourism customer is normally far from the service offered when making the decision to travel. For a better understanding of these important connections between consumer value and relationship marketing within the context of tourism, let us review what value research in tourism has already brought to academicians and practitioners.

## 10.3.   Value in Tourism: What has Already been Done

Conceptually, the relatively early proposal by Zeithaml (1988, p. 14) has remained one of the most universally accepted definitions of customer value: 'perceived value is the consumer's overall assessment of the utility of a product based on the perceptions of what is received and what is given'. This conceptualization has influenced a stream of tourism literature based on the 'get-versus-give' trade-off (e.g. Bojanic, 1996; Kashyap & Bojanic, 2000; Tam, 2000).

The study of value in tourism followed in the wake of the growing interest in service quality and satisfaction. The first scattered studies of value in tourism appeared in the 1990s. After 1999, a real stream of research with rigorous definitions and measurements of value emerged — extending to all types of tourism products, although destinations and hotels remained the most popular topics. Thus, empirical studies have now addressed the topic of consumer value in a wide range of tourism services: *destinations* (e.g. Babin & Kim, 2001; Chen & Chen, 2010; Chen & Tsai, 2007; Gallarza & Gil, 2006; Hutchinson, Lai, & Wang, 2009; Lee, Yoon, & Lee, 2007; Murphy & Pritchard, 1997; Murphy, Pritchard, & Smith, 2000; Sánchez, Callarisa, Rodriguez, & Moliner, 2006; Stevens, 1992; Um, Chon, & Ro, 2006); *hotels* and other *accommodations* (e.g. Bojanic, 1996; Hu, Kandampully, & Juwaheer, 2009; Jayanti & Ghosh, 1996; Kashyap & Bojanic, 2000; Nasution & Mavondo, 2008; Oh, 1999, 2000, 2003; Petrick, 2002); *restaurants* (e.g. McDougall & Levesque, 2000; Ryu, Han, & Kim, 2008; Tam, 2000; Yuan & Wu, 2008); *airlines* (e.g. Brodie, Whittome, & Brush, 2009); *cruises* (e.g. Duman & Mattila, 2005; Petrick, 2002, 2003, 2004); *packaged tour services* (e.g. Chen & Tsai, 2008; He & Song, 2009); *travel clubs* (e.g. Feng & Morrison, 2007); such *other attractions* as open-air theatres (e.g. Petrick, Morais, & Norman, 2001), rafting resorts (e.g. Walker, Backman,

Backman, & Morais, 2001) or food events (e.g. Kim, Kim, & Goh, 2011); and, in the non-profit sector, *voluntary service* in mega-events (e.g. Gallarza, Arteaga, Floristán, & Gil, 2009).

Methodologically, a *dual perspective* has guided empirical studies of value in tourism (Gallarza & Gil, 2006). Specifically, an *intervariable* approach uses means-end models for assessing relationships among value and other behavioural outcomes (e.g. Chen & Tsai, 2007; Oh, 1999, 2003; Tam, 2000), whereas an *intravariable* approach focuses on assessing the underlying dimensions of value (e.g. Cho & SooCheong, 2008; Martín-Ruiz, Gremler, Washburn, & Cepeda-Carión, 2008; Petrick, 2002; Sparks, Butcher, & Bradley, 2008).

### 10.3.1. The Intervariable Approach in Tourism-Value Measurement

The *intervariable* approach deals with the importance of relationships between service quality, satisfaction, perceived value and behavioural intentions. Although this approach has prompted a major stream of research for two decades, the precise nature of the relationships that exist between these constructs and the understanding of their effects on customer behaviour still remain key issues. Within this approach, value is studied jointly with service quality in early studies (e.g. Bojanic, 1996; Jayanti & Ghosh, 1996) and later with satisfaction and loyalty (e.g. Babin & Kim, 2001; Petrick, 2002). Value is often proposed as a complementary measure of satisfaction because 'satisfaction measurements give more information and are easier to interpret if they are backed by measurements of perceived value' (Petrick & Backman, 2002, p. 225). Thus, perceived value, service quality and satisfaction form a key conceptual and methodological triangle for research into tourism-related consumer behaviour. Further, a relatively broad consensus has evolved in the direction of extending the concept of value to embrace the antecedent, mediating and consequent relationships among quality, value and satisfaction. For a better understanding of this intervariable approach, the present review has been organized into Figure 10.1, where 24 works from this perspective (presented in chronological order) have been analysed in terms of their relevance to relationships among main behavioural constructs.

As Figure 10.1 shows, in means-end models within tourism services research, it is commonly understood that there is a positive relationship between perceived value and any loyalty-related behaviour, still assuming that value is of paramount importance to a correct understanding of behavioural intentions.

Although it is of clear importance in a relationship marketing approach to service settings that value perceptions have an effect on loyalty intentions, whether attitudinal (recommendation) or behavioural (repurchase), the main methodological issue concerns whether this effect is direct or must be mediated by satisfaction. In fact, within this *intervariable* approach lies the discussion of direct and indirect effects of service quality.

Satisfaction and value on tourists' repurchase intentions remains one or even *the* major concern and still awaits the emergence of a clear consensus. Specifically, the effect of service quality on loyalty is direct in the work on packaged tours by Gallarza and Gil (2006), but mediated by satisfaction in that by He and Song (2009). In the case of restaurants, Ryu et al. (2008) found that customer satisfaction partially mediates the relationship between perceived value and behavioural intention, whereas Tam (2000) claims that the direct value-to-intentions link is not significant so that service value influences repurchase intentions only via satisfaction in a fully mediated relationship. Recently, in the context of museums, the same issues have interested Hume (2011), who finds that both service quality and value are antecedents of repurchase intention, but with no intervening role for customer satisfaction.

In sum, important insights have appeared in the tourism-service literature, as represented most often by a chain of constructs from service quality to value to satisfaction to loyalty — repeat purchase and/or positive word of mouth (e.g. Chen & Chen, 2010; Chen & Tsai, 2007; Hutchinson, Lai, & Wang, 2009). And although researchers continue to accumulate knowledge concerning this particular chain, some would claim that the exact relationships among quality, value, satisfaction, loyalty and behavioural intentions remain unclear (e.g. Hume, 2011; Ryu et al., 2008), even while others amass precise evidence on the service quality–value–satisfaction–loyalty chain of effects (e.g. Chen & Chen, 2010). The implications of these issues for a relationship marketing perspective at a tourism firm are critical insofar as loyal customers are more likely than non-loyal customers to recommend other potential customers by acting as free word-of-mouth advertising agents. Knowing which is the strongest driver of this loyal customer — the best price–quality trade-off, the best value offer or a highly satisfying delivery — is crucial for tourism organizations that deal with once-in-a-lifetime tourists (remote destinations, exotic package tours and so forth).

### 10.3.2.  *The Intravariable Approach in Tourism-Value Measurement*

Related to the *intravariable* approach, in early studies, single-item value scales such as a simple value-for-the-money measure have been the norm (e.g. Bojanic, 1996; Kashyap & Bojanic, 2000; Murphy & Pritchard, 1997; Oh, 1999). More recently, however, multi-item measurement of tourism-service value has come to the fore (e.g. Al-Sabbahy, Ekinci, & Riley, 2004; Gallarza & Gil, 2006; Petrick, 2003; Sánchez et al., 2006). A multidimensional value perspective has seemed most appropriate in service contexts due to the importance of psychological and social aspects of consumption (Holbrook, 1999; Sheth, Newman, & Gross, 1991; Zeithaml, 1988). Further, tourism differs from other services because of the greater risk (vacations that take place only once a year) and uncertainty (new lands that remain unfamiliar). Consequently, the need for assessing emotions when dealing with any evaluative judgment in tourism becomes obvious. A purely functional perspective for measuring value is thus too simplistic for tourism-based consumption experiences. Hence, the richest recent approaches have emphasized 'sense', 'feel' and 'think' perceptions in restaurants (Yuan & Wu, 2008); have stressed emotional value, monetary price and non-monetary price in hotels (Nasution & Mavondo, 2008); or have focused on the hedonic-versus-utilitarian value of shopping when travelling (Diep & Sweeney, 2008).

In addition, the tourism experience is recognized as rich in social interactions, namely those between the tourist and the service provider, those between tourists and residents, and also those among tourists themselves. Principal approaches to value conceptualizations and measurements consider a social dimension when assessing value perceptions (Holbrook, 1999; Sheth et al., 1991). Thus, we stress the importance of including a social dimension in tourism-value measurements so as to better capture the essence and idiosyncrasy of the tourism experience. Recent empirical work on value has moved in this direction. For example, mutual relationships among tourists are researched by He and Song (2009) in packaged tour services, by Williams and Soutar (2009) in adventure tourism and by Nasution and Mavondo (2008) in hotels. Insights into loyalty behaviour, relevant to a relationship marketing approach, can stem form the social dimension — for example, in the case of travel clubs that enhance the social value of the tourism experience (Feng & Morrison, 2007). Also, because value is commonly understood as situational in nature (Holbrook, 1999), such changes from one time frame or from one location to another seem appropriate to evaluating a tourism service, where consumption occurs in a different context than usual. Comprehensive measurements of value perceptions in tourism may thus consider what is called an 'epistemic' or 'conditional' value when time and space of the experience matter. Additional aspects of value dimensionality in tourism appear in the work by Gallarza and Gil (2006) and by Cho and SooCheong (2008). Clearly, the task of providing measures of value in tourism highlights the need for embracing both cognitive and affective dimensions — as well as other possible approaches that focus on social, epistemic, ethical or conditional aspects of value.

## 10.4. Why Customer Value has Far-Reaching Implications as a Key Driver for the Competitiveness of Tourism Services

Contributions to customer value, while providing insights into the study of tourism management and touristic consumer behaviour, remain in a phase of conceptual and methodological development. In the following paragraphs, we highlight some of the reasons why further developments are yet to come in the area of value-related tourism services.

### 10.4.1. Value Compared to Satisfaction and Quality

Compared to service quality and satisfaction, customer value has two conceptual advantages. Considered together, these suggest that the strategic relevance of value in tourism and its academic interest may exceed those of the other related concepts.

First, the concept of perceived value facilitates an exploration of the multi-dimensionality of consumption in a comprehensive and varied experience such as tourism. Tourists may be influenced by different value dimensions and may be willing to sacrifice less salient values to maximize benefits from other dimensions. In this sense, the most recent value scaling attempts in tourism are meant to be valid for other services (e.g. Petrick, 2003; Sánchez et al., 2006; Sparks et al., 2008).

Second, tourism services (like all services) are inseparable (produced and consumed at the same time). However, because there is geographical separation between the decision to consume and the consumption event, this is an additional and sharper issue to consider in a correct approach to understanding the tourist. Unlike satisfaction, value can be assessed at two different moments in the experience (pre-purchase and post-purchase value). Very few works on value have empirically tested differences between expected and perceived values. Future research on touristic value should deal with this issue and should offer perspectives on how the expected value of a holiday can be understood by a manager in ways that help to build individualized experiences. In matching perceived value to desired value, information and communication technologies can help to create more finely tuned segmentation strategies — for example, via the interactive use of a hotel's web page, where consumers can design their own stay by combining different services or where they can engage in a pre-tour experience at a destination website.

Although the conceptual and methodological relationships between value, satisfaction and service quality have occupied the service-oriented researchers for more than three decades, the debate is not yet exhausted, as new insights continue to appear. See, for example, how the notion of image — very popular in the 1970s and 1980s among tourism researchers because of the geographical gap between the purchase decision and the consumption experience (Gallarza, Gil, & Calderón, 2002) — has recently reappeared as a key element in the quality–value–satisfaction–loyalty chain (e.g. Chen & Tsai, 2007, on destinations; Ryu et al., 2008, on restaurants; and Hu et al., 2009, on hotels). Although many studies have addressed the importance of service quality, satisfaction and perceived value, we believe that the conjoint study of their effect on perceived image (corporate image for hotels and restaurants or destination image for public tourism management) still remains a key issue.

### 10.4.2.   *Value Dimensionality Matches the Various Facets of a Tourism Experience*

Insofar as a consumer typically experiences several aspects of value simultaneously (Holbrook, 1999), destination-and-tourism services can be better understood if analysed in ways that recognize the multidimensionality of value — affective and cognitive, social and personal, and active and reactive (Gallarza & Gil, 2008; Martín et al., 2008). Thus, the heterogeneous nature of the tourism experience makes an analysis conducted via the value concept more plausible than one focused on satisfaction or quality. Further, we believe that the continuous interaction between producers and consumers during touristic services establishes a strong case for pursuing such new approaches to value as the so-called service-dominant logic (Vargo & Lusch, 2004; see also Chapter 15), which postulates a process of value co-creation. This approach has enhanced potential in the tourism sector because this industry involves composite services in which synergies can be obtained between multiple service providers. A touristic experience (see Part IV in this book for examples) is a lengthy process composed of inputs from numerous services so that the interactions between providers and consumers offer an interesting area of study from the viewpoint of the service-dominant logic. According to the aforementioned intravariable approach to value research, a multidimensional assessment of value co-creation — where new ideas from the service-dominant logic can help to explain the perceptions of value in the minds of consumers — can offer a source of competitive advantage. But a possible challenge to applying this approach may come from the multifarious nature of tourism services: *can we really imagine that all service providers of different specializations in the tourism system will actively work together and collaborate to improve the value of a touristic experience?* In that sense, the use of information technologies — geared toward capturing and reflecting the relationships between participants — can provide further insights for a truly customer-oriented tourism firm (Grewal et al., 2003; Ruiz-Molina, Gil-Saura, & Moliner-Velazquez, 2010; see also Chapter 19).

A combination of *intervariable* and *intravariable* approaches to measuring value in tourism services can shed light on the richness of the touristic experience, how its various elements are interrelated and how they can produce satisfaction and loyalty. In that sense, researchers may include not only a measurement of overall perceived value in structural models but also different value dimensions to understand the key determinants of customer satisfaction and loyalty. And managers should be aware of how different value dimensions (utilitarian and hedonic, social and individual, active and reactive) can interact with each other in a more synergistic way to produce better experiences that differentiate one offering from the others (e.g. emotional rewards in a restaurant combined with excellent service quality; time saving in an agile system for reservations, along with elegant and pleasurable customer care; or status-related aspects of belonging to a rewards club plus the best price deals for these more loyal customers).

### 10.4.3. Value as a Tool for Targeting and Positioning Tourism Products

For both marketing practitioners and researchers, the construct of perceived value has been identified as one of the most important aspects of the consumption experience (Cronin et al., 2000, p. 194; Holbrook, 1999, p. xiii). Value has been considered to be relativistic (Holbrook, 1999) — that is, personal, comparative and situational. From a managerial point of view, this means that value is linked to marketing strategies such as market segmentation-and-targeting and product differentiation-and-positioning.

**10.4.3.1. Segmentation and targeting** The highly personal nature of value perceptions (Holbrook, 1999) suggests that, according to the value-in-use theory, it is partly the consumer who determines the value of a touristic service. As theoretically stated by Holbrook (1999) and many others, value resides *not* in the product purchased (a particular destination) and *not* in the brand chosen (a specific hotel chain) but, *rather*, in the consumption experience derived, which is obviously unique and highly personal. Many valuable empirical proposals in the recent tourism literature have examined this issue in attempts to measure the value of an experience — among others, Yuan and Wu (2008) in coffee outlets as well as Chen and Chen (2010) in heritage sites. Subjective value orientations must be taken into consideration by managers in order to avoid any form of marketing myopia while reflecting their unique relationships with customers. The segmentation of tourists into homogeneous markets, according to differences and similarities in value orientations (social/individual, utilitarian/hedonic), allows for the comparisons between consumer groups and can assist management in formulating more customer-oriented marketing strategies. Tourism managers can have a strategic look into the value dimensionality, providing tourism organizations with a competitive edge in appealing to today's competitive and rapidly changing tourism consumers. In advertising, this greater understanding of consumers' values — cognitive for business travellers interested on efficiency (time and quality) and affective for pleasure travellers (pursuing hedonic and social values) — will suggest new ways to make an overall tourism experience more comprehensive and exciting.

**10.4.3.2. Differentiation and positioning** When translating the aforementioned relevance of value for marketing researchers into a competitive marketing approach for managers, we immediately recognize that competitiveness entails the value concept. That is, for a tourism company or a destination, the value of a strong brand lies in its competitive ability to attract and keep satisfied customers over time. However, 'this implies that the value behind the loyalty to one firm be greater than that of another, itself implying a comparison' (Oliver, 1999, p. 48). Within a relationship marketing approach, this comparison means that — once customers are attracted to starting a relationship with a given firm — they will be more likely to continue that relationship if they are consistently provided with a better offer than that from any competitor. This better offer is provided by the creation of better value (Anderson, 1995). The prescription for success is therefore to make this value offer as different as possible for as long a time as possible with respect to a particular target segment – that is, to establish a sustainable differential advantage. Consequently, the clear link between competitive advantage and value is very often emphasized insofar as maximal customer value serves as the key to gaining and maintaining a differential advantage (Day, 1999; Gale, 1994; Nilson, 1992).

In this sense, value can be seen as a definitive path toward improving a travel destination's competitive edge (Pechlaner, Smeral, & Matzler, 2002). Nevertheless, in other tourism-related contexts, this clear reasoning becomes less clear. Where hotels, airlines, attractions and restaurants have witnessed many attempts to reduce service heterogeneity by providing higher standards of flexible service, points of differentiation between competing firms have also been reduced (Palmer & Mayer, 1996). While homogeneity within a branded tourism chain has been enhanced, opportunities for product differentiation have also been reduced in the eyes of the tourism customer. An analysis of competitiveness via the value concept, defined earlier as multidimensional and experiential, must shed light on the provision of definitely different touristic experiences.

A viable positioning strategy, for instance, is the one derived from a value approach that comes from a deeper analysis of the value offered by the tourism firm, including the relevant trade-offs between benefits and costs (see, among others, 'Lower fares, fewer restrictions' at America West Airline or 'Fly cheaper' at Ryanair airline). Nevertheless, an abuse of the value trade-off, especially in promotional contents, may reveal problems in targeting and positioning. The problem may come when customers consider that the benefits of an offer do not compensate for its excessive price or, in the opposite way, when a low price depends on the sacrifice of important core benefits. Careful attention should also be given to promotional offers that seek to attract new customers by a deal that violates the value delivered to current customers. Customer loyalty is assured only as long as remaining with a firm gives extra benefits. Thus, tourism firms — for example, fast food restaurants or airlines — may attract price-sensitive customers by introducing a better balanced value offer while still preserving special treatment for the loyal ones. In that sense, future research is needed to shed light on the excessive use of promotional offers (i.e. 'best value offers') for a consumer who might be more interested in benefits other than price reduction (Gallarza & Gil, 2006).

All this reasoning reminds us how the value concept and its conceptual and methodological connections with loyalty behaviour must be continuously revisited in searching for excellence in the marketplace for tourism.

## 10.5.  Conclusion

The purpose of this chapter was to critically review the meaning and role of the notion of value in a tourism-related context for a relationship marketing-based approach. It did this through revising the role of value in relationship marketing, providing a state-of-the-art review on both conceptual and empirical research on customer value within the tourism literature, and outlining managerial implications of value in tourism services related to segmentation, differentiation and positioning.

First, this chapter reminds us how most of relationship marketing is based on a newly understood mindset that places value at the core of the contemporary approach to serving customers, emphasizing both the affective commitment to a service provider and the repeat-purchase or repatronage intentions. Both outcomes are fully studied, jointly or separately, in the consumer-marketing tourism literature, where perceived value is very often viewed as a positive influence on loyalty. However, unexploited insights in tourism B2B contexts remain when dealing with other stakeholders different from customer for an integrative view of tourism services.

The second aim of the chapter was to illustrate how tourism-related services are paradigmatically chosen by consumer behaviour researchers for studying value, either via an *intervariable* approach (links between value and other constructs such as quality, satisfaction and loyalty) or via an *intravariable* approach (dimensions of value applied to tourism services). Empirical studies since 2000 have addressed the topic of consumer value in a wide range of tourism services. Although new innovative tourism offers have recently been analysed, this type of *intervariable* value approach, interest in destinations and hotels still predominates. At any rate, perceived value, service quality and satisfaction form a key conceptual and methodological triangle for research into tourism-related consumer behaviour, and, although many authors provide precise evidence on the service quality–value–satisfaction–loyalty chain of effects, the discussion of direct and indirect effects of any of them on tourists' repurchase intentions awaits the emergence of a clear consensus. This issue, especially relevant in a relationship marketing approach, is crucial for tourism organizations that deal with once-in-a-lifetime tourists.

As for all service, a multidimensional value perspective has seemed most appropriate for assessing *intravariable* approaches in tourism. There is an obvious need for assessing emotions when dealing with value judgments, purely functional perspective value being too simplistic. A social dimension should be added, along with 'epistemic' or 'conditional' aspects when time and space of the experience matter. In fact, to fully capture the essence and idiosyncrasy of the tourism experience, there is still a concern by tourism researchers in establishing comprehensive measurements of value perceptions in tourism research.

This chapter has also sought to demonstrate that strategic relevance of value in tourism is higher than for other related concepts, and its academic interest may thus exceed those of service quality or satisfaction. Furthermore, the notion of image has recently reappeared as a key element in the quality–value–satisfaction–loyalty chain, although the conjoint study of the effect of all these constructs on perceived image still remains a key issue in tourism.

An additional fundamental point in this chapter was to make evident how both perceived value (in a consumer behaviour approach) and customer value (in a marketing management approach) are key drivers of competitiveness for tourism organizations' long-term viability. For better segmentation and targeting actions, managers should take subjective value orientations into consideration in order to avoid any form of marketing myopia. Furthermore, the clear link between competitive advantage and value has also been addressed, although this link is envisaged to be a better way for destinations than for hotels or restaurants that sometimes may use and abuse the so-called *best value* offers.

From an academic perspective we believe the next 5–10 years in tourism services researching will move toward adopting new conceptual mindsets, such as S-D logic or forthcoming approaches, because this industry involves composite services in which synergies can be obtained between multiple service providers. Contemporary tourism needs to be understood as a specific process within an experiential approach that seeks to maintain customers over time, and for this purpose, the concept of value, either in its classical view as a trade-off between benefits and costs or in more sophisticated experiential approaches, has far-reaching implications for tourism researchers and professionals.

## Acknowledgement

The authors are very grateful for the support of the project ECO2010-17475 of the Spanish Ministry of Science and Innovation.

## References

Al-Sabbahy, H., Ekinci, Y., & Riley, M. (2004). An investigation of perceived value dimensions: Implications for hospitality research. *Journal of Travel Research, 42,* 226–234.

Anderson, J. C. (1995). Relationships in business markets: Exchange episodes, value creation, and their empirical assessment. *Journal of the Academy of Marketing Science, 23*(4), 346–350.

Babin, B. J., & Kim, K. (2001). International students travel behaviour: A model of the travel-related consumer/dissatisfaction process. *Journal of Travel & Tourism Marketing, 10*(1), 93–106.

Bojanic, D. C. (1996). Consumer perceptions of price, value and satisfaction in the hotel industry: An exploratory study. *Journal of Hospitality and Leisure Marketing, 4*(1), 5–22.

Bolton, R. N., Kannan, P. K., & Bramlett, M. D. (2000). Implications of loyalty program membership and service experiences for customer retention and value. *Journal of the Academy of Marketing Science, 28*(1), 95–108.

Brodie, R. J., Whittome, J. R. M., & Brush, G. J. (2009). Investigating the service brand: A customer value perspective. *Journal of Business Research, 62*(3), 345–355.

Chaudhuri, A., & Holbrook, M. B. (2001). The chain of effects from brand trust and brand affect to brand performance: The role of brand loyalty. *Journal of Marketing, 65,* 81–93.

Chen, C.-F., & Chen, F.-S. (2010). Experience quality, perceived value, satisfaction and behavioural intention for heritage tourists. *Tourism Management, 31*(1), 29–35.

Chen, C.-F., & Tsai, D. (2007). How destination image and evaluative factors affect behavioural intentions? *Tourism Management, 28,* 1115–1122.

Chen, C.-F., & Tsai, M. H. (2008). Perceived value, satisfaction and loyalty of TV travel product shopping: Involvement as a moderator. *Tourism Management, 29,* 1166–1171.

Cho, M.-H., & SooCheong, S. J. (2008). Information value structure for vacation travel. *Journal of Travel Research, 47,* 72–83.

Chu, K.-M., & Shiu, C. (2009). The construction model of customer trust, perceived value and customer loyalty. *Journal of American Academy of Business, 14*(2), 98–103.

Cronin, J. J., Brady, M. K., & Hult, G. T. M. (2000). Assessing the effects of quality, value and customer satisfaction on consumer behavioural intentions in service environments. *Journal of Retailing, 76*(2), 193–218.

Day, G. S. (1999). *Market driven strategy. Processes for creating value* (2nd ed.). New York, NY: The Free Press.

Dick, A. S., & Basu, K. (1994). Customer loyalty: Toward an integrated conceptual framework. *Journal of the Academy of Marketing Science, 22*(2), 99–113.

Diep, V. C. S., & Sweeney, J. C. (2008). Shopping trip value: Do stores and products matter? *Journal of Retailing and Consumer Services, 15,* 399–409.

Duman, T., & Mattila, A. S. (2005). The role of affective factors on perceived cruise vacation value. *Tourism Management, 26,* 311–323.

Feng, R., & Morrison, A. M. (2007). Quality and value networks. Marketing travel clubs. *Annals of Tourism Research, 34*(3), 588–609.

Gale, B. T. (1994). *Managing customer value; creating quality and service that customers can see.* New York, NY: The Free Press.

Gallarza, M. G., Arteaga, F., Floristán, E., & Gil, I. (2009). Consumer behavior in a religious event experience: An empirical assessment of value dimensionality among volunteers. *International Journal of Culture, Tourism, & Hospitality Research, 3*(2), 165–180.

Gallarza, M. G., & Gil, I. (2006). Value dimensions, perceived value, satisfaction and loyalty: An investigation of university students' travel behaviour. *Tourism Management, 27*(3), 437–452.

Gallarza, M. G., & Gil, I. (2008). The concept of value and its dimensions: A tool for analysing tourism experiences. *Tourism Review, 63*(3), 5–20.

Gallarza, M. G., Gil, I., & Calderón, H. (2002). Destination image: Towards a conceptual framework. *Annals of Tourism Research, 29*(1), 56–78.

Gallarza, M. G., Gil-Saura, I., & Holbrook, M. (2011). The value of value: Further excursions on the role of customer value. *Journal of Consumer Behavior, 10,* 179–191.

Grace, D., & O'Cass, A. (2005). An examination of the antecedents of re-patronage intentions across different retail store formats. *Journal of Retailing and Consumer Services, 12,* 227–243.

Grewal, D., Iyer, G. R., Krishnan, R., & Sharma, A. (2003). The internet and the price–value–loyalty chain. *Journal of Business Research, 56,* 391–398.

Grönroos, C. (1997). From marketing mix to relationship marketing — Towards a paradigm shift in marketing. *Management Decision, 35*(4), 322–339.

He, Y., & Song, H. (2009). A mediation model of tourist's repurchase intentions for packaged tour services. *Journal of Travel Research, 47*(3), 317–331.

Holbrook, M. B. (1999). *Consumer value: A framework for analysis and research.* London: Routledge.

Hu, H.-H., Kandampully, J., & Juwaheer, T. D. (2009). Relationships and impacts of service quality, perceived value, customer satisfaction and image: An empirical study. *The Service Industries Journal, 29*(2), 111–125.

Hume, M. (2011). How do we keep them coming? Examining museum experiences using a services marketing paradigm. *Journal of Nonprofit & Public Sector Marketing, 23*(1), 71–94.

Hutchinson, J., Lai, F., & Wang, Y. (2009). Understanding the relationships of quality, value, equity, satisfaction and behavioral intentions among golf travelers. *Tourism Management, 30*(2), 298–308.

Jayanti, R., & Ghosh, A. (1996). Service value determination: An integrative perspective. *Journal of Hospitality and Leisure Marketing, 3*(4), 5–25.

Jensen, H. R. (1996). The interrelationship between customer and consumer value. *Asia Pacific Advances in Consumer Research, 2,* 60–63.

Kashyap, R., & Bojanic, D. (2000). A structural analysis of value, quality, and price perceptions of business and leisure travellers. *Journal of Travel Research, 39,* 45–51.

Kim, Y.-H., Kim, M. C., & Goh, B. K. (2011). An examination of food tourist's behaviour: Using the modified theory of reasoned action. *Tourism Management, 32*, 1159–1165.

Lee, C.-K., Yoon, Y. S., & Lee, S. K. (2007). Investigating the relationship among perceived value, satisfaction and recommendations: The case of the Korean DMZ. *Tourism Management, 28*, 204–214.

Lin, H.-H., & Wang, Y. S. (2006). An examination of the determinants of customer loyalty in mobile commerce contexts. *Information & Management, 43*, 271–282.

Martín-Ruiz, D., Gremler, D. D., Washburn, J. H., & Cepeda-Carión, G. (2008). Service value revisited: Specifying a higher-order, formative measure. *Journal of Business Research, 61*, 1278–1291.

McDougall, G. H. G., & Levesque, T. (2000). Customer satisfaction with services: Putting perceived value into the equation. *The Journal of Services Marketing, 14*(5), 392–410.

Murphy, P. E., & Pritchard, M. P. (1997). Destination price–value perceptions: An examination of origin and seasonal influences. *Journal of Travel Research, 35*(3), 16–22.

Murphy, P. E., Pritchard, M. P., & Smith, B. (2000). The destination product and its impact on traveller perceptions. *Tourism Management, 21*, 43–52.

Nasution, H. N., & Mavondo, F. T. (2008). Customer value in the hotel industry: What managers believe they deliver and what customer experience. *International Journal of Hospitality Management, 27*, 204–213.

Nilson, T. H. (1992). *Value-added marketing: Marketing management for superior results.* Berkshire, UK: McGraw Hill.

Oh, H. (1999). Service quality, customer satisfaction, and customer value: A holistic perspective. *International Journal of Hospitality Management, 18*(1), 67–82.

Oh, H. (2000). The effect of brand class, brand awareness, and price on customer value and behavioral intentions. *Journal of Hospitality and Tourism Research, 24*(2), 136–162.

Oh, H. (2003). Price fairness and its asymmetric effects on overall price, quality, and value judgements: The case of an upscale hotel. *Tourism Management, 24*, 397–399.

Oliver, R. L. (1999). Value as excellence in the consumption experience. In M. B. Holbrook (Ed.), *Consumer value: A framework for analysis and research* (pp. 43–62). London: Routledge.

Palmer, A., & Mayer, R. (1996). Relationship marketing: A new paradigm for the travel and tourism sector? *Journal of Vacation Marketing, 2*(4), 326–333.

Parasuraman, A., & Grewal, D. (2000). The impact of technology on the quality–value–loyalty chain: A research agenda. *Journal of the Academy of Marketing Science, 28*(1), 168–174.

Payne, A., Holt, S., & Frow, P. (2001). Relationship value management: Exploring the integration of employee, customer and shareholder value and enterprise performance models. *Journal of Marketing Management, 17*, 785–817.

Pechlaner, H., Smeral, E., & Matzler, K. (2002). Customer value management as a determinant of the competitive position of tourism destinations. *Tourism Review, 57*(4), 15–22.

Peck, H., Payne, A., Christopher, M., & Clark, M. (1999). *Relationship marketing. Strategy and implementation.* Oxford: Elsevier Butterworth-Heinemann.

Petrick, J. F. (2002). Development of a multi-dimensional scale for measuring the perceived value of a service. *Journal of Leisure Research, 34*(2), 119–134.

Petrick, J. F. (2003). Measuring cruise passengers' perceived value. *Tourism Analysis, 7*, 251–258.

Petrick, J. F. (2004). The roles of quality, value and satisfaction in predicting cruise passengers behavioural intentions. *Journal of Travel Research, 42*, 397–407.

Petrick, J. F., & Backman, S. J. (2002). An examination of golf travellers' satisfaction, perceived value, loyalty, and intentions to revisit. *Tourism Analysis, 6*(3–6), 223–237.

Petrick, J. F., Morais, D. D., & Norman, W. C. (2001). An examination of the determinants of entertainment vacationers' intentions to revisit. *Journal of Travel Research, 40,* 41–48.

Ravald, A., & Grönroos, C. (1996). The value concept and relationship marketing. *European Journal of Marketing, 30*(2), 19–30.

Ruiz-Molina, M. E., Gil-Saura, I., & Moliner-Velazquez, B. (2010). The role of information technology in relationships between travel agencies and their suppliers. *Journal of Hospitality and Tourism Technology, 1*(2), 144–162.

Ryu, K., Han, H., & Kim, T.-H. (2008). The relationship among overall quick–casual restaurant image, perceived value, customer satisfaction and behavioural intentions. *International Journal of Hospitality Management, 27,* 459–469.

Sánchez, J., Callarisa, L., Rodriguez, R. M., & Moliner, M. A. (2006). Perceived value of the purchase of a tourism product. *Tourism Management, 27,* 394–409.

Sheth, J. N., Newman, B. I., & Gross, B. L. (1991). Why we buy what we buy: A theory of consumption values. *Journal of Business Research, 22,* 159–170.

Sparks, B., Butcher, K., & Bradley, G. (2008). Dimensions and correlates of consumer value: An application of the timeshare industry. *International Journal of Hospitality Management, 27,* 98–108.

Stevens, B. (1992). Price value perceptions of travellers. *Journal of Travel Research, 31*(2), 44–48. Research notes and communications.

Tam, J. L. M. (2000). The effects of service quality, perceived value, and customer satisfaction on behavioural intentions. *Journal of Hospitality and Leisure Marketing, 6*(4), 31–43.

Um, S., Chon, K., & Ro, Y. (2006). Antecedents of revisit intention. *Annals of Tourism Research, 33*(4), 1141–1158.

Vargo, S. L., & Lusch, R. L. (2004). Evolving to a new dominant logic for marketing. *Journal of Marketing, 68,* 1–17.

Walker, J. T., Backman, K., Backman, S., & Morais, D. (2001). Using performance measurements to explore the influence of service quality dimensions on customer's perception of overall value of a nature based tourism outfitter. *Journal of Quality Assurance in Hospitality and Tourism, 2*(1/2), 49–68.

Williams, P., & Soutar, G. N. (2009). Value, satisfaction and behavioural intentions in an adventure tourism context. *Annals of Tourism Research, 36*(3), 413–438.

Yuan, Y. H., & Wu, C. K. (2008). Relationship among experiential marketing, experiential value, and customer satisfaction. *Journal of Hospitality and Tourism Research, 32*(3), 387–410.

Zeithaml, V. A. (1988). Consumer perceptions of price, quality, and value: A means-end model and synthesis of evidence. *Journal of Marketing, 52,* 2–22.

## Chapter 11

# Identifying the Major Determinants of Loyalty in Tourism

*Ana María Campón Cerro, José Manuel Hernández Mogollón and Helena Maria Baptista Alves*

## 11.1. Introduction

Tourism is a multidisciplinary research field of great interest. It has been studied using perspectives as diverse as geography, sociology, psychology, economics, business management or marketing. Based on a marketing perspective, an approach that may help tourism services is the relationship marketing approach. Organizations are becoming increasingly aware that survival and success are highly correlated with building successful long-term relationships with each customer (Lombard & Steyn, 2008). The creation of these relationships brings mutual benefits. For the customer, benefits include customized offers, reduced risk perception and time economies. For the company, customer loyalty, positive word of mouth and consequently greater returns may be cited (Reichheld, 1994).

However, for relationship marketing to succeed in the tourism sector, an active loyalty among tourists should be encouraged (Fyall, Callod, & Edwards, 2003). In this sense, to understand what generates loyalty in the tourism industry is challenging as this industry is composed of various services (accommodation, transport, food and beverage, travel agency, leisure activity, etc.) that prove very different even when in the same category, especially when talking about pleasure travelling. In the case of business travellers, a loyal customer might be one who chooses the same hotel chain, flies with the same airline or requires the services of the same travel agency whenever travelling. However, in the case of pleasure travellers, this definition of loyalty is not as straightforward as people search for diversity, particularly regarding destinations. In this sense, measuring loyalty in terms of repeated purchases is more difficult (Bigné, Sánchez, & Sanz, 2005). In these cases, loyalty is frequently measured by the willingness to return and recommend (Barroso, Martín, & Martín, 2007; Bigné & Andreu, 2005; Bigné, Sánchez, & Sánchez, 2001; Bigné et al., 2005; Bowen & Chen, 2001; C. Chen & Tsai, 2007; Chi, 2005; Chi & Qu, 2008; Faullant, Matzler, & Füller, 2008;

Strategic Marketing in Tourism Services
Copyright © 2012 by Emerald Group Publishing Limited
All rights of reproduction in any form reserved
ISBN: 978-1-78052-070-4

Hui, Wan, & Ho, 2007; Kandampully & Suhartanto, 2000, 2002; Matzler, Füller, & Faullant, 2007; Prayag, 2008), also accompanied by other indicators (e.g. the first choice, more benefits, feeling better, feeling proud or number of visits).

Given this difficulty in understanding loyalty, it is necessary to identify which factors generate loyalty in the tourism industry and what are the best methods for measuring it. Thus, this chapter takes on two objectives. The first is to identify the most significant factors predicting loyalty in tourism. To this end, a literature review regarding the loyalty of customers to destinations, accommodations and other relevant tourism products was carried out. The second objective is to further and deepen the study of relationship marketing and customer loyalty in the tourism industry, as illustrated in the reviews of Bigné (1996, 2004), Bigné, Andreu, Sánchez, and Alvarado (2008) and Oh, Kim, and Shin (2004). Specifically, the relevance of this work stems from the need to better understand the tourism loyalty process by approaching its determinants with the use of structural equation models in future studies. This work provides an insight into causal relationships between loyalty and the factors affecting its generation. This information is key to implementing relational strategies at the destination level. That would help achieve a loyal customer base that may improve profitability levels.

This chapter is divided into six sections. First, an introduction presents the chapter topic and objectives. The theoretical framework follows before setting out the method used to conduct the study. Then, results are reviewed and conclusions presented, with a final section detailing future research recommendations.

## 11.2. Relationship Marketing and Customer Loyalty: An Application to Tourism

The concept of relationship marketing was introduced by Berry in 1983 (Payne, 2000). He defined it as 'attracting, maintaining and — in multi-service organizations — enhancing customer relationships' (Berry, 2000, p. 150). Afterwards, he extended its scope to all stakeholders involved in enterprise–client interactions (E. Martín, 2005). The works by the Industrial Marketing and Purchasing (IMP) Group, the Nordic School of Services and other authors from the United Kingdom formed its original foundations. Since the 1990s, relationship marketing has been a burgeoning area in marketing theory (Christopher, Payne, & Ballantyne, 1994). This trend is driven by a newly competitive era characterized by the growing maturity, complexity, fragmentation and intensity of marketplace competition. At the same time, customers increasingly require individual and personalized services. This situation forces business to focus effort on building and maintaining relationships with the various parties involved in the exchange processes (Grönroos, 1999; Hunt & Morgan, 1994; Payne, 2000).

Since the last decade, researchers have been focusing their attention on studying the relationship marketing paradigm applied to new technologies and the Internet (e.g. Bai, Hu, & Jang, 2006; Dunn, Baloglu, Brewer, & Qu, 2009), and its application to various sectors such as banking (e.g. Leverin & Liljander, 2006), retailing (e.g. Meyer-Waarden, 2008), cellular phones (e.g. Johnson, Herrmann, & Huber, 2006) or tourism (see Table 11.1).

In practice, many companies have noticed that creating long-term relationships with customers and other companies provides a competitive advantage (Ganesan, 1994). Reichheld and Sasser (1990) estimated a company might be able to boost profits by between 25% and 85%, depending on the sector, by retaining 5% of their customers.

Saren and Tzokas (1998) suggest that repetitive purchases can be seen as evidence of the existence of a strong relationship. In this line, Oliver (1999, p. 34) defined loyalty as 'a deeply held commitment to rebuy or repatronize a preferred product/ service consistently in the future, thereby causing repetitive same-brand or same brand-set purchasing, despite situational influences and marketing efforts having the potential to cause switching behavior'. But some authors have moved away from this principle. They have argued for the need to conceptualize loyalty as a socio-psychological phenomenon, rather than a behavioural one (Saren & Tzokas, 1998). Customer retention does not automatically mean that customers remain loyal (Palmer & Mayer, 1996). Customers are loyal to a company for the value they receive (Reichheld, 1994), and for Hunt, Arnett, and Madhavaram (2006) relationships are the ones that contribute to the efficient and effective production of products and services of value to various market segments.

However, relationship marketing strategy should only be implemented in situations in which it contributes to achieving a sustainable competitive advantage over time (Morgan & Hunt, 1999) as the process of creating and maintaining relationships involves an investment in recurring opportunity costs (Bendapudi & Berry, 1997). To create and enhance loyalty, the most common tools are loyalty programmes. A loyalty programme is defined 'as a program that allows consumers to accumulate free rewards when they make repeated purchases with a firm. Such a program rarely benefits consumers in one purchase, but is intended to foster customer loyalty over time' (Liu, 2007, p. 20). A better understanding of loyalty programmes is necessary for researchers and managers to be able to focus on the most important performance predictors. That would help managers in designing loyalty programmes (Johnson et al., 2006). Many firms use relationship marketing instruments and loyalty programmes. For example, airlines encourage their travellers to accumulate air miles to get subsequent free flights. Hotels offer free rooms to customers who have already stayed a certain number of nights (Meyer-Waarden, 2008).

The tourism industry has been a frontrunner in the adoption of the relationship approach, yet the concepts of loyalty to destinations (Fyall et al., 2003) and acco-mmodations (Aksu, 2006) have received little attention in the literature. J. S. Chen and Gursoy (2001) pointed out that destinations currently face higher levels of competition. Hence, businesses relying on tourism need to understand what determines tourist destination loyalty (Pike, 2004, 2008). In the first place, one might ask whether a particular destination has the capacity to generate loyalty. Alegre and Juaneda (2006, p. 686) indicated that 'some tourism motivations would inhibit destination loyalty', such as the desire to break up the monotony of everyday

Table 11.1:  Ranking of constructs used and references (74).

| Constructs (*n*; %) | Destinations (42; 57%) | Accommodations (17; 23%) | Others (15; 20%) |
|---|---|---|---|
| Satisfaction (56; 76%) | Alegre and Cladera (2006, 2009), Barroso et al. (2007), Bigné et al. (2001, 2005), C. Chen and Tsai (2007), Chi (2005), Chi and Qu (2008), Cladera (2007), Gallarza and Gil (2006), L. Hernández, Solís, Moliner, and Sánchez (2006), Huang and Chiu (2006), Jang and Feng (2007), Kao (2007), K. Kim (2008), Kozak (2001), G. Lee (2001), J. Lee, Graefe, and Burns (2004, 2007), T. H. Lee (2009), D. Martín (2005), E. Martín (2005), Martínez, Novello, and Murias (2009), Mechinda, Serirat, and Gulid (2009), Mechinda, Serirat, Anuwichanont, and Gulid (2010), Petrick, Morais, and Norman (2001), Rodríguez del Bosque and San Martín (2008), San Martín (2005), Tian-Cole and Crompton (2003), Um, Chon, and Ro (2006), Vale, Moutinho, and Vale (2010), Yoon and Uysal (2005), Yüksel and Yüksel (2007), Yüksel, Yüksel, and Bilis (2010) | Back (2001), Bowen and Chen (2001), Chitty, Ward, and Chua (2007), Hu, Kandampully, and Juwaheer (2009), Kandampully and Suhartanto (2000, 2002), W. G. Kim and Cha (2002) Loureiro and Miranda (2006, 2008), Skogland and Siguaw (2004), Voces (2005) | Alén and Fraiz (2006), Alén, Rodríguez, and Fraiz (2007), Anuwichanont and Mechinda (2009), Bigné and Andreu (2004, 2005), Buracom (2002), Faullant et al. (2008), Kan, Yen, and Huan (2009), Li (2006), Li and Petrick (2008a), Matzler et al. (2007), Petrick (2004) |

| | | | |
|---|---|---|---|
| Quality (29; 39%) | Barroso et al. (2007), Bigné et al. (2001, 2005), C. Chen and Tsai (2007), Gallarza and Gil (2006), J. Lee et al. (2004, 2007), D. Martín (2005), E. Martín (2005), Murphy, Pritchard, and Smith (2000), Tian-Cole and Crompton (2003), Tian-Cole, Crompton, and Willson (2002), Um et al. (2006), Vale et al. (2010) | Choi and Chu (2001), Gould-Williams (1999), Hu et al. (2009), Lin (2005), Loureiro and Miranda (2006, 2008), Voces (2005) | Alén and Fraiz (2006), Alén et al. (2007), Alexandris, Kouthouris, and Meligdis (2006), Anuwichanont and Mechinda (2009), Buracom (2002), Li (2006), Li and Petrick (2008a), Matzler et al. (2007), Petrick (2004) |
| Image (25; 34%) | Barroso et al. (2007), Bigné et al. (2001, 2005), C. Chen and Tsai (2007), Chi (2005), Chi and Qu (2008), L. Hernández et al. (2006), Hui et al. (2007), T. H. Lee (2009), Li, Petrick, and Zhouk (2007), Mechinda et al. (2010), Prayag (2008), Rodríguez del Bosque and San Martín (2008), San Martín (2005), Sanz (2008), Vale et al. (2010) | Back (2001), Chitty et al. (2007), Hu et al. (2009), Kandampully and Suhartanto (2000, 2002), Loureiro and Miranda (2006, 2008) | Anuwichanont and Mechinda (2009), Faullant et al. (2008) |
| Value (15; 20%) | C. Chen and Tsai (2007), Gallarza and Gil (2006), G. Lee (2001), Mechinda et al. (2009, 2010), Murphy et al. (2000), Petrick et al. (2001), Vale et al. (2010) | Chitty et al. (2007), Choi and Chu (2001), Gould-Williams (1999), Hu et al. (2009) | Anuwichanont and Mechinda (2009), Petrick (2004), Petrick and Backman (2002) |

Table 11.1: (Continued)

| Constructs (*n*; %) | Destinations (42; 57%) | Accommodations (17; 23%) | Others (15; 20%) |
|---|---|---|---|
| Overall satisfaction (13; 18%) | Alegre and Cladera (2006, 2009), Baloglu, Pekcan, Chen, and Santos (2003), Chi (2005), Chi and Qu (2008), Cladera (2007), Hui et al. (2007), Martínez et al. (2009), Prayag (2008), Tian-Cole et al. (2002) | Choi and Chu (2001), Skogland and Siguaw (2004) | Matzler et al. (2007) |
| Trust (10; 14%) | Huang and Chiu (2006), Mechinda et al. (2010), Vale et al. (2010), Yen, Liu, and Tuan (2009) | W. G. Kim and Cha (2002), Loureiro and Miranda (2006, 2008), Sophonsiri (2008) | Anuwichanont and Mechinda (2009), Kan et al. (2009) |
| Emotions (9; 12%) | Rodríguez del Bosque and San Martín (2008), San Martín (2008), Vale et al. (2010), Yüksel and Yüksel (2007) | Shammout (2007) | Anuwichanont and Mechinda (2009), Bigné and Andreu (2004, 2005), Petrick (2004) |
| Related to destination characteristics (8; 11%) | Baloglu et al. (2003), J. S. Chen and Gursoy (2001), Gallarza and Gil (2006), Huang and Chiu (2006), Hui et al. (2007), Murphy et al. (2000), Um et al. (2006), Yüksel and Yüksel (2007) | — | — |
| Motivations (7; 9%) | Alegre and Cladera (2009), Cladera (2007), K. Kim (2008), Kao (2007), T. H. Lee (2009), Mechinda et al. (2009), Yoon and Uysal (2005) | — | — |

| Determinant | | | |
|---|---|---|---|
| Past experience/previous visits (6; 8%) | Alegre and Cladera (2006, 2009), J. S. Chen and Gursoy (2001), Cladera (2007), Kozak (2001), Petrick et al. (2001) | — | — |
| Price (6; 8%) | Hui et al. (2007) | Chitty et al. (2007), Kandampully and Suhartanto (2000, 2002) | Anuwichanont and Mechinda (2009), Petrick (2004) |
| Related to characteristics and services of a hotel (6; 8%) | — | Chitty et al. (2007), Choi and Chu (2001), Gould-Williams (1999), Kandampully and Suhartanto (2000, 2002), Tsaur, Chiu, and Huang (2002) | — |
| Disconfirmation (5; 7%) | Hui et al. (2007), Rodríguez del Bosque and San Martín (2008), San Martín (2005), Vale et al. (2010) | — | Bigné and Andreu (2004) |
| Tourist characteristics (4; 5%) | Alegre and Cladera (2006), G. Lee (2001), Mechinda et al. (2009) | Lin (2005) | — |
| Expectations (4; 5%) | Hui et al. (2007), Rodríguez del Bosque and San Martín, D. Martín (2005), E. Martín (2005), Vale et al. (2010) | — | |
| Related to relationship (4; 5%) | Yen et al. (2009) | W. G. Kim and Cha (2002), Shammout (2007) | Kan et al. (2009) |
| Cultural differences (3; 4%) | J. S. Chen and Gursoy (2001), Huang and Chiu (2006), Hui et al. (2007) | — | — |

Table 11.1: (*Continued*)

| Constructs (*n*; %) | Destinations (42; 57%) | Accommodations (17; 23%) | Others (15; 20%) |
|---|---|---|---|
| Participation (3; 4%) | K. Kim (2008), G. Lee (2001), J. Lee et al. (2007) | — | — |
| Attachment (3; 4%) | Mechinda et al. (2009), Yüksel et al. (2010) | — | Alexandris et al. (2006) |
| Commitment (3; 4%) | Yen et al. (2009) | Sophonsiri (2008) | Kan et al. (2009) |
| Overall image (3; 4%) | Li et al. (2007), Prayag (2008), Sanz (2008) | — | — |
| Value for money (3; 4%) | Alegre and Cladera (2009), Cladera (2007), Um et al. (2006) | — | — |
| Related to the characteristics and performance of the tourism establishment or place (3; 4%) | — | — | Alexandris et al. (2006), Faullant et al. (2008), Matzler et al. (2007) |

| Determinant | | | |
| --- | --- | --- | --- |
| Familiarity (2; 3%) | Mechinda et al. (2009, 2010) | – | – |
| Reputation (2; 3%) | – | Tsaur et al. (2002) | Anuwichanont and Mechinda (2009) |
| Safety (2; 3%) | J. S. Chen and Gursoy (2001), Huang and Chiu (2006) | – | – |
| Investment size (2; 3%) | – | – | Li (2006), Li and Petrick (2008a) |
| Attitude (2; 3%) | G. Lee (2001), T. H. Lee (2009), Jang and Feng (2007) | – | – |
| Novelty seeking (1; 1%) | | – | – |

life or to see new places, people, cultures and experiences. Barroso et al. (2007) defined four tourist segments that confirm the need tourists have for change. In addition, they discuss the significant differences between these segments depending on tourist intentions to return to or recommend the destination. In the same line, Zins (2001) suggests that owing to the unique nature of tourism, the application of conventional loyalty frameworks and metrics needs rethinking.

Therefore, more research on loyalty is needed (Chi & Qu, 2008; McKercher, Denizci-Guillet, & Ng, 2011). According to Chi and Qu (2008), it is necessary to gain a greater understanding of the concepts of loyalty and customer satisfaction, as well as other determinants and their interrelationships. Ndubisi (2007) stated that it is important to study the impact of relationship marketing determinants on customer loyalty. This knowledge enables better management of company–customer relationships and contributes to achieving higher customer loyalty levels. Therefore, a literature review focused on loyalty towards destinations, accommodations and other relevant tourism products was carried out. The aim is to gain a better understanding of how loyalty works at the destination level.

## 11.3.  Method

The literature review was developed taking into account the recommendations of R. Hernández, Fernández, and Baptista (2007). Content analysis as a technique for the collection, classification and study of information was also applied (Bigné, 1999). Research published in scientific journals and doctoral theses related to the study of the determinants of loyalty to destinations, accommodations and other relevant tourism products were collected and analysed. The main tourism management journals were reviewed. To carry out a more comprehensive review, the ISI Web of Knowledge, ProQuest, EBSCO, Scopus and Dialnet databases were searched. The result was a total of 74 relevant references (17.6% of the documents were doctoral theses, 16.2% were sourced from *Tourism Management*, 6.8% from the *Journal of Travel Research*, 5.4% from the *Journal of Travel & Tourism Marketing*, 5.4% from the *International Journal of Contemporary Hospitality Management*, 4.1% from the *Revista Europea de Dirección y Economía de la Empresa*, 4.1% from *Leisure Sciences*, 4.1% from *Annals of Tourism Research* and the remainder, 20.3%, were articles dealing with management and tourism).

## 11.4.  Constructs Used to Determine Tourist Loyalty

The literature review discusses 74 published articles and doctoral theses, proposing and developing models for the study of loyalty to destinations, accommodations and other relevant tourism products. Table 11.1 presents the constructs used in these studies in rank order. Satisfaction (76%), quality (39%) and image (34%) take the top three positions. Figure 11.1 shows the relative contribution of each construct in

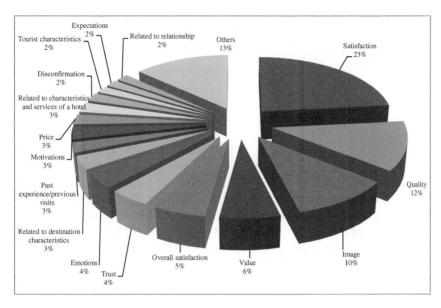

Figure 11.1: Relative contribution of each construct. *Note*: The category 'Others' includes the constructs that have been obtained up to three repetitions. They are cultural differences, participation, attachment, commitment, overall image, value for money, related to the characteristics and performance of the tourism establishment or place, familiarity, reputation, safety, investment size, attitude and novelty seeking.

relation to the other constructs analysed. Again, the high weighting of satisfaction (23%), quality (12%) and image (10%) is evident.

As seen in Table 11.1 and Figure 11.1, there are no significant differences between the constructs used for determining loyalty to destinations, accommodations and other relevant tourism products. Satisfaction is the most influential construct (shown in 76% of the studies examined, weighing 23% relative to the rest of the constructs used). It is followed by quality (39% and 12%, respectively), image (34%, 10%), value (20%, 6%) and overall satisfaction (18%, 5%).

Although some authors (e.g. McKercher et al., 2011; Saren & Tzokas, 1998) have argued for the need to conceptualize loyalty a behavioural as well as an attitudinal construct, based on these results it is possible to state that only few studies have analysed the construct in its totality. The literature analysed reveals that relational constructs have been left out, and there is a gap in studies on the relationship and its components. Only if the weightings of trust (incorporated into 14% of studies), other constructs related to the relationship (5%) and commitment (4%) were combined would relationships attain a middle position in the ranking. The only studies that display a relational orientation are those of Anuwichanont and Mechinda (2009), Kan et al. (2009), W.G. Kim and Cha (2002), Loureiro and Miranda (2006, 2008), Mechinda et al. (2010), Shammout (2007), Sophonsiri (2008), Vale et al. (2010) and

Yen et al. (2009). In total, only 10 of the 74 works reviewed here (14%) include the relational orientation. A vast number of the models analysed contain factors such as the intention to return (Alegre & Cladera, 2006, 2009; Choi & Chu, 2001; Cladera, 2007; Murphy et al., 2000; Petrick & Backman, 2002; Petrick et al., 2001; Um et al., 2006), future behavioural intentions (Alén & Fraiz, 2006; Alén, Rodríguez, & Fraiz, 2007; Baloglu et al., 2003; C. Chen & Tsai, 2007; Hu et al., 2009; T. H. Lee, 2009; J. Lee et al., 2004; Tian-Cole et al., 2002) or intended future behaviour (Tian-Cole & Crompton, 2003).

Regarding the loyalty construct, not all studies analysed deal with the construct as an explicit result of the model studied (64%). However, loyalty is examined implicitly through behavioural intentions (36%). In terms of the dimensionality of the construct, a single construct is often used (77% of cases for explicit loyalty and 74% for implicit loyalty) rather than the use of two, three or four dimensions. Regardless of whether studies examined loyalty either explicitly or implicitly, the most frequently deployed indicators were the intent to return and to recommend (64% and 56% of cases, respectively), whether on their own or accompanied by other items. Therefore, it is possible to conclude that there were no significant differences between the studies focusing on loyalty to destinations, accommodations or other travel products, whether the model results are explicit or implicit.

Using these results, and also the results of McKercher et al. (2011), which suggest that loyalty can be noted to different layers of tourism at the same time (e.g. destination and accommodation), a conceptual model to study loyalty at the destination and accommodation level is proposed here (see Figure 11.2). A hybrid model will capture loyalty to destinations and the companies operating within the

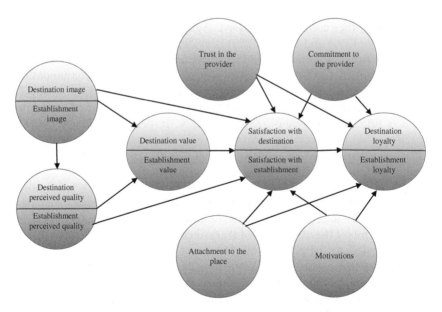

Figure 11.2: Proposed conceptual model.

destinations, such as accommodation facilities, while also containing the most commonly used constructs. For that reason, image, quality, value and satisfaction constructs were included. To highlight new relationships in the literature, it is important to focus on less studied factors, including relational constructs, such as commitment and trust on the provider, as well as attachment to the place and motivations. According to the results found by McKercher et al. (2011), relationships emerged as the second issue referred to by tourists when loyalty is scrutinized. In the proposed model, the casual links come from the results of several works (e.g. Alegre and Cladera, 2009; Faullant et al., 2008; Gallarza & Gil, 2006; L. Hernández et al., 2006; Kan et al., 2009; W. G. Kim & Cha, 2002; Loureiro & Miranda, 2006, 2008; Mechinda et al., 2009; Tian-Cole & Crompton, 2003; Yen et al., 2009; Yoon & Uysal, 2005). In this model, loyalty is proposed as an explicit construct.

## 11.5.  Conclusions

Given the stiff competition faced by tourism organizations and destinations, tools are needed to strengthen their competitiveness and positioning. These may be found in the relational approach to marketing and customer loyalty. Palmer (1994) emphasized that a successful marketing strategy should focus on winning new customers and then retaining them. Ndubisi (2007) stated that it is important to study the impact of the elements of a relationship marketing strategy on customer loyalty. The current chapter includes a literature review focusing on models proposed for studying loyalty to destinations, accommodations and other relevant tourism products. The results of this literature review may have important implications for advancing the study of loyalty. They serve as the foundations for discovering new relationships between constructs, as well as aiding in identifying new constructs. In addition, these results when applied to different contexts may improve knowledge with regard to this field, given the scarcity of previously existing research.

These results are the basis on which to build further research that will result in a deeper understanding of the factors nurturing loyalty to a destination and its services. Furthermore, they support the implementation of relational and customer loyalty strategies in destinations and tourism businesses.

The most outstanding result of this study is that the main constructs used in the literature as determinants of loyalty to destinations, accommodations and other travel products do not mutually differ. They are satisfaction, quality, image, value and overall satisfaction. Surprisingly, constructs related to relationship marketing such as commitment, trust and others have been barely used in these investigations whether loyalty is analysed either explicitly (64%) or implicitly (36%). Regarding metrics, these studies often use the intention to return and to recommend as indicators (64% and 56%, respectively), either alone or accompanied by other items to measure loyalty.

In light of these results, a hybrid model that captures the characteristics of the destinations and the companies operating within the destinations was proposed.

Causal relations between the most commonly used constructs (image, quality, value and satisfaction) and those related to relational strategy, commitment and trust were established. Attachment to the place and motivations were also incorporated in order to reflect emotional aspects related to destinations. As final construct of this model, an explicit loyalty construct was projected.

Nowadays, destinations are facing the toughest competition and most serious challenges in decades. But it may get worse in years to come. Therefore, obtaining a better understanding of why travellers become loyal to a destination and what drives that loyalty is vital (J. S. Chen & Gursoy, 2001; Chi & Qu, 2008). Destination marketers have to consider the practical implications of factors such as customer satisfaction, the quality and image of the destination and tourism establishments, value offered and so forth in enhancing loyalty. This would enable destination and establishment managers to know how to generate loyal customers, as well as how to implement and design relationship marketing strategies, such as loyalty programmes.

The tools of relationship marketing and activities have to be focused on enhancing customer satisfaction and loyalty. However, while it is impossible to control all determinants, some are susceptible to influence. They are, for instance, improving the image (e.g. with advertising), quality (e.g. certificates of quality) or value (creating and promoting tourism attractions and events). Both private and public actors are involved in the experiences offered to tourists. Therefore, destination organizations have to work together, in co-ordination and co-operation, to foster the desired loyalty objective. That loyalty can be enhanced by relationship marketing–based tools and the factors generating loyal customers. All facets of the strategy must be co-ordinated to create a positive post-purchase behaviour. An increase in the number of tourists loyal to a destination will improve its competitiveness and raise tourism-generated revenues.

## 11.6.   Limitations/Future Research Recommendations

The main limitations of this study result from the difficulty in conducting a comprehensive review. The literature on tourism management and marketing is highly concentrated in specific tourism-related publications, yet also widely dispersed throughout business management and marketing journals. Other limitations arose out of possible errors in subjectivity during the literature search, that is, in the process of identifying documents of interest or otherwise discarding them. At all times, the goal was to avoid errors by strictly following processes. Future research should focus on correcting any errors and expanding this topic.

Regarding future lines of research, it seems of interest to empirically validate not only the proposed model but also its application to different types of tourism. Although tourism is a high-contact service, there are very different types of tourism, namely rural tourism and luxury tourism. Therefore, it would be interesting to analyse how loyalty emerges in each type of tourism. Another focus of study could approach the loyalty construct and its dimensionality in different types of destinations, accommodations and tourism products, as Li and Petrick (2008b) did with cruise tourism. The goal should be to take advantage of past research and surpass the shortcomings in the literature, and at the same time provide relationship strategy management tools for tourism companies and destinations.

# References

Aksu, A. (2006). Gap analysis in customer loyalty: A research in 5 star hotels in the Antalya region of Turkey. *Quality & Quantity, 40*(2), 187–205. doi: 10.1007/s11135-005-5357-y

Alegre, J., & Cladera, M. (2006). Repeat visitation in mature sun and sand holiday destinations. *Journal of Travel Research, 44*(3), 288–297. doi: 10.1177/0047287505279005

Alegre, J., & Cladera, M. (2009). Analysing the effect of satisfaction and previous visits on tourist intentions to return. *European Journal of Marketing, 43*(5–6), 670–685.

Alegre, J., & Juaneda, C. (2006). Destination loyalty, consumers' economic behavior. *Annals of Tourism Research, 33*(3), 684–706. doi: 10.1016/j.annals.2006.03.014

Alén, M. E., & Fraiz, J. A. (2006). Evaluación de la relación existente entre la calidad de servicio, la satisfacción y las intenciones de comportamiento en el ámbito del turismo termal. *Revista Europea de Dirección y Economía de la Empresa, 15*(3), 171–184.

Alén, M. E., Rodríguez, L., & Fraiz, J. A. (2007). Assessing tourist behavioral intentions through perceived service quality and customer satisfaction. *Journal of Business Research, 60*(2), 153–160. doi: 10.1016/j.jbusres.2006.10.014

Alexandris, K., Kouthouris, C., & Meligdis, A. (2006). Increasing customers' loyalty in a skiing resort: The contribution of place attachment and service quality. *International Journal of Contemporary Hospitality Management, 18*(5), 414–425. doi: 10.1108/09596110610673547

Anuwichanont, J., & Mechinda, P. (2009). The impact of perceived value on spa loyalty and its moderating effect of destination equity. *Journal of Business & Economics Research, 7*(12), 73–89. Retrieved from http://journals.cluteonline.com/index.php/JBER/article/view/2368/2416.

Back, K. J. (2001). *The effects of image congruence on customer satisfaction and brand loyalty in the lodging industry.* Doctoral thesis, Pennsylvania State University, PA.

Bai, B., Hu, C., & Jang, S. (2006). Examining e-relationship marketing features on hotel websites. *Journal of Travel & Tourism Marketing, 21*(2/3), 33–48. doi: 10.1300/J073v21n02_03

Baloglu, S., Pekcan, A., Chen, S. L., & Santos, J. (2003). The relationship between destination performance, overall satisfaction, and behavioural intention for distinct segments. *Journal of Quality Assurance in Hospitality & Tourism, 4*(3/4), 149–165. doi: 10.1300/J162v04n03_10

Barroso, C., Martín, E., & Martín, D. (2007). The influence of market heterogeneity on the relationship between a destination's image and tourists' future behaviour. *Tourism Management, 28*(1), 175–187. doi: 10.1016/j.tourman.2005.11.013

Bendapudi, N., & Berry, L. (1997). Customers' motivations for maintaining relationships with service providers. *Journal of Retailing, 73*(1), 15–37. doi: 10.1016/S0022-4359(97)90013-0

Berry, L. (2000). Growing interest, emerging perspectives. In J. N. Sheth & A. Parvatiyar (Eds.), *Handbook of relationship marketing* (pp. 149–170). Thousand Oaks, CA: Sage Publications.

Bigné, J. E. (1996). Turismo y marketing en España. Análisis del estado de la cuestión y perspectivas de futuro. *Estudios Turísticos, 129*, 105–127.

Bigné, J. E. (1999). El análisis de contenido. In F. J. Sarabia (Ed.), *Metodología para la investigación en marketing y dirección de Empresas* (pp. 255–271). Madrid: Pirámide.

Bigné, J. E. (2004). Nuevas orientaciones del marketing turístico, de la imagen de destinos a la fidelización de los turistas. *Papeles de Economía Española, 102,* 221–235.

Bigné, J. E., & Andreu, L. (2004). Modelo cognitivo-afectivo de la satisfacción en servicios de ocio y turismo. *Cuadernos de Economía y Dirección de la Empresa, 21,* 89–120. Retrieved from http://www.acede.org/fotos/pdf/art102_21_05.pdf

Bigné, J. E., & Andreu, L. (2005). Emociones, satisfacción y lealtad de visitantes de museos interactivos. *Revista Europea de Dirección y Economía de la Empresa, 14*(2), 177–190.

Bigné, J. E., Andreu, L., Sánchez, I., & Alvarado, A. (2008). Investigación internacional en marketing turístico: Análisis de contenido sobre temas y metodologías. *Pasos, Revista de Turismo y Patrimonio Cultural, 6*(3), 391–398. Retrieved from http://www.pasosonline.org/ Publicados/6308/PS0308_1.pdf

Bigné, J. E., Sánchez, M. I., & Sánchez, J. (2001). Tourism image, evaluation variables and after purchase behaviour: Inter-relationship. *Tourism Management, 22*(6), 607–616. doi: 10.1016/S0261-5177(01)00035-8

Bigné, J. E., Sánchez, M. I., & Sanz, S. (2005). Relationships among residents' image, evaluation of the stay and post-purchase behavior. *Journal of Vacation Marketing, 11*(4), 291–299. doi: 10.1177/1356766705056626

Bowen, J. T., & Chen, S. L. (2001). The relationship between customer loyalty and customer satisfaction. *International Journal of Contemporary Hospitality Management, 13*(4/5), 213–219. doi: 10.1108/09596110110395893

Buracom, K. (2002). *The relationship between service quality and customer satisfaction in the formation of customer loyalty.* Doctoral thesis, University of South Australia, Adelaide, South Australia.

Chen, C., & Tsai, D. (2007). How destination image and evaluative factors affect behavioral intentions. *Tourism Management, 28*(4), 1115–1122. doi: 10.1016/j.tourman.2006.07.007

Chen, J. S., & Gursoy, D. (2001). An investigation of tourists' destination loyalty and preferences. *International Journal of Contemporary Hospitality Management, 13*(2), 79–85. doi: 10.1108/09596110110381870

Chi, C. G. Q. (2005). *A study of developing destination loyalty model.* Doctoral thesis, Oklahoma State University, OK.

Chi, C. G. Q., & Qu, H. (2008). Examining the structural relationships of destination image, tourist satisfaction and destination loyalty: An integrated approach. *Tourism Management, 29*(4), 624–636. doi: 10.1016/j.tourman.2007.06.007

Chitty, B., Ward, S., & Chua, C. (2007). An application of the ECSI model as a predictor of satisfaction and loyalty for backpacker hostels. *Marketing Intelligence & Planning, 25*(6), 563–580. doi: 10.1108/02634500710819941

Choi, T. Y., & Chu, R. (2001). Determinants of hotel guests' satisfaction and repeat patronage in the Hong Kong hotel industry. *The International Journal of Hospitality Management, 20*(3), 231–306. doi: 10.1016/S0278-4319(01)00006-8

Christopher, M., Payne, A., & Ballantyne, D. (1994). *Marketing relacional, integrando la calidad, el servicio al cliente y el marketing.* Madrid: Ediciones Díaz de Santos.

Cladera, M. C. (2007). *La repetición de la visita como variable clave en los destinos turísticos maduros.* Doctoral thesis, Universidad de les Illes Balears.

Dunn, G., Baloglu, S., Brewer, P., & Qu, H. (2009). Consumer e-loyalty to online travel intermediaries. *Journal of Quality Assurance in Hospitality & Tourism, 10*(1), 1–22. doi: 10.1080/1528008080802713751

Faullant, R., Matzler, K., & Füller, J. (2008). The impact of satisfaction and image on loyalty: The case of Alpine ski resort. *Managing Service Quality, 18*(2), 163–178. doi: 10.1108/09604520810859210

Fyall, A., Callod, C., & Edwards, B. (2003). Relationship marketing, the challenge for destinations. *Annals of Tourism Research, 30*(3), 644–659.

Gallarza, M. G., & Gil, I. (2006). Value dimensions, perceived value, satisfaction and loyalty: An investigation of university students' travel behaviour. *Tourism Management, 27*(3), 437–452. doi: 10.1016/j.tourman.2004.12.002

Ganesan, S. (1994). Determinants of long-term orientation in buyer–seller relationships. *Journal of Marketing, 58*(2), 1–19. doi: 10.2307/1252265

Gould-Williams, J. (1999). The impact of employee performance cues on guest loyalty, perceived value and service quality. *Service Industries Journal, 19*(3), 97–118. doi: 10.1080/02642069900000032

Grönroos, C. (1999). Relationship marketing: Challenges for the organization. *Journal of Business Research, 46*(3), 327–335. doi: 10.1016/S0148-2963(98)00030-7

Hernández, L., Solis, M. M., Moliner, M. A., & Sánchez, J. (2006). Tourism destination image, satisfaction and loyalty: A study in Ixtapa-Zihuatanejo, Mexico. *Tourism Geographies, 8*(4), 343–358. doi: 10.1080/14616680600922039

Hernández, R., Fernández, C., & Baptista, P. (2007). *Fundamentos de metodología de la investigación*. Madrid: McGraw-Hill.

Hu, H. H., Kandampully, J., & Juwaheer, T. D. (2009). Relationships and impacts of service quality, perceived value, customer satisfaction, and image: An empirical study. *The Service Industries Journal, 29*(2), 111–125. doi: 10.1080/02642060802292932

Huang, H. H., & Chiu, C. K. (2006). Exploring customer satisfaction, trust and destination loyalty in tourism. *Journal of American Academy of Business, 10*(1), 156–159. doi: 10.1002/jtr.731

Hui, T. K., Wan, D., & Ho, A. (2007). Tourists' satisfaction, recommendation and revisiting Singapore. *Tourism Management, 28*(4), 965–975. doi: 10.1016/j.tourman.2006.08.008

Hunt, S. D., Arnett, D. B., & Madhavaram, S. (2006). The explanatory foundations of relationship marketing theory. *Journal of Business & Industrial Marketing, 21*(2), 72–87. doi: 10.1108/10610420610651296

Hunt, S. D., & Morgan, R. M. (1994). Relationship marketing in the area of network competition. *Marketing Management, 3*(1), 19–28. Retrieved from http://proquest.umi.com/pqdweb?did=881906&sid=1&Fmt=3&clientId=21152&RQT=309&VName=PQD

Jang, S., & Feng, R. (2007). Temporal destination revisit intention: The effects of novelty seeking and satisfaction. *Tourism Management, 28*(2), 580–590. doi: 10.1016/j.tourman.2006.04.024

Johnson, M. D., Herrmann, A., & Huber, F. (2006). The evolution of loyalty intentions. *Journal of Marketing, 70*(2), 122–132. doi: 10.1509/jmkg.70.2.122

Kan, T. C., Yen, T. F., & Huan, T. C. (2009). Managing quality to influence loyalty. *Anatolia: An International Journal of Tourism & Hospitality Research, 20*(1), 75–85.

Kandampully, J., & Suhartanto, D. (2000). Customer loyalty in the hotel industry: The role of customer satisfaction and image. *International Journal of Contemporary Hospitality Management, 12*(6), 346–351. doi: 10.1108/09596110010342559

Kandampully, J., & Suhartanto, D. (2002). The role of customer satisfaction and image in gaining customer loyalty in the hotel industry. *Journal of Hospitality & Leisure Marketing, 10*(2), 3–25. doi: 10.1300/J150v10n01_02

Kao, C. (2007). *Travel motivation, satisfaction and destination loyalty: Taiwanese group package tourists visiting Australia school*. Doctoral thesis, University of Queensland, Queensland, Australia.

Kim, K. (2008). Analysis of structural equation model for the student pleasure travel market: Motivation involvement, satisfaction, and destination loyalty. *Journal of Travel & Tourism Marketing*, *24*(4), 297–313. doi: 10.1080/10548400802156802

Kim, W. G., & Cha, Y. (2002). Antecedents and consequences of relationship quality in hotel industry. *International Journal of Hospitality Management*, *21*(4), 301–471. doi: 10.1016/S0278-4319(02)00011-7

Kozak, M. (2001). Repeaters' behavior at two distinct destinations. *Annals of Tourism Research*, *28*(3), 784–807. doi: 10.1016/S0160-7383(00)00078-5

Lee, G. (2001). *Constructs of tourists' destination loyalty and market segmentation*. Doctoral thesis, Purdue University, IN.

Lee, J., Graefe, A. R., & Burns, R. C. (2004). Service quality, satisfaction, and behavioral intention among forest visitors. *Journal of Travel & Tourism Marketing*, *17*(1), 73–82. doi: 10.1300/J073v17n01_05

Lee, J., Graefe, A. R., & Burns, R. C. (2007). Examining the antecedents of destination loyalty in a forest setting. *Leisure Sciences*, *29*(5), 463–481. doi: 10.1080/01490400701544634

Lee, T. H. (2009). A structural model to examine how destination image, attitude, and motivation affect the future behavior of tourists. *Leisure Sciences*, *31*(3), 215–236. doi: 10.1080/01490400902837787

Leverin, A., & Liljander, V. (2006). Does relationship marketing improve customer relationship satisfaction and loyalty?. *International Journal of Bank Marketing*, *24*(4), 232–251. doi: 10.1108/02652320610671333

Li, X. (2006). *Examining the antecedents and structure of customer loyalty in a tourism context*. Doctoral thesis, Texas A&M University, TX.

Li, X., & Petrick, J. F. (2008a). Examining the antecedents of brand loyalty from an investment model perspective. *Journal of Travel Research*, *47*(1), 25–34. doi: 10.1177/0047287507312409

Li, X., & Petrick, J. F. (2008b). Reexamining the dimensionality of brand loyalty: A case of the cruise industry. *Journal of Travel & Tourism Marketing*, *25*(1), 68–85. doi: 10.1080/10548400802164913

Li, X., Petrick, J. F., & Zhouk, Y. (2007). Towards a conceptual framework of tourists' destination knowledge and loyalty. *Journal of Quality Assurance in Hospitality & Tourism*, *8*(3), 79–96. doi: 10.1080/15280080802080474

Lin, C. H. (2005). *Relationship between guest perceptions of service quality and customer loyalty in the hotel industry in south Florida*. Doctoral thesis, Lynn University, FL.

Liu, Y. (2007). The long-term impact of loyalty programs on consumer purchase behavior and loyalty. *Journal of Marketing*, *71*(4), 19–35. Retrieved from http://www.yupingliu.com/files/papers/liu_loyalty_program_effects.pdf.

Lombard, M. R., & Steyn, T. F. J. (2008). The relationship marketing practices of travel agencies in the Western Cape province. *South African Journal of Business Management*, *39*(4), 15–26. Retrieved from http://media.web.britannica.com/ebsco/pdf/729/35579729.pdf.

Loureiro, S. M., & Miranda, F. J. (2006). Calidad, satisfacción y fidelidad en el turismo rural: Un análisis hispano-portugués. *Papers de Turisme*, *40*, 49–66.

Loureiro, S. M., & Miranda, F. J. (2008). The importance of quality satisfaction, trust, and image in relation to rural tourist loyalty. *Journal of Travel & Tourism Marketing*, *25*(2), 117–136. doi: 10.1080/10548400802402321

Martín, D. (2005). *Determinantes estratégicos de la fidelidad del turista en destinos maduros*. Doctoral thesis, Universidad de La Laguna.

Martín, E. (2005). *Las corrientes de investigación dominantes en marketing en la última década.* Barcelona: Publicaciones de la Real Academia de Ciencias Económicas y Financieras.

Martínez, F., Novello, S., & Murias, P. (2009). Análisis de la lealtad de los turistas que visitan la ciudad de Santiago de Compostela. *Revista Galega de Economía, 18*(2), 1–15.

Matzler, K., Füller, J., & Faullant, R. (2007). Customer satisfaction and loyalty to Alpine ski resorts: The moderating effect of lifestyle, spending and customers' skiing skills. *The International Journal of Tourism Research, 9*(6), 409–421. doi: 10.1002/jtr.613

McKercher, B., Denizci-Guillet, B., & Ng, E. (2011). Rethinking Loyalty. *Annals of Tourism Research.* doi:10.1016/j.annals.2011.08.005.

Mechinda, P., Serirat, S., Anuwichanont, J., & Gulid, N. (2010). An examination of tourists' loyalty towards medical tourism in Pattaya, Thailand. *The International Business & Economic Research Journal, 9*(1), 55–70. Retrieved from http://journals.cluteonline.com/index.php/IBER/article/view/508/495

Mechinda, P., Serirat, S., & Gulid, N. (2009). An examination of tourists' attitudinal and behavioral loyalty: Comparison between domestic and international tourists. *Journal of Vacation Marketing, 15*(2), 129–148. doi: 10.1177/1356766708100820

Meyer-Waarden, L. (2008). The influence of loyalty programme membership on customer purchase behaviour. *European Journal of Marketing, 42*(1/2), 87–114. doi: 10.1108/03090560810840925

Morgan, R. M., & Hunt, S. D. (1999). Relationship-based competitive advantage: The role of relationship marketing in marketing strategy. *Journal of Business Research, 46*(3), 281–290. doi: 10.1016/S0148-2963(98)00035-6

Murphy, P., Pritchard, M. P., & Smith, B. (2000). The destination product and its impact on traveller perceptions. *Tourism Management, 21*(1), 43–52. doi: 10.1016/S0261-5177(99)00080-1

Ndubisi, N. O. (2007). Relationship marketing and customer loyalty. *Marketing Intelligence & Planning, 25*(1), 98–106. doi: 10.1108/02634500710722425

Oh, H., Kim, B. Y., & Shin, J. H. (2004). Hospitality and tourism marketing: Recent developments in research and future directions. *International Journal of Hospitality Management, 23*(5), 425–447. doi: 10.1016/j.ijhm.2004.10.004

Oliver, R. (1999). Whence consumer loyalty? *Journal of Marketing, 63*(4), 33–44. doi: 10.2307/1252099

Palmer, A. J. (1994). Relationship marketing: Back to basics? *Journal of Marketing Management, 10*(7), 571–579.

Palmer, A. J., & Mayer, R. (1996). A conceptual evaluation of the multiple dimensions of relationship marketing. *Journal of Strategic Marketing, 4*(4), 207–220. doi: 10.1080/09652549600000005

Payne, A. (2000). Relationship marketing, the U.K. perspective. In J. N. Sheth & A. Parvatiyar (Eds.), *Handbook of relationship marketing* (pp. 38–67). Thousand Oaks, CA: Sage Publications.

Petrick, J. F. (2004). The roles of quality, value, and satisfaction in predicting cruise passengers' behavioural intentions. *Journal of Travel Research, 42*(4), 397–407. doi: 10.1177/0047287504263037

Petrick, J. F., & Backman, S. J. (2002). An examination of the construct of perceived value for the prediction of golf travelers' intention to revisit. *Journal of Travel Research, 41*(1), 38–45. doi: 10.1177/004728750204100106

Petrick, J. F., Morais, D. D., & Norman, W. (2001). An examination of the determinants of entertainment vacationers' intentions to revisit. *Journal of Travel Research*, *40*(1), 41–48. doi: 10.1177/004728750104000106

Pike, S. D. (2004). *Destination marketing organisations.* Amsterdam, The Netherlands: Elsevier.

Pike, S. D. (2008). *Destination marketing: An integrated marketing communication approach.* Burlington, MA: Butterworth-Heinemann.

Prayag, G. (2008). Image, satisfaction and loyalty — The case of Cape Town. *Anatolia: An International Journal of Tourism & Hospitality Research*, *19*(2), 205–224.

Reichheld, F. F. (1994). Loyalty and the renaissance of marketing. *Marketing Management*, *2*(4), 10–22. Retrieved from http://proquest.umi.com/pqdweb?did=881899&sid=1& Fmt=3&clientId=21152&RQT=309&VName=PQD

Reichheld, F. F., & Sasser, E. (1990). Zero defections: Quality comes to services. *Harvard Business Review*, *68*(5), 105–111.

Rodríguez del Bosque, I., & San Martín, H. (2008). Tourist satisfaction, a cognitive–affective model. *Annals of Tourism Research*, *35*(2), 551–573. doi: 10.1016/j.annals.2008.02.006

San Martín, H. (2005). *Estudio de la imagen de destino turístico y el proceso global de satisfacción: adopción de un enfoque integrador.* Doctoral thesis, Universidad de Cantabria.

Sanz, S. (2008). Imagen global e intenciones futuras de comportamiento del turista de segunda residencia. *Revista Europea de Dirección y Economía de la Empresa*, *17*(4), 95–114. Retrieved from http://www.aedem-virtual.com/articulos/123686269200.pdf

Saren, M., & Tzokas, N. (1998). Some dangerous axioms of relationship marketing. *Journal of Strategic Marketing*, *6*(3), 187–196. doi: 10.1080/096525498346612

Shammout, A. B. (2007). *Evaluating an extended relationship marketing model for Arab guests of five-star hotels.* Doctoral thesis, Victoria University, Australia.

Skogland, I., & Siguaw, J. A. (2004). Are your satisfied customers loyal?. *Cornell Hotel and Restaurant Administration Quarterly*, *45*(3), 221–234. doi: 10.1177/0010880404265231

Sophonsiri, V. (2008). *Developing host–guest relationships in Thai tourist resorts.* Doctoral thesis, Victoria University, Australia.

Tian-Cole, S. T., & Crompton, J. L. (2003). A conceptualisation of the relationships between service quality and visitor satisfaction, and their links to destination selection. *Leisure Studies*, *22*(1), 65–80. doi: 10.1080/02614360306572

Tian-Cole, S. T., Crompton, J. L., & Willson, V. L. (2002). An empirical investigation of the relationships between service quality, satisfaction and behavioral intentions among visitors to a wildlife refuge. *Journal of Leisure Research*, *34*(1), 1–24. Retrieved from http://rptsweb.tamu.edu/crompton/Crompton/Articles/7.3.pdf.

Tsaur, S. H., Chiu, Y. C., & Huang, C. H. (2002). Determinants of guest loyalty to international tourist hotels – A neural network approach. *Tourism Management*, *23*(4), 397–405. doi: 10.1016/S0261-5177(01)00097-8

Um, S., Chon, K., & Ro, Y. (2006). Antecedents of revisit intention. *Annals of Tourism Research*, *33*(4), 1141–1158. doi: 10.1016/j.annals.2006.06.003

Vale, V., Moutinho, V., & Vale, J. (2010). Preditores e mediadores da satisfação e fidelização no destino turístico: um modelo cognitivo integrado. *Revista Turismo & Desenvolvimento* [*Journal of Tourism and Development*], *13/14*(1), 299–311.

Voces, C. (2005). *Modelización de la calidad de servicio y la lealtad del cliente en hostelería.* Doctoral thesis, Universidad de Santiago de Compostela.

Yen, T. F., Liu, H. H., & Tuan, C. L. (2009). Managing relationship efforts to influence loyalty: An empirical study on the sun ling sea forest and recreational park, Taiwan. *International Journal of Organizational Innovation*, *2*(2), 179–194. Retrieved from http://

www.ijoi-online.org/attachments/article/21/Microsoft%20Word%20-%20FINAL%20ISSUE %20VOL%202%20NUM%202%20FALL%202009.pdf#page=175.

Yoon, Y., & Uysal, M. (2005). An examination of the effects of motivation and satisfaction on destination loyalty: A structural model. *Tourism Management*, *26*(1), 45–56. doi: 10.1016/ j.tourman.2003.08.016

Yüksel, A., & Yüksel, F. (2007). Shopping risk perceptions: Effects on tourists' emotions, satisfaction and expressed loyalty intentions. *Tourism Management*, *28*(3), 703–713. doi: 10.1016/j.tourman.2006.04.025

Yüksel, A., Yüksel, F., & Bilis, Y. (2010). Destination attachment: Effects on customer satisfaction and cognitive, affective and conative loyalty. *Tourism Management*, *31*(2), 274–284. doi: 10.1016/j.tourman.2009.03.007

Zins, A. (2001). Relative attitudes and commitment in customer loyalty models: Some experiences from the commercial airline industry. *International Journal of Service Industry Management*, *12*(3), 269–294. doi: 10.1108/EUM0000000005521

Chapter 12

# Familiarity and Experience in Tourist Satisfaction and Loyalty Development

*Ramón Rufín Moreno, Cayetano Medina Molina, José Luis Roldán Salgueiro and Manuel Rey Moreno*

## 12.1. Introduction

Satisfaction and loyalty have become two of the main topics found in the literature on tourism marketing. It is generally assumed that should the managers of tourism organizations know the process of satisfaction and loyalty development, they would succeed in promoting a tourist destination, a hotel or any other activity pertaining to the tourism industry.

Several authors suggest that the best way to predict future consumer behaviour is to analyse former behaviour, given that while predictions made by consumers may prove to be fairly vague and superficial, achieved performance can cause a revision of those predictions and hence of expectations as well (Campo-Martínez, Garau-Vadell, & Martínez-Ruiz, 2010; Mazurski, 1989).

One of the concepts that explain the changes experienced by consumers based on past behaviour is the development of familiarity, which is the concept with the strongest influence on tourists' decision making (Baloglu, 2001; Bargeman & Van der Poel, 2006; Desai & Hoyer, 2000) because its increase reduces uncertainty concerning future purchases (Flavián, Guinaliu, & Gurrea, 2006).

In certain cases the terms familiarity and experience are used interchangeably given their similarities (Zhang, Ghorbani, & Cohen, 2007), but it is important to consider whether choosing certain formulas for their measurement would have an effect on the relationships that are being examined here. Therefore, the present chapter addresses the following issues:

- The role of familiarity/experience in the process of satisfaction and loyalty development
- The hypothetic differences between both constructs — familiarity and experience — when they are used in explaining tourist behaviour

## 12.2.   Satisfaction, Adjusted Expectations and Loyalty

### 12.2.1.   Cognitive Elements in Satisfaction Development: The Adjusted Expectations

Studying and analysing consumer satisfaction requires knowledge of the underlying processes behind its formation and particularly its relationship with expectations and disconfirmation (Oliver, 1997; Pieters, Koelemeijer, & Roest, 1995).

Most studies that analyse satisfaction development are based on the *expectancy disconfirmation paradigm*. According to Oliver (1980), consumers form their expectations before purchasing the good or service. After its use, they become aware of the achieved performance, and that performance level is compared to prior expectations. Thus, disconfirmation is usually measured according to the perceived discrepancies between the consumer's prior expectations and the performance obtained from the product (Oliver & DeSarbo, 1988; Yi & La, 2004).

According to Oliver and DeSarbo (1988), in a sense, the disconfirmation paradigm stems from two theories that account for satisfaction development according to consumers' greater sensitivity to expectations (assimilation theory) (Anderson, 1973) or to expectancy disconfirmation (contrast theory) (Oliver, 1997). Along these lines, a causal relationship appears to exist between disconfirmation and satisfaction (Bigné, Andreu, & Gnoth, 2005; Bowen, 2001; De Rojas & Camarero, 2008; Szymanski & Henard, 2001). Research concerning the effect of disconfirmation on loyalty is limited, although it has been confirmed in some cases (Bigné et al., 2005).

Despite broad acceptance and use of the theories mentioned above, Johnson, Nader, and Fornell (1996) argue that they are not entirely applicable to complex and infrequent services, since in those cases consumers are often unable to remember their prior expectations after consuming the good or service because the achieved performance could have affected them (Oliver & Burke, 1999; Pieters & Zwick, 1993). Other authors argue that, as a consequence of the disconfirmation paradigm, satisfaction will inevitably increase when expectations are reduced (Mechinda, Serirat, Anuwichanont, & Gulid, 2010).

Given that consumers' expectations are constantly changing, explanatory models for satisfaction development have to take this situation into account (Johnson, Anderson, & Fornell, 1995; Yi & La, 2004). That is why the application of *predictive expectations* in such cases is widely criticized (Yüksel & Yüksel, 2001). If what we analyse are expectations once the customer is actually experiencing the product or service, we must bear in mind *adjusted expectations,* namely those that are updated according to the new information that is acquired and that are affected by the satisfaction experienced by the consumer (Yi & La, 2004).

Above and beyond the potential controversy regarding the appropriate terminology for referring to expectations that are considered at different times, this issue has two important implications. The first concerns the limitation involved in measuring the factors that generate expectations after a service is provided. This limitation is often mentioned as a concern by the authors themselves (Rodríguez & San Martín, 2008; Rodríguez, San Martín, & Collado, 2006), given that if what the applied behaviour models consider are predictive expectations, the data required for measuring them should be collected before the consumer experience takes place (Johnson et al., 1995). Secondly, the use of adjusted expectations to explain consumer behaviour instead of prior expectations is relevant given the differing ways in which both types of expectations establish their causal relationships with satisfaction and loyalty.

Although early studies analysing the relationship between adjusted expectations and satisfaction suggested the existence of no relationship whatsoever (Johnson et al., 1996; Pieters et al., 1995), others later confirmed that adjusted expectations mediated the effect of consumer satisfaction on future purchase intention (Rufin, Medina, & Rey, 2012; Yi & La, 2004). Therefore, if what we intend to do is include the notion of the dynamic effect of expectations adjustment in the explanatory models, those expectations cease to be an antecedent of satisfaction and instead mediate its impact on loyalty.

### 12.2.2. Satisfaction and Loyalty

All the definitions of *customer satisfaction* describe the formation of satisfaction as a process; they define the key variables and the mechanisms of interaction of those variables and recognize that satisfaction is the final step of a psychological process. It is perceived as the final result of all activities carried out during the process of purchase and consumption and not only of observation and or direct consumption of the product or service (Oliver, 1997). All the reviewed definitions maintain, in one way or another, that satisfaction implies (Millán & Esteban, 2004) the existence of an objective that the consumer wishes to reach; the attainment (satisfaction) of this objective can only be judged by taking a standard of comparison as a reference, and the evaluation process of satisfaction implies the intervention of at least two stimuli: a result and a reference or standard of comparison. Giese and Cote (2000) defined satisfaction as a summary affective response of varying intensity with a time-specific point of determination and limited duration directed toward focal aspects of product acquisition and/or consumption.

Although there are many definitions of loyalty, loyalty is generally regarded as 'a deeply held commitment to re-buy or re-patronize a preferred product (or) service consistency, thereby causing repetitive same brand or same brand set purchasing, despite situational influences and marketing efforts having the potential to cause switching behavior' (Oliver, 1997).

Generally, loyalty has been measured in one of the following ways (Jacoby & Chestnut, 1978): (1) the behavioural approach, (2) the attitudinal approach and (3) the composite approach. The behavioural approach is related to consumers' brand loyalty and has been operationally characterized as sequence purchase, proportion of patronage or probability of purchase. This loyalty measurement does not attempt to explain the factors that affect customer loyalty. Namely, tourist loyalty to the products or destinations may not be enough to explain why and how they are willing to revisit or recommend these to other potential tourists. In the attitudinal approach, based on consumer brand preferences or intention to buy, consumer loyalty is an attempt on the part of consumers to go beyond overt behaviour and express their loyalty in terms of psychological commitment or statement of preference. Tourists may have a favourable attitude toward a particular product or destination, and express their intention to purchase the product or visit the destination. Thus, loyalty measures consumers' strength of affection toward a brand or product. Lastly, the composite or combination approach is an integration of the behavioural and attitudinal approaches. It has been argued that customers who purchase and have loyalty to particular brands must have a positive attitude toward those brands (Backman & Crompton, 1991; Yoon & Uysal, 2005).

*Repeat purchases or recommendations* to other people are most usually referred to as consumer loyalty in the marketing literature. In fact, customer loyalty is subdivided into two distinct types. The first of these are behaviour factors, which are due to strong loyalty and repeat purchases, etc. The second are attitude factors, which include brand preference, commitment and '*intention to buy*' (Lee, Lee, & Feick, 2001). The concept and degree of loyalty is one of the critical indicators used to measure the success of marketing strategy. Similarly, travel destinations can be considered as products, and tourists may revisit or recommend travel destinations to other potential tourists such as friends or relatives (Yoon & Uysal, 2005).

Researchers conduct new studies of loyalty by devoting more time to understanding customer satisfaction (Oliver, 1999). Both practitioners and academics understand that consumer loyalty and satisfaction are inextricably intertwined. In their efforts to elucidate the linkage between satisfaction and loyalty, many researchers have attempted to determine whether loyalty responses are related to the satisfaction component. Oliver (1999) insists that satisfaction is a necessary step in the formation of loyalty.

Several studies on the subject of tourist destinations confirm that satisfaction has a significant effect on loyalty (Chen & Tsai, 2007; Chi & Qu, 2008; Murphy, Pritchard, & Smith, 2000; Zabkar, Brencic, & Dmitrovic, 2010). However, although that relationship may appear to be intuitive, it varies significantly under different conditions, and thus we cannot assume that satisfaction necessarily implies revisit intention (Zeithaml, Berry, & Parasuraman, 1993). By the same token, it is important to consider the controversy as to whether satisfaction acts as an antecedent in the short run, but not in the mid- or long run, when novelty is the variable with the highest impact (Jang & Feng, 2007), or whether it actually has a short-term effect, whereas satisfaction has an effect in the long term (Bigné, Mattila, & Andreu, 2008). The origin of these differences can be traced back to the fact that visitors who revisit the destination in the short run are often less satisfied by perceived quality, and those who revisit show higher satisfaction levels (Tsiotsou & Vasioti, 2006a).

Jones and Sasser (1995) suggested that not all satisfied customers remain loyal, and Oliver (1997) argues that satisfaction is only the first step towards developing loyalty. Therefore, is it a necessary but not sufficient condition for revisiting a destination in the case considered here (Hong, Lee, Lee, & Jang, 2009). The reason for this phenomenon can be found in the fact that the relationship is moderated by certain consumer characteristics (Barroso, Martín, & Martín, 2007; Bigné et al., 2008; Sirayaka & Woodside, 2005), whereas demographic variables such as age and education can be good predictors of the level of satisfaction (Tsiotsou & Vasioti, 2006b).

Oliver (1999) defined loyalty as 'a deeply-held predisposition to repatronize a preferred brand or service consistently in the future, thereby causing repetitive same brand purchasing, despite situational influences and marketing efforts having the potential to cause switching behavior'. Attitudinal loyalty towards a destination is mainly driven by satisfaction, trust, perceived value, destination familiarity, as well as destination image, whereas behavioural loyalty is driven by familiarity (Mechinda et al., 2010; Mechinda, Serirat, & Gulid, 2009).

Since the personal feature with the strongest influence on decision making is the consumer's familiarity or level of experience (Bargeman & Van der Poel, 2006), which influences both the length of the decision-making process and the evaluations that are made (Söderlund, 2002), it is important to consider whether familiarity plays a moderating role in explanatory models for satisfaction and loyalty development.

## 12.3. Familiarity, Experience and Hindsight Bias

It is particularly relevant to analyse the concept of familiarity in the context of tourist destination visits because it allows for a different perception of its attributes (Brunner, Stöcklin, & Opwis, 2008). Destination familiarity is regarded as the consumer's perception of how much she or he knows about the attributes of the various choice alternatives being considered (Moorthy, Ratchford, & Talukdar, 1997). Familiarity with a destination can positively influence the perception of that destination — or of products/services provided by a particular destination (Mechinda et al., 2010). It is also important to bear in mind that familiarity has an effect on the sources of information that are used, since first-time visitors are more reliant on external sources such as informative brochures or thematic TV channels (Baloglu, 2001; Chen & Gursoy, 2004), whereas tourists revisiting a destination tend to rely on personal references and their own experience (Chen & Gursoy, 2004; Fuchs & Reichel, 2011). In addition, tourists returning to a destination exhibit different behaviour on their repeat visits, spending more money, participating in fewer activities and having longer visits (Lehto, O'Leary, & Morrison, 2004; Oppermann, 1997), independently of the time that may have elapsed since the prior experiences occurred (Pearce & Kang, 2009).

Although familiarity with a tourist destination has generally been measured as number of prior visits (Baloglu, 2001; Pearce & Kang, 2009) or to the degree of familiarity with the service provider that is perceived by the consumer (Flavián et al., 2006; Ha & Jang, 2010), the concept has been subject to a broad range of interpretations. When it is analysed in terms of services, familiarity reflects different situations ranging from prior encounters with the provider of the same or other services, to knowledge of the service based on sources of information (Alba & Hutchison, 1987; Söderlund, 2002), which leads to its conceptualization according to two fundamental dimensions: frequency of use and knowledge of the service (Baloglu, 2001).

In keeping with the concept's multiple interpretations, it is important to note that sometimes the terms 'familiarity' and 'experience' are used interchangeably (Zhang et al., 2007). Despite major similarities in their meaning, the formula used for their measurement differs. Hence, in the tourist sector, and depending on each specific case, what has been used to measure tourist experience is the number of trips per year (Söderlund & Gunnarson, 2000) or the number of hotel stays in the last two years (Hernández, Muñoz, & Santos, 2007).

The less experience tourists have, the more time and effort they will spend on seeking information (Bargeman & Van der Poel, 2006; Li, Cheng, Kim, & Petrick, 2008). However, the more experienced customers become, the less their evaluations are explained by previous attitudes (Hernández et al., 2007).

To determine the influence of familiarity and experience on the variables we examined, we must analyse their impact on the way expectations are adjusted. Although the expectations disconfirmation model implicitly assumes that people recall their original expectations (Oliver, 1980), the recollection of those predictions and the intentions associated with them are systematically biased by the outcome achieved (Pieters, Baumgartner, & Bagozzi, 2006). All of this is due to the process known as *hindsight bias*, which refers to people's tendency to exaggerate their capacity to have anticipated an event's occurrence once they already know its outcome (Arkes, Guilmert, Faust, & Hart, 1988; Hawkins & Hastie, 1990). The hindsight bias phenomenon is particularly relevant for products with emotional significance, such as visits to tourist destinations, and hence disconfirmation is determined by the discrepancy between hindsight expectations and perceived performance rather than by a comparison with predictive expectations (Zwick, Pieters, & Baumgartner, 1995).

Although hindsight bias has been observed both in experienced and inexperienced consumers alike (Arkes et al., 1988), its impact on expectations decreases as consumer familiarity grows (Christensen-Szalanski & William, 1991). It has been suggested that experienced individuals trust their own disconfirmation judgment more than inexperienced consumers, since their greater knowledge enables them to make more precise comparisons (Morgan, Attaway, & Griffin, 1996). Based on this information, the following hypotheses are posited.

**H$_{1a}$:** *Tourists' familiarity moderates the effect of disconfirmation on satisfaction.*

**H$_{2a}$:** *Tourists' experience moderates the effect of disconfirmation on satisfaction.*

**H$_{1b}$:** *Tourists' familiarity moderates the effect of disconfirmation on loyalty.*

**H$_{2b}$:** *Tourists' experience moderates the effect of disconfirmation on loyalty.*

Several studies suggest that familiarity moderates the relationship between satisfaction and loyalty (Ha & Jang, 2010; Kerstetter & Cho, 2004). Söderlund (2002) suggests that consumers who are familiar with a product tend to judge new experiences based on their prior expertise, making a more elaborate evaluation and having a greater awareness of their satisfaction. A high level of familiarity with the service is associated with more extreme responses from consumers in terms of satisfaction and repurchases intention (Li et al., 2008; Söderlund, 2002). Flavián et al. (2006) suggest that familiarity only affects loyalty among more experienced consumers. Conversely, Brunner et al. (2008) suggest that loyalty among scarcely experienced consumers is based to a greater extent on satisfaction. Based on this information, we posit the following:

$H_{1c}$: *Tourists' familiarity moderates the effect of satisfaction on loyalty.*

$H_{2c}$: *Tourists' experience moderates the effect of satisfaction on loyalty.*

Perceived performance systematically biases the recollection of prior expectations, and thus Oliver (1980) suggests the existence of a *revised attitude* based on achieved satisfaction, where the existence of a sequence between satisfaction, hindsight and post-purchase intention can be established. In fact, customers' expectations are the basis for their subsequent decisions (Pieters et al., 2006), which must be taken into account when considering the underlying relationships (Zwick et al., 1995). However, since familiarity has a decisive effect on the formation of expectations (Rodríguez et al., 2006), we posit the following (Figure 12.1):

$H_{1d}$: *Tourists' familiarity moderates the effect of satisfaction on adjusted expectations.*

$H_{2d}$: *Tourists' experience moderates the effect of satisfaction on adjusted expectations.*

$H_{1e}$: *Tourists' familiarity moderates the effect of adjusted expectations on loyalty.*

$H_{2e}$: *Tourists' experience moderates the effect of adjusted expectations on loyalty.*

## 12.4. Empirical Study

### 12.4.1. Measurement Scales and Field Work

In order to test the model explained in the present chapter, a field study was carried out in the cities of Cartagena de Indias (Colombia) and Seville (Spain) over the last

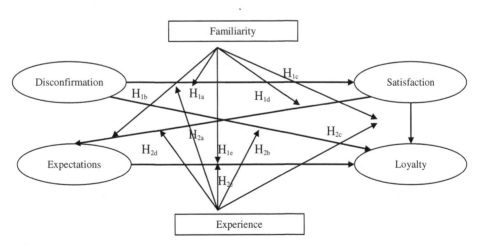

Figure 12.1: Research model.

quarter of 2008, with a survey questionnaire submitted to tourists in the city's old quarters. A total of 652 valid questionnaires were obtained.

The questionnaire used a seven-point Likert scale. Measurement of the satisfaction construct was drawn from Oliver (1997); loyalty was measured according to the scale proposed by Zeithaml et al. (1993); the scale for expectations was drawn from Murphy et al. (2000) and the scale for disconfirmation was the one used by Oliver and Burke (1999). Lastly, while familiarity was measured with a dichotomous variable (0 = destination not visited previously, 1 = destination visited previously), experience was measured according to the number of times the respondent travelled each year.

### 12.4.2. Analysis

The scales initially proposed for performing the statistical analysis were adaptations of scales that had been validated in previous studies and whose content we therefore could assume to be valid.

The statistical analysis of the behaviour of the constructs in the model was performed with variance-based structural equation modelling (SEM) (Reinartz, Haenlein, & Henseler, 2009) by applying the LISREL procedure. The maximum likelihood (ML) method of estimation and the two-stage testing process were developed with LISREL 8.53 (Jöreskog & Sörbom, 1996). Correlation matrices and standard deviations were used to test the hypothesized model. SEM is designed to evaluate how well a proposed conceptual model that contains observed indicators and hypothetical constructs explains or fits the collected data, and it also provides the ability to measure or specify the causal relationships among sets of unobserved (latent) variables, while describing the amount of unexplained variance (Figure 12.2).

The *t*-values of all the items under study were significant (Table 12.1), so these items were all kept to be used in the subsequent analysis (Jöreskog, 1993).

Covariance among the constructs that were included in the models, and the goodness of fit indexes of the constructs themselves, were also analysed (Table 12.2).

To make the study easier to read, the model for tourists who had not visited the destination previously was called not familiar with the destination, the one for repeat visitors was called high familiarity, for those who travelled less than four times a year was called low experience and those who travelled four or more times were referred to as high experience.

There is a strong similarity between the data obtained in the four models. In all four cases, the relationships between disconfirmation and satisfaction, between satisfaction and expectations, and between satisfaction and loyalty are significant. The only difference arises in the relationship between disconfirmation and loyalty, which is significant only in the model that represents the behaviour of tourists with a low level of experience, yet does not prove significant for revisiting tourists, nor for those with low level of experience.

The ability to detect the presence or absence of differences between groups and to estimate the strength of moderating effects are important in studies attempting to

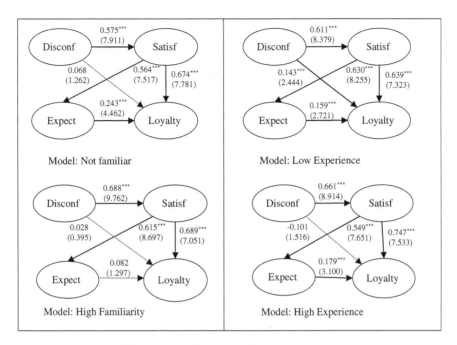

Figure 12.2: Structural model results.

show contingent effects (Qureshi & Compeau, 2009). The hypothesis in these types of multi-group models, aiming to compare the intensity of the differences between them, could actually be tested with a statistical comparison of the different path coefficients for the structural models for each one of the samples.

A multi-group analysis was also performed to find out if tourists' behaviour was consistent in the models in spite of measuring either familiarity or experience, since as indicated above both concepts are used sometimes as synonymous. For this purpose we applied the so-called between-group analysis using covariance-based SEM (Raykov & Marcoulides, 2006). This technique is referred as the covariance SEM approach (CSA). In CSA, measurement model invariance is tested first to see if the measurement models across the groups are comparable (Cheung & Rensvold, 2002). Once measurement equivalence is established or constrained to equality, the between-group structural equation model is tested. In the default model, all of the path coefficients are allowed to vary freely across the two groups (Qureshi & Compeau, 2009). Our findings show that there are no significant differences if one uses familiarity instead of experience in the models.

Several other conclusions can be drawn from this multi-group analysis. First and foremost, the existence of scarce differences in the behaviour of each one of the models in which familiarity and experience were analysed, based on the existence of prior visits or on the number of times the tourists travelled yearly. There is only one difference in each case. Thus, in terms of familiarity, it is the relationship between expectations and loyalty, which is stronger when the level of familiarity with the

Table 12.1:  Factor loading, standard error and t-value.

| | Not familiar with the destination | | | High familiarity | | | Low experience | | | High experience | | |
|---|---|---|---|---|---|---|---|---|---|---|---|---|
| | Loading | Standard error | t-value | Loading | Standard error | t-value | Loading | Standard error | t-value | Loading | Standard error | t-value |
| D1 | 0.720 | 0.051 | 14.160 | 0.644 | 0.054 | 11.867 | 0.583 | 0.052 | 11.185 | 0.789 | 0.0521 | 15.139 |
| D2 | 0.661 | 0.050 | 13.278 | 0.789 | 0.058 | 13.491 | 0.675 | 0.060 | 11.306 | 0.769 | 0.0475 | 16.170 |
| D3 | 0.675 | 0.056 | 11.965 | 0.805 | 0.053 | 15.298 | 0.770 | 0.058 | 13.351 | 0.710 | 0.0506 | 14.034 |
| D4 | 0.801 | 0.055 | 14.521 | 0.834 | 0.053 | 15.625 | 0.798 | 0.058 | 13.774 | 0.817 | 0.0515 | 15.844 |
| D5 | 0.790 | 0.054 | 14.539 | 0.778 | 0.052 | 15.104 | 0.758 | 0.058 | 13.148 | 0.794 | 0.0490 | 16.210 |
| D6 | 0.679 | 0.055 | 12.293 | 0.799 | 0.050 | 16.016 | 0.818 | 0.058 | 14.034 | 0.673 | 0.0461 | 14.589 |
| E1 | 0.790 | – | – | 0.883 | – | – | 0.809 | – | – | 0.862 | – | – |
| E2 | 0.726 | 0.059 | 12.250 | 0.749 | 0.062 | 12.121 | 0.667 | 0.066 | 10.177 | 0.843 | 0.0531 | 15.884 |
| E3 | 0.636 | 0.060 | 10.550 | 0.853 | 0.059 | 14.568 | 0.790 | 0.064 | 12.365 | 0.673 | 0.0556 | 12.104 |
| E4 | 0.713 | 0.056 | 12.733 | 0.895 | 0.055 | 16.391 | 0.797 | 0.058 | 13.780 | 0.811 | 0.0524 | 15.469 |
| E5 | 0.869 | 0.062 | 13.975 | 0.816 | 0.058 | 14.066 | 0.895 | 0.065 | 13.755 | 0.781 | 0.0541 | 14.451 |
| E6 | 0.688 | 0.055 | 12.507 | 0.767 | 0.056 | 13.817 | 0.846 | 0.059 | 14.343 | 0.606 | 0.0524 | 11.559 |
| S1 | 0.692 | – | – | 0.773 | – | – | 0.726 | – | – | 0.705 | – | – |
| S2 | 0.698 | 0.074 | 9.436 | 0.836 | 0.063 | 13.313 | 0.732 | 0.072 | 10.130 | 0.804 | 0.0711 | 11.303 |
| S3 | 0.817 | 0.074 | 11.004 | 0.727 | 0.066 | 11.012 | 0.810 | 0.074 | 10.934 | 0.746 | 0.0681 | 10.947 |
| S4 | 0.802 | 0.073 | 10.980 | 0.833 | 0.067 | 12.432 | 0.849 | 0.074 | 11.420 | 0.793 | 0.0691 | 11.477 |
| S5 | 0.752 | 0.073 | 10.339 | 0.820 | 0.066 | 12.403 | 0.830 | 0.074 | 11.270 | 0.736 | 0.0691 | 10.652 |
| C1 | 0.738 | – | – | 0.799 | – | – | 0.847 | – | – | 0.713 | – | – |
| C2 | 0.745 | 0.050 | 14.936 | 0.802 | 0.050 | 16.021 | 0.762 | 0.046 | 16.567 | 0.803 | 0.0533 | 15.057 |
| C3 | 0.736 | 0.050 | 14.850 | 0.877 | 0.046 | 18.860 | 0.865 | 0.049 | 17.566 | 0.737 | 0.0461 | 15.995 |
| C4 | 0.791 | 0.060 | 13.273 | 0.874 | 0.054 | 16.282 | 0.900 | 0.052 | 17.318 | 0.712 | 0.0611 | 11.638 |

Table 12.2: Covariance matrix of latent variables and goodness of fit of the models.

| | Satisfaction | Expectation | Loyalty | Disconfirmation |
|---|---|---|---|---|
| **Not familiar with the destination (NFI = 0.870; CFI = 0.886; RFI = 0.851; GFI = 0.727)** | | | | |
| Disconfirmation | **1.000** | – | – | – |
| Satisfaction | 0.564 | **1.000** | – | – |
| Expectation | 0.850 | 0.645 | **1.000** | – |
| Loyalty | 0.575 | 0.325 | 0.535 | **1.000** |
| **High familiarity (NFI = 0.914; CFI = 0.929; RFI = 0.902; GFI = 0.743)** | | | | |
| Disconfirmation | **1.000** | – | – | – |
| Satisfaction | 0.615 | **1.000** | – | – |
| Expectation | 0.759 | 0.517 | **1.000** | – |
| Loyalty | 0.688 | 0.423 | 0.537 | **1.000** |
| **Low experience (NFI = 0.915; CFI = 0.931; RFI = 0.903; GFI = 0.802)** | | | | |
| Disconfirmation | **1.000** | – | – | – |
| Satisfaction | 0.630 | **1.000** | – | – |
| Expectation | 0.827 | 0.617 | **1.000** | – |
| Loyalty | 0.611 | 0.385 | 0.595 | **1.000** |
| **High experience (NFI = 0.877; CFI = 0.891; RFI = 0.860; GFI = 0.670)** | | | | |
| Satisfaction | **1.000** | – | – | – |
| Expectation | 0.550 | **1.000** | – | – |
| Loyalty | 0.779 | 0.553 | **1.000** | – |
| Disconfirmation | 0.661 | 0.363 | 0.457 | **1.000** |

destination is low ($\chi^2_{185} = 248$). Conversely, in terms of experience, i.e. based on the number of times the tourists travelled yearly, the difference is found in the relationship between disconfirmation and loyalty ($\chi^2_{185} = 371$), the link being stronger in the case of those tourists with a low level of experience in travelling.

Although the variables that affect satisfaction and loyalty development in each case have been determined, to further pursue an analysis of the posited relationships, it is interesting to analyse the way in which the different variables influence loyalty, as a final dependent variable in the model. In order to do so, the origin of the explained variance of the loyalty construct was analysed to determine the extent to which the predictive variables contribute to its formation. The variance in an endogenous construct that is explained by another latent variable is determined by the absolute value of the result of multiplying the path coefficient by the corresponding correlation coefficient between the two variables (Calvo-Mora, Leal, & Roldán, 2006) (Table 12.3).

One can argue that differences exist in the way in which the different variables influence the explained variance of loyalty. Accordingly, we can establish how, regardless of the formula we use for measuring tourists' experience, satisfaction is the

Table 12.3: Explained variance analysis of loyalty.

| | Not familiar with the destination | High familiarity | Low experience | High experience |
|---|---|---|---|---|
| | $R^2 = 0.585$ | $R^2 = 0.474$ | $R^2 = 0.575$ | $R^2 = 0.493$ |
| Disconfirmation | 0.062 (11%) | 0.033 (7%) | 0.087 (15%) | 0.006 (1%) |
| Satisfaction | 0.371 (63%) | 0.365 (77%) | 0.361 (63%) | 0.372 (76%) |
| Expectations | 0.152 (26%) | 0.076 (16%) | 0.127 (22%) | 0.115 (23%) |

Table 12.4: Verification of the posited hypotheses.

| | Multi-group analysis |
|---|---|
| $H_{1a}$: *Disconfirmation → Satisfaction* | No |
| $H_{1b}$: *Disconfirmation → Loyalty* | No |
| $H_{1c}$: *Satisfaction → Loyalty* | No |
| $H_{1d}$: *Satisfaction → Expectations* | No |
| $H_{1e}$: *Expectations → Loyalty* | Yes |
| $H_{2a}$: *Disconfirmation → Satisfaction* | No |
| $H_{2b}$: *Disconfirmation → Loyalty* | Yes |
| $H_{2c}$: *Satisfaction → Loyalty* | No |
| $H_{2d}$: *Satisfaction → Expectations* | No |
| $H_{2e}$: *Expectations → Loyalty* | No |

variable that best explains loyalty development, and this effect grows as tourists' experience increases. Secondly, focusing on the influence of disconfirmation on loyalty, we can indeed suggest that it decreases as tourists' experience grows (Table 12.4).

Although our initial analyses showed an absence of differences in the model's behaviour, after further developing other analyses, we can consider their existence plausible in one of them. Our final results seem to suggest the existence of a different relationship between disconfirmation and loyalty in the case of experience, and between expectations and loyalty in the case of familiarity. Thus, we have support for $H_{1e}$ and $H_{2b}$. Conversely, we must reject the remaining posited relationships.

## 12.5.  Conclusions

Acquiring a deeper knowledge of how tourists' familiarity operates is essential for developing strategic marketing, as it is the variable with the strongest influence on consumer behaviour (Bargeman & Van der Poel, 2006; Desai & Hoyer, 2000). The present chapter analyses the moderating role of familiarity and experience in the explanatory model for tourists' satisfaction and loyalty development, and explores whether choosing one over the other (familiarity or experience) leads to differing results in the posited model.

Including adjusted expectations in the explanatory models for satisfaction and loyalty development enables us to overcome the limitation often imposed in this field of knowledge by measuring the factors that generate expectations once the service consumption had begun (Rodríguez & San Martín, 2008; Rodríguez et al., 2006). If what these models are attempting to use are the expectations that consumers have before the service is provided, these expectations ought to be measured before the consumption experience takes place (Johnson et al., 1995).

As far as methodological issues are concerned, we must bear in mind that the outcome of the analysis may be influenced by the fact that the results of the analysis of familiarity are often greater when the questionnaire, as occurred in our case, includes questions with neutral values instead of only positive or negative ones (Guibault, Bryant, Brockway, & Posavac, 2004).

An analysis of these results allows us to suggest the possibility of the model showing a similar behaviour regardless of the formula that we use to measure tourists' experience or the degree to which that experience is present. It appears that, generally speaking, the satisfaction and loyalty development process among tourists who have never visited the destination before is similar to that of those who only travelled a few times a year. In other words, it appears that disconfirmation has a strong influence on satisfaction, satisfaction has a strong influence on expectations and loyalty, and expectations, in turn, act as mediators between satisfaction and loyalty. Differing behaviour could also be identified based on tourists' familiarity or experience, given that among scarcely experienced or familiar tourists, disconfirmation has a significant effect on loyalty, and among those with a low level of travelling experience expectations have an effect on loyalty also.

If we focus on the analyses of individual relationships, beginning with the relationship between disconfirmation and satisfaction, the differences were only slight. However, what we could not verify was the appropriateness of the assumptions of Morgan et al. (1996), according to which experienced individuals are more confident in their own disconfirmation judgments. In fact, it seems that there is no effect of disconfirmation on loyalty either among those tourists who are familiar with the destination or among those with a high level of travelling experience.

The present chapter analyses a relationship that had previously scarce empirical support: the connection between disconfirmation and loyalty (Bigné et al., 2005; Rufín et al., 2012). Based on the obtained results, we can conclude that a significant, albeit weak relationship exists between disconfirmation and loyalty only among tourists with very limited experience. In addition, and continuing with this relationship, we observed that experience moderates the impact of disconfirmation on loyalty, which increases as tourists' experience decreases.

Analysing disconfirmation is rather interesting. While disconfirmation exerts a stronger influence on loyalty among scarcely experienced tourists, it has a stronger influence on satisfaction among those with greater familiarity or experience. In other words, disconfirmation has a shorter-term effect among tourists with greater experience or familiarity, and has a greater impact on mid- and long-term decisions as the tourist's degree of familiarity or experience decreases.

Examination of the relationships considered in the model shows that adjusted expectations do play a mediating role between satisfaction and loyalty for three of the models we analysed, but not in the case of the model representing the behaviour of those tourists with a high level of familiarity. Hence, including adjusted expectations in the model implies that disconfirmation is the only fundamental element in the process involved in satisfaction development. Overall, tourists' familiarity or experience regarding a destination has a limited impact on the behaviour of the relationships we have been considering in the present chapter.

Although Christensen-Szalanski and William (1991) suggest that expectations adjustment is less prevalent among familiar consumers, what we see is that this pattern is confirmed in the case of experience, but not in the case of familiarity. Furthermore, Söderlund (2002) suggests that experienced consumers attribute greater importance to adjusted expectations. However, our study could not show conclusive results in that respect given the fact that there are no significant differences in the case of experience. Conversely, it is in the case of familiarity that our findings seem to verify this last assertion.

Lastly, based on an analysis of the origin of the explained variance, and in line with Ha and Jang (2010) and Kerstetter and Cho (2004), we believe that familiarity, regardless of the formula used to measure it, has a certain influence on the relationship between satisfaction and loyalty. Contrary to the conclusions of Brunner et al. (2008), inexperienced consumers' loyalty is less reliant on satisfaction, and this reliance increases as consumers gain experience. According to several authors (Li et al., 2008; Söderlund, 2002), experienced individuals make a more elaborate assessment of their consumption experience and have a keener awareness of their satisfaction, and thus satisfaction has a greater influence on their loyalty.

If we consider both the fact that the greater the tourists' experience, the less their expectations will be adjusted when they visit the destination, and that for experienced tourists disconfirmation does not affect loyalty, we are faced with the key role that satisfaction plays in the development of loyalty towards previously visited destinations among tourists with high levels of familiarity or experience. Therefore, decision makers managing those destinations must make an effort to gain a thorough knowledge of the elements in the visits that have the greatest impact on satisfaction development.

In the case of tourists with scarce familiarity and experience, it is important to bear in mind the role of disconfirmation, given its significant influence on loyalty. If tourists have never been to the destination before, their adjusted expectations will have a greater influence on loyalty than in the case of experienced individuals; if they only travel a few times a year, satisfaction will lead to a greater adjustment of expectations. Since tourists with less experience and familiarity rely mostly on external sources for their decision making, promotional material developed by destinations and organizations operating in those destinations will benefit from generating realistic expectations capable of leading to a level of disconfirmation which in turn will lead to loyalty development.

Enhancing tourists' familiarity with destination can be a powerful tool for the managers of tourism organizations. Destination familiarity is regarded as the consumer perception of how much she or he knows about the attributes of various choice alternatives being considered (Vogt & Fesenmaier, 1998). Consumers can gain product knowledge from their previous experiences with the product, from the experiences of others, and by means of visual, verbal and sensory stimuli such as advertisements, newspaper/magazine articles and television programming (Brucks, 1985). Thus, prior product knowledge enhances one's internal memory and assists in the decision-making process (Gursoy & McCleary, 2004). Apart from advertising, tourism marketers should establish tourism information centres at every major tourist attraction. Upon visiting, tourists will be provided with all materials and information essential for them to benefit from their visit. Tourists should be able to access tourist information easily and free of charge, meaning that airports, bus terminals and train station should be fully equipped with such information. When tourists have useful and sufficient information, they are more confident and are more satisfied with their choice and are more likely to revisit, which is the main goal at stake. Additionally, when they are confident with their choice or familiar with the destination, they may want to introduce the destination to others (Mechinda et al., 2009, 2010).

Communication strategies can benefit from knowledge about tourists' familiarity also. Gursoy suggested that familiar and unfamiliar tourists are different in their information search behaviour. Communication approaches developed for unfamiliar travellers should provide simple information about the overall destination and a comparison between the destination and other destinations. Experienced travellers are more likely to utilize external information sources to gather information about the attributes of the destination than to use personal external information sources. Communication materials for such travellers should include detailed information about the destination and its key attributes (Mechinda et al., 2009, 2010).

# References

Alba, J. W., & Hutchison, J. W. (1987). Dimensions of consumer expertise. *Journal of Consumer Behavior, 13*, 411–454.

Anderson, R. E. (1973). Consumer dissatisfaction: The effects of disconfirmed expectancy on perceived product performance. *Journal of Marketing Research, 10*, 38–44.

Arkes, H. R., Guilmert, T. J., Faust, D., & Hart, K. (1988). Eliminating the hindsight bias. *Journal of Applied Psychology, 73*(2), 305–307.

Backman, S. J., & Crompton, J. L. (1991). The usefulness of selected variables for predicting activity loyalty. *Leisure Science, 13*, 205–220.

Baloglu, S. (2001). Image variations of Turkey by familiarity index: Informational and experiential dimensions. *Tourism Management, 22*, 127–133.

Bargeman, B., & Van der Poel, H. (2006). The role of routines in the vacation decision-making process of Dutch vacationers. *Tourism Management, 27*, 707–720.

Barroso, C., Martín, E., & Martín, D. (2007). The influence of market heterogeneity on the relationship between a destination's image and tourists' future behaviour. *Tourism Management, 28*, 175–187.

Bigné, J. E., Andreu, L., & Gnoth, J. (2005). The theme park experience: An analysis of pleasure, arousal and satisfaction. *Tourism Management, 26*(6), 833–844.

Bigné, J. E., Mattila, A. S., & Andreu, L. (2008). The impact of experimental consumption cognitions and emotions on behavioural intentions. *Journal of Service Marketing, 22*(4), 303–315.

Bowen, D. (2001). Antecedents of consumer satisfaction and dissatisfaction CS/D on long haul inclusive tours: A reality check on theoretical considerations. *Tourism Management, 22*(1), 49–61.

Brucks, M. (1985). The effects of product class knowledge on information search behaviour. *Journal of Consumer Research, 1*(12), 1–16.

Brunner, T. A., Stöcklin, M., & Opwis, K. (2008). Satisfaction, image and loyalty: New versus experienced customers. *European Journal of Marketing, 42*(9/10), 1095–1105.

Calvo-Mora, A., Leal, A., & Roldán, J. L. (2006). Using enablers of the EFQM model to manage institutions of higher education. *Quality Assurance in Education, 14*(2), 99–122.

Campo-Martínez, S., Garau-Vadell, J., & Martínez-Ruiz, M. (2010). Factors influencing repeat visits to a destination: The influence of group composition. *Tourism Management, 31*(6), 862–870.

Chen, C-F., & Tsai, D. C. (2007). How destination image and evaluative factors affect behavioral intentions? *Tourism Management, 28*, 1115–1122.

Chen, J. S., & Gursoy, D. (2004). Cross-cultural comparison of the information sources used by first-time and repeat travelers and its marketing implications. *International Journal of Hospitality Management, 19*(2), 191–203.

Cheung, G. W., & Rensvold, R. B. (2002). Evaluating goodness-of-fit indexes for testing measurement invariance structural. *Structural Equation Modeling, 9*(2), 233–255.

Chi, C. G-Q., & Qu, H. (2008). Examining the structural relationships of destination image, tourist satisfaction and destination loyalty: An integrated approach. *Tourism Management, 29*(4), 624–636.

Christensen-Szalanski, J. J. J., & William, C. F. (1991). The hindsight bias: A meta-analysis. *Organizational Behavior and Human Decision Processes, 48*(1), 147–168.

De Rojas, C., & Camarero, C. (2008). Visitors' experience. Mood and satisfaction in a heritage context: Evidence from an interpretation center. *Tourism Management, 29*, 525–537.

Desai, K. K., & Hoyer, W. D. (2000). The descriptive characteristics of memory-based consideration sets: influence of usage location frequency and usage location familiarity. *Journal of Consumer Research, 27*, 309–323.

Flavián, C., Guinalíu, M., & Gurrea, R. (2006). The influence of familiarity and usability on loyalty to airline journalistic services: The role of user experience. *Journal of Retailing and Consumer Services, 13*, 363–375.

Fuchs, G., & Reichel, A. (2011). An exploratory inquiry into destination risk perception and risk reduction strategies of first time vs. repeat visitors to a highly volatile destination. *Tourism Management, 32*(2), 266–276.

Giese, J. L., & Cote, J. A. (2000). *Defining consumer satisfaction.* Academy of Marketing Science Review. Retrieved from http://www.amsreview.org/articles/giese01-2000.pdf

Guibault, R. L., Bryant, F. B., Brockway, J. H., & Posavac, E. J. (2004). A meta-analysis of research on hindsight bias. *Basic and Applied Social Psychology, 26*(2&3), 103–117.

Gursoy, D., & McCleary, K. W. (2004). An integrative model of tourists' information search behavior. *Annals of Tourism Research, 31*(2), 353–373.

Ha, J., & Jang, SC. C. (2010). Perceived values, satisfaction, and behavioral intentions: The role of familiarity in Korean restaurants. *International Journal of Hospitality Management, 29*, 2–13.

Hawkins, S. A., & Hastie, R. (1990). Hindsight: Biased judgments of past events after the outcomes are known. *Psychological Bulletin, 107*(3), 311–327.

Hernández, R. S., Muñoz, P. A., & Santos, L. (2007). The moderating role of familiarity in rural tourism in Spain. *Tourism Management, 29*(5), 951–964.

Hong, S-k., Lee, S-W., Lee, S., & Jang, H. (2009). Selecting revisited destinations. *Annals of Tourism Research, 36*(2), 268–294.

Jacoby, J., & Chestnut, R. W. (1978). *Brand loyalty measurement and management.* New York, NY: Wiley.

Jang, S. C., & Feng, R. (2007). Temporal destination revisit intention: The effects of novelty seeking and satisfaction. *Tourism Management, 28*, 580–590.

Johnson, M. D., Anderson, E. W., & Fornell, C. (1995). Rational and adaptive performance expectations in a customer satisfaction framework. *Journal of Consumer Research, 21*(March), 695–707.

Johnson, M. D., Nader, G., & Fornell, C. (1996). Expectations, perceived performance, and customer satisfaction for a complex service: The case of bank loans. *Journal of Economic Psychology, 17*, 163–182.

Jones, T. O., & Sasser, W. E. (1995). Why satisfied customer defect. *Harvard Business Review, 73*(6), 88–99.

Jöreskog, K. G. (1993). Testing structural equation models. In K. A. Bollen, & J. S. Long (Eds.), *Testing structural equation models* (pp. 294–316). Newbury Park, CA: Sage.

Jöreskog, K. G., & Sörbom, D. (1996). *LISREL 8 User's Reference Guide.* Chicago, IL: Scientific Software.

Kerstetter, D., & Cho, M-H. (2004). Prior knowledge, credibility and information search. *Annals of Tourism Research, 31*(4), 961–985.

Lee, J., Lee, J., & Feick, L. (2001). The impact of switching costs on the customer satisfaction-loyalty link: mobile phone service in France. *Journal of Services Marketing, 15*(1), 35–48.

Lehto, X. Y., O'Leary, J. T., & Morrison, A. M. (2004). The effect of prior experience on vacation behavior. *Annals of Tourism Research, 31*(4), 801–818.

Li, X., Cheng, C-k., Kim, H., & Petrick, J. F. (2008). A systematic comparison of first-time repeat visitors via two-phase online survey. *Tourism Management, 29*, 278–293.

Mazurski, D. (1989). Past experience and future tourism decisions. *Annals of Tourism Research, 16*(3), 333–344.

Mechinda, P., Serirat, S., Anuwichanont, J., & Gulid, N. (2010). An examination of tourists' loyalty towards medical tourism in Pattaya, Thailand. *The International Business & Economic Research Journal, 9*(1), 55–70.

Mechinda, P., Serirat, S., & Gulid, N. (2009). An examination of tourists' attitudinal and behavioral loyalty: comparison between domestic and international tourists. *Journal of Vacation Marketing, 15*(2), 129–148.

Millán, A., & Esteban, A. (2004). Development of a multiple-item scale for measuring customer satisfaction in travel agencies services. *Tourism Management, 25*, 533–546.

Moorthy, S., Ratchford, B. T., & Talukdar, D. (1997). Consumer information search revisited: theory and empirical analysis. *Journal of Consumer Research, 23*(4), 263–277.

Morgan, M. J., Attaway, J. S., & Griffin, M. (1996). The role of product/service experience in satisfaction formation processes: a test of moderation. *Journal of Consumer Satisfaction, Dissatisfaction and Complaining Behavior, 9*, 104–114.

Murphy, P., Pritchard, M. P., & Smith, B. (2000). The destination product and its impact on traveler perceptions. *Tourism Management, 21*(1), 43–52.

Oliver, R. L. (1980). A cognitive model of the antecedence and consequences of satisfaction decisions. *Journal of Marketing Research, 17,* 46–59.

Oliver, R. L. (1997). *Satisfaction: A behavioural perspective on the customer.* New York, NY: McGraw-Hill.

Oliver, R. L. (1999). Whence consumer loyalty? *Journal of Marketing, 63,* 33–44.

Oliver, R. L., & Burke, R. R. (1999). Expectations processes in satisfaction formation. *Journal of Service Research, 1*(3), 196–214.

Oliver, R. L., & DeSarbo, W. S. (1988). Response determinants in satisfaction judgments. *Journal of Consumer Research, 14*(4), 495–507.

Oppermann, M. (1997). First-time and repeat visitors to New Zealand. *Tourism Management, 18*(3), 177–181.

Pearce, P. L., & Kang, M-h. (2009). The effects of prior and recent experience on continuing interest in tourist settings. *Annals of Tourism Research, 36*(2), 172–190.

Pieters, R., Baumgartner, H., & Bagozzi, R. (2006). Biased memory for prior decision making: Evidence from a longitudinal field study. *Organizational Behavior and Human Decision Processes, 99,* 34–48.

Pieters, R., Koelemeijer, K., & Roest, H. (1995). Assimilation processes in service satisfaction formation. *International Journal of Service Industry Management, 6*(3), 17–33.

Pieters, R., & Zwick, R. (1993). Hindsight bias in the context of a consumption experience. *European Advances in Consumer Research, 1,* 307–311.

Qureshi, I., & Compeau, D. (2009). Assessing between-group differences in information systems research: A comparison of covariance-and component-based SEM. *MIS Quarterly, 33*(1), 197–214.

Raykov, T., & Marcoulides, G. A. (2006). *A first course in structural equation modeling* (2nd ed.). Mahwah, NJ: Lawrence Erlbaum Associates.

Reinartz, W., Haenlein, M., & Henseler, H. (2009). An empirical comparison of the efficacy of covariance-based and variance-based SEM. *International Journal of Research in Marketing, 26*(4), 332–344.

Rodríguez, I., & San Martín, H. (2008). Tourist satisfaction. A cognitive-affective model. *Annals of Tourism Research, 35*(2), 551–573.

Rodríguez, I., San Martín, H., & Collado, J. (2006). The role of expectations in the consumer satisfaction formation process: Empirical evidence in the travel agency sector. *Tourism Management, 27*(3), 410–419.

Rufín, R., Medina, C., & Rey, M. (2012). Adjusted expectations, satisfaction and loyalty development in the case of services. *Service Industries Journal,* forthcoming. doi: 10.1080/02642069.2011.594874

Sirayaka, E., & Woodside, A. G. (2005). Building and testing theories of decision making by travelers. *Tourism Management, 26,* 815–832.

Söderlund, M. (2002). Customer familiarity and its effects on satisfaction and behavioral intentions. *Psychology & Marketing, 19*(10), 861–879.

Söderlund, M., & Gunnarson, J. (2000). *Customer familiarity and its effects on satisfaction and dissatisfaction.* SSE/EFI Working Papers Series in Business Administration (March) (2).

Szymanski, D. M., & Henard, D. (2001). Customer satisfaction: A meta-analysis of the empirical evidence. *Journal of the Academy of Marketing Science, 29*(1), 16–35.

Tsiotsou, R., & Vasioti, E. (2006a). Satisfaction: A segmentation criterion for "short term" visitors of mountainous destinations. *Journal of Travel and Tourism Marketing, 20*(1), 61–73.

Tsiotsou, R., & Vasioti, E. (2006b). Using demographics and leisure activities to predict satisfaction with tourism services in Greece. *Journal of Hospitality & Leisure Marketing, 14*(2), 69–82.

Vogt, C., & Fesenmaier, D. (1998). Expanding the functional tourism information search model. *Annals of Tourism Research, 25*(1), 551–578.

Yi, Y., & La, S. (2004). What influences the relationship between customer satisfaction and repurchase intention? Investigating the effects of adjusted expectations and customer loyalty. *Psychology & Marketing, 21*(5), 351–373.

Yoon, Y., & Uysal, M. (2005). An examination of the effects of motivation and satisfaction on destination loyalty: A structural model. *Tourism Management, 26*(1), 45–56.

Yüksel, A., & Yüksel, F. (2001). Comparative performance analysis: tourists' perceptions of Turkey relative to other tourist destinations. *Journal of Vacation Marketing, 7*(4), 333–355.

Zabkar, V., Brencic, M. M., & Dmitrovic, T. (2010). Modelling perceived quality, visitor satisfaction and behavioural intentions at the destination level. *Tourism Management, 31*, 537–546.

Zeithaml, V. A., Berry, L. L., & Parasuraman, A. (1993). The nature and determinants of customer expectations of service. *Journal of the Academy of Marketing Science* (Winter), 1–12.

Zhang, J., Ghorbani, A. A., & Cohen, R. (2007). A familiarity-based trust model for effective selection of sellers in multiagent e-commerce systems. *International Journal of Information Security, 6*, 333–344.

Zwick, R., Pieters, R., & Baumgartner, H. (1995). On the practical significance of hindsight bias: The case of the expectancy-disconfirmation model of consumer satisfaction. *Organizational Behavior and Human Decision Processes, 64*(1), 103–117.

# PART IV
# EXPERIENTIAL MARKETING

# Chapter 13

# Introduction to Experiential Marketing

*Ronald E. Goldsmith and Rodoula H. Tsiotsou*

## 13.1. Introduction

The hospitality and tourism industries are comprised of a wide variety of different
types of businesses, all of which much perform in a coordinated fashion to deliver a
consistent, unique, satisfying product to the consumer. The growing field of
destination management is well aware of this situation and seeks to create strategies
and managerial systems to achieve this goal. In addition, however, the unique nature
of this business also implies that destination managers must think carefully about
their 'product' and how it might differ from other industries. Because the ultimate
product of a tourist's visit is essentially the sum of the experiences, tourism services
managers must assume that they are the managers of these experiences in
cooperation with the suppliers of the experiences and the consumers who co-create
them. Consequently, the concepts described by 'experiential marketing' theory are
highly relevant to the task of managing tourism services (e.g. hotels, places,
destinations and transportations). This section of the book presents four chapters
describing current issues in experiential marketing for tourism. But to explain the
nature of experiential marketing, perhaps we should start with a general discussion
of consumer motivation, the larger context in which consumer needs and wants
are revealed, and how tourist experiences are the unique 'products' consumers want
to consume.

## 13.2. Consumer (and Thus Tourist) Motivations

Consumers buy products for the benefits or the service (Vargo & Lusch, 2004) they
deliver. Modern marketing thought is well aware of this truism because the major
argument it makes is that firms succeed when they create and deliver value to
customers in terms of the benefits or service their products provide. Firms are
counselled to be 'customer-centric', to put consumer needs and wants at the heart of
their businesses, to orient their operations and management culture around satisfying

Strategic Marketing in Tourism Services
Copyright © 2012 by Emerald Group Publishing Limited
All rights of reproduction in any form reserved
ISBN: 978-1-78052-070-4

customer needs. If customers participate actively by co-creating the product, by engaging with the brand and/or by commenting on it publically as they seek to improve and promote it, then this is all to the good. It is important, then, that firms understand the needs and wants of their customers in detail so that they can use their capabilities to work hand in hand with customers to deliver successful products. But what do customers want? Why do customers buy what they buy?

One way to answer this question is to consider the basic reasons that customers have for venturing into the marketplace and exchanging their resources of money, time and physical and cognitive energy for the firm's products. That is, we must distinguish consumer 'needs' from consumer 'wants'. Wants are the ways consumers learn through their life experiences to satisfy their needs. Needs are the fundamental motives that characterize all human behaviour, both in the marketplace and outside of it, while wants are specific ways to satisfy these needs learned during the life course in a specific time and place. Needs are few, but wants seem almost infinite in variety and amount. Needs are universal, but wants are highly specialized to time, place and circumstances.

Biologists and evolutionary psychologists famously propose that organisms must accomplish four tasks, the famous four F's (feeding, fighting, fleeing and mating), to be successful and so these tasks represent the fundamental motives. While not objecting to this proposal, marketing and consumer researchers (and others such as consultants) propose a variety of formulations. For example, Schwartz (1977, Ch. 3) described three fundamental drivers of consumer behaviour: *ego-related motives, emotional motives and rational motives*. Readers of research articles in marketing and consumer behaviour often see the motives stated as utilitarian or functional, hedonic and social. Lantos (2011) simply states that motives are either utilitarian or hedonic. Each scholar and manager develops his or her own list for the purpose at hand. Taking a broad view, Foxall and Goldsmith (1994) argue that the total view of the consumer as a social animal with a complex brain suggests that consumer motives can be grouped into six categories based on the different components that make up a human being, namely the biological, social, psychological, cognitive, hedonic and experiential (with perhaps a spiritual as well). Biological refers chiefly to the utilitarian and functional reasons people buy things. Social refers to the many social relationships that are important. Psychological describes motives grounded in the personality and symbolic nature of human life. Cognitive motives represent the activity of the curious and inquisitive mind. Hedonic motives are those driven by the five senses. Finally, experiential motives are related to feelings, emotions and moods.

This perhaps overlong introduction is meant to set the stage for discussions of the experiential reasons consumers buy goods, services and informational products. It acknowledges that any consumer behaviour can be simple in the motivational sense that a single motive drives it (e.g. eating ice cream for its hedonic pleasure) or complex when several motives drive it (e.g. eating ice cream for its hedonic pleasure combined the social goal of sharing food with a possible mate or friends or even as a reward to the ego for some accomplishment). Thus, the tourist visit is a complex product through which consumers satisfy several needs simultaneously. But the tourist product is best seen as predominantly an experiential product. Pine and Gilmore (1999) introduced the idea of the 'experience economy' to marketing management, arguing that managers should create value by seeing their products as experiences to be managed. In the hospitality and tourism context, experiential motives describe the benefits that tourists derive from learning about, experiencing and recounting their purchases of tourism products and services. As tourism managers learn that they compete with an increasingly growing variety of other tourism services nationally and globally, they must understand the tourists' motivations so that they can gain competitive advantage by distinguishing and uniquely positioning their offerings and by focusing on experiential benefits to give them this advantage (Tsiotsou & Ratten, 2010).

## 13.3. Experiential Marketing

Several definitions of experiential consumption and experiential marketing (or customer experience management, CEM) appear in the literature (Schmitt, 2010), as the chapters in this section attest. One exposition introduces the concept by contrasting experiential marketing with more traditional product marketing. According to Schmitt (2010), first, product marketing focuses on features and benefits of tangible goods, while experiential marketing focuses on customer experiences that occur when consumers encounter, undergo or live through situations that produce sensory, emotional, cognitive and behavioural effects. For example, while product marketers might emphasize the price or cleanliness of their hotel rooms, experiential marketers would stress the look and feel of the room and what it is like to stay there. Second, when product marketing focuses on narrow product categories, experiential marketing focuses on the broad situation (and its meaning) in which the products might be used. For example, rather than focus on selling the hotel room, the marketer would emphasize the role played by staying at the hotel in the total experience of visiting the destination. Third, product marketing sees consumers as rational decision makers, but experiential marketers appeal to the emotions involved in consuming the product. A destination is not just about going to a special place; that place entertains, stimulates and engages the visitor. Finally, instead of relying almost exclusively on analytical, quantitative and verbal methods to study consumer behaviour, experiential marketing (while not neglecting the analytical approach) is more eclectic and exploratory in its use of methods. Tourist destinations, for example, might be ideal topics for such fuzzy and esoteric research techniques as Zaltman's (2003) Metaphor Elicitation Technique, where researchers invite participants to create collages from magazine pictures and then tell elaborate stories about them, thereby providing insights into their motivations that would remain hidden from other types of research.

As tourism products are chiefly a type of service, they can be well described by the 'servicescape/environmental' model of services that considers all the interactions the customer has that create the service (tourism) experience. Thus, destinations share with all service products the features that distinguish services from tangible goods in that they are consumed within the context of a 'servicescape' containing all the experiential elements that make it up (Tsiotsou & Wirtz, 2012). According to

Lovelock and Wirtz (2011), servicescapes serve four purposes: (1) they engineer the consumer experience and shape consumer behaviour; (2) they convey the planned image of the firm and support its positioning and differentiation strategy; (3) they are part of the value proposition and (4) they facilitate the service encounter and enhance both service quality and productivity. Taken together, the interactions between tourists and the elements of the servicescape plus the cognitive and emotional reactions they stimulate in the tourists comprise the experience of the destination.

These experiential components have been described by different typologies (Schmitt, 2010), but a recent empirically derived scheme (Gentile, Spiller, & Noci, 2007) seems especially appropriate for tourism management (see Table 13.1).

Such typologies make explicit the dimensions of the experience from the customer/ tourist perspective, thus enabling tourism managers to enhance their strategies to create experiences that create value for tourists. In this perspective, the job of the managers is to design, intentionally produce (stage), organize, foresee, calculate, price (charge for) the experience (Stamboulis & Skayannis, 2003). Schmitt (2010) proposes a framework for CEM that starts with using the dimensions of customer/ tourist experience to first analyse the experiential world of the tourist to gain insights

Table 13.1: The dimensions of customer experience applied in tourism.

| Dimension | Description | Tourism example |
|---|---|---|
| Sensorial | The stimulation affects the senses; sight, hearing, touch, taste and smell; arouses pleasure, excitement, satisfaction or sense of beauty | Landscapes, architecture, music, food |
| Emotional | The stimulation affects moods, feelings or emotions | Theme park rides, tours, events |
| Cognitive | The stimulation stimulates thinking or conscious mental processes, engages creativity or changes ideas | Museums, art galleries, tours, performances |
| Pragmatic | The destination teaches a pragmatic art; doing something; learning a skill or craft | Arts and crafts camps; archaeological digs |
| Lifestyle | Affirms the system of values and beliefs of the customer; consumption/use reinforces or manifests values/beliefs | 'Voluntourism' — volunteer tourism, charity tourism, eco-tourism, social tourism |
| Relational | Socially oriented; use with other people or expression of social identity | group tours, family gatherings, reunions, clubs, sport tourism |

*Source*: Gentile et al. (2007).

that provide the basis for subsequent steps. Using the panoply of research methods available to them, interviews, focus groups, surveys and ethnographic methods, destination managers can learn how the tourist experiences the destination and how specific destination elements influence the experience. In step 2, the managers use these insights to build the experience platform, which includes the core experience and subsequent implementations. For example, learning how the destination experience affects emotions reinforces lifestyle choices, or social relations help managers coordinate the disparate stakeholders in the destination to yield a consistent, valuable product. Step 3 of the CEM framework is to implement the experience. Planning is easy; implementation is hard. This step is most like brand management, where the destination features are coordinated into a total brand experience including the 'look and feel' of the destination, its identity expressed through all the touchpoints with the tourist: advertising, web pages, brand communities social networks, visual elements and so forth. This task should involve all the destination manager's skills in decision making and execution. Moreover, managers must institutionalize and constantly monitor the experience platform to ensure that it remains relevant to the target segment(s) making up the core tourist customer(s). Updating and upgrading are likely to be needed. Finally, success in creating and implementing a successful experience platform provides the opportunity to innovate new tourist products, and because the tourist experience is co-created, customers/tourists should be involved as much as possible in all aspects of the programme, not just restricted to providing data in the initial steps.

Stamboulis and Skayannis (2003, p. 38) pointed out that while destination managers understood that they had to enrich the 'content of tourist services in combination with strategies of differentiation and customization', the nature of this content was poorly conceptualized. They argued that managers needed to understand that 'experience' is the content of destination's product and that, if they follow the recommendations of Pine and Gilmore (1999), they could better manage the tourist experience along four dimensions: entertainment, education, escapist and aesthetic. 'In an experience-based exchange the tourist enters into a multifaceted interaction with the actors and the setting of a narrative staged by the local community. Each individual experience is articulated through the four realms in a unique way' (Stamboulis & Skayannis, 2003, p. 38). Their recommendations, however, have not subsequently been taken as seriously by tourism managers as would be expected (Tsiotsou & Ratten, 2010), but tourism researchers have begun to study the unique elements of experiential tourism and report findings valuable to destination management.

## 13.4. Recent Research in Experiential Marketing in Hospitality and Tourism

The topic of experiential marketing in tourism has grown in importance in recent years. However, as the findings of a recent review of literature on the topic indicate, despite its importance, experience-related research remains an under-represented area in the tourism literature (Ritchie, Tung, & Ritchie, 2011). Ritchie et al. (2011) studied the articles published in major tourism journals between 2000 and 2009. From the 2645 published articles, only 263 focused on experiential tourism, representing 9.9% of total publications.

The available literature on experiential tourism focused on the personal and affective dimensions of tourists' experiences in natural settings (Schanzel & McIntosh, 2000), in hospitality services (McIntosh & Siggs, 2005) and heritage places (McIntosh, 2004), as well as the experiences of participants in high-risk adventure leisure activities (Arnould & Price, 1993; Celsi, Rose, & Leigh, 1993). Studies have examined the motivations of accommodation guests and report that possible different experiences are realized in different forms of accommodation (Johnston-Walker, 1999). McIntosh and Siggs (2005, p. 76) suggested that 'specialist accommodation establishments may be demanded for the experiences of comfort, luxury, uniqueness, history, host-guest interaction, and the more personal touches they can provide'. Their findings from in-depth interviews with 19 hosts and 30 guests at boutique accommodation establishments in Nelson in the South Island of New Zealand revealed that five key dimensions of the boutique accommodation experience exist as described by both hosts and guests. These were unique character, personalized, homely, quality and value added, while emotions were found to be an integral aspect of the boutique accommodation experience (McIntosh & Siggs, 2005).

In addition to the various settings in which the tourism experiences have been examined, a significant volume of the related literature has been focused on the determinants of the tourism experiences. Thus, an increasing research interest has been shown on the influence of mood and emotion on tourism services evaluations and experiences (Bigne & Andreu, 2004; Gnoth, Zins, Lengmueller, & Boshoff, 2000; Sirakaya, Petrick, & Choi, 2004; Zins, 2002). In their study, Schanzel and McIntosh (2000) found that 'viewing', 'proximity', 'authenticity' and the feelings of 'wonder' were significant determinants in characterizing bird-watching in New Zealand as an enjoyable, emotive and informative wildlife-viewing experience. Taken an experiential approach, Högström, Rosner, and Gustafsson (2010) describe a study of customer decision making for snowparks in Norway. They focused on the experiences of the tourists as the principle drivers of their choices. Employing the Kano model, the authors found that the physical service environment plays a significant role in creating the most attractive and satisfying experiences and affects destination image more than customers' interactions.

## 13.5. Conclusion

'Experiential marketing has become a cornerstone of recent advances in marketing with a great potential for its application in tourism marketing' (Tsiotsou & Ratten, 2010, p. 540). Although tourism services are high experiential services, it is surprising that the tourism marketing literature has not embraced yet this strategic orientation. Experiential marketing could assist tourism services in dealing with the fierce competition by differentiating their products/services and, therefore, gain competitive advantage. Moreover, given the difficulty in developing loyalty in tourism services (e.g. destinations and hotels) and because customer satisfaction is not just enough in developing loyal customers (Tsiotsou & Wirtz, 2012), experiential marketing provides the foundation for developing customer loyalty through customer delight. That is, by providing unique and highly emotional experiences, tourism services can achieve customer delight and, therefore, higher levels of loyalty. The four chapters in this section recount four unique perspectives on experiential marketing in hospitality and tourism and provide some useful insights to tourism academics and managers.

# References

Arnould, E. J., & Price, L. L. (1993). River magic: Extraordinary experience and the extended service encounter. *Journal of Consumer Research, 20,* 24–45.

Bigne, J. E., & Andreu, L. (2004). Emotions in segmentation. An empirical study. *Annals of Tourism Research, 31*(3), 682–696.

Celsi, R. L., Rose, R. L., & Leigh, T. W. (1993). An exploration of high-risk leisure consumption through skydiving. *Journal of Consumer Research, 20,* 1–23.

Foxall, G. R., & Goldsmith, R. E. (1994). *Consumer psychology for marketing.* London: Routledge.

Gentile, C., Spiller, N., & Noci, G. (2007). How to sustain the customer experience: An overview of experience components that co-create value with the customer. *European Management Journal, 25*(5), 395–410.

Gnoth, J., Zins, A., Lengmueller, R., & Boshoff, C. (2000). Emotions, mood, flow and motivations to travel. *Journal of Travel and Tourism Marketing, 9*(3), 23–34.

Högström, C., Rosner, M., & Gustafsson, A. (2010). How to create attractive and unique customer experiences. *Marketing Intelligence & Planning, 28*(4), 385–402.

Johnston-Walker, R. (1999). The accommodation motivations and accommodation usage patterns of international independent pleasure travellers. *Pacific Tourism Review, 3,* 143–150.

Lantos, G. (2011). *Consumer behavior in action: Real-life applications for marketing managers.* New York, NY: M.E. Sharpe.

Lovelock, C., & Wirtz, J. (2011). *Service marketing: People, technology, strategy* (7th ed.). Upper Saddle River, NJ: Prentice-Hall.

McIntosh, A. J. (2004). Tourists' appreciation of Maori culture in New Zealand. *Tourism Management, 25,* 1–15.

McIntosh, A. J., & Siggs, A. (2005). An exploration of the experiential nature of boutique accommodation. *Journal of Travel Research, 44,* 74–81.

Pine, B. J. I., & Gilmore, J. H. (1999). *The experience economy: Work is theatre & every business a stage.* Boston, MA: Harvard Business School Press.

Ritchie, B. J. R., Tung, V. W. S., & Ritchie, R. J. B. (2011). Tourism experience management research: Emergence, evolution and future directions. *International Journal of Contemporary Hospitality Management, 23*(4), 419–438.

Schanzel, H., & McIntosh, A. J. (2000). An insight into the personal and emotive context of wildlife viewing at the Penguin Place, Otago, New Zealand. *Journal of Sustainable Tourism, 8*(1), 36–52.

Schmitt, B. (2010). Key concepts of experience marketing. *Foundations and Trends in Marketing, 5*(2), 66–76.

Schwartz, E. L. (1977). Spatial mapping in the primate sensory projection: Analytic structure and relevance to perception. *Biological Cybernetics, 25*(4), 181–194.

Sirakaya, E., Petrick, J., & Choi, H. (2004). The role of mood on tourism product evaluations. *Annals of Tourism Research, 31*(3), 517–539.

Stamboulis, Y., & Skayannis, P. (2003). Innovation strategies and technology for experience-based tourism. *Tourism Management, 24*(1), 35–43.

Tsiotsou, R., & Ratten, V. (2010). Future research directions in tourism marketing. *Marketing Intelligence & Planning, 28*(4), 533–544.

Tsiotsou, R., & Wirtz, J. (2012). Consumer behavior in a service context (forthcoming). In V. Wells & G. Foxall (Eds.), *Handbook of new developments in consumer behavior.* Cheltenham, UK: Edward Elgar Publishing.

Vargo, S. L., & Lusch, R. F. (2004). Evolving to a new dominant logic for marketing. *Journal of Marketing, 68*(1), 1–17.

Zaltman, G. (2003). *How customers think.* Cambridge, MA: Harvard Business School.

Zins, A. (2002). Consumption emotions, experience quality and satisfaction: A structural analysis for complainers versus non-complainers. *Journal of Travel and Tourism Marketing, 12*(2/3), 3–18.

Chapter 14

# Tourist Experience Development: Designed Attributes, Perceived Experiences and Customer Value

*Lihua Gao, Noel Scott, Peiyi Ding and Chris Cooper*

## 14.1. Introduction

Contemporary consumers are increasingly seeking more experiences than products, and Pine and Gilmore (1998) have set out a vision for this new economic era — the experience economy — in which consumers look for affective memories, sensation and symbolism that combine to create a holistic and long-lasting personal experience. Within the tourism literature, it is widely accepted that tourism 'primarily sells a "staged" experience ... tourism's central productive activity [is] the creation of the touristic experience' (Sternberg, 1997, p. 952, 954). Tourism Australia, for example, has identified seven types of experiences that have the most potential to encourage international travellers to visit Australia and has based its international marketing on these, such as Aboriginal Australia, Outback Australia, or Food and Wine (Tourism Australia, 2011). Businesses as diverse as wine tasting centres, urban precincts and museums are rethinking their offerings to enhance the customer experience (Scott, Laws, & Boksberger, 2009). Hence, there is a need for managers of tourism businesses to consider how to design or develop their experiences to improve or increase customer value (CV).

The task of designing an experience to achieve a certain customer outcome is conceptually and practically difficult, not least because the academic concept of the experience is holistic and embedded in the customer's thinking. Thus, an experience is considered personal and involves and engages a tourist at different levels so as to create a holistic gestalt (Schmitt, 1999a). While 'an experience cannot happen without the consumer's involvement' (LaSalle & Britton, 2003, p. 29), managers may also seek to influence a tourist's experiences. Indeed, what tourism managers seek to do is to orchestrate how the set of interactions between their offerings and tourists occurs. There are of course limitations in the ability of managers to influence tourists' experiences as they may have no control over the pre- or post-experience stages and indeed research has noted that a tourist's satisfaction with an experience is affected by his or her prior mood (Huang, Scott, Ding, & Cheng, 2012). However, a manager may add or subtract tourist activities, staged effects, interactions and many other types of attributes to an experience process. Thus, the view of the experience from a management stager's perspective is different from that of the customer as it is seen as co-created and composed of discrete components (see the chapter by Part and Vargo in the present book). In this way we may determine the customers' perceived preference and evaluation, i.e. CV, which they place on experience attributes. This chapter therefore seeks to understand the theoretical linkage between experience attributes and CV.

## 14.2.  Theoretical Background

Four decades ago, Toffler (1970) predicted that a paradigm shift would affect goods and services and lead to the next stage of developed economies — experience industries. This prediction was subsequently matched by recognition of a 'growing quest on the part of ... consumers for immersion into varied experiences' (Firat, 2001, p. 113). Researchers began to move their foci from the 'world of products' to the 'world of experience' (e.g. Holbrook, Chestnut, Oliva, & Greenleaf, 1984; Holbrook & Hirschman, 1982), recognizing the importance of fantasies and feelings, and considering 'the actual unit of analysis is the individual consumption experience, not the respondent' (Havlena & Holbrook, 1986, p. 395). Experience became a key element in understanding consumer behaviour and a main foundation for economic and marketing thought (Caru & Cova, 2003; Holbrook, O'Shaughnessy, & Bell, 1990).

The concept of experience is used in a variety of academic disciplines and examined from a variety of viewpoints (Caru & Cova, 2003), and here we distinguish between a consumer and managerial perspective. The customer perspective draws on psychology and sociology to explore the emotional, symbolic and transformational significance of the experience for the individual involved. Themes in the research include a shift of emphasis from the rational to the emotional aspects of consumer decision making; a transition from satisfying needs to fulfilling aspirations, desires and dreams; and the role of the customer as an active participant rather than a passive consumer (Morgan, Elbe, & de Esteban Curiel, 2009).

On the other hand, the managerial perspective focuses on how organizations deliver experiences as part of an added-value offer (Ibid.). As an offering, experience is different from products, as products remain outside buyers, while experiences are inherently personal (Pine & Gilmore, 1999). However, an experience cannot generate spontaneously; only when customers have 'been *engaged* on an emotional, physical, intellectual or even spiritual level' (Pine & Gilmore, 1999, p. 12) is an experience constructed by them. In other words, experience is trigged by a special or designed context and shaped in the mind of customer who has been involved in the context. In this case, designed experience is to some extent *co-created* rather than attributable only to customers themselves, i.e. experience stagers can create a platform for customers who shape their own experiences. If this context is changed, customers' experiences may be affected. Therefore, both a customer perspective and a managerial perspective should be considered in the experience design process. This transformation of the view of the consumption experience also implies that traditional marketing offerings emphasizing the functional attributes and the quality of products are inadequate to create memorable experiences for customers (e.g. Gentile, Spiller, & Noci, 2007; Schmitt, 2003). In order to influence tourists' perceptions of experience and make them memorable, destination managers may change or enhance aspects of the offering that encourage tourists' involvements and hence provide added value (Berry, Carbone, & Haeckel, 2002; Oh, Fiore, & Jeoung, 2007).

## 14.3. The Definition of Experience

The term 'experience' has numerous different definitions. Some dictionaries such as the *Oxford English Dictionary* (Soanes & Stevenson, 2009) define experience as a noun, referring to a cognitive outcome, including knowledge and skill. Others, such as the *American Heritage Dictionary of the English Language* (Pickett, 2000), indicate that an experience is '[t]he feeling of emotions and sensations as opposed to thinking' and '... involvement in what is happening rather than abstract reflection on an event' (p. 625). The latter definition is a process-based one and considers experience as a verb. These diverse definitions of experience reflect the diverse ideas about experience in empirical research.

In marketing, the term 'experience' is considered ill-defined (Caru & Cova, 2003) and conceptual models do not offer 'a common terminology and a shared mindset' (Gentile et al., 2007, p. 39). The research roots of consumption experience can be traced back to the 1950s, when Abbott (1955) noted that:

> What people really desire are not products but satisfying experiences. Experiences are attained through activities. In order that activities may be carried out, physical objects or the services of human beings are usually needed ... People want products because they want the experience-bringing services which they hope the products will render. (pp. 39–40)

Three points are embodied in this quotation: first, the consumption of products or indeed destinations can lead to an experience; second, experience is the outcome of consumption; finally, people undertake consumption activities to obtain experiences. In this regard, experiences are the learned outcomes of consumption activities and relate to cognition.

Later researchers such as Schmitt (1999a) included emotion as a component; thus experience is 'a result of encountering, undergoing, or living through things. [They] provide sensory, emotional, cognitive, behavioural, and relational values that replace functional values' (p. 57). Schänzel and McIntosh (2000) defined experience as 'mental, spiritual and physiological outcomes' (p. 37) resulting from on-site recreational engagements. For these researchers, experience includes both emotional and cognitive outcome of activities but is a static concept. An experience has also been thought to be dynamic and associated with a process whose novelty may result in some response by consumers. For instance, Turner and Bruner (1986, p. 35) follow a distinction made by Dilthey (1976, p. 210) between 'mere experience' and 'an experience'. 'Mere experience' is simply the passive endurance and acceptance of events, referring to the outcome and regarded as a noun. 'An experience' has temporal or procedural structures, proceeding through distinguishable stages, and is regarded as a verb.

Other researchers such as Gupta and Vajic (2000) emphasized the interaction element of an experience. Here an experience occurs when a customer has any sensation or knowledge acquisition resulting from some level of interaction with different elements of a context created by a service provider. It is noteworthy that the word 'interaction' used in the definition implies that the consumer's role in creating experience has captured more attention from researchers (e.g. Addis & Holbrook, 2001; LaSalle & Britton, 2003). A customer's active participation involves co-creation of a unique experience (Prahalad & Ramaswamy, 2004) in which a business provides artefacts and contexts to enable them to shape their own experiences (Caru & Cova, 2003).

In short, used as a noun, experience is generally described as emotional, spiritual, psychological or learning outcomes resulting from a dynamic process of a person's involvement in activities. As a verb, experience is a transformation process that has happened in the past, embodies consumers' participation and leads to the aforesaid outcomes. For the purpose of this chapter, instead of accepting this distinction between experience as a noun and a verb, it will be considered as a total concept, referring to both *the experience processes* involving a person and *the psychological outcomes* resulting from a person's involvement. Therefore, an experience is 'a mental journey that leaves the customer with memories of having performed something special, having learned something or just having fun' (Sundbo & Hagedorn-Rasmussen, 2008, p. 83).

Even though they visit the same destination, it is notable that tourists' experiences vary, and not all tourists will obtain the same outcome: some will repurchase the product, some will be satisfied but purchase elsewhere and some will be neutral or negative about the experience performance. What tourists perceive is different from what stagers offer to them. Hence, we should distinguish between a managerial and customer perspective in designing an experience. This distinction should identify not only what can be provided by stagers and perceived by tourists in an experience process, but also allow an understanding of outcomes on which tourists evaluate the experience process offered to them. In the following sections, we accordingly discuss the attributes of an experience process and also a consumer's perception of the value of an experience.

## 14.4.  Attributes of an Experience Process

According to the above definition, experience is shaped in the minds of customers and depends highly on them (Ek, Larsen, Hornskov, & Mansfeldt, 2008). Surely, for these reasons, the roles of the supplier and receiver in the designed experience are correspondingly changed. *Consumers*, in the traditional service-oriented view, are rational decision makers, focusing on the functional 'features-and-benefits' (Williams, 2006, p. 485) of products, whereas experiential marketing views them as emotional beings, who are not merely passive consumers (receivers), but are creative, interactive agents (Richards & Wilson, 2006; Wearing & Wearing, 1996), focusing on achieving pleasurable and memorable experiences (Hudson & Ritchie, 2009; Zehrer, 2009). *Experience stagers*, although they cannot 'give' an experience per se to consumers, can respond to customers' demands by creating certain conditions in which input and opportunities are provided to enable each customer to shape their own experience, and differentiate the experience as against other competitors (Högström, Rosner, & Gustafsson, 2010). Thus, designed experience process is co-created by both experience stagers and customers (see Figure 14.1). In the experiential context that stagers create, customers have the chance to shape their own unique experience (Mossberg, 2007).

### 14.4.1. Customer and Manager Perspectives

In recent years, a consensus has emerged that characterizes experience as involving a multi-dimensional but 'holistic' evaluation by the consumer (e.g. Gentile et al., 2007; Schmitt, 1999b). Thus, from *a customer outcome or evaluation perspective (noun)*, an experience is a blend of many elements that have come together (Shaw & Ivens, 2002) to involve consumers emotionally, physically, intellectually and spiritually, so a variety of consumers' senses will be stimulated (Mossberg, 2007). As a result, from this perspective, the attributes of an experience include 'anything that can be perceived or sensed — or recognized by its absence' (Berry et al., 2002, p. 86) so long as it is recalled after the experience process is complete. Previous studies have explored various perceived experience attributes, such as atmosphere (e.g. Bitner, 1992; Heide, Lærdal, & Grønhaug, 2007), interaction with personnel and other

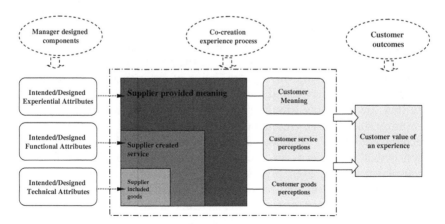

Figure 14.1: A model of a designed experience.

customers (e.g. Heide & Grønhaug, 2006; Mossberg, 2007), a theme or story (e.g. Mossberg, 2008; Nelson, 2009) and memorabilia or souvenirs (e.g. Ferdinand & Williams, 2010; Gordon, 1986).

Analysing experiences and identifying such evaluative attributes are typically done through interviews with customers and leads to typologies such as that of Carbone and Haeckel (1994), distinguishing between performance- and context-based attributes. Performance-based attributes relate to the function of a product and refer to 'technical skills performance' (Ellis & Rossman, 2008). In contrast to them, context-based attributes involve the multi-sensory environment in which experience is offered. They comprise two types: one involve 'mechanics', emitted by *things* (e.g. landscaping, graphics, scents and recorded music used in a heritage site); the other are 'humanics', emitted by *people*, and engineered by defining and choreographing the desired behaviour of employees involved in the customer encounter (Carbone & Haeckel, 1994). For instance, a tour guide plays the role of a source of information for tourists (Josiam, Mattson, & Sullivan, 2004), of path-finders and the mentors (Cohen, 1985), as well as of mediators between tourists and local scenes (Dahles, 2002), all of which help to orchestrate the experience.

From *a managerial perspective*, the design of an experience process must be distinct from the design of a product, otherwise when we discuss experiences we are just talking about products. Here we may draw on the distinction between 'mere experience' and 'an experience' discussed above. We consider that an experience as an offering is different from 'mere experience' and may be distinguished by special attributes, called experiential attributes, which concern emotions and refer to the features of products that encourage a set of interactions between consumer and the company or the company's offering (Addis & Holbrook, 2001; Caru & Cova, 2003) in harmony with different moments of contact or touchpoints (LaSalle & Britton, 2003; Shaw & Ivens, 2002), which can lead to consumers' active involvement in an experience.

In this perspective, the physical goods and functional service involved in the experience process are not completely unrelated to an experience. In service marketing, tangible goods can be viewed as embodying knowledge and activities (Normann & Ramírez, 1993). They may be 'appliances' (Vargo & Lusch, 2004a, p. 9) for service performance and can partly replace the direct service, as the 'importance of physical goods lies not so much in owning them as in obtaining the services they render' (Kotler, 1977, p. 8). Moving into design of experience, these 'appliances' are platforms not only for service but also for meeting higher-order needs (Rifkin, 2000), because they are 'artefacts, around which customers have experiences' (Prahalad & Ramaswamy, 2000, p. 84). Gutman (1982, p. 60) considered that goods are 'means' for reaching 'end-states', or 'valued states of being, such as happiness, security, and accomplishment'. In other words, people purchase goods for the benefit of owning them, displaying them, even experiencing them, such as key chains with iconic monuments or landmarks and local artefacts made from indigenous material. In these processes, goods can provide more benefits (including satisfaction, memories and so on) for people, which are beyond those associated with the basic functions of goods. Therefore, physical goods are 'platforms or appliances that assist in providing benefits ... [they can be] viewed as distribution mechanisms for services' (Vargo & Lusch, 2004a, p. 9), and a component of provision of benefits for experience.

Managers design experiences through choosing to include in the experience process a series of goods with technical attributes, services with functional attributes and meanings derived from experiential attributes. As discussed above, a goods component ('appliance') of an experience process may embody functional and/or experiential attributes as well as technical attributes. In Disney World, Cinderella's Castle, a striking replica of a medieval castle is provided for dinners. Employees are not only dressed in accurate replicas of medieval costumes, but also play the role of hosts from the medieval era, seating the guest, taking orders and serving food and beverages (Ellis & Rossman, 2008). All these elements construct an imaginary world for dinners.

Therefore, an experience outcome is not self-generated but induced, because it is derived from individually perceived episodes of a process that invoke emotional and cognitive responses. The outcome is then perceived holistically and 'integrated as a contingent type of value that stands side-by-side with utilitarian and socially expressive benefits, ... experiential benefits supplement the functional benefit contribution of an offering and possible even substitute it' (Kilian, 2009, p. 29). The designed experiences are *created* 'whenever a company intentionally uses services as the stage and goods as props to engage an individual' (Pine & Gilmore, 1999, p. 11) in a way that creates a memorable event. Therefore, on the one hand, products can be seen as the media used to involve customers in an experience, such as memorabilia, special ways of serving food and beverages; on the other hand, they are only part of an experience, such as visiting an exclusive golden bathroom, or visiting the Great Wall because of the Chinese saying 'One who fails to reach the Great Wall is not a hero'. In this case, a holistic experience is a combination of goods, service and experience; there are other components in an experience (i.e. experiential attributes) apart from those of the products, which can provide memorable sensations for consumers.

### 14.4.2. The Hierarchical Level of Experience Attributes

In many studies, quality is usually regarded as the result of a customer's subjective evaluation of a product (Eggert & Ulaga, 2002; Sweeney & Soutar, 2001). In this case, the dimensions used to evaluate quality are adopted for this chapter as the attributes of product in a holistic experience. Two dimensions can be identified: a technical or outcome dimension and a functional or process-related dimension (Grönroos, 2000; Parasuraman, Zeithaml, & Berry, 1985; Zeithaml, 1988). The former refers to what is delivered to consumers; the latter refers to how it is delivered. Furthermore, 'an experience cannot happen without the consumer's involvement' (LaSalle & Britton, 2003, p. 29). If there is intense physical and/or mental involvement with a product during its consumption, then it is increasingly likely to lead to a memorable experience. Therefore, the features of the product that encourage active involvement may be considered as experiential attributes. 'All of the outcomes of service processes are obviously part of the quality of experience' (Grönroos, 2000, p. 63), but the intensity, involvement and meaningfulness of the experience make it memorable. Through an experience, the objective world is perceived by and related to customers. A two-perspective hierarchy of attributes in an experience is presented in Figure 14.1.

On the left of Figure 14.1, we see the three levels or types of attributes that a manager would consider in designing an experience. *Technical attributes* refer that what is made for the customer or what the customer is left with physically, when service process and the experiential interactions are over, i.e. the concrete goods. For example, the postcard of a cultural heritage site. All these things are tangible and usually standardized. On the middle level are *functional attributes*, which refer that how to help consumer get the goods and how to help him experience the simultaneous 'production' and 'consumption' process, i.e. the services, for example, the service that allows a customer to send postcards to a friend at the exit of the cultural heritage site, or a video about the heritage site screened on site. Because these services are intangible, they are not totally the same when they are delivered each time, but may be similar for different interactive experiences. At the top level are *experiential attributes*, which are intended to provide a meaningful and hence memorable experience. Thus, the tangible goods and functional services are the media for an experience, but its meaning is increased and made memorable through enhancement and design. The more emotion is induced, or the customer actively involved, or the meaningfulness to them enhanced, the more the experience will be memorable.

In the middle of Figure 14.1, a consumer's perception is shown again at three levels, which are actually often considered as a holistic gestalt. As an ending of the experience process, the consumer has perceptions of the product as well as ascribing a meaning to it. If little or no meaning is identified then it is a 'mere' experience. If the meaning is intense, then we talk of 'an experience' and would generally consider that it provides the customer with value, showing on the right of Figure 14.1 and discussed in the next section.

## 14.5. Customer Outcomes — Customer Value of an Experience

'Customer value is the basic foundation for everything we do in marketing' (Holbrook, 2005, p. 46), and identifying and creating CV are regarded as essential prerequisites for long-term company survival and success (Huber, Herrmann, & Morgan, 2001; Porter, 1996). Researchers have constructed a number of models to understand CV (Payne & Holt, 2001), and two approaches may be identified, one focusing on perceived CV and the other on desired CV (Graf & Maas, 2008).

The initial studies of CV were based on the functional definition of value in terms of performance (quality) and outcome (benefits). For example, Monroe (1979) regards value as '… [a] cognitive trade-off between perceptions of quality and sacrifice' (Dodds, Monroe, & Grewal, 1991, p. 308). In many studies, quality is usually considered to be the result of a customer's subjective evaluation of a product, while benefits are assessed by consumers about their purchased products (Eggert & Ulaga, 2002; Sweeney & Soutar, 2001), and often are related to satisfaction.

However, many authors, from a consumer perspective, asserted that what customers perceive from a product may be not what they desire, in other words, perceived CV is different from desired CV. Here desired CV is conceptualized as a part of consumers' value system and relates to abstract value dimensions or consequences derived from specific performance characteristics (e.g. Holbrook, 1994; Woodruff, 1997). In his study, Woodruff (1997, p. 142) stated that:

> Customer value is a customer's perceived preference for and evaluation of those product attributes, attribute performances, and consequences arising from use that facilitate (or block) achieving the customer's goals and purposes in use situations.

Woodruff's definition of CV incorporates both desired and received value, and shows that customers' value judgments are subject and context-specific, determined within the constraints of a particular use situation, rather than product attributes, and emphasize those derived from customers' learned perceptions, preferences and evaluation.

The concept of CV in previous studies is related to the traditional goods-dominant logic of marketing, where value is produced by or embedded into a product (most of the time) and exchanged with a customer, i.e. value-in-exchange. In this case, customers are passive receivers, as they can only cognitively and rationally perceive or desire the delivered value of the product. With the research shift from the 'world of products' to the 'world of experience', a customer-centred perspective of the roles of suppliers and receivers in the value creation process developed (e.g. Edvardsson, Gustafsson, & Roos, 2005; Grönroos, 2006; Lusch, Vargo, & O'Brien, 2007; Vargo & Lusch, 2008). These authors consider that value is perceived and evaluated at the time of consumption.

For customers, products are no longer merely considered as categories of marketing offerings (Heinonen & Strandvik, 2009), but as perspectives on value creation. In other words, only when a customer is using a good, receiving a service or involved in an experience, is it possible for the value of the product, or experience, to be realized or evaluated by a customer, i.e. in the form of 'value-in-use' (*Ibid.*) or 'value-in-experience' (Turnbull, 2009). Sandström, Edvardsson, Kristensson, and Magnusson (2008) related value to the entire experience and defined it as 'the individual judgment of the sum total of all the functional and emotional experience outcomes' (p. 120). Hence, value is individual to every customer who has become an active value co-creator (Vargo & Lusch, 2004a, 2004b). In this chapter, we use a new term to describe CV of this type, *customer value of an experience* (CVE), since 'experiential value' appearing in some previous studies (e.g. Constantinides, 2004; Jeong, Fiore, Niehm, & Lorenz, 2009) is more likely to be regarded as one type of value rather than customers' perception of an entire experience.

There are numerous studies examining CV, but few relating to CVE (Yuan & Wu, 2008). Mathwick, Malhotra, and Rigdon (2001, 2002) considered that CVE was derived from 'interactions involving either direct usage or distanced appreciation of products and services' (2001, p. 41). The interactions provide the basis for relative preferences, i.e. CVE, held by the individuals involved (Holbrook & Corfman, 1985). CVE offers both extrinsic and intrinsic benefit (Babin & Darden, 1995; Crowley, Spangenberg, & Hughes, 1992; Mano & Oliver, 1993). Extrinsic benefit is usually derived from buying experiences that are utilitarian in nature, while intrinsic value is derived from the appreciation of the experience itself (such as a theatrical performance) (Mathwick et al., 2001). Furthermore, in a process of experience consumption, a customer can be either active or passive (Holbrook, 1994). The more active or participative a customer is, the higher the collaboration between the consumer and the marketing entity. Consumer collaboration is regarded as a necessary prerequisite to create a playful, game-like exchange experience (Deighton & Grayson, 1995). Given these view, Mathwick et al. (2001) presented a CVE scale, consisting of playfulness, aesthetics, customer return on investment, and service excellence.

We may notice that this CVE scale, similar to many previous studies, seeks to understand CV from a customer perspective. However, a one-side perspective is not suitable for either making marketing decisions or operationalizing the construct (Smith & Colgate, 2007), because experiences are co-created by both experience stagers and customers. Given this limitation, Smith and Colgate (2007) adopted a strategic marketing orientation and distinguished four major types of CV that can be 'created' by organizations:

- functional/instrumental value is concerned with the extent to which a product (good or service) has desired characteristics, is useful, or performs a desired function;
- experiential/hedonic value is concerned with the extent to which a product creates appropriate experiences, feelings and emotions for the customer;
- symbolic/expressive value is concerned with the extent to which customers attach or associate psychological meaning to a product;
- cost/sacrifice value is concerned with the transaction costs.

These types of CV are based on the identification of five major sources of value — information, products, interactions, environment and ownership, they are useful tools for managers to specify and illustrate value creation strategies, identify opportunities for new value creation propositions and suggest enhancements to the value propositions of existing products. These four types of CV are used in this chapter.

## 14.6.  Discussion, Conclusion and Further Research

In the above, we distinguished between the concept of experience as a process and as a meaningful psychological outcome resulting from a person's involvement. Only after a customer undergoes an experience process is the experience realized and able to be evaluated. Thus, an experience is 'a mental journey' (Sundbo & Hagedorn-Rasmussen, 2008, p. 83).

A rigorous framework has been developed based on this distinction that considers both a managerial and customer perspective of an experience. In this 'design' approach, an experience process is not self-generated but induced, and thus the manager can influence the outcome. Experience stagers cannot 'give' an experience to tourists, but they can create certain conditions providing opportunities for each tourist to create his or her own memorable experience. For experience stagers, it is important to identify the attributes that they can use or integrate into a 'platform' involving or interacting with tourists to affect their perceived value. The linkage between experience attributes designed by stagers, especially the experiential attributes, and tourists' perception of value is constructed in the following conceptual framework (see Figure 14.2).

One of the consequences of this model is that tourism managers should identify the value they add to an experience. If on a holiday to a resort island in the tropics, a couple share a romantic sunset and create a memory that they value for the rest of their lives, is the manager responsible or been involved in the design of this experience outcome? How much does the designer of a restaurant-based experiential process contribute to the value of the dining experience? These questions may be difficult to answer, but are derived from the conceptual framework developed.

In order to test this model, it is proposed to undertake qualitative research initially to identify the experience attributes of a process from a tourist and a managerial perspective, and seek to understand the linkage between them. This information will help to identify what different types of attributes are embodied in an experience rather than those in a product (i.e. experiential attributes). The research proposed will also seek to understand the different types of perceived value of an experience, and hence, through the linkage between the designed attributes and the perceived

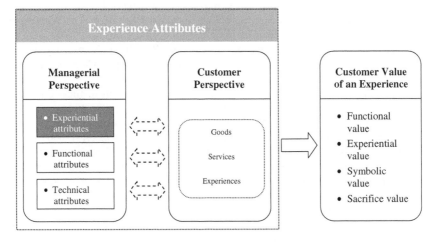

Figure 14.2: Conceptual framework.

attributes, the effect of designed attributes on tourists' perception of value can be identified.

Developing an understanding of how managers of all types of products (goods, services, destinations) design for experiential attributes is also considered as an important focus for subsequent researchers. The conceptual framework provided may be empirically tested in different contexts. The results will benefit tourism planners, managers and marketers in developing and designing offerings for tourists to create their experiences.

# References

Abbott, L. (1955). *Quality and competition: An essay in economic theory.* New York, NY: Columbia University Press.

Addis, M., & Holbrook, M. B. (2001). On the conceptual link between mass customisation and experiential consumption: An explosion of subjectivity. *Journal of Consumer Behaviour, 1*(1), 50–66.

Babin, B. J., & Darden, W. R. (1995). Consumer self-regulation in a retail environment. *Journal of Retailing, 71*(1), 47–70.

Berry, L. L., Carbone, L. P., & Haeckel, S. H. (2002). Managing the total customer experience. *MIT Sloan Management Review, 43*(3), 85–89.

Bitner, M. J. (1992). Servicescapes: The impact of physical surroundings on customers and employees. *Journal of Marketing, 56*(2), 57–71.

Carbone, L. P., & Haeckel, S. H. (1994). Engineering customer experiences. *Marketing Management, 3*(3), 8–19.

Caru, A., & Cova, B. (2003). Revisiting consumption experience: A more humble but complete view of the concept. *Marketing Theory, 3*(2), 267–286. doi: 10.1177/147059310300 32004

Cohen, E. (1985). The tourist guide: The origins, structure and dynamics of a role. *Annals of Tourism Research, 12*(1), 5–29. doi: 10.1016/0160-7383(85)90037-4

Constantinides, E. (2004). Influencing the online consumer's behavior: The Web experience. *Internet Research, 14*(2), 111–126.

Crowley, A. E., Spangenberg, E. R., & Hughes, K. R. (1992). Measuring the hedonic and utilitarian dimensions of attitudes toward product categories. *Marketing Letters, 3*(3), 239–249.

Dahles, H. (2002). The politics of tour guiding: Image management in Indonesia. *Annals of Tourism Research, 29*(3), 783–800. doi: 10.1016/s0160-7383(01)00083-4

Deighton, J., & Grayson, K. (1995). Marketing and seduction: Building exchange relationships by managing social consensus. *The Journal of Consumer Research, 21*(4), 660–676.

Dilthey, W. (1976). *Selected writings.* Cambridge, UK: Cambridge University Press.

Dodds, W. B., Monroe, K. B., & Grewal, D. (1991). Effects of price, brand, and store information on buyers' product evaluations. *Journal of Marketing Research, 28*(3), 307–319.

Edvardsson, B., Gustafsson, A., & Roos, I. (2005). Service portraits in service research: A critical review. *International Journal of Service Industry Management, 16*(1), 107–121.

Eggert, A., & Ulaga, W. (2002). Customer perceived value: A substitute for satisfaction in business markets? *Journal of Business & Industrial Marketing, 17*(2/3), 107–118.

Ek, R., Larsen, J., Hornskov, S. B., & Mansfeldt, O. K. (2008). A dynamic framework of tourist experiences: Space-time and performances in the experience economy. *Scandinavian Journal of Hospitality and Tourism, 8*(2), 122–140. doi: 10.1080/15022250802110091

Ellis, G. D., & Rossman, J. R. (2008). Creating value for participants through experience staging: Parks, recreation, and tourism in the experience industry. *Journal of Park and Recreation Administration, 26*(4), 1–20.

Ferdinand, N., & Williams, N. L. (2010). Tourism memorabilia and the tourism experience. In M. Morgan, P. Lugosi & J. R. B. Ritchie (Eds.), *The tourism and leisure experience: Consumer and managerial perspectives* (pp. 202–217). Bristol, UK: Channel View Publications.

Firat, A. F. (2001). The meanings and messages of Las Vegas: The present of our future. *M@n@gement, 4*(3), 101–120.

Gentile, C., Spiller, N., & Noci, G. (2007). How to sustain the customer experience: An overview of experience components that co-create value with the customer. *European Management Journal, 25*(5), 395–410.

Gordon, B. (1986). The souvenir: Messenger of the extraordinary. *The Journal of Popular Culture, 20*(3), 135–146. doi: 10.1111/j.0022-3840.1986.2003_135.x

Graf, A., & Maas, P. (2008). Customer value from a customer perspective: A comprehensive review. *Journal für Betriebswirtschaft, 58*(1), 1–20. doi: 10.1007/s11301-008-0032-8

Grönroos, C. (2000). *Service management and marketing: A customer relationship management approach* (2nd ed.). Chichester, UK: Wiley.

Grönroos, C. (2006). Adopting a service logic for marketing. *Marketing Theory, 6*(3), 317–333. doi: 10.1177/1470593106066794

Gupta, S., & Vajic, M. (2000). The contextual and dialectical nature of experiences. In J. A. Fitzsimmons & M. Fitzsimmons (Eds.), *New service development: Creating memorable experiences* (pp. 33–51). Thousand Oaks, CA: Sage.

Gutman, J. (1982). A means-end chain model based on consumer categorization processes. *The Journal of Marketing, 46*(2), 60–72.

Havlena, W., & Holbrook, M. B. (1986). The varieties of consumption experience: Comparing two typologies of emotion in consumer behaviour. *Journal of Consumer Research, 13*(3), 394–404.

Heide, M., & Grønhaug, K. (2006). Atmosphere: Conceptual issues and implications for hospitality management. *Scandinavian Journal of Hospitality and Tourism, 6*(4), 271–286.

Heide, M., Lærdal, K., & Grønhaug, K. (2007). The design and management of ambience — Implications for hotel architecture and service. *Tourism Management, 28*(5), 1315–1325. doi: 10.1016/j.tourman.2007.01.011

Heinonen, K., & Strandvik, T. (2009). Monitoring value-in-use of e-service. *Journal of Service Management, 20*(1), 33–51.

Högström, C., Rosner, M., & Gustafsson, A. (2010). How to create attractive and unique customer experiences: An application of Kano's theory of attractive quality to recreational tourism. *Marketing Intelligence & Planning, 28*(4), 385–402.

Holbrook, M. B. (1994). The nature of customer value: An axiology of services in the consumption experience. In R. T. Rust & R. L. Oliver (Eds.), *Service quality: New directions in theory and practice* (pp. 21–71). Thousand Oaks, CA: Sage.

Holbrook, M. B. (2005). Customer value and autoethnography: Subjective personal introspection and the meanings of a photograph collection. *Journal of Business Research, 58*(1), 45–61. doi: 10.1016/s0148-2963(03)00079-1

Holbrook, M. B., Chestnut, R. W., Oliva, T. A., & Greenleaf, E. A. (1984). Play as a consumption experience: The role of emotions, performance and personality in the enjoyment of games. *Journal of Consumer Research, 11*(2), 728–739.

Holbrook, M. B., & Corfman, K. P. (1985). Quality and value in the consumption experience: Phaedrus rides again. In J. Jacoby & J. C. Olson (Eds.), *Perceived quality: How consumers view stores and merchandise* (pp. 31–57). Lexington, MA: Lexington Books.

Holbrook, M. B., & Hirschman, E. C. (1982). The experiential aspects of consumption: Consumer fantasies, feelings, and fun. *The Journal of Consumer Research, 9*(2), 132–140.

Holbrook, M. B., O'Shaughnessy, J., & Bell, S. (1990). Actions and reactions in the consumer experience: The complementary roles of reasons and emotions in consumer behaviour. *Research in Consumer Behaviour, 4*, 131–163.

Huang, Y., Scott, N., Ding, P., & Cheng, D. (2012). Impression of Liusanjie: Effect of mood on experience and satisfaction. *International Journal of Tourism Research, 14*(1), 91–102. doi: 10.1002/jtr.829

Huber, F., Herrmann, A., & Morgan, R. E. (2001). Gaining competitive advantage through customer value oriented management. *The Journal of Consumer Marketing, 18*(1), 41–53.

Hudson, S., & Ritchie, J. R. B. (2009). Branding a memorable destination experience. The case of 'Brand Canada'. *International Journal of Tourism Research, 11*(2), 217–228.

Jeong, S. W., Fiore, A. M., Niehm, L. S., & Lorenz, F. O. (2009). The role of experiential value in online shopping: The impacts of product presentation on consumer responses towards an apparel web site. *Internet Research, 19*(1), 105–124.

Josiam, B. M. B. M., Mattson, M., & Sullivan, P. (2004). The historaunt: Heritage tourism at Mickey's dining car. *Tourism Management, 25*(4), 453–461. doi: 10.1016/s0261-5177(03)00126-2

Kilian, K. (2009). Experiential marketing and brand experiences: A conceptual framework. In A. Lindgreen, J. Vanhamme & M. B. Beverland (Eds.), *Memorable customer experiences: A research anthology* (pp. 25–44). Farnham, UK: Gower.

Kotler, P. (1977). *Marketing management: Analysis, planning, implementation, and control* (3rd ed.). Upper Saddle River, NJ: Prentice Hall.

LaSalle, D., & Britton, T. A. (2003). *Priceless: turning ordinary products into extraordinary experiences*. Boston, MA: Harvard Business School Press.

Lusch, R. F., Vargo, S. L., & O'Brien, M. (2007). Competing through service: Insights from service-dominant logic. *Journal of Retailing, 83*(1), 5–18. doi: 10.1016/j.jretai.2006.10.002

Mano, H., & Oliver, R. L. (1993). Assessing the dimensionality and structure of the consumption experience: Evaluation, feeling, and satisfaction. *The Journal of Consumer Research, 20*(3), 451–466.

Mathwick, C., Malhotra, N. K., & Rigdon, E. (2001). Experiential value: Conceptualization, measurement and application in the catalog and Internet shopping environment. *Journal of Retailing, 77*(1), 39–56.

Mathwick, C., Malhotra, N. K., & Rigdon, E. (2002). The effect of dynamic retail experiences on experiential perceptions of value: An internet and catalog comparison. *Journal of Retailing, 78*(1), 51–60. doi: 10.1016/s0022-4359(01)00066-5

Monroe, K. B. (1979). *Pricing: making profitable decisions*. New York, NY: McGraw-Hill.

Morgan, M., Elbe, J., & de Esteban Curiel, J. (2009). Has the experience economy arrived? The views of destination managers in three visitor-dependent areas. *Progress in Tourism and Hospitality Research, 11*(2), 201–216.

Mossberg, L. (2007). A marketing approach to the tourist experience. *Scandinavian Journal of Hospitality and Tourism, 7*(1), 59–74. doi: 10.1080/15022250701231915

Mossberg, L. (2008). Extraordinary experiences through storytelling. *Scandinavian Journal of Hospitality and Tourism, 8*(3), 195–210.

Nelson, K. B. (2009). Enhancing the attendee's experience through creative design of the event environment: Applying Goffman's dramaturgical perspective. *Journal of Convention & Event Tourism, 10*(2), 120–133.

Normann, R., & Ramírez, R. (1993). From value chain to value constellation: Designing interactive strategy. *Harvard Business Review, 71*(4), 65–77.

Oh, H., Fiore, A. M., & Jeoung, M. (2007). Measuring experience economy concepts: Tourism applications. *Journal of Travel Research, 46*(2), 119–132.

Parasuraman, A., Zeithaml, V. A., & Berry, L. L. (1985). A conceptual model of service quality and its implications for future research. *The Journal of Marketing, 49*(4), 41–50.

Payne, A., & Holt, S. (2001). Diagnosing customer value: Integrating the value process and relationship marketing. *British Journal of Management, 12*(2), 159–182. doi: 10.1111/1467-8551.00192

Pickett, J. P. (2000). *The American heritage dictionary of the English language* (4th ed.). Boston, MA: Houghton Mifflin.

Pine, B. J., & Gilmore, J. H. (1998). Welcome to the experience economy. *Harvard Business Review, 76*(4), 97–105.

Pine, B. J., & Gilmore, J. H. (1999). *The experience economy: Work is theatre & every business a stage.* Boston, MA: Harvard Business School Press.

Porter, M. E. (1996). What is strategy? *Harvard Business Review, 74*(6), 61–78.

Prahalad, C. K., & Ramaswamy, V. (2000). Co-opting customer competence. *Harvard Business Review, 78*(1), 79–87.

Prahalad, C. K., & Ramaswamy, V. (2004). Co-creation experiences: The next practice in value creation. *Journal of Interactive Marketing, 18*(3), 5–14. doi: 10.1002/dir.20015

Richards, G., & Wilson, J. (2006). Developing creativity in tourist experiences: A solution to the serial reproduction of culture? *Tourism Management, 27*(6), 1209–1223.

Rifkin, J. (2000). *The age of access: The new culture of hypercapitalism, where all of life is a paid-for experience.* New York, NY: J.P. Tarcher/Putnam.

Sandström, S., Edvardsson, B., Kristensson, P., & Magnusson, P. (2008). Value in use through service experience. *Managing Service Quality, 18*(2), 112–126.

Schänzel, H. A., & McIntosh, A. J. (2000). An insight into the personal and emotive context of wildlife viewing at the penguin place, Otago Peninsula, New Zealand. *Journal of Sustainable Tourism, 8*(1), 36–52.

Schmitt, B. (1999a). Experiential marketing. *Journal of Marketing Management, 15*(1–3), 53–67.

Schmitt, B. (1999b). *Experiential marketing: How to get customers to sense, feel, think, act, and relate to your company and brands.* New York, NY: Free Press.

Schmitt, B. (2003). *Customer experience management: A revolutionary approach to connecting with your customer.* Hoboken, NJ: Wiley.

Scott, N., Laws, E., & Boksberger, P. (2009). The marketing of hospitality and leisure experiences. *Journal of Hospitality Marketing & Management, 18*(2–3), 1–12.

Shaw, C., & Ivens, J. (2002). *Building great customer experiences.* New York, NY: Palgrave.

Smith, J. B., & Colgate, M. (2007). Customer value creation: A practical framework. *The Journal of Marketing Theory and Practice, 15*(1), 7–23.

Soanes, C., & Stevenson, A. (Eds.). (2009). *Concise Oxford English dictionary* (11th ed.). Oxford, UK: Oxford University Press.

Sternberg, E. (1997). The iconography of the tourism experience. *Annals of Tourism Research, 24*(4), 951–969. doi: 10.1016/s0160-7383(97)00053-4

Sundbo, J., & Hagedorn-Rasmussen, P. (2008). The backstaging of experience production. In J. Sundbo & P. Darmer (Eds.), *Creating experiences in the experience economy* (pp. 83–110). Cheltenham, UK: Edward Elgar Publishing.

Sweeney, J. C., & Soutar, G. N. (2001). Consumer perceived value: The development of a multiple item scale. *Journal of Retailing, 77*(2), 203–220. doi: 10.1016/s0022-4359(01)00041-0

Toffler, A. (1970). *Future shock*. London, UK: Bodley Head.

Tourism Australia. (2011). *Driving visitation to Australia using experience themes*. Retrieved from http://www.tourism.australia.com/en-au/documents/Corporate%20-%20Research/Experience_Fact_Sheet.pdf

Turnbull, J. (2009). Customer value-in-experience: Theoretical foundation and research agenda. *Australia and New Zealand marketing academy: Proceedings of the ANZMAC 2009 Melbourne conference, Melbourne*. Retrieved from http://www.anzmac.org

Turner, V. W., & Bruner, E. M. (1986). *The anthropology of experience*. Urbana, IL: University of Illinois Press.

Vargo, S. L., & Lusch, R. F. (2004a). Evolving to a new dominant logic for marketing. *The Journal of Marketing, 68*(1), 1–17.

Vargo, S. L., & Lusch, R. F. (2004b). The four service marketing myths: Remnants of a goods-based, manufacturing model. *Journal of Service Research, 6*(4), 324–335.

Vargo, S. L., & Lusch, R. F. (2008). Service-dominant logic: Continuing the evolution. *Journal of the Academy of Marketing Science, 36*(1), 1–10. doi: 10.1007/s11747-007-0069-6

Wearing, B., & Wearing, S. (1996). Refocussing the tourist experience: The flaneur and the choraster. *Leisure Studies, 15*(4), 229–243. doi: 10.1080/026143696375530

Williams, A. (2006). Tourism and hospitality marketing: Fantasy, feeling and fun. *International Journal of Contemporary Hospitality Management, 18*(6), 482–495.

Woodruff, R. B. (1997). Customer value: The next source for competitive advantage. *Journal of the Academy of Marketing Science, 25*(2), 139–153.

Yuan, Y. H., & Wu, C. (2008). Relationships among experiential marketing, experiential value, and customer satisfaction. *Journal of Hospitality & Tourism Research, 32*(3), 387–410. doi: 10.1177/1096348008317392

Zehrer, A. (2009). Service experience and service design: Concepts and application in tourism SMEs. *Managing Service Quality, 19*(3), 332–349.

Zeithaml, V. A. (1988). Consumer perceptions of price, quality, and value: A means-end model and synthesis of evidence. *The Journal of Marketing, 52*(3), 2–22.

# Chapter 15

# The Service-Dominant Logic Approach to Tourism Marketing Strategy

*Sun-Young Park and Stephen L. Vargo*

## 15.1. Introduction

As competition among tourism firms and destinations is ever increasing, a strategic approach to tourism marketing has become essential to success. Furthermore, the rapid changes in market conditions and technological advancements have called into question the traditional marketing approaches and their assumptions, which were developed, based on manufactured goods and suited for mass markets (Normann & Ramírez, 1993; Prahalad & Ramaswamy, 2004; Ramaswamy & Gouillart, 2010; Rust, Moorman, & Bhalla, 2010; Vargo & Lusch, 2004a), what Vargo and Lusch (2004a, 2008) call *goods-dominant (G-D) logic*. As Drucker (1980) warned, 'The greatest danger in times of turbulence is not the turbulence; it is to act with yesterday's logic'. Scholars from a wide array of business-related disciplines are increasingly recognizing the viability of an alternative to the traditional, G-D logic of exchange: *service-dominant (S-D) logic*.

We believe the S-D logic approach can provide an important basis for developing tourism marketing strategy that is more encompassing, adaptive and robust for changing market conditions. One key element of S-D logic is that value is co-created among social/economic actors, and value is actualized (co-created) and determined by the customer — rather than value being embedded in the offering by a firm (Vargo & Lusch, 2004a, 2008). The notion that value is co-created is especially applicable to tourism as social/cultural and economic phenomena concerning tourists, because various parties or entities are explicitly or implicitly involved in the varying phases of tourists' experience — from the multitude of daily stimulants for travel, vacation planning and actual travel experience in a tourism destination where tourists interact with employees, other tourists, local residents, etc., to reminiscing and sharing travel memories with friends, families and other social networks. The S-D logic approach can help tourism organizations recognize the joint roles of the organization, the tourist and these participants and elements in the value co-creation process in a larger picture, and shift the traditional focus on customers from the firm-centric, goods-centred perspective in understanding and facilitating relationship and experience. In this chapter, we discuss an overview of S-D logic and the implications of the S-D logic's key foundational premises (FPs) for tourism marketing strategy in setting marketing objectives, allocating resources and fostering competitive advantage, with a particular focus on understanding relationship and experience.

## 15.2.  Overview of Service-Dominant Logic

As noted, S-D logic, proposed by Vargo and Lusch (2004a, 2008), provides an alternative worldview of social and economic exchange to the traditional view, which they call G-D logic. G-D logic has provided the foundation of economics and business disciplines derived from it, including marketing and (at least initially) its sub-disciplines, such as services marketing, business-to-business (B2B) marketing and relationship marketing. G-D logic is rooted in Smith's (1776) notions of national wealth creation based on the export of tangible output, mostly manufactured goods, which became the foundation for economic philosophy and science. For Smith, creating surplus goods for trade was considered 'productive', whereas other social and economic actions were not, even though they were acknowledged to be essential to individual well-being (Vargo & Lusch, 2004a; Vargo & Morgan, 2005). Given this goods-centred definition of productive activity, over time, the term 'services' became defined by comparison, what goods are not: 'intangible products'. More recently, services have been conceptualized as being products with four distinguishing characteristics: intangibility, heterogeneity (cannot be standardized), inseparability of production and consumption, and perishability (cannot be inventoried for later sale) (Zeithaml, Parasuraman, & Berry, 1985), which are usually considered to be disadvantages, thus making services less desirable than tangible goods (Vargo & Lusch, 2004b).

S-D logic is represented by 10 FPs, as presented in Table 15.1. Central to under-standing S-D logic is understanding the meaning of service. In contrast to '*services*' (usually plural) being seen as a special class of goods, '*service*' (singular) is defined as a *process* (rather than a unit of output) of applying one's competences (knowledge and skills) for the benefit of oneself or another party and is seen as the common denominator of *all* social and economic exchanges. Goods remain important, but are seen as mechanisms for service distribution.

The S-D logic approach to tourism marketing is not just focusing on under-standing and trying to fulfil tourists' needs/wants but also engaging, collaborating with and learning from customers, and adopting these into the firm's process of service provision directly, in person, or indirectly, via goods. Accordingly, the S-D logic approach challenges the conventional focus of tourism marketing strategy, which is based on the conventional marketing approach, regarding the supplier's unidirectional role of creating and adding value, which is then delivered to tourists. Also, the S-D logic approach helps the tourism firm expand its market from narrowly defined 'target' markets that may desire the firm's attributes to dynamic markets that

Table 15.1: Foundational premises of service-dominant logic.

|  | Foundational premise (FP) | Explanation/justification |
|---|---|---|
| FP 1 | Service is the fundamental basis of exchange | The application of operant resources (knowledge and skills), 'service', is the basis for all exchange. Service is exchanged for service |
| FP 2 | Indirect exchange masks the fundamental basis of exchange | Goods, money and institutions mask the service-for-service nature of exchange |
| FP 3 | Goods are distribution mechanisms for service provision | Goods (both durable and non-durable) derive their value through use — the service they provide |
| FP 4 | Operant resources are the fundamental source of competitive advantage | The comparative ability to cause desired change drives competition |
| FP 5 | All economies are service economies | Service (singular) is only now becoming more apparent with increased specialization and outsourcing |
| FP 6 | The customer is always a co-creator of value | Implies value creation is interactional |
| FP 7 | The enterprise cannot deliver value, but only offer value propositions | The firm can offer its applied resources and collaboratively (interactively) create value following acceptance, but cannot create/deliver value alone |
| FP 8 | A service-centred view is inherently customer oriented and relational | Service is customer-determined and co-created; thus, it is inherently customer oriented and relational |
| FP 9 | All economic and social actors are resource integrators | Implies the context of value creation is networks of networks (resource integrators) |
| FP 10 | Value is always uniquely and phenomenologically determined by the beneficiary | Value is idiosyncratic, experiential, contextual and meaning laden |

*Source*: Vargo and Lusch (2008).

would recognize the proposed value by the firm and utilize their own resources to achieve their goals. This expansion is a critical shift in the basis for tourism marketing of defining the 'primary' customers, some of which may not be tapped when focusing on target markets to generate repeat patronage.

In the ensuing sections, we discuss S-D logic's FPs connected with the four major implications for tourism marketing strategy, as summarized in Table 15.2.

Table 15.2: A comparison of tourism marketing strategy approach: conventional versus service-dominant logic.

| | Conventional approach | Service-dominant logic approach |
|---|---|---|
| View of service | Unit of output comparable to goods: for example, two hotel services = a check-in service + a pick-up service | Process of applying one's competences for the beneficiary, using goods as mechanisms for service: for example, direct service (in person) — concierge service; indirect service (via goods) — hotel bed |
| View of tourists and marketing | Recipients of value[a] created, added and delivered by firms or destination marketing organizations — tourists' operant resources are exogenous to value creation, and often not considered | Participants, influencers, collaborators of value[b] co-creation and determination with their operant resources — tourists' operant resources are endogenous to value creation |
| | One-way marketing 'to' tourists via advertising, promotions, public relations — marketing programs that are acted upon tourists | Two-way marketing: directly or indirectly 'with' tourists who are constantly integrating their resources from various networks (e.g. other tourists, destination residents, media, etc.) that they influence or are influenced by |
| View of relationship | Repeat patronage: firm-centric | Much more than repeat patronage: association(s) between two or more parties through shared value and meaning — centred on a resource integrator (e.g. relationships between other tourists who share the same tour) |
| View of experience | Tourist's perceptions of isolated events with the firm (e.g. hotel check-in) or the sum of all events with the firm (e.g. hotel stay) | The experiencer's integration of events, meanings, identification, etc., of a full range of sources — market-facing (e.g. advertising and promotion by hotels), public (e.g. news about the destination politics, culture, online reviews) and private (e.g. family, friends) |

[a]Value-in-exchange.
[b]Value-in-use or value-in-context: value is realized during use and determined in the user context.

## 15.3. Tourism Service: From Output to Process

S-D logic's FPs 1, 2, 3 and 5 inform us that service is the common denominator of all social and economic activities and that goods are vehicles for service distribution. For instance, hotel room features are undoubtedly important, but tourists do not pay for the physicality of them but for the temporary use of the service they render (i.e. accommodation) and value (e.g. comfort, convenience, relaxation, self-image, socialization, etc.) is determined by the tourist depending on the situation. To the hotel, value would be the financial feedback (i.e. the received room use fee) and learning (e.g. the guest's complaints, compliments and/or word of mouth (WOM) to his or her social networks online and/or off-line), which would impact the hotel's future financial feedback. The guests' contribution to the value-co-creating experiences of other guests would also play a part in the hotel's value. This value is co-created between the hotel and the tourist during the tourist's actual usage of the room for his or her own goals and contextual circumstances, such as to sleep, to host a social gathering, to hold a business meeting and so forth (i.e. value-in-use). It also provides a platform for exploring, integrating and experiencing other resources, such as local attractions, meeting new people, etc.

In tourism, the dichotomy of tangible tourism goods (e.g. amenities, attractions and facilities) 'versus' tourism services (e.g. check-in, transportation and cultural performance) is often used, although it is not easy to dissect them. It is perhaps because of this difficulty, and arguably futile attempt, in separating what is actually exchanged in tourism that many different terms have been created, particularly for marketing purposes — adventure tourism, cultural tourism, sports tourism, wine tourism and so on, although each of these forms consists of a cornucopia of social/economic actors, interactions among them and various resources and phases, all contributing to value co-creation and tourists' experiences. This fragmented view of tourists' experiences based on the conventional separation of tangibles versus intangibles is often associated with tourism sectors (March, 1994), which may hinder marketing effectiveness of any tourism firm, because from the tourists' perspective, all these resources are part of their entire tourism experience.

With the S-D logic approach, the focus shifts from outputs to the processes of mutually beneficial interactions, and the participants and their resource integration for value co-creation. The focal role of the service provider is the participation in the creation of positive experiences with customers by making events and processes as seamless as possible. These processes can be direct or indirect, which Normann (2001) calls *relieving* (doing for) and *enabling processes* (facilitating self-service), respectively. For example, in the context of a travel agency business, the process is relieving or direct when the travel agents make travel arrangements, using their competences (i.e. knowledge and access to airline and hotel databases) on behalf of tourists, with minimum hassle and interactions. In contrast, it is enabling or indirect when the travel agents participate in the leisure tourist's resource integration by providing relevant information and materials (e.g. airport information, destination attractions and history) so that the tourist can enjoy the vacation planning process. In this case, the travel agency becomes one of the tourist's resources (e.g. friends, websites, magazines) to facilitate the tourist's positive vacation planning experience. Accordingly, 'a company's offerings have value to the degree that customers can use them as inputs to leverage their own value creation' (Normann & Ramírez, 1993, p. 74).

Reframing the tourism offerings in terms of their service potential, expressed through a value proposition that recognizes the firm's role as one of numerous sources of resources the tourist draws on to achieve desired value from experiences, can help tourism firms discover novel and unique ways of approaches to marketing strategy. This reframing might explain why Southwest Airlines has been successful when many other airlines struggle in the intensely competitive airline industry — while any airline can imitate Southwest Airlines' airplanes, uniforms or even the operational methods, its unique service and co-created value that benefit all involved constituents (the company, its employees, suppliers and customers) have yet to be effectively surpassed by competitors. It also implies that Southwest Airlines has been successful in proposing value (e.g. low-cost, fun air-transportation time) that helps its customers accomplish their own goals (e.g. business, leisure at the destination), and identified its role as one of the customers' resources.

## 15.4.   Tourists as Co-Creators, Not Recipients of Value

According to S-D logic's FPs 6, 7 and 8, the customer always co-creates value with the firm, and the firm can only propose value but cannot deliver it. The focus of service-centric strategy is no longer positioning a firm in a linear value chain but viewing the firm as part of an individual tourist's service system, in which various social/economic actors create value, as depicted in Figure 15.1. The service system is relatively self-contained, self-adjusting systems of resource-integrating actors connected by shared institutional logics and mutual value creation through service

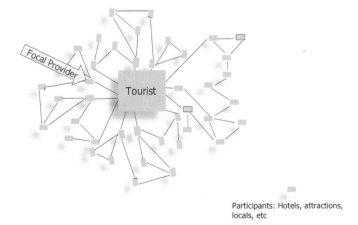

Participants: Hotels, attractions, locals, etc

Figure 15.1: The service system.

exchange (Vargo & Lusch, 2004a, 2008). That is, the individual tourist, not the firm, is central to the value creation process. Thus, S-D logic is 'inherently customer-oriented and relational' (Vargo & Lusch, 2008, p. 8), viewing customers as primary co-creators of value through resource integration and the firm as (often relatively minor) player in the customer's value creation process.

In addition, each resource integrator in value co-creation is a 'service system' (Vargo & Lusch, 2011; Vargo, Maglio, & Akaka, 2008). This wider systems view, akin to Normann and Ramírez's (1993) notion of 'value constellation', can enhance the understanding about tourism and tourist behaviour, as an important ingredient for effective marketing strategy. The implication is that tourism firms should re-evaluate the way they view themselves as 'producers' or 'providers' of value, and tourists as 'recipients' of value created and delivered to them.

Viewing producers apart from recipients is based on the manufacturing production model that tourism firms' marketing activities are 'value-added' through the firm's value creation chain. However, this segregation circumscribes the recognition of the tourists' rich capabilities, role and influence as contributors to value creation. Tourism offerings are not embedded with value and sold to tourists.

Value creation is interactional through dynamic networks, comprising various actors or entities (e.g. employees, the tourist, other guests, technologies). That is, value is created 'with' the tourist throughout the experience process and defined by individual tourists (experiencers), in the context of their own unique circumstances (e.g. personal values, life stage, culture) instead of determined by and flowing unidirectional from the firm to the tourist. All encounter points contribute to creating value or lack thereof. Therefore, tourism firms' goal is not to create value for tourists and others 'but to mobilize them to create their own value from the company's various offerings' (Normann & Ramírez, 1993, p. 69) by finding out ways to facilitate their own value co-creation by providing proper and adequate information and platforms for interactions.

Related to the idea that tourism firms can only propose but not add or deliver value, as tourists are co-creators, FP 10 of S-D logic advises that value is uniquely and phenomenologically determined by the tourist. Similarly, tourism firms cannot provide tourists with certain 'experiences', but they can facilitate them. This idea implies that the value of their offerings is not uniformly experienced by all or most tourists, and that tourists' individual circumstances (e.g. personal experience, background, contexts) may be significant in influencing their value interpretation. Tourists would not have the same experience even when encountering the same offering (e.g. visiting the same museum). The notion of S-D logic that value is phenomenological is supported by Anderson, Pearo, and Widener (2008), in an empirical study of the U.S. airline passengers in which they find that what matter to the passengers depend on situational variables. Also, Mittal and Kamakura (2001) find that satisfied customers' repeat purchase intention is moderated by individual characteristics. Whereas the contextual factors are usually considered as exogenous variables, they are endogenous to the value co-creation process within the framework of S-D logic.

Another implication is that tourism firms need to learn more about tourists' evaluation of their experiences and to rethink assessment. The conventional assessment typically involves satisfaction surveys, which ask customers to evaluate the firm's multiple attributes presumed to matter to them, based on valence (negative–positive) or level (low–high). In contrast, under the S-D logic's approach, the assessment would include customer value interpretations within the tourist's experience journey, namely the interactions with various entities (e.g. employees, the tourist's networks), taking into consideration the goals to be achieved within the particular context (Payne & Holt, 2001; Woodruff, 1997; Woodruff & Gardial, 1996). For instance, tourism firms should systematically monitor and integrate into their marketing the online reviews on various websites (e.g. TripAdvisor, Expedia, etc.), which reveal details of often unsolicited tourists' descriptions of their experiences. As in S-D logic's FP 10, these contextual elements may influence customer experience perceptions of a variety of service dimensions — employees, other customers, servicescape, etc. (e.g. Prebensen & Foss, 2010). With this deeper understanding, the focus of tourism marketing strategy can move towards facilitating the tourist's desired value in their usage context (value-in-use).

We argue that re-examining the tourist's role as value co-creators and the concept of value-in-use are particularly important for tourism marketers, because the fundamental motive for leisure travel is seeking new or different experiences while escaping the mundane environment (Bello & Etzel, 1985; Crompton, 1979; Iso-Ahola, 1982). No matter how highly satisfied, some or many tourists may not return to the same tourism firm or destination in search of other new experiences (Bowen & Shoemaker, 1998; Fyall, Callod, & Edwards, 2003). Similarly, Oh and Jeong (2010) argue that the hotel industry's conventional performance factors (i.e. room, service, price–value and cleanliness) are insufficient differentiators for developing marketing strategies pertinent to each hotel category, although they are good predictors of satisfaction. These findings indicate that guest satisfaction surveys are not able to capture the 'sources' of value-in-use, which in turn are the drivers of competitive advantage. Not only hotel managers and guests perceive value differently (Nasution & Mavondo, 2008), but also the *sources of value-in-use may differ* from those of proposed value (by the firm) that tourists consider in the decision-making phase. For instance, Dubé and Renaghan (2000) find the value sources identified by hotel guests 'during stay' include interactional aspects (e.g. customized service, personal recognition), which were not identified as important for hotel choice decision.

Another critical issue is customers' evaluations as to how well the value they want to achieve in the experience was accomplished, and how positive and influential their WOM will be to other tourists' perceptions and choices via their social networks. Accordingly, tourism firms should have a better understanding about value-in-use at each touch point to examine the drivers through dialogues and communications with tourists — who and what (operand and operant resources) are involved, what the context is, how the resources are processed to co-create value and how the value is evaluated and why. This examination can reveal which aspects of the tourist's experience are problematic and why, and what and how the tourism firm can add or exclude in its service provision and revise value proposition.

Tourism firms may also need to re-examine the notion that acquiring new customers is more costly than retaining existing ones (Reichheld & Sasser, 1990) in the tourism context, which views new and existing customers as passive receivers of or reactors to firms' marketing activities. In tourism, it may be that retention is better conceived of as managing positive and continued interactions with the tourist rather than extracting repeat purchase from the same tourist. That is because the wide-spreading availability and usage of social media may reinforce the importance of WOM and these can influence the perceptions and future choices of other potential tourists that the tourism firm or destination marketing organization is not currently 'targeting'. Accordingly, tourism marketers may need to shift the focus from customer loyalty based on repeat purchase intentions or actual patronage to relationship cultivation including customers' active advocacy — posting positive reviews, defending the firm towards other people's negative reviews, etc. Court, Elzinga, Mulder, and Vetvik (2009) find that the most powerful impetus for purchase is someone else's advocacy, indicating that many firms' marketing budgets are ineffectively spent at the stages where buyers' decisions are not influenced. This finding highlights what S-D logic emphasizes — value is co-created, not delivered by the firm to the customer, and that the customer actively integrates and utilizes resources. The conventional consumer behaviour based on the funnel metaphor — awareness leads to purchase — and marketing dollars spent on paid media to push the firm's offerings included in the consumer's awareness or familiarity set is no longer applicable in today's environment with a myriad of stimuli (Court et al., 2009; Rust et al., 2010). Thus, tourism firms should re-evaluate how and when their customers' decisions are influenced, redefine marketing goals and reallocate marketing budgets that might not have been traditionally considered.

## 15.5. Relationship: From Repeat Transactions to Interactions Among Service Systems

As discussed, the relationship that tourism marketers try to build based on repeat transactions may not be the most effective given the basic motives of tourists (seeking new and different experiences). Moreover, in S-D logic, relationship is much more than repeat patronage — that is, more multiple transactions intended to maximize the firm's profit in terms of customer lifetime value (Vargo, 2009). As explicated in S-D logic, the notion of value in this context, especially manifested by tourism firms' marketing programs, is value-in-exchange (i.e. focusing on the monetary value) and provider-centric. Relationship within S-D logic contains a mutual and comparable link between two or more parties of which association is evolving and adaptive. Relationship is, therefore, not limited to the firm–customer but encompasses all stakeholders in value creation, and there can be multiple levels of relationship.

For example, relationship can stem, often rather subtly, from shared meaning and values of those involved. The tourists can have relationship with one another, as well as with the tourist firms (including employees) and with local residents, simply on the basis of the desire to share similar experiences. In fact, this is likely to be a primary motivator of tourism. Tourist can also develop more direct relationships with the same parties, through the co-creation of value-providing experiences at the destination, sometimes subtly, just by creating context. Relationship can also occur over time, such as with repeat patronage, but it can also occur over time as tourists and others use experiences as contextual background for other future experiences. It is important for tourism service providers to recognize these and other levels of relationship meaning as they develop value propositions, including brand, for tourist. This recognition is also important because, intentionally or unintentionally, tourism firms create value propositions for ecosystem participants — employees, local residents, local attractions, etc., all of which impact the firm's ability to co-create valuable experiences for future tourists.

According to FP 9 of S-D logic, all social/economic actors are resource integrators, indicating that tourism firms, employees, tourists, destination residents and suppliers participate in value creation. Resources can be categorized as *operand resources* (those that must be acted upon to create value, e.g. goods, money, raw materials) and *operant resources* (those capable of acting on other resources to create value, e.g. knowledge and skills) (Vargo & Lusch, 2004a, 2008). Although collaborations among various tourism organizations (e.g. destination marketing organizations, non-profit organizations, private enterprises) are recognized to be critical, S-D logic can enrich and expand the network approach by the inclusion of tourists as one of the network entities to achieve marketing 'with' instead of 'to' tourists who integrate their own operant resources to achieve their goals — physical (e.g. mental endowment, energy, emotions, strength), social (e.g. family relationships, consumer communities, commercial relationships) and cultural (e.g. specialized knowledge and skills, history and imagination) (Arnould, Price, & Malshe, 2006).

Tourists can obtain information about a certain tour company via personal or online communications with those who have heard about or have had experience with it. The number, quality, depth and credibility of information sources can be plentiful. This might imply that it is insufficient to find out that most tourists use WOM as a major information source for choosing a particular tourism firm over other competitors. Due to technological advances and easily accessible and available information, tourists actively search for advice and reviews online as well as off-line. Tourists often exchange unsolicited or solicited information about tourism firms and destinations, which can determine their choice at all stages of decision-making process — prior, during, and post visit. Tourism marketers should integrate their understandings about the tourists' competences in this wider scope into marketing strategy, rather than treating them as peripheral information mainly to influence tourists' immediate decisions with short-term advertisements and promotions. Similar to the enlarged view of relationship in the S-D logic approach, experiences need to be understood as the tourist's integration of all his or her sources beyond the core service encounters with the tourism firm.

## 15.6. Experience: A Resource Integration Perspective

Experience refers to 'direct observation/perceiving of or participation in events' (Merriam-Webster.com), indicating that it is essentially integrative and holistic, because it involves concurrent processing of multiple senses and information. By centring on consumers' experiences, experiential marketing emphasizes sensory, emotional and relational aspects of purchase and consumption, rather than traditional marketing that focuses on product features and functions with the assumption that consumers make rational decisions (Pine & Gilmore, 1998; Prahalad & Ramaswamy, 2003; Schmitt, 1999). Experiential marketing, thus, expands firms' boundary of offering and competition (Schmitt, 1999). For example, a cruise line can offer not only relaxation opportunities but also unique entertainment and food, which enlarges competition bases beyond the cruise industry.

Similar to, but even more encompassing than, the treatment in experiential marketing, *experiences* in S-D logic are more than perceptions of isolated events with some entity (e.g. hotel check-in) or the sum of all events with that entity (e.g. hotel stay), which are often examined within the traditional marketing framework. They represent *the integration of events, meanings, identification, etc.*, of a full range of resources — market-facing (e.g. advertising and promotion by hotels), public (e.g. news about the destination politics, culture, online reviews) and private (e.g. family, friends). In the tourist's experience of Hawaii, shared experiences can also create relationships (e.g. 'I survived the road to Hana', travelling on a tour together). S-D logic provides a wider angle lens that allows one to see that the facilitation of relationships and experiences beyond what is directly related to a focal firm may be more important than what is normally considered as the tourist's core experience. For example, ease of getting to and checking into a hotel and ease of connecting with attractions, restaurants, etc., might be at least as important as rooms and beds. This principle implies that the tourism firm's allowing, if not facilitating and enabling, the tourist's resource integration is often as important as providing core service, and collaboration among service providers is necessary for the tourist experience.

As S-D logic's FP 4 states, when the tourism firm is able to extend its understanding of the tourist's experiences and relationships, the firm's knowledge and skills (how it reconfigures various actors' roles involved in the processes) become its operant resources, which will determine its competitive advantage. Proffering opportunities to tourists for them to utilize knowledge and skills to create value through experience can also overcome the potential discrepancy between the individual uniqueness and tourism marketing strategy developed based on the 'mean' satisfaction scores. This action would alleviate probable frustrations on the tourists' side, as they have a chance to customize their own experience based on their own value interpretation. Also, this would reduce the tourism firm's resource constraints from mass customization, and potential mistakes by 'targeting the middle ground'. Thus, strategy for tourism marketing should incorporate activities such as creating feasible platforms for interactions among those stakeholders and fostering continuous dialogue (Ramaswamy & Gouillart, 2010; Vargo & Akaka, 2009; Vargo & Lusch, 2008).

Tourism firms' marketing 'to' customers can often result in imitable and substitutable marketing strategies and activities. These similarities can then become self-destructive within the industry, as incumbents compete for the same or similar markets with lower prices, which was attested by the airline industry's intense battle in the 1980s and 1990s, leading to overcapacity, price wars and significant financial losses (Baily & Allen, 2005; Barla & Koo, 1999). Tourism firms can develop competitive advantage and create new markets, making current competition irrelevant (Christensen, Anthony, & Roth, 2004; Kim & Mauborgne, 2005) with tourism marketing strategy based on the S-D approach, particularly with the experiences that the firm can uniquely co-create with its customers. The focus of competitive advantage should be the competencies of the tourism firm in reconfigurating relationships and adaptability, because the fast changing environment implies that competitive advantage can quickly become a qualifier in the industry, and the firm's control usually presumed in the unidirectional marketing activities is being abated, while the tourist's power is rising. Thus, S-D logic can provide a good foundation for tourism marketing strategy to be continuously adaptable to changes.

## 15.7. Conclusion

The S-D logic approach offers a revised way of thinking tourism marketing strategy that has been based on the traditional G-D logic, towards a more integrated and collaborative way based on the relational and experiential nature of value creation and assessment. This allows the tourism firm to view itself as part of the tourist's total experience in the process of the tourist's resource integration, and to recognize the importance of not only focusing on providing its service but also understanding all the resource elements within the tourist's experience journey. Thus, the tourism firm can redefine its role as a reliever and/or enabler in the tourist's resource integration process, and collaborate with other participants (stakeholders) in value co-creation to facilitate the tourist's experience as seamless as possible.

Instead of separating tangibles and intangibles, tourism service can be viewed as a process of applying the firm's competences (knowledge and skills) for the tourist's benefits indirectly via goods or directly through interactions where service employees are often a critical part of the firm's competences. The concept of value shifts from value-in-exchange to value-in-use or value-in-context, and the scope of relationship and experience extend beyond the conventional and narrow boundary defined from the firm-centric view. Tourism firms and destination marketing organizations can propose value but cannot add it during production via value chain or deliver it to tourists for 'consumption'. Rather, value is co-created among tourism stakeholders through resource integration and service provision. Thus, tourists should be viewed no longer as recipients of value or targets but as value co-creators who participate in, influence and collaborate with the firm in relationship, utilizing their own resources. Furthermore, tourism marketing research with the S-D logic approach should be focused more on the in-depth understanding of tourists' integration of resources, participation (or non-participation) in the value creation process and interpretation of value under their own contextual circumstances. Throughout this procedure, tourism marketers can also learn more about tourists' networks and find more effective communication methods.

The focus of tourism marketing strategy should be to facilitate the experience sought by tourists at every touch point with the tourism firm by more thoroughly understanding the conditions fostering or prohibiting their participation in co-creation and finding out the firm's capabilities and limitations to develop its own competitive advantage. By formulating marketing strategy based on the S-D logic approach discussed in this chapter, tourism firms can find novel ways to be both competitive and collaborative (e.g. Shaw, Bailey, & Williams, 2011). Accordingly, this contemporary way of thinking about tourism marketing strategy may require unprecedented adjustments within the tourism firm. For example, as Rust et al. (2010) argue, tourism firms may need to consider 'reinventing the marketing department to customer department with a chief customer officer' who supervises customer-related functions within the firm (e.g. research, customer service) (p. 94).

More importantly, the S-D logic approach should be permeated throughout the firm not limited to one department, considering the entire tourist's experience and various social and economic actors involved in the process. As Chandler's (1962) classic strategic management model depicts, the changes in new technology and market conditions require re-evaluation and revision of strategy and structural change for effective implementation. To be consistent with the firm's overall strategy, to make relationship-focused marketing strategy work and to stay competitive, tourism firms might need to foster new organizational culture, reorganize the structure and modify performance measures from the offering to meaningful relationships and social contributions. These knowledge and skills will be the core competences and competitive advantage of the firm (Madhavaram & Hunt, 2008; Webster, 1992) and the basis for the firm performance (Kumar & Petersen, 2005).

Based on our discussion of the S-D logic approach to tourism marketing strategy, the following can be suggested for future directions of tourism research to enhance the understanding about tourist experiences, which can improve tourism marketing strategy. First, akin to the general marketing research, the premises of tourism marketing research should be re-examined and broadened. For example, tourists' resource integration role should be considered when devising a marketing plan as active resource integrators who are constantly and actively involved in co-creating their experience value. Accordingly, future research topics can include examining types and ways that tourists integrate resources; how and why (why not) they participate in value co-creation; and how they interpret and determine value-in-use within the context. Marketing research based on relationships and service systems should go beyond conventional marketing research, such as finding out tourists' characteristics to decide target segments who would be attracted to the attributes/features of the firm or destination, and/or designing marketing mix elements to meet tourists' needs/wants or expectations.

Second, a variety should be encouraged in tourism marketing research in terms of perspectives or approaches and research tools. Particularly, more use of inter-pretative methods is suggested, given that research on tourism experiences is limited, as Tsiotsou and Ratten (2010) also pointed out. In addition, one of the critical aspects of tourism marketing would be developing other marketing metrics that are different from the conventional repeat transactions or an average satisfaction score, but are more encompassing, holistic and reflective of tourist experience and co-created value.

As we are witnessing and perhaps will continue to see the unprecedented transformations in the business environment, tourism firms should be proactive by re-examining the evolving premises of their marketing strategy, for which S-D logic can be an important guide. The S-D logic approach broadens the boundary of tourism marketing strategy from the functional, linear, one-way, top-down, separated view of various tourism stakeholders to a more integrated, comprehensive view where the stakeholders' roles can be creatively redefined in the mutually beneficial and balanced ways, and the success of tourism firm's depends not only on profit but also on overall value it helps co-create in society.

# References

Anderson, S., Pearo, L. K., & Widener, S. K. (2008). Drivers of service satisfaction: Linking customer satisfaction to the service concept and customer characteristics. *Journal of Service Research, 10*(4), 365–381.

Arnould, E. J., Price, L. L., & Malshe, A. (2006). Toward a cultural resource-based theory of the customer. In R. F. Lusch & S. L. Vargo (Eds.), *The service-dominant logic of marketing: Dialog, debate and directions* (pp. 320–333). Armonk, NY: M.E. Sharpe.

Baily, E., & Allen, B. W. (2005). *Few survivors predicted: Why most airlines are caught in a tailspin.* Retrieved from http://knowledge.wharton.upenn.edu/index.cfm?fa=viewarticleandid=1124. Accessed on 20 October 2009.

Barla, P., & Koo, B. (1999). Bankruptcy protection and pricing strategies in the US airline industry. *Transportation Research, Part E, 35*, 101–120.

Bello, D. C., & Etzel, M. J. (1985). The role of novelty in the pleasure travel experience. *Journal of Travel Research, 24*(1), 20–26.

Bowen, J. T., & Shoemaker, S. (1998). Loyalty: A strategic commitment. *Cornell Hotel and Restaurant Administration Quarterly, 39*(1), 12–25.

Chandler, A. D., Jr. (1962). *Strategy and structure: Chapters in the history of the American industrial enterprise.* Cambridge, MA: MIT Press.

Christensen, C. M., Anthony, S. D., & Roth, E. A. (2004). *Seeing what's next: Using the theories of innovation to predict industry change.* Boston, MA: Harvard Business School Press.

Court, D., Elzinga, D., Mulder, S., & Vetvik, J. O. (2009). The consumer decision journey. *McKinsey Quarterly, 3*, 1–11.

Crompton, J. (1979). Motivations for pleasure vacation. *Annals of Tourism Research, 6*(4), 408–424.

Drucker, P. (1980). *Managing in turbulent times.* New York, NY: Harper Paperbacks.

Dubé, L., & Renaghan, L. M. (2000). Creating visible customer value: How customers view best-practice champions. *Cornell Hotel and Restaurant Administration Quarterly, 41*(1), 62–72.

Fyall, A., Callod, C., & Edwards, B. (2003). Relationship marketing: The challenge for destinations. *Annals of Tourism Research, 30*(3), 644–659.

Iso-Ahola, S. (1982). Toward a social psychological theory of tourism motivation: A rejoinder. *Annals of Tourism Research, 9*(1), 256–262.

Kim, W. C., & Mauborgne, R. (2005). *Blue ocean strategy: How to create uncontested market space and make the competition irrelevant.* Boston, MA: Harvard Business School Press.

Kumar, V., & Petersen, J. A. (2005). Using a customer-level marketing strategy to enhance firm performance: A review of theoretical and empirical evidence. *Journal of the Academy of Marketing Science, 33*(4), 504–519.

Madhavaram, S., & Hunt, S. D. (2008). The service-dominant logic and a hierarchy of operant resources: Developing masterful operant resources and implications for marketing strategy. *Journal of the Academy of Marketing Science, 36*(1), 67–82.

March, R. (1994). Tourism marketing myopia. *Tourism Management, 15*(6), 411–415.

Merriam-Webster Online Dictionary. (n.d.). Retrieved from http://www.merriam-webster.com/dictionary/experience

Mittal, V., & Kamakura, W. A. (2001). Satisfaction, repurchase intent, and repurchase behavior: Investigating the moderating effect of customer characteristics. *Journal of Marketing Research, 38*(1), 131–142.

Nasution, H. N., & Mavondo, F. T. (2008). Customer value in the hotel industry: What managers believe they deliver and what customer experience. *International Journal of Hospitality Management, 27*(2), 204–213.

Normann, R. (2001). *Reframing business: When the map changes the landscape.* New York, NY: Wiley.

Normann, R., & Ramírez, R. (1993). From value chain to value constellation: Designing interactive strategy. *Harvard Business Review, 71*(4), 65–77.

Oh, H., & Jeong, M. (2010). Evaluating stability of the performance–satisfaction relationship across selected lodging market segments. *International Journal of Contemporary Hospitality Management, 22*(7), 953–974.

Payne, A., & Holt, S. (2001). Diagnosing customer value: Integration the value process and relationship marketing. *British Journal of Management, 12*(2), 159–182.

Pine, B. J., II., & Gilmore, J. H. (1998). Welcome to the experience economy. *Harvard Business Review, July/August,* 97–105.

Prahalad, C. K., & Ramaswamy, V. (2003). The new frontier of experience innovation. *MIT Sloan Management Review, 44*(4), 12–18.

Prahalad, C. K., & Ramaswamy, V. (2004). Co-creating unique value with customers. *Strategy & Leadership, 32*(3), 4–9.

Prebensen, N. K., & Foss, L. (2010). Coping and co-creating in tourist experiences. *International Journal of Tourism Research, 13*(1), 54–67.

Ramaswamy, V., & Gouillart, F. (2010). Building the co-creative enterprise. *Harvard Business Review, October,* 100–109.

Reichheld, F., & Sasser, W. (1990). Zero defects: Quality comes to services. *Harvard Business Review, September–October,* 105–111.

Rust, R. T., Moorman, C., & Bhalla, G. (2010). Rethinking marketing. *Harvard Business Review, 88*(January/February), 94–101.

Schmitt, B. (1999). Experiential marketing. *Journal of Marketing Management, 15*(1–3), 53–67.

Shaw, G., Bailey, A., & Williams, A. (2011). Aspects of service-dominant logic and its implications for tourism management: Examples from the hotel industry. *Tourism Management, 32*(2), 207–214.

Smith, A. (1776). *An inquiry into the nature and causes of the wealth of nations.* London: W. Strahan and T. Cadell.

Tsiotsou, R., & Ratten, V. (2010). Future research directions in tourism marketing. *Marketing Intelligence & Planning, 28*(4), 533–544.

Vargo, S. L. (2009). Toward a transcending conceptualization of relationship: A service-dominant logic perspective. *Journal of Business & Industrial Marketing, 24*(5/6), 373–379.

Vargo, S. L., & Akaka, M. A. (2009). Service-dominant logic as a foundation for service science: Clarifications. *Service Science, 1*(1), 32–41.

Vargo, S. L., & Lusch, R. F. (2004a). Evolving to a new dominant logic for marketing. *Journal of Marketing, 68*(1), 1–17.

Vargo, S. L., & Lusch, R. F. (2004b). The four service marketing myths: Remnants of a goods-based, manufacturing model. *Journal of Service Research, 6*(4), 324–335.

Vargo, S. L., & Lusch, R. F. (2008). Service-dominant logic: Continuing the evolution. *Journal of the Academy of Marketing Science, 36*(1), 1–10.

Vargo, S. L., & Lusch, R. F. (2011). It's all B2B and beyond …: Toward a systems perspective of the market. *Industrial Marketing Management, 40*(2), 181–187.

Vargo, S. L., Maglio, P. P., & Akaka, M. A. (2008). On value and value co-creation: A service systems and service logic perspective. *European Management Journal, 26*(3), 145–152.

Vargo, S. L., & Morgan, F. W. (2005). Services in society and academic thought: An historical perspective. *Journal of Macromarketing, 25*(1), 42–53.

Webster, F. E., Jr. (1992). The changing role of marketing in the corporation. *Journal of Marketing, 56*(4), 1–17.

Woodruff, R. B. (1997). Customer value: The next source for competitive advantage. *Journal of the Academy of Marketing Science, 25*(2), 139–153.

Woodruff, R. B., & Gardial, S. F. (1996). *Know your customer: New approaches to customer value and satisfaction.* Cambridge, MA: Blackwell.

Zeithaml, V. A., Parasuraman, A., & Berry, L. L. (1985). Problems and strategies in services marketing. *Journal of Marketing, 49*(2), 33–46.

# Chapter 16

# Marketing the Rural Tourism Experience [*]

*Elisabeth Kastenholz, Maria João Aibéo Carneiro and
Carlos Peixeira Marques*

## 16.1. Introduction

Rural areas are increasingly investing in tourism as a form of economic diversification because their traditional economic activities are in decline. This investment
has led to growing competition among rural destinations, requiring innovative
strategies designed to help both destinations and individual tourism businesses to
compete effectively within a growing, but very demanding, international market
(Lane, 2009). An effective strategic approach to marketing the rural tourism
experience is especially essential for rural areas with scarce resources that seek
sustainable development. In this context, the 'rural features' of the territory and the
community visited play a significant role in any tourism experience that is designated
as 'rural' (Lane, 1994; Saxena, Clark, Oliver, & Ilbery, 2007). Additionally, the
experience must be integrated into a wider social, heritage and economic system in
order to also sustain the rural cultural economy (Kneafsey, 2001) and to try to
optimize the potentially powerful impacts tourism may produce. This chapter
suggests a focus on the 'total rural tourism experience' as the key selling point of any
rural tourism product/destination. The tourist experience concept has received
increasing attention in destination planning and marketing and is recognized as the
central element of tourist demand and satisfaction (Ellis & Rossman, 2008;
Mossberg, 2007; Stamboulis & Skayannis, 2003). This chapter discusses the total
experience, with reference to its main constituents, from the perspective of the
tourist, the service providers and host communities and the rural destination's
core resources, and suggests ways to enhance its overall quality yielding more
competitive and sustainable marketing strategies for rural destinations.

[*]This paper is integrated in a 3-year research project financed by the Fundação para a Ciência e
Tecnologia (co-financed by COMPETE, QREN and FEDER), 'The overall rural tourism experience and
sustainable local community development' (PTDC/CS-GEO/104894/2008), initiated in June 2010.

## 16.2.   The Concept and Role of Rural Tourism in Post-Modern Society

In the recent past, rural areas have experienced major transformations, mainly because they have lost many of their traditional *productive* functions and have gained increasing relevance for leisure and tourism *consumption* (Cavaco, 1995; OECD, 1994; Sharpley, 2002). Rural areas are increasingly conceptualized as multifunctional, with the integrative character of rural tourism being frequently suggested as a potential key for sustainable development (Lane, 1994; OECD, 1994; Saxena et al., 2007) capable of enhancing existing farming activities, while strengthening new functions of environmental and heritage protection. Rural tourism has, in fact, received increasing attention, not only from urban populations, for leisure and holiday purposes, but also from academics, politicians and investors, owing to its perceived business and development opportunities (Cavaco, 1995; Kastenholz & Sparrer, 2009; OECD, 1994; Ribeiro & Marques, 2002; Sharpley, 2005).

But what does *rural tourism* actually mean? Definitions vary from country to country, as do manifestations of rural tourism. It may be defined very broadly as the entire tourism activity in any rural area (OECD, 1994) or as a very specific tourism format, with some observers suggesting agriculture as a central element of this product (Cavaco, 1995). One may define rural tourism, as opposed to mass and resort/urban forms of tourism (Lane, 1994; OECD, 1994), as being characterized by features such as *small scale*, providing personalized contacts; the *traditional character* of service elements and environments (e.g. gastronomy or the physical *servicescape*); the presence of nature and agriculture; and the existence of traditional social structures, reflected in a specific way of life which tourists wish to discover (Kastenholz & Sparrer, 2009).

Urban populations in particular tend to perceive rural life mainly as *nature* and an *idyllically shaped reserve of* traditional ways of life (Figueiredo, 2009); as a symbol of the *good life* and the *authentic*, the antithesis of change and modernity; as an antidote to the anomie of urban life (Cawley & Gillmor, 2008); and as part of the nostalgia sought by post-modern tourists (Urry, 2002). However, rural tourists are not all the same (Frochot, 2005; Kastenholz, Davis, & Paul, 1999; Molera & Albaladejo, 2007), but rather a series of niche markets within a larger niche market (e.g. ecotourism, nature tourism, farm tourism, food and wine tourism) (Clemenson & Lane, 1997; Lane, 2009).

Rural tourism may thus be conceptualized as a complex economic and social activity, defined by a particular geographical, physical and human context, designed as *rural*, shaped by complex interdependencies, a high degree of diversity and continuous change, simultaneously influencing the development of the rural territories in which it occurs. The rural tourism experience is, in this context, lived as a complex reality by tourists and local residents alike, shaped by local resources and infrastructure, as well as by the specific rural tourism supply and eventually coordinated by a destination management/marketing organization, within a larger system of economic, cultural and social forces (see Figure 16.1).

Although the focus of this chapter is on the tourist, relevant interactions with all the above-mentioned elements of the system are included.

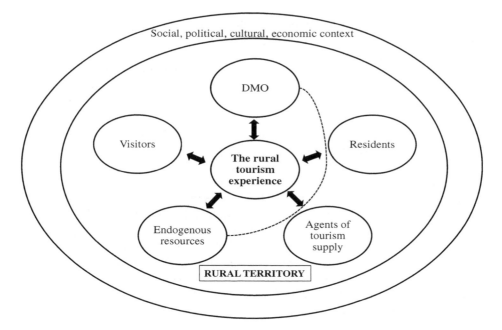

Figure 16.1: The overall rural tourism experience framework.

## 16.3. The Rural Tourism Experience as Lived by the Tourist

From the marketing perspective, the tourist experience should be seen and understood as a central topic, worthwhile studying in depth and focusing on when developing and managing tourism supply (Ellis & Rossman, 2008; Li, 2000; Mossberg, 2007; Stamboulis & Skayannis, 2003). Tourists seek, above all, appealing, unique and memorable experiences shaped by their prior expectations and the destination's image and products, as well as by its broader context and circumstantial occurrences. According to Gentile, Spiller, and Noci (2007), the experience of a product is personal and results from the interactions that the customer establishes with that product. These and other authors (e.g. Schmitt, 1999) also highlight the multidimensional character of the experience, arguing that the experience encompasses a range of components that include the stimulation of senses, the generation of emotions, cognitive processes and the development of relationships, among other elements. The tourist lives the experience subjectively, marked by primarily affective and symbolic facets. According to Otto and Ritchie (1996, p. 166), the tourist experience 'can be described as the subjective mental state felt by participants' implying holistic evaluations of affective expressions and representations of experiential, hedonic and symbolic benefits. This view is consistent with the earliest conceptualizations of consumer experience. For instance, Hirschman (1984) advocated this subjectivist perspective of consumption, stressing the role of the 'consumption experience', with 'experience seeking' defined as a composite of *cognition*, *sensation* and *novelty* seeking. Hirschman and Holbrook

(1982) centred on the enrichment of the dominant information processing approach in consumer behaviour research by raising issues such as product enjoyment, pursuit of pleasure, fantasies and play.

The so-defined consumption experience seems to be closely related to positive motivation and positive psychology in general. The positive outcomes that Hirschman and colleagues link to experience seeking result from the experience being a goal-directed activity, meeting experiential needs by providing some level of alertness, activity and challenge that enhances quality of life and self-esteem (Csikszentmihalyi, 2000). In contrast, passive escapist forms of spending free time are negative, in the sense that the only positive feelings generated in such situations result from their opposition to a demanding everyday life (Iso-Ahola, 1999). Regarding pleasure travel, positive psychology focuses on the balance between the need to explore new environments and the anxieties associated with high levels of novelty. In order to be intrinsically motivated to tourism, potential tourists must view the experience as *optimally challenging* and conducive to feelings of personal competence and achievement; perceive *autonomy and freedom* in engaging in the experience; and, above all, *enjoy* the experience itself, that is, 'just for the fun of it' (Iso-Ahola, 1999). *Relatedness* is another key element of self-determination, and Iso-Ahola (1999) notes that the regulation of social contacts, interaction and support are most important to pleasurable leisure experiences.

However, as Ryan (2002) notes, the simple fact of 'being away' may result in positive feelings because of its potential for engagement in novel/unusual experiences that one would not participate in at the home environment. This sense of contrast to normal life enhances the intensity of the experience lived by tourists. Research on typologies of the tourist experience also points out that a sense of opposition to the ordinary life of home pervades several modes of experience, contributing to their appeal. For example, Wickens (2002) identifies types of British mass tourists in Greece seeking the sun they do not have at home; the romance with a 'Greek God', which is only possible when 'Shirley Valentine' is able to forget the routines of work and domesticity; and the fantasized 'home', with a definitely better way of life than 'Lord Byron' could experience in England. Following that argument, the *rural* tourism experience should be enhanced by contrasting with normal *urban* life. When visiting rural destinations, tourists from urban areas tend to contrast the affective images of home and destination (Marques, 2005), and their positive experiences result from attractions and activities that may be seen as sensorially, symbolically or socially opposed to urban life.

Global tourism market research suggests that rural tourism experiences are increasingly sought (OECD, 1994; Ribeiro & Marques, 2002) for a variety of reasons (Frochot, 2005; Kastenholz et al., 1999; Molera & Albaladejo, 2007), with a dominant motivation being *closeness to nature*, either for relaxation, recreational and sportive outdoors activities or as a genuine nature experience. But also socialization with family and friends as well as local hosts and an interest in independently exploring a region and novelty seeking, as well as a more romantic search for the *rural idyll*, are relevant motives. The dimensions associated with the rural space thus reflect 'a set of meanings', valued and interpreted distinctively by distinct tourists, resulting in distinct experiences at the destination as well as images associated with it and subsequently reproduced (Lichrou, O'Malley, & Patterson, 2008).

For understanding the tourism experience at the destination level, the concept of a 'customer-activated services network' seems most appropriate, acknowledging the existence of a network that delivers diverse experience elements, in a sequence and manner determined by the tourist himself or herself (Gnoth, 2003). This network may be conceptualized to additionally include any kind of resources, facilities, spaces and people that may be perceived as part of the destination and 'activated' by the visitor. Since tourism supply is mostly provided by a large number and variety of small service firms, Zehrer (2009) suggests the focus on designing and managing appealing service experiences, if possible through synergistic cooperation, to achieve long-term competitiveness. The before-mentioned activation of the services network at the destination actually stresses the co-creation nature of tourism experiences permitting the consumer to obtain unique value in the context of a particular interaction between consumers and firms (Prahalad & Ramaswamy, 2004). Vargo and Lusch (2004, 2008) suggest the service-dominant logic as generally characterizing any market exchange and relation, with value creation conceptualized as interactive and networked by nature and the result being phenomenological, that is, individually lived and interpreted.

This rural tourism experience is restricted neither to the host–guest encounter at the lodging unit nor to the larger experience onsite. The entire tourist experience must be understood, which according to Aho (2001) commences with orientation and attachment as an enjoyable anticipation of the holiday and is prolonged after travel through memorabilia, networks and reflection on the experience. Here, *imagery* and *dreams* are crucial, since what tourists purchase, frequently at a physical, temporal and even cultural distance, are expectations of idealized experiences, with planning holidays involving fantasy, imagination and daydreaming, while the recall of the experience is a frequently embellished discourse and shared imagination of dream-like situations (Buck, 1993). The holistic rural tourist experience, therefore, must be understood as a complex and multifaceted phenomenon from the tourist's point of view, integrating a diversity of pre-, onsite and post-experiences related to visiting the rural area, with a series of sensorial, affective, cognitive, behavioural and social dimensions. The complex onsite experience is shaped by multiple features of the physical and human context, from which it takes elements that are often central attractors, but on which it simultaneously leaves impacts that require control and/or management when aiming at sustainable tourism development (Lane, 1994).

## 16.4. The Rural Tourism Experience as Lived and Shaped by the Community and Local Agents of Supply

Lane (1994) advocates that rural tourism should integrate the families living in rural areas and their traditions. Residents and service providers largely determine the tourist experience, through tourist–host interaction (Otto & Ritchie, 1996). Apart from the physical resources of a destination, attitudes, behaviours and skills of residents and service providers are also very important, especially to create competitive tourism supplies and experiences (Högström, Rosner, & Gustafsson, 2010). This social dimension of the experience is particularly relevant in rural tourism, where interest in regional culture, the way of life of local communities and interactions with hosts are most important (Kastenholz & Sparrer, 2009). Encounters between visitors and the host community (local residents and/or service providers) are identified as crucial elements of the tourist experience in Carmichael's study (2005) of wine tourism, and as the most memorable aspects of tourism experiences in Morgan and Xu's (2009) research.

Saxena et al. (2007) suggest integrated rural tourism (IRT) yielding sustainability as largely dependent on *endogeneity* — the development of rural tourism based on the area's resources and communities, who should be *empowered* and subsequently involved in the tourism development process. The latter, however, is seldom the case in rural destinations (Ilbery, Saxena, & Kneafsey, 2007). Additionally, brief and superficial host–tourist interactions prevail in many tourism contexts (Eusébio & Carneiro, 2010; Reisinger & Turner, 2002), eventually leading to a context-dependent sub-optimal tourist experience.

Interaction between residents and tourists varies in form, intensity and length, ranging from brief, non-verbal to much deeper contacts such as sharing meals, exchanging gifts or staying at a host's home (Jaworski, Ylänne-McEwen, Thurlow, & Lawson, 2003). The interaction that occurs between visitors and both the host community and service providers, as well as the way these encounters are enjoyed and interpreted, is influenced by factors such as the cultural differences between the actors, their openness to others, the hosts' dependency on tourism and their perceptions of tourism impacts (Morgan & Xu, 2009; Trauer & Ryan, 2005). Although cultural differences between tourists and hosts can be an attraction for tourists, they may also inhibit interaction, either by creating constraints due to communication barriers and insecurity feelings (Pizam, Uriely, & Reichel, 2000) or by provoking negative attitudes caused by envy, mistrust or the impression of being explored. Cultural difference is especially important in rural tourism, since most visitors come from urban centres with different cultural and socioeconomic backgrounds when compared to rural communities (Figueiredo, 2009). International tourism further adds to the complexity of the experience lived, and some degree of cultural proximity apparently results in a more satisfactory rural tourist experience, given the enhanced possibility of coping with novelty, communicating with residents and getting along (Kastenholz, 2010). In particular, host–tourist relationships where both parts are open and oriented to others result in increased respect, trust, mutual reciprocity and reinforced commitment to others (Trauer & Ryan, 2005).

Host communities, by contact with visitors, managing tourism businesses or simply being the 'focus of the eyes' of many visitors (Urry, 2002), thus assume a crucial role in the tourist experience, which is, indeed, 'co-created' by both hosts and guests (Carmichael, 2005; Morgan & Xu, 2009; Mossberg, 2007). Some major potential benefits of host–tourist interactions are cultural exchange (Uriely & Reichel, 2000) and the opportunity to socialize, valued by both tourists (Carmichael, 2005;

Morgan & Xu, 2009) and hosts (Pizam et al., 2000). Rural communities may offer visitors the opportunity to get to know the culture, way of life and characteristic products of the region (Albaladejo Pina & Díaz Delfa, 2005). Providing visitors the opportunity of participating in local community life (Heuman, 2005) and/or in farming is also an appealing and differentiating element of an IRT experience (Albacete-Sáez, Fuentes-Fuentes, & Lloréns-Montes, 2007; Kastenholz & Sparrer, 2009). Residents may also actively direct tourism experiences by acting as visitors' tour guides (Albacete-Sáez et al., 2007) or by managing recreational activities, such as cycling tours or barbeques, shared by hosts and guests, as in the case of Frisian Farms (Kastenholz & Sparrer, 2009).

Personalized encounters between the local people/culture and guests in rural accommodation units may, indeed, determine much of the quality of the tourist experience (Tucker, 2003). Here, tourists frequently seek relationships with hosts as a means to share the hosts' culture, hospitality and local knowledge. Hosts can, therefore, serve as *cultural brokers* (E. Cohen, 1988), overcoming language barriers (Albacete-Sáez et al., 2007) and facilitating access to a more complete rural tourism product (Kastenholz & Sparrer, 2009). This type of access is offered, for example, by rural tourism agents in the French 'accueil paysan' network (FNAP, n.d.) referring to the before-mentioned meanings frequently associated to a rural tourist experience — community integration, understanding and living of agriculture, traditions, history and integration of Man within Nature:

> The countryman welcomes you into his home, at his table, at the inn or a gîte in a rural setting ... He welcomes you amongst the animals and the countryside where he makes his living. He will share:
> - His knowledge of gardening, animal husbandry, wood cutting, country living;
> - His knowledge of rural life, its history, geography, economy;
> - His skill with the earth, plants and animals.
> 
> The countryman invites you to enjoy the rhythm of the seasons, of being 'at one with nature'.

However, a too close host–guest relationship may also lead to 'negative feelings of restriction and obligation from the point of view of the visitor, while hosts themselves may experience a sense of invasion of privacy' (Tucker, 2003, p. 88). Consequently, there the right balance between social exchange and autonomy/privacy is important (Kastenholz & Sparrer, 2009; Lynch, 2005; Tucker, 2003).

Residents, particularly the hosts of the accommodation units, are central to creating a friendly atmosphere at the destination, which is essential for the tourists' interest and willingness to explore it (Garrod, Wornell, & Youell, 2006; Uriely & Reichel, 2000). Heuman (2005) argues that, compared to 'commercial hospitality', 'traditional hospitality' has the advantage of tending to promote the protection of visitors by the hosts (e.g. providing more food or security beyond the mandatory) and to encourage non-monetary reciprocity — changes between hosts and visitors (e.g. gift giving, performing arts to visitors, lending objects to residents). This kind of hospitality is likely to promote important social exchanges, beyond economic exchanges, potentially enhancing the 'authentic' feeling of the rural tourism experience.


## 16.5.   The Role of Rural Tourism Destination Resources and Contexts

Crouch and Ritchie (1999) suggest *physiography*, including nature, landscape and climate, as a crucial qualifying determinant of visitor attraction and destination competitiveness. In tourism, the physical environment frequently is the most crucial element in the experience sought, having a powerful influence in tourists' satisfaction (Högström et al., 2010). This concept is most evident in the rural tourism context, where research reveals the particular relevance of nature and scenery as major destination attractors (Figueiredo, 2009; Frochot, 2005; Kastenholz, 2002). The resources at stake in this case are not confined only to the rural accommodation or to the locality visited, however important these central tourist experience sites are. The larger region is also relevant because rural tourists tend to explore the surrounding territories (Kastenholz & Sparrer, 2009). Regional horizontal (destination-covering) networks also contribute to the creation of successful tourism products by integrating local resources (Cawley & Gillmor, 2008). Apart from its relevance as a key attractor, the physical setting of the tourism experience, labelled by some as the 'experiencescape' (Mossberg, 2007), is an important conditioning element in any kind of tourism experience.

Another core attractor of rural tourism is cultural heritage (Crouch & Ritchie, 1999), in both its material and immaterial forms, particularly those elements that reveal the historic and traditional specificities of the community/territory visited and that may be signs of *authenticity* (Li, 2000), which may be both object-based and existential (Wang, 1999). Even if, compared to nature, the cultural dimension is not as relevant to all rural tourists, there is an opportunity for preserving elements of culture that otherwise may be condemned to disappear, despite being most distinctive attributes. Interestingly, it is particularly the dimension of 'living culture', ethnographic elements of the rural culture, that is most appreciated by rural tourists in North Portugal (Kastenholz, 2002). This study further identifies the items 'gastronomy' and 'friendly people' (residents) as a frequent positive association with the destination, both key resources in the rural tourism experience. Local resources do play a dual role, being both the central focus of tourist attraction and a fundamental element in the construction of community identity (Saxena & Ilbery, 2010), and need to be carefully integrated in an attractive and meaningful rural tourist experience (Kolar & Zabkar, 2010).


## 16.6.   Marketing the Rural Tourism Experience

To market this complex rural tourism experience successfully, we suggest a focus on the entire experience, in all its dimensions, its co-creative management in a network, around a theme and based on unique endogenous resources, as detailed next. We also emphasize the links between the overall experience and the destination's image, since, as noted by Baker (2007), destination branding involves masterminding not only the messages but also the experiences: 'each experience before, during and after the visit has a vital role in defining and delivering the promise that is inherent within the brand'.

### 16.6.1. Focus on the Tourist's Experience

The holistic tourist experience process may be initiated long before the travel begins and continue after the onsite experience, influencing memories, routine daily life post-travel and future travel experiences. Tynan and McKechnie (2009) identify a set of pre-experience activities, experience sources of value and post-experience outcomes that marketers should take into consideration in order to co-create the *experiencescape* with the tourist (Mossberg, 2007). Interaction is a key element in the process, as the intensity and quality of the tourist experience is affected by interaction with other tourists, the host population, service providers and other stakeholders. Interactions with individuals outside the tourism system, such as friends and relatives, also play an important role in the pre- as well as the post-experience. Interaction implies social resources that tourists mobilize in the production of their tourism experience, as they do with other types of resources, namely time, skills and goods (Andersson, 2007), whose successful use results in a sense of positive experience.

Destination image, particularly its affective dimension, is the key factor in the pre-experience determining the desire to engage in a rural tourism experience. Affective destination image is usually conceptualized and measured as affect beliefs, that is, expectations about potential affective consequences of experiencing the destination, but the process of choosing, of longing for a destination, may also involve large doses of imagination and fantasy (Goossens, 2000), and actual feeling experiences known as *anticipatory feelings* (J. B. Cohen, Pham, & Andrade, 2008). Such feelings, particularly those associated with vivid imagery, are part of the pre-experience, determine the way the destination is actually experienced, but also subsequent memories, involving mechanisms of reinterpretation and selective memory (Klaaren, Hodges, & Wilson, 1994; MacInnis & Price, 1990). Positioning a rural tourism experience should then induce positive anticipatory feelings that shape the way the potential tourist co-creates his or her own rural experience. As much as possible, those feelings should be related to affect beliefs that valorize the endogenous rural destination resources and features, and to the main strategic experiential modules (Schmitt, 1999) or value sources (Tynan & McKechnie, 2009), which involve sensory, affective, cognitive, physical and relational aspects of the holistic experience. However, it is also important to assure that the promotion of the destination is consistent with the reality of the territory and its ambience, portraying experiences that are likely to occur and avoiding the creation of unrealistic expectations that lead to tourists' dissatisfaction.

Regarding the onsite experience, the principal job of destination management organizations (DMOs) is to create the circumstances and the environment in which the tourist will have a positive experience (Mossberg, 2007), mainly by theming and staging the experience in a given environment (Müller & Scheurer, 2004). The feelings and perceptions relevant to the lived experience relate to the physical as well as the social environment affecting the tourists in their interactions, in each encounter in particular and with the rural area as a whole. *Sensory experiences* may involve any combination of the senses, with a profusion of smells, tastes, touches, sights and sounds being actionable for virtually any rural theme. The sensorial component was, indeed, the most important experience element in a study undertaken by Gentile et al. (2007), which included several products. *Cognitive experiences* engage the tourists creatively (Cloke, 2007; Schmitt, 1999) by enhancing their competence in a given subject and giving a sense of mastering the environment. *Physical experiences* focus on enhancing performance skills, mainly through challenging and exciting activities, such as mountain climbing, canoeing, horse riding or paragliding, as frequently offered in the rural tourism context. *Social experiences* enhance either relatedness or status and imply a social and symbolic meaning in the tourist performance, that is, a means of responding to the need to be accepted and respected by others. *Emotional experiences* are intense feelings that give a psychological meaning to sensory, cognitive, physical or social experiences. Any tourist experience needs to be emotional in order to correspond to pre-experience feelings and expectations and to be lasting post-experience outcomes (J. B. Cohen et al., 2008; Tynan & McKechnie, 2009). It also needs a *symbolic significance*, either embedded in traditional rural images or themes or in one of the new urban visions on the countryside, for example, as a space for adventure (Cloke, 2007).

As an example, we could mention crushing grapes with bare feet, a traditional winemaking process, which is packaged as a tourist experience at some port wine cellars, in Portugal. For most tourists, it is a novel sensory experience, intensely involving all the senses (Marques, 2005). However, it is also a physical performance very different from ordinary life, improving participants' footwork skills; it is a social experience, implying interaction with hosts from whom you learn and other guests with whom you team up to get the job done. Finally, it is even a cognitive experience, teaching much about winemaking. The experience can be a total learning package, including new activities, new forms of interaction and communication, plus the meaning of new smells and physical sensations. The way the supply network themes and stages this complex experience determines the type and intensity of feelings, which, in turn, determine their enjoyment of the experience, its future reliving and the potential evangelizing done by those tourists about the rural experience (Tynan & McKechnie, 2009). If, on the other hand, previous images influence the holistic experience, the feelings and meanings of the experience will also reshape the tourist's image of rurality and of the destination visited.

The *Enoteca* Douro, in Favaios (Portugal), is another good example of an attraction providing a rich and multisensory, cognitively and symbolically shaped experience of a wine destination. This *Enoteca* is an interactive wine museum where visitors can search information about wine; participate in a guided tour, oriented by the *Enoteca* owners and local farmers who emotionally engage in telling touching as well as romantic stories of their ancestors; watch robots disguised as wine workers trampling grapes and singing; taste several kinds of wine appreciating their tastes and smells; and finally purchase selected wines, if wished.

The creation of memorable experiences is, therefore, much associated with strong emotions at the time they occur. These memories will influence not only destination loyalty and place attachment but also post-visit experience sharing with family and friends (Martin, 2010), and more generally the visitors' quality of life through delightful recording of enjoyable and meaningful holiday experiences (Neal, Sirgy, & Uysal, 2004). The more intense these experiences, the more emotionally laden and associated with unique destination features, the higher the probability of enhancing place attachment, that is, a positive emotional relationship with the place visited and corresponding destination advocacy (Yüksel, Bramwell, & Yüksel, 2005). In this respect, encounters with hosts deserve particular attention, as human interaction represents a most relevant source of delightful experiences (Csikszentmihalyi & Wong, 1991). In addition, the physical settings, comprehending the landscape and the several servicescapes involved in the experience, should not only be pleasant to the senses but also emphasize the specificity of the rural site. Finally, material signs of the non-ordinary experience, namely souvenirs, permit more vivid memories of the experience through time, enriching the stories told to family and friends (Hu & Yu, 2007). Specially in rural destinations, rich in traditions and local products, these material signs of the experience must be recognized as relevant marketing tools.

### 16.6.2.   *Highlighting Unique Endogenous Resources*

For a successful differentiation of the product, to enhance overall destination appeal and the community's sense of identity (Crouch & Ritchie, 1999; Saxena & Ilbery, 2010) the most interesting, identifiable and unique destination resources, which may be the basis of meaningful themes, must be chosen. The certified German Landtourismus supply reveals a high degree of thematic specialization, differentiation and focalization on the tourists' expectations of their rural tourism experience, based on local and regional resources. Themes are apart from the general 'vacations on the farm', 'holidays in the saddle', 'vacations in the vineyard', 'holidays at country estates' and 'contentment on the country', the latter focusing on the taste of regional gastronomy (DLG, n.d.). These resources need to be carefully explored through attractive, if possible interactive interpretation, 'cultural brokerage' through hosts and through opportunities for tourists to get involved with themes, co-creating experiences and thereby enhancing the meaning and 'existential authenticity' of the overall experience (Curtin, 2010; Ellis & Rossman, 2008; Kastenholz & Sparrer, 2009; Kolar & Zabkar, 2010; Mossberg, 2007; Stamboulis & Skayannis, 2003), as in the case of the before-mentioned *Enoteca*. These elements, conceptualized as *countryside capital* (Garrod et al., 2006), permit the creation of a rural tourism product that valorizes endogenous destination features, sought by rural tourists for appealing, distinctive and significant experiences, and, if possible, valued by residents for place identity (Kneafsey, 2001; Saxena & Ilbery, 2010), yielding sustainable destination development.

### 16.6.3.   Theming and Co-Creative Experience Design

The identification of themes around which experiences are developed is a relevant tool both for integrating the diversity of rural tourism resources and services and for creating meaningful, consistent, appealing and distinctive tourism experiences (Mossberg, 2007). Themes 'authentically lived' (Wang, 1999) by tourists and meaningful to them further contribute to their increased knowledge of the rural destination and enhance their place attachment, probably increasing their destination loyalty. These themes, deeply rooted in the community's history and culture and highlighting the most sought countryside resources, such as nature and landscape, the 'rural way of life' and ambience, local traditions and products (Frochot, 2005; Kastenholz, 2002), simultaneously reflect and ideally strengthen the community's sense of identity. This feature may be most relevant for increasing the involvement of the local population when staging and co-creating appealing tourism experiences. For example, some traditional agriculture activities, particularly sowing and harvesting, involve large groups of villagers and represent opportunities to party and celebrate. In the Douro region of Portugal, vintages, although being the toughest labour time during the year, are always remembered by villagers as most joyful experiences, because of the opportunity to party with other people, playing, dancing, chattering, laughing and having food and drink together. Since the vintage is still a dominant activity in this wine region, local tourism promoters found that vintage heritage could be excellent for theming and co-creating harvest festivities. Nowadays tourists, villagers and professionals are involved in the 'traditional' vintage experience, much dependent on the co-creation of cultural activities and tourism services. Theming is also supported by large-scale events, such as the Douro Film Harvest, which, 'more than just a film festival, (...) is a major cultural and wine tourism platform' (DFH, 2011), based on the idea of 'harvesting' good films, directors, actors and composers who might subsequently use the Douro and its wine and cultural heritage as themes or background scenario in their cultural production.

Service providers in particular need to be sensitized and prepared for this co-creation process, directly involving tourists and hosts. Understanding customers and their needs (Trauer & Ryan, 2005), providing empathy and personalizing services are crucial (Noe, Uysal, & Magnini, 2010), particularly in rural tourism, where a familiar atmosphere is highly valued. Rural tourism lifestyle entrepreneurs may play an important role in this context (Ateljevic & Doorne, 2000), since they value most the lifestyle dimension of rural tourism, potentially understanding best the holistic rural experience sought by visitors. Finally, the possibility of co-creation of rural tourism products by tourism agents and creative industries (e.g. design, architecture, music, drama) (Mossberg, 2007) should also be explored, to promote creative development and innovation of tourism experiences in rural areas.

### 16.6.4.   Articulating the Overall Experience

Given the complexity of the rural tourism experience, networks among service providers should substantially improve visitors' experiences, resulting in a more coordinated service provision (Gnoth, 2003) and more attractive tourism products co-created by diverse, specialized supply agents (Mossberg, 2007). The provision of rural meals in lodging establishments, for example, may be complemented by visits to farms or traditional food production units (e.g. olive oil presses), if accommodation owners and infrastructure managers cooperate. Coordination would result in richer and more meaningful experiences of rural destinations. These initiatives, functioning via networks, are especially important in rural tourism, due to the fragmentation and small scale of rural tourism businesses (Cawley & Gillmor, 2008). Apart from the above-mentioned benefits of a better articulated supply system, networks of rural tourism providers permit the acquisition of 'critical mass' for more effective marketing action (Cai, 2002), resource sharing, continuous knowledge exchange, innovation and the development of social capital at the rural destination (Gibson, Lynch, & Morrison, 2005; Sharpley, 2005). Coordinating organizations, such as DMOs, promoting cooperation at the destination level (Dwyer & Kim, 2003), are of upmost importance in this context. In rural tourism destinations, characterized by a fragmented tourism supply of small tourism businesses, DMOs play a very important role in leading the development of tourism strategies that increase the rural destinations' competitiveness and that single suppliers usually do not develop owing to a lack of financial or knowledge resources. Cooperation in market communication, supported by a destination brochure or a destination web platform promoting and making available single businesses as well as the destination as a whole, is one of the examples of DMO's strategies.

The provision of a positive rural tourism experience also depends on the co-ordination between tourism suppliers and the 'gatekeepers' of the rural destinations, acting as intermediaries between the destination and its markets, providing information to both sides and creating expectations that determine the experience onsite (Ilbery et al., 2007). Both horizontal (at the destination level, articulating suppliers and resources) and vertical (reaching out to markets, e.g. through relational marketing approaches yielding specialized tour operators or familiarization trips, inviting and providing memorable experiences to travel writers and journalists) network coordination thus contribute to successful experience design and provision.

### 16.6.5. *Continuous Experience Monitoring*

Finally, it is of paramount importance to monitor the rural tourism experience over time. The way the tourist lives the experience onsite, the identification of determinants of attraction and enjoyment, and development of place attachment deserve particular attention. In addition, an understanding of the negative elements potentially 'killing the atmosphere' (Müller & Scheurer, 2004) is essential for continuously improving the experience setting.

## 16.7. Conclusions

Rural tourism is frequently suggested as a market opportunity, potentially enhancing sustainable development in rural areas. Not all rural areas, however, have the same potential, and increasing competition among rural tourism destinations and businesses requires a more professional design, management and marketing of rural tourism. Rural territories represent specific qualities that vary considerably from place to place, which in the era of globalization may be tourist attractions themselves. However, the question of how to proceed, to plan and manage successful rural tourism products that also contribute to sustainable destination development, is still a relevant issue.

The authors suggest developing competitive and sustainable destination marketing strategies, based on the key element of the tourism phenomenon — the rural tourism experience, which must be understood from the point of view of the tourist and the local community as well as considering the rural resources context that provides most of the ingredients of the rural experience sought. Its complex constitution must be well understood, so that it can be optimally planned and managed, particularly through co-creative experience designs (Mossberg, 2007) in partnership and network constellations, permitting integrated management and product development (Lane, 2009). Understanding the overall experience as an emotionally, sensorially and symbolically rich phenomenon, anchored in a common, appealing and distinctive theme, may be a powerful way to combine the pieces of the puzzle (Ellis & Rossman, 2008). The integration of all stakeholder groups at the destination (Gibson et al., 2005) and of the most relevant endogenous core resources and attractors, representing the territory's strongest comparative advantages (Crouch & Ritchie, 1999), should help provide a most unique, distinctive and possibly authentic rural tourism experience, while additionally enhancing sustainable rural tourism development.

The tourist experience may, thus, be considered a *new value attribute* (Pine & Gilmore, 1998) essential for developing successful rural tourism products and desti-nations. Based on a large variety of endogenous and territory-specific resources, meaningfully connected through interesting themes, distinct experiences may be designed that address a heterogeneous rural tourism market. The way these experi-ences are provided, staged and conditioned, with signs of the *authentic rural*, is a challenge for the community in its search of strengthened identity and new develop-ment opportunities, for local rural tourism providers, in search of sustainable profit generation, and for the tourist market, in search of authentic, pleasurable and significant experiences.

## References

Aho, S. K. (2001). Towards a general theory of touristic experiences: Modelling experience process in tourism. *Tourism Review, 56*(3/4), 33–37.

Albacete-Sáez, C. A., Fuentes-Fuentes, M. M., & Lloréns-Montes, F. J. (2007). Service quality measurement in rural accommodation. *Annals of Tourism Research, 34*(1), 45–65.

Albaladejo Pina, I. P., & Díaz Delfa, M. T. (2005). Rural tourism demand by type of accommodation. *Tourism Management, 26*(6), 951–959.

Andersson, T. D. (2007). The tourist in the experience economy. *Scandinavian Journal of Hospitality & Tourism, 7*(1), 46–58.

Ateljevic, I., & Doorne, S. (2000). 'Staying within the fence': Lifestyle entrepreneurship in tourism. *Journal of Sustainable Tourism, 8*(5), 378–392.

Baker, B. (2007). *Destination branding for small cities: The essentials for successful place branding*. Portland, OR: Creative Leap Books.

Buck, E. (1993). *Paradise remade: The politics of culture and history in Hawaii*. Philadelphia, PA: Temple University Press.

Cai, L. A. (2002). Cooperative branding for rural destinations. *Annals of Tourism Research, 29*(3), 720–742.

Carmichael, B. (2005). Understanding the wine tourism experience for winery visitors in the Niagara region, Ontario, Canada. *Tourism Geographies, 7*(2), 185–204.

Cavaco, C. (1995). Rural tourism: The creation of new tourist spaces. In A. Montanari & A. M. Williams (Eds.), *European tourism: Regions, spaces and restructuring* (pp. 127–149). Chichester: Wiley.

Cawley, M., & Gillmor, D. A. (2008). Integrated rural tourism: Concepts and practice. *Annals of Tourism Research, 35*(2), 316–337.

Clemenson, H. A., & Lane, B. (1997). Niche markets, niche marketing and rural employment. In R. D. Bollman & J. M. Bryden (Eds.), *Rural employment: An international perspective* (pp. 410–426). Wallingford, CT: CAB International.

Cloke, P. (2007). Creativity and tourism in rural environments. In G. Richards & J. Wilson (Eds.), *Tourism, creativity and development* (pp. 37–47). New York, NY: Routledge.

Cohen, E. (1988). Authenticity and commoditization in tourism. *Annals of Tourism Research, 15*(3), 371–386.

Cohen, J. B., Pham, M. T., & Andrade, E. B. (2008). The nature and role of affect in consumer behavior. In C. P. Haugtvedt, P. Herr & F. R. Kardes (Eds.), *Handbook of consumer psychology* (pp. 297–348). New York, NY: Lawrence Erlbaum Associates.

Crouch, G. I., & Ritchie, J. R. B. (1999). Tourism, competitiveness, and societal prosperity. *Journal of Business Research, 44*(3), 137–152.

Csikszentmihalyi, M. (2000). The costs and benefits of consuming. *Journal of Consumer Research, 27*(2), 267–272.

Csikszentmihalyi, M., & Wong, M. M.-H. (1991). The situational and personal correlates of happiness: A cross-national comparison. In F. Strack, M. Argyle & N. Schwarz (Eds.), *Subjective well-being: An interdisciplinary perspective* (pp. 193–212). New York, NY: Pergamon Press.

Curtin, S. (2010). Managing the wildlife tourism experience: The importance of tour leaders. *International Journal of Tourism Research, 12*(3), 219–236.

DLG. (n.d.). *Landtourismus: Urlaub auf dem Bauernhof*. Retrieved from http://www.landtourismus.de/443.html. Accessed on 30 July 2011.

Douro Film Harvest (DFH). (2011). *Who are we*. Retrieved from http://www.dourofilm harvest.com/en/sobreDFH.aspx. Accessed on 1 June 2011.

Dwyer, L., & Kim, C. (2003). Destination competitiveness: Determinants and indicators. *Current Issues in Tourism, 6*(5), 369–414.

Ellis, G. D., & Rossman, J. R. (2008). Creating value for participants through experience staging: Parks, recreation, and tourism in the experience industry. *Journal of Park and Recreation Administration, 26*(4), 1–20.

Eusébio, C., & Carneiro, M. J. (2010). Determinants of tourist–host interactions: A youth market analysis. Paper presented at the 5th world conference for graduate research in tourism, hospitality and leisure, Cappadocia, Turkey. *Anatolia: An International Journal of Tourism and Hospitality Research*.

Figueiredo, E. (2009). One rural, two visions — Environmental issues and images on rural areas in Portugal. *Journal of European Countryside, 1*(1), 9–21.

FNAP. (n.d.). *Accueil paysan: Home page*. Retrieved from http://www.accueil-paysan.com/ indexen.htm. Accessed on 15 April 2011.

Frochot, I. (2005). A benefit segmentation of tourists in rural areas: A Scottish perspective. *Tourism Management, 26*(3), 335–346.

Garrod, B., Wornell, R., & Youell, R. (2006). Re-conceptualising rural resources as countryside capital: The case of rural tourism. *Journal of Rural Studies, 22*(1), 117–128.

Gentile, C., Spiller, N., & Noci, G. (2007). How to sustain the customer experience: An overview of experience components that co-create value with the customer. *European Management Journal, 25*(5), 395–410.

Gibson, L., Lynch, P. A., & Morrison, A. (2005). The local destination tourism network: Development issues. *Tourism and Hospitality Planning & Development, 2*(2), 87–99.

Gnoth, J. (2003). Consumer activated services networks: Towards a dynamic model for tourism destinations. In *European Marketing Academy: Proceedings of the 32nd EMAC conference*, Glasgow, Scotland.

Goossens, C. (2000). Tourism information and pleasure motivation. *Annals of Tourism Research, 27*(2), 301–321.

Heuman, D. (2005). Hospitality and reciprocity: Working tourists in Dominica. *Annals of Tourism Research, 32*(2), 407–418.

Hirschman, E. C. (1984). Experience seeking: A subjectivist perspective of consumption. *Journal of Business Research, 12*(1), 115–136.

Hirschman, E. C., & Holbrook, M. B. (1982). Hedonic consumption: Emerging concepts, methods and propositions. *Journal of Marketing, 46*(3), 92–101.

Högström, C., Rosner, M., & Gustafsson, A. (2010). How to create attractive and unique customer experiences: An application of Kano's theory of attractive quality to recreational tourism. *Marketing Intelligence & Planning, 28*(4), 385–402.

Hu, B., & Yu, H. (2007). Segmentation by craft selection criteria and shopping involvement. *Tourism Management, 28*(4), 1079–1092.

Ilbery, B., Saxena, G., & Kneafsey, M. (2007). Exploring tourists and gatekeepers' attitudes towards integrated rural tourism in the England–Wales border region. *Tourism Geographies, 9*(4), 441–468.

Iso-Ahola, S. E. (1999). Motivational foundations of leisure. In E. L. Jackson & T. L. Burton (Eds.), *Leisure studies: Prospects for the twenty-first century* (pp. 35–51). State College, PA: Venture Publications.

Jaworski, A., Ylänne-McEwen, V., Thurlow, C., & Lawson, S. (2003). Social roles and negotiation of status in host–tourist interaction: A view from British television holiday programmes. *Journal of Sociolinguistics, 7*(2), 135–164.

Kastenholz, E. (2002). *The role and marketing implications of destination images on tourist behavior: The case of Northern Portugal*. Aveiro: University of Aveiro.

Kastenholz, E. (2010). "Cultural proximity" as a determinant of destination image. *Journal of Vacation Marketing, 16*(4), 313–322.

Kastenholz, E., Davis, D., & Paul, G. (1999). Segmenting tourism in rural areas: The case of north and central Portugal. *Journal of Travel Research, 37*(4), 353–363.

Kastenholz, E., & Sparrer, M. (2009). Rural dimensions of the commercial home. In P. Lynch, A. MacIntosh & H. Tucker (Eds.), *The commercial home: International multidisciplinary perspectives* (pp. 138–149). London: Routledge.

Klaaren, K. J., Hodges, S. D., & Wilson, T. D. (1994). The role of affective expectations in subjective experience and decision-making. *Social Cognition, 12*(2), 77–101.

Kneafsey, M. (2001). Rural cultural economy: Tourism and social relations. *Annals of Tourism Research, 28*(3), 762–783.

Kolar, T., & Zabkar, V. (2010). A consumer-based model of authenticity: An oxymoron or the foundation of cultural heritage marketing? *Tourism Management, 31*(5), 652–664.

Lane, B. (1994). What is rural tourism? *Journal of Sustainable Tourism, 2*(1), 7–21.

Lane, B. (2009). Rural tourism: An overview. In T. Jamal & M. Robinson (Eds.), *The SAGE handbook of tourism studies*. London: Sage.

Li, Y. (2000). Geographical consciousness and tourism experience. *Annals of Tourism Research, 27*(4), 863–883.

Lichrou, M., O'Malley, L., & Patterson, M. (2008). Place–product or place narrative(s)? Perspectives in the marketing of tourism destinations. *Journal of Strategic Marketing, 16*(1), 27–39.

Lynch, P. A. (2005). The commercial home enterprise and host: A United Kingdom perspective. *International Journal of Hospitality Management, 24*(4), 533–553.

MacInnis, D. J., & Price, L. L. (1990). An exploratory study of the effects of imagery processing and consumer experience on expectations and satisfaction. *Advances in Consumer Research, 17*(1), 41–47.

Marques, C. P. (2005, 8–10 December). Emotions, motivations and destination positioning. Paper presented at the international conference on destination branding and marketing for regional tourism development, Macau, China.

Martin, D. (2010). Uncovering unconscious memories and myths for understanding international tourism behavior. *Journal of Business Research, 63*(4), 372–383.

Molera, L., & Albaladejo, I. P. (2007). Profiling segments of tourists in rural areas of south-eastern Spain. *Tourism Management, 28*(3), 757–767.

Morgan, M., & Xu, F. (2009). Student travel experiences: Memories and dreams. *Journal of Hospitality Marketing & Management, 18*(2), 216–236.

Mossberg, L. (2007). A marketing approach to the tourist experience. *Scandinavian Journal of Hospitality & Tourism, 7*(1), 59–74.

Müller, H., & Scheurer, R. (2004). *Angebots-inszenierung in tourismus-destinationen*. Bern: Forschungsinstitut für Freizeit und Tourismus.

Neal, J. D., Sirgy, M. J., & Uysal, M. (2004). Measuring the effect of tourism services on travelers' quality of life: Further validation. *Social Indicators Research, 69*(3), 243–277.

Noe, F. P., Uysal, M., & Magnini, V. P. (2010). *Tourist customer service satisfaction: An encounter approach*. London: Routledge.

OECD. (1994). *Tourism strategies and rural development*. Unpublished manuscript. Paris, France.

Otto, J. E., & Ritchie, J. R. B. (1996). The service experience in tourism. *Tourism Management, 17*(3), 165–174.

Pine, J. B., & Gilmore, J. H. (1998). Welcome to the experience economy. *Harvard Business Review, 76*(4), 97–105.

Pizam, A., Uriely, N., & Reichel, A. (2000). The intensity of tourist–host social relationship and its effects on satisfaction and change of attitudes: The case of working tourists in Israel. *Tourism Management, 21*(4), 395–406.

Prahalad, C. K., & Ramaswamy, V. (2004). Co-creation experiences: The next practice in value creation. *Journal of Interactive Marketing, 18*(3), 5–14.

Reisinger, Y., & Turner, L. (2002). *Cross-cultural behaviour in tourism: Concepts and analysis.* Oxford: Butterworth-Heinemann.

Ribeiro, M., & Marques, C. (2002). Rural tourism and the development of less favoured areas — Between rhetoric and practice. *International Journal of Tourism Research, 4*(3), 211–220.

Ryan, C. (2002). From motivation to assessment. In C. Ryan (Ed.), *The tourist experience* (2nd ed., pp. 58–77). London: Continuum.

Saxena, G., Clark, G., Oliver, T., & Ilbery, B. (2007). Conceptualizing integrated rural tourism. *Tourism Geographies: An International Journal of Tourism Space, Place and Environment, 9*(4), 347–370.

Saxena, G., & Ilbery, B. (2010). Developing integrated rural tourism: Actor practices in the English/Welsh border. *Journal of Rural Studies, 26*(3), 260–271.

Schmitt, B. (1999). Experiential marketing. *Journal of Marketing Management, 15*(1–3), 53–67.

Sharpley, R. (2002). Rural tourism and the challenge of tourism diversification: The case of Cyprus. *Tourism Management, 23*(3), 233–244.

Sharpley, R. (2005). Managing the countryside for tourism: A governance perspective. In L. Pender & R. Sharpley (Eds.), *The management of tourism* (pp. 175–186). London: Sage.

Stamboulis, Y., & Skayannis, P. (2003). Innovation strategies and technology for experience-based tourism. *Tourism Management, 24*(1), 35–43.

Trauer, B., & Ryan, C. (2005). Destination image, romance and place experience — An application of intimacy theory in tourism. *Tourism Management, 26*(4), 481–491.

Tucker, H. (2003). The host–guest relationship and its implications in rural tourism. In D. L. Roberts & M. Mitchell (Eds.), *New directions in rural tourism* (pp. 80–89). Aldershot: Ashgate.

Tynan, C., & McKechnie, S. (2009). Experience marketing: A review and reassessment. *Journal of Marketing Management, 25*(5/6), 501–517.

Uriely, N., & Reichel, A. (2000). Working tourists and their attitudes to hosts. *Annals of Tourism Research, 27*(2), 267–283.

Urry, J. (2002). *The tourist gaze* (2nd ed.). London: Sage.

Vargo, S. L., & Lusch, R. F. (2004). Evolving to a new dominant logic for marketing. *The Journal of Marketing, 68*(1), 1–17.

Vargo, S. L., & Lusch, R. F. (2008). Service-dominant logic: Continuing the evolution. *Journal of the Academy of Marketing Science, 36*(1), 1–10.

Wang, N. (1999). Rethinking authenticity in tourism experience. *Annals of Tourism Research, 26*(2), 349–370.

Wickens, E. (2002). The sacred and the profane: A tourist typology. *Annals of Tourism Research, 29*(3), 834–851.

Yüksel, F., Bramwell, B., & Yüksel, A. (2005). Centralized and decentralized tourism governance in Turkey. *Annals of Tourism Research, 32*(4), 859–886.

Zehrer, A. (2009). Service experience and service design: Concepts and application in tourism SMEs. *Managing Service Quality, 19*(3), 332–349.

Chapter 17

# Destination Cross River

*Alvin Rosenbaum*

This case study examines the marketability of experiential products based on authenticity and visitor readiness to attract travellers to Cross River State (CRS) in southeastern Nigeria in sub-Saharan Africa (see Figure 17.1). During the period of study, 2008–2010, Africa experienced robust growth in international arrivals (UNWTO, 2005, 2011), while Nigeria tourism grew apace, but with most of its traffic coming from domestic airlift (FAAN, 2010).

For global tourism, customized products have advanced away from Fordist principles over the past 40 years, providing more personal involvement by travellers and a greater emphasis on service and customer relationships by suppliers (Addis & Holbrook, 2001; Högström, Rosner, & Gustafsson, 2010). A premise of the CRS project was to test the theory of competition through service and distinctive visitor experiences, concepts advanced as *service-dominant logic* (Lusch, Vargo, & O'Brien, 2007; Vargo & Lusch, 2004) and as experiential product development (Pine & Gilmore, 1999).

While targeting, messaging and tracking visitor preferences are all critical in marketing pioneer destinations, coordination for the assembly of marketable experiential products must come first (Addis & Holbrook, 2001). The challenge for CRS was the need to develop and promote place-based year-round customer experiences supported by quality services (Lusch et al., 2007). But since the inception of Cross River's tourism initiatives, its own story had been muted in favour of facilities investment far afield from the competitive advantages in CRS's cultural heritage and traditions (Cross River State, 2010). Management of service quality through various enhancement programmes and dynamic packaging options has changed with global consumption patterns (Zehrer, 2009) while the product and service offers in CRS remain fixed in outmoded concepts of innovation.

CDC Development Solutions (CDS), a Washington, DC based non-governmental, non-profit organization, introduced its Tourism Employment and Opportunity (TEMPO) project in CRS, from 2008 to 2010. The Federal Republic of Nigeria, with a loan from the World Bank, funded the project as a pilot to build and test a tourism development approach based on intensive survey research and value chain analysis,

Strategic Marketing in Tourism Services
Copyright © 2012 by Emerald Group Publishing Limited
All rights of reproduction in any form reserved
ISBN: 978-1-78052-070-4

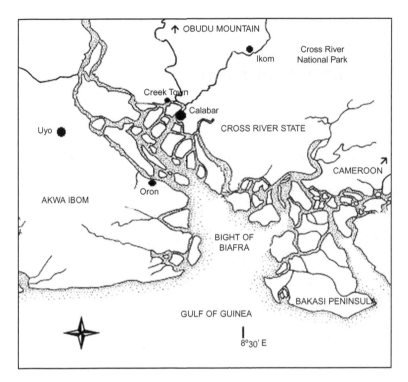

Figure 17.1: Cross River State in the Bight of Biafra region, Nigeria. Redrawn by the author after a map by Keith Scurr, University of Hull.

stakeholder engagement, grants for small business development services, experiential product development and capacity building over an 18-month period.

The TEMPO project created this demonstration in a destination isolated from international visitor flows to test the efficacy of Gilmore and Pine's experiential model and its utility for other emerging markets off the beaten track and with little or no history providing hospitality services beyond its own cultural community.

Tourism development had been at the core of the state government's strategy for development over the past decade (Ogunbiyi & Soyinka, 2007). CDS's TEMPO was developed to address sustainable tourism development and management in emerging markets and to assist destinations that already host substantial visitation for domestic and regional travellers, but seek to increase their exposure to international practices and markets with linkages that support a more structured and salubrious business environment.

Extensive visitor and business surveys were undertaken and a qualitative asset audit method was adapted from a schematic first developed by McKercher and du Cros (2002) for economic, destination and value chain analysis. This analysis informed product development initiatives specifically modelled for both retail and wholesale source markets in Nigeria's urban centres of Lagos, Abuja and Port Harcourt. Further, the model was formulated to meet the engagement's terms of reference to help build the capacity of the public sector's Cross River State Tourism Bureau (CRSTB) to support, rather than supplant, private sector initiative (Figure 17.2).

While TEMPO employed its own methodology, this case study is organized following the eight general principles of strategic authenticity and its 'Progression of Economic Value', summarized as 'commodities are fungible, goods tangible, services intangible, and experiences memorable' (Pine & Gilmore, 1999).

- Study your heritage: building on the past
- Ascertain market and industry positioning: surveying the immediate environment
- Gauge your trajectory: direction and speed
- Know your limits: being true and determining the destination's limits
- Stretch your execution capabilities: training and service delivery
- Scan the periphery: remedies, competitors and opportunities
- Formulate your strategic intention: differentiation
- Execute well: evaluation

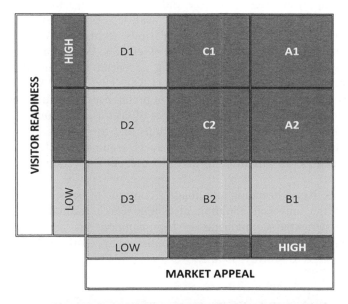

Figure 17.2: CDS's TEMPO Asset Audit. *Source*: McKercher and du Cros (2002).

## 17.1. Experiential Marketing of Tourism Destinations

Experiential marketing is the art of creating an experience where the result is an emotional connection to a person, brand, product or idea. Experiential marketing of tourism destinations has been driven by technology supporting mass customization and increased competition, where messages relating to feelings, fantasies and fun may overtake branding and place-based considerations (Holbrook & Hirschman, 1982).

Up until the mid-20th century, vacation activities in major destinations were typically organized and marketed by a few large travel companies and railroads such as Thomas Cook, American Express, Union Pacific, Orient Express and Compagnie Internationale des Wagons-Lits with the cost of modest place-based promotion campaigns shared with national governments. By 1958 the first commercially success- ful passenger jet service was launched by Pan American Airlines between New York and Paris, a milestone that began the process of both mass tourism and decen- tralization and specialization of tourism experiences, a gradual shift in the travel marketing canon from supply to demand (Pine & Gilmore, 1998; Richards, 2001; Vargo & Lusch, 2004).

The basis for experiential marketing of tourism destinations rests on the market- ability of its products and becomes possible when hotels, tour operators and attractions employ services as a stage and goods as props to engage visitors in a manner that creates a memorable event or vacation segment (Pine & Gilmore, 1998; Schmitt, 1999; Williams, 2000, 2002). Various techniques were famously first developed at Disneyland in the mid-1950s (Fjellman, 1992, chapter 3) and further delineated by promotion of festival shopping, adventure travel and those activities in consumption demand discussed by Urry (1995). Urry stated that contemporary tourism has passed into an increased range of preferences but with a decline in repeat visitation, encourages a proliferation of types of visitor attractions based on market research and supports alternative destinations and attractions and the growth in heritage, cultural and other experiential products, arguing as well that tourism blends the tourism experience with other forms of leisure, culture, retailing, education, sport and hobbies.

While place-based branding and imagery continue to be widely employed, parti- cularly with the universal adoption of online search technologies, selecting and perfecting experiential components in trip planning has been ascendant in the presentation of destination attributes and confirmed by sell-through, based on market research (Fodness & Murray, 1998).

### 17.1.1. The Subject of the Study

Among the world's regions sub-Saharan Africa has experienced 6.7% annual growth in international tourist arrivals from 2000 to 2010 even as its overall arrival numbers are small relative to other parts of the world at 30.7 million in 2010 (UNWTO, 2011). Nigeria as a West African destination hub for business and diasporic visits is well established even as it faces challenges to differentiate and project its competitive position for leisure travel for both international and regional arrivals. In sum, greater than 10% of all Africans live in Nigeria while the country only captures 2.2% of African cross-border tourism revenues and 2.9% of international tourism arrivals (UNWTO, 2011). Against these challenges Nigeria in 2009 had the largest domestic airlift in Africa with more than 10 million passenger arrivals (FAAN, 2010).

Tropical CRS in southern Nigeria, the subject of this case study, offers more than 2000 hotel rooms and a number of attractions, events and natural sites. Historically, public–private dialogue in CRS had been mainly dependent on the government's ability to support private sector activity rather than employing a shared risk, shared benefit model. Through a series of meetings with the TEMPO team followed by in-depth analysis, it became evident that Cross River's tourism industry required structural reorganization: the private sector needed to organize into an independent trade organization coordinated with the CRSTB, while the CRSTB and other public agencies needed to reorganize into a viable service unit to forge a better environment for collaboration.

In many ways the tourism potential of CRS was apparent at the commencement of TEMPO's efforts. The government had initiated a tourism promotion campaign that had begun coincident with the construction of Obudu Mountain Resort and Tinapa, a business resort and complex including a shopping centre, hotel, casino, waterpark, exhibition hall, film studio and event venue, developed under the direction of Donald Duke, CRS's governor from 1999 to 2007 (see Figure 17.3). According to Duke, Tinapa would put ₦300 billion (€1.46 billion) in circulation annually and would stimulate other industries: 'TINAPA is the land where the rich will come ... That's the story behind Monte Carlo ... The same principle applies to Las Vegas ... The same

Figure 17.3: TEMPO team member Jessica Ziegler (left) led a tourism stakeholders meeting, on 23 April 2009 at the Amber Hotel, Tinapa Business Resort, Calabar, Cross River State. All photographs by author.

Figure 17.4: The waterpark at Obudu Mountain Resort is reached by Africa's longest cable car system at 4 km. Obudu Mountain Resort is on a plateau at 1576 m above sea level on the Oshie Ridge of the Sankwala Mountains.

with Dubai … That's what Hong Kong was for China …' (Ogunbiyi & Soyinka, 2007) (see Figure 17.4).

As a part of this effort to turn Cross River into a competitive destination, Duke began a 'Clean and Green' programme. According to *The Economist* (2007), he changed Calabar, CRS's capital city, 'into a spotless city, planting trees and grass, making it the garden spot of Nigeria, if not West Africa'. And beyond the development in Calabar, nearly a million households in rural CRS were wired for electricity.

The missing link between investment and return at both Tinapa and Obudu was the actual delivery of memorable experiences, the combination of themed activities, timed events, the connections between place and activity that project a sense of authenticity and overall service quality.

Although Efik traders have done business along the Calabar and Cross Rivers for centuries, a service culture had been slow to develop. While Cross River's Efik, Ibibo, Annang and Oron people are friendly and welcoming, the idea of careers in the service trades was looked on as distasteful and the organization of most hospitality businesses has not been adequately informed by skills training and accepted trade practices (Amha & Ageba, 2006; Ashley, Boyd, & Goodwin, 2000; Egbaji, 2007). One particular difficulty in the improvement of services was that Tinapa and Obudu — massive facilities built and owned by the government — were not accountable to investors and did not maintain the normal business practice of monthly profit and loss and balance sheet statements.

Beyond these public investments was the rest of the Cross River tourism economy, burdened by frequent power interruptions, slow Internet connectivity and ill-trained and underpaid service workers. These obstacles created a shortage of good experiential products, combined with undeveloped or crumbling infrastructure at other visitor sites, an absence of intermediation for sales into source markets and gaps in standards and regulatory enforcement.

### 17.1.2. Building on the Past

Cross River and Old Calabar history provide important clues to its current culture and the challenges it faces in tourism development. CRS had very little experience offering commercial hospitality services prior to 2005, while most suppliers have little or no prior experience in the hospitality trade. The consequence in Cross River was a disconnect between investment and return with faulty feasibility studies presented to secure billions of naira for both public and private sector construction funding. To add to the problem, very little investment had been devoted in building workforce capacity or to experiential product development.

By contrast, Cross River's neighbours have taken a different approach in creating experiential travel products. Along Africa's West Coast, historic sites relating to the global slave trade are principal tourist attractions such as Ghana's Cape Coast Castle; the Gambia's James Island and the village of Albreda, claiming patrimony to *Roots'* Kunte Kinte; Badgery outside Lagos, Nigeria; Island of Gorée in Senegal and other trans-Atlantic slave trade sites up and down the coast. Cape Coast Castle, James Island and Island of Gorée have all been designated by UNESCO as World Heritage Sites.

With a grim past that carried through into the 1960s and 1970s — food shortages, civil war and a brutal military rule — CRS had understandably looked beyond its brutal history for ways to create a positive future for its tourism economy. CRS made a strategic decision nearly a decade ago to model its visitor products based on strategies developed for Dubai and similar shopping and luxury models rather than follow its West African neighbours that focused on their heritage after the success of Alex Haley's *Roots* (both book and television miniseries) bringing droves of African-American visitors to West Africa in the 1980s.

While it is only speculation that this opportunity continues for Cross River, its capital at Calabar has the historic sites to feature stories from its past as Nigeria's first capital, a prominent port in the West African 17th- to 19th-century slave trade to the Americas and as the African gateway for 19th-century Christian missions. Indeed, Calabar, a city-state once known as 'Old Calabar' (Akwa Akpa) in the Kalabari Kingdom, has been inhabited for 2 millennia and is where more than 1 million Africans were taken to the new world as slaves, 1701–1810, the largest single point of exit in Africa (Lovejoy & Richardson, 1999) (see Figure 17.5).

Cross River's safe, warm and personal environment blended with its citizens' appreciation of their rich cultural and religious heritage created an environment ripe for hospitality and memorable visitor experiences. In CRS interpretative approaches to create experiential products have not yet been considered strategic or beneficial to attract visitors, as heritage development and public history, in general, have not been incorporated into Nigeria's tourism offer.

Figure 17.5: The Old Calabar port is the historic heart of Cross River State but is
isolated from attractions and visitor services.

While the state enjoys a modern, popularly elected government, a chieftain culture
remains in parallel, as the Obong of Calabar, Treaty King and Grand Patriarch of
the Efiks, Ndidem of the Quas and the MuriMunene of the Efut (the tribal headsmen
of Greater Calabar), his high chiefs and councils still weigh in on many local civil
matters (Ighodaro, 2008). But as the Obong is important in many local matters, his
influence in public spending for heritage tourism development had not penetrated
the thinking among local officials who generally believe that Cross River's storied
history had little touristic value.

To provide a comparative analysis of positive visitor experiences, we may contrast
post-apartheid South Africa with post-colonial Nigeria — the two wealthiest sub-
Saharan countries — as measured by oil consumption, mobile phones, Internet
usage, imports, exports and GDP. As background, both South Africa and Nigeria
are ethnically diverse. Nigeria resisted European settlement as South Africa lured
immigration. By further contrast, Nigeria is Africa's largest exporter of oil while
South Africa is its largest importer. Nigeria is a model of transformation to conform
to its local cultures, while, as one scholar has observed, 'South Africa is the sub-
Saharan paragon of Westernization' (Mazrui, 2006).

There was an obvious chicken-and-egg problem in the introduction of experiential
products into the Nigerian offer. With a population of 76 million children under age 18,
Nigeria's education system in general had not had or applied the resources to directly
connect their students with their heritage, a primary motivation for governments to
invest in museums, historic preservation and other interpretive programmes for tourism.

To compare the visitor experience, South Africa's public and private projects such
as the Robben Island World Heritage Site, Constitution Hill, Soweto tours, District

Six Museum and other sites highlighting the country's progression from apartheid to freedom are among Africa's leading tourism attractions. Before 1994 and the ascendance of Nelson Mandela, both Nigeria and South Africa were *persona non grata* on the global leisure tourism stage. Over the past 30 years, international leisure arrivals to South Africa have grown 10-fold while Nigerian arrivals have remained relatively stagnant (UNWTO, 2005, 2011). With Mandela, South Africa created dynamic and successful activities generated by new and compelling sites and experiences while over the same period Nigeria's international leisure arrivals remained among the lowest per capita in the world.

Bold moves to build a tourism sector were led by Cross River's charismatic and progressive governor, adopting the oft-misquoted aphorism, 'If you build it they will come', assuming that the visitor experience would take care of itself. His vision sought to duplicate model projects in Dubai and Las Vegas without a complete understanding that Dubai's success was based on its pre-eminent position as a long-haul transfer hub between Europe and Asia while Las Vegas was in the State of Nevada, the only jurisdiction where casino gambling was permitted in the United States during its first two decades as a tourism Mecca. No effort was made to train a workforce or develop an activity pallet that would draw crowds, believing that shopping itself would draw the necessary traffic.

Nigeria, and specifically CRS, has not built on its past to create compelling visitor experiences, but has instead looked to faraway models with strikingly different traffic, landscape and demographic profiles. Because of the horrific past as a slave state, there was reason to believe that Nigerians avoid capitalizing on such a subject as a platform for leisure tourism. However, if the government focuses on the educational importance of promoting slave heritage as an experiential product, it may reap additional economic benefits.

Considering experiential tourism, should CRS focus on the historic preservation and presentation of Calabar along its waterfront? The question addresses a fundamental debate within local leadership and the positioning of its tourism offer. Based on TEMPO's survey of 1200 visitors in early 2009, the largest visitor group to Calabar was from its own territory, CRS (population 3.5 million) and neighbouring Awka Ibom State (4.0 million) and Cameroon, followed by Lagos and other southern Nigerian states. Visitors lack a variety of 'things to do' as a leading criticism of the CRS offer, and despite various past efforts, very few international or West African regional visitors find their way to Calabar.

In both interviews and social situations, the author found that Calabar residents are steeped in both tribal-ethnic and religious observances that create a secure, welcoming hospitality environment. However, the destination was without significant place-based products, arts and crafts or music to promote. One exception was the spicy local cuisine featured in a few successful local restaurants serving mostly the local population.

A consequence was a tug-of-war between old and new with elected officials having the financial leverage to move traditional observances to the backstage as they have introduced new forms of ritual, promoting a tourism product dominated by the state's large December event, Carnival Calabar, modelled on the Trinidad and

Figure 17.6: A signal event in 2009 was a gala at the Tinapa Film Studio to unveil the Calabar Festival logo (now called Carnival Calabar), promoting sponsorships to Nigerian corporations.

Tobago Carnival, an event with much greater focus and investment than for its own authentic and localized Leboku (see Figure 17.6).

Leboku, an annual three-week New Yam Festival celebrated in Cross River's town of Ugep, honours the earth goddess and ancestral spirits, ushering in peace, good health and prosperity (Oladoyin, 2008). It had not been promoted outside the jurisdiction of Cross River, and by the author's personal observation at Leboku in 2009, it appeared that the audience was local. In discussion with a local tour operator, the perceived differences between the Carnival Calabar and Leboku are dispositive of the central thesis presented here: Carnival Calabar was public and touristic, organized to attract visitors from other places, while Leboku in 2009 was traditional and therefore considered more 'private', imbedded into community culture but not planned to accommodate outsiders (see Figure 17.7).

While CRS has a compelling history and distinctive culture, its tourism products have tended towards entertainment rather than edification, a potential problem in creating a competitive advantage and, not incidentally, added value to its educational system.

### 17.1.3.  Positioning

CRS is a terminus (rather than a hub) on Nigeria's border with Cameroon at the frontier of the Niger River Delta region (see Figure 17.8). Airlift from Lagos and Abuja, ferries to Akwa Ibom and Cameroon and paved roads into Cross River end

Figure 17.7: The three-week ancient and authentic Leboku is the annual New Yam Festival celebrated in Ugep, Cross River State honouring the earth goddess and ancestral spirits. A highlight of Leboku is a performance poetry and dance contest among Leboku maidens.

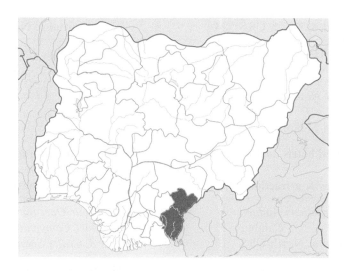

Figure 17.8: Cross River State is at the frontier of the oil-producing Niger River Valley of Nigeria (southwest) and bordering Cameroon (southeast) with access to the sea at the Calabar River (south) and Obudu Mountain Resort (north). Wikimedia Commons.

there, limiting in-transit traffic. Positioning of Cross River for experiential products was based on its survey research, weighing visitor preferences, the visitor readiness of its suppliers and their products' marketability. Visitors were surveyed at hotels, the airport, Port of Calabar and Obudu Mountain Resort and a profile was developed capturing party size, length of stay, transportation mode, activities, spending level and purpose of visit.

The survey of tourism suppliers employed eight different survey instruments for:

- Hotels and commercial lodging facilities
- Food and beverage facilities
- Sites and attractions
- Transport businesses
- Retail businesses and handicrafts
- Entertainment
- Tour guides and interpreters
- Tour operators (Table 17.1)

Table 17.1: TEMPO Asset Audit results summary for Cross River State.

### Cross River State Tourism Asset Audit

### 480

| A. Hotels | | C. Food & beverage establishments | |
|---|---|---|---|
| *Hotels Audited In-Depth* | | *Food & Beverage Establishments Audited In-Depth* | |
| Calabar | 86 | Calabar | 73 |
| Central & North CRS | 24 | Central & North CRS | 14 |
| Total Hotels Audited In-Depth | 110 | Total Food & Beverage Est. Audited In-Depth | 87 |
| *Additional Hotels Audited* | | *Additional F&B* | |
| Calabar | 112 | Calabar | 44 |
| Central & North CRS | 39 | Central & North CRS | 13 |
| **Total hotels audited** | **261** | **Total food & beverage audited** | **144** |
| **B. Sites & attractions** | | **D. Support businesses** | |
| *Sites & Attractions Audited* | | *Tour Guides & Tour Operators Audited* | 10 |
| Calabar | 15 | *Transport Companies Audited* | 13 |
| Central & North CRS | 10 | *Arts & Crafts Shops Audited* | 27 |
| **Total sites & attractions audited** | **25** | **Total support businesses audited** | **50** |
| | | **Total assets audited** | **480** |

Sustained by offshore oil revenues in the Gulf of Guinea, Cross River's primary employment generators have been with the public sector resulting in a robust informal economy after the nearly three decades of military control that followed the Biafran War (1967–1970), fought at Cross River's doorstep and finally ending with the democratic election of President Olusegun Obasanjo in 1999 and Governor Donald Duke.

Calabar's first modern hotel, The Mirage, was developed by High Chief Edem Duke, remarking that the key to earnings is a combination of customer satisfaction and improved products, including presentation, packaging and pricing. His hotel opened in the late 1980s, with many others to follow, including those owned by the government.

But on TEMPO's arrival in 2009 there were virtually no data on which to develop a strategy to fill those hotel rooms. The TEMPO team spent more than two months on data collection, and then organizing survey data into an asset audit including a scoring and grading system developed by the TEMPO team. This approach differed from most traditional tourism market research efforts in that it separately evaluated and scored *marketability* and *visitor readiness* of each business and attraction and across the entire spectrum of products. By contrast, most destinations in emerging markets do not qualitatively score individual sites, properties and services under these criteria to determine the best product mix for tailored packaged offerings and promotion into source market segments.

The TEMPO analysis also included reviews of two 2005 marketing surveys, including visitor estimates by KPMG and a demand survey conducted by Gendel Associates, both of Johannesburg. The TEMPO positioning statement presented the following findings:

- Based on a lack of experiential products and reputational issues at the national level, international leisure arrivals have been inconsequential.
- An experiential model for product development and promotion requires organization and testing.
- The capacity of existing small and medium business enterprise (SME) required substantial remediation and training.
- Trust between the public and private sectors required new collaboration strategies and a new business model.
- Participants in the tourism value chain needed to develop a destination management organization (DMO).
- A distribution system needed to be organized and tested.

One outcome of TEMPO's findings was the development of experiential themes by stakeholders, embracing education, escapist entertainment and the aesthetic — ideas that included the development of five packaging themes based on data analysis and intensive stakeholder engagement in a strategic planning process:

- Faith-based music
- Events and festivals
- Entertainment

- Obudu Mountain Resort and nature
- Meetings and conferences

Although Nigeria continues to promote its destinations at international trade events, the leisure product, as developed in CRS, has not been suitable to attract many visitors beyond its own borders and the immediate neighbouring states. Repositioning the product offering was developed to provide opportunities for CRS to increase visitation from a wider circle of source markets and with targeted marketing efforts.

### 17.1.4.   Direction and Speed

The salient variable in donor-supported tourism development at a pioneer destination is a workforce experienced in meeting minimum global hospitality standards and a scope of work that can be completed within an allotted time frame. Due to a lack of investment in recruitment, technical assistance and skills training, CRS's human resources have suffered, leading to difficulties in creating a positive visitor experience. However, if these issues were addressed, the resulting product could enable the visitor to have a positive experience, both fundamental to building a good reputation through word of mouth, media relations, online social networking and, ultimately, sustainable sell-through.

More than ₦100 billion (€500 million) was invested by state government to build Tinapa Business Resort, Obudu Mountain Resort and Cable Car and a Marina complex but without concomitant investments in human resources. Additional private investment in hotels, branch banks, buses and other facilities anticipated substantial increased traffic that had not materialized. Hospitality companies and other professional investors in the trade made very few CRS investments prior to 2009. But for those outside the industry who did invest, they made overly optimistic income and employment projections to their bankers and shareholders.

While the CRS government had devoted substantial resources to economic development, its promotion to entrepreneurs for investment projects has tended to be generic (e.g. an amusement park, a monorail, a new downtown retail centre), rather than specific to its cultural and natural assets.

### 17.1.5.   Limitations

There were constraints on the World Bank's 2009 CRS project, styled as the Tourism Industry Supply Chain Development Program, designed as a pilot and limited to an 18-month effort with start-up in the midst of disappointments, delays and a lack of trust between public sector officials and private sector stakeholders. CDS's TEMPO devoted more than three months to its assessment process, followed by weeks of stakeholder consultations to formulate a strategy to improve quality standards and increase capacity both for private sector players and within the CRSTB. This work was followed by a competitive grant programme with 61 applicants vying for 10 business development contracts valued at €300,000, awarded to local Nigerian providers for training, a familiarization (FAM) trip, marketing materials and website development, short message service (SMS) marketing, media relations, service training, service incentives and an entertainment component. TEMPO also provided workshops on data collection, online information, and booking and settlement systems. The challenges of experiential product development also required lessons in both service delivery and distribution, the prerequisites of an effective tourism programme.

Virtually all of these efforts moved beyond local trade practices. In CRS and for Nigeria in general there was limited experience at collaboration and cooperation among SMEs and between SMEs and public agencies. Beyond collaborative trust were the problems across the value chain including on-time delivery of services, conventional costing/pricing and yield strategies, market research and prospect targeting.

There are systemic limitations to Cross River's tourism programme including security issues on the roads leading to Cross River from the nearby oil states of the Niger River Valley, an inadequate national electric power grid creating daily extended blackouts and geographic and political isolation from global markets.

### 17.1.6. Service Delivery

In Cross River, direct interaction between hosts and guests had been either formal or limited, with remediation needed at the skills level among reception and wait staff, their managers and facility owners. Where guest contact was limited, such as building maintenance and housekeeping, the quality of services was relatively high and guest complaints were rare. Beyond lodging, slow-to-very-slow table service and unavailable or limited menu choices at restaurants as well as a lack of awareness of international standards are common. Two examples are that few restaurants provide brewed coffee and there is a lack of club soda at most bars.

As a pilot, TEMPO and the project's grantees conducted training for 189 hotel workers, more than 40 musicians and entertainers and two-dozen craft workers related to decorum and presentation, up-selling, service delivery and attitude.

A very significant obstacle in addressing minimum service standards was the problem of continuous electric power from the national grid, creating dining room service gaps and forcing hotels and restaurants to spend significant sums on supplemental electric power from massive diesel generators, creating operational difficulties in properly maintaining refrigerated food stores and many basic guest services.

But while the people of Cross River have had little exposure to service industry good practices, their innate hospitality was well known and appreciated throughout Nigeria. In Lagos and Abuja, many, if not most, of the middle class had visited Cross River at least once and both the press and their readers comment on its good qualities of friendliness, a safe and clean environment and an appealing landscape.

### 17.1.7. Remedies, Opportunities and Competition

A tourism production system (Britton, 1991) incorporates several economic sectors and includes a wide variety of SME producers. The system embraces (1) activities aimed at producing and selling travel and tourist products; (2) the social groups, cultural features and physical components that serve as tourism attractions; and (3) the ordering institutions and bodies set up to regulate commercial behaviour and social externalities associated with such production.

TEMPO was designed to help achieve a sustainable tourism production system to meet both visitor expectations and competitive returns on investment following traditional techniques. These processes were organized to specifically address challenges and bottlenecks in pioneer markets that typically lag in the adoption of global SME business practices and UNWTO guidelines for public tourism agencies.

The TEMPO schematic (Figure 17.9) was developed to organize tasks, sequencing and linkages that, according to Britton's definition, 'regulate commercial behaviour and social externalities'. In this context *standardize* may be a more appropriate term than *regulate* given that most of the activity should be private sector coordinated,

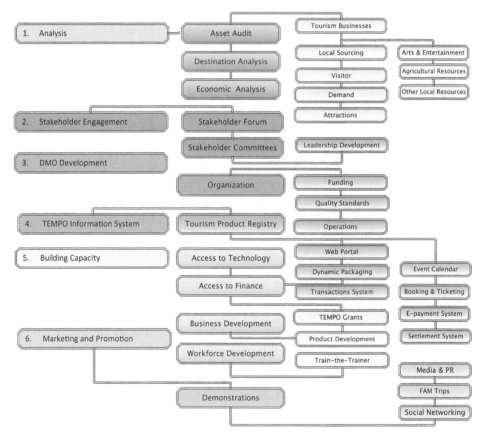

Figure 17.9: The TEMPO project in Cross River State was organized into a tourism production system with significant remedial processes indicated before experiential products may be effectively marketed to visitors.

driven or sanctioned. While public policy, master planning and regulation play a role, the TEMPO approach was focused on business-to-business and business-to-consumer activity and, only secondarily, business-to-government activity, even as many bilateral and multilateral donor projects tend to be oriented around public sector–driven initiatives.

The reason for this shift of stakeholder focus was based on research into the actual cost–benefit of donor interventions and reliable indicators for job creation and economic growth in the tourism sector. One important factor in the TEMPO model that was prototyped at Cross River was the development of a tourism product registry and its migration into a content management system for information, booking and settlement systems.

A serious challenge for the local offer in both passive and experiential packages across 60 vendors in CRS was promotional pricing and appropriate settlement during a 2010 campaign promotion for the destination's lowest occupancy month. The TEMPO team found that pricing for rooms, meals and activities was typically not based on customer value but on sunken and operational costs, with SME owners reluctant to provide promotional pricing for packaged products either for distressed inventory or during low occupancy periods.

In a 30-day market test (14 February to 15 March 2010) promotional and commissionable pricing of experiential packaged products were tested in the Nigerian source markets of Lagos, Abuja and Port Harcourt. Brokerage by travel agents in those markets was introduced providing 17% commissions for sell-through and settlement. While 30 travel agents and travel writers attended a three-day FAM trip to Calabar and Obudu Mountain Resort, only three agents actually sold products to customers because, as they stated, they knew little about Nigeria and heretofore had only sold travel for outbound trips to places such as Dubai, London and Atlanta.

The competitive opportunities presented to the travel trade during this promotion period included new experiential activities, up-selling, yield management, online booking and settlement systems, in-depth information to travellers, both passive and active guest participation, decentralized entertainment at new venues and a rewards programme for recognized outstanding guest services.

TEMPO was designed as a World Bank pilot in CRS as an example and template for the rest of Nigeria and for other emerging markets to help identify bottlenecks and challenges in the tourism and hospitality value chain for SMEs and to provide approaches to address these issues for future growth and new job opportunities. The following are several areas where significant advances were made through TEMPO and Cross River stakeholder efforts, including:

1. Four hundred and eighty suppliers were selected and interviewed and 1200 visitor surveys were completed to create a baseline for tourism data.
2. Two hundred and seventy-two supplier surveys were confidentially scored and ranked to gain market intelligence.
3. Workshops with 67 CRS tourism businesses were conducted including proposals for public–private partnerships.

4. A Business Development Services Grant Program generated 61 proposals and 10 grants with a value of €307,000, creating more than 350 paid training opportunities.
5. TEMPO conducted a train-the-trainer programme for service quality. Each of the 14 trainers provided 40 hours of training to 189 frontline hotel and restaurant managers and workers.
6. A promotional campaign was conducted with 16 hotels and their restaurants, 5 independent restaurants, 8 transportation and car hire companies, 29 entertainers, 9 church choirs and 30 craft producers.
7. The media relations effort reached 65 national news outlets with 4.25 million total exposures.
8. The value of local in-kind contributions of hotel, restaurant and transport products was 92.7 million naira (€452,237).
9. Thirty resellers were introduced to CRS through a FAM trip organized by TEMPO.
10. The concept of a DMO and booking service was introduced to the Nigerian tourism industry.
11. Local sources for produce and other food stuffs procured by hotels and restaurants were surveyed and introduced into the hospitality value chain.
12. IBM assisted TEMPO through its Corporate Service Corps, facilitated through CDS's International Corporate Volunteer programme to create www.crossriverquality.com generating 1333 unique visitors, 1.63 visits per unique visitor and 39.39 hits per visit (a total of 211,911 hits) over a 30-day period.

While benchmarks set by the donor exceeded their expectations, the fundamental challenge to increase visitor arrivals, lengths of stay and pocket spending may be met with an increased number of experiential products and the delivery of better quality services.

### 17.1.8.  *Differentiation*

The 2010 CRS public sector promotion, product development, operational subsidies and maintenance budgets for its substantial network of properties was approximately 1 billion naira (€6.75 million), not including debt service. Based on TEMPO surveys, only one in five Cross River visitors stay in hotels, with the remainder visiting friends and relatives (VFR). To differentiate Cross River, the issue to address was the creation of products and the identification of markets that increase leisure arrivals beyond December's Carnival Calabar for the rest of the year. TEMPO recommendations have also included a focus on educational and volunteer markets with both cultural and natural packaged products and the ability to reach those markets through information technology.

CDS's TEMPO marketing approach introduced the concept of incorporating local food specialties into menu offerings, increased use of electronic booking and payment systems and the advantages of yield pricing in packaged products. At the conclusion of CDS's engagement it had also introduced Google Maps to CRS resulting in the first small city in sub-Saharan Africa to be fully geocoded with tourism points of interest.

Across Nigeria there are perhaps two-dozen hotel properties managed to an international standard (e.g. Hilton, Starwood, Protea, African Sun) across a resident population of 150 million. Small independent hotels have not had the training resources or experience to adequately differentiate from their competition through experiential products and sustainability principles, until recently only providing cash-in-advance accommodations, limited credit card acceptance and few packaged products.

In sum, a focus on all the prerequisites for packaging experiential products was a key driver of the TEMPO intervention and the significant differentiator for CRS as a distinctive West African and Nigerian destination. Understanding the bottle-necks and deficits across the whole tourism supply chain and providing remedial attention to these problem areas are essential for Cross River's future leisure offer.

## 17.2.  Conclusion

Beyond Carnival Calabar, marketable products based on new experiential com-ponents — particularly entertainment, pilgrimage, health and sport — have not yet attracted a sustainable domestic customer base that is only now beginning to consider travel within Nigeria as an organized leisure activity (as opposed to business meetings or VFR). But as noted here, a shift in marketing from supply to demand requires adjustments in capacity, products and messaging.

Even as the promotion of Cross River Quality's 2010 packages achieved more than 4 million impressions online, through newspaper features and SMS text messaging, few suppliers or consumers were ready to compare traditional offers (air, hotel, transfers) against experiential packages, a necessary shift in both supply and demand.

The TEMPO pilot in CRS testing the marketability of experiential products to attract domestic travellers confronted several challenges, some that were anticipated and others that came as a surprise. The lessons learned from the pilot may be incorporated in follow-up activities when a longer-term intervention is initiated, including:

1. A DMO should be formed with workable destination and content management systems.
2. Online information, booking and payment systems should be made available.
3. For meetings, incentives, conferences and exhibitions (MICE) packages as a target product, promotion timing must be better planned to meet normal scheduling cycles.
4. Nigerian travel agents require more education about Nigerian destinations.
5. The low wage culture is typically responsible for inadequate service quality.

Adequate human resources administration and training are essential to the introduction of experiential products. While these trends should favour pioneering destinations, many emerging markets are struggling with the development of experiential products and service quality standards that remain substantially foreign and difficult to interpret in settings where the delivery of the basics of international hospitality norms is a work in progress and remains uneven and underdeveloped. In Nigeria, newly elected President Goodluck Jonathan in 2011 named Cross River's High Chief Edem Duke as Nigeria's Minister of Culture, Tourism and National Orientation, who is now specifically charged with advancing cultural product development and investment across the country and at international meetings.

## Acknowledgements

The author wishes to thank CDC Development Solutions CEO, Deirdre White, and recognize the tireless efforts of the TEMPO team leadership Jessica Ziegler, Ausmus Marburger and Jane Nsunwara and IBM volunteer consultants Scott Jenkins, Ryan Fanzone and Tim van den Heede.

## References

Addis, M., & Holbrook, M. B. (2001). On the conceptual link between mass customization and experiential consumption: An explosion of subjectivity. *Journal of Consumer Behaviour, 1*(1), 50–66. Retrieved from http://dx.doi.org/10.1002/cb.53

Amha, W., & Ageba, G. (2006). Business development services (BDS) in Ethiopia: Status, prospects and challenges in the micro and small enterprise sector. *International Journal of Emerging Markets, 1*(4), 305. Retrieved from ABI/Inform Complete. Retrieved from http://www.proquest.com

Ashley, C., Boyd, C., & Goodwin, H. (2000). Pro-poor tourism. Putting poverty at the heart of the tourism agenda. *ODI Natural Resource Perspectives, 51*, 1.

Britton, S. G. (1991). Tourism, capital, and place: Towards a critical geography of tourism. *Environment and Planning D: Society and Space, 9*, 451–478. Retrieved from http://dx.doi.org/10.1068/d090451

Cross River State. (2010). *Official website of the Cross River State government.* Retrieved from http://www.crossriverstate.gov.ng

The Economist. (2007). Big men, big fraud and big trouble. *The Economist, 383*(8526), 55–57. Retrieved from ABI/INFORM Complete. Retrieved from http://www.proquest.com

Egbaji, S. (2007). *Tourism development in Nigeria: The Cross River experience* (pp. 98–102). Lagos, Nigeria: El-Sapphire.

FAAN. (2010). *Federal Airport Authority of Nigeria.* Retrieved from http://www.faannigeria.org/statistics

Fjellman, S. M. (1992). *Vinyl leaves* (Chapter 3). Boulder, CO: Westview.

Fodness, D., & Murray, B. (1998). Tourist information search. *Annals of Tourism Research, 37*(2), 108–119.

Högström, C., Rosner, M., & Gustafsson, A. (2010). How to create attractive and unique customer experiences: An application of Kano's theory of attractive quality to recreational tourism. *Marketing Intelligence & Planning, 28*(4), 385–402.

Holbrook, M. B., & Hirschman, E. C. (1982). The experiential aspects of consumption: Consumer fantasies, feelings, and fun. *Journal of Consumer Research, 9*(2), 132–140. Retrieved from http://dx.doi.org/10.1086/208906

Ighodaro, J., (2008). *Nigeria: Bassey ekpo bassey emerges new obong of Calabar.* Vanguard. Retrieved from http://allafrica.com/stories/200804071297.html. Accessed on 20 February 2011.

Lovejoy, P. E., & Richardson, D. (1999). Page trust, pawnship, and Atlantic history: The institutional foundations of the Old Calabar slave trade. [Unnumbered] of 337. Also, Slavery Record. *Liberator (1831–1865)*; May 26, 1832; 2, 21. Both retrieved from *American Periodical Series Online.* Retrieved from http://www.proquest.com

Lusch, R. F., Vargo, S. L., & O'Brien, M. (2007). Competing through service: Insights from service-dominant logic. *Journal of Retailing, 83*(1), 5–18.

Mazrui, A. (2006). *A tale of two Africas: Nigeria and South Africa as contrasting visions.* London: Adonis & Abbey.

McKercher, R., & du Cros, H. (2002). *Cultural tourism: The partnership between tourism and cultural heritage management.* Binghamton, NY: Haworth Press.

Ogunbiyi, Y., & Soyinka, O. (2007). *Doing the right thing: The Donald Duke story.* Ibadan: Bookcraft.

Oladoyin, D. (2008). *Cross River State's tourism drive through the Leboku Festival.* Tourism ROI. Retrieved from http://www.tourismroi.com/InteriorTemplate.aspx?id=29054&terms=leboku

Pine, B. J., & Gilmore, J. H. (1998). Welcome to the experience economy. *Harvard Business Review, July/August,* 97–105.

Pine, B. J., & Gilmore, J. H. (1999). *The experience economy* (p. 171). Boston, MA: Harvard Business School Press.

Richards, G. (2001). The experience industry and the creation of attraction. In *Cultural attractions and European tourism.* Wallingford, Oxfordshire: Cabi Publishing.

Schmitt, B. H. (1999). Experiential marketing. *Journal of Marketing Management, 15*(1), 53–67. Retrieved from http://dx.doi.org/10.1362/026725799784870496

UNWTO. (2005). *United Nations World Tourism Organization, Tourism Market Trends 2004.* Retrieved from www.unwto.org

UNWTO. (2011). *United Nations World Tourism Organization, Tourism Highlights 2010.* Retrieved from www.unwto.org

Urry, J. (1995). *Consuming places.* London: Routledge.

Vargo, S. L., & Lusch, R. F. (2004). Evolving to a new dominant logic for marketing. *The Journal of Marketing, 68*(1), 1–17.

Williams, A. J. (2000). Consuming hospitality: Learning from postmodernism. In C. Lashley & A. Morrison (Eds.), *In search of hospitality.* Oxford: Butterworth-Heinemann.

Williams, A. J. (2002). *Understanding the hospitality consumer.* Oxford: Butterworth-Heinemann.

Zehrer, A. (2009). Service experience and service design: Concepts and application in tourism SMEs. *Managing Service Quality, 19*(3), 332–349.

# PART V
# E-MARKETING

Chapter 18

# An Overview of the Main Innovations in E-Marketing

*Maria Elena Aramendia-Muneta*

## 18.1. Introduction

The purpose of this introductory chapter is to present the main innovations in e-marketing, as well as to contribute to the theoretical basis and effects those innovations may have on the tourism industry. Innovations in this area affect not only the traditional way of conducting business, that is, selling and buying, but they also represent a new approach on how customers are viewed, turning them into the focal point of the online environment.

The rapid evolution of online markets and their impact on business compel firms to provide a quick response to the ongoing changes. The number of Internet users increases from day to day, but there is still a large market to be tapped, as Figure 18.1 shows. For the strategic management of tourism products, this growth implies considerable opportunities to use the Internet to connect with customers, attract them to targeted destinations and develop their loyalty.

Although Asia represents 42% of the world's Internet user base, its penetration rate is still very low and so it is a market with high potential to attract new users. North America is the leader in Internet penetration; however, it has only 13.5% of the user base. Europe is the second most representative area in the world, but its Internet penetration rate is nearly 20% lower than that of North America. The data seem to suggest that North America, Europe and Asia are the most attractive markets for e-tourism, taking into account their user base and penetration rates.

The Internet is an important source of information for consumers and a formidable channel of communication for advertisers (Faber, Lee, & Nan, 2004). Moreover, Internet advertising is a viable medium, which is constantly on the increase (Silk, Klein, & Berndt, 2001). According to eMarketer (June 2010), online advertising is the only means of promoting business that is set to grow in the next few years. In 2009, e-advertising represented 11.9% of total advertising revenues, and in 2014 the share is expected to reach 17.2%. Table 18.1 and Figure 18.2 show past data and estimates of e-advertising revenues.

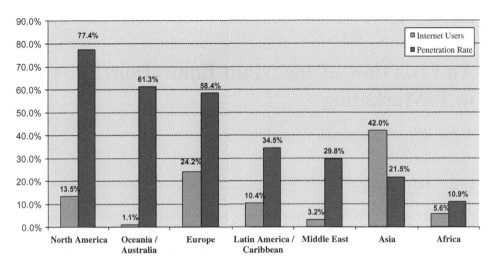

Figure 18.1: Internet users and world Internet penetration rates. *Source*: Internet World Stats (2010).

Table 18.1: E-advertising revenues and annual growth.

|  | Revenues billions ($) | Percent change |
|---|---|---|
| 2008 | 54.2 |  |
| 2009 | 55.2 | 2.0 |
| 2010 | 61.8 | 11.9 |
| 2011 | 68.7 | 11.1 |
| 2012 | 79.0 | 15.0 |
| 2013 | 87.4 | 10.6 |
| 2014 | 96.8 | 10.8 |

*Source*: eMarketer (June 2010).

From 2008 to 2014, e-advertising revenues will almost double, and starting from 2010, they will experience a steady growth rate of over 10% each year. The charts seem to suggest that a great potential in e-advertising for the tourism industry remains largely unexplored, and so this sector should be well aware of how effective e-marketing can be in this line of business.

Increasing numbers of Internet users all over the world and the boom in e-advertising suggest that the tourism industry should elaborate online marketing strategies to provide a prompt response to take advantage of these changes. This chapter highlights the relevance the role consumers and new ways of communication play in the tourism sector and tries to present ways tourism firms can readjust their strategies to the present market so as to be competitive.

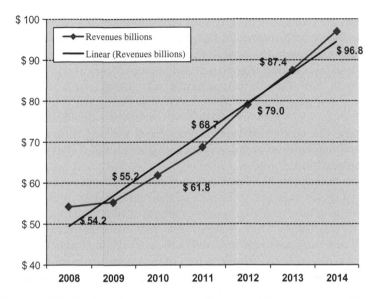

Figure 18.2: E-advertising revenues. *Source*: eMarketer (June 2010).

## 18.2. Innovation in E-Marketing and Its Impact on the Tourism Industry

Most research has focused on the impact of the online environment on businesses, but there has been little research into the main innovation developments in this field according to tourism industry sources. The main innovations can be broken down into two main areas: customers and new ways of communication.

As regards customers, the spread of networking technologies has brought with it collective consumer innovations that are taking on new forms and are transforming the nature of consumption and work, as well as society and marketing. From the point of view of innovation, virtual environments incorporate customers as partners in creating and testing products so that they contribute to the innovation process itself. Thus, virtual environments embody a customer-centred approach.

Community Based Innovation (CBI) has taken into consideration new methods to make use of the potential of online communities and integrates their members into the process of developing new products (Füller, Bartl, Ernst, & Mühlbacher, 2004). Within these communities, new e-tribes are formed as a result of the creative collective innovation of its members, which stems from inner motivation (Kozinets, Hemetsberger, & Schau, 2008). Active participation strengthens the member's sense of belonging to a given online community, which, in turn, spurs members to share their opinions (Qu & Lee, 2011). Geocollaborative portals are a good example of the contribution of CBI, where the community supports decision processes through the use of technology (Sigala, 2010).

Enterprises are well aware of the power of the Internet as a means of creating new added-value for their costumers. In fact, the Internet fosters new ways of interacting and relating to customers (Sawhney, Verona, & Prandelli, 2005). Hence, firms that promptly adopt this innovative approach will be pioneers in attracting new consumers. An example of how the tourism industry may benefit from adapting to these innovations in trying to reach a wider client base is clearly reflected in the Google + community, a new social network which has experienced a significant growth in 2011. Unfortunately, the number of tourism enterprises availing themselves of this new approach to doing business is not very meaningful yet, but it is expected to increase widely in the near future.

Social networking sites like Facebook are real e-tribes, and as they have become so enormously popular, they are well aware of their potential to reach a wide user base and to innovate in advertising campaigns without shedding the social component of those sites (Evans, 2009). Thus, it seems clear that social networks cannot miss the opportunity and potential to get involved in the e-marketing business. Being part of a community has always been an integral part of the Internet user base, but research has not so far defined what being part of that community means, nor has it delved into the many and varied needs of its members (Wang, Yu, & Fesenmaier, 2002).

Electronic Word of Mouth (eWOM) communication is one of the mainstays of the tourism industry because it attracts new customers and is also an indicator of how satisfactory the services provided are (Godes & Mayzlin, 2004). Goldsmith and Horowitz (2006) highlighted that eWOM has far reaching effects on sales of a wide range of goods and services, because it has a direct impact on firm's reputation. Consumers' information is more valuable than advertising, and eWOM is ranked as one of the most important information sources for consumers in their purchase choice. eWOM should be viewed as a potentially cost-effective means for the tourism industry, because this sector is selling intangible products (Litvin, Goldsmith, & Pan, 2008).

There is much concern in the tourism industry about anti-branding, websites that focus on negative information. These sites harm the brand value and stimulate consumer anti-consumption and, consequently, firms experience a negative change in their return on investment (ROI). In general, anti-branding campaigns target well-established firms (Krishnamurthy & Kucuk, 2009). The cruise tourism sector has become very popular in Europe in the last decade. In 2009, more than 4.8 million passengers embarked on a cruise from a European port, a 3.2% increase over 2008 (European Cruise Council, 2010). Prospective cruise travellers put their faith in information gleaned from the Internet, especially when it comes to personal attention and quality of services provided by a given company. Some anti-branding campaigns focus on the nationality of customers as a very important factor and highlight how some of them are discriminated against in the treatment they receive based solely on their country of origin (CO). In fact, CO seems to be an important informational cue for cruise passengers, and CO effects are stronger than the brand effects (Ahmed, Johnson, Ling, Fang, & Hui, 2002).

Travel blogs contribute to influence traveller's choice, as the information they provide often forms the foundations of purchase decisions, be they negative or positive

(Buhalis & Law, 2008; Zehrer, Crotts, & Magnini, 2011). Travellers act at the same time as creators and consumers of information throughout the Internet, giving rise to a collective intelligence (Sigala, 2008). Travel blogs turn out to be real customer feedback through inexpensive media, called consumer-generated media (CGM), and must be taken into consideration as a means of tourism marketing communication (Litvin et al., 2008; Mack, Blose, & Pan, 2008; Pan, MacLaurin, & Crotts, 2007; Yoo & Gretzel, 2008, 2011). Most vacationers read and use online information for their holiday choices; however, that information is most often generated by a small number of users who wish to share their opinions (Bronner & de Hoog, 2011; Yoo & Gretzel, 2011).

Blogs, social networks, virtual communities (e.g. Facebook, Twitter), wikis, and in general, file-sharing media like YouTube are part of the so-called social media websites (Pan et al., 2007). Social media in the online tourism domain are playing such a major role as to influence results returned by search engines. Actually, search engines take travellers directly to social media sites because they are viewed as important sources of information (Xiang & Gretzel, 2010). When conducting a search for a well-known hotel company, search engines rank Twitter or Facebook hits high up in the organic search as most consumers seem to have more confidence in information provided by social networks rather than that provided by a firm's official site.

Regarding the new ways of communication, online advertising has significantly transformed the service provided by the advertiser. There are three aspects to be considered when it comes to innovative advantages: first, the Internet has proved efficient in reaching individual users and getting feedback from those same users, so that ads can be more specifically targeted to those users. Second, the Internet has made it possible to develop highly efficient intermediation markets for advertising; this is clearly shown in the keyword bidding system that is transforming advertising. Finally, the Internet has enabled specialization as traditional publishers have been able to merge content provision with selling advertising space to advertisers (Evans, 2009).

Search engine providers face the problem of revenue generation as users expect free content, while advertisers need to attract the interest of searchers. To meet the expectations of both parties, search engines providers introduced paid search, that is, the use of text advertisements based upon search topic (Laffey, 2007). This kind of promotion is cheaper than other more traditional means of advertising, and tourism SMEs can compete on an equal footing with other firms that have at their disposal larger financial resources to advertise their own brand of business.

The most innovative and best-known campaigns involve 'search-based advertising', in which advertisers and consumers are matched based on the 'keywords' that people enter into search engines (Murphy, Hofacker, & Mizerski, 2006). The use of content network ads is increasing on a daily basis; according to comScore, the Google Content Network reached 80% of global Internet users and each day there are more than 6 billion ad impressions across hundreds of thousands of websites (Google, 2009). As most tourism firms spend over half of their budget on advertising (Tsiotsou, 2006), the Internet offers new, cheaper opportunities, especially for SMEs, to expand their market share, providing more competitiveness and saving part of their budget to bolster other areas of their business and keeping distribution costs low (Tsiotsou & Vlachopoulou, 2011).

Not only does search-based advertising influence searchers, but it also has a great impact on display advertising. Most firms are investing in search engine optimization (SEO) and this affects directly Web 2.0. Web 2.0 contributes to customer empowerment and has a crucial effect on consumer behaviour (Constantinides & Fountain, 2007; Sigala, 2008). For example, agrotourism is a growth tourism sector, but most enterprises in this sector are SMEs. They are under the false impression that they can kick-start their business just by creating a website, completely disregarding how user-friendly their site is, not even taking into consideration how important proper ranking is for their business. More often than not, they blame the Internet when the root of the problem is their ill-advised approach to the Internet and its potential exploitation and benefits. According to Evans and Parravicini (2005), a lower proportion of SMEs use Web to take bookings directly.

Using Web 2.0 increases tourism revenues, but Schegg, Liebrich, Scaglione, and Ahmad (2008) suggest that most enterprises in the tourism sector are at an early stage in applying Web 2.0 technologies to their business. However, there is much concern because at present Web 2.0 is being upgraded to Web 3.0. Web 3.0 provides more accurate information than its predecessors do, and tourism firms could offer more intelligent and connected data (Weidong, 2010). Web 3.0 is the result of combining Web 2.0 with the semantic web (web of meaning), where it is possible for the consumer to find information according to their needs (Wahlster & Dengel, 2006). This way, the data are linked and readily available to all participants.

Figure 18.3 outlines the different phases the Web has gone through since its inception. It is noticeable that while most websites in the tourism industry are still using Web 1.0 (Individual Intelligence) or Web 2.0 technologies (Collective Intelligence), they should be updating to Web 3.0 (Knowledge Internet). It is also important to point out that there is an under-utilization of the possible technologies and information and communication technologies (ICTs) that can be applied in a tourism firm (Tsiotsou & Ratten, 2010).

The information-intensive nature of the tourism industry suggests there is an important role to be played by Internet and Web technology in the promotion and marketing of destinations (Doolin, Burgess, & Cooper, 2002). It is worth highlighting the usefulness of interactivity to measure the relative maturity of tourism-related websites.

Figure 18.3: Different phases of the Web since its inception.

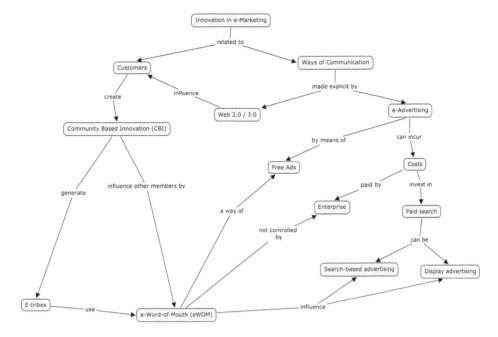

Figure 18.4: A concept map of innovation in e-tourism marketing.

## 18.3. Summary

All the theoretical explanations of innovation in online marketing affecting the tourism industry mentioned above have been coupled with a very useful tool, the so-called Concept Maps (CM). According to Novak and Cañas (2008), concept maps 'are graphical tools for organizing and representing knowledge'. CMs are an enormously useful tool to organize information and to provide new insights into that same information. It is also widely considered as an educational and counselling tool to analyse cognitive structure (Novak & Gowin, 1984). Although CM have proved their value in carrying out marketing research (Joiner, 1998), they have been used very little in tourism marketing strategy.

CM can help firms to recognize inner flows and whether they are acting according to the present market development and they expose the main strategic strengths and weaknesses, either to lend support to their marketing strategies or to acknowledge their shortcomings and failures and to immediately correct them.

Figure 18.4 illustrates the main innovations in e-tourism marketing and their interconnections by means of CM, as explained above.

This CM summarizes the main innovations to be applied in a firm operating in the tourism sector. In the first place, e-tourism focuses on customers, and customers create CBI and influence other members drawing from their experiences (eWOM). Tourism firms have to take advantage of the opportunities for communication that the Internet offers, be it by designing creative websites or profiting from e-advertising to appeal to customers. Finally, the nexus between the two approaches is the fact that consumers in the context of tourism have the power of generating independent means of network persuasion not controlled directly by firms themselves.

The distribution aspect of e-marketing is crucial for the tourism industry. In fact, Internet as channel revolutionized the way of buying and selling; for example, it dramatically changed how people book flights. However, as everything can be bought and sold on the Internet, the new means of communication IT provides spur consumers to buy on the Internet. The tourism industry frequently launches innovative campaigns that also contribute to increasing their offline sales at a later stage. This chapter aims at summarizing how ITs influence the tourism sector.

# References

Ahmed, Z. U., Johnson, J. P., Ling, C. P., Fang, T. W., & Hui, A. K. (2002). Country-of-origin and brand effects on consumers' evaluations of cruise lines. *International Marketing Review, 19*(3), 279–303.

Bronner, F., & de Hoog, R. (2011). Vacationers and eWOM: Who posts, and why, where and what? *Journal of Travel Research, 50*(1), 15–26.

Buhalis, D., & Law, R. (2008). Progress in information technology and tourism management: 20 Years on and 10 Years after the Internet — The state of eTourism research. *Tourism Management, 29*(4), 609–623.

Constantinides, E., & Fountain, S. J. (2007). Web 2.0: Conceptual foundations and marketing issues. *Journal of Direct, Data and Digital Marketing Practice, 9*(3), 231–244.

Doolin, B., Burgess, L., & Cooper, J. (2002). Evaluating the use of the web for tourism marketing: A case study from New Zealand. *Tourism Management, 23*(5), 557–561.

eMarketer. (2010). *Worldwide ad spending.* Retrieved from http://www.emarketer.com/Report.aspx?code=emarketer_2000710.

European Cruise Council. (2010). *The cruise industry.* Retrieved from http://www.europeancruisecouncil.com/content/contribution_of_cruise_tourism_to_the_economies_of_europe_2009.pdf

Evans, D. S. (2009). The online advertising industry: Economics, evolution, and privacy. *Journal of Economic Perspectives, 23*(3), 37–60.

Evans, G., & Parravicini, P. (2005). Exploitation of ICT for rural tourism enterprises. The case of Aragon, Spain. In D. Hall, I. Kirkpatrick & M. Mitchell (Eds.), *Rural tourism and sustainable business* (pp. 103–118). Cleveland, UK; NY, USA; Ontario, Canada: Multilingual Matters Ltd. Available at http://books.google.es/books?id = lzikHgcCxdoC&pg = PA103&dq = exploitation + of + ICT + for + rural + tourism + enterprises&hl = es&sa = X&ei = ZaRXT9vVKKGr0QW7-PTNDQ&ved = 0CDgG6Q6AEwAA#v = onepage&q = exploitation%20of%20ICT%20for%20rural%20tourism%20enterprises&f = false

Faber, R. J., Lee, M., & Nan, X. N. (2004). Advertising and the consumer information environment online. *American Behavioral Scientist, 48*(4), 447–466.

Füller, J., Bartl, M., Ernst, H., & Mühlbacher, H. (2004). Community based innovation: A method to utilize the innovative potential of online communities. *Proceedings of the 37th Hawaii international conference on system sciences 2004*, IEEE, Kona, HA.

Godes, D., & Mayzlin, D. (2004). Using online conversations to study word-of-mouth communication. *Marketing Science, 23*(4), 545–560.

Goldsmith, R. E., & Horowitz, D. (2006). Measuring motivations for online opinion seeking. *Journal of Interactive Advertising, 6*(2), 3–14.

Google. (2009). *CPA performance trends on the Google content network*. Retrieved from http://static.googleusercontent.com/external_content/untrusted_dlcp/www.google.com/en//ads/research/gcnwhitepaper/whitepaper.pdf

Internet World Stats. (2010). *Internet usage statistics*. Retrieved from http://www.Internet worldstats.com/stats.htm. Accessed on 3 December 2010.

Joiner, C. (1998). Concept mapping in marketing: A research tool for uncovering consumers' knowledge structure associations. *Advances in Consumer Research, 25*, 311–322.

Kozinets, R., Hemetsberger, A., & Schau, H. J. (2008). The wisdom of consumer crowds: Collective innovation in the age of networked marketing. *Journal of Macromarketing, 28*(4), 339–354.

Krishnamurthy, S., & Kucuk, S. U. (2009). Anti-branding on the Internet. *Journal of Business Research, 62*(11), 1119–1126.

Laffey, D. (2007). Paid search: The innovation that changed the web. *Business Horizons, 50*, 211–218.

Litvin, S. W., Goldsmith, R. E., & Pan, B. (2008). Electronic word-of-mouth in hospitality and tourism management. *Tourism Management, 29*(3), 458–468.

Mack, R. W., Blose, J. E., & Pan, B. (2008). Believe it or not: Credibility of blogs in tourism. *Journal of Vacation Marketing, 14*(2), 133–144.

Murphy, J., Hofacker, C., & Mizerski, R. (2006). Primacy and recency effects on clicking behavior. *Journal of Computer-Mediated Communication, 11*(2), 522–535.

Novak, J. D., & Cañas, A. J. (2008). *The theory underlying concept maps and how to construct them*. Technical Report IHMC CmapTools 2006-01 Rev 01-2008. Florida Institute for Human and Machine Cognition. Retrieved from http://cmap.ihmc.us/Publications/ResearchPapers/TheoryUnderlyingConceptMaps.pdf

Novak, J. D., & Gowin, D. B. (1984). *Learning how to learn*. Cambridge: Cambridge University Press.

Pan, B., MacLaurin, T., & Crotts, J. C. (2007). Travel blogs and the implications for destination marketing. *Journal of Travel Research, 46*(1), 35–45.

Qu, H., & Lee, H. (2011). Travelers' social identification and membership behaviors in online travel community. *Tourism Management, 32*(6), 1262–1270.

Sawhney, M., Verona, G., & Prandelli, E. (2005). Collaborating to create: The Internet as a platform for customer engagement in product innovation. *Journal of Interactive Marketing, 19*(4), 4–17.

Schegg, R., Liebrich, A., Scaglione, M., & Ahmad, S. F. S. (2008). An exploratory field study of web 2.0 in tourism. In P. O'Connor, W. Höpken & U. Gretzel (Eds.), *Information and communication technologies in tourism 2008* (pp. 152–163). Wien: Springer-Verlag.

Sigala, M. (2008). Web 2.0, social marketing strategies and distribution channels for city destinations: Enhancing the participatory role of travelers and exploiting their collective intelligence. In M. Gascó-Hernández & T. Torres-Coronas (Eds.), *Information communication technologies and city marketing: Digital opportunities for cities around the world* (pp. 1244–1273). Hershey, PA: Information Science Publishing.

Sigala, M. (2010). Measuring customer value in online collaborative trip planning processes. *Marketing Intelligence & Planning, 28*(4), 418–443.

Silk, A. J., Klein, L. R., & Berndt, E. R. (2001). The emerging position of the Internet as an advertising medium. *Netnomics, 3*(2), 129–148.

Tsiotsou, R. (2006). Current trends and practices of Greek travel agencies: Human resource management, marketing and use of new technologies. *Proceedings of the international tourism conferences*, European Tourism Association (June 15–17, 2006), Heraklio, Greece (pp. 1–14).

Tsiotsou, R., & Ratten, V. (2010). Future research directions in tourism marketing. *Marketing Intelligence & Planning, 28*(4), 533–544.

Tsiotsou, R., & Vlachopoulou, M. (2011). Understanding the effects of marketing orientation and e-marketing on services performance. *Marketing Intelligence & Planning, 29*(2), 141–155.

Wahlster, W., & Dengel, A. (2006). *Web 3.0: Convergence of Web 2.0 and the semantic web.* Technology Radar, II, 0. German Research Center for Artificial Intelligence (DFKI).

Wang, Y., Yu, Q., & Fesenmaier, D. R. (2002). Defining the virtual tourist community: Implications for tourism marketing. *Tourism Management, 23*(4), 407–417.

Weidong, W. (2010). *Study on hotel marketing strategy under Web 3.0. International conference on e-business and e-government*, 07–09 May, 2010, ICEE, Guangzhou, China (pp. 138–140).

Xiang, Z., & Gretzel, U. (2010). Role of social media in online travel information search. *Tourism Management, 31*(2), 179–188.

Yoo, K.-H., & Gretzel, U. (2008). What motivates consumers to write online travel reviews? *Information Technology & Tourism, 10*(4), 283–295.

Yoo, K.-H., & Gretzel, U. (2011). Influence of personality on travel-related consumer-generated media creation. *Computers in Human Behavior, 27*(2), 609–621.

Zehrer, A., Crotts, J. C., & Magnini, V. P. (2011). The perceived usefulness of blog postings: An extension of the expectancy-disconfirmation paradigm. *Tourism Management, 32*(1), 106–113.

Chapter 19

# Information and Communication Technologies in Tourism: A Comparison for Travel Agents, Hotels and Restaurants

*Irene Gil-Saura, María-Eugenia Ruiz-Molina and Gloria Berenguer-Contrí*

## 19.1. Introduction

Investing in information and communication technologies (ICTs) is an important strategic decision for tourism companies, especially for small and medium-sized businesses, since it usually involves substantial firm resources. Literature on tourism marketing has emphasized that companies in this industry should use technology in an effective way to immediately satisfy customer desires and needs, adding value across their information systems, and thus avoiding the risk of being relegated to price competition (Olsen & Connolly, 2000). In general, technology might contribute to the overall effectiveness of the tourism company (Chatzipanagiotou & Coritos, 2010) and supports the globalization of the tourism industry by providing effective tools for suppliers to develop, manage and distribute their offerings worldwide (Buhalis, 1998).

Notwithstanding, the relationship between the use of ICT and tourism business performance remains unclear. For instance, research on the impact of e-marketing on tourism business performance reports contradictory findings (Tsiotsou & Vlacho-poulou, 2011). Thus, while most tourism companies appreciate their website as a useful tool to differentiate from competition and attract new customers, some studies reveal that e-marketing activities do not exert a direct influence on small hotels' performance (Coviello, Winklhofer, & Hamilton, 2006) and technology is not among the most important performance determinants for small tourism businesses (Komppula & Reijonen, 2006).

Nevertheless, ample evidence attests to the benefits of ICTs for tourism companies, which include improvements in efficiency and customer service, among others (e.g. Law & Jogaratnam, 2005). Tourism companies implement not only a wide array of technological solutions, such as hardware, software and network

Strategic Marketing in Tourism Services
Copyright © 2012 by Emerald Group Publishing Limited
All rights of reproduction in any form reserved
ISBN: 978-1-78052-070-4

connectivity but also more specific tools for e-procurement, business integrated processes, electronic marketing and sales, customer relationship management (CRM) and ICT solutions related to C2C communications (Buhalis, 1998; Buhalis & Law, 2008; eBusiness W@tch, 2006).

Since ICT involves committing firm resources, there is a need to adjust investment to what is strictly necessary. Therefore, ICT solutions that fit a tourism company are expected to differ across business type. In this vein, this chapter aims at analysing the relative importance of several ICT solutions for different types of tourism companies, i.e. travel agencies, hotels and restaurants.

In order to achieve this aim, we conducted a survey to collect data directly from companies. In particular, we distributed personal surveys to managers of travel agencies, hotels and restaurants in the main Spanish cities. Spain is the third tourism destination in the world in number of tourism arrivals (UNWTO, 2009), and companies directly related to tourism represent more than 10% of total GDP and employment (INE, 2010). These figures illustrate the importance of the tourism industry in the Spanish economy and the importance of ensuring competitiveness of the companies in this industry.

In this way, this study intends to identify the major factors to take into account when prioritizing the implementation of certain technological solutions by tourism companies, assuming the peculiarities associated to each business type, i.e. travel agencies, hotels and restaurants. In particular, in order to shed light on practitioners' decisions regarding ICT investment, in the present chapter we aim to go further with academic work through the consideration of the following questions:

1. *Are there differences in the intensity of use of ICT solutions by different types of tourism businesses?* We understand that travel agencies, hotels and restaurants differ in the tasks developed as well as the importance of the establishment atmosphere in customer perceptions. Therefore, we expect that they use different ICT solutions, and even if they use the same solutions, they differ in the intensity of use of such technologies.
2. *Are there differences in the assessment of pros and cons of ICT use by different tourism businesses?* We determine if travel agencies, hotels and restaurants differ in their perceptions about the advantages and disadvantages of ICT solutions.

The results of this research are also expected to provide managerial implications for ICT providers so that they may develop specific solutions and catalogues for each type of company. In view of the relative importance provided by travel agents, hotels and restaurants to the advantages and disadvantages of ICT solutions, technology providers may be empowered to develop sales propositions to target more effectively each market segment.

Although this research is limited to the Spanish tourism industry, since Spain as a tourism destination is one of the most important at world level, we expect to provide orientations that may be also valid for tourism companies operating in other countries. In particular, the results of this study may be especially relevant for emerging tourism destinations such as China or India, as they are expected to follow the same trend of ICT implementation as the consolidated tourism destinations in Europe and America (Huang, 2006; Ma, Buhalis, & Song, 2003).

## 19.2. ICT and the Tourism Industry

ICT includes 'all forms of technology utilized to create, capture, manipulate, communicate, exchange, present, and use information in its various forms (business data, voice conversations, still images, motion pictures, multimedia presentations, etc.)' (Ryssel, Ritter, & Gemunden, 2004, p. 198). Regarding the use of ICT in tourism businesses, several academics have analysed technology from both conceptual and empirical perspectives. Table 19.1 summarizes the main contributions in the literature about ICT and tourism business.

Analysing the use of ICT in the tourism industry involves considering both the demand (i.e. tourism businesses) and the supply side (i.e. ICT providers). Next, we discuss the more common topics researched.

Several studies in the hospitality industry focus on the implementation of ICT solutions by tourism businesses, as well as the advantages and disadvantages of technology (Buick, 2003; eBusiness W@tch, 2006; Galloway, 2007; Irvine & Anderson, 2008; Law & Jogaratnam, 2005; Lee et al., 2003; Ma et al., 2003; Martínez et al., 2006; Observatorio, 2007a, 2007b; Sancho, 2004). Most of these studies assess specific technology solutions such as the Internet (Baloglu & Pekcan, 2006; Chung & Law, 2003; Galloway, 2007; Jeong et al., 2003; Ma et al., 2003; Murphy et al., 2003; Zafiropoulos & Vrana, 2006), data mining (Magnini et al., 2003), CRM (Piccoli et al., 2003; Stockdale, 2007), self-service technologies (Stockdale, 2007) and in-room ICT solutions in hotels (Wolff, 2005). This interest for some ICT solutions may be explained by the unequal development of technologies in the tourism industry. Thus, in spite of the high level of Internet implementation by tourism companies (eBusiness W@tch, 2006; Observatorio, 2007a, 2007b), ICT investment in this industry is quite unequal (Martínez et al., 2006), especially for some technologies such as ambient intelligence (Manes, 2003), i.e. electronic sensitive environments able to respond to the presence of people, providing customized added-value services and energy savings at the same time (Nizic, Karanovic, & Ivanovic, 2008).

The main research topics in the literature on ICT in the tourism industry are the use of the Internet, online marketing policies (e.g. dynamic pricing, social networks, blogging) and e-commerce. The rapid development of Internet users has motivated most of tourism organizations to implement Internet technologies as part of their marketing and communication strategies (Buhalis & Law, 2008).

In this sense, literature has evidenced the wide range of ICT solutions implemented by tourism businesses, especially by hotels (Buhalis & Law, 2008; eBusiness W@tch, 2006; Law & Jogaratnam, 2005; Observatorio, 2007b). These solutions include hardware and software, network connectivity technologies, business integrated processes, electronic marketing and sales solutions, information systems for providers and CRM. In addition to this, several technologies have been developed for enhancing

Table 19.1: Summary of literature review on ICT in tourism businesses.

| Author (year) | Paper type | ICT | Business type | Research topic |
|---|---|---|---|---|
| Brathwaite (1992) | Conceptual | Several ICTs | Several types | ICT and value chain |
| Buhalis (1998) | Conceptual | Several ICTs | Several types | ICT use by tourism companies |
| Crotts and Turner (1999) | Conceptual | Several ICTs | Travel agencies | Trust and commitment |
| Medina and García (2000) | Empirical | Several ICTs | Hotels | Relationship hotel–travel agency |
| Olsen and Connolly (2000) | Conceptual | Several ICTs | Several types | ICT-induced changes |
| Kim, Han, and Lee (2001) | Empirical | Relational marketing ICT | Upscale hotels | Relational marketing effects |
| Kim and Cha (2002) | Empirical | Relational marketing ICT | Upscale hotels | Hotel–guest relationship quality |
| O'Connor and Frew (2002) | Conceptual | ICT-based distribution systems | Hotels | ICT influence on distribution systems |
| Paraskevas and Buhalis (2002) | Empirical | Several ICTs | Hotels | Reasons for collaboration with ASP |
| Buick (2003) | Empirical | Several ICTs | Hotels | ICT implementation and use |
| Chung and Law (2003) | Empirical | Hotel website | Hotels | Hotel website performance |
| Jeong, Oh, and Gregoire (2003) | Empirical | Hotel website | Hotels | Hotel website quality and consequences |
| Lee, Barker, and Kandampully (2003) | Empirical | Several ICTs | Hotels | ICT implementation and service quality |
| Ma et al. (2003) | Conceptual | ICT and Internet | Several types | ICT and Internet adoption |
| Magnini, Honeycutt, and Hodge (2003) | Conceptual | Data mining | Hotels | Use and limitations of data mining |
| Manes (2003) | Conceptual | Ambient intelligence | Several types | Uses of ambient intelligence |
| Minghetti (2003) | Conceptual | Several ICTs | Several types | Perceived value |

Table 19.1: (*Continued*)

| Author (year) | Paper type | ICT | Business type | Research topic |
|---|---|---|---|---|
| Murphy, Olaru, Schegg, and Frey (2003) | Empirical | Hotel website and e-mail | Hotels | Use of hotel website and e-mail |
| O'Connor (2003) | Empirical | Online distribution | Hotels | Online pricing |
| O'Connor and Piccoli (2003) | Conceptual | Global distribution systems (GDS) | Hotels | GDS use by hotels |
| Piccoli, O'Connor, Capaccioli, and Alvarez (2003) | Conceptual | CRM | Hotels | CRM use: pros and cons |
| Law, Leung, and Wong (2004) | Empirical | Internet | Travel agencies | Impact of Internet on travel agencies |
| Law and Jogaratnam (2005) | Empirical | Several ICTs | Hotels | ICT use |
| Wolff (2005) | Conceptual | In-room ICT | Hotels | Use of in-room entertainment ICT |
| Baloglu and Pekcan (2006) | Empirical | Internet | Upscale hotels | Website design |
| eBusiness W@tch (2006) | Empirical | Several ICTs | Several types | ICT implementation |
| Huang (2006) | Empirical | B2B ICT | Travel agencies | Strategic B2B alliances |
| Kim, Lee, and Yoo (2006) | Empirical | Several ICTs | Upscale restaurants | Relationship quality and results |
| Martínez, Majó, and Casadesús (2006) | Conceptual | Several ICTs | Hotels | ICT use: pros and cons |
| Tsaur, Yung, and Lin (2006) | Empirical | Several ICTs | Travel agencies | Wholesale–retail travel agencies' relationships |
| Vrana and Zafiropoulos (2006) | Empirical | Internet | Travel agencies | Attitudes towards Internet adoption |
| Wu and Chang (2006) | Empirical | Internet | Travel agencies | e-Trust |

Table 19.1: (*Continued*)

| Author (year) | Paper type | ICT | Business type | Research topic |
|---|---|---|---|---|
| Zafiropoulos and Vrana (2006) | Empirical | Internet | Hotels | Website assessment |
| Galloway (2007) | Conceptual | Broadband Internet access | Rural hotels | Broadband Internet access: pros and cons |
| Kothari, Hu, and Roehl (2007) | Case study | e-Procurement | Hotels | e-Procurement |
| Moliner, Sánchez, Rodríguez, and Callarisa (2007) | Empirical | Several ICTs | Travel agencies | Relationship quality |
| Observatorio (2007a) | Empirical | Several ICTs | Rural hotels | ICT implementation: pros and cons |
| Observatorio (2007b) | Empirical | Several ICTs | Hotels | ICT implementation: pros and cons |
| Sigala (2007) | Empirical | Internet | Travel agencies | Internet impact on B2B relationships |
| Stockdale (2007) | Conceptual | e-CRM and SSTs | Several types | Tourist trust and loyalty |
| Bigné, Aldás, and Andreu (2008) | Empirical | Several ICTs | Travel agencies | Antecedents of ICT adoption |
| Buhalis and Law (2008) | Conceptual | Several ICTs | Several types | Implications of ICT |
| Campo and Yagüe (2008) | Empirical | Several ICTs | Tour operators | Perceived quality, satisfaction and loyalty |
| Garau and Orfila-Sintes (2008) | Empirical | Internet | Hotels | Internet impact on B2B relationships |
| Huang (2008) | Empirical | e-Commerce | Travel agencies | e-Loyalty in B2B relationships |
| Irvine and Anderson (2008) | Empirical | Several ICTs | Hotels | ICT use |
| Nasution and Mavondo (2008) | Empirical | Several ICTs | Hotels | Perceived value |
| Thao and Swierczek (2008) | Empirical | Internet | Travel agencies | Internet use and B2B relationships |
| Karadag, Cobanoglu, and Dickinson (2009) | Empirical | Several ICTs | Hotels | Decisions on IT investment |

Table 19.1: (*Continued*)

| Author (year) | Paper type | ICT | Business type | Research topic |
|---|---|---|---|---|
| Guadix, Cortés, Onieva, and Jesús Muñuzuri (2010) | Empirical | Technology revenue management system | Hotels | Inventory management |
| Lin and Lee (2010) | Empirical | Online reservation systems | Hotels | Impacts of online reservation systems |
| Minghetti and Buhalis (2010) | Conceptual | Several ICTs | Several types | Unequal access and use of ICT |

the guest experience in the hotel or in the restaurant, such as cable TV, DVD, piped music, ambient intelligence or touch screen in the hall of the hotel.

Regarding travel agencies, the literature has focused on the use of the Internet (Law et al., 2004; Vrana & Zafiropoulos, 2006; Wu & Chang, 2006), e-commerce (Huang, 2008) and ICT solutions enabling B2B relationships with wholesale travel agencies and tour operators (Bigné et al., 2008; Crotts & Turner, 1999; Huang, 2006; Moliner et al., 2007; Sigala, 2007; Thao & Swierczek, 2008; Tsaur et al., 2006).

Among the benefits derived from ICT implementation by companies, the business literature has pointed out significant improvements in internal processes that ultimately contribute to customer service improvements. In particular, it has been argued that ICT positively affects internal efficiency through important savings in terms of time, communication costs and personnel expenses; greater reliability, accurateness and error reduction; as well as increases in productivity through the automation of labour-intensive tasks (Ellram, La Londe, & Weber, 1999; Lowson, 2001). More specifically, in the tourism industry, various technological applications are aimed at increasing internal efficiency, knowledge of the needs, behaviours and preferences of their customers, capturing and managing new customers, and improving customer experience in the establishment (Buhalis & Law, 2008; Frew, 2000; Minghetti, 2003).

In spite of its advantages, ICT solutions are less intensively implemented in independent and small and medium-sized tourism companies than in larger ones (Buick, 2003; Galloway, 2007; Main, 2001; Paraskevas & Buhalis, 2002). There is also evidence about the underutilization of the potential of the ICT implemented in tourism companies (Hensdill, 1998; Martínez et al., 2006; Tsiotsou & Ratten, 2010). In other words, tourism companies, and hotels in particular, do not make full use of their technologies. Additionally, given the variety-seeking behaviour of tourists and low probability of repeat visits (Inman, 2001; Van Trijp, Hoyer, & Inman, 1996), tourism companies may feel discouraged when it comes to investing in technologies targeted towards them.

Nevertheless, travel agencies and restaurants deliver their services not only to tourists but also to the local demand. In this sense, ICT investments may also profit these companies, especially restaurants, in view of the significant influence of the restaurant atmosphere and extra services on perceived quality, customer satisfaction and repeat visits (Dulen, 1998; Susskind & Chan, 2000). In addition, highly satisfied tourists are more likely to repeat their visit and to generate positive word-of-mouth (Anderson, 1998) and e-word-of-mouth communication (Kim & Cha, 2002; Kim et al., 2001; Litvin, Goldsmith, & Pan, 2008).

Furthermore, practitioners and academics disagree regarding the optimum ICT investment by companies. Thus, while ICT practitioners state that higher levels of ICT investment are always better than lower levels, academics posit that 'good' technology is the 'suitable' technology (Palmer & Markus, 2000), avoiding the risk of 'over-engineering' (Sethuraman & Parasuraman, 2005). Although ICT investments are crucial for tourism companies to adapt to the environment and to maintain competitiveness (Magnini et al., 2003), they might require scarce financial resources not always easily available, especially for small independent businesses (Orfila-Sintes, Crespí-Cladera, & Martínez-Ros, 2005). In this regard, some ICT solutions should be prioritized (Minghetti, 2003).

In a position between the 'higher levels are always better' and the 'what is suitable', application service providers (ASP) have been recommended for tourism businesses, especially for small and midsize companies (Paraskevas & Buhalis, 2002). These organizations enable the delivery and management of applications and computer services through remote data centres, thus providing an affordable ICT infrastructure with low investment.

## 19.3.   Research Method

In order to achieve the proposed objectives, a survey was conducted through personal interviews with managers or owners of tourism firms. The survey aims at obtaining information regarding the intensity of use of ICT solutions by travel agencies, hotels and restaurants, as well as their assessment of pros and cons of technology used with their main group of customers. Table 19.2 exhibits the main characteristics of our sample.

To elaborate the questionnaire for the survey, the items regarding the intensity of use of the ICT of the different ICT solutions were extracted and adapted from Buhalis (1998), Buhalis and Law (2008), eBusiness W@tch (2006) and Observatorio (2007a, 2007b). The items used to measure reasons for and against using ICT were extracted from Observatorio (2007a, 2007b). All items of the questionnaire are measured in a 5-point Likert scale, ranking from 1 (strongly disagree) to 5 (strongly agree).

The database of travel agencies, hotels and restaurants was obtained from secondary information. In particular, the main travel agencies and hotels were selected according to their NACE (i.e. National Classification of Economic Activities) and TEA (i.e., Tax on Economic Activities) codes obtained from SABI (Iberian

Table 19.2: Sample description.

| | |
|---|---|
| Study population | Travel agencies (10,779) |
| | Hotels (12,290) |
| | Restaurants (63,728) |
| Geographical scope | Spain |
| Sample size | 309 retail travel agencies (2.867% of study population) |
| | 200 hotels (1.627% of study population) |
| | 150 restaurants (0.002% of study population) |
| Travel agencies' characteristics | *Main activity of the travel agency*: |
| | - Retailer: 278 (89.97%) |
| | - Wholesaler: 31 (10.03%) |
| Hotels' characteristics | *Category*: |
| | - Three stars: 90 (45.0%) |
| | - Four stars: 83 (41.5%) |
| | - Five stars: 27 (13.5%) |
| Restaurants' characteristics | *Average menu price*: |
| | - Less than €20: 18 (12.0%) |
| | - €20–39: 37 (24.7%) |
| | - €40–59: 74 (49.3%) |
| | - More than €60: 21 (14.0%) |
| | *Restaurant profile*: |
| | - Innovative cuisine: 35 (23.3%) |
| | - Traditional cuisine: 97 (64.7%) |
| | - Restaurant chain: 18 (12.0%) |
| Sample design | Personal survey to business owners/managers |
| Data collection period | June 2009 to April 2010 |
| Statistical techniques | Descriptive analysis |
| | Analysis of variance (ANOVA) |
| Statistical software | SPSS version 17.0 |

Accounting Analysis System), an Informa database that contains the annual reports of the most important Spanish and Portuguese companies, in terms of total sum of the assets in the company's balance sheet. In the case of hotels, this information was validated and completed with the directory Visiting Spain,[1] since SABI provides no information about hotel category. Data were collected in the three main Spanish cities

---

1. http://www.visitingspain.es

(Madrid, Barcelona and Valencia), as well as Alicante, the capital of Costa Blanca, one of the main areas in terms of number of tourist arrivals.

The sample of restaurants was obtained from several restaurant directories, i.e. Guía Vergara (Vergara, 2006), www.verema.com, www.guiarepsol.com, www. viamichelin.es, www.guiasrestaurantes.com, www.laotraguia.com, www.gourmets. net (Gourmetour) and www.mesalibre.com. Restaurants in Valencia and its metropolitan area were selected. Regarding the travel agencies, hotels and restaurants that agreed to participate in our study, as can be observed from Table 19.2, the final samples include a wide variety of companies in terms of their profile in order to enhance sample representativeness.

For all the items measuring ICT use and reasons for and against the use of technology, ANOVAs are run to identify in which items travel agencies, hotels and restaurants differ. A principal component analysis has been performed for the items measuring reasons for and against using ICT and the Cronbach reliability coefficient has been computed for these scales to measure their reliability.

Finally, in order to identify certain groups of ICT products that are commonly used together, we applied a cluster analysis considering as key variables the different types of ICT solutions. First, the hierarchical method was used to delimit the number of conglomerates. Next, as it was not expected that groups are included in other groups, a *K*-means non-hierarchical clustering method was selected. Nevertheless, this method requires a number of *a priori* clusters for the initial analysis, as well as centroids, which are provided by the hierarchical analysis previously carried out (Punj & Stewart, 1983).

## 19.4. Results for Spanish Travel Agencies, Hotels and Restaurants

In order to assess the use of ICTs in travel agencies, hotels and restaurants, mean values were calculated for each ICT solution in each tourism business type. To test the existence of significant differences, analysis of variance (ANOVA for items and MANOVA for constructs in bold) and Tukey *post hoc* multiple comparison tests were performed (Table 19.3).

The results suggest that some ICT solutions are widely adopted in the tourism industry regardless of the type of company. Desktop PCs, point of sale terminals and Internet connection show high levels of use in all business types, although significant differences are observed across them. In general, hotels are the tourism companies using more intensively hardware, connectivity and software solutions, while restaurants show the lowest scores. In contrast, some devices, such as digital phone communications and electronic cash, are more intensively used by restaurants in comparison to other tourism businesses.

Regarding the intensity of use of CRM, communications with customers, advertising and online order reception ICT solutions, results are shown in Table 19.4.

Again, while some ICT solutions are widely implemented by all tourism companies (e.g. personal phone customer service, customer service by e-mail), others

Table 19.3: Intensity of use of hardware, connectivity and software: ANOVA analysis.

| | $F$ | $p$-Value | Differences across groups[a] |
|---|---|---|---|
| Hardware | **23.21** | **0.00** | |
| Desktop PC | 43.37 | 0.00 | 1–3, 2–3 |
| Laptop PC | 4.56 | 0.01 | 1–2 |
| Server | 23.24 | 0.00 | 1–3, 2–3 |
| Hardcopy system | 15.37 | 0.00 | 1–3, 2–3 |
| PDA | 4.74 | 0.01 | 1–3, 2–3 |
| Digital phone communications | 27.66 | 0.00 | 1–2, 1–3, 2–3 |
| Mobil phone communications | 2.92 | 0.06 | 1–2 |
| Fax | 144.27 | 0.00 | 1–2, 1–3, 2–3 |
| Switchboard | 125.51 | 0.00 | 1–2, 1–3, 2–3 |
| Digital camera | 19.19 | 0.00 | 1–2, 2–3 |
| LCD screen | 17.96 | 0.00 | 1–2, 2–3 |
| Touchscreen | 14.47 | 0.00 | 1–2, 1–3 |
| Digital terrestrial television | 76.82 | 0.00 | 1–2, 1–3, 2–3 |
| DVD | 10.27 | 0.00 | 1–2, 2–3 |
| Electronic cash | 39.92 | 0.00 | 1–2, 1–3, 2–3 |
| Point of sale (POS) terminal | 2.36 | 0.10 | – |
| Domotic systems | 19.68 | 0.00 | 1–2, 2–3 |
| Connectivity | **44.89** | **0.00** | |
| Internet connection through BRI/ISDN/ADSL/cable/others | 41.83 | 0.00 | 1–3, 2–3 |
| Virtual private network (VPN) | 92.76 | 0.00 | 1–2, 1–3, 2–3 |
| Wireless Internet (Wi-Fi) | 85.76 | 0.00 | 1–2, 1–3, 2–3 |
| Bluetooth | 8.04 | 0.00 | 1–3 |
| Worldwide Interoperability (WiMAX) | 9.38 | 0.00 | 1–2, 1–3 |
| Software | **16.96** | **0.00** | |
| Office software | 39.44 | 0.00 | 1–3, 2–3 |
| Design software | 27.45 | 0.00 | 1–2, 1–3, 2–3 |
| Security systems | 17.74 | 0.00 | 1–3, 2–3 |
| Electronic invoicing | 8.94 | 0.00 | 1–3, 2–3 |
| Specific departmental solutions | 18.82 | 0.00 | 1–2, 1–3, 2–3 |
| Data analysis and report and project management | 35.90 | 0.00 | 1–2, 2–3 |
| Simulators | 23.26 | 0.00 | 1–2, 2–3 |

[a]The Tukey *post hoc* multiple comparison test was used to test for the significance of differences between types of tourism businesses. Only the statistically significant differences between groups at the 5% level are shown.

are scarcely used (e.g. automatic speech recognition). Additionally, significant differences are observed across tourism business type. Generally speaking, hotels most intensively use ICT solutions, while restaurants make the least intensive use.

The low use of Web 2.0 communities is remarkable. Although surveys were collected during 2009 and 2010, results may have experienced a substantial change, since the use of virtual communities by companies — especially social networks — may have increased dramatically in the last year, according to the explosive growth in the number of members of the most popular virtual communities (Inside Facebook, 2011).

Furthermore, an important characteristic of ICT is that technology/communication products are often sold or purchased in bundles. In order to identify certain groups of ICT products that are commonly used together, a cluster analysis was performed. As a result of this analysis conducted with the data of all tourism businesses, two groups of ICT solutions were identified. In general terms, the first group gathers the main basic ICT solutions (e.g. desktop, server, fax, office software, etc.), while the second group includes the most sophisticated ones (e.g. touch screen, WiMAX, simulators, etc.), as shown in Table 19.5.

Notwithstanding, some technologies that are considered as advanced by some types of tourism companies seem to be very basic for a specific group of businesses. In this sense, when replicating the cluster analysis for each type of business company independently (i.e. travel agents, hotels and restaurants), although most of ICT solutions are grouped in the same clusters as for the total sample, some discrepancies emerge.[2] Thus, for instance, while for the total sample CRS and GDS are included in cluster 2, for travel agencies these are considered as basic (cluster 1). Similarly, call centres and own booking system are considered as basic by hotels. In contrast, switchboards and virtual area networks are included in the second cluster for restaurants, while considered as elementary by travel agencies and hotels.

Differences observed in the intensity of use of the different ICT solutions may be explained not only by the peculiarities of the tasks developed by the different companies but also by the business manager perceptions about the advantages and disadvantages of ICT solutions. Therefore, respondents were asked about their assessment of the reasons for and against using ICT solutions. Results for reasons for using ICT solutions are shown in Table 19.6.

Consistently with the greater use of ICT applications by hotels and travel agencies in comparison to restaurants, it is noted that the former appreciate at a greater extent the benefits of technology in their relations with their suppliers and customers. All benefits are positively assessed by all business types, since scores for all items are above the midpoint of the scale.

Finally, we analysed a number of reasons against using ICT solutions by tourism companies. Results are displayed in Table 19.7.

---

2. Table 19.5 shows coincidences of each type of tourism business with the total sample between brackets.

Table 19.4: Intensity of use of ICTs for customer relationship management and communications: ANOVA analysis.

| | *F* | *p*-Value | Differences across groups[a] |
|---|---|---|---|
| Customer relationship management (CRM) | **17.16** | **0.00** | |
| Customer information systems (CIS) | 32.08 | 0.00 | 1–2, 1–3, 2–3 |
| E-mail marketing/direct marketing | 40.97 | 0.00 | 1–2, 1–3, 2–3 |
| Viral marketing | 12.80 | 0.00 | 1–2, 1–3, 2–3 |
| Loyalty programme | 45.89 | 0.00 | 1–2, 1–3, 2–3 |
| Communications with customers | **30.67** | **0.00** | |
| Personal phone customer service | 4.63 | 0.01 | 1–2 |
| Call centre | 55.15 | 0.00 | 1–2, 1–3, 2–3 |
| Automatic speech recognition | 3.01 | 0.05 | – |
| Customer service by fax | 111.76 | 0.00 | 1–2, 1–3, 2–3 |
| Customer service by e-mail | 47.35 | 0.00 | 1–2, 1–3, 2–3 |
| Advertising | **13.87** | **0.00** | |
| Promotional CD/DVD | 50.30 | 0.00 | 1–2, 2–3 |
| Informative website | 29.76 | 0.00 | 1–2, 2–3 |
| Informative e-brochure | 24.39 | 0.00 | 1–2, 2–3 |
| e-Magazine | 15.14 | 0.00 | 1–2, 2–3 |
| Multimedia solutions (3D, virtual tour) | 27.42 | 0.00 | 1–2, 1–3, 2–3 |
| Online order reception | **34.03** | **0.00** | |
| Own booking system without payment facilities | 184.30 | 0.00 | 1–2, 1–3, 2–3 |
| Own booking system with payment facilities | 158.79 | 0.00 | 1–2, 1–3, 2–3 |
| Computerized reservation system (CRS) | 147.40 | 0.00 | 1–2, 1–3, 2–3 |
| Global distribution system (GDS) | 151.57 | 0.00 | 1–2, 1–3, 2–3 |
| Booking system of tourist destinations | 185.64 | 0.00 | 1–3, 2–3 |
| Dynamic packages | 129.24 | 0.00 | 1–3, 2–3 |
| Electronic distribution to corporate customers | 101.72 | 0.00 | 1–2, 1–3, 2–3 |
| m-Commerce | 58.87 | 0.00 | 1–2, 1–3, 2–3 |
| Searchers and metasearchers | 126.90 | 0.00 | 1–3, 2–3 |
| Price comparison/predictors | 126.63 | 0.00 | 1–2, 1–3, 2–3 |
| Auction websites | 35.11 | 0.00 | 1–2, 1–3, 2–3 |
| Web 2.0 virtual communities | 44.28 | 0.00 | 1–2, 1–3, 2–3 |

[a]The Tukey *post hoc* multiple comparison test was used to test for the significance of differences between types of tourism businesses. Only the statistically significant differences between groups at the 5% level are shown.

Table 19.5: Cluster analysis results.

| Cluster 1 | Cluster 2 |
| --- | --- |
| Desktop PC (TA, H, R) | Laptop PC (TA, H, R) |
| Server (TA, H, R) | PDA (TA, H, R) |
| Hardcopy system (TA, H, R) | Digital camera (TA, H, R) |
| Digital phone communications (TA, H, R) | Touchscreen (TA, H) |
| Mobil phone communications (TA, H, R) | Digital terrestrial television (DTT) (TA, R) |
| Fax (TA, H) | DVD (TA, H, R) |
| Switchboard (TA, H) | Electronic cash (TA, H, R) |
| LCD screen (TA, H, R) | Bluetooth (TA, H, R) |
| Point of sale (POS) terminal (TA, H, R) | Worldwide Interoperability (WiMAX) (TA, H, R) |
| Domotic systems (TA, H, R) | Simulators (TA, H, R) |
| Internet connection (TA, H, R) | Viral marketing (TA, H, R) |
| Virtual private network (VPN) (TA, H) | Loyalty programme (TA, H, R) |
| Wireless Internet connection (red Wi-Fi) (H) | Call centre (TA, R) |
| Office software (TA, H, R) | Automatic speech recognition (TA, R) |
| Design software (H) | Promotional CD/DVD (TA, R) |
| Security systems (TA, H, R) | e-Magazine (TA, H, R) |
| Electronic invoicing (TA, H, R) | Multimedia solutions (TA, H) |
| Specific departmental solutions (TA, H) | Own booking system without payment facilities (TA, R) |
| Data analysis and report and project management (TA, H) | Own booking system with payment facilities (TA, R) |
| Customer information systems (CIS) (TA, H) | Computerized reservation system (CRS) (R) |
| E-mail marketing/direct marketing (TA, H) | Global distribution system (GDS) (R) |
| Personal phone customer service (TA, H, R) | Booking system of tourist destinations (H, R) |
| Customer service by fax (TA, H) | Dynamic packages (H, R) |
| Customer service by e-mail (TA, H, R) | Electronic distribution to corporate customers (TA, H, R) |
| Informative website (TA, H, R) | m-Commerce (TA, H, R) |
| Informative e-brochure (TA, H) | Searchers and metasearchers (H, R) |
| | Price comparison/predictors (H, R) |
| | Auction websites (TA, H, R) |
| | Web 2.0 virtual communities (TA, H, R) |

TA, travel agency; H, hotel; R, restaurant.

Table 19.6: Reasons for using ICT: ANOVA analysis.

| | $F$ | $p$-Value | Differences between groups[a] |
|---|---|---|---|
| Utilitarian reasons for using ICT ($\alpha = 0.849$) | 9.75 | 0.00 | |
| IT facilitates and expedites the purchasing process | 35.18 | 0.00 | 1–2, 1–3, 2–3 |
| IT solutions enable better monitoring and standardization of the purchasing process | 33.54 | 0.00 | 1–2, 1–3, 2–3 |
| I can access information anytime, anywhere | 22.19 | 0.00 | 1–2, 1–3, 2–3 |
| IT solutions provide the opportunity for more benefits (more information access to special promotions, …) than the traditional way with less effort | 28.65 | 0.00 | 1–3, 2–3 |
| IT offers me security, reliability, accuracy and protection against risk | 25.46 | 0.00 | 1–2, 1–3, 2–3 |
| Using IT solutions, any task requires less effort | 12.99 | 0.00 | 1–3, 2–3 |
| IT allows me to obtain a proof of the transaction to facilitate claims if necessary | 33.63 | 0.00 | 1–2, 1–3, 2–3 |
| IT solutions allow me to avoid employee interaction | 4.23 | 0.02 | 2–3 |
| Hedonic reasons for using ICT ($\alpha = 0.734$) | 11.29 | 0.00 | |
| I love having a choice (between using and not using IT solutions) | 5.01 | 0.01 | 1–3 |
| I have a good time using IT solutions; they are a good entertainment | 5.10 | 0.01 | 1–2 |

*Principal component results*: KMO, 0.852; determinant, 0.037; Bartlett's test of sphericity (significant level), 0.000; explained total variance, 55.85%.
[a]The Tukey *post hoc* multiple comparison test was used to test for the significance of differences between types of tourism businesses. Only the statistically significant differences between groups at the 5% level are shown.

Scores for almost all items are below the midpoint of the scale, showing the little importance of ICT disadvantages for tourism business managers. Those expressing the highest concerns about ICT solutions are restaurants. Regarding the different items, the biggest problem for all companies is missing personal touch with their counterparties.

Table 19.7: Reasons against using ICT: ANOVA analysis.

|  | *F* | *p*-Value | Differences between groups[a] |
|---|---|---|---|
| Reasons against using ICT ($\alpha = 0.784$) | 16.40 | 0.00 | |
| I am not familiar with technology in general | 7.85 | 0.00 | 1–3 |
| I have to invest too much time in learning and managing IT solutions | 42.86 | 0.00 | 1–2, 1–3, 2–3 |
| This technology is not available for all products yet | 7.83 | 0.00 | 1–2, 1–3 |
| I have difficulty solving problems that may arise/I do not feel sure | 7.07 | 0.00 | 1–3, 2–3 |
| I miss personal contact | 12.04 | 0.00 | 1–2, 1–3 |

*Principal component analysis results*: KMO, 0.808; determinant, 0.151; Bartlett's test of sphericity (significant level), 0.000; explained total variance, 58.24%.
[a]The Tukey *post hoc* multiple comparison test was used to test for the significance of differences between types of tourism businesses. Only the statistically significant differences between groups at the 5% level are shown.

## 19.5.   Conclusions

In Spanish tourism companies, the level of use of ICT solutions in their relationships with providers and customers is generally high. Notwithstanding, differences across business type (i.e. travel agencies, hotels and restaurants) and technology solutions are observed. In reply to our first research question (*Are there differences in the intensity of use of ICT solutions by different types of tourism businesses?*), excepting some specific solutions (e.g. electronic cash), hotels use ICT more intensively in their business processes while, in contrast, restaurants use these solutions less, in agreement with Observatorio (2007a, 2007b). This difference might be explained by several factors. First, the services provided by a hotel are heterogeneous, and the final product, as a combination of these services, is complex. Thus, ICT solutions may yield important efficiency gains. Additionally, in hotel service delivery the points of interaction with the customer are manifold before, during and after the tourist stay. Consequently, hotels might use several technological tools to deliver high-quality services and guarantee customer satisfaction.

On the other hand, the lower use of ICT in restaurants may be because most of these companies are independently owned (88% of our restaurant sample vs. 67% of the hotel sample) and smaller than hotels. Therefore, restaurants may have scarce financial resources to invest in ICT solutions. This is consistent with Galloway (2007), who identifies availability of expertise for implementation and maintenance of ICT as a supply side barrier to a small firm's adoption.

With regard to the second question (*Are there differences in the assessment of pros and cons of ICT use by different tourism businesses?*), our results allow us to conclude that, consistently with the more intensive use of ICT solutions by hotels and travel agencies, these are the companies that appreciate to a greater extent the benefits of technology and neglect the disadvantages of ICT solutions. In particular, travel agencies and hotels highly appreciate the utilitarian reasons for using ICT, e.g. the ability of ICT to facilitate, expedite, monitor and standardize the purchasing process. Although the benefits of ICT seem to be widely known by tourism companies, some have concerns about missing the personal touch through the use of technology.

In sum, this evidence is in the line of Sethuraman and Parasuraman (2005), so that it supports the convenience of adapting technology to the company's needs. Differences in the use and assessment of ICT solutions across hotels, travel agencies and restaurants may be explained by the duration of the interactions between these companies and their customers. Therefore, since the length of the stay is longer and the use of the company's facilities by the customer is more intensive in hotels in comparison to travel agencies and restaurants, the former should invest in technology at a greater extent in comparison to the latter.

Additionally, the obtained results allow us to extract a set of managerial implications. First of all, from the company's point of view, it is desirable to adapt technology to business characteristics and points of interaction with customers. Therefore, ICT providers should prioritize those applications that are most valued by tourism businesses. Since the general advantages of ICT solutions seem to be widely recognized by tourism companies, ICT providers should concentrate on developing and explaining special features for the specific needs of each tourism business.

On the demand side, tourism companies should consider the features that are considered by customers as 'expected product' (i.e. ICT solutions that are basic, offered by almost all companies of this type, such as desktop PC, phone communications, point of sale terminal or Internet facilities) and 'increased product' (i.e. sophisticated ICT solutions whose absence is not missed by customers, but, when implemented, might add value to the service provided, e.g. touch screen, in-room DVD, loyalty programme).

Thus, our results provide evidence about the impact of ICT in different tourism subsectors, as well as about the reasons for and against using technology in tourism companies. These topics have been pointed out as important research directives (Tsiotsou & Ratten, 2010) and, in this sense, we expect that our findings have shed light on these issues.

Nevertheless, the obtained evidence allows us to suggest new further research lines. In this sense, the results obtained in this study should be considered as a first exploratory stage in the assessment of the most suitable technology solutions for each tourism business. The following step should be to assess the impact of ICT on customer satisfaction and loyalty. Finally, it may be useful to analyse the advantages and disadvantages of different ICT solutions by each type of tourism company depending on their profile, category or specialization, since differences in ICT are expected across hotels or restaurants in different categories and travel agencies depending on their target market (e.g. individuals or businesses). In this way, the design of specific actions may be facilitated to overcome initial customers' reluctance to new ICT solutions and encourage their use of these technologies.

## Acknowledgement

This research has been financed by the Spanish Ministry of Education and Science (Projects ref.: SEJ2007-66054/ECON and ECO2010-17475).

## References

Anderson, E. W. (1998). Customer satisfaction and word of mouth. *Journal of Service Research, 1*(1), 5–17.

Baloglu, S., & Pekcan, Y. A. (2006). The website design and Internet site marketing practices of upscale and luxury hotels in Turkey. *Tourism Management, 27*(1), 171–176.

Bigné, J., Aldás, J., & Andreu, L. (2008). B2B services: Adoption in travel agency supply chains. *Journal of Services Marketing, 22*(6), 453–464.

Brathwaite, R. (1992). Value-chain assessment of the travel experience. *Cornell Hotel and Restaurant Administration Quarterly, 33*(5), 41–49.

Buhalis, D. (1998). Strategic use of information technologies in the tourism industry. *Tourism Management, 19*(5), 409–421.

Buhalis, D., & Law, R. (2008). Progress in information technology and tourism management: 20 years on and 10 years after the Internet — The state of eTourism research. *Tourism Management, 29*(4), 609–623.

Buick, I. (2003). Information technology in small Scottish hotels: Is it working? *International Journal of Contemporary Hospitality Management, 15*(4), 243–247.

Campo, S., & Yagüe, M. J. (2008). Tourist loyalty to tour operator: Effects of price promotions and tourist effort. *Journal of Travel Research, 46*(3), 318–326.

Chatzipanagiotou, K. C., & Coritos, C. D. (2010). A suggested typology of Greek upscale hotels based on their MrkIS: Implications for hotels' overall effectiveness. *European Journal of Marketing, 44*(11/12), 1576–1611.

Chung, T., & Law, R. (2003). Developing a performance indicator for hotel websites. *International Journal of Hospitality Management, 22*(1), 343–358.

Coviello, N. E., Winklhofer, H., & Hamilton, K. (2006). Marketing practices and performance of small services firms: An examination in the tourism accommodation sector. *Journal of Service Research, 9*(1), 38–58.

Crotts, J. C., & Turner, G. B. (1999). Determinants of intra-firm trust in buyer-seller relationships in the international travel trade. *International Journal of Contemporary Hospitality Management, 11*(2/3), 116–123.

Dulen, J. (1998). Dazzling by design. *Restaurants and Institutions, 108*(30), 40–49.

eBusiness W@tch. (2006). *ICT and e-business in the tourism industry* (Retrieved from http://www.ebusiness-watch.org/studies/sectors/tourism/tourism.htm). Brussels: European Commission.

Ellram, L. M., La Londe, B. J., & Weber, M. M. (1999). Retail logistics. *International Journal of Physical Distribution and Logistics Management, 29*(7/8), 477–494.

Frew, A. J. (2000). Information and communications technology research in travel and tourism domain: Perspective and direction. *Journal of Travel Research, 39*(2), 136–145.

Galloway, L. (2007). Can broadband access rescue the rural economy? *Journal of Small Business and Enterprise Development, 14*(4), 641–653.

Garau, J. B., & Orfila-Sintes, F. (2008). Internet innovation for external relations in the Balearic hotel industry. *Journal of Business and Industrial Marketing, 23*(1), 70–80.

Guadix, J., Cortés, P., Onieva, L., & Jesús Muñuzuri, J. (2010). Technology revenue management system for customer groups in hotels. *Journal of Business Research, 63*(5), 519–527.

Hensdill, C. (1998). Hotels technology survey. *Hotels, February*, 51–76.

Huang, L. (2006). Building up a B2B e-commerce strategic alliance model under an uncertain environment for Taiwan's travel agencies. *Tourism Management, 27*(6), 1308–1320.

Huang, L. (2008). Exploring the determinants of e-loyalty among travel agencies. *Service Industries Journal, 28*(2), 239–254.

INE. (2010). *Spanish National Institute of Statistics*. Retrieved from http://www.ine.es

Inman, J. J. (2001). The role of sensory-specific satiety in attribute-level variety seeking. *Journal of Consumer Research, 28*(1), 105–120.

Inside Facebook. (2011). *Official webpage*. Retrieved from http://www.insidefacebook.com

Irvine, W., & Anderson, A. R. (2008). ICT (information communication technology), peripherality and smaller hospitality businesses in Scotland. *International Journal of Entrepreneurial Behaviour and Research, 14*(4), 200–218.

Jeong, M., Oh, H., & Gregoire, M. (2003). Conceptualizing web site quality and its consequences in the lodging industry. *International Journal of Hospitality Management, 22*(2), 161–175.

Karadag, E., Cobanoglu, C., & Dickinson, C. (2009). The characteristics of IT investment decisions and methods used in the US lodging industry. *International Journal of Contemporary Hospitality Management, 21*(1), 52–68.

Kim, W. G., & Cha, Y. (2002). Antecedents and consequences of relationship quality in hotel industry. *Hospitality Management, 21*(4), 321–338.

Kim, W. G., Han, J. S., & Lee, E. (2001). Effects of relationship marketing on repeat purchase and word of mouth. *Journal of Hospitality and Tourism Research, 25*(3), 272–288.

Kim, W. G., Lee, Y.-K., & Yoo, Y.-J. (2006). Predictors of relationship quality and relationship outcomes in luxury restaurants. *Journal of Hospitality and Tourism Research, 30*(2), 143–169.

Komppula, R., & Reijonen, H. (2006). Performance determinants in small and micro tourism business. *Tourism Review, 61*(4), 13–20.

Kothari, T., Hu, C., & Roehl, W. S. (2007). Adopting e-procurement technology in a chain hotel: An exploratory case study. *International Journal of Hospitality Management, 26*(4), 886–898.

Law, R., & Jogaratnam, G. (2005). A study of hotel information technology applications. *International Journal of Contemporary Hospitality Management, 17*(2), 170–180.

Law, R., Leung, K., & Wong, J. (2004). The impact of the Internet on travel agencies. *International Journal of Contemporary Hospitality Management, 16*(2), 100–107.

Lee, S.-C., Barker, S., & Kandampully, J. (2003). Technology, service quality, and customer loyalty in hotels: Australian managerial perspectives. *Managing Service Quality, 13*(5), 423–432.

Lin, Y.-L., & Lee, T. J. (2010). The impacts of the online reservation system in London city hotels. *Journal of Hospitality Marketing and Management, 19*(1), 82–96.

Litvin, S. W., Goldsmith, R. E., & Pan, B. (2008). Electronic word-of-mouth in hospitality and tourism management. *Tourism Management, 29*(3), 458–468.

Lowson, R. H. (2001). Retail operational strategies in complex supply chains. *International Journal of Logistics Management, 12*(1), 97–111.

Ma, J. X., Buhalis, D., & Song, H. (2003). ICTs and internet adoption in China's tourism industry. *International Journal of Information Management, 23*(6), 451–467.

Magnini, V. P., Honeycutt, E. D., Jr., & Hodge, S. K. (2003). Data mining for hotel firms: Use and limitations. *Cornell Hotel and Restaurant Administration Quarterly, 44*(2), 94–105.

Main, H. (2001). The expansion of technology in small and medium hospitality enterprises with a focus on net technology. *Information Technology and Tourism, 4*(3/4), 167–174.

Manes, G. (2003). The tetherless tourist: Ambient intelligence in travel and tourism. *Information Technology and Tourism, 5*(4), 211–220.

Martínez, J., Majó, J., & Casadesús, M. (2006). El uso de las tecnologías de la información en el sector hotelero. In *Proceedings VI Congreso Turismo y Tecnologías de la Información y las Comunicaciones Turitec*.

Medina, D., & García, J. M. (2000). Successful relationships between hotels and agencies. *Annals of Tourism Research, 27*(3), 737–762.

Minghetti, V. (2003). Building customer value in the hospitality industry: Towards the definition of a customer-centric information system. *Information Technology & Tourism, 6*(2), 141–152.

Minghetti, V., & Buhalis, D. (2010). Digital divide in tourism. *Journal of Travel Research, 49*(3), 267–281.

Moliner, M. A., Sánchez, J., Rodríguez, R. M., & Callarisa, L. (2007). Relationship quality with a travel agency: The influence of the postpurchase perceived value of a tourism package. *Tourism and Hospitality Research, 7*(3/4), 194–211.

Murphy, J., Olaru, D., Schegg, R., & Frey, S. (2003). Swiss hotels' web-site and e-mail management: The bandwagon effect. *Cornell Hotel and Restaurant Administration Quarterly, 44*(1), 71–87.

Nasution, H. N., & Mavondo, F. T. (2008). Customer value in the hotel industry: What managers believe they deliver and what customer experience. *International Journal of Hospitality Management, 27*(2), 204–213.

Nizic, M. K., Karanovic, G., & Ivanovic, S. (2008). Importance of intelligent rooms for energy savings in the hotel industry. *Tourism and Hospitality Management, 14*(2), 323–336.

Observatorio de las Telecomunicaciones y la Sociedad de la Información — Entidad Pública Empresarial Red.es. (2007a). *Diagnóstico tecnológico del sector de turismo rural*. Retrieved from http://www.conocimientoytecnologia.org/pdf/gestion_conocimiento/orsi/estudios_actualidad/8_diag_trural_2007.pdf

Observatorio de las Telecomunicaciones y la Sociedad de la Información — Entidad Pública Empresarial Red.es. (2007b). *Diagnóstico tecnológico del sector hotelero*. Retrieved from http://www.ontsi.red.es/empresas/articles/id/434/diagnostico-tecnologico-del-sector-shotelero-junio-2006.html

O'Connor, P. (2003). Room rates on the Internet — Is the web really cheaper? *Journal of Services Research, 1*(1), 57–72.

O'Connor, P., & Frew, A. (2002). The future of hotel electronic distribution: Expert and industry perspectives. *Cornell Hotel and Restaurant Administration Quarterly, 43*(3), 33–45.

O'Connor, P., & Piccoli, G. (2003). Marketing hotels using global distribution systems — Revisited. *Cornell Hotel and Restaurant Administration Quarterly, 44*(5/6), 105–114.

Olsen, M. D., & Connolly, D. J. (2000). Experience-based travel: How technology will change the hospitality industry. *Cornell Hotel and Restaurant Administration Quarterly, 41*(1), 31–40.

Orfila-Sintes, F., Crespí-Cladera, R., & Martínez-Ros, E. (2005). Innovation activity in the hotel industry: Evidence from Balearic Islands. *Tourism Management, 26*(6), 851–865.

Palmer, J. W., & Markus, M. L. (2000). The performance impacts of quick response and strategic alignment in specialty retailing. *Information Systems Research, 11*(3), 241–259.

Paraskevas, A., & Buhalis, D. (2002). Outsourcing IT for small hotels: The opportunities and challenges of using application service providers. *Cornell Hospitality Quarterly, 43*(2), 27–39.

Piccoli, G., O'Connor, P., Capaccioli, C., & Alvarez, R. (2003). Customer relationship management — A driver for change in the structure of the US lodging industry. *Cornell Hotel and Restaurant Administration Quarterly, 44*(4), 61–73.

Punj, G., & Stewart, D. W. (1983). Cluster analysis in marketing research: Review and suggestions for application. *Journal of Marketing Research, 20*(2), 134–148.

Ryssel, R., Ritter, T., & Gemunden, H. G. (2004). The impact of information technology deployment on trust, commitment and value creation in business relationships. *Journal of Business and Industrial Marketing, 19*(3), 197–207.

Sancho, A. (2004). *Innovación, especialización, diversidad y competitividad en el sector turístico de la Comunidad Valenciana.* Generalitat Valenciana: Consellería de Empresa, Universidad y Ciencia.

Sethuraman, R., & Parasuraman, A. (2005). Succeeding in the Big Middle through technology. *Journal of Retailing, 81*(2), 107–111.

Sigala, M. (2007). Investigating the internet's impact on interfirm relations. Evidence from the business travel management distribution chain. *Journal of Enterprise Information Management, 20*(3), 335–355.

Stockdale, R. (2007). Managing customer relationships in the self-service environment of e-tourism. *Journal of Vacation Marketing, 13*(3), 205–219.

Susskind, A. M., & Chan, E. K. (2000). How restaurant features affect check averages. *Cornell Hotel and Restaurant Administration Quarterly, 41*(6), 56–63.

Thao, H. T. P., & Swierczek, F. W. (2008). Internet use, customer relationships and loyalty in the Vietnamese travel industry. *Asia Pacific Journal of Marketing and Logistics, 20*(2), 190–210.

Tsaur, S.-H., Yung, C.-Y., & Lin, J.-H. (2006). The relational behavior between wholesaler and retailer travel. *Journal of Hospitality and Tourism Research, 30*(3), 333–353.

Tsiotsou, R. H., & Ratten, V. (2010). Future research directions in tourism marketing. *Marketing Intelligence and Planning, 28*(4), 533–544.

Tsiotsou, R. H., & Vlachopoulou, M. (2011). Understanding the effects of market orientation and e-marketing on service performance. *Marketing Intelligence and Planning, 29*(2), 141–155.

UNWTO. (2009). Retrieved from http://unwto.org/facts/menu.html

Van Trijp, H. C. M., Hoyer, W. D., & Inman, J. J. (1996). Why switch? Product category level explanations for true variety seeking behavior. *Journal of Marketing Research, 33*(3), 281–292.

Vergara, A. (2006). *Anuario gastronómico de la Comunidad Valenciana 2007.* Valencia: Edicions Gratacels.

Vrana, V., & Zafiropoulos, C. (2006). Tourism agents' attitudes on internet adoption: An analysis from Greece. *International Journal of Contemporary Hospitality Management, 18*(7), 601–608.

Wolff, C. (2005). Guest-centered entertainment. *Lodging Hospitality*, *61*(6), 38–40.

Wu, J.-J., & Chang, Y.-S. (2006). Effect of transaction trust on e-commerce relationships between travel agencies. *Tourism Management*, *27*(6), 1253–1261.

Zafiropoulos, C., & Vrana, V. (2006). A framework for the evaluation of hotel websites: The case of Greece. *Information Technology and Tourism*, *8*(3–4), 239–254.

# Chapter 20

# Exploring the Potential of Travel Reviews: Implications for Strategy Formulation and Implementation

*Antonella Capriello*

## 20.1. Introduction

Social media now play a central role in the sharing of experiences and exchanging of information in 'virtual communities' (Litvin, Goldsmith, & Pan, 2008; Sigala, 2010; Wang, Yu, & Fesenmaier, 2002). Huang, Shen, Lin, and Chang (2007) indicate that self-expression, life documenting, commenting and information seeking are the determinants of the motivation and behaviours of bloggers.

Assuming a service-centric perspective, consumers can determine value and participate in its creation through the process of co-production (Vargo & Lusch, 2004, 2008). The advent of information technologies has been instrumental in establishing innovation collaborations with consumers (Lusch, Vargo, & O'Brien, 2007). Armed with these new tools, consumers have the opportunity to communicate directly with firms and interact with them in co-production processes through sharing ideas and co-design (Prahalad & Ramaswamy, 2004). Virtual community partners can also be treated as firm alliances in the co-creation of value as these online communities are based on shared enthusiasm for, and knowledge of, a specific consumption or related group of activities influencing online brand reputation (Kozinets, 1999).

Previous studies concerning consumer storytelling and travel blogs represent a compelling approach to mining consumer sentiments, since online information and digital word of mouth are rich data sources that measure the actual behaviours of consumers and tourism enterprises (O'Connor & Murphy, 2004). Stories and storytelling allow understanding consumer psychology (Escalas & Stern, 2003; Holt, 2003; Woodside, Sood, & Miller, 2008) and provide a substantial amount of information that is stored and retrieved from visitors' stories (Woodside, Cruickshank, & Dehuang, 2007). By making use of this approach, marketing researchers can gain insights into customer experiences in a way that is less costly, time consuming and intrusive than focus groups and personal interviews (Kozinets, 2002).

From a strategic marketing perspective, user-generated content from TripAdvisor to Twitter provides a new opportunity to understand customer perceptions and preferences, supplying information that can be incorporated and integrated with data from existing customer surveys.

Online travel reviews are not only a vital source of feedback within a wider marketing strategy framework but also a form of word-of-mouth message that can increase the visibility of tourism and travel firms beyond other advertising campaigns. The growing importance of travel reviews also requires identifying innovative e-marketing strategies to enhance the experiences of tourists and to customize offerings.

With a focus on delightful and terrible experiences, this chapter aims to uncover the role of travel reviews and the implications for e-marketing strategies as well as contribute to tourism and travel literature in relation to previous studies focused on the concept of customer delight in blog postings (Crotts & Magnini, 2011; Magnini, Crotts, & Zehrer, 2011).

## 20.2.  Travel Reviews for Strategic Marketing

Online feedback mechanisms have considerable implications for a wide range of strategic marketing activities such as customer acquisition and retention, brand building, product development and quality assurance (Dellarocas, 2003). Travel reviews can be instrumental for strategic marketing in connection with the idea of exploring own content for the following purposes.

### 20.2.1.  Online Marketing Communication Processes

Travel reviews represent an online word-of-mouth message enabling complementary promotional actions in relation to editorial contents from tourist boards. Dickinger (2011) reports that user-generated content appears to be highly trustworthy and shows high levels of integrity. Travel reviewers progressively achieve greater online credibility as customers have the opportunity to express the utility of travel opinions. From this perspective, travel and tourism marketers need to reconsider the criteria for allocating advertising budgets in relation to the emerging importance of consumer-generated content.

Online opinions also facilitate marketing campaigns that are more focused on target markets. For example, online travel agencies (OTAs) such as booking.com employ banners reporting customer experiences to increase the visibility of selected hotel properties on their own websites.

### 20.2.2.  Online Visibility and Reputation-Building Processes

Travel reviews contribute to reputation-building processes and promote brand identity in the travel and tourism sector. In accordance with consumer opinions,

TripAdvisor lists the best and worst hospitality and tourism services, assigning quality awards for specific categories.

A Facebook fan page can be instrumental in spreading positive word of mouth. As prior guests, Facebook fans can be engaged in describing their travel experiences and contribute to establishing an online brand community (Mackenzie, 2011). Customers can provide affordable testimonials in terms of a positive word-of-mouth message, disseminating it through personal online networks. A Facebook fan page also helps engage people with similar lifestyles who create effective word of mouth among their friends and a Facebook friend's recommendation may have greater standing in comparison to unknown reviewers (Chu & Choi, 2011).

Consumers can also spread negative word of mouth in connection with unsatisfactory experiences. They may oppose or contest destinations and the marketing and management values of tourism and travel firms. On the 'Visit Japan 2010' Facebook page, users posted videos and pictures on its wall, asking Japan to stop killing whales and dolphins, requesting people to boycott Japan until the nation has addressed this issue (Chong, 2010). Customers can also establish online counter-brand communities (Kozinets & Handelman, 2004). An example of an opposing virtual community is the Facebook page 'I hate Ryanair' with over 4000 fans. By sharing own terrible customer experiences, in this case of the airline, the fans spread negative word of mouth.

Online communication strategies need to be focused on the overall online reputation scores located on leading social media sites. For example, a marketing agency, ReviewPro, offers web-based analytical tools that allow hotels to efficiently aggregate, organize and manage their online reputation by tracking more than 60 travel review websites.

### 20.2.3. *Product Design and Positioning*

Travel reviews contain relevant data on customer preferences to capture sources of customer satisfaction and delight. Pan, McLauren, and Crotts (2007) explored visitor opinions related to Charleston, USA, and posted on leading travel blogs to gain insights into the destination image including the strengths and weaknesses being communicated. The results show that attractions are Charleston's main strength while weaknesses concern car travel, weather, food, and parking and road signs. The described limitations suggest significant recommendations in terms of tourist destination planning and development.

Comparing travel reviews in mature and emerging destinations, Magnini et al. (2011) identify factors such as room design, hotel facilities, and food and location that explain customer delight. They also disclose an inference of customer origin (domestic or international tourists) on preferences.

With a focus on farmstay experiences in four destinations (Australia, Italy, the United States and the United Kingdom), Capriello, Mason, Davis, and Crotts (forthcoming) categorize customer likes and dislikes in accordance with the contents of reviews. This study indicates that the comfort and cleanliness of the room, the quality of food and beverages, and the availability of attractive things to do and see on both the farm and in the surrounding community are important from the guests' perspective.

Travel review contents also help marketers to analyse destination competitiveness, in both local and global marketplaces. As evidence of this, Crotts, Davis, and Mason (2009) demonstrate that travel reviews provide qualitative data that allow identifying key drivers of guest satisfaction influencing firm competitive positions in a specific area.

### *20.2.4. Quality Assurance Processes*

Travel reviews are complementary sources of information to guest comment cards and surveys that provide a valuable source of customer feedback on market performance (Crotts et al., 2009). Franchisors in the tourism and travel sector need to consider the franchisees' online reputation to maintain brand quality standards and customer expectations (Dendler, 2011).

Online opinions should also induce destination marketers to reflect on regional competitiveness, since this assessment is particularly useful in implementing measures to enhance the quality of service provision in tourist destinations (Capriello et al., forthcoming). For example, if travel reviewers frequently report an inconsistency of the star ranking system in relation to their expectations and previous experiences in other tourist areas, destination managers need to re-examine the criteria for assigning star categories (Crotts et al., 2009; Magnini et al., 2011).

## 20.3. Understanding Customer Experiences in Travel Reviews

The customer experience originates from a series of interactions between a customer and a product, company or part of its organization, provoking a reaction (La Salle & Britton, 2003; Shaw & Ivens, 2005). La Salle and Britton (2003) reveal the importance of enabling the customer to experience all instances of the relationship with a company in an excellent way. This concept should not be limited to some pre-purchase activity, nor to some post-purchase activity (the assessment of satisfaction), but includes a series of other activities that influence consumer decisions and future actions (Carù & Cova, 2003). Arnould, Price, and Zinkhan (2002) divide the experience into four stages, including recalling the consumption experience through storytelling processes.

Relationship marketing emphasizes the relevance to firms of establishing long-term relationships and to consider customers as valid contributors to the production process (Groönroos, 1995). Customer relationship management (CRM) is an instrumental approach to create, develop and enhance relationships with targeted customers and is often associated with utilizing information technology to implement marketing strategies (Gummesson, 1999). Customer loyalty depends on trust and commitment, but these dimensions can vary from one individual to another

(Blois, 1997). Thus, a better understanding of firm relationships with customers can only come about by analysing consumers' individual experiences (Addis & Holbrook, 2001).

In the case of travel reviews, Barsky and Honeycutt (2010) underline that individuals who had an exceptionally either good or bad experience are more inclined to post a review. Delightful and terrible experiences are effective constructs to explore customer experiences in online opinions.

## 20.4. Delightful and Terrible Experiences

In view of the fact that e-word-of-mouth messages influence firm and destination performance and online reputation, customer opinions have significant implications on the willingness/unwillingness to recommend and in turn to influence consumer decision processes (Chevalier & Mayzline, 2006; Sen & Lerman, 2007). Positive reviews affect consumer intention to buy, whereas negative reviews seem to have less influence in travel decision-making processes (Vermeulen & Seegers, 2009). This evidence does not mean that negative reviews are harmless. Zehrer, Crotts, and Magnini (2011) demonstrate that multiple negative blog postings on TripAdvisor increase the probability of not purchasing a product.

In service marketing literature, the concept of delight is based on the expectancy–disconfirmation model (R. L. Oliver, 1980) and relates to the idea of comparing perceived performance with prior expectations. The comparison of both elements can generate three situations: (a) slight performance deviation that is considered normal; (b) disconfirmed performance, which is considered plausible, but experienced infrequently; (c) disconfirmed performance, which is highly unlikely based on past experience. This latter consideration can be associated with a status of delight. R. Oliver, Rust, and Varki (1997) demonstrate that delight is a function of surprisingly high positive disconfirmation.

The construct of 'delight' also has a more affective basis than satisfaction (Berman, 2005) and is associated with feelings of 'surprise', 'joy' and 'pleasure' in service encounters (Arnold, Reynolds, Ponder, & Lueg, 2005; R. Oliver et al., 1997; Rust & Oliver, 2000). Other descriptors include happy, glad and cheerful.

Outcomes of delight relate to the intention to repurchase the product (Holbrook & Hirschman, 1982). Crotts and Magnini (2011) identify a strong positive correlation between the status of delighted customers and the willingness to recommend/ repurchase the product. They also reveal that this propensity is higher for this category when compared to satisfied customers.

The concept of a 'terrible experience' is based on service encounters generating a negative set of emotions. Negative emotions are expected to generate a dissatisfaction condition. Zeelenberg and Pieters (2004) associate this idea with two specific emotions: regret and disappointment. The authors consider that regret stems from a wrong consumer decision and is typically associated with self-blame. In a travel review, the expression of regret can induce consumers to stress their wrong hotel selection with negative consequences on online marketing communication. Disappointment instead stems from disconfirmed expectation and is typically associated with blaming others or the circumstances (Zeelenberg et al., 1998). Zeelenberg and Pieters (2004) demonstrate that a condition of disappointment produces negative word of mouth and a tendency to complain. The feeling of anger may result not only in complaining but also in a malicious attempt to damage the service provider. Online communication enables different forms of this latter type of behaviour to intentionally spread bad rumours about the service provider.

For tourism marketers, a key issue is to understand the factors explaining the delightful and terrible experiences reported in travel reviews. In the services sector, Bitner (1990) examined favourable and unfavourable service encounters based on the customer's perspective, ascertaining that both satisfactory and unsatisfactory incidents could be attributed to one or more of the following three main types of employee behaviours: (a) how employees responded to service delivery failure; (b) how the employee responded to customer needs and requests; (c) unprompted or unsolicited employee actions. Arnold et al. (2005) adopted this approach to analyse customers' delightful and terrible experiences in retailing services. They formulate a theoretical framework where customer delight and outrage can be explained in relation to interpersonal relationships with employees and non-interpersonal factors associated with product provision. The empirical findings also indicate: (a) the interpersonal factors refer to situations when the source of delightful/terrible experiences is associated with the actions of service providers; (b) factors such as interpersonal efforts, interpersonal engagement, problem resolution, interpersonal distance and ethics in business practices influence the relationship between frontline employees and customers; and (c) non-interpersonal factors concern the product in relation to expected acquisition and value.

## 20.5.   Travel Reviews and Content Analysis: An Exploratory Study

### 20.5.1.   *Content Analysis and Text Mining*

Content analysis and text mining are a dominant approach to analysing user-generated content (Banyai & Glover, forthcoming). In the current study this research approach helps expose factors explaining delightful and terrible experiences in travel reviews.

For illustrative purposes, a sample of 240 travel reviews was collected following the reported research strategies. First, consistent with the idea of employing the concept of 'customer delight' in analysing the travel reviews, a focus group with linguistic and marketing experts was organized who identified a list of adjectives describing a delightful stay in a hospitality property. This list includes the following elements: amazing, awesome, beautiful, delightful, enjoyed, fantastic, happy, magic, magnificent, marvellous, ideal, idyllic, surprised, superb, stunning, terrific and wonderful. Second, the study also addresses the factors explaining 'customer outrage' and this construct was based on failed service encounters with implications for customer behavioural responses (Zeelenberg & Pieters, 2004) and recurrent patterns associated with a 'terrible experience' (Arnold et al., 2005). The same focus group also produced a list of adjectives describing a dissatisfying experience. The list includes the following terms: annoyed, disappointed, disgusting, horrific, regretful and terrible. Third, a word search was performed in order to identify travel reviews containing the above-mentioned adjectives associated with either delight or dissatisfaction through interrogating three travel review websites. The research assistants performed several controls in order to exclude the presence of any expressions that could change the meaning of a sentence.

A sample of 240 travel reviews was constructed including 50% delightful and 50% terrible experiences. The data were collected with a view to obtaining a variation in terms of the nature of the tourism service industry, destinations and the nationality of travel reviewers. This research strategy enables conducting a more comprehensive analysis of customer experiences in different settings. A manual text mining operation was then undertaken to identify both key drivers of customer delight and factors explaining customer dissatisfaction following the categories offered in previous studies (Arnold et al., 2005). Content analysis was also performed in order to investigate the construct of willingness or unwillingness to recommend. A search of the narrative was performed to determine the relationship between the nature of experiences ('delightful' or 'terrible') and the willingness/unwillingness to recommend.

A second analysis was carried out on the Facebook fan pages of 50 hospitality properties to isolate a sample of compliments and complaints. This strategy was oriented to produce a more comprehensive understanding of customer participation via social media.

### 20.5.2. Delightful and Terrible Experiences in Travel Reviews

The data analysis confirms the potential of customer delight to explain positive word-of-mouth responses and the significant relationship between standard expressions of customer delight identified in the focus group and willingness to recommend.

The sources of delightful experiences are mainly associated with two causes: personal interactions with employees and non-interpersonal factors that consumers perceive as sources of higher levels of quality service. It is important to underline that in each narrative analysed four factors were normally reported in the categories examined that influence customer experience.

Table 20.1 summarizes the factors, reporting their frequency in the cases analysed. In assessing the interpersonal factors, favourable service encounters depend on employees' efforts to offer a high level of assistance from the booking stage to the departure stage. The staff needs to be extremely friendly and nice, interacting with the clientele without being too pushy while paying attention to personal needs. Problem solving capabilities are associated with the idea of anticipating specific needs (e.g. to send back lost personal items to customers without a prior request, to supply

Table 20.1: Critical factors explaining delightful experiences.

|  | Frequency | % |
|---|---|---|
| **1  Interpersonal factors — employees** | | |
| Interpersonal effort (helpful) | 54 | 14 |
| Interpersonal engagement (friendly, nice, welcoming, hospitable) | 33 | 8 |
| Problem resolution (corrected a situation/attention to any request) | 22 | 5 |
| Interpersonal distance (non-pushy–non-intrusive) | 3 | 1 |
| Skills and knowledge | 8 | 2 |
| **2  Non-interpersonal factors — product** | | |
| Higher expected acquisition | 24 | 6 |
| Higher level of technical product quality | | |
| Hotel design–maintenance–decor | 21 | 5 |
| Amenities–facilities | 46 | 11 |
| Food and beverage service | 55 | 13 |
| Room design and provision | 59 | 14 |
| Housekeeping | 26 | 6 |
| Location | 42 | 10 |
| Atmosphere | 22 | 5 |
| | 415 | 100 |

extra information to customers, etc.). Additional competences are required to correct critical situations with special offers (upgraded rooms, special gifts, discounts). Skills and knowledge are mainly connected with mastering foreign languages as well as dominance of tourist information on the area.

Non-interpersonal factors focus on the service product and represent a strong signal to practitioners indicating that they cannot ignore basic elements such as product design and investment in property renovation. Customers identify higher expected value in relation to firm price policy (e.g. customer receiving a price discount or perceiving to have obtained a bargain by spending the vacation in a specific property) or service quality (e.g. clients underline a higher level of provision in relation to the star category). A higher level of technical quality is associated with the need for governing the tangible aspects of the service product such as service design, provision of amenities and facilities, and location. Services such as the cleaning and food and beverage provision are considered a further priority. The atmosphere also contributes to the quality of the experience, normally described as relaxing and welcoming.

The data analysis confirms the potential of customers' terrible experiences to explain negative word-of-mouth messages, and the significant relationship between the standard expressions of customer outrage and willingness to recommend. It is important to underline that in each analysed narrative three factors were reported in the categories examined generating customer outrage. The critical incidents in service encounters are associated with two groups of causes generating customer outrage: interpersonal relationships with employees and non-interpersonal factors associated with the service product feature. Table 20.2 reports a detailed analysis of these groups.

With regard to the first group, interpersonal relationships can fail for the following reasons:

(a) Lack of interpersonal efforts concerns situations where the staff ignores specific requests from the clientele; travel reviews frequently report the term 'unhelpful' staff.

(b) Lack of interpersonal engagement refers to a condition where reviewers report that employees exhibited rude and unfriendly behaviour or ignored their needs.

(c) Lack of problem resolution relates to the travel narratives in which employees demonstrate rigid behaviour without going beyond the rules or are reluctant to respond to customers' specific needs. These situations frequently occur in managing the check-in and check-out stages (clients waiting at reception after an intercontinental flight or airport transfer) and/or customers' specific needs (travellers with children).

(d) Lack of ethics includes a group of factors associated with dishonest behaviour in relation to the terms and conditions. This situation is frequently associated with

Table 20.2: Critical factors explaining terrible experiences.

|  | **Frequency** | **%** |
|---|---|---|
| **1  Interpersonal factors — employees** | | |
| Lack of interpersonal effort (not at all helpful) | 14 | 4 |
| Lack of interpersonal engagement (unfriendly, rude, ignored) | 28 | 9 |
| Lack of problem resolution (would not go beyond the rules) | 12 | 4 |
| Lack of ethics (dishonesty) | 29 | 9 |
| Lack of skills or knowledge | 16 | 5 |
| **2  Product** | | |
| Lack of expected acquisition (could not find what they were looking for) | 27 | 8 |
| Lack of expected value | 15 | 5 |
| Lack of technical product quality | | |
| *Design–maintenance–decor* | 42 | 13 |
| *Service–activities–facilities* | 25 | 8 |
| *Food and beverage* | 23 | 7 |
| *Room design–provision* | 46 | 14 |
| *Housekeeping* | 30 | 10 |
| *Atmosphere* | 22 | 4 |
| | 329 | 100 |

booking, payment and cancellation policies that generate a negative perception of services offered and business ethics.

(e) Lack of skills and knowledge is associated with mastery of foreign languages, which frequently represent a barrier in dealing with international clientele.

With a focus on service product, lack of unexpected acquisition relates to the situation where the service fails with respect to three relevant issues: (a) service provision in an affiliated property is not coherent with brand quality standards; (b) property and service provision are not consistent with the declared star category; (c) effective property and service provision significantly contradict the advertising material.

Lack of expected value describes a condition where the property seems to be overpriced in comparison to service levels, and guests demonstrate regret at having selected a specific property.

Lack of technical quality reflects limited service provision, since the property demonstrates failure in the basic principles of technical quality (maintenance and renovation, amenities and facilities, room design and provision).

A second analysis considers compliments and complaints on the Facebook fan pages of selected hospitality properties. Table 20.3 reports some comments from the clientele.

The analysis of compliments confirms the key drivers of customer delight reported in the aforementioned study while the content also underlines potential new ideas regarding travel packages (friend reunions, honeymoons). In dealing with compliments, firms interact more with customers in comparison to the behaviours observed in travel review websites. The enhancement of customer participation is also achieved with selected strategies to elicit consumer storytelling processes by promoting content focusing on guest vacation photos and vacation memories. Customer engagement is also stimulated with requests for advice from specific market segments (travellers with kids and/or pets). Complaints instead focus on factors describing terrible experiences, but indicate the need to align the current provision to specific customer needs. In this situation, firms adopt some form of direct interaction to redress customer outrage and forestall the spread of a negative word-of-mouth message.

## 20.6.  Travel Reviews and E-Marketing

The study demonstrates that travel reviews can contribute to innovative e-marketing approaches with implications for strategy formulation and implementation, calling for firm policies to manage customer feedback.

### 20.6.1.  *Implications for Strategy Formulation*

With a focus on customer knowledge, the preceding study reports that travel reviews contain valuable information to better understand customer needs, interests, behaviours and characteristics in relation to service encounters. Marketers

Table 20.3: A sample of compliments and complaints.

---

**Compliments**

Great Room ... delicious breakfast ... fabulous hosts with some of our close friends
who stayed during that period with their kids

... it was the honeymoon we never thought we would have ...

The friendliest hotel on the planet, they always make me feel like family when I come
here

The rooms are soothingly beautiful and the price for this hotel is as wonderful

Gorgeous hotel for 30th birthday celebration

... had an amazing stay! The grounds, staff and amenities exceeded all expectations

... Food & Wine Coma ... A stellar experience

... it was like paradise there ... friendly people from the front desk to cleaning people

... it was the perfect retreat to rest my mind and body in the newly refurbished,
beautifully presented spa ...

**Complaints**

You don't want to pay for the resort fees. I don't even use the services or anything
related to these fees. Why don't you bill me for the services that I use?

Somebody broke into hotel room and cut my luggage with a knife ... . Hotel does not
accept responsibility

No refrigerator in the rooms ... you have to go to the lobby. No one wants to call
someone to bring ice to own room

I was treated extremely rudely ... by the manager no less! I've been a ... customer for
many years, but if that's how they treat people I'm rethinking staying there .... I've
stayed at this particular one for the past 4 or 5 years, but will NEVER stay there
again

I tried to reach someone online, but I found no email to contact, and I will not call
again!

... Kicked out of the hotel because of numerous complaints

Just arrived at the HH hotel, very disappointed to find the old L. bath products and
not the P (the new one)

Nothing worse than pet-friendly hotels for people with allergies ... believe me!!!!

---

can employ the data to establish innovative marketing actions that influence
customer experience and retention. By tracking customer complaints about the
service via Facebook (e.g. disappointment about a bath product as reported in Table
20.3), travel and tourism managers can immediately act in terms of service recovery.
A similar approach is adopted by KLM Airlines with a pilot programme called
'KLM Surprise' to reward their customers at certain airports who check in on
Foursquare. KLM employees collect information from social media accounts such as
Twitter, Facebook and Foursquare, identify an individual gift for customers, locate
them in the airport terminal and deliver a surprise gift to them, sharing this
information on KLM's Facebook page and Twitter account (Kotadia, 2010).

Guest opinions can also support marketing segmentation processes by identifying new emerging needs (as in Table 20.3, critical issues in developing pet friendly packages). They can aid the implementation of targeted products and customer care relationship programmes to meet individual needs and wants. The data can help design customized promotional marketing programmes to improve the effectiveness of communicating with each customer.

Customer engagement with travel reviews is based on the idea of collecting and storing customer preferences and/or eliciting content on memorable experiences. User-generated content can contribute to innovation processes, as consumers can express their own ideas that help identify new products and to customize existing services in innovative ways. For example, in the current study, delightful experiences are also associated with special events (honeymoons, birthday celebrations, friend reunions) and the key drivers can potentially support the development of special package offers. This aspect is relevant to diversify the service provision and reduces dependence on identified sectors.

Delightful and terrible experiences in travel reviews highlight the importance of service design, moving from the simple concept of 'value for money' to the idea of interacting with customers to provide unique and valuable occasions. From this perspective, mining consumer sentiments enables discovering key factors of customer delight that have considerable implications on guest retention and brand loyalty. As reported in the study, customer compliments and complaints on a Facebook fan page can be instrumental in establishing real connections between the values of the organization and customers. For example, for travel and tourism firms relying on repeat business with high levels of retention, customer opinions and online forms of communication can enhance direct marketing communications and sustain customer loyalty.

### 20.6.2.  Implications for Strategy Implementation

As travel reviews are a form of online advertising messages based on guest experience, they imply the promotion of efficiency and effectiveness in business processes and the pursuit of operational excellence in tourist destinations. The findings have underlined that customer opinions have significantly empowered front-office employees to deliver a valuable experience. This empirical evidence is crucial and requires reformulating human resource policies in terms of recruitment, training actions and incentive programmes while employees need to move beyond traditional tasks and co-share organizational values (Zehrer, 2009).

The terrible experiences reported, instead, call for a reflection on operational processes and business practices to improve firm performance. This element is particularly relevant to global tourist operators to maintain and promote brand reputation processes across their affiliated units (e.g. travel agency networks). As such, social media require defensive strategies to protect the brand image against external attacks.

Guest feedback represents an input for investment decisions, since factors explaining customer outrage also highlight the importance of monitoring maintenance and renovation needs to preserve the star category and/or brand quality standard. The current study also indicates that marketing communications should avoid setting unreal expectations. Advertising communications that create too many expectations could risk guest disappointment on arrival. Marketing policies need to manage the guest experience rather than investing in unfocused advertising campaigns. Managers can also benefit from negative travel reviews to establish a service recovery programme. From this perspective, an emerging organizational need is to create a taskforce to examine and effectively deal with guest feedback by removing traditional barriers between departments (Public Relations, Marketing, Sales and Human Resources). Internal online forums among departments discussing blog postings, travel reviews, comments and complaints in social media can help identify innovative solutions.

### 20.6.3.   *Implications for Firm Policies*

The results also identify the importance of implementing guidelines for monitoring, responding to or acting on guest reviews. Through constant analyses of travel reviews managers can observe the evolution of the firm's online reputation and analyse specific issues over time. The results suggest integrating e-marketing strategies with the principles of customer participation to foster firm reputation-building processes.

With the advent of social media, firms need to interact with customers, responding to reviews in real time given that guest comments can significantly affect revenues. A response to a positive review is a way of encouraging prior guests to spread their positive word of mouth through travel websites. The response should cultivate customer intention to revisit the property and enhance brand loyalty.

In the current study, only 16% of travel reviews concerning terrible experiences shows a response to negative reviews on travel review websites. This result appears to indicate low control of the dissemination of negative word-of-mouth messages influencing own online reputation. The response to a negative review should primarily focus on assuring the travelling public that the issue is being addressed and the tourism service firm is dedicated to customer service. Although customer outrage frequently means an unsatisfied client and service failure in the service provision, managers' responses are also instrumental in showing respect towards guest opinions as well as concern for the reasons behind the service failure and to identify forms of redress.

To contrast the impact of negative word-of-mouth messages, a defensive strategy is required to encourage reviews directly via the website and spread positive messages through the social media channels (DeGeorge, 2011). In order to prevent negative customer comments, tourism and travel managers need to dedicate more attention to talking to guests during their stay to identify possible reasons of dissatisfaction and effective ways to solve them (Dendler, 2011).

The enhancement of online reputation also depends on encouraging and stimulating guest review comments. A strategy is required to encourage customers reporting positive experiences on guest comment cards to leave positive comments online and/or report those guestbook comments via the Facebook fan page (Dendler, 2011). The CRM system can implement electronic cards to ask guests for reviews while the firm's online visibility can be improved by concentrating publically accessible travel reviews on websites, effortlessly increased by users and easily indexed by search engines (Starkov & Mechoso Safer, 2011).

## 20.7. Conclusions

This chapter aims to expose the potential of travel reviews in analysing consumer experiences, and to identify the implications for e-marketing strategies in the tourism and travel sectors.

The study contributes to extending current understanding of delightful and terrible experiences in travel reviews, while previous studies focused on customer delight (Crotts & Magnini, 2011; Magnini et al., 2011). Factors influencing customer experiences were identified, extending the application of Arnold et al.'s (2005) study in the travel and tourism sectors.

For practitioners, the study proposes best practices in managing the tourism experiences in order to produce positive word of mouth. The current analysis considers user-generated content as a convenient way to capture customer experiences and measure destination performance on marketplaces. Assuming a service-centric perspective, the results also allow reflecting on the importance of human resources to achieve a delightful experience since interpersonal relationships with the clientele strongly influence the quality of a vacation. In analysing terrible experiences, interpersonal factors aid in understanding how employees can more effectively interact with customers. This finding is relevant to tourism and travel managers, indicating the need for improvement opportunities in frontline employee training and recruitment procedures. As concerns service design, the empirical evidence allows verifying which tangible and intangible resources need to be monitored in marketing and managing tourism service firms. The results create a more comprehensive framework on how to concentrate financial efforts in order to create delightful experiences.

Focusing on the findings, a proactive marketing strategy is required to redesign the CRM approach, since user-generated content has implications on strategy formulation and implementation. Future challenges may lead to a fundamental shift in travel and tourism marketing strategies with marketers needing to work in a multichannel marketing environment where destination websites, e-mail marketing and social media have a synergetic relationship in terms of online communication strategies. In this emerging context, online marketing strategies to enhance customer engagement and participation need to be monitored to estimate the implications on destination performance.

# References

Addis, M., & Holbrook, M. B. (2001). On the conceptual link between mass customisation and experiential consumption: An explosion of subjectivity. *Journal of Consumer Behaviour*, *1*(1), 50–66.

Arnold, M., Reynolds, K., Ponder, N., & Lueg, J. (2005). Customer delight in a retail context: Investigating delightful and terrible shopping experiences. *Journal of Business Research*, *58*(8), 1132–1145. doi: 10.1016/j.jbusres.2004.01.006

Arnould, E., Price, L., & Zinkhan, G. (2002). *Consumers*. New York, NY: McGraw-Hill.

Banyai, M., & Glover, T. D. (forthcoming). Evaluating research methods on travel blogs. *Journal of Travel Research*. doi:10.1177/0047287511410323

Barsky, J., & Honeycutt, R. (2010, 13 September). *Balance your feedback strategy*. Retrieved from http://www.hospitalitynet.org/news/4048255.html

Berman, B. (2005). How to delight your customers. *California Management Review*, *48*(1), 129–151.

Bitner, M. J. (1990). Evaluating service encounters: The effects of physical surroundings and employee responses. *Journal of Marketing*, *54*(April), 69–82.

Blois, K. (1997). When is a relationship "a relationship"? In H. G. Germunden, T. Ritter & A. Walker (Eds.), *Relationships and networks in international markets* (pp. 53–64). Oxford: Pergamon.

Capriello, A., Mason, P., Davis, B., & Crotts, J. C. (forthcoming). Farm experiences in travel reviews: A cross-comparison of three approaches. *Journal of Business Research*. doi:10.1016/j.jbusres.2011.09.018.

Carù, A., & Cova, B. (2003). Revisiting consumption experience: A more humble but complete view of the concept. *Marketing Theory*, *3*(2), 267–286. doi: 10.1177/14705931030032004

Chevalier, J., & Mayzlin, D. (2006). The effect of word of mouth on sales: Online book reviews. *Journal of Marketing Research*, *43*(3), 345–354. doi: 10.1509/jmkr.43.3.345

Chong, S. (2010, 5 April). *How to promote tourism through social media*. Retrieved from http://www.penn-olson.com/2010/04/05/how-to-promote-tourism-through-social-media/

Chu, C.-S., & Choi, S. M. (2011). Electronic word-of-mouth in social networking sites: A cross-cultural study of the United States and China. *Journal of Global Marketing*, *24*(3), 263–281. doi: 10.1080/08911762.2011.592461

Crotts, J. C., Davis, B., & Mason, P. (2009). Measuring guest satisfaction and competitive position: Application of stance analysis to blog narratives. *Journal of Travel Research*, *48*(2), 139–151. doi: 10.1177/0047287508328795

Crotts, J. C., & Magnini, V. (2011). The customer delight construct: Is surprise essential? *Annals of Tourism Research*, *38*(2), 719–722. doi: 10.1016/j.annals.2010.03.004

DeGeorge, L. (2011). *HeBS digital perspective: Lessons from the TripAdvisor vs. Google controversy?* Retrieved from http://www.hotelnewsresource.com/article51985.html

Dellarocas, C. (2003). The digitization of word of mouth: Promise and challenges of online feedback mechanisms. *Management Science*, *49*(10), 1407–1424. doi: 10.1287/mnsc.49.10.1407.17308

Dendler, E. (2011). *ReviewPro guide: A basic guide to managing online reviews for hotels*. Retrieved from http://www.reviewpro.com/basics-managing-online-reviews-hotels-4982

Dickinger, A. (2011). The trustworthiness of online channels for experience- and goal-directed search tasks. *Journal of Travel Research*, *50*(4), 378–391. doi: 10.1177/0047287510371694

Escalas, J. E., & Stern, B. B. (2003). Sympathy and empathy: Emotional responses to advertising dramas. *Journal of Consumer Research*, *29*(4), 566–578. doi: 10.1086/346251

Groönroos, C. (1995). Relationship marketing: The strategy continuum. *Journal of the Academy of Marketing Science, 23*, 252–254. doi: 10.1177/009207039502300404

Gummesson, E. (1999). *Total relationship marketing.* Oxford: Butterworth.

Holbrook, M. B., & Hirschman, E. C. (1982). The experiential aspects of consumption: Consumer fantasies, feelings, and fun. *Journal of Consumer Research, 9*(2), 132–140.

Holt, D. B. (2003). What becomes an icon most? *Harvard Business Review, 81*(3), 43–49.

Huang, C. Y., Shen, Y. Z., Lin, H. X., & Chang, S. S. (2007). Bloggers' motivations and behaviours: A model. *Journal of Advertising Research, 47*(4), 472–480.

Kotadia, H. (2010, 27 November). *KLM surprise: Is it social CRM?* Retrieved from http://hkotadia.com/archives/3591

Kozinets, R. V. (1999). E-tribalized marketing? The strategic implications of virtual communities of consumption. *European Management Journal, 17*(3), 252–264. doi: 10.1016/S0263-2373(99)00004-3

Kozinets, R. V. (2002). The field behind the screen: Using netnography for marketing research in online communities. *Journal of Marketing Research, 39*(1), 61–72.

Kozinets, R. V., & Handelman, J. M. (2004). Adversaries of consumption: Consumer movements, activism, and ideology. *Journal of Consumer Research, 31*(3), 691–704. doi: 10.1086/425104

La Salle, D., & Britton, T. A. (2003). *Priceless: Turning ordinary products into extraordinary experiences.* Boston, MA: Harvard Business School Press.

Litvin, W. L., Goldsmith, R. E., & Pan, B. (2008). Electronic word-of-mouth in hospitality and tourism management. *Tourism Management, 29*(3), 458–468. doi: 10.1016/j.tourman.2007.05.01

Lusch, R. F., Vargo, S. L., & O'Brien, M. (2007). Competing through service: Insights from service-dominant logic. *Journal of Retailing, 83*(1), 5–18. doi: 10.1016/j.jretai.2006.10.002

Mackenzie, J. (2011, March). *ReviewPro guide: A hotel guide to Facebook.* Retrieved from http://www.reviewpro.com/guides/en/ReviewPro-Guide-to-Facebook.pdf

Magnini, V., Crotts, J. C., & Zehrer, A. (2011). Understanding customer delight: An application of travel blog analysis. *Journal of Travel Research, 50*(5), 535–545. doi: 10.1177/0047287510379162.

O'Connor, P., & Murphy, J. (2004). Research on information technology in the hospitality industry. *International Journal of Hospitality Management, 23*(5), 473–484. doi: 10.1016/j.ijhm.2004.10.002

Oliver, R., Rust, R., & Varki, S. (1997). Customer delight: Foundations, findings and managerial insight. *Journal of Retailing, 73*(3), 311–336. doi: 10.1016/S0022-4359(97)90021-X

Oliver, R. L. (1980). A cognitive model of the antecedents and consequences of satisfaction decisions. *Journal of Marketing Research, 17*(4), 460–469.

Pan, B., McLauren, T., & Crotts, J. (2007). Travel blogs and their implications for destination marketing. *Journal of Travel Research, 46*(1), 35–47. doi: 10.1177/0047287507302378

Prahalad, C. K., & Ramaswamy, V. (2004). Co-creation experiences: The next practice in value creation. *Journal of Interactive Marketing, 18*(3), 5–14. doi: 10.1002/dir.20015

Rust, R., & Oliver, R. (2000). Should we delight the customer. *Journal of Academy of Marketing Science, 28*(1), 86–94. doi: 10.1177/0092070300281008

Sen, S., & Lerman, D. (2007). Why are you telling me this? An examination into negative consumer reviews on the web. *Journal of Interactive Marketing, 21*(4), 76–94. doi: 10.1002/dir.20090

Shaw, C., & Ivens, J. (2005). *Customer experience management: A revolutionary approach to connecting with your customer.* Hoboken, NJ: Wiley.

Sigala, M. (2010). Measuring customer value in online collaborative trip planning processes. *Marketing Intelligence & Planning, 28*(4), 418–443. doi: 10.1108/02634501011053559

Starkov, M., & Mechoso Safer, M. (2011, June). *HeBS digital perspective. The future is now: The emergence of the customer engagement channel in hospitality.* Retrevied from http://www.hebsdigital.com/articles/recentarticles.php

Vargo, S. L., & Lusch, R. F. (2004). Evolving to a new dominant logic for marketing. *The Journal of Marketing, 68*(1), 1–17.

Vargo, S. L., & Lusch, R. F. (2008). Service-dominant logic: Continuing the evolution. *Journal of Academy Marketing Science, 36*(1), 1–10. doi: 10.1007/s11747-007-0069-6

Vermeulen, I. E., & Seegers, D. (2009). Tried and tested: The impact of online hotel reviews on consumer consideration. *Tourism Management, 30*(1), 123–127. doi: 10.1016/j.tourman.2008.04.008.

Wang, Y., Yu, Q., & Fesenmaier, D. R. (2002). Defining the virtual tourist community: Implications for tourism marketing. *Tourism Management, 23*(4), 407–417. doi: 10.1016/S0261-5177(01)00093-0

Woodside, A. G., Cruickshank, B. F., & Dehuang, N. (2007). Stories visitors tell about Italian cities as destination icons. *Tourism Management, 28*(1), 475–496. doi: 10.1016/j.tourman.2005.10.026

Woodside, A. G., Sood, S., & Miller, K. E. (2008). When consumers and brands talk: Storytelling theory and research. *Psychology & Marketing, 25*(2), 97–145. doi: 10.1002/mar.20203

Zeelenberg, M., & Pieters, R. (2004). Beyond valence in customer dissatisfaction: A review and new findings on behavioural responses to regret and disappointment in failed services. *Journal of Business Research, 57*(4), 445–455. doi: 10.1016/S0148-2963(02)00278-3

Zeelenberg, M., van Dijk, W. W., van der Pligt, J., Manstead, A. S. R., van Empelen, P., & Reinderman, D. (1998). Emotional reactions to the outcomes of decision: The role of counterfactual thought in the experience of regret. *Organizational Behavior and Human Decision Processes, 75*(2), 117–141. doi: 10.1006/obhd.1998.2784

Zehrer, A. (2009). Service experience and service design: Concepts and application in tourism SMEs. *Managing Service Quality, 19*(3), 332–349. doi: 10.1108/09604520910955339

Zehrer, A., Crotts, J. C., & Magnini, V. (2011). The perceived usefulness of blog postings: An extension of the expectancy–disconfirmation paradigm. *Tourism Management, 32*(1), 106–113. doi: 10.1016/j.tourman.2010.06.013

Chapter 21

# Mobile Marketing in Tourism Services

*Shintaro Okazaki, Sara Campo and Luisa Andreu*

## 21.1. Introduction

In recent years, tourism destinations are becoming more and more competitive at a national as well as an international level (Bornhorst, Ritchie, & Sheehan, 2010), while the tourism industry is increasingly fragmented with many different suppliers (Leiper, 1990; Richards, 2002); location-specific attractions and products are the raw materials that differentiate the destination. A wide range of natural, cultural and experiential differences make individual locations truly unique and attractive. As a result, the dominant model of tourism production seems to be shifting from Fordist *mass tourism* to post-Fordism (Urry, 1990).

Given this shift, the fate of destinations depends on a more innovation-oriented tourism policy (Keller, 2004). In particular, the use of information and communications technology (ICT) is crucial, because it contributes towards efficiency, productivity and competitiveness improvements of both inter-organizational and intra-organizational systems (Dwyer, Edwards, & Mistilis, 2009). The ICT adds value to tourism services and products because it supports the development of industry networks — particularly among airlines, car rentals and hotel chains. In a well-developed ICT system, the whole tourism value chain is covered in terms of information on destinations, accommodation, transportation, package tours and services (Barnes, Mieczkowska, & Hinton, 2003; Rayman-Bacchus & Molina, 2001), while the actual process and availability of such services is always updated (Buhalis & Licata, 2002).

In recent years, mobile device is increasing its importance as an ICT tool, especially for consumers who seek flexible, specialized and easily accessible products (Bruner & Kumar, 2005). Here, 'mobile device' includes 'conventional' mobile phones, smartphones, PDA, tablet PC, palm tops as well as vehicle fitted devices. This chapter specifically focuses on smartphones because leading brands in a highly competitive market — in particular, iPhone, Android and Blackberry — have revolutionalized the usability of mobile device, mainly due to the introduction of multifunctional touch screens. The major benefit of the smartphone is its unprecedented utility: ubiquity

(Watson, Pitt, Berthon, & Zinkhan, 2002). Ubiquity can be defined as the flexibility in time and space (Okazaki, 2006). For example, users can access Internet — through 3G or Wi-Fi — at any time at any place, to receive detailed, up-to-date location-based information on the availability and prices of products. This ability also facilitates direct communication between tourists and producers (e.g. hoteliers, air carriers, tour operators, etc.). In 2000, Pröll and Retschitzegger acknowledged that mobile access to Internet content and services by means of mobile devices, such as cellular phones, was becoming an interesting possibility, both for the tourism information provider and for tourists on the move.

This chapter focuses on the use and adoption of mobile tourism support systems. Our intention is to provide an overview of available applications and their current usage. In what follows, we first describe a theoretical framework by which we attempt to explain a diverse range of applications in use. Then, we conclude the chapter with some implications to both scholars and practitioners.

## 21.2. Mobile Tourism Marketing Framework

Given rapid advances in many ICT tools, one may wonder why mobile device is so special for tourism marketing. However, at the same time, one may raise a question: how mobile services are and/or may be used in tourism (marketing) contexts? Our response to this question lies in the uniqueness of mobile handsets, characterized by their portability, mobility and 'always-on' capacity. Such uniqueness would enable travellers to access information based on a specific location regardless of time constraints. To further relate such uniqueness to tourism marketing, this chapter proposes a framework summarizing contemporary and foreseeable marketing challenges in tourism, which serves as a reference point for our later section.

Figure 21.1 shows our mobile tourism marketing framework. Here, we conceptualize marketing using mobile-based tourism services as a three-phase model: (1) pre-travel information search for tourism planning, (2) on-site information search for travel execution and (3) post-travel feedbacks for online consumer review. This information search behaviour and feedback mechanism is based on general consumer behaviour theory, which has widely been applied in many fields of marketing (Hawkins, Best, & Coney, 2001). Pre-travel search corresponds to pre-purchase search in general consumption, which 'occurs in response to the activation of problem recognition' (Hoyer & MacInnis, 2001, p. 210). For example, when consumers decide to travel for their vacations, they often visit travel agencies, search the Internet, talk to friends or read travel guides. With mobile device, potential tourists can use wireless Internet and related applications to make better pre-travel decisions. On-site information search occurs after arrival of travel destinations. This corresponds to ongoing search in general consumption, which is on a regular and continuous basis after all relevant decisions have already been made. In fact, this on-site information and travel execution is the most important area in mobile tourism marketing, because travellers are normally unfamiliar with the destination sites and often need

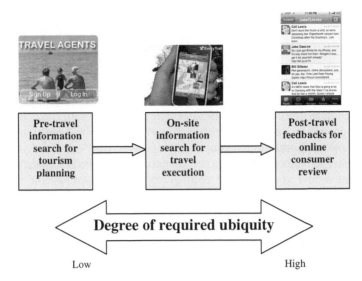

Figure 21.1: Mobile tourism marketing framework. *Source*: Own elaboration.

information that is not foreseen before the travel. Furthermore, such information search or execution occurs at unexpected times and places, thus requiring greater ubiquitous capacity. In this regard, travel advertisers and marketers could take advantage of highly functional smartphones, sending invitations and coupons for tourist attractions, such as museums, historical spots, restaurants, stores or travel dealers. WLAN or Bluetooth can be used to transmit such information that is easily captured by tourists without assuming additional costs. Finally, post-travel feedbacks can be given through online consumer reviews, such as TripAdvisor or Twitter. Such feedbacks activate consumers' motivation to engage in electronic word of mouth (eWOM), which is increasingly important in tourism marketing in recent years.

### 21.2.1. Conceptualization of Ubiquity

Although the complete conceptualization of ubiquity is beyond the scope of this chapter, it is important to provide its clear picture in mobile services. Ubiquity has been identified as one of the most important benefits in mobile-based telecommunication technology (Watson et al., 2002). The time–space perspectives stem from the work of Hägerstrand (1970) at the University of Lund, Sweden. He focused on the organization of activities into temporal and spatial terms that can be employed to define the performance of human activities. This was the very first step of so-called *time geography*, an attempt to stress factors associated with the spatial and temporal spread of innovations within particular environments. Because we strongly believe that Hägerstrand's works may provide a key to better understand the very basic nature of ubiquity concept, we describe his theory in detail below.

Hägerstrand (1970) argues that the importance of spatial factors is demonstrated for interpersonal communications, whereby most influence is transferred within local social systems or the 'neighbourhood effect'. According to him, both terrestrial and social distance barriers impede diffusion, in that human activities form environments that have a hierarchical ordering to the extent that those who have access to power in a superior domain frequently use this to restrict the set of possible actions permitted inside subordinate domains. On this basis, Hägerstrand (1970) developed the basics of the time-geographic notation in order to have a means to keep track of both the spatial and the temporal dimensions simultaneously.

In Hägerstrand's theory, there is a 'time–space' entity called 'domain'. In a domain, activities and events are under the control and influence of specific individuals or organizations. The ability of an individual or an organization to navigate through the domain depends on three time–space constraints that characterize information technology: coupling, capability and time–space zones. Coupling constraints requires the user's presence at a specific time and place. That is, individuals must join other individuals or organizations in order to form production, consumption, social and other activity bundles. Capability constraints, which refer to the user's resources and ability to overcome spatial separation at a specific moment, circumscribe the amounts of time needed to take care of physiological necessities and hence limit the distance (space) that an individual can cover within a given time-span within given transport technologies. Finally, authority constraints become important when several activities are pretended to be packed into a limited space. Authority constraints subsume those limited-space activities in terms of rules, laws, economic barriers and power relations that determine who does or does not have specific access to specific domains at specific times at specific spaces.

Based on Hägerstrand's time geography and activity theory, Miller (2005) conceptualizes a *people-based* perspective of geographic information systems (GIS) for theoretical and applied transportation and urban analysis. In his seminal essay 'What about People in Geographic Information Science?' he argues that a prior *place-based* perspective was developed in an era when data were scarce, computational platforms weak and questions simpler, and ignores the basic spatiotemporal conditions of human existence and organization. However, such a view is no longer tenable because drastic changes in transportation and telecommunication systems had altered the nature of space and time. Thus, Miller (2005) contends that researchers should extend their place-based perspective in GIS to encompass a people-based perspective. According to him, the world is 'shrinking', because transportation and communication costs dropped drastically over the last two centuries. The world is 'shrivelling', because relative differences in transportation and telecommunications costs are increasing at most geographic scales. The world is also 'fragmenting', because people and activities are becoming disconnected from location. A people-based perspective is more suitable for answering questions of access, exclusion and evolution in a shrinking but shrivelling and fragmenting world.

In Miller's (2005) theory, individuals differ with regard to the transportation resources and information technology available to overcome the constraints imposed by space–time anchor points. That is, we possess different levels of accessibility to resources, opportunities and support networks in key anchor points of our life, such as home and work locations. This seems extremely relevant to our ubiquity concept, in terms of accessibility or one's ability to overcome time–space constraints.

Similarly, based on Hägerstrand's time geography theory, Yu and Shaw (2008) claim that mobile phones now serve as the navigation mode in virtual space to carry out a growing number of activities:

> One important change introduced by the modern ICT is that we now live in a more flexible and dynamic environment of conducting activities. For example, mobile phones have freed us from the fixed locations of landline phones to stay in touch with other people. This removes the spatial constraints imposed by the landline phones. We now can purchase plane tickets on the Internet anytime in a day even when travel agency offices are closed. This eliminates the temporal constraints, as well as the spatial constraints, of visiting a travel agency office during fixed business hours and at a particular physical location. Modern ICT also provide us with additional flexibility of choosing the ways that an activity is performed. We now have more choices of conducting activities either in physical space (e.g., shopping at a local store), in virtual space (e.g., shop-ping on the Internet), or with a combination of both virtual and physical activities (e.g., price comparisons on the Internet followed by a physical trip to a local store). (p. 141)

Generally, our social practices prescribe the precise time and place of events, resulting in general maximum distance limits between activity sites (e.g. home and work). In this light, Janelle (2004) explains the temporal and spatial constraints that affect our everyday lives, in association with biological, social and technological factors. Technology allows consumers to extend these distance limits by reducing the amount of time required to perform a given task or to move between the places. Such advances in technology also enable multitasking capability in our everyday lives. By the same token, Yu and Shaw (2008) developed a temporal dynamic segmentation model in which each space–time path is treated as a linear feature with a starting time and an ending time. This model consists of a space–time path that traces multiple physical and virtual activities in a three-dimensional space–time system. Of particular interest to our conceptualization, this model permits multiple activities or multitasking by overlapping with each other on a space–time path. Multitasking can be defined as the simultaneous conduct of two or more activities, during a given time period (Kenyon, 2008). This multitasking capability seems to be a key to understanding what ubiquity enables us to perform with mobile device.

A basic assumption underlying multitasking is that two or more activities must be spatially co-present. For example, we may want to make a plane ticket reservation at a travel agency while visiting a dentist for check-ups. We cannot undertake both activities because we cannot be in two locations simultaneously. However, the availability of mobile ticketing would change the situation of such co-presence, as it 'brings' the activity to us, rather than we needing to physically travel to the activity. It is mobile telecommunication capability that can overcome spatial barriers to force the spatial co-presence of activities, and thus can enable a simultaneous conduct at a single location. Through such virtual mobility, activities that traditionally require physical movement can now be freely performed, regardless of the physical location of the person undertaking the activity. Thus, virtual mobility can create accessibility opportunities. In addition, virtual mobility can overcome temporal barriers to participation, both enabling and overcoming the need for temporal co-presence. A great benefit of mobile telecommunication activities is that they can be conducted at any time (Kenyon, 2008).

### 21.2.2.  Cases of Mobile Tourism Marketing Applications

Thanks to a rapid proliferation of smartphones worldwide, a diverse range of tourist applications have been introduced in conjunction with mobile technology. For our pedagogic purpose, this section mainly aims to explicate the conceptual definitions and actual 'hand-in' examples based on our mobile tourism marketing framework. Thus, what follows is comprised of three sections: pre-travel information search for travel planning, on-site information search for travel execution and post-travel feedback for online consumer review.

#### 21.2.2.1.  Pre-travel information search for travel planning
*Ticketing and reservation*   The technological development of smartphones has allowed firms to implement more convenient ways of ticketing. Many tourism companies, such as travel agencies online, tour operators, flight search engines, airlines, hotels, etc., have begun to use, or have developed, mobile-based applications that allow purchasing and/or reservations through smartphones. A project led by dotMobi[1] aims at developing customized applications for mobile devices. In collaboration with leading mobile operators, network and device manufacturers, and Internet content providers (such as Ericsson, Microsoft, Nokia, Telecom, Samsung Electronics, T-Mobile, Movistar, Visa, Vodafone, etc.), dotMobi created a consortium based in Dublin (Ireland), which promotes the use of a mobile website with the domain name .'mobi' (hence dotMobi). The company ensures that services and sites developed around .'mobi' are optimized for its use on mobile devices, and therefore all applications listed on the page work correctly when the user accesses with any mobile telephone. Iberia airline, for example, has its domain .'mobi' (see Figure 21.2) where the user can book flights, check in or use other services available online.

Sol Meliá, Spain's leading hotel company, is one of the leading tourist companies to employ mobile telephony in their services. The first phase of their implementation

---

1. http://mtld.mobi/

Figure 21.2: Iberia services with 'dotMobi' domain. *Source*: App Store.

was the launch of a unique online booking portal for mobile terminals, which exceeded, according to the company, 1 million hits in nine months. At the beginning of 2010, it also launched three free booking applications for most popular smartphones on the market: iPhone, Blackberry and Android. After downloading these applications, customers can access their loyalty programme account and quickly make a hotel reservation in any of the more than 300 hotels of Sol Meliá in the world. In addition, this system, through the use of global positioning system (GPS), will allow users to easily locate a hotel nearby.

According to the press release of Sol Meliá,[2] the Director of Distribution and Electronic Commerce, David Wright said, 'We wanted to open up access to reservations by phone to different platforms on the market so that our customers can find us easily'. As demonstrated with the launch of mobile portal, Sol Meliá is strongly committed to innovation in creating new services that allow users to make their reservations as they prefer.

***QR code check in***   The bi-dimensional (2D) image codes or image recognition-based codes represent a large amount of data owing to a higher density compared with the one-dimensional (1D) bar codes, which include PDF-417, Quick Response (QR) code and Data Matrix. In comparison with 1D bar code, most 2D image codes encode high-density data for representing a larger amount of data within a smaller

---

2. http://prensa.solmelia.com/

size, but 2D image codes have more complex code structures. This is a revolutionary way to enter information on a mobile phone, so there is no longer need for using the mobile phone keypad, and it is only necessary to focus on the code with the camera phone to download the information. The most representative 2D image code in terms of mobile Internet service is the QR code. This system was created by Japanese corporation Denso Wave in 1994 and can store extensive information in an array of points or a 2D bar code. QR is characterized by three squares that are in the corners that allow detection of the reader position (in this case the phone). QR codes could contain a diverse range of information, including website URLs, e-mail addresses, product images and coupons, among others. Since a QR code reader is now often preinstalled in mobile phones, it has become more and more popular in Japan. According to a recent survey, as much as 88.4% of mobile users have a QR code reader with their mobile devices, and 83.6% have actually used and accessed QR codes (Impress RD and Mobile Content Forum, 2007).

There are different types of 2D codes apart from QR code, such as Data Matrix code, BIDI code or BeeTagg. In addition, companies are beginning to develop new configurations of more creative 2D codes. For example, Figure 21.3 shows an operational QR code created by Japanese advertising agency SET and designed by Takashi Murakami for Louis Vuitton brand. This code allows access from the mobile device to the Louis Vuitton website.[3] Data Matrix code is a 2D coding system with a high reliability reading, since, thanks to their redundant information systems and error correction, the code can be read with low-contrast mobile cameras and even when 20–30% of the code is damaged. The code consists of black and white cells, where each cell represents one bit of information.

On the other hand, BeeTagg code developed by Swiss company Connvision[4] has, when compared to other codes, the peculiarity of designing and introducing colour logos or pictures inside. The most popular 2D code in Spain is called BIDI (whose acronym comes from 'dimensional' or '2D'), marketed by the company Movistar. The difference between BIDI and other codes such as the QR lies in the method of configuration and costs. QR code is an open-source technology, and, therefore, its creation, download and reading are free; BIDI code, however, is not free. To read it, it is necessary to download a free program — for Movistar's customers — but at a cost to customers of other companies. This program is compatible with most popular smartphones on the market and in many cases already comes preinstalled on the terminal. Once installed, you must open the application and turn your mobile phone camera on. By pointing the camera to the code, if the code is valid, the application will recognize and capture the image, and the phone will activate or perform what the BIDI is encoded for, for example, accessing a promotional website or coupon. While downloading the application is free in some cases, its use is associated with a cost, which depends on the rate established by the mobile network operator.

---

3. http://lvmonogram.jp/store
4. http://www.convision.com

Figure 21.3: Different types of 2D codes. *Note*: From left to right, BIDI code, QR code, Data Matrix code and BeeTagg code. Courtesy: Códigos QR.

There are many uses and applications of QR codes for the marketing of tourism services. They are very useful for providing tourist information about a city, monument or place to visit. For example, an information panel may include a QR code — whatever the format is — which would enable users to access specific information about the site or monument they are visiting.

It can also be used to develop mobile marketing programmes or customer loyalty. In the first case, the codes can be placed in advertisements in newspapers, magazines, billboards or even tangible products, so that the user can download product information, coupons, discounts or promotions. In the second case, users can display QR codes as personal identification. This allows the company to streamline purchasing processes and customer registration and the user can easily enjoy the benefits associated with loyalty programmes.

The most common use in the tourism sector is air travel or rail check-in services using QR codes. By accessing the airline/rail company website with the mobile phone, it detects the terminal type and allows the consumer to book and buy tickets. Then, the website sends a SMS to the mobile phone with the boarding pass. The SMS includes a QR code with the boarding pass information that can be read by the terminal gates at airports or railway stations.

#### 21.2.2.2. On-site information search for travel execution

*Museum guide support* New-generation smartphones have revolutionized the way we visit museums. In the first mobile service implemented in museums, visitors could call a mobile phone number in order to receive information about a particular artwork or send SMS for downloading guides. However, in recent years, these services have been replaced with new — and much more interactive — applications that use cutting-edge mobile technology. The use of Bluetooth or 2D codes for sending guides to the mobile phone in the museum is an increasingly popular practice. The use of Bluetooth would be a passive form of information retrieval, as a museum visitor activates the function to detect the Bluetooth emitter with the mobile phone. By contrast, the 2D code reading would be an active form of information retrieval for the user. Those visitors interested in specific information can seek and read the code, which could increase their satisfaction. Canadi, Höpken, and Fuchs (2010) conducted an experiment in the Mercedes Benz museum regarding the download of information with QR codes and found a very positive evaluation by the users.

A service widely used by art galleries and museums is the podcast, audio and video content on a particular topic. A typical service runs in 15–30 min and usually requires a registration to download the content on their mobiles. In recent years, some museums have begun to implement custom-made and interactive multimedia guides. Among those, one of the finalists in the 2004 Imagine Cup (Microsoft-sponsored technological ideas competition) was 'VAMOS: the museum of the future'[5] which was designed by students of the Polytechnic University of Valencia (Spain). The VAMOS stands for 'Virtual Assistant for Museum Occasional Sightseeing' and aims at enhancing and customizing museum visits via mobile device. The program allows museum visitors to choose, using their PDA, the routes in the museum according to their preferences and available time. With this information, in seconds, the visitor could access through his or her mobile a map and a guide to the paintings and rooms to visit in the custom route, with an explanation of each painting in a multimedia format guide.

In the same way, the MOMO project — developed by FutureLab (research group of Department of Information Systems and Computing of the Polytechnic University of Valencia) and funded by Microsoft — has developed applications for using interactive multimedia guides in museums' mobile devices. This application was used in the 100 handheld computers available to the public in the 2009 exhibition 'Sorolla: A Vision of Spain' organized by Bancaja, which acted as interactive mobile guides.[6] Currently, augmented reality, which is a technology cluster that allows real-time overlay of images and data of each object visited in the museum, is increasingly used. This technology allows the development of highly interactive and dynamic educational projects, where visitors can 'touch, feel and see' the picture or slip into the historical context in which it was created. In 2011, the Civil War through Augmented Reality Project was launched (HistoriQuest[7]). It was conceived by several public educators by the Institute of Social Studies of the Pennsylvania State University with a desire to offer more interactivity to students and the general public visiting historical sites. The objective of the project is to develop and implement augmented reality services (with tablet personal computers) related to the American Civil War in Pennsylvania, to allow the general public a chance to experience the applications.

Figure 21.4 shows a HistoriQuest application; when pointing with the mobile device, you can see a body of a Confederate States soldier in the town of Gettysburg on one of the first days of the invasion in 1863. At the application where the body was found, the mobile application triggers a CSI investigation, of sorts, where Gettysburg visitors can follow clues through various points of interest in the town.

---

5. http://www.imaginecup.com
6. http://obrasocial.bancaja.es/cultura/exposiciones/exposicionesficha.aspx?id = 203
7. http://www.historiquest.com; http://acwarproject.wordpress.com

Figure 21.4: Mobile application in HistoriQuest with augmented reality. *Source*:
Watters (2011).

The success of the historical tourist routes in game format is proven in research by
(Kim & Schliesser, 2008).

***Cultural tourism guide*** As in cultural guides for museums, mobile technology applied
to cultural tourism guides differs in complexity. It can range from standard guides that
a user downloads from a web or from a tourist information point by sending and
receiving a SMS to Bluetooth services, or 2D codes. However, a trend in the touristic
areas is the design of customized tour guides that combine location (GPS) with other
technologies such as augmented reality. These new ways of understanding visits
have been proven in different studies such as Kramer, Modsching, and Hagen (2008),
which shows that when using custom guides, the places visited and length of visit were
not different from when using traditional guides, but the tourist satisfaction increases.
For example, with these applications, the traveller could focus a building with his or
her mobile device camera and the application would play an opera of the theatre,
provide data for a monument or reconstruct, in a real time, a historical monument as it
was centuries ago. Furthermore, in augmented reality the user can tag any image or
sound, and share his or her experience with other users. There is a huge potential for a
funnier and more interactive visit to the city.

The Museum of London has promoted an application called Streetmuseum™ that
allows an interactive visit to London (2011). The idea is to combine a visit to the
streets of London with interactive historical data. Once the users are *geolocated*,
when the user points his or her camera to a given area, data and historical photos of
the place will be shown on the screen (see Figure 21.5).

Some applications for next-generation devices, such as Layar or TwittARound,
exploit these technologies for visits to outdoor areas, cities, landscapes, etc. Layar is
designed as a system of 312 different layers, each including different information, as
tweets nearby, information on homes for sale, nearby restaurants, reviews, etc.
TwittARound, however, is the application designed for iPhone devices and/or

Figure 21.5: Streetmuseum™ © Museum of London. *Source*: Museum of London (2011).

Figure 21.6: Layar (left) and TwittARound (right) applications. *Source*: Layar and TwittARound.

compatible mobile phones. When an individual focuses with the mobile to a particular place, he or she can see and check all those tweets that are published in real time around the location (see Figure 21.6).

***Bluetooth spots*** Bluetooth name comes from Harold Bluetooth, the English name translation for Danish and Norwegian king, Harald Blatand. This application is an industrial specification for wireless personal area networks (WPANs) that enables voice and data transmission between different devices through a short-distance radio-frequency link. It is specially designed to low consumption and short-distance coverage devices, being mainly aimed at simplifying communications and data synchronization between mobile and fixed computer devices without using cables.

The 'Bluetooth Special Interest Group (SIG)', created by some leading telecommunication companies (mainly Ericssom, Intel, Ienovo, Microsoft, Motorola, Nokia and Toshiba), is in charge of Bluetooth wireless technology development and marketing.

The Bluetooth-enabled devices can communicate between them when in range. Communications are carried out through radio frequency, which means that devices do not have to be paired and could be in separate rooms, even with obstacles, if transmission power allows. The transmission power changes with the devices and fluctuates between 1 and 100 m; however, regardless of their coverage range, the devices are always compatible.

Bluetooth possibilities for marketing tourist services are almost limitless. Below we highlight three specific capacities that have great potential for tourism marketing:

(1) This technology eliminates the cable connection need between devices, as well as between fixed and mobile devices. Thus, cellular phone users can download through Bluetooth touristic information from a specific terminal or devices strategically located. For example, a traveller could visit a touristic information point, a museum or any interest place and download maps, guides or useful information to his or her mobile devices.

(2) This technology allows information exchange (such as files, business cards, appointments, etc.) between its users. This means that any tourist can transmit, quickly and at no cost, the information he or she has downloaded to his or her cellular phone to other tourists, which, in its turn, facilitates efficient information spreading.

(3) A usual application lies in promotion and advertising campaigns to Bluetooth-active mobile devices when they enter into a delimited range area. In this way, a tourist service such as restaurants, bars or point of interest could send information, promos, discounts, etc., to potential customers. This service's main disadvantage is that the customer does not grant permission to receive information in his or her devices and, thus, it could be considered an intrusive practice. This application can also work as remote controls (e.g. 'Sony PlayStation 3' and 'Wii' incorporate Bluetooth technology). The technology can also be used in hotel room key systems, entrance doors to museums or entertainment events or act as electronic purses for paying any service.

***Global positioning system*** GPS is a global satellite navigation system that allows the location of an object position in any place of the world with an accuracy that varies from centimetres to few metres. It was developed by the US Defense Department, which operates a network of 24 satellites synchronized to cover the earth surface, called NAVSTAR. The GPS system is designed to calculate the position of any point in space coordinates ($x$, $y$, $z$) based on a calculation (using the triangulation method) of the distances from a minimum of three satellites whose location is known (Sonnenberg, 1988).

A GPS system for mobile phones has been developed through A-GPS system that sends the antenna identification and the phone position to an external server when the terminal is turned on. The process can reduce the location and positioning time from several minutes to seconds. The disadvantage is that a phone connection with an associated cost is needed, except in Wi-Fi-enabled mobile models.

The GPS application for mobile phones is particularly common in last-generation mobile phones and PDAs. Its use ranges from simple user location to many tourist services such as searching of restaurants, hotels, shows, etc. For example, the Spanish tourism portal[8] has developed the first online tool that integrates GPS technology to create custom travel guides. The users can design their own free travel guide establishing the coordinates of different landmarks on the map; they can identify the places with icons and pictures, and share this information with friends in social networks such as Facebook or Twitter. Moreover, each tourist point of interest is available to other users so they can share their feedback and participate with their own experiences. This system has been used in other tourist sites[9] where the user is presented with numerous preset routes and where he or she can create his or her route. Then, the user can export the route to the mobile phone or PDA for future reference as a multimedia book. Once finished the route, visitors can share their experiences on the web including photos, comments, etc.

The Tourism Promotion Plan of the Government of Catalonia, Spain, has developed another interesting application, called Geo-Xating,[10] which aims at promoting tourism in this region. This application is a geocaching-based implementation, developed to promote tourism[11] The website offers 10 hiking paths each of which contains 3–4 points that participants should visit, check the information and answer questions to find a 'treasure chest' and participate in the prize draw.

Furthermore, data based on GPS location presents important opportunities in terms of tourism research (Shoval & Isaacson, 2007). It allows researchers to discover the attractions of an area and to describe the pattern of tourist movements, and information that cannot be known with other databases (Ahas, Aasa, Mark, Pae, & Kull, 2007). This information allows us to accurately quantify the demand for a city or town at any time, in order to develop tourism local plans and business strategies; longitudinal studies also allow to identify tourism trends, to analyse the visits that occur at a particular area attraction and/or to measure the effectiveness of a show or event (Ahas, Aasa, Roose, Mark, & Silm, 2008). It has also been applied to tourism market segmentation (Tchetchik, Fleischer, & Shoval, 2009).

---

8. http://www.turismoespanagps.com
9. http://www.gps.huescalamagia.es
10. http://www.geoxating.cat
11. A high-tech treasure hunting game played throughout the world by adventure seekers equipped with GPS devices. The basic idea is to locate hidden containers, called geocaches, outdoors and then share your experiences online.

**21.2.2.3. Post-Travel Feedbacks for Online Consumer Review Sites**   Social media are becoming increasingly important as information sources for travellers. This new channel of communication offers individuals the ability to distribute information via blog sites or specific product review sites (Sparks & Browning, 2011). Many of them assist consumers in posting and sharing their travel-related comments, opinions and personal experiences, which then serve as information for others (Xiang & Gretzel, 2010). The content of reviews may vary depending on the product attributes being evaluated.

Many online consumer review sites comprise a product review or assessment platform, along with some social networking functions. The reviews can be either positive or negative but usually require the user log in or identification. Many reviewers provide a numerical rating of the product as part of the review process. Consumers, who find information that can potentially influence their purchase decisions (Sparks & Browning, 2011), tend to make referrals to other users on the site.

Popular online consumer review sites, such as TripAdvisor (Figure 21.7), Foursquare, Gowalla, Tripwolf, VirtualTourist, and IgoUgo, include not only comprehensive travel-specific information but also capability of quick circulation of their feedbacks or opinions through eWOM. Prior research defines eWOM as any positive or negative statement digitally disseminated and circulated by potential, actual or former customers about a product or company (Hennig-Thurau, Gwinner, Walsh, & Gremler, 2004). Because travel and tourism services are intangible and cannot be

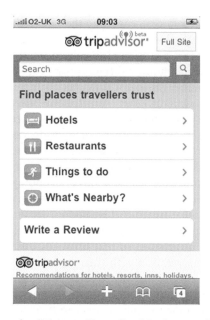

Figure 21.7: TripAdvisor for iPhone. *Note*: On this site, tourists could post their own experiences, feedbacks and evaluations, which turn into pivotal information source for the others. *Source*: Tripadvisor.com.

evaluated before consumption, the recommendations of individuals who have experienced the service become a pivotal part of the decision-making process (Litvin, Goldsmith, & Pan, 2008). With these online information sources, consumers are able to access opinions not only from close friends, family members and co-workers but also from strangers from all over the world who may have used a particular product or service in question (Pan, MacLaurin, & Crotts, 2007).

According to PhocusWright (2009), 9 out of 10 cybertravellers read (and trust) online reviews on tourism services (hotels, restaurants and destinations). Additional functions of these online consumer review sites are linked with the capability of *geolocalization* with which tourists could seek recommendations for the nearby travel spots or restaurants while they are travelling. Consequently, from a business perspective, tourism marketers cannot ignore the role of these sites in distributing travel-related information (Sparks & Browning, 2011; Xiang & Gretzel, 2010).

## 21.3. Concluding Remarks

This chapter proposes a mobile tourism marketing framework. The framework consists of pre-travel, on-site and post-travel information behaviour. Based on this, we described several practical cases based on actual applications in use. Several implications can be drawn in terms of use of smartphones in tourism marketing.

First, location-based services can be the key that holds the successful implementation of this ICT. The obvious reason is that travellers' main concern is how to find the popular tourist spots. This has been a serious issue when they are the first-time visitors. Although traditional (i.e. paper-based) tourism guides have been the main information source, this can change as an increasing number of practical applications are now available for smartphone users. GPS and Bluetooth significantly improve the flexibility of time and place when tourists are on the move or in transition from one place to another. The worldwide penetration of 'Wi-Fi hot spots' would further increase cross-border usability of these technologies as mobile Internet connection would not be impeded by cost factors.

Second, at the same time, the use of mobile technology will likely be combined with traditional media. For example, QR codes will serve as a bridging tool between traditional media and mobile Internet. This coding technology greatly enhances the ease of information retrieval. More and more travel agencies insert QR codes in their pamphlets, leaflets or even websites, so that browsing customers scan the image and get quick access to the information with their mobile device. In this way, travellers will also gain freedom to choose the way to retrieve or search information, according to their time and space flexibility and emergent needs. In this light, mobile-based tourism support opens a door to multichannel tourism services.

In addition, code-based check in has converted in a quick, efficient and practical solution for many airline as well as railway companies. This tool could significantly improve a cue-waiting time, and the accuracy of passengers' information retrieval.

Probably similar service can be implemented in different fields of tourism, such as museum/monument entrance, city tour pass and public transportation card, among others.

Third, more enhanced mobile tourism support may be extended to the capability of financial transaction. For example, a prepaid rechargeable RFID smart card system, such as FeliCa and its application, Suica, can be a practical example that has become a standard payment system in Japan. In particular, Suica enables users to register any major credit card for its use, thus greatly enhancing ticketing capability for travellers. This can be easily integrated into booking and reservation applications in smartphones.

In short, this chapter recognizes the increasing importance of mobile device, in particular, smartphones, in terms of tourism marketing. Strategic planning will be needed among tourism firms — agencies, tour operators, airline companies and hotels, among others — and these firms should offer practical and easy-to-use mobile applications in order to accommodate sophisticated needs for more ubiquitous tourism experiences.

## Acknowledgement

This research was funded by a grant from the Spanish Ministry of Science and Innovation (National Plan for Research, Development and Innovation ECO2011-30105).

## References

Ahas, R., Aasa, A., Mark, Ü., Pae, T., & Kull, A. (2007). Seasonal tourism spaces in Estonia: Case study with mobile positioning data. *Tourism Management*, *28*(3), 898–910.

Ahas, R., Aasa, A., Roose, A., Mark, U., & Silm, S. (2008). Evaluating passive mobile positioning data for tourism surveys: An Estonia case study. *Tourism Management*, *29*(3), 469–486.

Barnes, D., Mieczkowska, S., & Hinton, M. (2003). Integrating operations and information strategy in ebusiness. *European Management Journal*, *21*(5), 626–634.

Bornhorst, T., Ritchie, J. R. B., & Sheehan, L. (2010). Determinants of tourism success for DMOs & destinations: An empirical examination of stakeholders' perspectives. *Tourism Management*, *31*(5), 572–589.

Bruner, G. C., II., & Kumar, A. (2005). Explaining consumer acceptance of handheld Internet devices. *Journal of Business Research*, *58*(5), 553–558.

Buhalis, D., & Licata, M. C. (2002). The future etourism intermediaries. *Tourism Management*, *23*(3), 207–220.

Canadi, M., Höpken, W., & Fuchs, M. (2010). Application of QR codes in online travel distribution. In P. O'Connor, W. Hopken, & U. Gretzel (Eds.), *Information and communication technologies in tourism 2008: Proceedings of the international conference in Innsbruck, Austria* (pp. 215–227).

Dwyer, L., Edwards, D., Mistilis, N., Roman, C., & Scott, N. (2009). Destination and enterprise management for a tourism future. *Tourism Management, 30*(1), 63–74.

Hägerstrand, T. (1970). What about people in regional science? *Papers of the Regional Science Association, 24,* 1–12.

Hawkins, D. I., Best, R. J., & Coney, K. A. (2001). *Consumer behavior: Building marketing strategy* (9th ed.). New York, NY: McGraw-Hill.

Hennig-Thurau, T., Gwinner, K. P., Walsh, G., & Gremler, D. D. (2004). Electronic word-of-mouth via consumer-opinion platforms: What motivates consumers to articulate themselves on the Internet? *Journal of Interactive Marketing, 18*(1), 38–52.

Hoyer, W. D., & MacInnis, D. J. (2001). *Consumer behavior* (2nd ed.). Boston, MA: Houghton Mifflin Company.

Impress R&D and Mobile Content Forum. (2007). *Keitai hakusho.* Mobile white paper. Tokyo: Impress R&D (in Japanese).

Janelle, D. G. (2004). Impact of information technologies. In S. Hanson & G. Giuliano (Eds.), *The geography of urban transportation* (3rd ed., pp. 86–112). New York, NY: Guilford.

Keller, P. (2004). Conclusions of the conference on innovation and growth in tourism. Paper presented at the conference on innovation and growth in tourism, Lugano, Switzerland.

Kenyon, S. (2008). Internet use and time use the importance of multitasking. *Time & Society, 17*(2/3), 283–318.

Kim, H., & Schliesser, J. (2008). Adaptation of storytelling to mobile entertainment service for site-specific cultural and historical tour. In P. O'Connor, W. Hopken, & U. Gretzel (Eds.), *Information and communication technologies in tourism 2008: Proceedings of the international conference in Innsbruck, Austria* (pp. 97–108). New York, NY: Springer.

Kramer, R., Modsching, M., & Hagen, K. T. (2008). Development and evaluation of a context-driven, mobile tourist guide. *International Journal of Pervasive Computing and Communications, 3*(4), 378–399.

Leiper, N. (1990). Tourist attraction systems. *Annals of Tourism Research, 17*(3), 367–384.

Litvin, S. W., Goldsmith, R. E., & Pan, B. (2008). Electronic word-of-mouth in hospitality and tourism management. *Tourism Management, 29*(3), 458–468.

Miller, H. J. (2005). What about people in geographic information science? In P. Fisher & D. Unwin (Eds.), *Re-presenting geographical information systems* (pp. 215–242). New York, NY: Wiley.

Museum of London. (2011). *Explore online.* Retrieved from www.museumoflondon.org.uk/Resources/app/you-are-here-app/index.html on September 21, 2011. Accessed on 2 July 2011.

Okazaki, S. (2006). What do we know about mobile Internet adopters? A cluster analysis. *Information & Management, 43*(2), 127–141.

Pan, B., MacLaurin, T., & Crotts, J. C. (2007). Travel blogs and the implications for destination marketing. *Journal of Travel Research, 46*(1), 35–45.

PhoCusWright. (2009). *PhoCusWright's European consumer travel trends survey.* Sherman, CT: PhoCusWright.

Pröll, B., & Retschitzegger, W. (2000). Discovering next generation tourism information systems: A tour on TIScover. *Journal of Travel Research, 39*(2), 182–191.

Rayman-Bacchus, L., & Molina, A. (2001). Internet-based tourism services: Business issues and trends. *Futures, 33*(7), 589–605.

Richards, G. (2002). Tourism attraction systems: Exploring cultural behavior. *Annals of Tourism Research, 29*(4), 1048–1064.

Shoval, N., & Isaacson, M. (2007). Tracking tourists in the digital age. *Annals of Tourism Research*, *34*(1), 141–159.

Sonnenberg, G. J. (1988). *The global positioning system: Radar and electronic navigation* (6th ed.). London: Butterworth-Heinemann.

Sparks, B. A., & Browning, V. (2011). The impact of online reviews on hotel booking intentions and perception of trust. *Tourism Management*, *32*(6), 1310–1323.

Tchetchik, A., Fleischer, A., & Shoval, N. (2009). Segmentation of visitors to a heritage site using high-resolution time–space data. *Journal of Travel Research*, *48*(2), 216–229.

Urry, J. (1990). *The tourist gaze: Leisure and travel in contemporary societies*. London: Sage.

Watson, R. T., Pitt, L. F., Berthon, P., & Zinkhan, G. M. (2002). U-commerce: Expanding the universe of marketing. *Journal of the Academy of Marketing Science*, *30*(4), 333–347.

Watters, A. (2011). *Augmented reality field trips & the 150th anniversary of the U.S. Civil War*. ReadWriteWeb, top story. Retrieved 1 September 2011 from www.readwriteweb.com/archives/augmented_reality_field_trips_the_150th_anniversar.php. Accessed on 1 May 2011.

Xiang, Z., & Gretzel, U. (2010). Role of social media in online travel information search. *Tourism Management*, *31*(2), 179–188.

Yu, H., & Shaw, S. L. (2008). Exploring potential human activities in physical and virtual spaces: A spatio-temporal GIS approach. *International Journal of Geographical Information Science*, *22*(4), 409–430.

# Epilogue

Managers in the tourism industry today face many challenges. Three of the most important are (1) an increasing intensity in competition, (2) the variety of technological changes they encounter and (3) growing consumer sophistication among tourists. The increasing intensity of competition comes from the growing number of international destinations that seek to attract the tourist dollar and in the form of new types of tourism products (e.g. rural tourism). The appearance of new technologies of all types, especially information and communication technologies (ICT), has many implications for tourism management. These include the consumer side, where consumers increasingly use the Internet to locate and evaluate destinations, create their own bookings and schedules, and interact with other consumers before, during and after their visit; as well as the B2B or supplier side where technology is also becoming more and more important to the management of tourism businesses as it enables managers to both coordinate the delivery of their products. Given these important challenges, how can tourism managers best respond? Finally, consumers are becoming more familiar with and adept in using new technologies, especially social media, to interact with both tourism destinations as well as other tourists.

The purpose of the present book was to provide a forum for marketing scholars and practitioners in the tourism industries to present their latest thoughts and results to guide tourism managers towards these challenges. The fundamental idea is that the marketing response should be strategic in nature, that is it should begin by clearly establishing the goals of the marketing efforts, develop detailed plans for achieving those goals and incorporate the latest concepts in strategic tourism management into those plans. In doing so, the recommendation seems to be to build on proven strategic marketing initiatives derived from other industries and adapt them to the tourism context. Thus, the strategic marketing approach takes the formulation of the tasks of marketing management popularized by Philip Kotler (Research → Segmentation, Targeting, Positioning → Marketing Mix → Implementation → Control) and builds on it in several ways.

Marketing management models, however, are only the starting point for a strategic tourism marketing perspective in tourism. Tourism sectors present unique challenges that require specific adaptations to their special circumstances. For example, tourism destinations are characterized by multiple partners in the delivery of the tourism product, including often the participation of the residents of the destination. Destinations have organic images that must be accounted for by the managers who seek to market a specific image that is both attractive to tourists and distinguishes one destination from another. More so than many other products, the role of customer co-creating is a core element in the ultimate outcome of the destination's consumption. Thus, marketing strategies for tourism products must involve multiple partners in both their development and implementation; they must strive to create and project realistic and genuine images of the destination; and they must involve the customer to an extent unfamiliar to most marketing managers in the co-creation of the brand.

The first part of the book dealt with *Target Marketing* and presented new approaches to segmenting and targeting the tourism market. The second part addressed *Branding* in the tourism industry, especially branding destinations, a key success factor in the modern tourism environment. Part III explained the important idea of *Managing Relationships* with tourists as an essential element of a contemporary strategic tourism marketing plan. In this regard, tourism managers are somewhat behind the curve, but are quickly adopting the latest strategies and technologies that enable them to establish genuine, long lasting relationships with tourists that both enhance their competitive positions and improve the tourism experience for their customers. Part IV described an especially important element of modern strategic marketing for tourism, the need to view the product as an experience, so that *Experiential Marketing* should be a core element of any strategy. Finally, Part V somewhat capped off the preceding sections by introducing several approaches to electronic marketing. *E-Marketing* is one of the most recent orientations that tourism marketers can use strategically to accomplish their goals. The readings in this part discuss a range of ICT that both managers and consumers use in the relationship building process. These five areas of strategic marketing were chosen as topics because they represent some of the most rapidly developing aspects of marketing strategy and because they are particularly appropriate for the tourism context.

If tourist services are to survive the fierce competitive and financially difficult global environment of the twenty-first century they must learn how to satisfy customers' needs and desires through the systematic application of strategic marketing management. A lack of work on strategic marketing issues in tourism has been identified in the literature (Bagnall, 1996; Riege & Perry, 2000; Tsiotsou & Ratten, 2010). The purpose of the present book has been to help fill this gap in the literature by providing recommendations for tourism managers. Moreover, this review reveals several new topics for further research and development by both scholars and practitioners.

With regard to segmentation in the tourism industries, one topic for future research would be how tourism managers can use the latest analytic techniques available to them to gain important insights into the market structure of the customer environment. The increasing availability of ICT and their spreading use in the tourism industries will make available to managers large amounts of data on consumers that was not available to them prior to the implementation of these technologies. Managers will have to learn how to analyse this data to discover unique segments of potential tourists. In addition, social network data will also likely be an excellent source of insights into tourism consumers' behaviour that can be used for segmentation, targeting and brand building.

As the chapters in this part of the book attest, there is little research in brand building in the tourism industries other than the more generic studies of branding for services and the domain specific studies of destination image. The brand image of a destination is an especially complex entity, far more complex than that of a package good or even a consumer durable. This is because destinations are comprised of so many different elements, so many different firms participate in creating the destination product and because of the key role the subjective tourist experience plays in the co-creation of the experience. Brand building for tourist destinations, especially as these efforts employ the newly available tools of social networking, should become a key topic of research for the future.

How best to use the increasingly sophisticated tools of customer relationship management to build relationships is a crucial area for further study. As the ICTs become more commonplace, their use will become not just an element for competitive advantage, but a ticket to entry for any firm wishing to keep up with the competition. Researchers can aid tourism management by studying how these technologies can be best integrated into the overall marketing management strategy and by identifying both ways to improve them and overcome any barriers to their adoption by as many managers as possible.

One of the most stimulating aspects of the material covered in this book is the exciting opportunities the concept of experiential marketing brings to the management of tourism industries. Theodore Levitt is famous for posing the fundamental question, 'what business are you in?' The query is especially applicable to tourism because it is becoming increasingly obvious that these businesses do not sell locales, destinations, air tickets, rooms or beaches, they sell a total experience that the tourism can co-create and retain as a valuable memory.

Finally, the part devoted to E-Marketing reminds us that as society changes, marketers of all stripes must change along with it. As consumers become more 'social' and connected with each other, marketers must learn how to participate in this social exchange to build their brands and relationships with customers. This is no less true for the tourism industries, especially because tourism activities constitute such a popular and pleasant content for so much social exchange. If tourism marketers can learn how to integrate themselves effectively into these conversations, they will go a long way toward building the relationships they so value with customers.

In reality, we can see that all the topics covered in this book exist not as discrete silos of information, but form part of an overall pattern of strategic marketing for tourism. They are interrelated in that decisions made for any of them can affect the other areas, so that what is needed, and this is not a novel concept, is an integrated strategy directed towards specific organizational goals in which each aspect, segmentation, branding, relationship management, the experiential product and e-marketing, is consistent with the others. A huge challenge for the tourism managers, but one worthy of the effort to achieve it. It is hoped that the chapters presented in this book make a real contribution to helping both managers and researchers reach their shared goals.

Ronald E. Goldsmith

# References

Bagnall, D. (1996). Razor gang creates tourism jitters. *The Bulletin, 25*, 46.

Riege, A. M., & Perry, C. (2000). National marketing strategies in international travel and Tourism. *European Journal of Marketing, 34*(11/12), 1290–1304.

Tsiotsou, R., & Ratten, V. (2010). Future research directions in tourism marketing. *Marketing Intelligence & Planning, 28*(4), 533–544.

# Appendix

## Global Tourism Organisations

| Organization | Website |
|---|---|
| World Tourism Organization (WTO) | http://www.unwto.org |
| World Travel and Tourism Council (WTTC) | http://www.wttc.org |
| World Bank (WB) | http://www.worldbank.org/ |
| International Air Transport Association (IATA) | http://www.iata.org |
| International Association of Antarctic Tour Operators (IAATO) | http://www.iaato.org |
| International Civil Aviation Organization (ICAO) | http://www.icao.int |

## Regional Tourism Organisations

| Region | Organization | Website |
|---|---|---|
| Caribbean | Association of Caribbean States | http://www.acs-aec.org |
| | Caribbean Tourism Organization | http://www.onecaribbean.org |
| Europe | European Travel Commission | http://www.etc-corporate.org |
| | Eurostat | http://ec.europa.eu/eurosta |
| Scandinavia | Scandinavian Tourist Boards | http://www.goscandinavia.com |
| South Pacific | South Pacific Tourism Organization | http://www.south-pacific.travel/ |
| | Pacific Asia Travel Association | http://www.pata.org |
| | Association of South East Asian Nations | http://www.aseansec.org |

## National Tourism Organisations

| Country | Organization | Website |
|---------|-------------|---------|
| Albania | Institute of Statistics | http://www.instat.gov.al/ |
| Algeria | Office National des Statistiques | http://www.ons.dz/-Tourisme-.html |
| Antigua and Barbuda | Ministry of Tourism | http:// www.tourismantiguabarbuda.gov.ag http://www.ab.gov.ag |
| Argentina | National Institute of Statistics and Census | http://www.indec.mecon.gov.ar/ |
| Australia | Tourism Australia Tourism Research Australia | http://www.tourism.australia.com http://www.ret.gov.au/TOURISM/ TRA/Pages/default.aspx |
| Austria | Statistik Austria | http://www.statistik.at/web_en/ statistics/tourism/index.html |
|  | Tourism Austria | http://www.austria.info/ |
| Bahamas | Tourism Today | http://www.tourismtoday.com |
|  | Department of Statistics | http://statistics.bahamas.gov.bs/ key.php?cat=86 |
| Barbados | Ministry of Tourism | http://www.tourism.gov.bb |
|  | Totally Barbados | http://www.totallybarbados.com |
| Belgium | Statistics Belgium | http://statbel.fgov.be |
| Bonaire | Department of Economic and Labour Affairs | http://www.bonaireinsider.com/pdfs/ 20070525-BonaireTourismStatistics- 2006-Complete.pdf http://www.bonaireeconomy.org/ tourism_statistics.html |
| Botswana | Ministry of Wildlife, Environment and Tourism | http://www.mewt.gov.bw |
| Brazil | Brazil Tourism | http://www.braziltour.com |
| Bulgaria | Bulgarian Tourism Chamber | http://www.btch.org |
| Cambodia | Ministry of Tourism | http://www.mot.gov.kh |
| Canada | Tourism Canada | http://uk.canada.travel/ |
|  | Transport Canada | http://www.tc.gc.ca/eng/menu.htm |
| Cayman Islands | Department of Tourism | http://www.caymanislands.ky |
| China | China National Tourism Office | http://www.cnto.org |
| Colombia | Ministerio de Comercio, Industria y Turismo | http://www.mincomercio.gov.co |

| Country | Organization | Website |
|---|---|---|
| **Croatia** | Croatia National Tourism Board | http://business.croatia.hr/en-GB/ Croatian-national-tourist-board |
| **Cuba** | Cuba Tourist Board in Canada | http://www.gocuba.ca/client/home/ index.php |
| **Cyprus** | Cyprus Tourism Organisation | http://www.visitcyprus.com |
| **Czech Republic** | CzechTourism | http://www.czechtourism.cz |
| **Denmark** | Tourism Denmark | http://www.visitdenmark.com/ siteforside.htm |
| | Statistics Denmark | http://www.dst.dk/HomeUK/Guide/ search.aspx?search=tourism |
| **Dominica** | Ministry of Tourism & Legal Affairs | http://tourism.gov.dm |
| **Egypt** | Egyptian Tourism Federation | http://www.etf.org.eg |
| **Estonia** | Visit Estonia | http://www.visitestonia.com |
| **Finland** | Finnish Tourism Board | http://www.mek.fi |
| **France** | Ministère de l'Economie, de l'Industrie et de l'Emploi | http://www.tourisme.gouv.fr |
| **Georgia** | Department of Tourism and Resorts | http://www.dotr.gov.ge |
| **Germany** | German National Tourism Board | http://www.germany-tourism.de |
| **Greece** | Greek National Tourism Organization | http://www.visitgreece.gr |
| **Honduras** | Secretariat of Tourism | http://www.iht.hn |
| **Hong Kong** | Hong Kong Tourism Board | http://partnernet.hktourismboard.com |
| **Hungary** | Hungarian National Tourism Office | http://www.hungary.com |
| **Iceland** | Icelandic Tourism Board | http://www.ferdamalastofa.is |
| **India** | Ministry of Tourism | http://www.tourism.gov.in/ |
| **Indonesia** | Ministry of Culture and Tourism | http://www.budpar.go.id |
| **Ireland** | Tourism Ireland | http://www.tourismireland.com/ Home/about-us.aspx |
| | Failte Ireland | http://www.failteireland.ie |
| **Israel** | Israel Ministry of Tourism | http://www.goisrael.com/ Tourism_Eng/Pages/home.aspx |
| **Italy** | Italian Tourism Board | http://www.enit.it http://www.ontit.it/ont/ |

| Country | Organization | Website |
|---|---|---|
| | ONT: national observatory on tourism | |
| **Jamaica** | Jamaica Tourism Board | http://www.jtbonline.org/ tourism_jamaica/default.aspx# |
| **Japan** | Japan Tourism Marketing Co. | http://www.tourism.jp |
| **Jordan** | Ministry of Tourism and Antiquities | http://www.tourism.jo |
| **Kenya** | Experience Kenya | http://www.experiencekenya.co.ke |
| | Ministry of Tourism | http://www.tourism.go.ke |
| **Korea** | Visit Korea | http://kto.visitkorea.or.kr |
| **Libya** | General Board of Tourism and Traditional Industries | http://www.libyan-tourism.org/ List.aspx?ID=95 |
| **Lithuania** | Lithuania Tourism Department | http://www.tourism.lt |
| **Malawi** | Visit Malawi | http://www.visitmalawi.mw |
| **Malaysia** | Tourism Malaysia | http://www.tourism.gov.my |
| **Maldives** | Ministry of Tourism, Arts and Culture | http://www.tourism.gov.mv/ |
| **Malta** | Malta Tourism Authority | http:// www.maltatourismauthority.com/ page.aspx?id=105 |
| **Mexico** | Secretaria de Turismo | http://www.sectur.gob.mx |
| **Mongolia** | Ministry of Road, Transport and Tourism | http://www.mongoliatourism.gov.mn |
| **Morocco** | Forum Marocain du Tourisme | http://www.tourismemaroc.com |
| **Myanmar** | Ministry of Hotels and Tourism | http://www.myanmartourism.org/ tourismstatistic.htm |
| **Namibia** | Namibian Tourism Board | http://www.namibiatourism.com.na |
| **Nepal** | Ministry of Tourism and Civil Aviation | http://www.tourism.gov.np |
| **Netherlands** | Netherlands Board of Tourism and Conventions | http://www.nbtc.nl |
| **New Zealand** | Ministry of Tourism | http://www.tourismresearch.govt.nz/ |
| **Norway** | Visit Norway | http://www.innovasjonnorge.no |
| **Panama** | Autorida de Turismo Panama | http://www.atp.gob.pa |
| **Peru** | Ministerio de Comercio Y Turismo | http://www.mincetur.gob.pe |
| **Philippines** | Department of Tourism | http://www.visitmyphilippines.com |
| **Poland** | Institute of Tourism | http://www.intur.com.pl |

| Country | Organization | Website |
|---|---|---|
| **Portugal** | Instituto Nacional de Estatistica | http://www.ine.pt |
| **Romania** | Romanian National Tourist Office | http://www.romaniatourism.com/ronto.html |
| **Serbia** | National Tourism Organization of Serbia | http://www.serbia.travel/ |
| **Singapore** | Singapore Tourism Board | http://www.stb.com.sg/ |
| **Slovakia** | Ministry of Economy and Construction | http://www.economy.gov.sk |
| **Slovenia** | Slovenian Tourism Board | http://www.slovenia.info |
| **Spain** | Tourism Institute of Spain | http://www.tourspain.es/en/HOME/ListadoMenu.htm?Language=en http://www.spain.info/ |
| **Sri Lanka** | Sri Lanka Tourism Development Authority | http://www.sltda.lk |
| **Sweden** | Ministry of Tourism | http://www.visitsweden.com/sweden/ |
| **Switzerland** | Swiss National Tourism Office | http://www.myswitzerland.com |
| **Syria** | Ministry of Tourism | http://www.syriatourism.org |
| **Taiwan** | Tourism Bureau, Ministry of Transportation and Communications | http://admin.taiwan.net.tw |
| **Thailand** | Tourism Authority of Thailand | http://www2.tat.or.th |
| **Turkey** | Turkish Culture & Tourism Office | http://www.gototurkey.co.uk/ |
| **UK** | Visit Britain | http://www.visitbritain.org |
| **USA** | US Travel Association | http://www.ustravel.org |
| **Vietnam** | Vietnam National Administration of Tourism | http://www.vietnamtourism.gov.vn |
| | Vietnam Travel | http://www.vietnamtravel.org |
| **Yemen** | Yemen Tourism Promotion Board | http://www.yementourism.com |

## Listservs in Tourism

| Organization | Website |
| --- | --- |
| **Association of American Geographers (AAG) — Recreation, Tourism and Sport Specialty Group** | rtsnet@yahoogroups.com |
| **Association for Tourism and Leisure Education (ATLAS)** | list@atlas-euro.org |
| **CAUTHE (Council for Australian Tourism and Hospitality Education)** | cauthe@lists.uq.edu.au |
| **Dark Tourism Forum** | http://www.jiscmail.ac.uk/cgi-bin/ webadmin? SUBED1=dark-tourism&A=1 |
| **International Geographical Union (IGU) Tourism Commission** | tourismgeography@yahoogroups.com |
| **Irish Tourism and Hospitality Research List** | DIT-TSM-HOSP- IRL@LISTSERV.HEANET.IE |
| **Listourism-and-hospitality** | http://www.jiscmail.ac.uk/lists/lis-tourism- and-hospitality.html |
| **Network on Travel and Tourism History** | H-TRAVEL@H-NET.MSU.EDU |
| **SPRENET** | SPRENET@LISTSERV.UGA.EDU |
| **Strategic Management in Tourism** | SM-tourism@yahoogroups.com |
| **Tourismanthropology** | http://www.jiscmail.ac.uk/cgi-bin/ webadmin? SUBED1=tourismanthropology&A=1 |
| **TRINET** | http://www.tim.hawaii.edu/timlistserv/ about_trinet.aspx |

# Index

Accommodations, 38, 39, 105–106, 164, 165, 172, 174, 175, 212, 253, 254, 339
Active value, 226
Activity segmentation, 22, 26
Adjusted expectations, 186–189, 197
Affective commitment, 147–148, 157
Affective *vs.* cognitive values, 80, 89
Ambient intelligence, 36, 301, 305
Android, 339, 345
*A posterior* segmentation, 21
*A priori* segmentation, 3, 21, 308
Assimilation theory, 186
Attitudinal intentions, 151
Attribute-based items, 98, 100, 101, 104, 105
Attributes, 215, 218–226
Authenticity, 129, 212, 254, 257, 265, 267
Authority constraints, 342
Automatic speech recognition, 310, 311

B2B, 150, 232, 305
B2B marketing, 232
BeeTagg code, 346, 347
Behavioral intentions, 66
Behavioral outcomes, 66
Beneficiary, 233, 234
Benefits, 4, 5, 6, 11, 12, 19, 31, 37, 40, 83, 95, 97, 139, 142, 154, 157, 163, 207, 209, 219, 221, 222, 242, 259, 273, 294, 299, 313, 315, 347
Benefit segmentation, 19, 22, 26
Best value offer, 152, 157, 158
BIDI code, 346, 347
Bi-dimensional (2D) code, 345, 346, 347, 349
Blackberry, 339, 345
Bluetooth, 341, 347, 349
Bluetooth Special Interest Group (SIG), 351
Bluetooth spots, 350–351
Bootstrapping, 26
Brand architecture, 53, 63, 67, 72–74
Brand awareness, 55, 56, 96, 99

Brand development, 51, 53–54, 57, 58, 96, 97, 110
Brand identity, 53, 54, 57, 58, 96, 322
Brand image, 29, 53, 55, 98, 99, 103, 332
Brand knowledge, 55, 96, 111
Brand performance factors, 97
Brand personality, 121, 134
Business integrated processes, 300, 301

C2C communications, 300
Cable TV, 303
Call centre, 310, 311
Capability constraints, 342
CBBE dimensions, 96, 99, 111
Chain of effects, 152, 158
City Communication, 66
Co-create, 35
Co-creation, 142, 144, 145, 231, 321
    experiencescape, 254, 255
    experiential marketing, 207–212, 268, 321
    overall rural tourism experience, 258
    tourist experience, 235, 242
    *see also* Experience
Collaboration, 32, 56, 57, 58, 103, 106, 144, 224, 240, 241, 279
Commitment, 58, 147–148, 165, 173, 175, 187–188, 252, 324
Communication technologies, 36, 43, 154, 294, 299
Community. *See* Host communities
Competences, 232, 235, 240, 242, 243, 328
Competing destination, 12, 31
Competition strategy, 18, 30
Competitive advantage, 3, 5, 10, 11, 12, 13, 18, 19, 21, 22, 27, 31, 133, 139, 148, 155, 156, 158, 165, 209, 213, 232, 238, 241, 242, 243, 265, 274
Competitive differentiation, 118, 129, 130, 131, 133

Competitiveness, 51, 52, 148, 153, 156, 157,
    158, 175, 251, 254, 259, 294, 300, 306,
    324, 339
Complexity, 70, 72, 74, 81, 95, 98, 120, 121,
    126, 164, 252, 258, 349
Components of value, 148
Composite services, 155, 158
Computerized reservation system (CRS),
    311, 312
Conceptual research, 148, 151, 157
Conditional value, 153
Consequences, 36, 106, 110, 148, 223,
    225, 326
Consequent relationships, 151
Consumer behaviour, 82, 97, 143, 148, 151,
    153, 158, 185, 197, 208, 209, 210, 216,
    239, 294, 340
Consumer behaviour assessments, 148
Consumer decision-making process, 147,
    216, 325
Consumer value, 147, 148, 150, 158
Consumption, 19, 36, 37, 39, 64, 97, 98, 111,
    117, 124, 129, 130, 141, 147, 152, 154,
    156, 187, 197, 198, 209, 216, 217, 221,
    223, 232, 241, 242, 248, 249, 250, 265,
    268, 272, 291, 321, 324, 340, 342, 354
Consumption values, 119, 129, 130
Content analysis (CA), 84, 86, 89, 122, 124,
    134, 172, 326–330
Contingent effects, 193
Contrast theory, 186
Coordination mechanisms, 57
Coupling constraints, 342
Created image, 131
Cruise, 38, 44, 88, 89, 142, 241, 292
Cultural brokerage, 257
Cultural tourism guide, 349–350
Customer advocacy, 239
Customer-based destination brand equity
    model (CBDBE), 102–109, 111, 112
Customer experience, 209, 210, 215, 238, 265,
    305, 321, 322, 323, 324–325, 327, 334
Customer information systems (CIS), 311,
    312

Customer loyalty, 97, 99, 110, 142, 147,
    157, 163, 164, 175, 187, 188, 239, 324,
    332, 347
Customer orientation, 19
Customer relationship management (CRM),
    140, 143, 145, 300, 324
Customer retention, 142, 147, 165
Customer value, 104, 140, 147, 148, 153, 157,
    158, 215, 216, 238, 281

Data analysis and report and project
    management, 312
Data-driven segmentation, 22, 25, 29
Datamatrix code, 346, 347
Data mining, 301, 302
Definition, 52, 53, 63, 64, 66, 98, 110–111,
    118, 119, 140, 145, 150, 187, 209, 217,
    218, 222, 223, 232, 248, 280, 344
Delight, 213, 323, 327
Delightful experiences, 257, 322, 325–330,
    332
Demand-side, 51–59, 315
Desired positioning, 92
Desktop PC, 308, 309, 312, 315
Destination attributes, 95, 98, 99, 101, 102,
    104, 105, 106, 109, 110, 268
Destination Brand, 70
    assessment, 56
    development, 51–58
Destination brand equity, 95, 102–103
Destination branding, 98
    objectives, 120, 126
    specificities, 120, 126
Destination governance, 51, 56–58
Destination image, 52, 55, 79–92, 117,
    118, 119, 121, 128, 131, 133, 134,
    154, 323
    affective, 255
    dimensions, 255
    responses, 82
Destination management organization
    (DMO), 51, 105, 255, 277
Destination personality, 121
Destination selection, 79

Destinations, 35, 51, 52, 53, 80, 81, 83, 89, 97–99, 104, 105, 110, 117, 121, 130, 131, 134, 142, 175–176, 207, 231, 265, 266, 268, 294, 323, 327, 332

Determinants, 147–148, 163, 172, 175, 212, 254, 299

Diamantina, 118, 122, 123–126, 130, 131, 132, 133

"mineiridade" Stereotype, 125, 126, 127

Differentiation, 5, 44, 80, 96, 121, 148, 156–157, 211, 282–283

Digital camera, 309, 312

Digital phone communications, 308, 309, 312

Digital Terrestrial Television (DTT), 312

Direct effects, 110

Direct links, 122

Disappointment, 278, 325, 326, 331, 333

Dissonant view of India, 92

DMOs, 53, 56, 57, 58, 255, 259

Domain, 64, 110, 143, 293, 342, 344, 345

Domotic systems, 309, 312

DVD, 305, 309, 311, 312, 315

Efficiency, 3, 133, 156, 299, 305, 314, 332, 339

Electronic cash, 308, 309, 312, 314

Electronic distribution to corporate customers, 312

Electronic invoicing, 309, 312

Electronic marketing and sales, 300, 301

e-Magazine, 311, 312

e-mail marketing/direct marketing, 311, 312, 334

Embeddedness, 57

Emerging markets, 266, 277, 281, 284

Emotional value, 129, 152–153

Emotions, 12, 40, 45, 91, 98, 101, 105, 109, 110, 119, 129, 142, 144, 152, 155, 158, 168, 176, 190, 208, 209, 210, 211, 212, 216, 217, 218, 220, 221, 240, 241, 249, 256, 257, 260, 268, 325

Empirical research, 42, 75, 148, 217

Employees, 39, 105, 150, 220, 221, 231, 236, 237, 238, 239, 240, 242, 326, 329, 332, 334

Enabling process, 235

Endogenous resources. *See* Tourism resources

Epistemic value, 44, 153, 158

e-procurement, 300, 304

Ethical value, 38, 153

Evaluative judgments, 152

e-word-of-mouth, 306, 325

Exchange, 36, 37, 39, 44, 45, 46, 164, 211, 223, 231, 232, 235, 237, 252, 253, 259, 301, 351

Expectancy disconfirmation paradigm, 186

Expected value, 154, 330

Experience

co–creation, 142, 144, 145, 218, 231, 237, 239, 242, 243, 251, 258, 321

experiencescape, 254, 255

experiential marketing, 207–212, 219, 241, 268, 321

overall rural tourism experience, 247, 249

tourist experience, 92, 111, 190, 207, 210, 211, 215–224, 241, 243, 247, 249, 252, 253, 254, 256, 260

Experiencer, 234, 237

Experiential attributes, 220, 221, 222, 225, 226

Experiential consumption, 209

Experiential model for product development, 277

Experiential product development, 265, 266, 271, 279

Experiential tourism, 211, 212, 273

Express Travel & Tourism, 84

External marketing, 51, 54, 58

Extrinsic *vs.* Intrinsic values, 224

Facilitating process, 40, 143, 231, 241, 253

Familiarity, 69, 173, 185–196, 197, 198, 239

Fast food restaurants, 157

Favourable Service Encounters, 326, 327

"Feel" perceptions, 95, 152

FeliCa, 355

Festivals, 88, 89, 132, 258, 268, 274, 275, 277

Firm-centric perspective, 231, 234, 242

Foreign tourists, 82, 85

Functional destination attributes, 95, 105, 106, 109, 110
Funding strategies, 56

General models for images in tourism, 117
Geographic information systems (GIS), 342
Get *vs.* give trade off, 150
Global distribution system (GDS), 310, 311
Global positioning system (GPS), 345, 351–352
Goods, 95, 139, 208, 209, 216, 220, 222, 231, 232, 235, 240, 242, 255, 267, 292
Goods-dominant logic, 223
Government of India representations, 84, 85, 86

Hamburg, 63, 66, 67, 68, 69, 70, 71, 72, 73
Hardcopy system (USB memory, portable hard disk), 309, 312
Hedonic value, 224
Heritage, 12, 80, 82, 85, 86, 89, 97, 124, 156, 212, 220, 222, 247, 248, 254, 265, 268, 271, 272, 273
Heterogeneity, 156, 232
  of tourism services, 156
Hindsight bias, 189–191
Historic preservation, 272, 273
Host communities, 247, 252
Host-guest encounters, 251
Hotels, 39, 41, 142, 143, 150, 153, 154, 156, 158, 165, 213, 241, 268, 276, 278, 279, 282, 299, 301, 305, 306, 308–314, 323, 344, 352
Human extensibility, 342

Identity, 53, 54, 55, 56, 57, 58, 81, 82, 91, 96, 119, 120, 211, 254, 257, 258, 260, 322
Image, 5, 12, 13, 29, 52, 54, 55, 66, 70, 72, 80, 98, 101, 117–118, 119, 120, 123, 125, 126, 131, 132, 154, 158, 174, 175, 176, 249, 255, 301, 323, 345, 346, 349, 354
Image formation process, 55
Incredible India campaign, 83, 86, 90
India, 79–92, 300
Indian government representations, 84, 85

Indian public representations, 84
Indian tourism identity, 91
Indian travel magazines, 89
Indirect effects, 38, 151, 158
Indirect links, 38, 158
Induced agents, 80, 81, 84, 90
Induced image, 80, 119, 120, 123, 126, 128, 130, 131
Information and communications technology (ICT), 36, 154, 294, 299–314, 339
Informative e-brochure, 311, 312
Innovation, 36, 97, 110, 139, 144, 258, 259, 265, 289–295, 321, 332, 339, 345
In-room ICT solutions, 301
Inseparability, 117, 232
Intangibility, 117, 120, 232
Intangible destination attributes, 104, 110
Intangible products, 232, 292
Interaction effect, 216
Interactions, 6, 23, 35–44, 98, 105, 130, 153, 187, 209, 210, 212, 216, 218, 235, 237, 239, 241, 250, 251, 252, 255, 256, 257, 279, 313, 324, 330
Intermarket segmentation, 4, 11
Internal marketing, 56
International market segmentation, 4
Internet, 20, 28, 35, 36, 41, 82, 83, 140, 143, 164, 272, 289, 290, 292, 293, 295, 296, 301, 303, 306, 313, 340, 343, 344, 346, 354
Intervariable approach, 151–152, 158
iPhone, 339, 345, 349, 353

Layar, 349, 350
LCD screen, 307, 310
Linear structural equation modelling, 106
Location-based services, 36, 354
Long-term viability, 147, 158
Loyal customers, 144, 152, 163, 164, 176, 213
Loyalty, 54, 97, 98, 99, 101, 102, 104, 105, 109, 110, 111, 142, 144, 145, 147, 148, 149, 150, 151, 152, 153, 154, 155, 157, 158, 163–172, 175, 176, 185–191, 192, 195, 196, 197, 198, 213, 239, 258, 289, 315, 332, 347

Loyalty programme, 144, 165, 176, 311, 312, 345, 347

Manufactured goods, 231, 232
Marketability, 265, 268, 276, 277
Marketing myopia, 156, 158
Marketing strategies, 3, 5, 44, 45, 140, 148, 155, 156, 165, 175, 231–244, 260, 295, 322, 334
Market segmentation, 3–4, 6–10, 11, 17–32
m-commerce, 311
Means-end models, 149, 151
Measurements, 41, 67, 95–112, 151–153, 191–192, 193
Measuring place brands, 67–68
Media relations, 278, 279
Mediating, 81, 151, 198
Memorable, 104, 217, 221, 222, 257, 271, 332
Meta-comparison, 99
Methodological links, 148
MICE, 86, 88
Ministry of Tourism, 83, 84
Mobile device, 339–340, 344, 346, 348
Mobile phone communications, 343, 347, 352
Mobile phones, 339, 343, 346, 347, 352
Mobile tourism support systems, 340
Models, 40, 97, 99–102, 122, 149, 151, 174, 186, 192, 193, 195, 197
Moderating effects, 192
MOMO project (MuseO MOvil), 348
Monetary price, 153
Motivations, 11, 22, 92, 98, 101, 175, 207–209, 212
Multidimensionality of consumption, 154
Multidimensional value perspective, 193
Multi-group analysis, 193
Multi-item measurement, 152
Multimedia solutions (3D, virtual tour), 311
Museum guide support, 347–349
Museums, 20, 152, 215, 273, 347–348, 349

National level government representations, 85–86
Network, 36, 57, 68, 69, 240, 251, 259

Network analysis, 67, 68, 69
Network centrality, 57
Network density, 57
Networks
    rural networks, 251, 254, 256, 259
    service networks, 251
Non-monetary price, 153

Once-in-a-lifetime tourists, 152, 158
One-dimensional (1D) code, 345
Online order reception, 308, 311
Operand resource, 240
Operant resource, 233, 240, 241
Organic image, 80, 119
Orientalism, 81, 91
*Outlook Traveller*, 84
Output, 235–236

Packaged tours, 152, 153
Palm tops, 339
Paradigm shift, 147, 216
Pattern matching technique, 122
PDA, 309, 339, 352
Perceived value, 147, 148, 150, 151, 154, 155, 225
Perceptions Based Market Segmentation (PBMS), 18, 21, 28–29
Performances, 97, 101, 105, 165, 186, 190, 191, 220, 222, 243, 256, 275, 299, 302, 325
Perishability, 232
Personal phone customer service, 311, 312
Photoethnography, 121, 122, 128, 134
Pioneer destinations, 265, 278
Piped music, 305
Place brand (definition), 63, 64–67
Place brand centre, 63, 73
Place brand perception, 66, 67–68
Place identity, 53, 257
Place marketing (definition), 64
Place selling, 64
Places of memory, 130
Platform, 20, 41–42, 211, 220, 225, 237
Podcast, 348

Point of sale (POS) terminal, 308, 309, 312, 315

Positioning, 5–6, 12–13, 20, 23, 24, 29, 30, 51, 52, 53, 89, 91, 156–157, 255, 274–278, 323–324

Postcolonial discourse, 91

Posteriori segmentation, 21

Post-hoc segmentation, 3, 10

Post-purchase value, 154

Potential customers, 152, 351

Predictive expectations, 186, 190

Prepaid rechargeable RFID smart card system, 355

Pre-purchase value, 154, 340

Price–quality tradeoffs, 152

Price-sensitive customers, 157

Pricing differentials, 281

Process, 40, 55, 58, 74, 118–119, 218–222, 235–236, 322–323, 324

Product design and positioning, 323–324

Projective techniques, 134

Promoted image, 120

Promotional CD/DVD, 311

Promotion media of developing world destinations, 81

Psychological and social aspects of consumption, 152

Public protest, 72

QR (Quick Response) code, 345

Quality, 24, 45, 99, 101, 104, 105, 153–154, 167, 176, 221, 222, 253, 265, 324, 328, 330

Radio frequency identification (RFID), 355

Reactive value, 154, 155

Recommend, 41, 75, 325, 327

Recommendation, 19, 24, 35, 106, 141, 142, 172, 176, 188–189, 354

Regret, 325

Relationship, 44, 45, 51, 56–57, 96, 97, 99, 101, 110, 139–140, 163, 186, 187, 197, 198, 234, 239–240, 243, 311

Relationship marketing, 139–145, 147–159, 164–172, 175, 176

Repatronage intentions, 147, 148, 157

Repeat behaviour, 111, 142, 188, 239–240, 306

Repeat purchase, 55, 111, 147, 188–189, 239

Repeat purchase/repeat patronage, 157, 233

Repositioning, 5, 12

Representative dissonance, 79–92

Reputation building processes, 322–323

Residents, 37, 39, 64, 65, 70, 72, 73, 120, 122, 130, 131, 240, 251–252, 253

Resource integration, 235, 240–242

Resources, 53, 57, 88, 105, 144, 208, 235, 236, 237, 238, 240, 247, 252, 254, 255, 257, 259, 260, 278, 300

Rewards clubs, 155

Rural development, 247, 248, 249, 252, 259, 260

Rural idyll, 250

Rural tourism, 247–260
    integrated rural tourism, 176

Sacrifices, 154, 157

Sales image, 120

Satisfaction, 10, 37, 38, 41, 51, 54, 79, 92, 98, 101, 102, 104, 109, 110, 120, 142, 151, 152, 153–154, 155, 158, 166, 172–173, 175, 176, 185–199, 238, 243, 304, 314, 315, 324

Searchers and metasearchers, 309

Second economy, 45, 46

Security systems, 309, 312

Segmentation, criteria, 4, 6, 21–22

Self-concept theory, 121

Self-image, 119, 120, 131

Self-service technologies, 301

Semiotic analysis, 82

"Sense" perceptions, 152

Service distribution, 232, 235

Service-dominant logic, 231–244
    foundational premises, 233

Service ecosystem, 240

Service encounter, 39, 210, 325, 326, 327, 329

Service providers, 35, 39, 54, 140, 147, 155, 157, 158, 189, 218, 235, 240, 247, 251, 252, 258, 326

Service quality, 10, 151, 152, 154, 158

Services, 6, 13, 22, 36, 39, 40, 41, 65, 82, 95, 96, 97, 98, 111, 139, 147–159, 163, 186, 189, 197, 207, 209, 212, 220, 221, 222, 224, 235–236, 242, 251, 258, 265, 270, 271, 279, 325, 326, 327, 328, 329, 330, 332, 333, 334, 340, 347, 348, 351, 354

Services marketing, 95, 111, 112, 220, 232, 325

Shareholders, 150, 278

Short-range radio frequency communication, 351

Short text messaging (SME), 279, 293, 294

Situational, 153, 155, 165, 187

Smartphones, 339, 344, 345, 347, 354, 355

Smith, Adam, 232

Social and economic actors, 231, 235, 236, 240, 243

Social and economic exchanges, 232

Social interactions, 35–46

Social media, 13, 36, 143, 239, 293, 321, 331, 332, 333, 334

Social network, 36, 40–44, 145, 211, 238, 292, 293, 301, 310

Social networking, 36, 44, 292, 353

Social value, 119, 153, 156

Sold image, 120

Source markets, 11, 267, 271, 278, 281

South Africa, 8, 144, 272, 273

Southwest Airlines, 236

Stakeholders, 12, 19, 51, 52, 53–54, 55, 56, 57, 58, 63, 64, 65, 66, 67, 69, 71, 74, 75, 103, 104, 117–134, 140, 150, 164, 211, 241, 242, 244, 260, 266, 269, 277, 278, 281

Stakeholders of tourist trade, 122

Statewide level government representations, 84, 86–89

Stereotype, 70, 86, 90, 91, 120, 121, 125, 126, 128, 129, 134

Story, 92, 220, 265, 269

Storytelling, 321, 324, 330

Strategic marketing, 3, 17, 18–21, 23, 28, 31, 79, 92, 196, 224, 322–324

Suica, 355

Supply. *See* Tourism supply

Supply chain, 44, 46, 283

Supply. *See* Tourism supply

Supply-side, 51–59

Sustainable development, 38, 247, 248, 259

Sustainable tourism, 251, 266, 280

Synergies, 66, 155, 158

Tablet PC, 339

Target groups (internal/external), 63, 65, 66, 67, 68, 69, 70, 71, 72, 73, 74

Targeting, 4, 11–12, 17, 20, 21, 28, 145, 155, 156, 157, 158, 239, 265, 279

Targeting strategies, 241

Target marketing, 3–13

TEMPO. *See* Tourism Employment & Opportunity

Terrible experience, 322, 325–326, 327–330, 332, 333, 334

Theme, 84–85, 86, 88, 89, 91, 92, 122, 123, 124, 127, 128, 133, 216, 256, 257, 258, 260, 277

Theming, 256, 258

"Think" perceptions, 152

Ticketing and reservation, 344–345

Time geography, 341, 342, 343

Time–space entity, 342

Time–space perspectives, 341

Touchscreen, 309, 312

Tourism, 3–13, 17–31, 35–46, 52, 53, 56, 57, 63–75, 79, 82, 83, 90, 92, 95–109, 110, 111, 117–133, 139–145, 153–157, 163–176, 185, 199, 207, 209, 210, 211–212, 215, 231, 233, 235, 236, 243, 247, 249, 250, 251–252, 254, 258, 260, 265, 266, 267, 268, 269, 271, 272, 273, 277, 279, 280, 282, 283, 284, 290, 292, 293, 294–296, 299, 300, 301, 305–306, 308, 314, 315, 321, 322, 326, 331, 332, 334, 339–354

Tourism Australia, 11, 12, 215

Tourism destination, 4, 12, 17, 21, 24, 27, 29, 31, 35, 39, 53, 55, 83, 95, 97–99, 98, 99, 109, 110, 111, 112, 117–133, 259, 260, 268–283, 300, 339

Tourism Employment & Opportunity (TEMPO), 265, 266, 267, 269, 276, 277, 278, 279, 280, 281, 282, 283

Tourism experience, 128, 142, 145, 153, 154–155, 156, 158, 235, 247–259, 334, 355

Tourism firm, 4, 10, 12, 13, 44, 143, 148, 152, 155, 231, 232, 235, 236, 237, 238, 239, 240, 241, 242, 282, 292, 293, 294, 332, 355

Tourism industry supply chain development programme, 278

Tourism marketing strategy, 140, 231–242, 244, 295

Tourism organization, 11, 148, 152, 156, 158, 175, 185, 231, 240, 301

Tourism preferences, 3, 13, 37, 41, 42, 43, 265, 268, 322, 348

Tourism production system, 279–280

Tourism product registry, 281

Tourism resources, 258
  endogenous, 97, 99, 106, 237, 257, 260

Tourism segmentation, 10, 20, 25, 35

Tourism supply, 249, 251, 259
  accommodation, 53, 80, 105, 110, 118, 150, 163, 164, 165, 172, 174, 175, 212, 235, 253, 254, 259, 283, 339
  lifestyle entrepreneurs, 258
  service providers, 35, 39, 54, 140, 155, 158, 240, 247, 251, 252, 255, 258, 306, 326

Tourist behaviour, 185, 237

Tourist publicity, 52, 120, 123, 125, 128

Tourists' experience, 110, 191, 195–196, 197, 198, 212, 215, 218, 231, 235

Traces of discrepancy, 91

Travel clubs, 150, 153

Travel experiences, 36, 37, 38, 80, 231, 255, 323

Trust, 58, 145, 175, 189, 190, 252, 277, 324

TwittARound, 349, 350

Ubiquity, 339–340, 341, 343

Uni-dimensional (1D) code, 12, 345

User-generated content, 13, 322, 332, 334

Utilitarian value, 153

Vacation, 22, 27, 29, 37, 38, 152, 231, 236, 268, 293, 330

Value-added tax, 237

Value chain, 36, 144, 236, 242, 265, 266, 277, 279, 281, 339

Value co-creation, 231, 235, 237, 242, 243

Value determination, 187

Value dimensions, 154, 155, 223

Value for money, 97, 101, 102, 104, 109, 110, 173, 332

Value-in-context, 234, 242

Value-in-exchange, 223, 234, 239, 242

Value interpretation, 237, 238, 241

Value-in-use, 110, 111, 112, 156, 223, 234, 235, 238, 242, 243

Value-in-use theory, 156

Value proposition, 5, 210, 224, 236, 238, 240

Values, 5, 11, 35, 37, 39, 40, 43, 53, 59, 95, 98, 99, 101, 104, 105, 106, 108, 109, 110, 118, 119, 121, 129, 140, 142, 144, 147–157, 173, 195, 197, 209, 210, 215, 218, 220, 222–224, 232, 233, 234, 235, 236, 237, 240, 241, 242, 251, 272, 274, 281, 282, 292, 321, 332, 339
  cost/sacrifice, 224
  experiential/hedonic, 224
  functional/instrumental, 224
  symbolic/expressive, 224

Value scaling, 154

VAMOS (Virtual Assistant for Museum Occasional Sightseeing), 348

Viral marketing, 311, 312

Virtual Community, 321, 323

Virtual Private Network (VPN), 309, 312

Visitor readiness, 265, 276, 277

Voluntary services, 151

Web 2.0 virtual communities, 309, 310

Wireless Internet connection (WI-FI), 309, 312, 340, 352, 354
Wireless local area networks (WLANs), 341
Word-of-mouth (WOM), 54, 66, 139, 140, 143, 145, 152, 163, 235, 278, 292, 304, 321, 322, 323, 325, 326, 328, 330, 333, 334

World Bank, 265, 278, 281
World Wide Interoperability (WiMAX), 309, 310, 312

Yield pricing, 282